TRADE POLICY

IN THE 1980s

TRADE POLICY

IN THE 1980s

Edited by

William R. Cline

Institute for International Economics

Washington, DC
1983
Distributed by
MIT Press/Cambridge, London

Dr. William R. Cline is a Senior Fellow at the Institute for International Economics. He was formerly a Senior Fellow at the Brookings Institution; Deputy Director for Development and Trade Research at the US Treasury Department; Ford Foundation Visiting Professor in Brazil and Assistant Professor at Princeton University; and is currently Professorial Lecturer at Johns Hopkins University School for Advanced International Studies.

INSTITUTE FOR INTERNATIONAL ECONOMICS
C. Fred Bergsten, Director
Kathleen A. Lynch, Director of Publications
Rosanne Gleason, Publications Assistant

The Institute for International Economics was created, and is principally funded, by The German Marshall Fund of the United States.

The views expressed in this publication are those of the authors. The publication is part of the research program of the Institute, as endorsed by its Board of Directors, but does not necessarily reflect the views of individual members of the Board or Advisory Committee.

Library of Congress Cataloging in Publication Data
Main entry under title:

Trade Policy in the 1980s.
    "Papers prepared for "Trade Policy in the 1980s," a conference held at the Institute for International Economics in Washington, June 23–25, 1982."

    Bibliography.
    Includes index.
    1. Commercial policy—Congresses. 2. Commerce—Congresses. I. Cline, William R. II. Institute for International Economics (U.S.)
HF1410.5.T7 1983   382'.3   83–4310

ISBN 0–88132–008–1
ISBN 0–262–03099–3 (MIT Press)

Contents

ix

Preface

Impressive postwar progress toward trade liberalization has faltered since the mid-1970s. Despite significant agreements in the 1974–79 Tokyo Round of trade negotiations, new or more severe protection has emerged in important products such as textiles and apparel, steel, and automobiles. Protection and subsidization of agricultural trade remains a contentious issue. The severe world recession of 1980–82 intensified protectionist pressures. In addition new trade issues face the international community, including restrictions on trade in services, high technology trade, and trade distortions through direct investment incentives.

In June 1982 the Institute for International Economics held a conference to examine past and prospective trade issues and to consider the proper design for trade policy in the 1980s. The Institute's POLICY ANALYSES IN INTERNATIONAL ECONOMICS 3, published before the November 1982 General Agreement on Tariffs and Trade (GATT) meeting of trade ministers, synthesized the policy findings of that conference. This volume reports the conference proceedings in full, with additional comments on the outcome of the GATT Ministerial.

The Institute for International Economics is a private nonprofit research institution for the study and discussion of international economic policy. Its purpose is to analyze important issues in that area, and to develop and communicate practical new approaches for dealing with them.

The Institute was created in November 1981 through a generous commitment of funds from the German Marshall Fund of the United States. Financial support has been received from other private foundations and corporations, including a grant from the Rockefeller Foundation in support of the conference on which this volume is based. The Institute is completely nonpartisan.

The Board of Directors bears overall responsibility for the Institute and gives general guidance and approval to its research program— including identification of topics that are likely to become important to international economic policymakers over the medium run (generally, one to three years) and which thus should be addressed by the Institute. The Director of the Institute, working closely with the staff and outside Advisory Committee, is responsible for the development of particular projects and makes the final decision to publish an individual study.

The Institute hopes that its studies and other activities will contribute to building a stronger foundation for international economic policy around the world. Comments as to how it can best do so are invited from readers of these publications.

C. Fred Bergsten
Director

CHAPTER 1

Introduction and Summary

William R. Cline

The international trading system is under great pressure, and seems likely to remain under great—or greater—pressure for the foreseeable future.

Background

The level of world trade is declining substantially for the first time in the postwar period because of the stagnation in the world economy. Unemployment is at its highest levels since the 1930s in virtually every industrial country and seems unlikely to decline very much unless economic growth recovers much more rapidly than most forecasters expect. Many developing countries have raised additional trade barriers to reduce their external deficits and enable them to continue servicing their huge external debts.

The United States has additional problems. A severely overvalued dollar has undermined American competitiveness in world trade, and its bilateral deficit with Japan has soared to record levels despite the domestic recession. The Trade Adjustment Assistance program, which for twenty years provided an alternative to import relief for trade-affected workers and firms, has been largely dismantled. As a result of these pressures, the current US administration—despite its undoubted preference for free markets including open international trade—has implemented new import barriers in four major industries (autos, textiles and apparel, sugar, steel) during its first two years in office.

These pressures have severely strained international economic relations. At the political level, recent trade disputes have heightened tensions between the United States and Europe. The decision of the Reagan administration to prohibit the use of US technology for construction of the Soviet-European gas pipeline provoked angry official

European responses, including denials of American authority to impose such restrictions on the US-licensed technology of firms based in Europe. In November 1982, the United States rescinded its restrictions in exchange for a general agreement with West European allies on East–West trade. Prospective US actions on steel triggered European threats of retaliation against US agricultural products and a more aggressive European position on the illegality of the Domestic International Sales Corporation (DISC) program, which defers US taxes on American export earnings, before a negotiated settlement on steel was reached in mid-October 1982. The perennial debate over European Community (EC) agricultural subsidies has intensified with growing EC penetration of traditional US markets.

Trade friction with Japan has also been acute. Frustrated by the record bilateral trade deficit with Japan, US legislators have threatened a new brand of aggressive "reciprocity" legislation that would employ threats of market closure as leverage to obtain unilateral liberalization abroad and have pushed "local content" bills that could virtually halt US imports of Japanese automobiles.[1] The EC has taken an unprecedentedly sweeping case against Japan to the General Agreement on Tariffs and Trade (GATT), charging essentially that the entire Japanese economic system is a huge trade barrier. As on previous occasions in the past decade, Japan has tried to defuse the growing conflict by announcing lists enumerating new steps in unilateral trade liberalization—without much effect in stilling the foreign criticism.

Irritants have also grown in North–South trade. The general tightening in 1981 of the Multi-Fiber Arrangement (MFA) controlling trade in textiles and apparel, and new protection in sugar, have affected developing countries' export prospects at a time when their need is acute for foreign exchange to make payments on heavy external debt. Emerging trade conflicts with the developing countries include frustration in the North with extremely high protection in the South, as well as trade-distorting requirements on the investment of multinational corporations in the developing countries.

Behind these unfolding conflicts lies a more general background of macroeconomic conflict. At the last two economic summit conferences, and throughout most of 1981 and 1982, the high level of

---

[1] William R. Cline, *"Reciprocity": A New Approach To World Trade Policy?*, POLICY ANALYSES IN INTERNATIONAL ECONOMICS, no. 2 (Washington: Institute for International Economics, September 1982). This study also appears as chapter 4, this volume.

US interest rates—with its resulting aggravation of global recessionary pressure and pressure on other countries' exchange rates—was a central issue of international discord. As already noted, the world has been experiencing its most serious recession since the 1930s. In this environment, trade conflicts have tended to escalate from the business-as-usual economic track to the higher profile political track.[2]

Even on "purely economic" grounds, recent trends in international trade are disturbing. There is a real risk of significant increases in beggar-thy-neighbor policies, as country after country seeks to defend itself against the severe economic problems of the day and even to export its unemployment to others. The "new protectionism" since the late 1970s has imposed both new subsidies to exports and important new barriers to imports, and in some sectors (especially textiles and apparel) protection was already high.

In broad terms, the process of progressive trade liberalization that marked most of the postwar period, and contributed importantly to its record of economic success, reached a turning point in the mid-1970s. Since then, creeping protectionism in new forms, such as "voluntary" export restraints and orderly marketing agreements, has countered (and probably more than offset) the further liberalization achieved, including the results to date of tariff and nontariff agreements reached in the 1974–79 Tokyo Round of trade negotiations. To be sure, the trade glass is no more completely empty than it is full; broad trading opportunities remain available and the system on balance is still relatively open. But the level in the glass has shown disturbing declines in recent years. In addition to import protection, subsidies and "national industrial policies" are increasingly used to enhance countries' international competitive efforts.

Recognizing the threat to the open trading system, in June 1982 the Institute for International Economics held a conference on "Trade Policy in the 1980s" to review the recent directions of trade policy and its likely course over the years ahead, and to try to develop a sensible approach for current and future policy. Such a review was especially timely because a meeting of the trade ministers of the member countries of the GATT—the "GATT Ministerial"—was scheduled for November 1982. The last ministerial meeting had been held in Tokyo in 1973, when the ministers agreed to launch the seventh and largest Multilateral Trade Negotiation (MTN) of the

[2] Richard N. Cooper, "Trade Policy is Foreign Policy," *Foreign Policy* (Winter 1972–73), pp. 18–36, provides the classic analysis of this two-track distinction.

postwar period, the "Tokyo Round" (1973–79). The ministerial meeting in 1982 could have been a crucial event for responding to the pressures facing the international trading system and could have set the terms of reference for trade policy for the next several years. In the end, the accomplishments of the ministerial meeting were modest, as discussed in the final chapter of this volume.

Research on a wide range of trade topics was commissioned for the conference from leading academic and business experts, and from former government officials who had played major roles in past trade negotiations. Conference participants included experts from US labor unions and from academic, research, and international institutions in Europe, Canada, Japan, and several developing countries.

This volume presents the papers and proceedings of the conference and, in a final chapter, draws on its analyses and discussions to recommend a policy approach to trade issues in the 1980s. The papers prepared for the conference address the principal areas of trade policy that currently face policymakers or seem likely to emerge in the coming decade. To establish the general policy setting for the more specific issue areas, the first group examines several key conceptual issues: the relationship of exchange rate misalignments to protectionist pressure; the recent push away from the tradition of most-favored-nation treatment in favor of "reciprocity legislation" in the United States; the functioning of GATT; and the array of current threats to the multilateral trading system. The roles of the major international players are examined next, with analyses of the forces for both protection and continued liberal policies in the United States, Europe, and Japan.

The major unresolved trade issues of the past are then reviewed with respect to policies on subsidies and unfair trade, safeguards, and trade adjustment and with respect to the leading problem sectors: agriculture, textiles, automobiles, and steel. The final group of papers explores new issues that have begun to emerge and could emerge in the 1980s: trade in services, trade-related investment issues, high technology trade, and the potential effects of complete tariff elimination.[3]

The remainder of this introductory chapter summarizes the findings of the conference papers and, on some of the most controversial issues, adds my own views or those of conference discussants. The

---

[3] A useful recent review of many of these issues is provided in Gary C. Hufbauer, *US International Economic Policy 1981: A Draft Report* (Washington: Georgetown University Law Center, 1982).

final chapter of this volume develops the principal policy options that emerge from the stock-taking of trade policy that the studies presented here provide, and recommends a specific course of action to respond to the pressures on the trading system that seem likely to continue.[4]

The Setting

In the postwar period, international trade has been a dynamic source of economic growth. From 1950 through 1975, merchandise trade of industrial countries grew at an average rate of 8 percent annually, contributing importantly to historically high growth rates, averaging over 4 percent.[5] Moreover, the relation between trade and growth has an accelerationist feature, attributable in part to the high responsiveness of imports to income growth (income elasticity) as well as inventory behavior for traded goods. When economic activity in the countries in the Organization for Economic Cooperation and Development (OECD) is rising by more than 1.5 percent to 2 percent per year (all numbers in volume terms), the nonoil imports of those countries (which account for over 60 percent of world trade) tend to grow about three times as fast.[6] Under such circumstances, which prevailed throughout the postwar period until quite recently, there is a virtuous circle between economic growth and trade: increased growth stimulates even faster growth of trade, which stimulates more economic expansion, and so on.

When OECD growth dips below 1.5 percent, however, a similar negative cycle takes over because OECD (and hence world) trade tends to decline at a multiple of the shortfall in growth. When OECD business activity shows zero growth, for example, nonoil trade tends to decline by about 5 percent. Such a fall in trade further erodes

[4] Earlier versions of Chapters 1 and 22 of this volume appeared as a monograph summarizing the conference and proposing policy strategies for the GATT Ministerial and beyond. C. Fred Bergsten and William R. Cline, *Trade Policy in the 1980s*, POLICY ANALYSES IN INTERNATIONAL ECONOMICS, no. 3 (Washington: Institute for International Economics, November 1982).

[5] William R. Cline, "Long-Term Change in Foreign Trade Policy," US Congress, Joint Economic Committee, *Special Study on Economic Change, Vol. 9, The International Economy: US Role in a World Market* (Washington: US Government Printing Office, 1980), p. 188.

[6] Based on regression analysis in C. Fred Bergsten and William R. Cline, "Overview: Trade Policy in the 1980s," chapter 2, this volume.

national economies, producing a further decline in trade, and so on. We are now witnessing just such a negative spiral, which stands in sharp contrast to all previous postwar experience and is reminiscent of the early 1930s. Such a situation, of course, fosters sharply increased pressures for trade restrictions—which would steepen the downward spiral.

Reductions in protection achieved through international trade negotiations played a major role in the rapid growth of trade and income. Early postwar negotiations cut tariffs substantially, the Kennedy Round (1964–67) cut them further by about one-third, and the Tokyo Round (1975–79) established codes of behavior on nontariff barriers (NTBs) and achieved additional tariff cuts. Average tariffs on dutiable industrial products after the Tokyo Round are only 4.4 percent for the United States, 4.7 percent for the EC, and 2.8 percent for Japan.[7] As tariffs have come down, however, NTBs have become relatively more important.

Recent Trends in Protection

The overview paper for the conference reviews recent trends in protection and the forces causing these trends.[8] In the mid-1970s the steady progress toward lower protection reached a turning point. Since that time, international trade has been increasingly affected by the "new protectionism." Because of GATT obligations "binding" lower tariffs, protection has taken other forms, including "voluntary" export restraints on supplier countries, orderly marketing agreements (OMA), and, increasingly important, government intervention through subsidies and other means, sometimes aimed at investment decisions rather than trade per se, with indirect but potentially enormous effects on trade.

The worldwide inflation of 1973 prompted a surge of import liberalization that took protection to new postwar lows. In the United States, quotas on steel, oil, meat, and sugar were eliminated in 1973–74, and similar reductions in protection occurred in other industrial countries seeking to moderate high inflation by making imports cheaper. In fact, a number of countries erected export controls to try to reduce inflationary pressures during this period, but most of those measures

---

[7] GATT, *The Tokyo Round of Multilateral Trade Negotiations: II Supplementary Report* (Geneva: GATT, 1980), p. 33.

[8] Bergsten and Cline, chapter 2, this volume.

were short-lived and thus did not have lasting effect on the trading system.

By 1977, however, the tides of protectionism began to rise again, partly in a delayed response to the world recession of 1974–75 and partly due to renewed exchange rate misalignments. In the 1977 renewal of the Multi-Fiber Arrangement, the EC substantially tightened its import restrictions on textiles and apparel. In the same year the United States negotiated orderly marketing agreements limiting exports of footwear from Korea and Taiwan, while Canada and the United Kingdom imposed footwear quotas.

In steel, the EC adopted a rationalization plan that imposed import quotas beginning in 1977. In 1978 the United States began a trigger price mechanism (TPM) of accelerated antidumping procedures that provided some degree of protection for steel.[9] In electronics, the United States negotiated orderly marketing agreements on color television sets from Japan in 1977 and from Korea and Taiwan in 1979. France, Italy, and the United Kingdom also imposed quotas on television sets in the late 1970s. In 1979 and 1980 Canada, the United Kingdom, and Germany increased their protection of shipbuilding in the form of higher subsidies.

A striking feature of the new protectionism of the late 1970s was its concentration in the same product sectors in several industrial countries: textiles and apparel, steel, television sets, footwear, and shipbuilding. This pattern reflected not only the similar ailing conditions of these industries in most of the industrial countries but also the "ricochet" dynamics of protection whereby, when one group of countries raises barriers, a second group fears that its markets will be inundated by diverted supply and implements protection of its own.

In 1981–82 a second wave of the new protectionism arrived, in the midst of even deeper world recession and an even more severe bout

---

[9] Because it was based on antidumping enforcement, the TPM was arguably an instrument for fair trade rather than a protective device. But it eliminated the legal burden of the petitioner to submit meaningful evidence that the foreign firm was selling below its cost or its home-market price, placing all of the legal burden on the foreign supplier and acting thereby as a nontariff barrier of the harassment variety. It also occasioned a surge mechanism for specialty steel, whereby dumping procedures were initiated without evidence of dumping solely on the basis of observed increases of imports. Nonetheless, the protective effect of these measures was certainly less severe than that of the EC quotas or the earlier program of "voluntary restraints" on steel sales to the United States (1969–74).

of currency imbalances. This time automobiles were affected, as the United States induced a voluntary quota of 1.68 million vehicles per year on Japanese exports (about 20 percent of the expected 1981 market). Canada and Germany followed suit with automobile protection, while other EC countries already had protection on Japanese automobiles, ranging from substantial (United Kingdom) to extreme (France and Italy). Also in 1981, the renewal of the Multi-Fiber Arrangement further tightened this protective régime. And in 1982 the United States adopted sugar quotas and negotiated "voluntary" quotas with the EC on steel products. The only contrary trend was US termination of quotas on television sets and footwear (in 1981), where the stakes are much smaller than in the combined sectors of automobiles, steel, sugar, textiles, and apparel.

Against the clear trend toward nontariff barrier (NTB) protection since the mid-1970s, there is the liberalizing trend of the phase-in of Tokyo Round tariff cuts and the (largely untapped, but perhaps sizable) potential of the new NTB codes. However, tariffs are being cut only from an average of 7 percent to 4.7 percent (for industrial countries) over the course of the decade, a very modest liberalization although tariff cuts will be more significant for some sectors and may be especially important for exports from developing countries. On balance, the trend in the past five years has been at best ambiguous and, more probably, toward a net increase in protection—especially when defined broadly to include trade-distorting subsidies and government aids.

The pressures for protection have clearly risen even more sharply than actual protective measures. In the United States, there have been serious legislative proposals for an aggressive style of "reciprocity" enforced by threats of retaliation and for "local content" requirements for automobiles. A growing list of specific industries is petitioning for import relief.

So far, however, both protectionist pressures and the actual net balance of protectionist actions have failed to show up in a serious retrenchment of international trade. It is true that world trade has stagnated recently: the real volume of world trade rose only 1.5 percent in 1980, did not rise at all in 1981, and declined in 1982. More significantly, nonoil imports into the OECD declined by 2.5 percent in 1981 and probably fell further in 1982. But statistical regressions in the overview paper indicate that these declines are fully explained by the reduction in world growth. For every percentage point decline in the OECD growth rate, nonoil imports into the OECD decline by 3 percent; and it requires growth of 1.5 percent just to keep imports from falling. This pattern, estimated for data covering 1961–81, explains the decline in industrial countries' trade in 1981 without any additional room for attributing the decline to more severe protection. As noted above, the estimates do suggest that trade will remain stagnant until normal growth is restored in the industrial countries—and that pressure on the trading system will thus remain acute.

The rise of protectionist pressures since the mid-1970s derives from both long- and short-term economic influences. Two long-term factors tending toward protectionism have been the decline in US economic hegemony and the rise in economic interdependence. Following a long-term decline in the US share in the world economy and world trade in the postwar period, the United States is now in a weaker position to provide global economic leadership. Similarly, rising interdependence has heightened the role of imports as a source of adjustment pressure on domestic industry. From 1953–54 to 1979–80, imports of goods and services as a share of GNP rose from 4.3 percent to 10.6 percent in the United States; an average of 16.8 percent to 22.2 percent in England, France, and Germany; and 11.8 percent to 14.9 percent in Japan.[10] Expressed as a percentage of the relevant set of tradable goods and services, imports are even higher.

Unemployment has been a major cause of protectionist pressure. When unemployment is high, adjustment to increased imports is more difficult; the demand for protection from labor, and the degree of governmental sympathy for supplying protection, both increase. The "new protectionism" of the late 1970s followed closely the severe world recession of 1974–75 and the recent wave of protection in automobiles and steel is clearly related to the devastated level of activity in these sectors during the global stagnation of 1980–82.

Against the long- and short-term pressures for protection other forces favor trade liberalization. They include concern about inflation (as indicated by the notable liberalizing in 1973–74 for anti-inflationary purposes), the growing importance of exports to all industrial countries (notably including the United States), and the role of foreign policy considerations in tempering disputes with allies. In addition, the existence of an ongoing round of multilateral trade negotiations acts broadly as a liberalizing force and indirectly as an obstacle to protectionist backsliding. The hypothesis of "dynamically unstable trade policy" holds that the trade régime either moves forward toward liberalization or backward toward protection, and an

[10] International Monetary Fund, *International Financial Statistics,* May 1978 and April 1982.

MTN helps the trade policy "bicycle" keep its forward-moving momentum.

Costs of Protection

The new protectionism has continued to mount despite the wide body of theory and evidence that protection and trade-distorting subsidies are economically costly. Moreover, with the anemic economic growth of recent years, these additional costs make it even harder to achieve acceptable increases in living standards. Protection against imports directly increases costs to consumers by raising the domestic price, and reducing the availability, of products the country imports. Protection and subsidies reduce the economic potential of a country by inducing producers to shift resources from items it can produce efficiently to those in which it is inefficient. These losses of "static" efficiency from sacrifices of consumer benefits and the misallocation of resources were recognized by economists as early as two centuries ago when Adam Smith analyzed them.

Protection also has dynamic costs. It stifles competitive pressures for technological change. By worsening inflation through raising important prices, it tends to cause macroeconomic losses as policymakers are forced to accept more recession to bring down inflation. By reducing specialization it limits the potential for achieving economies of large-scale production.

The costs of protection are especially high for consumers. In the late 1970s American consumers paid an estimated $58,000 annually per job saved by protection of specialty steel, television sets, and footwear[11]; this would equate to about $92,000 annually per job at 1982 prices. European consumers paid approximately $11 billion yearly for the protection of European farm products ($17 billion at 1982 prices)[12]; and American consumers pay an estimated $12 billion yearly for the protection of textiles and apparel.[13] The "static" costs of protection to the nation as a whole are lower than these consumer costs because part of the consumer loss is a transfer to domestic producers in the form of higher profits. But the nation's net economic costs from protection are nevertheless substantial, especially when dynamic effects are included.

---

[11] Robert W. Crandall, "Federal Government Initiatives to Reduce the Price Level," *Brookings Papers on Economic Activity,* 1978, p. 431.

[12] *World Development Report 1981* (Washington: World Bank), p. 33.

[13] Martin Wolf, "Textile Pact: The Outlook," *New York Times,* 12 January 1982.

To be sure, the calculus of trade policy must include attention to adjustment costs. If a surge in imports causes displacement of domestic workers, their unemployment during the transition to a new activity represents a direct personal loss as well as a loss in production to the economy. (Whether the corresponding idling of fixed capital equipment is a social loss is a moot point, because judged by new international criteria it has lost its "social opportunity cost" value if it has become outmoded.) Nonetheless, the economic benefits estimated for trade liberalization usually exceed by far these adjustment costs. Appropriate adjustment programs can help ensure not only that the economic cost of adjustment is reduced but also that displaced workers receive equitable compensation for trade policies that benefit the economy at large but in the first instance place the burden disproportionately upon them.[14]

Import controls that protect workers in a single industry inherently displace workers in other industries. Such a result can occur as other countries retaliate via trade restrictions or are simply unable to buy as much abroad because of the cutback in their own export earnings arising from the controls in the importing country. More broadly, however, effective import controls stimulate an appreciation of the exchange rate of the restricting country. This in turn reduces its export competitiveness and stimulates imports in uncontrolled sectors. At best, import controls in a single industry thus redistribute unemployment rather than protect total employment.

Despite its costs, significant protection exists in industrial countries in several major product sectors, especially agriculture, textiles and apparel, steel, automobiles, footwear, consumer electronics, and shipbuilding. The main political explanation for protection, in the face of its substantial economic costs, is that well-organized special interest groups of business and labor in import-affected industries are able to obtain the political support needed for protection. In part, this is possible because the corresponding losses to consumers are more thinly dispersed, and their interests are largely unorganized. In addition, the "infant-industry" motive and, in some cases, national

---

[14] The current and future benefits from tariff cuts in the Tokyo Round of trade negotiations are estimated at 50 to 100 times as large as adjustment costs for the major industrial countries. William R. Cline, Noboru Kawanabe, T. Kronsjo, and Thomas Williams, *Trade Negotiations in the Tokyo Round: A Quantitative Assessment* (Washington: Brookings Institution, 1978), pp. 232–33. See also the calculation by Martin Wolf concerning current restraints on textile and apparel imports, cited below.

security considerations, lead some countries to protect new industries they wish to develop (especially high technology industries such as computers and aircraft), frequently in the form of special subsidies or other state intervention.

Exchange Rates and Protection

The conference paper by Bergsten and Williamson[15] deals with what appears to be an important additional source of periodic protectionist pressure over the last decade: the misalignment of exchange rates. When the exchange rate is overvalued, a country's products become less competitive in international markets. Imports widen their inroads and exports lose market shares abroad. The demands for domestic protection increase.

Ironically, protectionist pressures may also be created in a country with an undervalued exchange rate. Industries that build up capacity on the basis of exports made artificially competitive by an undervalued rate may find they have excess capacity when the exchange rate returns to a more normal level. At that time they may press for import restrictions or export subsidies—with some justification, since their capacity was built under erroneous price signals deriving from government policy, the functioning of the international monetary system, or both.

The authors address the question of what it means for exchange rates to be under- or overvalued under the present system of floating exchange rates. They identify the "fundamental equilibrium exchange rate" as the rate that, over the longer run, would make the country's external (current account) deficit or surplus consistent with its long-run tendency toward capital inflow (as in developing countries) or outflow (as in mature industrial countries, especially those with high savings rates). The "market exchange rate" can differ from fundamental equilibrium because of poor information, because current economic circumstances are unrepresentative of longer-run conditions, and because the market rate can be dominated for extended periods by factors (such as interest rate differentials and international political disturbances) which are unrelated to underlying economic relations.

[15] C. Fred Bergsten and John Williamson, "Exchange Rates and Trade Policy," chapter 3, this volume.

Bergsten and Williamson cite evidence of protectionist pressure associated with overvaluation. The highly restrictive Mills and Burke-Hartke bills of the early 1970s, as well as the initiation of US import controls for steel and a major broadening of the controls on textiles and apparel, coincided with severe overvaluation of the dollar toward the end of the fixed rate system. In 1977–78 the dollar was overvalued (after the 1975 recession depressed imports, producing a temporary US current account surplus) while the Japanese yen was undervalued (partly because Japan bought dollars to keep the yen from rising), and major trade conflict between the United States and Japan erupted again. The pattern repeated itself in 1981–82 when, relative to the yen, the dollar has risen over 50 percent from its 1978 trough. Once again trade conflict with Japan was intense; voluntary export quotas were imposed on Japanese automobiles, and Congress considered a spate of bills calling for retaliation and aimed mainly at Japan.[16]

For policy purposes, there are three main implications. First, trade policymakers must integrate their efforts with those of monetary authorities. The divorce between the two sets of policymakers is striking, both in terms of domestic bureaucracies (trade ministries versus finance ministries and central banks) and international institutions (GATT versus the International Monetary Fund). Second, domestic economic policies must take their exchange rate consequences much more carefully into account. The recent dollar-yen imbalance has resulted to a considerable degree from opposing macroeconomic policy mixes, for example, with the United States running a relatively loose fiscal and tight monetary mix while Japan has had broadly the opposite combination. Third, reforms in the international monetary system may be needed to reduce the risk and degree of exchange rate misalignment. At a minimum, increased policy coordination is required. More fundamentally, monetary reform moving toward the adoption of "target zones" or "reference" exchange rates warrants intensified consideration. In some cases, capital controls (for example, on outflows from Japan, or more general interest equalization taxes) could prove necessary.[17]

[16] Details on this issue can be found in C. Fred Bergsten, "What To Do About the US-Japan Economic Conflict," *Foreign Affairs*, vol. 60, no. 5 (Summer 1982).

[17] See John Williamson, *The Exchange Rate System,* POLICY ANALYSES IN INTERNATIONAL ECONOMICS, no 7. (Washington: Institute for International Economics, forthcoming 1983).

GATT and the Multilateral System

The conference papers by John H. Jackson and Harald B. Malmgren examine the adequacy of GATT and the present threat to the multilateral system.[18] Underlying this issue is a fundamental tension among the United States, which seeks to reduce government intervention in international trade and production decisions, and several other major countries, which see rising governmental intervention as necessary to guide the increasingly severe adjustment process. GATT is the multilateral institution charged with moderating such trade conflict. Jackson emphasizes that there is an inherent conflict between reliance on rules versus the exercise of power diplomacy in the GATT. Smaller nations favor the approach of rule making, while the EC tends to seek to exercise power in the GATT based on its economic and political weight. The United States is ambivalent, having the weight to pursue power diplomacy but committed by tradition to developing rules and adhering to them—though, as noted below, it does not in practice always stick to these principles.

Malmgren develops the theme further, maintaining that GATT is neither a judicial body nor an agency for enforcement. Instead, it is the "cumulative effect of negotiations." Perceptions of it as a judicial body cause many observers to conclude that GATT has failed when a particular trade rule is broken. Rather, according to Malmgren, departure from GATT rules usually reflects prior inability to reach full agreement among negotiating countries.

Both Jackson and Malmgren fault the United States and the EC for undermining the GATT, in several ways. First, they (together with Japan and perhaps Canada) dominate the GATT so much that other members feel they have little meaningful voice. In quadrilateral meetings, often not even in Geneva, the big four have made deals that are presented to other members as *faits accomplis*. Second, both the United States and the EC avoid going to the GATT when they find it convenient, working out bilateral resolutions of their conflicts, thereby leaving the impression that GATT is of little relevance. Third, both the United States and EC have pointedly ignored some major GATT rulings. The United States has refused to give up the DISC, despite a GATT panel's finding that it violates the subsidies code; the EC has ignored GATT rulings on protection in sugar. Fourth, in

---

[18] John H. Jackson, "GATT Machinery and the Tokyo Round Agreements," and Harald B. Malmgren, "Threats to the Multilateral System," chapters 5 and 6, respectively, this volume.

Malmgren's opinion, the recent EC case brought in GATT against Japan (under Article XXIII, "nullification and impairment" of former tariff liberalization) is so sweeping (attacking the very way of doing business in Japan) that it amounts to an abuse of the GATT, an exercise in bringing an essentially imprecise and ill-defined complaint in order to demonstrate that GATT cannot act so that there will be justification for actions outside the GATT.

Jackson's review of dispute settlement within the GATT suggests that the record is not as bleak as often assumed, however. Under GATT's Article XXIII, about one-half of a total of 159 cases were settled or withdrawn before a GATT panel report was issued; of the others, GATT members approved of the panel finding in nearly all cases, and there were only eight in which the offending country refused to comply with the finding.

Jackson considers it premature to judge the effectiveness of the new codes on nontariff barriers negotiated in the Tokyo Round. The first formal panel procedures under an MTN code began only in March 1982. However, Jackson foresees conflicts between the codes and the underlying GATT. Some of the codes, especially on subsidies and government procurement, can be interpreted as excluding non-signatories from their benefits: certainly the United States and the EC signed these codes with such limited coverage in mind, as an incentive to get countries to accept the obligations of the codes. But Article I of the GATT assures members of "most-favored-nation" (MFN) treatment—equal to that given to any other GATT member— and the GATT members in November 1979 reaffirmed that the new MTN codes did not deny members any other GATT privileges, explicitly citing those from Article I.

Malmgren proposes a strategy to strengthen the GATT. He rejects the idea that its rules should be rewritten to legitimize restrictive practices now outside the GATT (even if hopeful clauses to moderate the practices are included), and thus he opposes a new safeguards code allowing selective protection against individual suppliers (now illegal under GATT; see the discussion of safeguards below). Instead, he advocates a revitalization of the existing GATT provisions, especially Article XIX on temporary "safeguard" protection in response to import injury. In particular, he proposes the establishment of a GATT Surveillance Committee to monitor all trade restrictions. The committee would assemble information on trade barriers, not only from complaints cited by countries encountering barriers, but also at the initiative of the GATT Secretariat itself. (Without a specific mandate to do so, GATT staff cannot on their own assemble an inventory of restrictions because there would be howls of protest from the offending countries.) In Malmgren's approach, a GATT armed with a committee and mandate for surveillance could then require statements from protecting countries of how and when they intended to phase out the protection.

"Reciprocity" and Retaliation

As an example of the present threat to the multilateral trading system as expressed in the GATT, in the spring of 1982 several bills calling for trade "reciprocity" were introduced in the US Congress. These bills called for retaliatory US protection against countries not granting market access "substantially equivalent" to that in the United States. My own conference paper evaluates this possible new approach to trade policy.[19]

The "new reciprocity" would be aggressive rather than passive as in the past: it would impose new trade barriers as a threat, rather than merely refraining from extending new liberalization to nonreciprocating countries. In past negotiations the United States and other countries have sought a broadly reciprocal balance of liberalization, but the new approach would make judgments of reciprocity not on the basis of *changes* in protection but on the current *level* of protection.

The fundamental premise of the new reciprocity movement—that US markets are far more open than foreign markets—is doubtful. The "coverage" of manufactured goods by major nontariff barriers in recent years has extended to nearly one-third of the US market (including textiles, apparel, automobiles, steel, footwear, and television sets), a figure comparable to that in some European countries and higher than that in other industrial countries—although some foreign barriers, such as French and Italian quotas on Japanese automobiles, are clearly more severe than those in the United States. In the specific case of Japan, a large bilateral surplus with the United States has provoked congressional ire, but market access cannot be judged by bilateral balances—for example, the EC has a large deficit with the United States. Data on tariffs, quotas, current account balances, and imports relative to GNP reveal no clear evidence of excessive protection in Japan except in agriculture. (The conference paper by Gary R. Saxonhouse, summarized below, reaches a similar conclusion via a wholly different methodology.) Low manufactured imports reflect the heavy reliance of Japan on raw materials imports.

---

[19] Cline, "Reciprocity," chapter 4, this volume.

Most important, an undervalued yen and overvalued dollar have been the major source of the periodic surges in Japan's surplus (including with the United States) and precipitated numerous allegations of unfair Japanese practices because of resulting trade pressure.

The "new reciprocity" would involve a watershed departure from US trade practice over the last sixty years of unconditional most-favored-nation treatment. Imposing protection against a country judged nonreciprocal would mean discriminating among suppliers. This approach would violate a fundamental principle of the GATT, set forth in Article I (MFN treatment). Notably, in 1922 the United States moved from conditional to unconditional MFN because of unfortunate past experience with demands from other trading partners for equal treatment whenever a new bilateral treaty was signed. In the postwar period the exceptions to unconditional MFN have been for purposes of trade creation (for example, free trade areas) or economic assistance to developing countries (the Generalized System of Preferences, GSP), and it is not clear that even the new MTN codes will eventually deviate from unconditional MFN. In contrast, "aggressive reciprocity" would be an exception to unconditional MFN that could often lead to trade suppression, not trade creation.

From a pragmatic standpoint, the worst flaw of aggressive reciprocity is that it frequently might fail to open foreign markets. If it did fail, a minimum result would be new protection of the US market—which would be costly in itself. At worst, the sanction of new protection would induce counterretaliation abroad, reducing US exports. Retaliatory escalation is familiar from the trade wars of the 1930s. Although retaliation has been more limited in the postwar period (for example, the "chicken war" between the United States and the EC), the atmosphere is currently heavily charged with potential for retaliatory escalation. The confrontations with Europe over the Soviet pipeline and on steel have already led to threats of retaliation by the EC.

The analysis of chapter 4 does consider the possibility that the growing similarity of factor endowments and technological levels among industrial countries causes comparative advantage to be relatively arbitrary across a range of manufactured goods, giving undue advantage in selected sectors to countries where governments intervene with special support. Under these conditions trade performance becomes less a matter of inherent comparative advantage and more one of determination by the type of strategic behavior associated with imperfectly competitive markets. A "level playing field," with international rules of behavior, becomes especially important where comparative advantage is arbitrary. This theme runs through several of the individual issue areas examined in the conference, especially subsidies, trade-related investment issues, and high technology trade (including the more general issue of whether national industrial policy can be compatible with equitable international trading practices). Nevertheless, to address this and other problems of commercial practice, policies other than "reciprocity" threats are preferable: revitalization of negotiations to counter "impairment and nullification" under GATT Article XXIII, use of other GATT provisions, new negotiations on services and trade-related investment issues (which are key concerns of the reciprocity movement), and perhaps bilateral and sectoral negotiations. However, expectations of gains should not be great if the United States is unprepared to offer what has always been the relevant bargaining chip in the past: further liberalization of its own market.

The Players

The conference considered the strains on the international trading system caused by the policies and practices of each of the major actors: the European Community, Japan, and the United States. The discussion also included the role of the developing countries. To sharpen the focus, the authors were requested to concentrate on the protectionist practices of the country in question.

The European Community

Gardner Patterson, formerly a high official of the GATT, saw four basic causes of protectionism in the EC: the structure of EC decision making; the Community's preference for bilateral and sectoral arrangements; its traditional tendency toward discriminatory treatment; and its resistance to international dispute settlement procedures.[20]

The EC must deal with individual members before it can deal with the outside world. Any member can veto an action considered a matter of national interest. This structure is biased toward protection. Logrolling contributes; each country supports protectionist requests of others in return for support of its own requests.

In agriculture, despite early EC protestations to the contrary, a watertight protective régime has evolved whereby prices are set on the basis of the costs of the least efficient producer, and the resulting

---

[20] Gardner Patterson, "The European Community as a Threat to the System," chapter 7, this volume.

excess production is exported with subsidies. As a result, although the EC was a net importer of grains, sugar, dairy products, and beef in the early 1970s, it is now a net exporter. Similarly, the EC has led the way in recent tightening of protection on textiles and apparel. Left to itself the EC Commission would choose less protection, but the member countries have delegated less authority to it in recent years.

Bilateral trade deals can have adverse effects on third countries but the EC has favored them. As both Malmgren and Patterson note, the United States, the EC, and Japan increasingly have reached private deals, often imposing them on other GATT members during the Tokyo Round (and leading the developing countries to protest the results, although they are certainly among the major beneficiaries of the overall outcome). Sectoral arrangements also tend toward protectionism, creating vested interests that turn temporary measures permanent. Yet the EC tends to favor sectoral arrangements such as those in textiles and apparel, steel, shipbuilding, electronics, and automobiles.

The EC tradition of discrimination is deeply engrained. The Community itself is a preferential economic community. Following earlier practice it extends special preferences to its associated overseas states (under the Lomé convention), discriminating especially against Latin America. Exercising their GATT rights, Great Britain, France, Italy, and Belgium refused MFN treatment to Japan when it joined the GATT in 1956, relenting later only on the condition of selective safeguards against Japanese goods. The EC has special protection against Eastern Europe. And in the Tokyo Round, the EC torpedoed the safeguards code by insisting on the right to apply safeguard protection on a selective basis, in effect discriminating against developing countries (and Japan).

The United States

Rodney de C. Grey, the Canadian Ambassador for the Tokyo Round, begins with the assignment to identify practices of the United States that cause problems for the trading system.[21] He criticizes the growing shift from a régime of fixed protection through tariffs to one of flexible "contingent protection" through administrative procedures. He recalls that the United States helped initiate this drift in

---

[21] Rodney de C. Grey, "A Note on US Trade Practices," chapter 8, this volume.

the early 1960s when its increasing use of antidumping measures (imposing penalties on goods exported at a lower price than in the exporter's home market) induced negotiators in the Kennedy Round to adopt an antidumping code. Rather than reduce antidumping as a protective device, codifying its administrative procedures had the effect of authorizing all signatories of the code to use the varied procedural devices drafted into the code, perversely making the instrument more restrictive than before.

Turning to sectoral practices, Grey notes the irony that it was the United States that first insisted on a GATT waiver for protection of certain of its agricultural products, setting a precedent the Europeans and others have since exploited in the extreme. Grey recalls that the United States also inaugurated the international régime of protection in textiles and apparel when the Kennedy administration had to accede to protectionist demands of the textile sector to secure its neutrality in passage of the legislation authorizing the Kennedy Round. As in the case of the agricultural waiver, the United States was soon outdone by the Europeans in textile protection.

In steel, Grey criticizes the trigger price mechanism as too "complex" and "bizarre" to be sustained by the weak base of antidumping, itself an inadequate substitute for policies designed to deal with longer term sectoral adjustment. He anticipates further stages of protection to follow the collapse of the TPM and imposition of countervailing and antidumping duties—as does indeed seem already to be the case, in light of the US–EC deal of October 1982—and argues that approaching the problem of steel through the safeguard Article XIX of GATT would have been better.

In the case of automobiles, Grey notes that US protection is much less severe than that in the United Kingdom, France, and Italy. He maintains that the United States created an unnecessary embarrassment for itself because its own domestic laws on escape clause action are more stringent than the GATT safeguard rules in Article XIX. Because the US escape clause law requires demonstration that imports are a major cause of the industry's difficulties, and recession was clearly more important, the International Trade Commission rejected action while the US political process eventually pressured Japan into accepting voluntary quotas. In the case of the Domestic International Sales Corporation (DISC), the United States is more culpable; it first delayed GATT panel proceedings, then disputed and refused to comply with the findings. More generally, however, Grey does not "attach the major share of the blame" to the United States for protectionism. He concludes that if there is to be leadership for halting or reversing protectionist drift, it will have to come from the United States.

Japan

The conventional wisdom holds that Japan is highly protective. Accordingly, the terms of reference for the conference paper on Japan called for not only an enumeration of Japanese protection but also a balanced overall evaluation of its severity in international perspective. Gary Saxonhouse, a University of Michigan expert on the Japanese economy, notes the presence of 22 agricultural quotas (including those on beef and oranges) but cites only 5 industrial quotas (on charcoal briquettes and four leather product categories).[22] He enumerates the usual nontariff barriers in Japan: restrictions on imports by state-trading companies (tobacco, salt, livestock, Nippon Telephone and Telegraph); burdensome procedures for customs evaluation and for meeting health and environmental standards; and Japan-specific safety standards. However, Saxonhouse considers the Japanese implementation of Tokyo Round agreements, and especially further commitments made early in 1982, to have eliminated most barriers of this genre, at least in nonagricultural products. This assessment appears to be broadly confirmed by the failure of surveys of American businessmen in Japan to find pervasive patterns of major NTB protection.[23]

The main thrust of Saxonhouse's analysis is that the Japanese economy is much less closed than is conventionally believed. Japan has accelerated its Tokyo Round tariff cuts to completion in 1983 with an average tariff of 2.9 percent; when the corresponding cuts are completed in 1987, US tariffs will average 4.4 percent, and tariff averages will range from 5.2 percent to 6.9 percent in the EC. Japan has fewer quotas than France and Benelux, and they are concentrated in agriculture. According to Saxonhouse, the highest estimates of the global impact of removal of Japanese import barriers are in the range of $2 billion to $3 billion, small even when compared to the size of the bilateral Japanese surplus with the United States alone.

Despite the paucity of overt barriers, Japan's manufactured imports are low: only 22 percent of total imports and 2 percent of GNP. One

---

[22] Gary R. Saxonhouse, "The Micro- and Macroeconomics of Foreign Sales to Japan," chapter 9, this volume.

[23] American Chamber of Commerce in Japan (ACCJ), "Report on 1981/82 Trade-Investment Barrier Membership Survey" (Tokyo: ACCJ, March 8, 1982).

approach is to seek an explanation of low manufactured imports in Japanese institutions that are "illiberal" from a foreign perspective. These include: a major governmental role in formulating industrial policy; government intervention in financial markets; large, bank-centered industrial groups; trading companies that dominate distribution and foreign trade; legislation perpetuating an inefficient distribution system; pervasive use of cartels; treatment of labor as a fixed cost; and delayed implementation of liberalization in capital markets, yen internationalization, competitive procurement, and the service sector.

But Saxonhouse rejects this possible explanation. Instead, he argues that Japan's manufactured imports are consistent with normal trade factors. His econometric work on cross-country trade patterns shows that Japan's low manufactured imports can be explained by capital stock, labor force, geographic location, and natural resource endowment. Special "country" terms in statistical tests (evidence of protective effects) show up in only 4 percent of Japan's trade, compared with 10 percent for Italy and 16 percent for France. High-quality labor, poor natural resources, and great distance from trading partners are the driving forces behind Japan's low manufactured imports. Thus, there is little room left for liberalization of trade practices or institutions to make much difference.

Saxonhouse explains the paradox of "illiberal" institutions yet a normal trade pattern (in light of underlying economic variables) by arguing that Japan's various "illiberal" institutions simply act as substitutes for more liberal institutions abroad, with little if any net impact on Japan's trade. Official industrial policy in Japan substitutes for stronger equity markets in the United States. Government intervention in banking offsets the power of bank-centered industrial groups. Government-sponsored cooperation among firms in research and development compensates for the highly firm-specific nature of technical training and absence of informal exchange among experts. Government aid to biotechnological research is minimal compared to funds poured into this research by US equity markets.

Saxonhouse argues, that exchange rate misalignment is a more potent cause of trade friction than overt and covert protection in Japan. Substantial econometric work has demonstrated that Japan's trade (especially exports) responds sharply to the value of the yen. The current undervaluation of the yen (and resulting trade conflict) has resulted largely from worldwide political and economic uncertainties, reinforcing the "safe haven" role of the dollar, and from high US interest rates and low Japanese interest rates—a consequence of opposite mixes between monetary and fiscal policy. These developments make the dollar scarce and the yen abundant, setting their prices accordingly. But there are obstacles to correction. With depressed world markets, Saxonhouse argues that Japanese exporters welcome a depreciated yen. A high bankruptcy rate inhibits a policy of increasing interest rates. Japanese banks, forced to buy government bonds, oppose higher deficits.

However, Saxonhouse criticizes the illiberal financial market practices that also help keep interest rates low (such as restrictions on commercial and housing financing). He advocates greater freedom for international use of the yen, citing limitations on the issuance of yen-denominated bonds by foreign companies. There is a large latent demand for the yen as a transactions medium that would boost the value of the yen if restrictions on foreign holdings of yen were relaxed. Thus, Japanese monetary policies deepen the exchange rate misalignments that in turn intensify trade frictions. However, the legendary heavy hand of Japanese protectionism is more myth than fact if Saxonhouse's diagnosis is correct.

The Developing Countries

Other important players in international trade policy include Canada, certain other industrial countries (for example, Switzerland introduced the tariff-cutting formula adopted in the Tokyo Round), and the developing countries as a group. Although the developing countries often were bypassed by the big four (United States, EC, Japan, and Canada) in the MTN (as emphasized by Malmgren and others), their voice was decisive on certain issues, especially in development of the "framework" code that gave ongoing legitimacy to tariff preferences, and in rejection of a safeguards code embodying selectivity.

The negotiating position of the developing countries in the 1960s emphasized extension of generalized tariff preferences by industrial countries. In the 1970s, under the tutelage of the United Nations Conference on Trade and Development (UNCTAD), their viewpoint toward MFN tariff reductions in the Tokyo Round was at best initially ambivalent or negative because of the fear that preference margins would be eroded—even though most analyses indicated export gains for developing countries as the result of Tokyo Round tariff cuts by industrial countries.[24]

---

[24] See for example William R. Cline, Noboru Kawanabe, T. Kronsjo, and Thomas Williams, *Trade Negotiations in the Tokyo Round*, pp. 220–24.

An inherent limitation on the bargaining strength of developing countries in past rounds of trade negotiations has been the lack of liberalization offers of their own to serve as bargaining chips. Indeed, the traditional concept has been that developing countries provide "automatic reciprocity" because they spend virtually all of the foreign exchange they earn on imports, largely from the industrial countries. While broadly true, this traditional concept has meant a lack of bargaining power.

In the 1980s the principal trade issues for developing countries will no longer be tariff preferences, which generate only very modest benefits (especially if evaluated by their impact at the margin, considering that many developing countries have already reached the export ceilings allowed for duty-free entry). The single most important trade issue will be the maintenance of their current degree of access to world trade markets. The risk is that markets may progressively close.[25] The other salient issues will be trade liberalization by developing countries themselves, "graduation" of middle-income countries to a status where they assume at least some of the trade practice responsibilities of industrial country GATT members, trade-related investment performance requirements (discussed below), and South–South trade.

Experience since the late 1960s has shown that outward-looking policies favor higher growth than inward-looking development based on import substitution behind high trade barriers. Because many developing countries have high protection, their most astute strategy for the 1980s would probably be along the following lines. They would seek to liberalize imports for the purpose of improving efficiency in their own economies. But in doing so, they would take advantage of this intention by entering negotiations with the industrial countries to obtain further liberalization in northern markets in return. And the bargaining objectives need not be limited to marginal goals such as the (partial) maintenance of generalized preferences. Instead, developing countries prepared to undertake major liberalization of their own could bargain for reductions in the truly significant protection

---

[25] However, projections suggest that even rapid growth in manufactured exports from developing countries can be accommodated with relatively little induced increase in protection in industrial countries, on the basis of statistical estimates relating sectoral protection to import penetration, size of labor force, and other variables. William R. Cline, "Exports of Manufactures from Developing Countries: Performance and Prospects for Market Access" (Washington: Brookings Institution, 1982; processed).

that affects them in markets in the North: in particular, quotas on textiles and apparel; tariffs (and in some cases voluntary export restraints) on footwear, leather goods, and other consumer nondurables; steel protection; protection of sugar, beef, and other agricultural products; and tariffs more generally in areas where higher tariffs on processed goods (tariff escalation) discourage the development of processing of raw materials.

The United States has suggested a "North–South" round of trade negotiations, although this proposal was broadly rejected by developing countries at the GATT Ministerial. For the future, if the industrial countries are truly prepared to consider liberalization of some of the most politically sensitive sectors such as textiles and agriculture, the gains from such a round could be highly attractive for the South. But if all the North has to offer is nonelimination of preferences or nonimposition of new protection otherwise to be erected in the name of "reciprocity," the developing countries may understandably have reservations about a North–South round.

At the same time South–South trade could be a central element in a strategy for the 1980s. As J. Michael Finger noted in the conference discussion, by opening their markets to each other the developing countries would obtain access to the world's fastest growing market—their own. This process would have greater focus, however, if their liberalization were preferential in favor of trade with each other; otherwise the industrial countries would probably be the South's main suppliers of increased imports of manufactures previously protected.

Conference participant Carlos Diaz-Alejandro raised pointed questions about the current North–South trade strategy of at least some industrial countries. He criticized the "extravagant demands" for liberalization and graduation by the newly industrialized countries (NICs) at a time when their balance of payments and debt-servicing capacity are under severe pressure. He also criticized the undifferentiated attack on developing countries' export subsidies, considering that these subsidies largely serve to offset overvalued exchange rates and export disincentives from the domestic protective structure rather than to confer a net competitive advantage. He noted that these very measures had resulted from the process of moving from inward- to outward-looking policies in the 1960s and early 1970s, a process encouraged by the World Bank and bilateral aid agencies. The alternative route to the same end through complete import liberalization simply turned infeasible after the oil shock and world recession of the mid-1970s. Nonetheless, for the longer term Diaz-Alejandro advocated fuller integration of developing countries into the trading system through graduation, although he criticized the push for lib-

eralization of services as intrusive in sensitive domestic areas—as
shown by the notable absence of proposals for free trade in the
services of migrant labor.

Issues from the Past

Today's trade problems divide into two broad categories: unresolved problems from the past and emerging new areas of trade
conflict. This section discusses three major thematic issues from the
past: subsidies, safeguards, and adjustment assistance. The next section examines the product sectors with problems from the past (agriculture, textiles and apparel, steel, and automobiles), and the subsequent section considers new issue areas for the future (services,
trade-related investment, high technology trade, and tariff elimination).

Subsidies

An underlying cause of trade conflict is the (probably growing)
tendency of government intervention in economic activity. Gary Clyde
Hufbauer provides a comprehensive review of trade subsidy issues.[26]
He cites the upward drift of all subsidies relative to GNP in industrial
countries in the past three decades, noting that this ratio is lowest in
the United States, where it has declined since the late 1960s. Export
credits (generally subsidized) cover an average of approximately 45
percent of exports in Japan, France, and the United Kingdom, but
only about 10 percent in the United States, Germany, and Canada.
One school of thought (European) considers subsidies to be second-
best corrections to the market that should be penalized only when
they cause injury; another (US) considers them to be generally undesirable, efficiency-reducing distortions resulting from special interest groups. The Tokyo Round subsidies code is a compromise

---

[26] Gary Clyde Hufbauer, "Subsidy Issues After the Tokyo Round," chapter
10, this volume. This analysis is expanded in Gary Clyde Hufbauer and
Joanna Shelton-Erb, *Subsidies in International Trade* (Washington: Institute
for International Economics, forthcoming 1983).

between these two conceptions.[27] The code has two tracks. On the first, a country may impose "countervailing duties" against another country's "domestic" or export subsidies if they cause "material injury," a relatively high threshold of damage associated with falling sales and employment, rising import shares, and a price-depressing effect of imports. On the second track, there can be multilateral authorization of countervailing duties or other offsetting measures when the subsidy in question is clearly an export subsidy, even though the threshold of injury is low ("adverse effects") and the subsidizing country can avoid such action only by disproving that any such "adverse effects" exist—which is quite difficult to do.

By long GATT tradition, agricultural subsidies enjoy looser control, and their heavy use by the EC is near the top of the US agenda for future negotiations. They are not subject to remedy unless they garner "more than an equitable share of world trade" based on a "previous representative period" (GATT Article XVI:B), a condition difficult to demonstrate despite some tidying up of definition in the Tokyo Round.

The subsidies code allows differentiation for developing countries. In return, at least the United States expected (and from Brazil received) commitments to phase out export subsidies; but US acceptance (for foreign policy reasons) of an empty pledge by Pakistan and US acquiescence to Indian membership in the code with only a best-efforts commitment (following a skirmish on India's MFN rights) have eroded the substance of the developing-country commitment.

Export credit subsidies have been regulated in the OECD, and the subsidies code adopts by reference those limitations on interest rate subsidies. The OECD has recently raised interest rate floors and "graduated" the Soviet Union and other upper middle-income countries to the highest interest rate tier. Moreover, if long-term interest rates return to more normal levels, the current OECD rates would essentially eliminate interest subsidies. Other problems remain, however, notably the economically ludicrous practice of stating the interest rate floor without regard to the currency or its rate of inflation,

---

[27] The Tokyo Round subsidies code essentially represented a bargain whereby the United States accepted the general GATT practice of applying countervailing duties only when injury exists (a requirement previously absent under US "grandfather clause" rights) in exchange for European acceptance of the principle that subsidies, ostensibly for domestic purposes, are also subject to countervailing if they cause trade injury.

giving an advantage to the more inflationary countries (because a given nominal interest rate floor means a lower real interest rate for them).

Tax rebates are a source of contention. GATT practice of allowing rebates of indirect, but not direct, taxes gives the impression of unfairness to US exporters, considering the greater reliance on direct taxes in the United States than abroad. The DISC, declared an export subsidy by GATT, has been defended by the United States under the dubious argument that its total effect does not exceed the degree of stimulus to exports presented by other (for example, European) countries' overall tax practices.[28] This argument invites country harmonization to the lowest common denominator of trading practice and ignores the fact that the exchange rate—at least in principle—provides overall balance. At any time Canada and Europe could impose countervailing duties against the DISC, but so far they have preferred to hold the issue in abeyance for leverage against a strong US stand on their own subsidies. DISC is the American Achilles' heel in the debate on subsidies.

The definition of a "domestic subsidy" and an "export subsidy" remains a divisive issue. Upstream subsidies are another area of dispute, with the EC maintaining that subsidies on inputs (coking coal for steel, wheat for pasta) are not subject to countervailing if they do not reduce the price of the final product below the world price. Proper calculation of the size of a subsidy, if any, from state capital equity is another issue. A consensus is emerging that subsidies for general research are not troublesome but that major subsidy programs "targeting" new fields (biogenetics, semiconductors) are.

Hufbauer proposes that the agricultural subsidy standards be made equivalent to those for manufactures; that GATT parties develop a listing of domestic subsidies that are potentially subject to countervailing; and that countries agree to open up their administrative proceedings to petitioners from abroad to address the problem of export subsidies to third-country markets.

One conceptual issue warrants further comment. Implicitly, there is little agreement on whether countervailing duties against subsidies (and for that matter antidumping duties) are protective devices or whether they are legitimate measures for ensuring "fair" trade. Rodney Grey argues that the countervailing-antidumping issue is protec-

---

[28] In recent months, however, the Office of the US Trade Representative has made some gestures in the direction of modifications of DISC to make it more consistent with the GATT. *Washington Post*, 28 July 1982.

tionist-administered trade, and the European position broadly has been that US application of these instruments (at least on steel) amounts to protection.

But conceptually there need be no protectionist content to countervailing and antidumping. Indeed, their *absence* would invite protection in the system in the form of trade distortions implemented on the side of subsidization rather than import barriers. After all, the essence of protection is the distortion of the allocation of resources and production. Analytically, it is only the application of countervailing and antidumping measures in arbitrary and unqualified ways, including procedures that discourage foreign exports because of the threat of unfair application, that can make them "protectionist."[29] The conflict over perception of these measures as protectionist as opposed to legitimate is nowhere more visible than in the recent case of steel, as discussed below.

Safeguards

No subject stirred more heated debate at the conference than the issue of whether there should be a new safeguards code permitting "selective" application of protection against individual countries whose exports are causing injury. Alan William Wolff, a former deputy special US Trade Representative (USTR), presented a paper arguing that such a code, with appropriate controls, should be negotiated.[30]

Article XIX provides the only legitimate protective action under GATT.[31] This escape clause or "safeguard" provision allows protection, on an MFN basis, when an unforeseen increase in imports causes or threatens serious injury. The importing country must offer compensation to the exporting country by liberalizing other products, or else the exporting country may impose retaliatory protection.

Wolff describes the drift of US practice away from Article XIX since 1975 in negotiating orderly marketing agreements for specialty steel, leather footwear, and color television sets, and a voluntary

---

[29] The US practice, since 1974, of finding dumping when the sale is below average cost, though at the same price as in the supplier's domestic market, is essentially protectionist in that it fails to recognize that normal marginal-cost pricing practices may lead to price below average cost in a recession.

[30] Alan Wm. Wolff, "The Need for New GATT Rules to Govern Safeguard Actions," chapter 11, this volume.

[31] The Multi-Fiber Arrangement, which provides a form of international legitimacy to protection of textiles and apparel, involves an explicit waiver by all parties of their rights and obligations under GATT Article XIX.

export restraint on Japanese automobiles. Wolff notes that the EC has never used Article XIX much, resorting to other protective devices, and Japan has never used the clause because, in his opinion, its economy is already impenetrable to imports.[32]

Wolff enumerates the failures of Article XIX that have caused countries to avoid it. The article lacks multilateral procedures. It must be applied to all suppliers on an MFN basis, causing intense pressure for removal by a wide group of countries. The article calls for compensation or, lacking that, authorizes retaliation. Non-GATT agreements with exporters may appear less protective to the public. For EC members, Article XIX may mean awkward involvement of the EC Commission rather than state-to-state dealings.

Proper reform of Article XIX might bring the various protective measures back within the auspices of GATT. Opponents of reform fear that to be acceptable to some important countries it would necessarily have to legitimize more severe protection and they note that, at least at present, the article exercises moral suasion because of the stigma of applying safeguard protection outside its sanction. The debate is essentially whether the GATT should be altered to permit practices that seem to abound outside its domain, in an effort to apply "safeguards against safeguards," or whether it is better to leave a higher GATT standard observed substantially in the breach.

The crux of this debate is whether "selectivity" should be allowed and under what conditions. In the Tokyo Round, selectivity was an absolute precondition to a safeguards code from the standpoint of the Europeans; the United States was reluctantly prepared to accept it in order to bring the wide range of voluntary export controls and similar measures under international control; and the developing countries strongly resisted selectivity. Wolff argues that "selective actions can be more reasonable than MFN actions." He cites the case of footwear, when the EC insisted that US protection not extend to them because the problem was caused by East Asian countries. He argues that under a reformed system, the older, larger established suppliers and new entrants with minimal market shares should be able to have trade unaffected if they are not a cause of the problem.

It may be noted, however, that except under unusual circumstances, Wolff's defense of selectivity seems to give inadequate attention

---

[32] Wolff's perception of Japanese restrictiveness, which is widespread, is challenged by the papers by Saxonhouse and Cline. Cline, "Reciprocity," and Saxonhouse, "The Micro- and Macroeconomics of Foreign Sales to Japan," chapters 4 and 9, respectively, this volume.

to the concept of fungibility. If a product supplied by a traditional source is suddenly also offered by a new source, the two sources of supply are fungible (or substitutable); in economic terms there is no basis for distinguishing between them. In exceptional cases the products from alternative sources may not be close substitutes (for example, perhaps some low-cost footwear from developing countries and high-fashion footwear from Europe), but more typically substitutability does exist (steel from alternative sources, automobiles from Japan and those from Germany). To discriminate by source generally biases markets in favor of past suppliers, discriminating against new supply (usually from developing countries). And this discrimination is much more severe than that resulting from imposition of MFN quotas (although even they involve somewhat disproportionate cutbacks for the most rapidly growing suppliers because of reversion to market shares in a base period).

Export markets can usefully be viewed as a sort of "international commons." When this commons becomes overcrowded, there is no reason for the traditional suppliers to have prior claim to it at the expense of new suppliers. Moreover, selectivity removes broad-based pressures for avoiding the import restriction (and terminating it, once adopted), and it places the smaller countries with little retaliatory power at the mercy of larger countries or trading blocs. Commenting on Wolff's paper, Robert E. Baldwin saw greater danger in accepting selectivity than in allowing continuation of the current unsatisfactory situation. He noted that selective controls would eventually lead to more generalized protective régimes as other countries not discriminated against increased their exports. In sum, it would seem that at best selectivity should be approached as an evil, if a necessary one for successful negotiations, not as a desirable feature in its own right.

Wolff's prescription for a safeguards code includes objective criteria to determine when selectivity is appropriate, which could mitigate some of the concerns about the overall concept: rising market shares; the product differs from those not controlled, an attempt to deal with the problem of substitution; an equity clause would extend restrictions to other suppliers if they took advantage of the situation. But he considers the conditions set forth by the developing countries in the Tokyo Round for finally accepting selectivity to be too rigid. He also calls for multilateral surveillance, with a mandate for GATT to seek out and publicize all trade restraints; the continuation of compensation or sanctions against the safeguarding country; and comprehensive coverage of all safeguard-like measures.

There was virtual unanimity at the conference that safeguard actions should be regulated, and brought within the GATT. It is clear that the present nonsystem fosters protectionist actions undertaken without procedural restraints or any meaningful international surveillance. In short, there is a compelling need to develop "safeguards on safeguards." But there is also a strong risk that the wrong kind of new agreement on the topic would simply legitimize a large measure of the current, objectionable pressures—including a license to apply safeguards selectively.

The safeguards issue is a paradigm of a fundamental theme running through many other trade issues: is it strategically better for the system to attempt new negotiated agreements, or is the trade environment such that any new agreements capable of negotiation might make trade on balance more protected rather than liberalizing it?

Adjustment Assistance

Open markets are easier to maintain if there are credible alternatives to protection for cushioning the adjustment of domestic firms and workers to imports. Yet in the United States the traditional instrument for this purpose, trade adjustment assistance (TAA), has been virtually discarded.

J. David Richardson reviews US experience with TAA.[33] He finds that it worked relatively well in the early 1970s in terms of the equity goal of assisting displaced workers. However, he argues that by the late 1970s it had become discredited because it was acting as a vehicle more for political patronage than adjustment (as shown by the quadrupling of its budget to accommodate automobile workers just before the 1980 election) and thus that its budget did not survive a change in the governing party. But the conventional critique that TAA failed to promote adjustment is inaccurate. Richardson argues that certification for TAA acted as a signaling device to firms and workers to avoid entry into affected sectors. And adjustment would have been far worse under the alternative of protection.

Considering likely trends in the 1980s, Richardson anticipates a moderate increase in adjustment problems. High real interest rates may reduce human capital formation even as labor demand shifts toward greater human capital requirements. The robotics revolution may cause adjustment strain, though less than is commonly thought because it is likely to be dispersed across many sectors, avoiding concentration of displacement. Based on trends in capital income—

---

[33] J. David Richardson, "Worker Adjustment to US International Trade: Programs and Prospects," chapter 12, this volume.

an indicator of cross-sector differences in expansion—jobs may be expected to decline in low technology industries. However, demographics will be more favorable, with a decline in the 15-to-24 year age group and a deceleration of growth in the population above 65 years.

The market mechanism is not fully effective in promoting labor adjustment. Special programs for workers affected by trade are necessary, according to Richardson, because of the greater unanticipated shocks in trade-related sectors. One may add that special trade-related programs are needed to carry out income transfers that enable a political response permitting society at large to gain from more open trade. In view of possibly rising adjustment problems, Richardson recommends consideration of a new TAA program, with greater emphasis on adjustment and less on compensation than before. New approaches could include employment subsidies for workers permanently (but not temporarily) displaced by trade; loan and insurance programs for retraining permanently trade-displaced workers; and extension of unemployment benefits for workers displaced by trade, provided that their former firms and the remaining employed workers share the cost.

Agriculture

Trade problems from the past include conflicts in specific major product sectors. Of these, agriculture has faced perhaps the most chronic and severe protectionism. Dale Hathaway, a former under secretary for international affairs and commodity programs of the US Department of Agriculture, reviews trade issues in agriculture.[34] He first notes that trade in grains and meat has grown rapidly despite protection (especially in the EC and Japan); that export shares of developing countries have declined (except in cotton) while those of industrial countries have risen; and that the developing and the socialist countries have sharply increased their shares of food imports.

Hathaway attributes the old problems in agricultural trade to government intervention in agriculture in every market economy through price supports, purchase programs, health restrictions, and so forth, typically for the purpose of transferring income to farmers. These

[34] Dale E. Hathaway, "Agricultural Trade Policy for the 1980s," chapter 13, this volume. For a discussion of the late 1982 flare-up in the controversy between the United States and the European Community over agricultural subsidies, see chapter 22.

domestic programs inherently lead to trade restrictions (quotas, levies, tariffs, bans), yet GATT has failed to come to grips with the
domestic policies and has focused on the secondary (and hard to
measure) issue of the degree of distortion of world market shares.
Instead, Hathaway proposes outright recognition that countries will
intervene domestically and a search for rules on particular domestic
policy instruments that will reduce trade distortions. But he is not
optimistic, because countries are reluctant to subject domestic food
policies to international negotiations; and in any event he sees these
old problems as affecting a decreasing portion of trade.

New problems focus on the growing role of centralized state trade,
which is far more prevalent for agriculture than for manufactures.
Socialist countries are increasingly important buyers, as are state
entities in Japan and many developing countries. State selling agencies
control grain exports in Canada, Australia, and Argentina. In Hathaway's opinion state trading violates free market principles, and it is
outside the GATT.[35]

Government trading adds to the instability already caused by "old"
agricultural trade problems. Thus, recent price declines for grains
have reflected weakening demand as socialist and developing countries have less foreign exchange for food purchases, while the wheat
boards of Canada and Australia have expanded exports rather than
building stocks. Yet US attention has focused on blaming EC export
subsidies rather than recognizing the role of centralized trading. Both
the old and new distortions place the burden of adjustment to fluctuations on the few open systems left, especially that of the United
States.

Hathaway cites possible distortions from increasingly popular bilateral long-term agreements providing for a minimum guaranteed
level of sales, such as that between the United States and the Soviet
Union. Such agreements can impose the burden of adjustment to
fluctuations on nonparticipants. Hathaway recommends GATT discussions on acceptable practices under long-term agreements. He is
not sanguine about international commodity agreements, noting the
breakdown of the 1978–79 negotiations on wheat. The EC sought
world price supports to buttress its internal programs; the United

[35] If state planners used market signals, centralized trading would not
necessarily distort trade (although it would add an element of monopoly
power). But typically planners try to insulate domestic prices from world
market fluctuations, so that their actions do not parallel private market
results.

States, Canada, Australia, and Argentina sought price and trade stabilization agreements to spread the burden of adjustment and costs of stockpiling more evenly; middle- and low-income importers sought supply assurance and food aid, respectively. The conflicting goals led to stalemate.

Although Hathaway lays out the ideal action—negotiations on permissible *domestic* farm programs and introduction of GATT controls on long-term agreements and perhaps other aspects of state trading— he holds little hope of adoption of these reforms because of the political sensitivity of agriculture, not only from the political strength of the farm bloc but also because of the primacy of concerns about food security.

Textiles and Apparel

As in agriculture, protection has long been entrenched in textiles and apparel, an all-important sector for developing countries (accounting for 30 percent of their manufactured exports despite the pervasiveness of import controls). Martin Wolf reviews the experience of this sector, which has been under restrictive international agreements with GATT-excepted status for two decades.[36] In 1962 the United States led the creation of the international Long-Term Arrangement (LTA) on cotton textiles. The Kennedy administration owed the textile sector a reward for electoral support and acquiescence in the launching of the Kennedy Round; it sought to "share the burden" of textile imports with Europe; and it hoped to establish some room for growing developing-country exports in the face of still more protective legislation that threatened domestically. Wolf judges that the LTA worked relatively well: it treated new suppliers fairly generously and exempted many products, especially man-made fibers. In 1974, the MFA replaced the LTA; in it the United States secured coverage of man-made fibers and in exchange offered the promise of relatively liberal growth in quotas: 6 percent annually. A crucial feature of both the LTA and the MFA was that they restricted only the imports from developing countries (and, initially, Japan); the United States and Europe did each other the favor of exempting their own products from the quota restrictions, on the grounds that they did not create "market disruption," in one of the sorrier episodes of power-dominated international economic relations.

---

[36] Martin Wolf, "Managed Trade in Practice: The Implications of the Textile Arrangements," chapter 14, this volume.

By the time of the 1977 renewal of the MFA, recession had increased protectionist pressures in Europe, and the EC led the way toward tighter protection. The protective vice closed tighter in the 1981 renewal, which allows the quotas of dominant suppliers to be cut back, permits quota increases below 6 percent, and limits full utilization of previously underutilized quotas. In its new agreement with Hong Kong, the United States has allowed growth of only 0.5 percent annually on two-thirds of the items and no more than 2 percent annually on the others.

The economics of the sector would lead to a greater share of production in developing countries. It is labor intensive, accounting for 12 percent of employment but only 7 percent of output in manufacturing in the industrial countries. Import penetration is still modest; in 1979 imports from developing countries accounted for only 9.6 percent of consumption in the industrial countries, and even in the more affected subsector of clothing the figure was only 14 percent. Industrial countries dominate trade in textile yarns and fabrics, while the developing countries have managed to establish strong comparative advantage only in clothing, cotton and jute textiles, and knitted carpets.

The MFA has been effective in restricting trade, at least for the United States. There are fewer square-yard equivalents of textile and apparel imports into the United States today than in 1971. After the EC tightened restrictions in 1977, its imports from developing countries grew at only 2.2 percent annually. Ironically, for the EC, the MFA has not choked off textile imports but has diverted them from developing-country suppliers to the United States and Italy in particular. Total EC textile and apparel imports have grown at 10.3 percent annually since 1976. US textile imports have grown slowly, however, because high tariffs hold down imports from countries not covered by the MFA.

Based on detailed Canadian data, Wolf finds that the present discounted value over future years of the losses to society (after deducting transfers to producers) are $430,000 per textile job gained, whereas the maximum private cost of adjustment to the worker, if instead the job were sacrificed, is only $5,000 (Canadian dollars). Wolf's calculations do suggest, however, that free trade in textiles could require considerable adjustment: from 1980 to 1990 employment in the sector is not expected to rise in industrial countries, but it would fall by one-third if trade were freed.

Wolf concludes that the experience of textiles shows that a sectoral system of discriminatory practice can only develop in the direction of greater restrictiveness. The political dynamics forcing this trend are these: domestic producers are bought off by protection; exporters from industrial countries enjoy exemption from protection; and exporters from established developing-country suppliers enjoy the benefits of assured market share against newcomers. Only consumers and smaller, new developing-country suppliers lose. Wolf argues that the textile experience shows that new régimes such as a selective safeguards code should be avoided, because they will only increase the resort to protection through such measures.

Steel

Protection in steel is more recent than that in agriculture and textiles. Ingo Walter examines the economic forces that have led to steel protection in the United States and Europe.[37]

High wages demanded by monopoly labor, and the willingness of oligopoly firms to grant them in the expectation of passing on higher costs to consumers, have driven US steel wages from a level equal to the manufacturing average in the 1950s to 63 percent above the average in 1980, even while steel workers' productivity fell from 21 percent to only 3 percent above the manufacturing average during the same period. US firms, unable to attract much equity capital because of erratic earnings, have invested relatively little, leaving them with aging plants that have not incorporated important technological changes. Environmental and health costs absorbed 17 percent of capital outlays in the 1970s. And, according to Walter, management has been poor. For all these reasons, steel imports grew from 5 percent of US consumption in the 1950s to 18 percent in 1978, and in recent years US steel prices have averaged one-fourth to one-third above prices of imports from Japan and Europe.

The American steel industry has reacted by pressing for protection. With its large number of workers, geographical concentration, and the argument of national security importance on its side, it has political receptivity to protection; and with high fixed capital costs and little incidence of diversification in its firms, it has an incentive to seek protection rather than adjust. In 1968 through 1974 the United States imposed voluntary export restraints on Japanese and European steel. After brief liberalization, by 1976 the industry was pressing suits against foreign subsidies and dumping. To ward off these suits, the Carter administration devised the trigger price mechanism to

[37] Ingo Walter, "Structural Adjustment and Trade Policy in the International Steel Industry," chapter 15, this volume.

initiate fast-track investigations on foreign steel selling below a Japanese-based reference price, a measure that had some protective effect against efficient producers because of its increased risk to steel importers and the questionable nature of its "fair value" estimates.

Although the United States appears to have secured a freeze on imports from Japan, according to Walter (who notes that all sides deny such a tacit agreement exists), the TPM was a license to dump for the more inefficient European producers (whose costs are higher than the Japanese cost on which the trigger price is based). At the same time, recession and imports helped drive US steel production to only 43 percent of capacity by late 1982, and employment from 403,000 in 1970 to 285,000 in 1981. Imports had reached 26 percent of consumption by early 1982. The steel industry finally brought massive countervailing duty and antidumping suits in 1982 against firms in Europe and some other countries, causing the administration to end the TPM (as its predecessor had done briefly on a similar occasion in 1980) and calling forth bitter US-European trade conflict. Walter argues that the US industry's true purpose was to force the administration to obtain voluntary export quotas from Europe, which it finally did in October.

For their part, European countries have in the past sustained obsolete steel plants for social reasons, leading to operating losses and heavy subsidies. German firms and some small Italian producers have been efficient, but the nationalized steel industries of the United Kingdom, France, Italy, and Belgium have not. From 1975 through 1980 the EC progressively tightened controls on imports, prices (at first), and production (subsequently).

Japan's efficient production is a sharp contrast. It derives from large scale of operation (Japan had 34 blast furnaces with capacity over 2 million tons in operation or under construction in 1977, while the United States had only 3), construction after important technological changes had occurred (bulk carriers, basic oxygen furnaces, continuous casting, computer control), and the combination of deep-water ports with sharply falling transport costs in the 1960s. But Japan is already shifting to high value-added specialties, while comparative advantage is moving to new producers in developing countries (Korea, Taiwan, Brazil, Mexico) where costs of labor and raw materials are lower.

Walter argues that some adjustment is already taking place as production scales down in the United States and Europe and shifts to developing countries. In the longer run Walter foresees a leaner steel industry, with US production trimmed by approximately 20 percent and concentrated around the Great Lakes. He sees the medium-term pressures for protection as so strong, however, that he reluctantly concludes that an international steel agreement is needed to set rules of the game (including strict time limits on protection), despite the risks that it would turn into another MFA.

Walter does not address the alternative strategy of relying instead on the "fair trade" remedies of countervailing duties and antidumping. In principle these measures need not be "protectionist." In the recent US–EC conflict, the EC has claimed that countervailing duties should not be charged because the subsidies are for the purpose of reducing steel production and achieving adjustment, and the computation of subsidies from government-owned firms stands in considerable doubt. A more desirable solution to the steel problem than a new international agreement would be simply the implementation of countervailing duties and antidumping fees on a more widely agreed (and presumably less extreme) basis.

But instead the drama of steel has turned out in that most familiar of endings, the voluntary export restraint. In October 1982, member governments of the EC agreed to limit their exports of 11 carbon steel products and alloys to an overall average of 5.12 percent of the US market (a reduction from 6 percent) until December 1985—with specific subceilings for individual categories, as in the MFA. They also accepted in principle a ceiling of 5.9 percent market share on pipe and tube steel (where the EC market share in the United States is currently 11 percent), although an adamant Germany won a concession that this provision was not binding but instead subject to further negotiation. In return, the US steel firms dropped their legal complaints against European subsidies and dumping.[38]

The new agreement has helped soothe US-EC trade relations but holds potential for a far more protectionist outcome than would have been the result if normal countervailing and antidumping duties had been imposed. Already the EC has proposed that European steel imports be cut back by more than 10 percent in 1983 to make room domestically for steel displaced from the US market, passing the protectionist consequence along to countries such as Brazil and South Korea.[39] Already the US steel industry has announced a campaign to restrict imports from Japan on grounds that EC protection against Japan has diverted Japanese steel to the US market. In short, the initial steps toward a new régime of international quotas in steel seem well under way. Far from being a harmless substitute of one form of

[38] *Washington Post,* 22 October 1982.
[39] *Journal of Commerce* (October 25, 1982).

fair trade enforcement for another, the new quota arrangement seems highly likely to inaugurate a renewed period of more severe protection in steel.

Automobiles

The most recent major sector to join the ranks of protected trade is the automobile industry, long a redoubt of free trade (among firms and, until the mid-1960s, even labor). Robert B. Cohen examines the forces that have brought protection in the sector.[40]

The US share of world automobile production fell from 65 percent in 1965 to 20 percent in 1980, while Japan's share has surged from near zero to 27 percent, and that of semi-industrial countries (especially Spain, Brazil, Mexico, Poland, and South Africa) has risen from 2 percent to 15 percent. Western Europe has shifted from being a net exporter to a net importer of automobiles.

The share of compact cars in the US market has risen from 39 percent in 1972 to 66 percent in 1980. Given a sustained Japanese share of 40 percent in compact cars, imports from Japan have risen accordingly, to about one-fifth of total US consumption in 1981. Major retooling has been taking place for the downsizing of automobiles, requiring heavy capital outlays and establishing new and higher volumes as the threshold for efficient scale.

US producers have lost ground to the Japanese for several reasons. Labor costs per hour are twice as high in the United States as in Japan ($18.00 versus $9.00 per hour). Even if wages were identical, Japan would have an advantage because its labor requirements per car are much lower (90 man-hours per car compared to 140 man-hours in the United States).

High Japanese performance reflects special government and bank support to the industry in the 1960s, including special tax treatment and access to foreign exchange for technology and equipment. Late development facilitated use of modern technology. Labor relations are good; low-cost supply of components is available from small suppliers; and robotization has begun to cut labor costs. US firms, lulled by high profits in the 1960s and early 1970s, were slow to respond to the trend toward small cars. (It should be added that the distortion of low US gasoline prices during the mid-1970s contributed to this inadequate response.) In 1981–82 an undervalued yen and overvalued

---

[40] Robert B. Cohen, "The Prospects for Trade and Protectionism in the Auto Industry," chapter 16, this volume.

dollar made the competitive disadvantage of US automobiles even worse. One econometric study finds that the exchange rate changes from 1980 to 1981 alone caused an increase of US imports of transportation equipment by $4 billion.[41]

Cohen emphasizes that the basic strategic response of the US automobile industry to the Japanese challenge is to internationalize production. General Motors will rely on a Japanese partner to supply an entire line of compact cars. By 1983, one-third to one-half of all engines in US-produced automobiles will be from abroad, especially from Mexico and Brazil. Cohen notes that lower labor costs are not a major source of savings from these components. New plants do permit greater efficiency but, in addition, foreign export subsidies, tax concessions, domestic content rules, and other performance requirements play an important role in countries such as the United Kingdom, Mexico, and Brazil—raising important trade policy questions, which are addressed below in the discussion of trade-related investment issues. Internationalization of investment and production reflects the desire to establish strategic positions in regional markets and to enter large and attractive, but protected, markets in the newly industrialized countries (NICs). Cohen notes that the degree of future internationalization will depend on the degree of flexibility of domestic labor.

The 1981 US "voluntary" export restraint on Japanese automobiles, set at 1.68 million cars per year, followed the decision by the International Trade Commission that protection was not warranted under safeguard legislation because recession and changing taste, not imports per se, were the main causes of the industry's plight. Breaking with a free trade tradition, Ford Motor Company had requested a quota of 1 million cars. With both industry and labor pushing for protection, and given the importance of the automobile industry, policy escalated from the technical to the political track. New protection followed suit in Germany and other countries, and highly protective régimes already existed in Italy, France, and the United Kingdom.

Cohen suggests that imports could reach 45 percent of the US market by 1984 if the voluntary export restraints are lifted. The labor movement has spearheaded a new tier of protection against that day, in the form of proposed requirements of up to 90 percent in local

---

[41] Alan V. Deardorff and Robert M. Stern, "The Sectoral Impact of the Recent Appreciation of the US Dollar" (Ann Arbor: University of Michigan, 1982; processed).

content for automobiles sold in the United States. This measure would force Japan to cut back exports sharply. Estimates of the employment effects of the measure range from 800,000 jobs added or saved, according to the AFL-CIO, to approximately 150,000 jobs according to certain government studies. However, not even the low estimates take into account the loss of export jobs in other sectors that may be expected if Japan retaliates (or, although in smaller numbers, even if it does not retaliate but instead the yen declines further as its external balance is adversely affected). Automobile prices might rise by 10 percent, causing one-third of a percent increase in consumer prices; and the United States could be locked into inefficient production.

Cohen concludes that, despite intense protectionist pressures, the strong dynamic toward internationalization to maintain competitiveness will push the automobile industry toward a free trade policy in the medium- and longer-term, avoiding an MFA-type outcome in the industry. That judgment is supported so far by the opposition of industry leaders to the local content bill.[42] In testimony on the bill in September 1982, they focused on the importance of the yen-dollar exchange rate and opted instead for continuation of the "voluntary" restraints for another year. Although the local content bill did pass the House in the lameduck session of 1982, most observers doubted it could pass the Senate in the Ninety-eighth Congress.[43]

New Issues

The experience of the last two years has highlighted the fact that much unfinished business remains in the traditional issue and product areas despite progress in the Tokyo Round. In addition, new issue areas are gaining prominence. The final group of conference papers focused on services, high technology, investment, and tariff elimination.

[42] See testimony before the Subcommittee on International Trade of the House Ways and Means Committee, on September 24, 28, and 29, 1982 respectively, Phillip Caldwell of Ford Motor Company, Roger Smith of General Motors, and Paul Tibet of American Motors Company.

[43] Even the House bill included an amendment ruling out application of the law in a way contrary to international obligations (*Washington Post,* 16 December 1982). Considering that Article III, paragraph 5 of the GATT prohibits such "mixing" restrictions, the House version must be considered a defeat for the local content movement.

Services

William Diebold and Helena Stalson examine the services sector, a central concern of the United States in its call for new negotiations.[44] Services have remained largely outside GATT trading rules. Trading concerns center on insurance, accounting, consulting, design, advertising, transportation, communications, banking, motion pictures, art and music, legal and health services, and education.

The central problems in services are the denial of right to establishment and, once established, burdensome licensing and certification requirements, limits on the range of services that may be provided, requirements on nationality of employee, limits on foreign equity, and discrimination in government contracts, as well as more restrictive licenses and higher fees than for national firms.

Some international efforts to regulate trade in services already exist. GATT itself contains a clause (unfortunately allowing domestic quotas) on motion pictures. The government procurement code covers services linked to delivery of products. There is an OECD code on invisibles, though it is riddled with exceptions. The OECD also has committees dealing with shipping, telecommunications, insurance, tourism, and financial markets. International agreements have long governed shipping, aviation, and communications, and UNCTAD has been active on shipping (although its rules tend to restrict rather than liberalize trade). New negotiations in services would have to take these arrangements into account.

The central objective of the US initiative in services is to achieve international acceptance of the principle that trade in services, like trade in goods, should be liberalized. Diebold and Stalson suggest that there is less consensus about the gains from freer trade in services than there is about trade benefits in goods. There is uncertainty about which countries would stand to gain the most from liberalization. But the reasons to act now, they suggest, include not only a lengthy list of impediments to services trade compiled by USTR (and the authors recommend that foreign countries compile similar lists on US practices) but also the possibility that technological change will open up new service-trading opportunities that might be accorded free trade if action were prompt enough to precede the entrenchment of vested interests.

---

[44] William Diebold, Jr., and Helena Stalson, "Negotiating Issues in International Services Transactions," chapter 17, this volume.

The authors call attention to questions about the US initiative on services. They note that services linked to national security, such as communications, airport control, and even banking, are unlikely candidates for liberalization (at least in some dimensions). While judging the US market to be relatively open to trade in services, they recall US restrictions (American ownership of radio and telegraph services, limitation of coastal shipping to US vessels, possible restrictions in the construction industry).

Diebold and Stalson dwell on alternative approaches to negotiations. Considerable progress could be made by extension of the GATT code on technical standards. Alternative negotiating approaches include: application of the existing GATT, with a declaration that its principles apply to services, use of nullification and impairment, and use of the NTB codes; adoption of a new code for services; adoption of a "standstill" agreement to avoid new restrictions in services; establishment of a complaints procedure, with GATT authorized to collect complaints about barriers; improvement of the OECD efforts; and bilateral agreements.

The US government has concentrated much attention on liberalization of services. This emphasis reflects the fact that although trade in services is substantial, representing nearly one-fifth of world trade in goods and services (including capital earnings),[45] it remains outside the GATT even though it faces nontariff barriers similar to those in merchandise trade. Attention to services also reflects the emergence of new trade in services (such as apply to data transmission) and the likely rapid growth of services associated with high technology trade (as pointed out by discussant Bela Balassa). Finally, a tactical focus on services may reflect the fact that those who would oppose a new round of trade negotiations, on grounds that there is nothing left to negotiate after the Tokyo Round, cannot make this argument with respect to the important new areas it left largely untouched: services, high technology trade, and trade-related investment. These considerations notwithstanding, many experts have questioned the concentration of efforts for further extension of trade liberalization into new areas even while major protective barriers continue to plague the more traditional areas of trade in goods. Chapter 22 returns to this issue of negotiating strategy.

[45] According to discussant Bela Balassa, the Office of USTR estimates this share at 17.2 percent in 1980, compared with 16.8 percent in 1974.

Trade-Related Investment Issues

Trade can be distorted not only by tariffs and NTBs but also by investment decisions taken under the influence of incentives or requirements that distort trade. A. E. Safarian considers this emerging area of trade conflict.[46]

Many governments make their permission for entry or expansion by foreign firms conditional on performance requirements. Some of these, such as minimum export targets, maximum import ceilings, or limits on balance of payments effects, clearly affect trade. Others, such as those on technology transfer and job maintenance, may do so only indirectly. A 1977 survey by the Department of Commerce found that 14 percent of all US foreign investment, and 29 percent of such investment in developing countries, was subject to performance requirements.

But these data reflect the historical stock of investment and may understate current practices; one US industry-labor group maintains that 18 of the 20 largest recipient countries of US foreign investment levy performance requirements on exports and imports. Among industries, automobiles are especially affected, subjected first to import and local content restrictions and later to export requirements. Canada's Foreign Investment Review Agency (FIRA) is concerned with spurring Canadian ownership but its criteria for investment include additional exports and the use of local inputs. Much less transparent requirements in Europe typically include trade and balance of payments targets.

Some sectors are simply closed to foreign investment: defense, finance, transportation, media, and sometimes natural resources. Foreign firms also sometimes face discriminatory treatment relative to national firms in taxation, subsidies, access to local finance, government procurement, and regulation.

Government tax concessions, subsidies, tariff exemptions, and other incentives distort the country allocation of investment. In the Commerce Department survey, 26 percent of firms reported receiving such incentives. According to some studies, however, these incentives are not very effective in altering investment decisions, partly because of widespread competition among countries in offering them.

Countries impose requirements, discriminatory treatment, and incentives for several reasons. Many developing countries feel a need

---

[46] A. E. Safarian, "Trade-Related Investment Issues," chapter 18, this volume.

to offset perceived monopoly bargaining power of multinational corporations, for example, regarding corporate decisions to limit (or prohibit) exports by their foreign subsidiaries. Even in industrial countries, including the United States, foreign ownership is an issue. Some countries seek to capture markets without using more direct trade restrictions or violations; some generally pursue an interventionist ideology.

Among past international efforts to police investment requirements and incentives, the most successful is that among the members of the EC, although even there conflicts have existed (as in the insistence of France before 1980 on the right to reject corporate takeovers by partner-country firms). There are OECD codes on liberalization of capital movements and on investment by multinational firms, but they do not include the developing countries, lack effective sanctions, and have many loopholes.

Of various policy strategies possible, Safarian recommends extension of the GATT to cover trade-related investment issues (probably in a new code). Following the NTB experience, governments would submit lists of complaints about each others' practices and would then negotiate on what practices to eliminate. Safarian strongly recommends concentration on directly trade-related performance requirements and incentives (implying that those who see the next phase of negotiations as an occasion to break open foreign investment opportunities more generally may be asking too much considering the stout resistance that may be expected). He also suggests the industrial countries set their own house in order before pressing the developing countries to change their practices.

High Technology Trade

As industrial countries adjust to the loss of comparative advantage at the lower end of the technological spectrum (for example, clothing, footwear) they should in principle be moving on to new, technologically sophisticated products (the "product cycle" hypothesis). Yet many observers are concerned that because of preemptive government intervention, some industrial countries are staking out a larger share in future exports of these goods than would result from the workings of market based comparative advantage alone—despite the fact that the new high technology goods should be uniquely amenable to open trading régimes, because as "sunrise" rather than "sunset" industries they have not developed the vested interests in protection found in declining industries. John Diebold, of the Diebold Group,

Inc., considers policy toward the "information industry" as a case study of industrial and trade policy in high technology goods.[47]

Diebold defines the information technology industry as including semiconductors, office equipment, computers, telecommunications, and associated services (including information processing and programming). He estimates that in 1981 shipments of the industry reached approximately $170 billion in the United States, with a positive trade balance of $9 billion. Because of its pervasive implications for quality of products (for reasons including the use of computer control in production processes and the incorporation of minicomputers in products ranging from automobiles to sewing machines), Diebold considers the industry to be the key determinant of competitiveness in coming decades.

Japan, several European countries, and some developing countries have adopted conscious policies toward the information industry— often with arguments of an infant industry nature—while the United States has continued a laissez faire approach. Japan has had the most effective policy, reflecting a conscious decision that its comparative advantage lies in knowledge-intensive industries. The government, together with business, banks, and universities, has selected products for promotion, allocated tasks among firms, identified critical research needs, and implemented a multitude of small financial benefits. Whereas the US capital market lends to numerous small firms in new technology, in Japan government financial support has gone to large integrated firms that could use their "deep pockets" from earnings in other products to sustain low-cost penetration of foreign markets in new high technology products, as Diebold maintains occurred in the 16K and 64K RAM (random access memory) semiconductor chips.

France has had an active policy on high technology but has been much less effective in translating scientific advances into commercial success. In 1974 the government forced the sale of the telecommunications subsidiaries of IT&T and Ericsson (Swedish), completing French control of the industry. The government has obliged the public telephone and telegraph entities to buy large quantities of sophisticated new communications terminals to achieve large-scale production and low cost, although this program has proved to be overambitious. And a new French program in microcomputers could encounter falling world prices from rapid advances already made in this field.

---

[47] John Diebold, "The Information Technology Industries: A Case Study of High Technology Trade," chapter 19, this volume.

US policy toward high technology industry has been inadequate, in Diebold's opinion. Regulation has failed to keep pace with technology. New technology has outdated legislation from the 1930s making communications a monopoly industry. A 1956 legal decision kept American Telephone and Telegraph out of the computer business, while firms in foreign countries have been able to take advantage of equipment convergence in computers and telecommunications. US leadership in the space launch and satellite industry has eroded because of an absence of US industrial objectives compared with concrete industrial policies in Europe and Japan. Diebold maintains that, except for special cases such as the Boeing 707, US technological development from defense contracting is not a sufficient compensation for national policies abroad, because rigid design specifications for defense are inappropriate for commercial products.

Diebold argues for a more conscious US industrial policy in high technology goods. He cites the Apollo Space Project and the Communications Satellite program as examples of past US success that could serve as a model for future efforts. Aspects of the Japanese Ministry of Trade and Industry (MITI) approach could be incorporated, including administrative guidance and financial support. Experts could identify the crucial research needs in specific areas (for example, personal portable communications). A new policy would revise regulations in line with technological change. It would adjust antitrust guidelines to permit joint efforts in research and development. It could provide special depreciation incentives to take account of low profitability and the short product cycle in high technology goods. A new policy would review adequacy of patent protection (for example, in computer programs). Diebold urges that the United States press foreign governments to increase market access, and itself use countervailing and antidumping duties to ensure fair trade in US imports.

For other countries (especially developing countries), Diebold recommends careful consideration of the true costs of pursuing high technology goods and examination of their relation to comparative advantage. He also advocates a cut in the 17 percent EC tariff on integrated circuits (the level is 4 percent for the United States and Japan).

Diebold's essay raises the recurrent question of whether the United States should have a conscious industrial policy. It also at least suggests that the effect of such policies abroad is to protect foreign markets from US exports and unduly promote foreign export penetration into the US market. One approach is to respond in kind with new US industrial policies; another (not completely alternative) is to seek new international understandings on what constitutes acceptable trade practice in high technology industries.

Tariff Elimination

All trade negotiations in the past have included tariff reductions. Even though post-Tokyo Round tariffs are low on average, there might still be significant economic gains from further liberalization and it might be useful in terms of political dynamics for a future negotiation to incorporate complete elimination of tariffs. Deardorff and Stern examine the economic implications of tariff elimination.[48]

They first emphasize that tariffs, though low, have a considerable dispersion, with high tariffs in sectors such as textiles, wearing apparel, and footwear, so that in many cases effective protection (protection on value added as opposed to raw material inputs) can be relatively high. They also emphasize that today NTBs provide considerably more protection than tariffs and that many of the most severe NTBs were not liberalized in the Tokyo Round.

Deardorff and Stern apply their previously developed quantitative trade model to estimate the effects of tariff elimination, and conclude that the result would be an increase of 3.9 percent in total trade, although the exports of developing countries would change little.[49] The gross change in employment (shifted from existing jobs because of increased imports) would range from 0.16 percent of the labor force in the United States to 0.85 percent in Europe. Economic welfare would rise on balance by over $600 million annually at 1976 prices, although some countries would experience welfare losses because of changes in terms of trade or input costs. (Freer trade would tend to raise prices of traded goods because of increasing demand for them, and these changes would not be uniform across industries and countries.) However, the estimates capture only the static welfare effects, and dynamic effects (stimulus to investment and technological

---

[48] Alan V. Deardorff and Robert M. Stern, "The Economic Effects of Complete Elimination of Post-Tokyo Round Tariffs," chapter 20, this volume.

[49] However, the latter finding was rejected by Balassa in his commentary, partly on the basis of his analysis that tariff protection by industrial countries on industrial goods imported from developing countries was about twice as high as suggested by the aggregate data, and because he considered export supply elasticities of developing countries to be much higher than assumed in the Deardorff-Stern model.

change, for example) could be larger. Consumer prices would decline slightly.

For the United States, job increases from tariff elimination would be concentrated in agriculture, transport equipment, chemicals, and machinery. Job losses would be concentrated in textiles and apparel, and employment would decline in nontradable sectors as consumers shift demand to imported goods. Overall, however, employment effects would be relatively small.

The broad implication of the Deardorff-Stern study is that the impact of tariff elimination would be relatively small because tariffs are already low. These results confirm the widespread impression that it is nontariff barriers, not tariffs, that pose the major obstacle to trade today. Indeed, the major argument against an elimination of tariffs is that it would prompt the initiation of new (or intensification of existing) NTBs to substitute for them. Again, there arises a central theme: does negotiation of *gross* trade liberalization really produce *net* trade liberalization, or is policy in this area sufficiently fungible that new barriers quickly replace—or even exceed—old ones under current conditions?

Policy Implications

Jagdish Bhagwati, Richard Cooper, and W. Max Corden derive policy inferences in their panel concluding the conference.[50] Reaffirming the desirability of an open trading régime, especially in light of the postwar record of the contribution of trade to growth (including in the South), Bhagwati emphasizes three themes. On MFN versus selectivity, he maintains that amending GATT Article XIX to permit selectivity would undermine the current ability of OECD policymakers to resist protectionist pleas on grounds of their violation of GATT. On reciprocity and subsidies, he notes that economists' traditional complacence over any bargains foreigners might wish to offer failed to consider systemic effects. Subsidies and dumping distort world efficiency. They offend the sense of fairness, inviting protectionist response. The threshold of tolerance to unfair trade has been declining, and, according to Bhagwati, there is an implicit social contract whereby efficiency gains from outside the society are rejected despite their benefits to some groups if they come at the expense of

---

[50] "Toward a Policy Synthesis: Panel Discussion," chapter 21, this volume.

serious losses by other groups—while such gains are accepted if they come from inside.

Immigration policy is a prime example. At the minimum policy analysts must reject arguments that can be used by special interest groups in this area, such as the fallacy that because ex post a bilateral deficit exists with Japan the general complaints against invisible Japanese barriers must be true. More subtly, tempting arguments that subsidies are tolerable also open a Pandora's Box because of the difficulty of drawing the line around what is acceptable.

Finally, on the new issues Bhagwati recognizes that, because its comparative advantage is shifting away from manufacturing toward services, for the United States liberalization in this area could be attractive. But he is wary of premature negotiations, in view of the intensity of national political concerns (as the taboo on migrant labor as an item for services negotiations illustrates). Instead, he would concentrate efforts on reestablishing GATT norms in textiles and apparel and in agriculture, and on encouraging the newly industrializing countries to move toward reciprocity in reducing their own barriers. Efforts should focus on righting old lapses, not extension of GATT into new areas.

W. Max Corden criticizes US and European paranoia on Japan, especially in the tendency to base policy on bilateral trade balances. He notes that the world should be appreciative of Japan's high savings rate, which helps keep world interest rates down although it causes a high current account balance. On exchange rates he concludes that patience is necessary to await the eventual corrections, and that attention must be paid to fundamental correction through fiscal and monetary policy. Nonetheless, he attributes the bulk of protection to domestic recession, not exchange rate misalignment. Accepting the need to temper free trade ideology with realism, Corden sees three alternative strategies: adoption of complex rules to eliminate current loopholes—as favored by the United States but resisted by Europe and Japan; decentralized complex negotiations leading mainly to bilateral bargains; and, his preferred option, simple rules. He proposes his own: abolition of quotas, voluntary export restraints, and tariffs; permission of subsidies except those that obviously distort trade; and allowance of only temporary and transparent safeguards.

Richard N. Cooper contends that the approaches represented by the conference are too incrementalist. He attributes protectionist pressure to global recession and, more fundamentally, to the growing trend of the public to hold the government responsible for economic conditions. One partial solution would be to reduce public expectations. Seeking a less incrementalist approach, Cooper advocates free trade in industrial products, perhaps with highly constrained escape clauses, among all interested countries. He defends conditional MFN policy (but not aggressive reciprocity) as a means of overcoming the free rider problem and extending open trade for a subgroup of countries beyond the limits accepted by general GATT membership. On generalized preferences he favors limitation to only the poorest countries. In services he sees such a disparate category of activities, with many already covered by one régime or another, that a piecemeal approach is necessary instead of a broad negotiation, although multilateral fact-gathering would be useful. Finally, Cooper urges movement toward an exchange rate régime involving target zones.

In the concluding chapter of this volume, C. Fred Bergsten and I attempt to develop a trade policy strategy for the 1980s based on the analysis of the Conference.[51] We first outline a blueprint for a "constrained ideal" of the trading system in the 1980s. This ideal calls for an immediate standstill on any new protection and gradual phasedown of existing protection. GATT should be strengthened, with its staff increased and with a specific mandate to compile and publicize existing trade barriers. A major round of new trade negotiations should be launched, dealing with both the unresolved issues from the past and new issue areas. Developing countries should be incorporated more fully into the trading régime, with liberalization of their own imports in exchange for industrial-country liberalization in products of vital interest to them, including textiles and agriculture. Subsidy policy should provide a clearer demarcation of practices that are permissible and those that are not; remedies should be administered in a way that enforces fair trade but does not go further toward actual protection; and agricultural subsidies should be treated like those in manufacturing. Any new safeguards code should have strict multilateral controls on selectivity (including agreement by the exporting country) and provisions for the phasing down of protection within a specific time period. Safeguard protection should be in the form of tariffs, not quotas or voluntary export restraints, and the revenue of these tariffs should be earmarked for adjustment programs in the industry in question.

The constrained ideal for the 1980s includes a move in agriculture toward restructured domestic farm programs that cause minimum interference with international trade, for example by reliance on income maintenance, acreage set-asides, or other programs rather than

---

[51] C. Fred Bergsten and William R. Cline, "Conclusion and Policy Implications," chapter 22, this volume.

on price supports that cause surplus production and result in the subsidization of exports. New norms for state trading would also be desirable. In textiles and apparel, the trade régime of the late 1980s should move toward dismantling of the MFA. Safeguard protection in textiles and apparel would then face the same tests (such as injury) and time limitations expected of all other industries. Such safeguard protection as remained would move to an MFN basis instead of being concentrated on developing countries. In steel, the challenge will be to avoid a new MFA-like régime of quotas, and to phase out the recent US quotas against the European Community. In automobiles, efforts to establish local content requirements should be resisted; and quotas against Japan should be phased out in the United States, the European Community (especially in France, Italy, and the United Kingdom, where protection is the most severe), and Canada.

The constrained ideal would include a new régime for services, probably on the basis of new codes regulating nontariff barriers. It would include new rules of the game limiting investment performance requirements that distort trade. It would encompass a broader understanding among nations about the types of industrial policies that are acceptable, especially those affecting high technology industries. And in the constrained ideal, all tariffs would be eliminated, addressing the problem of trade distortion through tariff escalation.

To achieve the transition to a reformed international trading régime, Bergsten and I propose a four-point program.

First, there would be an immediate standstill on further protection. Violators would be obliged to extend compensation or face retaliation. The GATT trade ministers would meet annually to review the standstill. For its part, in order to adhere to the standstill, the United States would implement adjustment assistance rather than new protection whenever escape clause actions were in order under US law.

Second, the major nations would agree to launch a new Multilateral Trade Negotiation. Trade policy has the unstable dynamics of a bicycle: either it moves forward toward greater liberalization or it topples over into protection. The presence of a negotiation enables authorities to respond to protectionist requests with the argument that the problems in question are under negotiation. More fundamentally, broad negotiations will be required to achieve the broad reform outlined here. The new MTN should address both the old issues, including trade conflict in agriculture, textiles and apparel, steel, and automobiles, as well as the new issues: services, high technology trade, and trade-related investment issues. Tariff reductions (perhaps with negotiations on the phasing of their elimination) should be included as a familiar staple of negotiations.

Third, a revitalized program of adjustment assistance is essential if US trade policy is to remain open. It could be financed at least in part from tariff revenues, including those from tariffs imposed for safeguard protection. Nontariff barriers should be converted to tariffs for this purpose. Improved adjustment programs are required, more focused on labor adjustment and less susceptible than in the past to political manipulation.

Fourth, policy making in trade and in international money should be linked. Misaligned exchange rates cause protectionist pressure. Domestic policy-making bodies in the respective spheres of trade and monetary policy should coordinate their decision-making processes, as should the GATT and the International Monetary Fund. International monetary reform in the direction of "reference" exchange rates or "target zones" is also probably necessary.

The GATT Ministerial meeting in November 1982 could have inaugurated a far-reaching program such as this. But the prevailing mood, and especially the European Community's, was that given high unemployment no significant new initiatives toward liberalization could be undertaken. The ministers did achieve a mild standstill agreement, pledging to avoid new restrictions that violate international rules; but the commitment contained no enforcement mechanisms. The ministers agreed to develop a safeguards code in special negotiations through 1983. Falling far short of US objectives of policing agricultural export subsidies, they agreed merely to establish a committee to carry out a two-year study on agricultural issues. And, salvaging at least a remnant of the centerpiece of the US program, they agreed that GATT would coordinate preliminary studies by industrial countries on trade in services. The ministerial yielded no results at all on investment issues, high technology trade, and the new round of North-South negotiations that had been proposed by the United States.

Our concluding chapter proposes reconvening the GATT Ministerial by 1984 or early 1985, to review progress on the modest set of agreements reached in November 1982 and, more importantly, to initiate in earnest the type of program for major trade reform outlined here.

PART I

The Setting

Historical, institutional, and conjunctural factors condition the prospects for trade policies in the 1980s. C. Fred Bergsten and I examine the general background to trade policy in chapter 2, focusing on the theoretical basis for open trade, trends in protection, its costs, and the forces favoring protection on one hand and liberalization on the other. Exchange rate misalignment is a special cause of protectionist pressure that has emerged periodically in the last decade. In chapter 3, C. Fred Bergsten and John Williamson examine the relationship between exchange rate misalignment and protectionist pressure, and set forth a concept of fundamental equilibrium exchange rate that involves conscious policy measures (particularly, coordination of national monetary and fiscal policies) to guide the market rate back toward the equilibrium rate when the two diverge.

An important recent movement that must be taken into account as part of the policy environment is the push for "reciprocity" in trading relations. Fostered by the perception that foreign markets are more closed than the home country markets, this approach would use the threat of new protection to force liberalization abroad. This approach has been introduced in numerous recent bills submitted to the US Congress, and even in the United Kingdom officials have cited it as justification for considering new restrictive measures against several countries.[1] In chapter 4, I examine this policy approach.

The institutional environment is a major factor determining the prospects for trade policy. The General Agreement on Tariffs and Trade (GATT) is under criticism for ineffectiveness, most lately because of the limited progress achieved at the November 1982 GATT ministerial meeting. In chapter 5, John Jackson, a noted legal scholar in international trade, examines the capacity of GATT to deal with trade conflicts, and in particular the workings of GATT machinery

---

[1] Including the United States, Japan, South Korea, Spain, Brazil, and East Europe. *Journal of Commerce*, 2 November 1982.

after the new codes negotiated in the Tokyo Round. Harald Malmgren, formerly a Deputy US Special Trade Representative, completes
the review of the institutional setting with a discussion, in chapter 6,
of the current threats to the multilateral system, and of the structural
forces causing these threats.

Altogether the panorama of the political economic environment
for trade policy is sobering. The greatest underlying threat stems from
the severe global recession and the protectionist pressures stirred by
high unemployment. Even so, in a historical perspective the international trading régime remains relatively open. The challenge to
policymakers is to halt the erosion of this openness that began in the
mid-1970s, and to shore up and extend the coverage of this open
trading régime.

CHAPTER **2**

Trade Policy in the 1980s: An Overview

C. Fred Bergsten and William R. Cline

As Western policymakers face decisions that may set the course of trade relations for the rest of this decade, and beyond, most remain committed to the principle of an open trading system (as reaffirmed once more at the Versailles summit). The major contribution of trade liberalization to postwar economic growth is generally accepted. From 1950 through 1975, merchandise trade of the industrial countries grew at an average of 8 percent annually in real terms, acting as a leading sector to help produce historically high real growth rates of GDP averaging 4.4 percent.[1]

An important reason for the rapid growth in trade flows was the liberalization achieved in successive rounds of trade negotiations, including the Dillon Round in 1960–61 and the Kennedy Round in 1964–67 (which cut tariffs by about one-third). The formation of free trade areas in Europe (the European Economic Community, EEC, and the European Free Trade Association, EFTA) liberalized trade dramatically for the member countries, and also expanded world trade generally (since most analyses show that their trade creation exceeded their trade diversion).[2] The Tokyo Round of trade negotiations (1973–79) not only cut tariff's further but established important new codes for the elimination (or regulation) of nontariff barriers—such as discriminatory government procurement and application of technical

---

[1] William R. Cline, "Long-Term Changes in Foreign Trade Policy of the United States," in US Congress, Joint Economic Committee, *Special Study on Economic Change: Vol. 9, The International Economy: US Role in a World Market* (Washington: Government Printing Office, 1980), p. 189.

[2] See for example Bela Balassa, ed., *European Economic Integration* (Amsterdam: North-Holland, 1975), ch. 3.

standards, and subsidization of exports. Just as the waves of protectionism in the 1930s (which carried the average US tariff to 50 percent) prolonged and deepened world depression, postwar trade liberalization helped stimulate growth.

The Issues

Only three years after the conclusion of the Tokyo Round, however, the pressures for protectionism are high and, in the opinion of some, higher than at any other time in the postwar period.[3] Despite its clear adherence to market principles and thus free trade, even the Reagan administration in the United States in its first two years in office took substantial trade restrictive steps in four major industries: autos, textiles, sugar, and steel. Record postwar levels of unemployment, increasingly fierce competition from Japan and the newly industrializing countries (NICs) and exchange rate misalignments are among the factors cited by those seeking to limit the growth of world trade—or even roll it back. It has been suggested often that world trade policy is "at a crossroads," but such a characterization of the early 1980s may be reasonably accurate. To provide background for analysis of the wide range of trade policy issues examined in the conference, this study outlines the evolution of the international trading system in recent years, reviews the premises underlying trade policy in the past three decades, and evaluates the force of the pressures pushing both toward and against protectionist approaches in the current setting.

The Case for Free Trade

One reason why officials have remained committed to liberal trade in principle, despite strong protectionist pressures, is that the grounding of free trade in economic theory is relatively well understood. The basic case for free trade remains the same as formulated two centuries ago by Adam A. Smith and, later, David Ricardo: by the law of comparative advantage, it benefits nations to produce domestically the goods in which they are relatively more efficient and to import those goods in which they are relatively less efficient. Essentially, free trade provides a wider array of products from which to choose, and lower real costs than if all products were produced

---

[3] As judged, for example, by US Trade Representative William S. Brock and several private sector experts. *Wall Street Journal,* 5 January 1982.

only at home. This fundamental point is obvious when imports of bananas or coffee into the United States are considered, but it also applies to the whole range of goods (and services). The opportunity for lower priced supply through imports became especially germane in the 1970s, when inflation became a pervasive problem throughout the world.

There are other elements in the economic argument for free trade. Economies of scale are easier to achieve through production for an international market (as with aircraft and computers), especially for smaller countries. The output-suppressing and price-raising distortions of monopoly power are tempered by the competition provided from imports in an open trading régime. The incentive to adopt new technology and the pressure to achieve greater efficiency generally are greater if the industry is exposed to the rigors of international competition (*X*-efficiency).

The only generally recognized theoretical arguments against free trade on economic grounds are those concerning the need to develop important industries, and the use of an optimal tariff to improve a country's terms of trade (export price relative to import price) through depressing demand for the foreign country's product. But most industries in the industrial countries can hardly claim infant status, since scale and capital markets in those countries are sufficient to obviate the need for government intervention, and even in developing countries the argument has more often been abused than used wisely.[4] And optimal tariff protection is generally regarded as either not applicable (small countries) or not feasible without provoking foreign retaliation that in the end leaves both countries worse off than before.[5]

There are also three quasi-political arguments against free trade. One is the straightforward case for protecting industries that are essential for national security purposes. A second is social risk aversion; a country may wish to insure against fluctuations by ensuring a domestic food supply through protection, for example (although if the country or grouping is large enough that such policies lead to disruption of external markets through subsidized exports of resulting

---

[4] See for example Anne O. Krueger, *Foreign Trade Régimes and Economic Development: Liberalization Attempts and Consequences* (Cambridge, Mass.: Ballinger, 1978).

[5] Harry Johnson's case, whereby the protecting country is better off even after foreign retaliation, requires special assumptions about the country's trade elasticities that are unlikely to apply. Harry G. Johnson, *International Trade and Economic Growth,* (Cambridge, Mass.: Harvard University Press, 1967).

surpluses, the nation may expect foreign retaliation). The third is the case for erecting (or maintaining) barriers in sectors where such barriers exist in other countries in an effort to force liberalization abroad. As set forth in the conference paper on reciprocity (chapter 4, this volume), however, such protection carries direct welfare costs, runs considerable risk of foreign retaliation, and can easily be abused as an excuse for outright protectionism.

Several important assumptions must, however, be met in practice to validate the standard conceptual case for free trade.[6] Prices must accurately reflect social opportunity costs. An important possible violation of this assumption occurs when there is unemployment. With unemployment, the social opportunity cost of domestic resources employed in producing the protected good may be sufficiently low that elimination of protection does not achieve the standard benefit from reallocation of scarce resources (instead, the resources released may go unutilized). It does not necessarily follow, however, that protection is appropriate if there is unemployment. Macroeconomic tools may be more appropriate for addressing unemployment than is protection, which tends to get locked in for long periods. Even in the face of protracted unemployment, protection may be a poor remedy because it invites counter-protection by foreign countries, leading to a downward spiral in demand and activity in the export sector and worsening the problem of unemployment itself (as in the Great Depression).

Another assumption of the standard case is that the income distribution effects of free trade have been resolved satisfactorily. Trade liberalization benefits the factors used intensively for exports and hurts those used intensively for production of import substitutes. Because free trade offers net gains for the nation as a whole, it is potentially possible to redistribute income so that any losses to one factor are offset by compensation paid from the gains of another factor. In the case of industrial countries, free trade tends to benefit skilled labor, injure unskilled labor, and have favorable effects on capital (or ambiguous effects on capital, given the Leontief paradox for the United States).[7] If adequate provision for compensation is

---

[6] See Richard N. Cooper, "Economic Assumptions of the Case for Liberal Trade," in C. Fred Bergsten, ed., *Toward a New World Trade Policy: The Maidenhead Papers* (Lexington, Mass: Lexington Books, 1975), pp. 19–32.

[7] Leontief found that, contrary to theory, US exports relied more heavily on labor inputs while US imports relied more heavily on capital imports, despite the greater abundance of capital than of labor in the United States.

not made, free trade may be questioned on grounds of distributional equity, given the lower income level of unskilled labor than of skilled labor and owners of capital.

Similarly, the case for trade liberalization assumes that the present discounted value of factor adjustments to freer trade is less than that of the benefits of liberalization. Most analyses suggest that liberalization benefits far exceed adjustment costs. For example, in the Tokyo Round the present value of liberalization benefits was an estimated 50 times as large as labor adjustment costs for the United States, and as high as 100 times for Japan.[8] It is at least possible, however, that liberalization benefits would not exceed adjustment costs. Both for the purpose of reducing adjustment costs by making factors more mobile, and to address the issue of distributional equity, programs of adjustment can play a vital role in bringing reality closer to the standard assumptions underlying the case for free trade.

Equilibrium in the balance of payments is another underlying assumption of the case for free trade. In today's environment of flexible exchange rates, this translates into an assumption of equilibrium relationships among currencies. Free trade merely heightens distorted resource allocation when the exchange rate is seriously overvalued or undervalued for an extended period of time, as will be elaborated below and in chapter 3, this volume.[9]

Cost and Transfers from Protection

The empirical side of the case for free trade is the high cost of existing levels of protection to consumers as well as the substantial net welfare cost to the economy even after allowing for the benefits to producers of higher prices. Table 2.1 summarizes various recent estimates of consumer costs and net welfare costs imposed by protection. Systematic and comprehensive estimates of the costs of pro-

---

W. W. Leontief, "Factor Proportions and the Structure of American Trade: Further Theoretical and Empirical Analysis," *Review of Economics and Statistics*, vol. 38 (Nov. 1956), pp. 342–97. However, subsequent researchers have found that if skilled labor (which the United States does have in abundance) is separated from unskilled labor, this paradox disappears.

[8] W. R. Cline, et al., *Trade Negotiations in the Tokyo Round* (Washington: Brookings Institution, 1978), pp. 232–33. In chapter 14 of the present volume, Martin Wolf cites alternative estimates for Canadian textiles that are in the same range.

[9] C. Fred Bergsten and John Williamson, "Exchange Rates and Trade Policy," chapter 3, this volume.

TABLE 2.1 COSTS OF PROTECTION

Country	Source	Product	Restriction
United States (1975–77)	Crandall	sugar	1977 variable tariff
	Crandall	carbon steel	1976 quota on specialty steel
	Crandall	meat	
	Crandall	TV sets	a.
	Crandall	footwear	a.
	Wolf (1981)	textiles:	tariffs
	Wolf (1981)	textiles:	quotas
	Cline et al. (c. 1977)	all	tariffs cut in Tokyo Round
	Magee (c. 1971)	all	all tariffs
	Magee	oil, sugar, textiles, steel, meat, dairy	quotas
European Community	World Bank	agriculture	common agricultural policy
Sweden	World Bank	shipbuilding	subsidies
Japan	World Bank	beef	quotas

n.a.   Not available.
Sources: Robert W. Crandall, "Federal Government Initiatives to Reduce the Price Level", *Brookings Papers on Economic Activity* 1978:2, p. 431; W.R. Cline, *et al.*, *Trade Negotiations in the Tokyo Round* (Washington, DC: Brookings Institution, 1978), p. 230; Stephen P. Magee, "The Welfare Effects of Restrictions on U.S. Trade", *Brookings Papers on Economic Activity* 1972:3, p. 666–73; Martin Wolf, "Textile Pact: The Outlook", *New York Times*, Jan. 12, 1982; and World Bank, *World Development Report 1981*, p. 33.
a. Initial US ITC recommendations. Actual orderly marketing agreements negotiated not subject to comparable analysis.
b. Estimate is 78 percent of corresponding gains for 60 percent tariff cut.
c. At 1977 prices, inflated by US wholesale price index.

tection are not available, but these analyses suggest that the costs are significant. In the late 1970s US consumers paid approximately $12 billion annually as the result of protection on textiles alone and European consumers paid an even larger amount (at current prices) because of higher agricultural prices (and taxes to finance subsidies) attributable to the EEC Common Agricultural Policy. Although protection is usually imposed for the purpose of protecting jobs, Table 2.1 shows that the consumer costs per job saved are typically quite high—on the order of $50,000 and more in 1977 prices.

	Annual costs (million dollars)		Consumer cost per job
	Consumer	Welfare	
	660	57	n.a.
	1,254	106	62,700
	400–800	5–19	n.a.
	500	116	54,526
	1,200	75	57,143
	9,000	n.a.	n.a.
	2,000–4,000	n.a.	n.a.
	n.a.	1,300 gain[b] static	n.a.
		6,700 gain[b] total	
	n.a.	890[c]	n.a.
	n.a.	6,400[c]	n.a.
	11,000	n.a.	n.a.
	n.a.	n.a.	50,000
	(consumer pays eight times world price)		n.a.

Welfare costs to the economy as a whole are lower than consumer costs of protection, because much of the consumer cost is merely a transfer from consumers to producers. However, the welfare costs of protection are also large. At 1977 prices, Magee's estimates of welfare costs of US protection in 1971 amount to over $7 billion yearly.[10] In their analysis of Tokyo Round tariff cuts, Cline, Kawanabe, Kronsjo, and Williams estimated the resulting annual welfare gains at nearly $7 billion for the United States (including not only static gains but also dynamic effects and induced macroeconomic effects from an improved trade-off between inflation and unemployment).[11]

[10] Stephen P. Magee, "The Welfare Effects of Restrictions on US Trade," *Brookings Papers on Economic Activity 1972:3,* pp. 645–701.

[11] Note however that other authors, focusing on static welfare effects, have calculated smaller gains. See Robert E. Baldwin, "Trade and Employment Effects in the United States of Multilateral Tariff Reductions" (Washington, 1975; processed); and A. V. Deardorff and Robert Stern, "An Economic Analysis of the Effects of the Tokyo Round on the United States and

The scant evidence available on import prices also suggests that direct savings are available to consumers from relatively low-priced imports. On the basis of a sample survey carried out by the Survey Research Center of the University of Illinois, Cline calculated that in 1978 imports of consumer merchandise (excluding autos) from Asia and Latin America were cheaper than domestic US products of comparable quality by an average of 16 percent. The difference ranged as high as 24 percent for footwear and 30 percent for television sets, goods subject to quotas that prevented American consumers from buying as much as they wished. The study concluded that, including imports from all areas, import prices averaged 10.3 percent below domestic US prices, providing consumers a direct saving of over $2 billion annually without considering the extra costs that would occur from increased prices of domestic goods if import supply were curtailed).[12]

In sum, although the empirical estimates are imperfect, the available evidence indicates that the consumer and welfare costs of existing protection are substantial, and that there are important direct consumer benefits from the availability of relatively low-priced imported goods. Correspondingly, the trade liberalization achieved in the Tokyo Round provided significant welfare gains.

In addition, all of these estimates substantially understate the potential consumer and welfare benefits from trade liberalization. As discussed below, history reveals that trade policy is additional restrictions as well as the benefits from reducing the tariff or nontariff barriers themselves. These "opportunity gains" cannot be quantified, of course, but probably add substantially to the economic benefits from trade liberalization.

Trends in Trade Policy

Despite these analytical conclusions, however, and despite the broad trend toward trade liberalization during most of the postwar period, there have been interludes of renewed protection and even more

---

the Other Major Industrialized Countries," MTN Studies, no.5, Subcommittee on International Trade, Finance Committee, US Senate, 96th Cong., 1st sess., June 1979.

[12] William R. Cline, *Imports and Consumer Prices: A Survey Analysis* (Washington: American Retail Federation, 1979), pp. 19 and 27. The survey examined a total of 4,300 observations on 168 products with detailed specifications, in four US cities.

extensive episodes of protectionist pressures—particularly in the early 1980s.

The most conspicuous sector is that of textiles and apparel. The Long Term Arrangement (LTA) had regulated trade in cotton textiles since 1962, when it was adopted in the face of import competition from Japan and some developing countries (in part, as a quid pro quo for for US textile industry's acquiescence in the legislation authorizing US participation in the Kennedy Round). By 1974, the successor Multi-Fiber Arrangement (MFA) extended the quota régime to textiles and clothing of woolen and man-made fibers (which had already been constrained by voluntary export restraints for Japan, Korea, Hong Kong, and Taiwan), increasing the scope of protection. The renewal of the MFA in 1977 led to tighter restriction, mainly at the insistence of the EEC (where looser restrictions than in the United States had diverted trade under the first MFA). In bilateral agreements under the 1977 MFA, quota growth was typically more limited than under the previous MFA. At the end of 1981 the MFA was extended, and once again the conditions represented a ratcheting toward a still tighter protective régime, this time seemingly allowing for actual reductions in some quotas.[13]

More general protectionist pressures can also be observed, however, particularly over the last 15 years. In the United States, "voluntary" restraint agreements on steel and meat were sought and negotiated in 1968. In 1970 the US House of Representatives passed the "Mills bill," which would have imposed quotas at the 1967–69 level on most items where the level of import penetration accounted for 15 percent or more of domestic consumption and was rising rapidly. Shortly thereafter, the AFL-CIO and some US industries actively pushed the Burke-Hartke bill, that would have reduced US imports in a wide range of products to a quota set at the 1965–69 level and limited these imports to a fixed share of domestic consumption thereafter (a cutback of about 3 percent from the level of total 1971 imports).[14]

---

[13] For discussion of textile protection through the 1977 MFA, see Donald B. Keesing and Martin Wolf, *Textile Quotas Against Developing Countries* (London: Trade Policy Research Centre, 1980).

[14] C. Fred Bergsten, "Future Directions for US Trade Policy," in C. Fred Bergsten, ed., *The Maidenhead Papers*, pp. 341–69. In passing, it should be noted that the US Congress almost never actually passes legislation to protect a particular sector; the last such instance was the Meat Import Act of 1964. Administrations frequently succumb to the threat of legislative action, however, and implement such protection through administrative devices.

By 1973, worldwide concern over inflation contributed to a temporary swing toward trade liberalization. During 1973–74, the United States terminated its quota (or "voluntary" restraint) protection on petroleum, sugar, meat, and steel, four areas that represented a major portion of the total costs of protection to the US economy.[15] (Sugar protection re-emerged in 1977 as the United States imposed a form of variable tariff to offset the difference between world and domestic target prices, and via import quotas in early 1982. Steel protection also resumed, arguably from 1978 but certainly in late 1982, as discussed below.) Similar unilateral liberalization occurred in other countries. Indeed, during the height of inflationary concern a number of cases arose in which governments restricted exports rather than imports, as in the case of the temporary embargo on US exports of soybeans—which amounted to seeking to export inflation, just as traditional protection represents an attempt to export unemployment.[16] Government intervention, broadly defined, thus declined by considerably less in this period than did protection against imports.

Following the oil shock of 1974 (with its ensuing balance of payments pressures), and in 1975 the most severe decline in global economic activity since the 1930s, the trend reversed toward what has come to be called "the new protectionism." At the same time that negotiators in Geneva were bargaining on tariff cuts and new codes on nontariff barriers (NTBs), new protectionist measures were adopted in a strikingly similar core group of industries in several major industrial countries.

In addition to textiles, already noted, other sectors prominently affected by the new protectionism involved steel, television sets, footwear, ships, and automobiles.

In steel, since late 1977 the European Community (EC) has pursued a rationalization plan that has cut back production capacity and imposed bilateral import quotas. US "voluntary" quotas on steel be-

---

[15] Magee estimated that, in 1971, annual welfare costs of US tariffs were about $500 million, while annual welfare costs of quotas (petroleum, sugar, steel, textiles, meat, and dairy) amounted to $3.6 billion. Considering that Magee estimates welfare costs of $1.5 billion from petroleum quotas, $403 million for sugar quotas, $211 million for steel quotas, and $4 million for meat, approximately 45 percent of all US protection (by size of welfare cost) was eliminated in 1973–74 through elimination of these four quota régimes. Magee, "Welfare Effects."

[16] For a contemporary account see C. Fred Bergsten, *Completing the GATT: Toward New International Rules to Govern Export Controls* (Washington: British–North American Committee, 1974).

ginning in 1969 were terminated in 1974 in response to inflationary concerns (although orderly marketing agreements, OMA, limited imports of specialty steel from 1976 through 1980). Later, however, the United States devised a trigger price mechanism (TPM), which was begun in 1978 and, after suspension in 1980, renewed in September 1980 to invoke "fast-track" investigations of dumping if imported steel were sold below a benchmark price based on Japanese production costs (before again being suspended, in the face of a rash of antidumping and countervailing duty complaints, in early 1982). This mechanism might be considered technically nonprotective if antidumping legislation is considered nonprotectionist. However, because the 1974 US Trade Act contains an approach whereby (contrary to normal practice under the General Agreement on Tariffs and Trade, GATT) selling below average cost is defined as dumping even if the sales price is the same at home and abroad, and in view of special acceleration of investigations in the event of a surge in steel imports, the TPM is most realistically viewed as a quasi-protectionist measure.[17] In any event, the TPM was superseded by a new "voluntary" restraint agreement, at least for US-European trade, in late 1982.

Protection in footwear emerged in the late 1970s. The United States reached orderly marketing agreements with Korea and Taiwan in 1977, but allowed the restrictions to expire in 1981. Canada imposed a global quota on footwear in 1976 and moved to bilateral "voluntary" agreement in late 1977. The United Kingdom imposed quotas on footwear from Taiwan in 1977 and a voluntary export restraint on footwear from Korea beginning in 1979. In electronics, the United States negotiated OMAs on color television sets with Japan in 1977 and Korea and Taiwan in 1979, allowing expiration for Japan in 1980 and for Korea and Taiwan in 1981. Bilateral quotas on television sets (mainly against Japan, Taiwan, and Korea) existed in the late 1970s in France, Italy, and the United Kingdom.

In shipbuilding, protection has taken the form of domestic subsidies in Canada, the United Kingdom, and Germany. In 1979 and 1980, public assistance to shipbuilding increased substantially. Depressed conditions in the industry reflect not only the business cycle but also overexpansion of oil tanker capacity prior to the oil price shock of 1973–74.[18]

[17] Steel protection is described in S. J. Anjaria, Z. Iqbal, L. L. Perez, and W. S. Tseng, *Trade Policy Developments in Industrial Countries* (Washington: International Monetary Fund, 1981), pp. 13–15.

[18] Anjaria, et al., *Trade Policy Developments,* p. 12.

Automobiles are among the products not liberalized at the Community level in the EC, and some member countries have long protected their markets against Japanese imports. Japanese automobiles have been limited to 3 percent of the market in France and fewer than 3,000 units in Italy, and (through an industry-to-industry agreement) 11 percent of the market in the United Kingdom.[19] In 1981 the United States induced Japan to adopt voluntary export quotas; Canada and Germany swiftly followed suit.

A striking feature of the new protectionism is that it has focused on the same limited set of sectors in most of the major industrial countries (textiles, steel, electronics, footwear, shipbuilding, automobiles). Similarly, in most cases it has been concentrated on supply from Japan and the newly industrializing countries. The similarity of protective measures across countries indicates that there are global forces at work affecting industrial countries with relatively similar economic structures, rather than predominantly special national problems.

Figure 2.1 portrays the path of major NTB protection in the past 15 years in the United States. The figure is designed to give an intuitive, rather than quantitative, impression of the overall trend of NTB protection in this period. Beside each product affected by a major NTB, a rectangle indicates the time span covered by protection (horizontal axis). The height of the rectangle indicates the importance of the product in domestic consumption (proportional to its share in total manufacturing apparent consumption).[20] The rectangle is shaded if the NTB in question is considered severe (having a high tariff-equivalent), and unshaded if the NTB is moderate.

The impressions that emerge from figure 2.1 are the following: textile-apparel protection has been a constant, although it has probably increased in intensity; during the period 1974–76 there was probably a reduction in total NTB protection, after the phase-out of quotas on steel, oil, meat, and sugar; and by 1977 and after there was probably an increase in total NTB protection. In 1981, the phasing-out of protection on television sets and footwear was more than offset by

---

[19] Ibid., p. 22, and European Parliament, *Report on the European Automobile Industry*, 15 December 1980, Document 1-673/80.

[20] Calculated from the data base on trade and production for 1978 developed in William R. Cline, "Exports of Manufactures from Developing Countries: Performance and Market Access" (Washington: Brookings Institution, 1982; processed). For petroleum, meat, and sugar, the proportionate size of domestic consumption is based on Magee, p. 669.

FIGURE 2.1   MAJOR US NONTARIFF BARRIERS, 1967–82

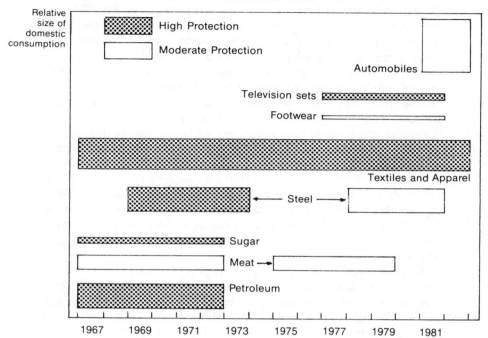

new (albeit mild) protection in the heavily weighted automobile sector.

Similar patterns appear to have applied to other major countries, although ambiguity about beginning dates (for example, in automobile protection) makes it more difficult to constuct corresponding chronograms. In any event, an accurate measurement of the level of NTB protection would require estimation of the tariff-equivalent of each major NTB. More empirical work is needed on this subject.

If figure 2.1 is representative, there appears to have been an increase in the degree of NTB protection since the mid-1970s (although the degree of this protection compared to, say the mid-1960s or around 1970, is highly uncertain). At the same time, however, the Tokyo Round has inaugurated a further phasing-in of tariff reductions, following the Kennedy Round reductions completed in 1973. The Tokyo Round cut average tariffs on industrial products for the United States, Canada, Japan, EC, and five other European countries from 7 percent to 4.7 percent (import-weighted, or from 10.4 percent to 6.4 percent, simple average). The tariff cuts are generally to be phased in by equal installments from 1980 through 1987.[21] However, the problem of tariff escalation by stage of production remains; post-Tokyo Round tariffs will average 0.3 percent on raw materials, 4 percent on semi-manufactures, and 6.5 percent on finished manufactures. Moreover, because sensitive items such as textiles already had high tariffs and tended to be granted greater exceptions from the standard tariff-cutting formula, tariffs are apparently more disperse after the Tokyo Round than before, at least for the United States; the intended tariff harmonization gave way to disharmonization.[22]

Overall, the trend in protection over the last several years has been at best ambiguous, and more probably toward intensification. There was a fairly sharp but brief import liberalization during 1973–75, in response to inflationary concerns (but with some interventions to limit exports); a growing incidence of major NTBs since the mid-1970s; and a restrictive phase beginning in 1980, when the phase-in of Tokyo Round tariff cuts were probably inadequate (because of their small magnitudes) to offset tighter protection in automobiles, textiles, sugar, and now steel.

Nonetheless, it would appear that the pressures for protection since the mid-1970s have increased relatively more than has actual protection. In broad historical terms, moreover, the entire period since the mid-1960s has been one of relatively liberal trade, especially when compared with high protection of the 1930s. We will turn shortly to the outlook for protectionist and liberalizing pressures, after briefly reviewing the actual course of the level of world trade itself.

Recent Trade Stagnation

The aggregate data on world trade flows do not reflect any substantial increase in protection. To be sure, the real volume of world trade did not rise at all in 1981 and rose only by 1 percent in 1980. According to GATT, the dollar value of world trade in 1981, approximately $2 trillion, was actually 1 percent lower than in 1980 because of a decline in average trade prices, reflecting the strengthening of the dollar in the exchange markets.[23] In view of the protec-

---

[21] GATT, *The Tokyo Round of Multilateral Trade Negotiations: II, Supplementary Reports* (Geneva: General Agreement on Tariffs and Trade, 1980), pp. 4, 6, 33.

[22] Robert F. Baldwin, "The Political Economy of US Import Policy" (University of Wisconsin, 1981; processed), pp. 199–200.

[23] GATT, "International Trade in 1981 and Present Prospects," Press Release, GATT/1313, 23 March 1982.

tionist pressures, especially since the mid-1970s, it is tempting to attribute some of the slowdown in world trade growth to increased protection. However, a closer analysis suggests that virtually all of the slowdown can be explained by softer demand for imports associated with slower economic growth.

Table 2.2 (page 76) presents data on the deflated value of nonoil imports into the countries in the Organization for Economic Cooperation and Development (OECD) from 1961 through 1980[24] (in constant 1975 dollars) as well as the corresponding figures for annual growth in such imports and real GDP growth for the OECD countries. These estimates indicate that nonoil imports for the OECD actually fell by 0.4 percent in 1980 and by 2½ percent in 1981, when real GDP rose a bare 1.3 percent and 1.0 percent respectively.[25]

Figure 2.2 (page 78) summarizes table 2.2 in a diagram relating OECD trade growth to real GDP growth, with the data grouped into five periods: 1962–66, 1967–73 (excluding 1971 for reasons of the discontinuity between the alternative price indexes), 1974–75 (two years of world recession), 1976–79, and 1980–81 (two years of very low OECD growth; see table 2.2). It is clear from figure 2.2 that variation in real import growth is well explained, among these five periods, by real GDP growth. However, the slowdown in import growth in 1980 and 1981 is fully explained by low GDP growth: the observation for the average of these two years lies directly on the

---

[24] A deflator for these imports has been constructed as follows: from 1961 through 1970, the IMF unit value index for imports into industrial countries is used. For 1972 to 1981 this index becomes unusable for nonoil imports because of the extreme rise in oil prices and their importance in the total import price index. Instead a weighted average of the export unit value for industrial countries and nonoil developing countries is used as the deflator for nonoil imports into industrial countries. The weights, 0.819 and 0.181 respectively, are based on the share of nonoil developing countries in estimated nonoil imports of industrial countries in 1975 and 1980. IMF, *Direction of Trade Statistics Yearbook,* 1974–80.

[25] The 1981 trade and growth figures are from GATT. The analysis assumes that the GATT figure for decline in total import volume for industrial countries (2½ percent) also applies to nonoil imports by the OECD. If anything, the bias is probably toward understatement of trade growth, because oil import volume appears to have declined by considerably more than 2½ percent. If nonoil imports declined by less, then there would be higher trade growth than predicted by the trend line discussed below, reinforcing the conclusion than trade in 1980–81 was not abnormally low given the slow rate of economic growth.

line relating trade to growth, leaving no unexplained decline in trade growth to be attributed to protection.[26]

In addition, nonoil imports for the world as a whole in 1980–81 have shown positive growth (4½ percent in 1980 and 2½ percent in 1981, in real terms), with the main thrust of import growth coming from the Organization of Petroleum Exporting Countries (OPEC) and the nonoil developing countries (but also positive growth in the socialist block).[27] The divergence between the industrial countries and the rest of the world highlights the fact that it is the recession in the developed countries that has acted as the main drag on trade and the world economy.

[26] Using the 1961–81 data in table 2.2, the following regression was estimated:

$$g_m = -4.6 + 3.14 g_Y; \ \overline{R}^2 = 0.77$$
$$ (2.6) \ \ (7.9)$$

where:

g_m *is* percentage growth of real nonoil imports, and g_Y *is* percentage growth of GDP (t-statistic in parentheses). The equation predicts a decline of trade by 0.5 percent in 1980 and 1.5 percent in 1981, approximately the performance actually observed.

Note that the relatively high explanation of trade achieved by income raises a conceptual issue concerning the proposition at the beginning of this study that trade liberalization has stimulated trade and growth in the postwar period. If trade can be well explained by income, it might be argued that there is little room left for an independent role of liberalization causing trade causing growth. Under this interpretation, rapid growth in trade, at least after 1960, would be the consequence, not the cause, of high domestic growth. The impact of trade liberalization on growth was probably greater during the early postwar period as the high barriers created during the 1930s and wartime period were dismantled. Even the results of such a model might tend to understate the trade impact of negotiations for trade liberalization. As noted in the text, history shows that steady trade liberalization is needed to avoid successful efforts by protectionist interests.

Ideally, a more complete model would show (1) trade as a function of income and protection, and (2) the feedback effect of higher trade growth on higher income growth. The net impact of liberalization on growth would then be given by the change in trade explained by reduced (and avoided) protection, as applied to the feedback relationship of trade on growth. Our expectation is that a more sophisticated model along these lines would bear out both that (1) liberalization in 1950–73 explained a considerable portion of trade growth and (2) this trade growth made a significant contribution to income growth.

[27] GATT, "International Trade," p. 2.

In short, despite the public impression of a severe increase in protectionist pressures, and despite the seeming drive toward increased protection since the late 1970s, the slow import growth of 1980 and 1981 is explained by low growth of income. No extra reduction in trade growth appears to be attributable to higher protection. The point is underlined by noting the position of 1974–75 in figure 2.2. At that time, although protection had, if anything, changed somewhat toward liberalization (at least temporarily), trade fell by much more than in 1980–81. The reason, as predicted accurately by the trade-growth relationship, lay in the severe slowdown in economic growth.

It is noteworthy that the relationship in figure 2.2 shows that a certain level of OECD growth must be achieved before trade growth is positive. Below 1½ percent GDP growth, nonoil imports decline instead of growing. Also, trade is highly sensitive to economic activity. For each percentage point rise in GDP growth, nonoil imports rise by more than three percentage points. An income elasticity of imports of more than three reflects the higher responsiveness of trade to income over the business cycle than on a long-term basis; by comparison, the long-run apparent income elasticity of imports is only 2.0.[28]

The Sources of Protectionist Pressure

The key issue, however, is the future course of world trade and trade policy. The recent historical record, as indicated above, has been a drift toward protection since the mid-1970s, even though no sharp decline in trade attributable to protection (as opposed to income) has yet shown up in aggregate trade data.[29] The pressures to

---

[28] The long-run elasticity is obtained by regressing the logarithm of real nonoil imports on the logarithm of an index of real GDP. The resulting regression ($R2 = 0.99$) has an elasticity of 1.966 (t-statistic $= 40.8$) for the period 1974–81 and, adding an interactive dummy term (coefficient 0.026, t-statistic $= 5.4$), 1.993 for 1961–73. Note that the income elasticity is a hybrid that also incorporates the effects of (outward) supply shifts in trade.

[29] Note, however, that at the level of industry detail the impact of protection on trade is evident. For example, in real terms US imports of footwear from Korea and Taiwan fell from 30 percent annual growth in 1971–77 to − 1.5 percent in 1978–81 when orderly marketing agreements (OMAs) were imposed; US imports of TV sets from Korea and Taiwan grew at 26 percent annually from 1970 to 1978 but declined by 1.2 percent annually in 1979–81 under OMAs; and EC imports of apparel from Hong Kong, Korea, and Taiwan grew at 17 percent annually from 1971 to 1977 but at only 6 percent from 1978 to 1980 after the first tightening of the Multi-Fiber Arrangement. William R. Cline, "Exports of Manufactures," ch. 2.

TABLE 2.2   NONOIL IMPORTS AND REAL GDP GROWTH, OECD, 1961–81

Year	Oil imports (billion dollars)	Nonoil imports (billion dollars)	Nonoil import price deflator[a] (1975 = 100)
1961	4.88	59.94	42
1962	5.90	69.70	41
1963	6.57	76.51	41
1964	7.41	87.76	42
1965	8.06	97.41	43
1966	8.49	109.46	43
1967	9.92	115.34	43
1968	11.24	131.83	43
1969	12.24	154.37	44
1970	14.16	182.30	46
1971	18.71	200.97	51[b]
1972	22.07	238.24	56
1973	31.82	325.13	69
1974	95.52	426.73	92
1975	92.86	425.63	100
1976	113.09	492.04	102
1977	126.94	562.96	111
1978	133.59	667.92	124
1979	191.59	846.93	143
1980	278.28	975.46	164
1981	n.a.	n.a.	159

n.a.   Not available.
Sources: OECD, *Trade Series C*; OECD *Economic Outlook* December 1981, pp. 4, 131; GATT, Press Release 1313, 25 March 1982; IMF, *International Financial Statistics*.
a. 1961–70: import unit value index, industrial countries; 1976–81: weights average of export unit value indexes, industrial countries (weight 0.819) and nonoil developing countries (weight 0.181); 1971–75, average of the two series.
b. New series not comparable with previous years.
c. GATT estimates.
d. GATT estimates for total imports in industrial countries.

restrict trade are quite evident, but also revealed by the recent past are pressures to liberalize trade further (or at least to avoid new restrictions). A large number of factors enter both sides of the equation. Full understanding of their complex interaction is a necessary basis for formulating a trade policy for the 1980s.

The analysis presented here is intertemporal, i.e., it will seek to assess why net pressures for protectionist or liberalization have changed over time.[30] Its goal is to provide an analytical framework encom-

---

[30] By contrast, most of the previous literature concerns cross-section analyses of protection across industries. See Cline, "Exports of Manufactures."

Real nonoil imports (1975 billion dollars)	Real GDP growth (percentage)	Growth of real nonoil imports (percentage)
142.7	4.8	n.a.
170.0	5.3	19.13
186.6	4.8	9.76
209.0	6.3	12.00
226.5	5.2	8.37
254.6	5.3	12.41
268.2	3.7	5.34
306.6	5.8	14.32
350.8	5.4	14.42
396.3	3.6	13.00
n.a.	3.8	n.a.
425.4	5.3	7.94
471.2	6.1	10.77
463.8	0.9	−1.57
425.6	−0.4	−8.24
482.4	4.9	13.35
507.2	3.7	5.14
538.6	3.8	6.19
592.3	3.4	9.97
594.8	1.3	−0.4
n.a.	1.0[c]	−2.5[d]

passing all of the key variables that determine the direction of trade policy, as a framework within which judgments can be made about that direction both now and in the future. The analysis will center on the experience of the United States, in light of its central role in the trading system (and the comparative advantage of the authors), but its conclusions could and should be tested against the empirical record in other countries as well. We will first consider the forces for restriction, which can be grouped under five headings: unemployment, increased import penetration, increased government intervention in general, international monetary considerations, and trade policy itself. We will use the terms "protection" and "restriction" largely interchangeably, usually meaning them to encompass export subsidies and general governmental intervention in trade policy as well as import relief per se.

Unemployment

Conventional wisdom suggests that *high levels of unemployment* are the single most important source of protectionist pressures. Both

FIGURE 2.2 RELATIONSHIP BETWEEN IMPORTS AND GDP GROWTH (OECD
            COUNTRIES, NON-OIL IMPORTS AT 1975 CONSTANT PRICES)

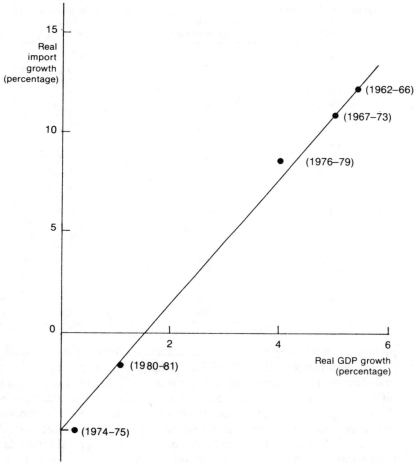

economic and political pressures to limit the impact of all sources of
pressure for adjustment, whether arising from domestic or foreign
sources, are intensified by high levels of joblessness. The postwar
record levels of unemployment in 1981–82 have contributed greatly
to new protection in steel and automobiles, and to broader pressures
for additional import relief.

There are counter examples, however. Congress passed the Trade
Expansion Act of 1962, which authorized the trade liberalization of
the Kennedy Round, with US unemployment ranging between 5.5

percent and 6 percent, a rate lower than in the recessions of 1958 and 1960–61 but much higher than in most of the preceding decades. The most severe protectionist pressures of the postwar era, until now, culminating in House passage of the "Mills bill" in 1970 and substantial support for the Burke-Hartke bill in 1971–72, began while unemployment was around 3.5 percent, the lowest level in the United States since the Korean War. (In this instance, the overvalued dollar seems to have dominated the influence of low unemployment.) And the US Senate passed the Trade Act of 1974 authorizing US participation in the Tokyo Round as unemployment was rising sharply toward a new postwar high of almost 9 percent.

The issue here is the degree to which the textbook concept of *adjustment* works in actual practice. The unemployment rate, or the change in it, reflects the scope for "adjustment"—the ability of the economy to provide new jobs for workers displaced by imports. If these workers can readily find alternative work, particularly of a more rewarding character, pressures to restrict imports are presumably mitigated to a substantial extent. A rapidly growing economy creates more new job opportunities for workers displaced by imports than any conceivable jobs program or direct governmental effort. However, the degree of worker mobility is a separate, additional factor in determining the import of unemployment or trade policy—and J. David Richardson argues, in chapter 12, that such mobility is likely to decline in the United States in the years ahead, as has already happened in Europe, intensifying the pressures for protection at any given level of joblessness.

The protectionist impulse provided by unemployment in a single country is magnified when the entire world economy is experiencing slow or stagnant growth, as in the early 1980s. Under those circumstances, many (or all) countries look to increased exports to stimulate at least a modicum of economic recovery. As noted above, however, the aggregate level of world trade shrinks under such circumstances. Hence all countries are seeking to expand their sales in a contracting market. This intensification of pressure heightens the likelihood of protectionist successes.

However, the presence or absence of direct governmental efforts to mitigate the adjustment impact of trade flows would also seem to be important—both for their real impact in providing jobs or for compensating displaced workers, or both and for the policy importance of indicating governmental concern for the problem and an effort to do something about it. Most countries have aggregate manpower policies, but the United States does not. For the past twenty years in the United States, this effort has occurred primarily via the program of Trade Adjustment Assistance (TAA). The "success" of TAA, perhaps measured by the number of workers it assisted, should thus be another counterbalance to the intensification of protectionist pressures deriving from import-induced unemployment.[31]

Economic Interdependence

Although high levels of unemployment undoubtedly add to the pressures to restrict trade, other factors clearly play a major role in determining US trade policy. One longer-term structural factor is the growing interdependence of the world economy and more rapid transmission of economic change across national boundaries.

The rapid export growth in recent years of Japan and some of the NICs is a specific component of this increased pace of change. Greater competitive pressure from those countries follows to a considerable degree from their increased share in world manufacturing production, largely the consequence of their high overall economic growth rate. From 1960 to 1980, the share of developing countries in world manufacturing production rose from 6.9 percent to 10.2 percent.[32] From 1969 to 1978, the share of world production of automobiles rose from 11.3 percent to 19.0 percent in Japan and from 1.0 to 1.7 percent in Brazil; steel, from 15.7 to 17.1 percent in Japan and from 3.0 to 5.1 percent in Brazil, Korea, and India combined; and television sets, from 0.2 to 8.0 percent in Korea.[33] Trade performance has accompanied production performance. Japan's share in the manufactured exports of the five largest industrial countries grew from 9 percent in 1960 to 17.7 percent in 1979 (while the US share fell from 32.7 to 24.6 percent and that of the United Kingdom from 21.5 to 13.2 percent).[34]

While rising production and exports of manufactures by competitor countries need not imply heightened protectionist pressures, as shown

---

[31] See J. David Richardson, "Worker Adjustment to US International Trade: Programs and Prospects," chapter 12, this volume. On the other hand, the sizable budgetary expenditures which emerged for TAA in recent years—in some sense, a measure of its "success"—contributed to its rejection by both the Reagan administration and the Congress.

[32] United Nations Conference on Trade and Development (UNCTAD), *Trade and Development Report, 1981*, p. 100.

[33] United Nations, *Yearbook of Industrial Statistics,* 1978, vol. 2; and International Iron and Steel Institute, *World Steel in Figures,* 1981, and *Yearbook of Steel Statistics*, 1980. Steel data are for 1970 and 1980.

[34] Calculated from United Nations, *Yearbook of International Trade Statistics,* 1963 and 1979.

by the smoother-than-expected process of economic integration in Europe, close analysis would probably show that the trade of Japan and the NICs with the industrial countries tends to be interindustry (exports in different product sectors from imports) rather than intraindustry, and therefore more conducive to protectionist response in the sectors affected by imports than in the case of the largely intraindustry trade among European countries (and between North America and Europe). Thus, for the United States in 1980 a measure of sectoral specialization (ranging from zero for complete sectoral trade balance—or intraindustry trade—to 1 for complete one-way sectoral specialization—or interindustry trade) showed higher interindustry trade in manufactures with Japan (0.71) and the developing countries (0.58) than with Western Europe (0.35).[35]

Rising interdependence may be seen directly in the share of imports in the overall US economy, or in the goods sector thereof. These ratios have been rising steadily, and suggest a secular rise in the pressure of imports on the US economy and thus on both jobs and corporate profits. (The share of *exports* to GNP has also been rising steadily, and this factor will be considered below as a source of *liberalizing* pressure.) The growing penetration of imports into the US economy is probably an important factor in adding to pressures to restrict, both on a secular basis and when there are periodic jumps in the penetration level.[36]

---

[35] Based on calculations at the level of two digits of the Standard International Trade Classification. The measure used here is:

$$\frac{\Sigma |X_i - M_i|}{\Sigma (X_i + M_i)}$$

where:
X_i, M_i are exports and imports in sector i.

With trade balanced in each sector (intraindustry trade) the numerator is zero. With trade exclusively one-way in each sector, the numerator equals the denominator. OECD, *Statistics of Foreign Trade*, Series B, 1980. However, although intraindustry trade is less pronounced with developing countries than among industrial countries, it has shown a rising share over time even in North–South trade, according to comments by Bela Balassa, Part IV, this volume.

[36] For exceptionally open economies, such as the Netherlands, a very high ratio of imports to GDP may be a *liberalizing* indicator because it proxies the country's heavy dependence on trade and futility of protectionism. The sign of this particular variable may thus reverse beyond some threshold level.

From 1953–54 to 1979–80, the share of imports of goods and services in GNP rose from 4.3 percent to 10.6 percent in the United
States, 22.1 to 27.0 percent in the United Kingdom, 14.7 to 17.8
percent in Germany, 13.6 to 21.8 percent in France, and 11.8 to 14.9
percent in Japan.[37] The general trend toward opening national economies has meant broader exposure to competition from imports (especially as foreign supply shifted outward), setting the stage for greater
protectionist pressures from those industries in which the increase in
imports was most concentrated and in which there was little rise in
exports to provide an offsetting, trade-oriented attitude.

In terms of a political-economic analysis of protection, the demand
for protection by such industries (as represented, for example, by the
potential rewards to them of lobbying for protection) shifted outward
as the potential rents from protection grew along with the relative
size of imports. Unless the political supply of protection were to shift
compensatingly toward less protection, the expected result would be
more protection in such sectors.

In support of this hypothesis, several recent studies show that,
across industries, import penetration (imports relative to apparent
consumption) is associated with higher protection. For example, Cline
has demonstrated that the presence of protection for a specific industry in the manufacturing sector can be predicted with reasonable
accuracy by linking (1) the political influence (and economic importance) of the industry as measured by its total level of employment
and (2) the ratio of import penetration that it faces.[38]

In principle, one could construct a related aggregate measure for
the entire economy by summing for all industries (for example,
weighting each industry's import penetration ratio by its share in
employment). Such a step is in fact necessary if we are to draw any
conclusions at the aggregate level from industry-specific developments, because many of the episodes of industry-specific protection in
the United States—particularly concerning textiles and agricultural
products—have occurred in isolation from any broader trends in the
same direction. Indeed, some of these restrictive steps, especially in
the case of textiles but also regarding carpets and glass in 1962, have
been explicit trade-offs to permit new trade liberalization to proceed.[39]

---

[37] International Monetary Fund, *International Financial Statistics*, May
1978 and April 1982.

[38] W. R. Cline, "Exports of Manufactures," ch. 2.

[39] On the other hand, there is an "equity" case for protecting additional
industries once a single industry is accorded such relief (unless that industry's

Government Intervention

The apparent inclination in many countries to increase the degree of *governmental intervention in the economy* is another secular trend with repercussions on trade. Particularly in Europe, there seems to be a long-term rise in governmental involvement—at least as measured by its share of national GDPs.[40] Recent changes have perhaps been most drastic in France—but the goal of the Mitterrand government to "recapture the domestic market does not sound too different from the proposals of the Giscard government for "organized free trade."

In addition, governments have been increasingly prepared to directly subsidize or otherwise support ailing industries from the past (such as shipbuilding and steel), new industries viewed as essential for development of the country's technological capability (computers, electronic components, aircraft), and agriculture (where, in addition to intervention in Europe and Japan, there exists direct state trading in the socialist countries and many developing countries). Intervention in the technologically dynamic industries is further complicated by the role of defense spending; in response to US charges of unfair trade, foreign advocates of government intervention reply that high technology industries in the United States have long enjoyed an unfair advantage themselves as the consequence of high US defense expenditures. While it is difficult to gauge the extent and trend in government intervention, the direction appears to be broadly toward greater involvement and resulting trade conflicts.

To be sure, countervailing trends have been launched in some countries, most notably under the Reagan administration in the United States and the Thatcher government in the United Kingdom. However, those intended changes have not yet led to fundamental changes in some key sectors—as indicated by continuing subsidies to American

---

case is judged to be wholly unique, as with automobiles in the recent past). The "Mills bill" of 1970, for example, included a "basket provision" to provide relief for any industry facing a certain import penetration ratio, primarily because of the House's desire to provide for other industries once having voted explicit quotas for textiles and footwear.

[40] For the OECD countries see *OECD Economic Outlook*, Dec. 1981, t. R8–R9, pp. 138–39. The total OECD ratio of government outlays to GNP rose steadily from 28.4 percent in 1960 to 37.9 percent in 1978, with the EEC total rising from 32.1 percent to 46.2 percent. There has been a *decline* in the ratios since 1975, however, for the United States, United Kingdom, Canada, and Germany.

farmers, British Leyland, British Steel, and so on. However, there has been continued resort to government intervention with direct effects on trade in addition to the more general subsidies, e.g., the auto and steel voluntary export restraints (VERs) and sugar import quotas in the case of the United States, bans on coal imports and foreign competition for computer sales to the Inland Revenue Service in the case of Britain. Increased *dirigism* in general is thus another factor to consider in assessing the sources of protectionist pressure.

International Monetary Factors

Another basic assumption underlying traditional trade theory is the existence of balance of payment equilibrium. Under today's system of flexible exchange rates, this assumption emphasizes the need for currency equilibrium. Prolonged deviation from balance of payments or exchange rate equilibrium, or both, thus can be expected to add to pressures for trade restrictions.

At least three aspects of international monetary affairs may have an important impact on trade flows and trade policy.[41] First, *the existence of sizable balance of payment deficits* may lead countries to limit imports simply to conserve foreign exchange. Article XII of the GATT in fact permits the application of import barriers (in the form of quotas) for balance of payment purposes.[42]

A large number of major developing countries, including Mexico and Brazil, are carrying out such policies at present. Examples of similar activities by industrial countries are less frequent, but have certainly occurred: the United States, United Kingdom, and Canada all applied sizable import surcharges during the latter stages of the

---

[41] In principle, there is a fourth monetary element which should have a trade liberalizing effect: the existence of large debt obligations by exporting countries (e.g., Brazil and Mexico) to importing countries (e.g., the United States), which should induce the latter to avoid trade restrictions which would hamper the ability of the debtors to repay. The debt crisis which broke in late 1982 reminds us of this phenomenon, which was widely discussed as "the transfer problem" in the interwar period. However, there are few signs that this clearest economic relationship has had much impact on trade policy.

[42] On the other hand, the existence of payments deficits may provide creditor countries or institutions with the leverage to insist on trade liberalization by the deficit country, at least over time. The IMF traditionally includes such requirements in its funding packages, and frequently seeks currency realignments by borrowing countries sufficient to obviate the need for continued restrictions.

Bretton Woods system of fixed exchange rates, and Italy has periodically employed prior import deposit schemes to bolster its trade
balance (and soak up domestic liquidity). Such episodes have tended
to be temporary, and less prevalent since the widespread advent of
flexible exchange rates. Nevertheless, their use can have an important
impact on world trade.

Second, it is often argued that the *volatility of flexible exchange
rates*—especially as experienced in practice—fosters protective trade
policies due to the uncertainties which result for pricing, investment
returns, and competitive positions. Increased transaction costs arise
as traders are forced to buy forward cover and otherwise hedge against
unexpected effects on their earnings from changes in currency relationships.[43]

Third, and probably most significant, is the impact of *misaligned
exchange rates* on trade flows and trade policy. A country with a
currency that is overvalued, in terms of the country's underlying
competitive position vis-à-vis its major trading partners, will face an
across-the-board disadvantage in trading internationally because its
prices in both exporting and import-competing industries will be above
equilibrium levels by the amount of the overvaluation. As a result,
a wide range of its industries—going well beyond those normally
facing intense competitive pressure from abroad—will be inclined to
seek relief from imports and subsidies for exports, with some degree
of justification because of the jeopardy into which they have fallen
as a result of their country's international monetary policy.

Of course, currency overvaluations are always corrected eventually. Governments are not always prone to relax protection once it

---

[43] However, little evidence has been addressed to support this contention.
A more subtle issue relates to the impact of US accounting practices, formerly
FASB 8 and now FASB 52, on the reported earnings of US firms. Combined
with fluctuating exchange rates, these practices tend to produce severe volatility in reported earnings. Their main effect comes via the translation into
dollars of firms' *earnings* in other countries, however, which derive mainly
from the activities of their foreign subsidiaries. The impact on US *trade,*
therefore, depends on whether the foreign direct investment itself produces
additional US trade or substitutes for it. The most extensive studies of the
issue suggest that the net impact is small; see C. Fred Bergsten, Thomas O.
Horst, and Theodore H. Moran, *American Multinationals and American
Interests* (Washington: Brookings Institution, 1978), especially chapter 3. So
there is little reason to believe that flexible rates have much impact on trade
via dollars earned abroad—in addition to doubts as to whether the accounting
practices, bothersome and noneconomic as they are, have significant impact
on the level of such investment itself.

has been granted, however, even when the original justification for the protection no longer exists. The classic case in the United States is the Domestic International Sales Corporation (DISC) system of export tax incentives, initiated at the height of dollar overvaluation in 1971 but maintained through subsequent export boom and balance of payments surpluses. At about the same time, import controls were adopted for noncotton textile products and steel. The former have been retained ever since, despite the shift of the textiles (as opposed to apparel) sector into sizable trade surplus, and steel controls remained in force well beyond the restoration of US balance of payments and currency equilibrium. Periodic currency overvaluation may thus have a ratchet effect in adding to a country's level of import restrictions (and export subsidies) over time, in addition to generating periodic pressures for temporary intervention.

Import restrictions may also result, paradoxically, from currency undervaluations. A country with an underpriced currency, in terms of underlying competitive positions, will frequently seek to exploit its international competitive advantage by investing heavily in export- and import-substituting industries, as did Germany and Japan during at least the late 1960s and early 1970s. When the undervaluation is eliminated, however, as it eventually must be, some of those investments will no longer produce competitively. As a result, the industries involved may seek and receive protection—again, having been misled by the price signals emanating from their countries' international economic policies.[44]

There is thus a double asymmetry in terms of the impact of exchange rate misalignments on trade flows and trade policy: they may cause an upward ratchet in the level of protection in any individual country that suffers periodically from overvaluation, and they may cause an upward ratchet in the level of worldwide restrictions by generating pressures for such steps (albeit at different times) in countries with both overvalued and undervalued currencies. This topic is sufficiently important that it is considered separately in chapter 3.[45] Suffice it here to note that there appears to be a high correlation in the United States between the direction of trade policy and the international position of the dollar:

[44] It is also possible that currency undervaluation may have permitted more rapid liberalization of import controls, as in Germany in the 1950s and Japan in the early 1970s and early 1980s.

[45] C. Fred Bergsten and John Williamson, "Exchange Rates and Trade Policy," chapter 3, this volume.

- Dollar equilibrium permitted steady liberalization throughout the 1950s and early 1960s, even when unemployment (as noted above) was at high levels.
- The growing dollar overvaluation of the late 1960s and early 1970s coincided with the deepest protectionist pressures of the postwar period, despite modest levels of unemployment.
- The restoration of dollar equilibrium, via the devaluations of 1971 and 1973, along with the new focus of macroeconomic policy on inflation, corresponded to the extensive unilateral trade liberalization of 1973–74 and passage of the Trade Act of 1974 despite a level of unemployment not seen since the 1930s.
- Renewed dollar overvaluation in 1975–76 correlated with a renewal of protectionist pressures, culminating in several new restrictive measures.
- The restoration of dollar equilibrium in 1978–79 supported a dramatic improvement in the US trade position and overwhelming congressional support for the Trade Act of 1979, ratifying the Multilateral Trade Negotiations (MTN).
- The contemporary onset of the most severe dollar overvaluation since the collapse of the Bretton Woods system, along with new highs in the unemployment rate, clearly relate to the renewal of major pressures for import relief.

Indeed we can see from this perspective a fundamental conflict within US international economic policy throughout much of the postwar period. While attempting to remain firmly on the path of liberal trade, and indeed leading the world in the direction of ever greater liberalization, the United States for extended periods did nothing to promote the underlying equilibrium in exchange rate relationships which is an essential precondition for liberal trade. During the last five years or so of the Bretton Woods system of fixed exchange rates, the United States in fact actively resisted either parity changes or greater flexibility of the exchange rate system. Since early 1981, the United States has rejected both internal policy changes and exchange market intervention despite the reemergence of a clearly overvalued dollar. Greater consistency of its international monetary approach with its trade policy will be essential for any sustained success of a liberal trade effort by the United States, and thus probably for the world.

Trade Policy

The ability of trade policy itself to cope with current and prospective problems, at both the national and international levels, has an important impact on whether liberalizing or restrictive tendencies will dominate. An inability of trade policy to respond effectively to the problems perceived as significant for a country's trade position will tend to push that country's policy itself in a restrictive direction. Trade policy is thus heavily affected by previous trade policy and perceptions thereof.

One reason for this interrelation is the extensive degree of *policy interdependence* among nations in the trade area. The concept of economic interdependence is by now widely recognized and understood. It is less widely realized, however, that there is also an enormous amount of policy interdependence. Restrictive trade action by any significant nation increases the prospect of similar action by other countries, both in the same industry (due to the fear of trade diversion) and in unrelated industries (due to the general tendency toward restrictions which is implied).[46]

The most obvious recent example of this phenomenon arose in the automobile sector, as indicated above. Similar ping-pong action occurred earlier in steel, where the United States imposed restraints partly because of the fear of diversion due to European restraints—which then Europe tightened in response. A similar pending problem lies in the investment area, where pressures are growing for US imposition of performance requirements—particularly in the auto sector—or even institution of a US Foreign Investment Review Agency (à la Canada's) because of the local content rules, minimum export quotas, and overall screening procedures employed by other important countries such as Canada, Mexico, and Brazil.

This policy interdependence functions at both the bilateral and multilateral levels. If an imbalance is perceived in the overall trading relationship between two countries, the aggrieved party will often tend toward restrictive devices to "right the balance." More broadly, countries viewed as "free riders" on a relatively open trading system—without themselves contributing to its openness, or in fact even maintaining far greater restrictions than their trading partners—will become particular targets of retaliatory proposals. Such perceptions

---

[46] One aspect of policy interdependence, highlighted by the recent debt crisis, can have trade-liberalizing effects: the ability of creditor countries (such as the United States) and international institutions (such as the IMF) to require reductions in trade barriers by debtor countries (such as Mexico, specifically regarding its export subsidy system) as a quid pro quo for the needed financial assistance, perhaps by implementing exchange rate corrections sufficient to obviate continued need for the restrictions.

in the United States, primarily vis-à-vis Japan but also regarding Canada and some of the NICs (such as Mexico), in fact lie behind much of the push for "reciprocity" legislation.[47]

"Multilateral policy interdependence" refers to *the effectiveness of the multilateral institutions*, notably the GATT but the Organization for Economic Cooperation and Development (OECD) and others as well, in handling their responsibilities to manage the world trading system. If the major trading nations are unable collectively to formulate and enforce a trading régime that is widely viewed as both effective and equitable, protectionist pressures in individual countries will be enhanced.

This issue is quite important at the moment. Elements in both the United States and Europe appear to believe that the current GATT rules are ineffectual in defending their interests in such areas as agriculture and dumping, respectively. There is a growing sense that the adjudication system of the GATT is woefully feeble, and unable to implement even the rules on the books. At least in the United States, concern is widespread that new rules are needed to deal with such issues as services and trade-related investment problems if the GATT is to retain its relevance in the 1980s and beyond. Many developing countries justify their departure from international trading norms on the view that the GATT rules are unfair to them, having been created primarily by and for the industrial nations.[48]

Beyond these specific manifestations of trade policy itself, and perceptions thereof, lie several broader policy trends that would seem to add, perhaps significantly, to the prospect for trade restrictions. One is the apparently increasing tendency to use *trade restrictions for foreign policy or national security reasons* or both—again, like the balance of payments, an area where restrictions are permitted under the GATT. Such restrictions sometimes take the form of export controls, as in the case of US and Coordinating Committee (COCOM) limitations on sales to the Soviet Union and other communist countries. They sometimes take the form of import controls, as in the EC sanctions against Argentina in early 1982—which were perhaps easier

---

[47] As discussed by Cline in chapter 4, this volume. Another element of this problem is the wholly unsatisfactory definition of "reciprocity" used in international trade negotiations, which makes it quite easy for proponents of protectionist measures to argue that their country made a bad bargain in the previous "round." See C. Fred Bergsten, "Future Directions for US Trade," pp. 347–50.

[48] See chapter 5 by John H. Jackson, this volume.

to adopt because most of Argentina's sales to the EC consisted of textile products, shoes, and steel.

It is always difficult to quantify the value of trade blocked by a policy action, but the amount involved in these cases may be quite substantial. Estimates by the Reagan administration suggested that a successful US effort to delay completion of the Siberian gas pipeline, for example, would deny the Soviet Union export earnings of $6 billion to $8 billion annually. Argentine exports to the EC have been running at about $2 billion a year. Increasing use of these techniques, in an effort to promote the foreign policy or national security goals, or both, of the countries undertaking them, would subtract considerably from the level of world trade (and, presumably, welfare as defined in conventional economic terms).

Another possibly crucial, policy issue affects the extent of protectionist pressure: the existence or nonexistence of a *multilateral trade negotiation*. It is widely recognized that trade policy is dynamically unstable. Absent a major liberalizing initiative, the omnipresent pressures for protection are more likely to succeed. In the past, such initiatives were manifest primarily through a multilateral negotiation and the attendant domestic authorizing legislation. The existence of such a negotiation, based on an explicit legislative mandate in pursuit of a broadly defined national interest in freer trade, provided both substantive reason and political justification for avoiding new restrictions—which would run contrary to the purpose of the negotiation, and could even undermine prospects for its success because of the policy interdependence outlined above.

Again, the empirical record suggests some importance for this factor. Between the Dillon and Kennedy Rounds, substantial pressures for new import restrictions—a number of which were successful—emerged. Immediately after the conclusion of the Kennedy Round, pressures that had been bottled up for at least part of its duration again erupted, at least three of which (steel, meat, and subsequently textiles) were successful. Pressures again erupted during the 1975–76 lull in MTN activities, and after the conclusion of the MTN in early 1979.

Directly related to the prospects for generating multilateral trade negotiations is *leadership of the economic system*. In the early postwar period, the large external surplus of the United States and its large share of gross world product, along with the relatively small impact of external events on the US economy, made the United States the natural leader of the system with the occasional costs that the role entailed. Thus, the United States was willing to support European economic integration for foreign policy reasons even though the Common Market meant some diversion of trade away from US exports. Similarly, in the 1950s and early 1960s, the United States tolerated high protection in Japan and developing countries in recognition of their scarcity of foreign exchange.

As the US share of world production has fallen, as its external position shifted from chronic surplus to frequent deficit, and as the consequences of trade have become more crucial for the US economy itself, the United States has lost its hegemony in the world economy. Especially after the devaluations of the dollar in 1971 and 1973, US policy has been conceived more and more in terms of achieving symmetrical opportunities for US exporters ("fair trade") and less in terms of the need to accept short-run costs in the name of long-run improvement of the global economic system. This shift in policy environment has meant on balance a more protectionist tendency in the United States, much as an earlier shift of similar proportions dramatically altered the world leadership role of the United Kingdom.

Thus, a large number of factors tend to promote the adoption of new trade restrictions, at least in the United States. At the same time, a number of factors push in the opposite direction—toward trade liberalization, or at least opposition to protection. We turn next to an assessment of those countervailing forces.

The Sources of Antiprotectionist Pressure

Just as there are a number of forces pushing in the direction of trade protection, a number of forces oppose any such tendencies. In fact, these forces often push in the direction of further trade liberalization—which, as noted above, is probably necessary if protection, of at least a creeping variety, is to be avoided. We will group these antiprotectionist, or proliberalization, forces under five headings: inflation, increasing export dependency, trade policy factors, overall foreign policy, and the intellectual foundations underlying this policy area.

Inflation

The advent of concern about inflation as the widespread focus of economic policy throughout the world produces a substantial transformation in trade policies. When unemployment is unambiguously the chief target of economic policy, efforts to export unemployment—including through import barriers and export subsidies—are a natural derivative. When inflation becomes the primary problem, however, it fosters efforts to export inflation—which implies import liberalization and, perhaps, export controls (as well as competitive currency appreciation rather than depreciation). Most political leaders have recognized that import barriers exacerbate inflationary pressures by limiting the supply of goods available to a country, and that reduction of such barriers can be a useful—even critically important—tool in combating such pressures.[49]

This transformation became most obvious during 1973–74, when many key countries experienced a rapid jump into double-digit inflation for the first time in the postwar period. Their response via trade policy, as indicated above, encompassed a wide range of unilateral reductions in tariffs and import quotas—in the United States, including total elimination of quotas (or "voluntary" export restraints on sales to the United States) in oil, steel, sugar, and meat. Some of the traditionally most protectionist countries, including Australia, Canada, and Japan, cut their tariffs unilaterally. All this occurred despite the runup to a major multilateral negotiation (the Tokyo Round), during which period countries normally husband their protective devices with particular zeal in order to extract maximum return for the eventual liberalization thereof.

However, the world trade implications of such a policy shift are not wholly positive. Along with the liberalization of imports come controls on exports, exemplified by (but going far beyond) the US embargo on exports of soybean and other agricultural products in 1973. World trade (and its beneficial effects) presumably suffers equally from controls that limit it from the export as well as import side (although export controls tend to be much more temporary than import controls). Hence inflation, while typically supportive of freer trade, can also pose a restrictive threat when it moves to extreme levels and/or completely dominates unemployment as a policy concern. In today's environment, there will be a constant tug between the restrictive pressures emanating from concerns about unemployment and the antirestrictive counterpressures emanating from continuing concern about inflation.

Moreover, as pointed out by Juergen B. Donges in his comments at the conference, rapid inflation *in a single country* can push that country into balance of payments deficit and thus, as noted above, intensify its protectionist pressures. The issue here is whether the shifting focus of economic policy toward inflation is widely general-

---

[49] Over time, of course, inflation can lead to unemployment by requiring the adoption of restrictive macroeconomic policies. This discussion addresses only the short-run impact of each on trade policy.

ized around the world, as in 1973–74, or whether it is limited to one or a few countries; protection will be deterred in the former case, while it may be promoted in the latter.

One specific aspect of anti-inflation concern bears mention: the widely felt need to cut budget deficits. Expenditure cuts in pursuit of this goal can of course include cuts in export subsidies, as with the significant reductions in lending by the US Export-Import Bank during 1981–82. Thus the protectionist implications of the general trend toward greater government intervention, outlined above, have at least a partial counterweight in the pressure to cut government spending to fight inflation.[50]

Export Dependency

A second antiprotectionist force in most countries is the growing dependence of their economies on exports, which has proceeded pari passu with the growing dependence on imports cited above. Taken in combination with the high and growing degree of policy interdependence, as already discussed, export interests represent a substantial countervailing force against import controls.

In the United States, this force has been surprisingly strong. The primary political response to the record US trade and current account deficits of 1977–79, in fact, was a major push to expand exports rather than to retard imports. The main pressure within Japan to liberalize its import régime, of course, is the fear that its exports will otherwise be further restricted abroad. The interests of French agricultural exporters and German manufacturing exporters sustained the initial, and continuing, adherence to free trade within the EC.

There is also an important relationship between this particular antiprotectionist force and the state of a country's exchange rate, as outlined in the previous section. Sustained currency overvaluation mutes both the export capability of a country and the zeal of its export community to support freer trade, and thus renders (or even negates) this particular countervailing force. Again, there is clear interaction among the different factors affecting the net direction of a country's trade policy.

[50] In principle, the desire to cut budget deficits also enhances the appeal of raising tariffs to increase government revenues leaving aside the question of whether increased tariffs would really raise government revenues, after all their effects played through, this propensity is unlikely to have much impact in practice—at least in the industrial and advanced developing countries—because of the tiny contribution of tariffs to the overall revenue base.

Trade Policy

We noted above that several facets of trade policy and the international trading system, such as perceived shortcomings in their ability to provide fair treatment for all countries, can promote protectionist pressures. At the same time, however, at least two trade policy phenomena generally help defend against such pressures.

One is the existence of the GATT system itself. The rules and institutions of the GATT were created for this very purpose, of course, and have generally been viewed as largely successful in achieving their basic purpose. Major questions have now been raised, however, both about the relevance of the rules to contemporary trade problems and about the effectiveness of the organization in implementing the rules that do exist. A separate paper for this conference addresses the issue, which is a critical part of the overall picture.[51]

However, the shortcomings of the GATT system—in both coverage and implementation—generate antiprotectionist as well as protectionist pressures. The reason is that certain countries, most frequently the United States, periodically wish both to expand the coverage of the GATT rules (to NTBs via the Tokyo Round, to services and investment-related trade issues now) and improve its enforcement record. These policy objectives typically produce proposals for new multilateral negotiations or other initiatives, which are generally viewed as much more difficult—perhaps impossible—to achieve if the same country is itself taking protectionist, i.e., antisystemic, actions at the same time. Indeed, countries seeking a freer trade environment have typically used the existence of, or even the need for, such a negotiation as a key component of their negative responses to most domestic pressures for new restrictions.

There is, however, a contrary view which suggests that systemic changes can best be achieved by adopting a "tough" trade policy including the institution of new restrictions—which are, perhaps, then to be bargained away in pursuing the broader objectives. Such reasoning lies behind at least some of the contemporary support in the United States for "reciprocity" legislation. It may also lie behind such specific proposals as those for local content rules in the automobile industry, on the view that international rules to limit such practices will prove negotiable only if the United States itself adopts similar practices first.

It is impossible to make a definitive judgment as to which of these approaches is more accurate, given the highly political and psycho-

---

[51] See chapter 5 by John H. Jackson, this volume.

logical nature of the dynamics involved. There are at least three reasons, however, to suppose that an antiprotectionist attitude is more likely than a protectionist approach to achieve desired systemic changes. First, at the conceptual level, Cline shows in his game-theoretic analysis of the "reciprocity" issue that most of the possible outcomes of that strategy are unlikely to produce their avowed objectives of reducing foreign barriers to US exports—and may frequently have the opposite effect. Second, at the empirical level, US leadership of virtually all of the postwar systemic reforms has coincided with a basically open US trading policy—albeit a policy which, on several occasions, did explicitly provide protection for a domestic industry (notably textiles and apparel) to assure domestic support for the overall policy. Third, the rising degree of policy interdependence in today's trading world—as outlined above—strongly suggests that, in light of the domestic politics in most nations, restrictive actions by any major country are more likely to trigger similar action elsewhere than to induce liberalizing responses. Hence the desire for systemic changes, and further liberalization in new areas, seems on balance to represent an antiprotectionist force.

Foreign Policy

Another policy area that pushes most countries in the direction of freer trade, or at least the avoidance of protectionism, is overall foreign policy. Trade issues rank high on the agendas of most countries, so that steps taken by others which hurt their trade can be significantly damaging to overall relations between them. Worse yet, in this context, would be any steps by a country that disrupted the entire trading system and thus generated substantial costs for a wide range of others.[52]

The one exception to this generalization, as noted above, lies in the overall relationship between unfriendly—or even enemy—countries. At the extreme, hostilities between nations have usually (though not always) been accompanied by economic warfare between them, including complete trade embargos. Short of hostilities, prolonged tensions (of the "cold war" variety) have also produced trade barriers such as the long-standing COCOM (and tighter US) limitations on East-West trade.

At the same time, however, such tensions solidify relationships within the respective alliance systems and thus tend to dampen the

---

[52] The classic statement is by Richard N. Cooper, "Trade Policy is Foreign Policy," *Foreign Policy*, no. 9 (Winter 1972–73).

proclivity of members of such systems to enact trade (or other) barriers against each other. There is thus a correlation between the degree of international political tension at any point in time and the degree to which overall foreign policy promotes freer trade, which nets against each other the induced tendencies for friendly and hostile countries to promote economic exchange in light of the extant international political situation.

Ideology

The final factor that pushes steadily in the direction of freer trade, and which in a sense underlies all the others, is the widespread acceptance of the theory of international trade and trade policy which was summarized at the outset of this chapter. The intellectual consensus in this area is in fact quite rare, at least within the realm of economic policy; Keynesians, monetarists, so-called supply-siders, and virtually all other schools of thought agree on the virtues of open trade.

As with all areas of economics, however, there are differing degrees of adherence to it in practice—as suggested in the discussion of government intervention in the previous section, where a Reagan or Thatcher have very different views from a Mitterrand. Nevertheless, even most protectionist initiatives begin by paying homage to the theory of free trade before going on to try to justify an exemption in their particular case—reinforcing the notion that it is very difficult to fight at least the idea of free trade.

Conclusion

Strategies for responding to the overall trade problems of the 1980s will have to respond to the forces generating pressures for new restrictions, in part by appealing to (and strengthening) the forces opposing such pressures and pushing for further liberalization. Some of the issues are structural in nature, and can be affected by trade (or other) policies only over an extended period of time: import-penetration ratios for the economy as a whole and individual industries; the export dependence of the economy as a whole; the role of government in the economy; and foreign policy relationships. Some of the issues go well beyond trade policy, and presumably will not be greatly affected by trade concerns: the aggregate level of unemployment and changes therein, the pace of inflation, and the overall role of government. The exchange rate is often viewed as distinct from trade policy as well, but we have argued that it should be integrated with trade policy.

Hence, trade policy can probably affect the outcome most directly by addressing the following issues:

- the extent of exchange rate overvaluation, if any
- trade adjustment assistance or its equivalent
- the level of trade restrictions in major trading partners
- the existence or absence of trade-liberalizing negotiations, inter alia to deal with these restrictions
- the institutional effectiveness of the GATT in coping with existing and future international trade problems, including perceptions thereof.

A strategy based on these conclusions would thus focus on three areas: eliminating current exchange rate misalignments, most notably the overvaluation of the dollar, and seeking to institute a more effective monetary system to minimize such realignments in the future; improving domestic programs of adjustment to imports, particularly trade adjustment assistance in the United States; and launching a new multilateral trade negotiation which would seek both reduction in trade barriers in all countries and improved performance by the GATT itself in monitoring and managing the international trade system. Separate chapters of this volume address in detail the dollar exchange rate and international monetary system, TAA, the functioning of the GATT, and trade barriers in each of the key regions. This paper will therefore conclude simply with a few thoughts about possible policy packages that might enable the world to avoid a significant onset of new trade restrictions in the 1980s, and perhaps even push in the direction of opening the world economy further to international trade flows.

At their most ambitious level, such packages would have to include several major components:

- changes in domestic macroeconomic configurations, such as the US and Japanese mixes of fiscal and monetary policy, both to help restore equilibrium exchange rates (by sharply narrowing the present disparity between US and foreign, notably Japanese, interest rates) and to promote reduced unemployment levels in all countries (since high real interest rates around the world, deriving from high US rates, are probably the single greatest deterrent to growth and increased employment at present)
- changes in domestic microeconomic policies, to address directly the problems of specific industries (e.g., automobiles) and to provide more effective assistance for workers displaced by imports

• improvements in the international monetary system to reduce the overshooting (and perhaps volatility) of exchange rates, to avoid the buildup of renewed currency misalignments in the future
• constant efforts to implement the MTN codes effectively, both to limit substantive trade disputes which will otherwise continue to fester (e.g., regarding agriculture and subsidies) and to enhance procedurally the GATT as a credible institutional manager for the system
• a new "round" of major multilateral negotiations, to deal with the "new" trade issues of the 1980s (e.g., services, investment-related problems, high technology) as well as to resolve the carryover issues from the MTN (e.g., safeguards and broader North-South questions).

A policy package for the future is set forth in greater detail in the final chapter of this volume. To be sure, components of any such package could be adopted in isolation—and would still help to maintain an open trading system, though perhaps not as effectively as if the several steps were pursued together. In addition, there are alternative means to proceed; "carryover" and/or "new" issues could be negotiated case-by-case rather than in the context of any broader package. Whatever specific approach is chosen, however, the major trading countries will have to address the array of issues outlined here as they plan world trade policy—and their own—for the 1980s and beyond. If they wish to resist effectively the pressures to reverse the steady expansion of world trade and liberalization of trade policy over the past three decades, new initiatives along the lines suggested will almost certainly turn out to be needed.

CHAPTER 3

Exchange Rates and Trade Policy

C. Fred Bergsten and John Williamson

Trade policy has traditionally been associated with tariffs, quotas, export subsidies, and other nontariff distortions. Relatively little attention has been paid to the impact of exchange rates on trade policy, despite widespread analyses by international monetary economists of their impact on trade flows. This paper argues that the continued failure to link the trade and monetary aspects of international economic exchange is a major mistake, in terms both of diagnosing the policy problems which now confront the trading system and of dealing with those problems in the foreseeable future.

Misaligned Currencies and Trade Protection

The bifurcation between money and trade, at both the analytical and policy levels, is understandable yet strange. It is understandable for three reasons. First, different officials and, usually, different ministries are responsible for monetary and trade matters in most countries. Different institutions, the International Monetary Fund (IMF) and the General Agreement on Tariffs and Trade (GATT), bear such responsibilities at the international level. The degree of coordination between these groups waxes and wanes over time, depending upon the individuals who man them, but there are few systematic interlinkages. Hence there is no assured method to coordinate monetary and

The authors are indebted to Paul Armington, Max Corden, William R. Cline, Rachel McCulloch, and participants in the Institute's conference for comments on a previous draft; the usual caveats apply.

trade policies, either in national capitals or internationally.[1] Even within the academic world, few economists specialize in both trade and monetary affairs and are thus in a position to recognize the relationships between them.

Second, there is a legitimate difference between the focus of trade policy on the *level* of trade flows and the focus of exchange rates (and international monetary policy, more broadly) on trade *balances*. As long as trade negotiations are reciprocal in practice as well as in principle, trade policy has a neutral impact on the trade balance. Similarly, the balance of payments adjustment process addresses the problem of the trade balance rather than the trade level. In this sense, it is both logical and desirable that trade and monetary policy be assigned to different targets.

But the main reason why the money-trade relationship has been so ignored is probably the widespread assumption that the international monetary system will not permit the existence of substantial exchange rate misalignments for prolonged periods. This is indeed a generally accepted objective of international monetary arrangements, but in practice—as we shall see shortly—the record is quite spotty. Sizable disequilbria have developed, and persisted for substantial periods. Nevertheless, the assumption of balance of payments equilibrium—at least over time—explains much of the bifurcation between trade and monetary considerations.

This bifurcation is strange, however, because exchange rates demonstrably do deviate substantially from their equilibrium paths for substantial periods of time, and because the basic case for liberal trade rests upon the assumption inter alia of balance of payments equilibrium, hence equilibrium exchange rates. If the exchange rate conveys price signals to producers and consumers which are incorrect

---

[1] Proposals to remedy this situation are made in chapter 22, this volume. Among the relatively rare public statements on the topic by officials are C. Fred Bergsten (while Assistant Secretary of the Treasury for International Affairs), "Trade and Money: The Need for Parallel Progress," a speech presented to the French-American Chamber of Commerce, New York, 20 June 1978, reprinted in *The International Economic Policy of the United States: Selected Papers of C. Fred Bergsten, 1977–1979* (Lexington, Mass.: D.C. Heath and Co., 1980), pp. 177–82; and Anthony M. Solomon, "Making the Necessary Linkage Between Money and Trade Policies," remarks before the Center for International Business, Dallas, 8 April 1981.

reflections of the underlying economic relationships, significant distortions can result for production, hence trade.[2]

Persistent overvaluation of a country's exchange rate will, of course, adversely affect the country's price competitiveness in international trade (in both goods and services). Exports will be discouraged and imports will be encouraged. The tradable goods sector of the economy, as a whole, will be disadvantaged with resulting distortions in the distribution of domestic output. The current account will shift adversely, financed via private capital inflows or a decline in the country's external reserves. The amounts of money involved can be quite sizable; for the United States, the typical analysis suggests that the merchandise trade balance declines by about $3 billion for every percentage point decline in US international price competitiveness.[3]

From the standpoint of trade policy, the chief implication is the (additional?) pressure that is generated for protectionist measures.[4] Export- and import-competing firms and workers will tend to seek help from their governments to offset these distortions, which undermine their ability to compete, with some degree of legitimacy since the distortions are accepted—in some cases, even fostered—by those governments. Coalitions in support of trade restrictions will be much easier to form, and much broader in their political clout, because no longer will only the most vulnerable firms and workers be seeking help—and no longer will the countervailing pressures from successful

[2] The argument is summarized in Richard N. Cooper, "Economic Assumptions of the Case for Liberal Trade," in C. Fred Bergsten, ed., *Toward a New World Trade Policy: The Maidenhead Papers* (Lexington, Mass.: D. C. Heath and Co., 1975), especially pp. 21–23. Note that the analysis in this paper focuses on *misalignments* of exchange rates vis-à-vis their underlying equilibrium levels, rather than on the *volatility* of fluctuating rates. Some observers have argued that fluctuations per se discourage international trade in general, and may also generate protectionist pressure by increasing the uncertainty of competing internationally; most analyses of the issue have found little evidence of such effects, though there is some empirical support as reported in John Williamson, *Exchange Rate Rules* (London: Macmillan, 1981), p. xvii.

[3] The latest evidence is in Alan V. Deardorff and Robert M. Stern, "The Sectoral Impact of the Recent Appreciation of the US Dollars," (University of Michigan, April 1, 1982; processed). Their analysis suggests a similar ratio for the European Community as a group, and a ratio for Japan of $1 billion per percentage point.

[4] For a broader compilation of the factors that promote protectionist pressures, see chapter 2, this volume by C. Fred Bergsten and William R. Cline.

exporters be as effective. As we shall see below, overvaluation of the dollar has proved to be an accurate "leading indicator" of trade policy in the United States—perhaps the most accurate of all such indicators—in the postwar period.

The protectionist impact of an overvalued currency, moreover, may persist beyond the duration of the overvaluation itself. Once adopted, protection is frequently maintained long after its initial cause (or justification) has passed. A return to currency equilibrium, or even "reverse overshooting" to undervalued levels, may not produce elimination of restrictions implemented to offset a previous overvaluation. Exchange rate oscillations may thus produce a ratchet effect on protection, raising it during (the inevitably reversible) periods of overvaluation but failing to undo it when equilibrium is restored.

In the United States, three cases in point come to mind. The clearest is the Domestic International Sales Corporation (DISC) tax incentive for exports, adopted at the height of dollar overvaluation in 1971 but retained ever since through periods of export boom and payments surplus. A second is the extension of textile import controls to cover synthetic fibers, also in the early 1970s, which persist despite the shift of that sector (as opposed to apparel), along with the overall US current account, into substantial surplus. A third case is steel, where import restraints were also adopted in the wake of dollar overvaluation in the late 1960s and maintained well beyond the restriction of exchange rate equilibrium and payments balance.

Paradoxically, undervalued exchange rates may also generate protectionist pressures.[5] A country with an undervalued currency should become more willing to *lower* its trade barriers, especially if it could get other countries to do so as well and thereby exploit its competitive advantage. (This factor may have been important in inducing unilateral import liberalization in Germany in the 1960s and Japan in the early 1970s and early 1980s.) However, resources may be induced to enter export- and import-competing industries solely because of the artificially favorable competitive position generated by undervaluation, as in Germany and Japan during the prolonged period of DM and yen undervaluation in the late 1960s and early 1970s. When

---

[5] If deliberately sought in order to preserve the size of the tradable goods sector, currency undervalution may also be regarded as a *form* of protectionism. See W. M. Corden, "Exchange Rate Protection," in Richard N. Cooper, et al., eds., *The International Monetary System Under Flexible Exchange Rates: Global, Regional and National* (Cambridge, Mass.: Ballinger, 1982), pp. 17–39.

the undervaluation subsequently disappears, those industries may then have to seek import restrictions or subsidies to avoid sharp cutbacks in their operations (including bankruptcies). Again, they would have some legitimacy in making such a request if the creation of those industries (or their expansion) was in fact due primarily to the currency misalignment.

Currency misalignments can thus have a doubly asymmetrical effect on trade policy. On the one hand, overvaluation (directly) and undervaluation (when reversed over time) can both generate pressures for trade restrictions and subsidies. On the other hand, a return to equilibrium will not necessarily offset the tendencies toward protection caused by an initial position of overvaluation—while a return toward equilibrium from an initial position of undervaluation is a possible trigger for protectionist pressures.

Exchange rate disequilibrium can thus have a substantial impact on trade policy, pushing it in the direction of increased restrictions. The extent of this problem, of course, will depend on the extent and duration of the currency disequilibrium. The protectionist pressures will be most severe if substantial misalignments persist for prolonged periods.

On the Concept of the Equilibrium Exchange Rate

The thesis presented in this paper rests on the concept of "misalignment," implying a deviation of the exchange rate from its equilibrium value. But there is more than one concept of the "equilibrium exchange rate," and it is therefore essential to be clear as to which concept is being used. The three concepts distinguished below have all appeared in the literature: fundamental equilibrium, current equilibrium, and market equilibrium.

Fundamental Equilibrium

This term is intended to connote the obverse of "fundamental disequilibrium," the criterion for an exchange rate change under the Bretton Woods system. Although the term was never formally defined, the IMF's report on the exchange rate system in 1970 implied that fundamental disequilibrium was a situation in which a country could not expect to generate a current account balance to match its underlying capital flow over the cycle as a whole without, on the one hand, depressing its income below "internal balance" or imposing trade controls for payments purposes or, on the other hand, importing inflation.[6] Conversely, therefore, the equilibrium exchange rate is that which is expected to generate a current surplus or deficit equal to the underlying capital flow over the cycle, given that the country is pursuing "internal balance" as best it can and not restricting trade for balance of payments reasons.

This concept is what is generally meant by "the rate justified by fundamentals." It is also what people usually have in mind when they describe rates as "overvalued" or "undervalued"—and it is so used throughout this paper. It relates to the real rather than the nominal exchange rate. In general, one expects the fundamental equilibrium rate to change only occasionally, e.g., when there is a major and permanent shift in the terms of trade or in the country's relationship to the international capital market, or else gradually, e.g., as a consequence of differential productivity growth vis-à-vis the country's trading partners.

Estimates of whether a rate is in fundamental equilibrium require judgments that in practice contain subjective elements regarding cyclical adjustment, the underlying capital flow, and trade elasticities. As a result, skeptics deny any hope of identifying the fundamental equilibrium rate. The concept certainly has a normative element, inasmuch as what constitute the "underlying capital flow" and "internal balance" depend on the macroeconomic policy regarded as appropriate.

Current Equilibrium

This term is intended to indicate the rate that would obtain if markets had full knowledge of all relevant facts, including elements unrelated to "the fundamentals" which determine the fundamental equilibrium rate. The current equilibrium rate will depend inter alia upon the path of interest rates, which in turn depends on the stance of macroeconomic policy and the state of the business cycle, and, given risk aversion, on net asset positions vis-à-vis the rest of the world. The current equilibrium rate varies around the fundamental equilibrium, depreciating below it at the start of a recession when future interest rates are expected to be low (so as to generate a yield-equalizing appreciation during the period when domestic interest rates are actually low).[7] This is the concept of equilibrium that is in the

[6] *The Role of Exchange Rates in the Adjustment of International Payments* (Washington: International Monetary Fund, 1970).

[7] R. Dornbusch, "Expectations and Exchange Rate Dynamics," *Journal of Political Economy* (December 1976).

minds of economists who model the behavior of exchange rates. It is apparently also sometimes what is meant by "the rate justified by fundamentals"; clarity would be served if those who use this phrase in the future would specify whether they are referring to what we have termed the fundamental equilibrium rate or to the current equilibrium rate.

Given that knowledge is not perfect, one has to interpret the concept of the current equilibrium rate in a rational expectations sense, as the rate that would be expected to equalize yields (in the simple case of risk neutrality) on the basis of currently available information. The current equilibrium rate therefore adjusts in response to relevant news, which may concern the state of the cycle or macroeconomic policy as well as the real changes that alter the fundamental equilibrium rate. The current equilibrium rate refers to a nominal rather than a real rate.

Market Equilibrium

This is simply the exchange rate that would clear the market in the absence of official intervention. It is easy to identify the presence of equilibrium in this sense, since the objective fact of nonintervention implies that the rate is in equilibrium. Conversely, absence of equilibrium is signified by the presence of heavy intervention, reserve borrowing, or policy changes designed to sustain the rate.

If markets were rational, in the sense of always selecting the unique stable trajectory, then the market equilibrium would necessarily coincide with current equilibrium. That is why market enthusiasts equate intervention with a policy of distorting the rate away from equilibrium. But note that even someone who accepts it as axiomatic that the government cannot expect systematically to outsmart the market might believe there was a case for the government to modify its macroeconomic policy in order to limit the deviation of current and market rates from fundamental equilibrium. An *additional* possible justification for "market meddling" would be a belief in the existence of such market irrationalities as (extrapolative expectations formation leading to) speculative runs, for under those conditions the market equilibrium deviations from current (as well as fundamental) equilibrium.

The market equilibrium rate clearly refers to a nominal rate and, like current equilibrium, responds to relevant news. Some believe that it also responds to irrelevant news.

If the only criterion relevant to choosing an exchange rate target were its effect on trade flows and trade policy, it is obvious that one would target on fundamental equilibrium.[8] But one of the main traditional arguments for exchange rate flexibility is the additional independence it is supposed to give to macroeconomic policy. One degree of independence can in fact be secured without the rate's departing from fundamental equilibrium, namely, the accommodation of differential inflation. However, in other respects—for example, in order to pursue an anticyclical monetary policy at variance with that of the rest of the world, or to reduce the rate of inflation through a restrictive monetary policy—the exercise of policy independence requires a change in the real interest rate, which will necessarily lead to a deviation of the current equilibrium rate from the fundamental equilibrium rate.

Exchange rate targeting therefore involves a basic choice between seeking to avoid distortions to trade flows on the one hand and gaining additional freedom for monetary policy on the other. It is of course possible to visualize compromise strategies, in which both the desire to keep the exchange rate in the vicinity of fundamental equilibrium and the desire to vary interest rates out of tune with the international norm play a role. The classic version of such a compromise strategy is the "band proposal," under which the parity is set at fundamental equilibrium while the band around it provides scope for the current equilibrium rate to vary around parity to accommodate the interest rate variations deemed desirable in the light of the cyclical situation.[9]

---

[8] It is important to recognize that a policy of seeking to maintain fundamental equilibrium cannot be considered a case of "exchange rate protection" as that term is used by Corden, "Exchange Rate Protection." Exchange rate protection à la Corden arises when the exchange rate is maintained at a rate depreciated relative to the welfare-maximizing level so as to increase the real income of the tradable sector, or a lagging part of the tradable sector. A common reason for countries' adopting a policy of exchange rate protection is, according to Corden, the "Dutch disease," which stems from rapid expansion of a leading part of the tradable sector, typically due to exploitation of resource discoveries (Dutch gas, North sea—or other—oil, Australian minerals). The high productivity in the leading sector leads to appreciation of the real exchange rate and adverse effects on the rest of the tradable sector, which therefore lobbies for exchange rate protection. This is clearly not the same thing as a policy of seeking to avoid demand-managment policies (or shifts in portfolio preferences) leading to adverse shifts in competitiveness and trade flows.

[9] See R. I. McKinnon, "Monetary Theory and Controlled Flexibility in the Foreign Exchanges," *Essays in International Finance*, no. 84 (Princeton, NJ: Princeton University, 1971), for the classic exposition and G. N. Halm, "The 'Band' Proposal: The Limits of Exchange Rate Variations," *Special*

The Impact of Misalignments on Trade Flows

There is a long literature in international monetary economics on the impact of exchange rate changes on trade flows, dating back to some of the earliest applications of econometrics in the 1940s. Much of the early evidence tended to suggest that the effect was weak, nonexistent, or even perverse, and the phrase "elasticity pessimists" was coined to describe those who accepted this evidence at face value.

However, Orcutt[10] argued that there were technical reasons for expecting the elasticity estimates to be biased toward zero, and subsequent work seems to have justified this view. In particular, the use of distributed-lag models permitted the recognition of high long-run elasticities in conjunction with low short-run elasticities, which has for many years been taken as the stylized fact about the response of trade flows to changes in relative prices. Although elasticity pessimism lives on here and there, a typical result for the long-run price elasticity of demand for the manufactured exports of a medium-sized industrial country would be something like -1.5 or -2.[11]

During the 1960s a number of studies attempted to estimate separately "exchange-rate elasticities" and "tariff elasticities," the former representing the impact on trade flows of exchange rate changes

---

Papers in International Finance, no. 6 (Princeton, NJ: Princeton University, June 1965), for the first modern proposal of this idea.

[10] Guy H. Orcutt, "Measurement of Price Elasticities in International Trade," *Review of Economics and Statistics,* vol. 32 (May 1950), pp. 117–32.

[11] A recent review of findings in this area is Robert M. Stern, Jonathan Francis, and Bruce Schumacher, *Price Elasticities in International Trade* (Toronto: Macmillan of Canada, 1976). A contrary view is stated in Richard Blackhurst and Jan Tumlir, *Trade Relations Under Flexible Exchange Rates,* GATT Studies in International Trade, no. 8, September 1980; however, their own analyses recognize the importance of exchange rate changes for trade balances in Germany, Japan, France, and Switzerland and reject such importance for the United States and Italy only by rejecting the well-established time lags between price and volume changes (pp. 25–27). Blackhurst and Tumlir are correct, however in asserting that changes in GNP have greater effects on trade than exchange rate changes, that the latter can have lasting impact only if supported by proper domestic policies, and that "exchange rate fluctuations in no way reduce the importance of efforts to liberalize world trade," (p. 13).

and the latter the impact of tariff changes.[12] The stylized fact emerged that tariff elasticities were substantially larger, by a factor of two or three, than exchange rate elasticities. The usual explanation of this empirical regularity was the greater confidence presumably felt by traders that tariff changes would result in "permanent" changes in competitiveness.

In comparing the relative importance of tariff and exchange rate changes, however, it must be recognized that there has been a much greater degree of fluctuation in exchange rates than in tariffs during the postwar period. The celebrated trade liberalization of the Kennedy Round, for example, which is widely referred to as a 35 percent reduction, cut tariffs by an average of only 4–5 percentage points for the United States and European Economic Community (EEC) and about 7 percentage points for Japan and the United Kingdom.[13] By contrast, real effective exchange rates[14] frequently change by such amounts within very short periods of time—and remain further away from their underlying equilibrium paths (by as much as 10–20 percent) for extended episodes, as noted below. Hence the economic impact of exchange rate changes may at times substantially exceed the impact of tariff changes, even if tariff elasticities are in fact a good bit higher than exchange rate elasticities.

As to the future, tariffs remaining after the Multilateral Trade Negotiations (MTN) cuts will average about 4–6 percent in each of the major industrialized trading areas. Their complete elimination would then be overshadowed by the fluctuations which frequently occur, and the misalignments which periodically persist, in exchange rates. This is not to say that further trade liberalization would not be

[12] For example see Lawrence B. Krause, "United States Imports, 1947–1958," *Econometrica,* vol. 30 (April 1962), pp. 221–38, and Mordechai E. Kreinin, "'Price' vs 'Tariff' Elasticities in International Trade—A Suggested Reconciliation," *American Economic Review,* vol. 57, no. 4 (September 1967), pp. 891–94.

[13] Ernest Preeg, *Traders and Diplomats* (Washington: Brookings Institution, 1970), pp. 208–11. Cuts on some individual products, of course, were higher—though none of the major categories for these countries changed by more than 10 percentage points.

[14] The "real effective exchange rate" is the proper measure of a country's currency for these purposes. It (1) weights a country's exchange rate in terms of the currencies of its major trading partners (to make it "effective" rather than bilateral) and (2) adjusts for differences in domestic price movements between the country and its trading partners (to make it "real" rather than nominal).

significant, of course, but that shifts in trade balances are likely to be more influenced by changes in exchange rates than in tariffs (although changes in other forms of protection may well be more important in certain sectors).

The evidence therefore indicates that changes in real effective exchange rates have significant effects on international trade flows—and, through trade, on key domestic economic variables such as output, employment and prices. Deardorff and Stern[15] have made the following estimates of the effects of each percentage point of exchange rate change for the major trading areas (between the second quarters of 1980 and 1981):

TABLE 3.1   EFFECTS OF EXCHANGE RATE CHANGE, MAJOR TRADING AREAS

	Price level (percentage)	*Unemployment*	*Trade balance (dollars)*
United States	0.3	70,000	3 billion
European Community	0.4	100,000	3 billion
Japan	0.5	40,000	1 billion

These estimates suggest that a 20 percent overvaluation could raise unemployment by 1.4 million in the United States or 2 million in Europe, while a similar undervaluation could add 6 percent to the price level in the United States, 8 percent in Europe and 10 percent in Japan.

The Impact of Misalignments on Trade Policy

It would be surprising if such sizable effects on trade flows, output, unemployment and inflation did not have an impact on policy. What is perhaps surprising is that so much of the impact has been on *trade* policy rather than on *monetary* policy, at least in the last decade. But the historical record suggests that in the United States this has indeed been the case.

Severe misalignments emerged in the final years of the Bretton Woods system for several major currencies—the dollar and pound were overvalued, the DM and yen undervalued. As revealed by the realignments which became unavoidable in 1971 and 1973 (and earlier

---

[15] Deardorff and Stern, "The Sectoral Impact of the Recent Appreciation of the US Dollar."

for sterling), these disequilibria exceeded 15 percent to 20 percent for a number of major exchange rates.

Flexible exchange rates were then widely adopted, and subsequently authorized by amendments to the IMF Articles of Agreement. Though not widely articulated at the time, trade policy concerns were an important motivation behind the US push for both the parity realignments of 1971 and 1973 and the systemic shift to flexible rates. The growing dollar overvaluation of the late 1960s and early 1970s had contributed heavily to protectionist pressures in the United States—as manifest by the adoption of new import restrictions in three major industries (textiles, steel, meat), House passage of the "Mills bill" in 1970 and widespread support for the Burke-Hartke proposals in 1971–72. Basic monetary changes were correctly deemed to be essential to avoid substantial risk of fundamental change in the direction of US trade policy, as well as for broader monetary and domestic macroeconomic reasons.

Since flexible rates were expected to avoid prolonged disequilibrium, it became natural to assume that monetary phenomena would no longer create problems for trade policy. If anything, the rapid equilibration of payments imbalances which they promised—and in fact achieved in several cases in the mid-1970s, particularly regarding the United States and Japan—seemed to strengthen the international environment for a liberal trading system.

By 1976, however, Bergsten was already noting that "major disturbances [had] returned to the international monetary system. . . [raising] particularly serious problems for trade policy."[16] Japan was intervening heavily to avoid appreciation of the yen, and thus sowing the seeds for its huge surpluses of 1977–78—which triggered major new trade problems.[17] The dollar again became substantially overvalued in the exchange markets for at least two years.

The current situation is even more troublesome, as it becomes clear that exchange rates may respond for prolonged periods much more to interest rate differentials and international political events than to underlying competitive relationships. As is well known, the dollar has now been substantially overvalued for some time—perhaps on the order of 15 percent to 20 percent, as in the final phase of fixed exchange rates. From the dollar lows of late 1978 to its highs of mid-

---

[16] C. Fred Bergsten, "Let's Avoid a Trade War," *Foreign Policy*, no. 23 (Summer 1976), p. 26.

[17] As detailed below, this is the clearest case in recent times of "exchange rate protection" as defined by Corden in the article cited above.

and late-1982, the dollar rose by a trade-weighted average of 25–30 percent against the other major currencies (and by 40–50 percent against the yen and DM). Over that same period, US inflation averaged about the same as that of the other major countries (and was 15 to 20 percentage points higher than in Germany and Japan). Even allowing for some dollar undervaluation in late 1978 and the roughness of the concepts involved, the dollar became overvalued by perhaps 15 percent to 20 percent on average and by substantially more against the yen and DM. The yen and perhaps to a lesser extent the DM, again became substantially undervalued.[18]

The case of the United States graphically depicts the impact of exchange rate misalignments on trade policy. The three postwar periods of most severe protectionist pressures in the United States— the early 1970s, 1976–77, and the present—followed promptly upon periods of overvaluation of the dollar:

- the growing dollar overvaluation of the late 1960s and early 1970s, subsequently revealed in the the devaluations totaling more than 20 percent in 1971 and 1973, coincided with the deepest protectionist pressures of the postwar period as noted above (despite modest levels of aggregate unemployment)
- the restoration of dollar equilibrium via the devaluations of 1971 and 1973, along with the new focus of macroeconomic policy on inflation, corresponded to extensive unilateral US trade liberalization in 1973–74 and passage of the Trade Act of 1974 authorizing further liberalization via the MTN, despite a level of unemployment not seen since the 1930s
- renewed dollar overvaluation in 1975–76, which required a depreciation of about 15 percent in 1977–78, correlated with renewal of protectionist pressure and the adoption of several new restrictive measures (steel trigger price mechanism, TPM; shoes; sugar)
- the restoration of dollar equilibrium in 1978–79 supported a dramatic improvement in the US trade position and overwhelming congressional support for the Trade Act of 1979, ratifying the MTN

[18] The details are in C. Fred Bergsten, "The Costs of Reaganomics," *Foreign Policy*, no. 44 (Fall 1981), and "The Villain is the Overvalued Dollar," *Challenge*, vol.25, no. 1 (March-April 1982). Rough calculations of purchasing power parity, with a March 1973 base, can be inferred from Morgan Guaranty, *World Financial Markets* (January 1983), p. 12, which imply for November 1982 a dollar overvalued by about 23 percent and a yen undervalued by about 20 percent.

• the contemporary onset of the most severe dollar overvaluation since the collapse of the Bretton Woods system, along with the new highs in the unemployment rate, clearly contribute to the renewal of major pressures for import relief.

The impact of exchange rates on trade policy is even more evident in the bilateral relationship between the United States and Japan over the past dozen years.[19] This relationship is now experiencing its third period of major conflict. The first of these episodes led to the US import surcharge of August 1971, viewed in Japan as the second of the "Nixon shocks" aimed at that country, and a US threat to invoke the "Trading with the Enemy Act" against its chief Pacific ally.[20] The second episode produced major US pressure on Japan during 1977–78 to boost its domestic growth rate, with lasting effect on Japanese confidence in its American connection and immediate impact on the political career of the current prime minister.[21] The third, current, episode promises to be the nastiest yet—with the United States joined as *demandeur* by the European Community, with racist overtones already creeping into the rhetoric, with frustration on both sides of the Pacific, and with obvious spillover to the reemerging issue of security relations between the two countries.

There are a number of ongoing, even structural, problems in the US-Japan economic relationship which must be addressed through the conventional tools of trade policy. However, exchange rate misalignments have been present in each of the three crisis periods, and go far to explain the difficulties that have arisen on each occasion. In each instance, the yen became substantially undervalued—dramatically improving Japan's competitiveness around the world. The huge swings in trade and current account balances which marked each episode, and which triggered the sharp intensification of US-Japan hostility, can be traced primarily to these exchange rate movements, although the Japanese delay in expanding demand was also an important element in the surplus in 1977–78.

By the beginning of the 1970s, the parities of the dollar and yen—which had been set in 1933 and 1949, respectively—were clearly out

[19]   This analysis is drawn from C. Fred Bergsten, "What to Do About the US-Japan Economic Conflict," *Foreign Affairs*, vol. 60. no. 5 (Summer 1982).

[20]   The best published account is in I. M. Destler, Haruhiro Fukui, and Hideo Sato, *The Textile Wrangle: Conflict in Japanese-American Relations, 1969–1971* (Ithaca and London: Cornell University Press, 1979).

[21]   For an excellent analysis of this period see I. M. Destler and Hideo Sato, *Coping with US-Japanese Economic Conflicts* (Lexington, Mass.: D. C. Heath and Co., 1982), especially chapter 6.

of line with the underlying economic relationships between those
countries and between them and the rest of the world. With the onset
of US inflation from the mid-1960s, stemming from the Vietnam war
and simultaneous expansion of Great Society programs, the dollar
became substantially overvalued, as already noted. With the dramatic
expansion of economic capacity and productivity in Japan, the yen
became substantially undervalued.

The results began to accumulate in 1968–69 and accelerated rapidly
to the first postwar crisis in US-Japan economic relations in 1970–
71. Japan began to run steady and growing external surpluses. The
US current account balance slipped into deficit for the first time in
the postwar period. Japan's bilateral surplus with the United States
expanded sevenfold from 1966–67 to 1971–72.

One result was the most intense pressure for trade protection in
the United States of the entire postwar period, at least until the
present. The Mills bill, which passed the House of Representatives
in 1970, would have placed numerical limits on import penetration
in virtually every industry. The proposed Burke-Hartke bill, which
would have drastically curtailed both US imports and foreign investments, was the source of widespread congressional interest and
support during 1971–72. For the first time, the bulk of the pressure
was aimed at Japan. Exchange rate misalignment had entered the
picture as a major source of difficulty between the United States and
Japan.

There is no need to speculate about whether the exchange rates
had become severely misaligned. Despite the historical antipathy of
both countries to parity changes, the realignments of 1971 and 1973
devalued the dollar and revalued the yen: the yen appreciated in
terms of the dollar by over 30 percent. It was finally understood by
both countries that such changes were essential to preserve an open
trading system as well as to avoid the repeated bursts of international
monetary instability which were eroding the entire global economic
system.

These exchange rate realignments achieved their objective. In 1973,
before the onset of the first oil crisis, Japan had returned to global
balance and the United States to modest surplus. The bilateral merchandise account, on which the oil shock had little direct impact,
returned during 1973–75 to the much lower levels of 1969–70. Adjustment had occurred and the first major episode of US-Japan economic conflict receded into history.

In 1975–76, however, a renewed exchange rate misalignment began
to develop. The dollar appreciated substantially because the United

States ran large current account surpluses during that period, although these surpluses (especially in 1975) were due primarily to the depth of the US recession—which was far sharper than in Japan or other major countries. This, reinforced by the delayed recovery in Japan, sowed the seeds for a renewed deterioration of the US competitive position and the record deficits which ensued in 1977–78.

Meanwhile, Japan committed one of its most serious policy errors of the entire postwar period. Arguing that its renewed current account surpluses were transitory phenomena, attributable solely to the cyclical situation, Japan intervened massively in the foreign exchange markets throughout 1976 to block significant strengthening of the yen. The result, as Bergsten predicted at the time,[22] was a renewed undervaluation of the yen and massive Japanese surpluses in 1977–78—including a fivefold rise in the bilateral surplus with the United States.

This juxtaposition of developments produced the second outbreak of major US-Japan economic tensions, in 1977–78. Again, the main culprit was a severe misalignment in the exchange rate between the two currencies. Again, a correction of that misalignment—which began to occur from early 1977, when the Carter administration successfuly insisted that Japan let the yen rate respond to market forces—was the crucial factor which eased the tension. By 1979 and 1980, the United States returned once more to global surplus and Japan—hit also by the second oil shock—moved into sizable deficit.

For a third time, however, the pendulum swung too far. Beginning in early 1981, the peculiar policy mix of the new US administration produced record levels of real interest rates, huge movements of capital into the dollar and a currency probably as overvalued as in the final stages of the Bretton Woods system.

From its lows of late 1978 to its highs of August 1981 and June and November 1982, the dollar rose by about 50 percent against the yen. Meanwhile, Japanese inflation ran about 20 percentage points less than US inflation. The price competitiveness of the United States in world trade thus deteriorated by about 70 percent vis-à-vis Japan within about three to four years.

A new crisis would inevitably follow—and it did, reaching levels

[22] See his testimony before the House Banking Committee on June 3, 1976, and the Joint Economic Committee on October 18, 1976, both reprinted in *Managing International Economic Interdependence: Selected Papers of C. Fred Bergsten, 1975–1976* (Lexington, Mass.: D.C. Heath and Co., 1977), chapters 5 and 6, as well as Bergsten, "Let's Avoid a Trade War."

of tension not seen for a decade. The global US current account deteriorated substantially in real terms throughout 1981 and 1982, and sharply in current dollars in the second half of 1982, despite the deep domestic recession and sharp reduction in oil imports. Indeed, this decline in the external accounts was more important than the housing or auto slumps in pushing the US economy into the 1981–82 recession.

On the other side of the Pacific, Japan moved back into global surplus. The bilateral imbalance in favor of Japan soared to record levels. All these developments seem likely to become even worse in 1983, as dollar overvaluation and yen undervaluation persist; their full effects take up to two years to appear, so the die is cast by the exchange rate configuration of 1982 for continued major trouble.

Analysis of the turbulent recent history of US-Japan economic conflict thus points to the exchange rate relationship between the dollar and the yen as the single most critical variable. To be sure, high unemployment in the United States (as at present) intensifies the problem. Japan's continuing "propensity not to import" and periodic export surges do so as well. More rapid US productivity growth, if not matched by concomitant improvement in Japan, could help resolve the problem. So could increased Japanese spending on housing and other social infrastructure. Cyclical disjunction, as in 1977–78, can make things worse. All these aspects of the overall problem must be addressed continuously.

But the major problem lies in the monetary realm. Hence any serious effort to remedy the US-Japan problem must address the underlying causes of the severe misalignments which have periodically emerged between dollar and yen. In view of the critical importance of the US-Japan relationship to the global trading system, such remedies will also be crucial to its future stability.

Strategies of Exchange Rate Management

Although the above evidence relates to the United States and the US-Japanese bilateral relationship, and it would be desirable to examine whether misaligned exchange rates can help explain trade policies in other countries as well, the experiences examined suffice to create a prima facie case for believing that trade policy considerations should be accorded a major role in shaping exchange rate policy. This section of the paper considers, albeit briefly, whether and how a government that wished to maintain its exchange rate in the vicinity of fundamental equilibrium could hope to achieve that objective.

The basic analytical point is implicit in the distinction made earlier between current equilibrium and fundamental equilibrium: if one wishes to drive the market rate toward fundamental equilibrium, one has to be prepared to orient macroeconomic policy, and specifically monetary policy, to that end. Both Hume's price-specie-flow mechanism and the monetary approach to the balance of payments imply that there is no reason to doubt the possibility of achieving a particular target for the nominal exchange rate *provided* that monetary policy is systematically devoted to that end. There are three broad ways in which that might be done: by pegging with supportive monetary policies, by floating with target zones or reference rates, or by imposing capital controls.

Pegging with Supportive Monetary Policies

The most certain way to achieve a target for maintaining fundamental equilibrium (or the real exchange rate) would be to intervene to whatever extent was necessary in support of the nominal rate needed to achieve the desired real rate on the basis of current price levels, and ensure that the domestic monetary consequences of the intervention were (at least partly) unsterilized. The nominal rate to be achieved by intervention would crawl in line with the inflation differential, and might also be adjusted (presumably also on a crawling basis) to offset the effects of differential productivity growth and to induce any underlying change in competitiveness regarded as desirable in the interests of payments adjustment. Nonsterilization of intervention would require countries to adhere to prespecified domestic credit expansion (DCE) targets, as has been urged by McKinnon.[23] As McKinnon points out, if a group of countries adopts such a policy, the result (abstracting from differences in reserve requirements) is to ensure that their *collective* money supply actually grows at the rate implied by the sum of the DCE targets and is independent of intervention policies, despite the fact that individual national money supplies will depend on intervention.

---

[23] R. I. McKinnon, "On Securing a Common Monetary Policy in Europe," Banca Nazionale del Lavoro *Quarterly Review*, March 1973. However, in his case the intervention is urged in support of fixed nominal rates rather than fixed real rates.

Floating with Target Zones or Reference Rates

Pegging the nominal rate at the level needed to achieve the real target rate involves accepting and announcing an obligation to prevent the market rate from deviating by more than a specified amount (the margin) from the central rate. An alternative strategy involves adopting a central rate or target zone, but not accepting any obligation to defend it. By definition, therefore, the rate floats. (The central rate or target zone might or might not be publicly acknowledged or announced.)

Under such an approach, the goal would to be avoid clearly "incorrect" rates rather than to try to maintain exactly "correct" rates. Intervention, backed up by monetary policy, could be systematically directed toward pushing the market rate toward the central rate. One version of such an approach is that intervention should endeavor, but not guarantee, to keep the rate within some zone, which might or might not be expressed as margins around a central rate. Another version is the "reference rate proposal," under which any intervention must always be such as to push the rate toward the central rate, but without any guarantee that there will be intervention at all—and certainly without any guarantee of sufficient intervention to establish a market rate within any particular margin of the central rate. Under either proposal, the central rate or target zone could crawl on the same principles as if it were pegged. The effectiveness of such intervention policies in keeping the rate close to target (the central rate or zone) would depend not merely on the scale of the intervention, but also—more importantly—on whether the intervention was sterilized or not.

Capital Controls

Aside from intervention and monetary policy, the other main instrument for seeking to manipulate exchange rates is capital controls.[24] In light of the huge outflows from Japan which resulted from its liberalization of capital markets in late 1980, compounded by interest rate differentials disadvantageous to the yen, Bergsten has urged a sharp cutback in Japanese capital exports (through "admin-

---

[24] In recent years, the main advocate of using capital controls (in the form of "real interest equalization taxes") to influence exchange rates has been Dornbusch. See his memorandum on monetary policy to the House of Commons Select Committee on the Treasury and Civil Service (London: Her Majesty's Stationery Office, 17 July 1980).

istrative guidance") and massive foreign borrowing by the Japanese government to push the yen to a more appropriate level—a proposal motivated directly by concern over the trade implications of the current undervaluation of the yen.[25] Doubts about capital controls have traditionally stemmed from two sources: their distorting effects on resource allocation, and the ease with which they can be circumvented in a highly integrated world economy ("money is fungible").[26]

The Impact of Managed Exchange Rates

Suppose that one or another, or some combination, of the three monetary options were successful in the proximate aim of maintaining the nominal exchange rate deemed desirable on grounds of competitiveness. It remains to consider: whether achievement of a nominal target can ensure achievement of the target real rate and whether that might seriously destabilize the domestic economy.

With regard to the first issue, the answer would clearly be no if the nominal rate were held constant. However, the proposals considered here involve the nominal rate crawling to maintain competitiveness at the target level. That is clearly possible—but it does incur the second danger, of destabilizing the domestic economy. Specifically, if the competitiveness target were fixed at a level which implied a real wage lower than the labor force was willing to accept, the enforcement of that target would result in accelerating inflation. This

[25] See Bergsten, "What to Do About the US-Japan Economic Conflict."

[26] For the sake of completeness, it should also be mentioned that, in principle, target levels of competitiveness could be pursued by the use of comprehensive border tax adjustments to offset the effects of deviation of the exchange rate from its fundamental equilibrium level. There are, however, formidable objections to such a course of action. First, border tax adjustments are never comprehensive; at best they tend to cover only visible trade, at worst some sectors secure exemption (e.g., because of the perceived inequity of taxing essential imports). Second, it may be difficult to secure the prompt withdrawal of such protection even when no longer merited by an exchange rate misalignment. Third, the volatility of exchange rates coupled with the lag between placing an order and shipment may result in traders' facing inappropriate and inequitable border taxes. Fourth, the taxes will influence the current account in a way that may push exchange rates further away from their desired levels and thus have a perverse effect on the underlying situation. For these reasons we believe that the option of border tax adjustments—unlike the three monetary options discussed previously—should be eliminated from further consideration.

is precisely the same result as occurs if a government tries to peg the unemployment rate at a level below the natural rate, or to peg the interest rate at a level below its natural rate. Any attempt at macroeconomic management can be counterproductive if the real variables are targeted at disequilibrium levels; whether one concludes that macro management should be abandoned depends on whether or not one trusts governments to pick sensible targets, and modify them in time to avoid disaster when conditions change.

There are other ways in which pursuing exchange rate targets could be destabilizing. Pursuit of a constant nominal target that involves a severe real misalignment can of course be seriously destabilizing, as Britain found out after 1925 and other countries have discovered since. Pursuit of inconsistent targets by the major countries would obviously be a recipe for disaster; even if the targeted exchange rates were internationally consistent, the system could have an inflationary or deflationary potential unless the target rates of DCE were coordinated to ensure an appropriate world rate of monetary growth. One may therefore conclude that a redirection of policy toward maintaining exchange rates close to fundamental equilibrium would require more effective international coordination, as well as more responsible and responsive national policy making, than has been customary.

Conclusions

It is clear from the analysis presented here that trade policy in the 1980s, and beyond, could proceed much more smoothly under a more effective international monetary régime—and may not be able to proceed in a liberal direction at all unless such a régime, with supportive policies in at least the major countries, can be developed. Prolonged deviations of exchange rates from fundamental equilibrium can and do generate protectionist pressures, from countries with both overvalued and undervalued currencies. Considerable asymmetries compound the problem and fail to achieve much, if any, in the way of countervailing pressures in the other direction.

The postwar record reveals that trade policy in the United States, at least, has been substantially affected by the existence of equilibrium or disequilibrium in the exchange rate of the dollar. US-Japan economic conflict, which is central to global trade policy as a whole, has been particularly disrupted by the frequent recurrence of yen-dollar misalignments. The advent of flexible exchange rates has failed to assure the degree of equilibrium in currency relationships that is essential if liberal trade policies are to prevail; indeed, recent misalignments, particularly for the dollar and yen, may be as great as existed in the final breakdown stages of the Bretton Woods system of fixed parities.

Hence any comprehensive strategy for trade policy in the 1980s must encompass a monetary component, as well as working on the more traditional elements of commercial affairs. It is clearly possible, in principle, both to define "fundamental equilibrium" for exchange rates and to fashion an exchange rate régime which would avoid deviations from such levels significant enough to cause serious trade distortions (and thus protectionist pressures). Considerable work will be needed to design and negotiate such a system in practice, but the importance of the issue counsels an early start.

CHAPTER 4

"Reciprocity": A New Approach To World Trade Policy?

William R. Cline

More than thirty bills have been introduced in the Ninety-seventh Congress calling for US government action to achieve "reciprocity in foreign trade," or, as this term is used in these proposals, access to foreign markets comparable to that in the United States. US reciprocity objectives in the past meant seeking reciprocal *changes* in protection in trade negotiations; the new approach seeks reciprocity in the *level* of protection *bilaterally* and over a certain *range of goods*. The principal proposals envision US retaliation in the form of higher protection against any foreign country that does not grant comparable market access to US exports. Whether or not any of these bills pass, the surge of congressional interest in this approach marks what may be a watershed in US commercial policy and requires a reexamination of that policy. Reciprocity enforced by retaliation would violate the fundamental principle of unconditional most-favored-nation (MFN) treatment followed by the United States for the last sixty years, and would risk trade wars through counter-retaliation.

Critics of the new reciprocity, especially those in the foreign official community, maintain that it is thinly disguised protectionism. Ironically, key sponsors of reciprocity legislation consider it a preferable alternative to protection, one that is designed to address trade pressures by increasing US export opportunities rather than extending the network of barriers to US imports. Indeed, groups normally most

Note: Originally published as *Reciprocity: A New Approach to World Trade Policy?* POLICY ANALYSES IN INTERNATIONAL ECONOMICS, No. 2. Washington: Institute for International Economics, September 1982.

inclined to support proposals for import barriers have not been enthusiastic about this legislation; for example, the AFL-CIO contends
that it "diverts attention from the real problem" of excessive imports.[1]
Nonetheless, the risk is high that a protectionist outcome would result
from a strategy of reciprocity based on the threat of retaliation.

The new reciprocity movement has appropriated the term to a
narrow usage focusing on equivalent market treatment, in some cases
even for limited ranges of goods. In the more traditional conception
of the term, reciprocity has meant a broad balance between the reduction in trade barriers offered by the United States and the liberalization secured from other major trading partners in negotiations,
or reciprocity "at the margin" on a basis of all products considered
together. US trade policy has always been built around this broader
concept of reciprocity, and its achievement has been not only a goal
but also in good measure an accomplishment of the succession of
postwar trade negotiations. The new reciprocity movement focuses
instead on reciprocity of the resulting outcome, and tends to base
judgments on sectoral grounds rather than recognize an overall balance. It also tends to seek bilateral reciprocity of trade outcome,
focusing on countries that have a bilateral surplus with the United
States while not taking into account US bilateral trade surpluses with
other areas.

The basic policy issue is how the reciprocity objective of US policy
should be defined. In short, has the trading environment reached a
point where the United States should begin an aggressive campaign
to demand liberalization by other countries, either in the aggregate
or in specific sectors, by brandishing threats of retaliation whenever
the United States unilaterally decides that the current balance of
opportunities is "unfair"? Would US interests, and world interests,
be served by this approach?

Before turning to detailed analysis of the new reciprocity movement, some of its most important aspects warrant special mention.

First, there is a strong *sectoral* theme to the push for reciprocity.
Many of the proposed bills have called for reciprocal or symmetric
treatment in individual product sectors such as telecommunications
or high technology. The omnibus bills also have a sectoral nature in
that they refer implicitly only to those broad product sectors where

---

[1] *Washington Post*, 7 May 1982.

the United States is "competitive,"[2] and it is difficult to see how equal market access would be judged without reference to some specified range of products. Nonetheless, these broader bills represent a second (and, by mid-1982, dominant) track of the reciprocity movement that is multisectoral, specifically acknowledges that reciprocity need not mean symmetry of market access in a narrow sector, and recognizes that retaliation need not be confined to the specific sector where the grievance is found.

Second, a major objective of the reciprocity movement is to open up foreign markets in *services and foreign investment*, two areas that have been largely outside the trading rules of the General Agreement on Tariffs and Trade (GATT).

Third, the new reciprocity is *unilateral* in nature. As such, it would usually involve the unilateral scrapping by the United States of trade commitments agreed previously in negotiations. This reneging on US obligations, without international authorization, would be likely to precipitate foreign *retaliation*.

Fourth, the new reciprocity would force the complying foreign country into a position of either defaulting on its own MFN obligations to third parties or else making a new unilateral concession available to all—thereby discarding a bargaining chip for future negotiations. It is unclear whether even the reciprocity advocates would want foreign countries to make special liberalizing exceptions that applied to the United States but no other country.

Fifth, the push for reciprocity may well reflect an attempt to deal with what could be a growing phenomenon of *"arbitrary comparative advantage."* In some manufacturing products, the traditional bases for trade specialization—such as differences in relative national availabilities of labor, capital, skilled labor, and technological sophistication—may no longer dominate (as industrial and some developing countries become more similar in these attributes), while other traditional determinants of trade (such as natural resource endowment) may not be germane. In such products, the pattern of trade specialization may be arbitrary, and factors such as noncompetitive firm behavior and government intervention may determine which country prevails. In such products, the need for a "level playing ground" is

---

[2] In introducing his bill (S. 2094) Senator John Danforth (R-Mo.) stated its purpose as: "To achieve the same degree of access to foreign markets for competitive US exports, services and investment that we accord to other countries." *Congressional Record*, vol. 128 (11), p. 5.

especially acute. These themes of the reciprocity movement are discussed in greater detail below (including Appendix 4.B), after an examination of the premises, principles, and likely outcome of the new reciprocity approach to trade policy.

Unequal Market Access?

The premise underlying the proposed reciprocity legislation is that, after decades of US leadership in trade liberalization, "the result is an American market with comparatively few import barriers while foreign markets are protected by a variety of restrictions."[3] Hence, the United States has lost its bargaining chips, and legislation providing the sanction of retaliation would restore them.

The widespread perception that the US market is substantially more open than foreign markets has little empirical support, at least for manufactured products. Tariffs after the Tokyo Round are at approximately the same (low) levels in the United States, Europe, Canada, and Japan. In the late 1970s and early 1980s, the product sectors protected overtly by major nontariff barriers (NTBs, such as those on textiles and apparel, footwear, television sets, and Japanese automobiles; and the trigger price mechanism [TPM] or quotas in steel) covered 34 percent of the market for US manufactures, 10 percent for Canada, 20 percent for Germany, 32 percent for France, 34 percent for Italy, 22 percent for the United Kingdom, and 7 percent for Japan.[4]

The extent of market coverage does not reveal the severity of protection on the products in question, of course. For example, the degree of protection on Japanese automobiles is undoubtedly higher in Italy (where fewer than 3,000 units annually are permitted), France (where the limit is 3 percent of the market) and the United Kingdom (11 percent of the market) than in the United States, where the limit of 1.68 million units represents approximately 20 percent of the market.[5] Similarly, European quotas on steel imports have been more

---

[3] Ibid., p. 1.

[4] Weighting by each sector's share in total apparent consumption in manufacturing. William R. Cline, "Exports of Manufactures from Developing Countries: Performance and Prospects for Market Access" (Washington: Brookings Institution, 1982; processed).

[5] Shailendra J. Anjaria, Zubair Iqbal, Lorenzo L. Perez, and Wanda S. Tseng, *Trade Policy Developments in Industrial Countries* (Washington: International Monetary Fund, July 1981), pp. 13–15; and Andrew Loewinger,

restrictive than the trigger price mechanism used in the United States in 1978–81. Moreover, the "trade coverage" of overt nontariff barriers does not capture the influence of discriminatory government procurement or of disguised barriers such as administrative guidance, cultural factors, and noncompetitive practices—influences that may be especially important in Japan.

Nonetheless, it is a sobering fact that the available empirical evidence on nontariff barriers, much of it based on a comprehensive compendium by GATT, does show that the portion of the market covered by nontariff barriers in the United States is comparable to or wider than in other major industrial countries. At the very least, this evidence implies that, contrary to the usual premise behind reciprocity legislation, there can be no automatic presumption that the United States has a substantially more open market than those of its major trading partners.

If the conventional wisdom of greater market access in the United States is suspect for manufactures, it is closer to the mark in agriculture. Europe's Common Agricultural Policy (CAP) and Japan's quotas on meat, rice, citrus fruits, and other agricultural items are substantially more restrictive than the protection of US agriculture (limited mainly to meat, dairy products, and sugar).[6] However, the main thrust of the new reciprocity approach concerns perceived imbalances in access to markets for manufactured goods, not agricultural products.

But the real basis for the current perception of unequal access stems not from a careful analysis of protection itself, but primarily from growing frustration over the US bilateral trade deficit with Japan, which reached $16 billion in 1981[7] and is expected to hit $20 billion to $22 billion in 1982. Broadly, the reciprocity movement has been prompted almost exclusively by the persistent and (periodically resurfacing) perception that Japan keeps its market closed through a variety of devices. Indeed, some observers view the proposed reciprocity bills as part of a ritualized process whereby the US executive branch uses the threat of congressional action to extract Japanese

---

"Automobile Trade," in Gary Clyde Hufbauer, ed., *US International Economic Policy 1981: A Draft Report* (Washington: Georgetown University Law Center, 1982), pp. 4–11.

[6] See, for example, William R. Cline, Noboru Kawanabe, T.O.M. Kronsjo, and Thomas Williams, *Trade Negotiations in the Tokyo Round: A Quantitative Assessment* (Washington: Brookings Institution, 1978), ch. 4–5.

[7] *Survey of Current Business*, vol. 62(5) (May 1982), pp. 5–17.

concessions, but averts such legislation once concessions are obtained.[8]

Because so much of the impetus for reciprocity legislation comes from the frustration over Japan's perceived protection, a brief review of the evidence is in order.[9] It is generally agreed that, although Japan used protection for infant-industry development in the early postwar period, by now Japan's tariffs and overt NTBs in industry are as low as, or lower than, those of the United States. Agricultural quotas remain a problem, but do not appear to be the chief focus of congressional frustration. The immediate cause of the conflict is Japan's large bilateral surplus with the United States: in the words of Senator Robert Dole (R-Kan.), "reciprocity should be assessed not by what agreements promise but by actual results—by changes in the balance of trade and investment between ourselves and our major economic partners."[10]

Surely bilateral trade balances cannot be the criterion for trade equity. It must be recalled that the United States runs a large surplus with Europe, but US policymakers would be incensed if Europeans cited this fact as evidence that the US market is more closed than the European market.

A more relevant question is whether Japan has run a total current account surplus that is disproportionately large. A large chronic surplus could reflect high protection. In fact, however, from 1973 through 1981 Japan's current account balance was negative in five years and

---

[8] See Emilio Collado III, "Reciprocity Legislation," in Hufbauer, ed., *US International Economic Policy 1981*, ch. 5. On the other hand, some experts believe that, in the past, Japan has liberalized only in response to pressure and that the actual passage of reciprocity legislation would facilitate future bargaining with Japan. I.M. Destler, "How Not to Negotiate: Some Thoughts on Our Current Trade Flap with Japan," in US Congress, House, Committee on Foreign Affairs, 97th Cong., 2d sess. *Government Decision Making in Japan, Implications for the United States,* report of a workshop organized by the Subcommittee on Asian and Pacific Affairs of the Committee on Foreign Affairs, the Woodrow Wilson International Center for Scholars of the Smithsonian Institution, and the Congressional Research Service of the Library of Congress, March 16, 1982 (Washington: US Government Printing Office, 1982).

[9] An in-depth examination of the case of Japan, and of the structural features of its economy leading to its trade profile, appears in Gary R. Saxonhouse, "The Micro- and Macroeconomics of Foreign Sales to Japan," chapter 9, this volume.

[10] Robert Dole, "Reciprocity in Trade," *New York Times*, 22 January 1982.

positive in four. In the period before exchange rate floating, Japan's average current account surplus was relatively high (1.52 percent of GNP in 1968–72, although Japan had deficits in the early 1960s), but from 1973 to 1981 Japan's current account surplus was actually lower on average relative to GNP than those in the United States and Germany (0.15 percent versus 0.16 percent and 0.46 percent, respectively).[11]

More sophisticated critics point not to bilateral trade balances but to Japan's low ratio of manufactured imports to GNP as evidence of protection. In 1979 Japan's imports of manufactures were only 2.3 percent of GNP, compared with 3.1 percent in the United States and 8.8 percent in Germany.[12] However, the increase in oil prices inevitably drove Japan to a trading structure involving large surpluses in manufactures to compensate—by pure accounting necessity—for large deficits in primary products. Relatively low manufactured imports as a share of GNP should come as no great surprise.

On the other hand, Japan's share of total imports (not just manufactures) in GNP lies fully within the international pattern. In the period 1973–81, Japan's imports of all goods and services averaged 13.4 percent of GNP, intermediate between 9.1 percent in the United States and 25.3 percent in Germany (as would be expected considering that these two economies are larger and smaller, respectively, than the Japanese economy). Moreover, the 40 percent rise in imports relative to GNP for 1973–81 over the period 1968–72 was also intermediate between those in the United States (65 percent) and Germany (28 percent).[13] Thus, whether the criterion is the current account position over time, the average surplus relative to GNP, or average imports relative to GNP, Japan's profile shows no marked signs of excessive protection.

[11] Calculated from OECD, *Economic Outlook*, vol. 30 (Dec. 1982), p. 143 and IMF, *International Financial Statistics* (Yearbook 1981 and April 1982). The comparison is not biased by rising oil prices: from 1972 to 1980 the rise in the share of oil in imports was approximately 21 percentage points for both Japan (from 16.5 percent to 37.4 percent) and the United States (from 4.0 percent to 25.1 percent), although for Germany the rise was only 10 percentage points. Ibid.

[12] Calculated from OECD, *Statistics of Foreign Trade*, Series A (June 1982), pp. 30-32; IMF, *International Financial Statistics* (July 1982). Manufactures are defined here as Standard International Trade Classification (SITC) categories 5 through 9.

[13] Calculated from IMF, *International Financial Statistics,* various issues.

The few sophisticated econometric studies of Japanese imports have failed to document any systematic bias toward a protected economy. In one statistical model relating manufactured imports to variables such as factor availabilities (capital, labor, human capital), distance, and resources (oil, iron ore, land), Gary R. Saxonhouse finds that Japan's import profile is well explained by the underlying economic variables and shows no tendency toward downward bias from protection (indeed, some other industrial countries show more bias).[14]

There is, to be sure, a considerable anecdotal (or "eyewitness") tradition insisting that Japanese protection is severe and takes many indirect forms, from abuse of technical standards (such as time-consuming inspection of individual automobiles, or required changes in electrical cords for appliances) to cultural factors (distaste for imports, an antiquated distribution system). However, a close examination of this tradition suggests that it is not a persuasive indictment of Japanese practices; for example, sample surveys of US and other importers in the Japanese market show much lower incidence of complaints than would be expected from the anecdotal stereotypes.[15] Moreover, there are anecdotes that point in the opposite direction. For example, Coca-

---

[14] Gary R. Saxonhouse, "Evolving Comparative Advantage and Japan's Imports of Manufactures" (Ann Arbor: University of Michigan, 1982; processed).

[15] Saxonhouse, "The Micro- and Macroeconomics of Foreign Sales to Japan, chapter 9, this volume."

Note that a recent survey by the American Chamber of Commerce in Japan (ACCJ) does not reveal pervasive trade barriers in the perception of the American business community in Japan (questions about the presence of such barriers typically show only a minority of affirmative replies). The report acknowledges in the preface that "perceived failure of the American business community to come forward with specifics has led many within the Japanese community to question the reality of the nontariff barrier problem and to assert that the Japanese market is, in fact, essentially open." The survey does show that US banking, insurance, and transportation firms operate under special difficulties such as foreign exchange controls and restrictions applied more severely to foreign than domestic firms; also, government procurement is considered discriminatory by respondents from the transportation and technology industries but is generally not a major problem for enterprises in nine other industries. American Chamber of Commerce in Japan, "Report on 1981/82 Trade-Investment Barrier Membership Survey" (Tokyo, March 8, 1982), and "US-Japan Trade and Investment," ACCJ Position Papers (prepared for presentation in Washington, May 18–22, 1982; processed).

Cola is the largest selling soft drink in Japan, Schick is number one in the razor market, and Nestlés holds 70 percent of the instant coffee market.[16]

Perhaps the most intriguing critique is that industrial organization in Japan leads to systematic restriction of imports. A recent study of the semiconductor industry maintains that even after the Japanese government had liberalized trade and investment in the sector in 1976, the oligopolistic structure of Japan's industry limited imports.[17] Over 60 percent of the consumption of semiconductors in Japan is by the six largest Japanese electronics and computer firms producing semiconductors (reflecting their vertical integration). Much of their production of semiconductors is traded among them in a pattern of specialization. The study acknowledges that the decline of the share of imports in consumption of semiconductors from 31 percent in 1975 to 22 percent in 1978 may be "straightforward import substitution," but judges that more likely it is the result of collaborative action among Japanese firms after their mastery of the relevant technology. Although this analysis fails to answer why one Japanese firm would sacrifice profits by purchasing from another rather than from cheaper foreign supply, it is conceivable that at least in some product sectors Japanese oligopoly structure restrains imports (although the argument has more appeal for intermediate products such as semiconductors than for final consumer goods).

In general, however, there is little systematic, empirical evidence that Japan protects its market substantially more than the United States does its own. A salient point to recognize is that the trade conflicts with Japan have risen sharply in intensity during three periods over the past decade, coinciding with periods when the yen was undervalued (1970–71, 1976–77, 1981–82).[18] Yet protection is a continuous process, so there should have been no discontinuity in trade conflict if the true problem were underlying Japanese protection. All the evidence points to the exchange rate, not continuous protection, as the main source of difficulty. Today's trade problems with Japan seem to be driven mainly by an overvalued dollar and undervalued

[16] *Wall Street Journal,* 28 June 1982.

[17] Michael Borrus, James Millstein, and John Zysman, *International Competition in Advanced Industrial Sectors: Trade and Development in the Semiconductor Industry,* study prepared for the Joint Economic Committee, 97th US Cong., 2d sess. (Washington: US Government Printing Office, 1982).

[18] This point is developed at length in C. Fred Bergsten and John Williamson, "Exchange Rates and Trade Policy," chapter 3, this volume.

yen (resulting broadly from a tight-money, loose-fiscal-policy mix in the United States and the opposite mix in Japan).

Although perceived protection by Japan is the motivating force behind most of the reciprocity bills, practices in other countries would surely be challenged on the basis of similar impressions of excessive protection. Canada's Foreign Investment Review Agency (FIRA) would be a natural target, and in this case the premise of lower "market access" abroad than in the United States appears warranted (although Canadians maintain that FIRA's controls on investment are transparent while similar controls are exercised by many countries through opaque administrative means).

Brazil and Mexico are countries that probably would be high on the list of targets for application of reciprocity pressure. Both have high protection and both actively affect the pattern of international trade through local content and export requirements in their agreements with multinational corporations.

The cases of Mexico, Brazil, and other developing countries are complicated, however. Their "reciprocity" tends to be automatic at the aggregate level, because their need for foreign exchange is so great that they tend to spend whatever amounts of it they can earn. They are not accumulating large idle reserves; indeed, they have rapidly built up sizable foreign debts. Their tariff and quota protection and investment requirements distort the composition of imports, but the level of their imports is essentially determined by their export earnings (and capital inflows). To force compositional changes in their industrial structure would benefit some US exporters but hurt others because, if Brazil (for example) imported more automobiles, it would have less foreign exchange left to import wide-bodied aircraft.

Moreover, Brazil, Mexico, and some other newly industrialized countries (NICs) can legitimately point to the argument of infant industries to justify some of their protection, considering that their domestic markets are large enough for potential economies of scale and that they have an increasingly sophisticated base of skilled labor. Over the longer run, better rules of the game will have to be worked out for trade with the newly industrialized countries. However, now is hardly the time to impose additional pressure on exports from Mexico and Brazil, considering their high external debt (much of it held by American banks) and their already severe balance of payments problems.

When the burden of proof is placed on the contention that the major industrial trading partners of the United States are vastly more protectionist than the United States itself, the proof is found wanting; and protection by the NICs, especially those in severe balance of payments difficulty, raises an essentially different set of issues. Thus, the fundamental premise of reciprocity legislation—that comparable market access in foreign countries does not now exist—is weak.

Discrimination versus Unconditional MFN

Even if that evidence is weak, some legislators feel it is time for US trade policy to "get tough." However, a move to a policy of attempting to force foreign liberalization through the threat of retaliation would almost inevitably violate the principle of unconditional most-favored-nation treatment that has been the foundation of trade negotiations for decades and is stated in Article I of the GATT:

> . . . any advantage, favor, privilege or immunity granted by any contracting party to any product originating in or destined for any other country shall be accorded immediately and unconditionally to the like product originating in or destined for the territories of all other contracting parties.[19]

If the United States (or any other country adopting reciprocity legislation) applied retaliatory action against another country because of "unequal access" to that country's market, treatment would no longer be uniform across suppliers, and unconditional MFN would be violated. This violation would occur despite protestations of some authors of reciprocity bills that their approach is consistent with the GATT (and, in the case of a key proposal, the original language stated that, somehow, action would "take account of the obligations of the United States under any trade agreement.")[20]

In historical terms such a sharp break from unconditional MFN would represent a watershed change in US policy, and a reversion to the conditional MFN practiced by the United States when it was a developing nation and a newcomer to world trade. Unconditional MFN was the norm in European trade as early as the fifteenth and sixteenth centuries (initially, for countries covered by treaties, and later, for all supplier countries); it emerged as each country sought in bilateral negotiations to ensure that it would not be granted lesser opportunities than other countries. As a new nation finding difficulty breaking into foreign markets, the United States adopted conditional

---

[19] General Agreement on Tariffs and Trade (1947, as amended), in John H. Jackson, *Legal Problems of International Economic Relations, Documents Supplement* (St. Paul, Minn.: West Publishing Co., 1977), p. 4.

[20] The Danforth Bill, S. 2094, as originally submitted.

MFN in its first treaty (with France) in 1786, and pursued a policy of setting high tariffs for negotiating purposes, making extension of MFN conditional on the granting of reciprocal concessions.[21] Europe turned toward the US pattern in the early nineteenth century but, influenced by liberalism, returned to unconditional MFN by the late nineteenth century.

After World War I, with US manufactures much in demand in Europe, the United States adopted a policy of unconditional MFN (under authority in the Tariff Act of 1922—echoing one of Woodrow Wilson's 14 points—and by provisions in the Tariff Agreements of 1934). Thus, the dominant nation in world trade—England in the nineteenth century, the United States after World War I—has tended to support unconditional MFN, not surprisingly given the dominant country's favorable position for taking advantage of the general liberalization of trade markets. However, it was not merely commercial dominance that led to US support for unconditional MFN. In an important study written by the eminent trade economists F.W. Taussig and Jacob Viner, among others, the US Tariff Commission noted in 1919 that the past US practice of conditional MFN had caused "frequent controversies" as signatories of existing agreements claimed the benefits of new agreements concluded with third parties.[22]

The United States later insisted on unconditional MFN in the foundation of the GATT, and in a multilateral context the principle came to mean in broad terms that discrimination would be avoided. The essential logic was that "in the long run all countries will suffer from

---

[21] Under conditional MFN, if country A grants a concession to country B in exchange for a given concession, A extends the concession to another country, C, only if C grants a corresponding concession. Under unconditional MFN, C obtains the concession without granting one of its own.

[22] "The evidences show that the conclusion of reciprocity treaties is likely to lead to claims from States outside the agreement which, if granted, will defeat the purposes of the treaties, and which, if not granted, occasion the preferring of a charge of disloyalty to treaty obligations. The practice of making reciprocity treaties requires the conditional construction of the most-favored-nation clause. But the use by the United States of the conditional interpretation of the most-favored-nation clause has for half a century occasioned, and, if it is persisted in, will continue to occasion frequent controversies between the United States and European Countries." US Tariff Commission, *Reciprocity and Commercial Treaties* (Washington: US Government Printing Office, 1919), p. 42.

the inevitable distortion of trade patterns which will arise out of discrimination, even though they may be temporary beneficiaries."[23]

While adhering in principle to unconditional MFN, the postwar trade negotiations have generally managed to follow a reciprocity principle. Tariff concessions on an MFN basis have been worked out among principal suppliers with an eye to ensuring broad reciprocity. Some argue that in economic terms MFN has in practice been conditional because the products submitted for tariff liberalization have systematically been selected such that they came primarily from countries that offered tariff concessions in return, and tariff cuts might have been more limited had this not been the case.[24]

In the opinion of the US executive branch in documentation preceding the Trade Act of 1974, "adherence to MFN, however qualified as time passed, deserves a good deal of the credit" for the enormous growth of world trade in the postwar period.[25] Although thorough studies on the effect of MFN (conditional or otherwise) do not exist, perhaps a sense of its importance may be gleaned from a comparison of US trade with those socialist countries that enjoy MFN status against trade with those that do not. In 1979, exports to the United States from non-MFN East Germany and USSR averaged 0.055 percent of their GNP, while for MFN-status Yugoslavia and Poland the figure was 0.56 percent, 10 times as high.[26] Thus, the level of protection facing non-MFN countries appears to be sufficiently high to reduce their market access considerably relative to MFN suppliers.

Deviation from unconditional MFN has long been permitted by special exceptions in the GATT for customs unions and free trade areas, in the belief that these tended to liberalize trade, and for

[23] Quoted from John W. Evans in J.H. Jackson, *Legal Problems of International Economic Relations: Cases, Materials and Text,* 1977, p. 517. The discussion here also draws on US Congress, Senate, Committee on Finance, *Executive Branch GATT Studies*, no. 9, 93d Cong., 2d sess., Committee Print (Washington: US Government Printing Office, 1974).

[24] J. Michael Finger, "Trade Liberalization: A Public Choice Perspective," in Ryan C. Amacher, Gottfried Haberler, and Thomas D. Willett, eds., *Challenges to a Liberal International Economic Order* (Washington: American Enterprise Institute, 1979).

[25] *Executive Branch GATT Studies* (Washington: US Government Printing Office, 1974), p. 4.

[26] Calculated from *Direction of Trade Statistics* (Yearbook 1981), pp. 380–82, and 1980 *World Bank Atlas: Population, Per Capita Produced, and Growth Rates,* p. 16.

government procurement. The US-Canadian automobile agreement is an exception authorized by GATT waiver.

In recent years, the erosion of unconditional MFN has grown. The Generalized System of Preferences (GSP) was a major departure from MFN. So is the proposed new US Caribbean Basin Initiative. The NTB codes of the Tokyo Round, especially those on subsidies and government procurement, were conditional upon signatory status (although there is serious dispute as to whether these codes will in the end stand up against challenge that they violate the right to unconditional MFN stated in Article I of the GATT).[27] Fearing the consequences for nonsignatory developing countries, the United Nations Conference on Trade and Development (UNCTAD) has warned against the trend toward conditional MFN (although it was the leading supporter of the GSP).[28] More drastic departures from unconditional MFN have occurred in the Multi-Fiber Arrangement (MFA) and in the voluntary export restraints that have emerged outside the context of GATT.

Despite these instances of erosion of the principle, unconditional MFN still governs the bulk of trade today. For the United States, the exceptions of Canadian automobiles, textiles and apparel, the GSP, and Eastern bloc trade account for only 10 percent of total imports.[29]

[27] For an argument that the Codes are not in violation of GATT because the NTBs in question concern legitimate countermeasures that are inherently discriminatory among countries, see Gary Clyde Hufbauer, Joanna Shelton-Erb, and H.R. Starr, "The GATT Codes and the Unconditional Most-Favored-Nation Principle," *Law and Policy in International Business*, vol. 12, no. 1 (1980), pp. 59–93. Nevertheless, the United States recently backed down in a countervailing duty case in the face of India's contention that the US interpretation of the code violated GATT Article I.

[28] United Nations Conference on Trade and Development, "Multilateral Trade Negotiations, Conference decision 132(V)," TD/3(xxiv)/SC1/Misc.1, Statement of the Director of the Manufactures Division, 3d meeting of the Sessional Committee I, Geneva, March 9, 1982.

[29] In 1980 total US imports were $253 billion. Non-MFN imports were: $7.6 billion, Canadian automobiles; $9.5 million, textiles and apparel; $7.3 billion, GSP; and $780 million, non-MFN countries of the socialist bloc. IMF, *Direction of Trade Statistics* (Yearbook, 1981); OECD, *Statistics of Foreign Trade, Series C* (1980); and Office of the US Trade Representative. Note that for textiles and apparel and Eastern bloc trade, a low share of trade may mean confirmation of a trade-distorting effect instead of evidence that departure from MFN is minor. On the other hand, there is a trade-increasing influence from the other departures from MFN: Canadian automobiles and GSP.

For the European Community (EC) the fraction is considerably higher, although less so if EC members are treated as a single bloc and only their trade with outsiders is considered—leaving their free trade arrangements with the European Free Trade Association (EFTA), textile-apparel arrangements, GSP, Lomé Convention preferences (for African, Caribbean, and Pacific developing economies), and Eastern bloc trade as their main exceptions to unconditional MFN. For its part, Japan has almost complete adherence to unconditional MFN, although it does have GSP. Whatever the effect of departures from unconditional MFN on actual trade values, they have not become dominant for trade policies. The NTB Codes of the Tokyo Round are the most important major recent policy development leading away from unconditional MFN. Yet it is ambiguous whether even these agreements depart from the principle. To be sure, an important element in achieving their negotiation was the perception, both by Europe and by the United States, that only signatories—countries undertaking the disciplines of the Codes—would receive their benefits. However, in November 1979 the Contracting Parties to GATT specifically reaffirmed that the Codes did not affect "existing rights" under GATT, including MFN rights under Article I. Some legal experts maintain that the November 1979 agreement and Article I of the GATT will require that members of the various MTN Agreements extend the same benefits to nonsignatories that they offer to each other under these codes.[30] Indeed, in 1981 the United States backed down in a confrontation with India over this issue in the case of the subsidy code.[31]

There is a more fundamental distinction between the NTB codes and the new brand of reciprocity proposals, however. Whether or not the NTB codes departed from unconditional MFN, they were

[30] John H. Jackson, "GATT Machinery and the Tokyo Round Agreements," chapter 5, this volume.

[31] The United States had initially rejected India's membership in the subsidies code on grounds that India's offered reduction in export subsidies was inadequate. When, on these grounds, the United States then refused to apply its new injury test to the Indian products, India argued that nonrecognition of its code membership and failure to apply the injury test would violate its MFN rights under Article I of the GATT. The United States then agreed to recognize Indian membership in the code on the basis of an Indian "best endeavors" agreements to limit export subsidies. Bureau of National Affairs, *Import Weekly*, "US Accepts India as a Country Under the Agreements for Subsidy Code, GATT Case Dropped," ITIM, vol. 97, no. 5 (October 7, 1981).

multilateral and *trade-creating* in nature. They embraced most of the major trading nations and on balance surely will cause more trade creation than trade diversion or suppression. The new reciprocity movement, to the contrary, would be bilateral in nature; and, as will be analyzed below, the chances are high that application of the new reciprocity approach would more often result in trade suppression (with new protection by all parties) rather than trade creation.

In sum, by the adoption of reciprocity legislation based on the threat of retaliation the United States would enter new, unknown territory in departure from unconditional MFN by moving from a passive form—the withholding of concessions—to an active or aggressive form—the imposition of new trade barriers. Policymakers should be fully aware of the fundamental break with at least six decades of US trading practice that this step would involve. To be sure, the door to the reciprocity-retaliation approach is already open a crack as the result of section 301 of the Trade Act of 1974 as amended in 1979 (and its precursor, section 252 of the Trade Expansion Act of 1962), which authorize the President to retaliate against a foreign practice that "is unjustifiable, unreasonable, or discriminatory and burdens or restricts US commerce."[32] But 301 cases have been minor, and a broad mandate from reciprocity legislation to seek out and (if necessary) retaliate against foreign protection considered "unequal" to domestic is much broader and more aggressive than section 301's surgical provisions for "unfair" trade.[33]

Dynamics of Retaliation

If the first fundamental point to recognize about reciprocity through retaliation is that it is a radical change in US trade policy, the second is that it opens up the Pandora's box of counterretaliation or trade wars.

[32] US PL 93–618, January 3, 1975, as amended by PL 96-39, July 26, 1979.

[33] There have been a total of 31 cases under section 301 since its enactment. Of these, 17 have been settled, and 14 are pending. The President has taken action on only one case, concerning Canadian broadcast advertising (for which "mirror treatment" legislation, requested by both Presidents Carter and Reagan, is pending). Leonard Weiss, "Reciprocity" (Washington: American Society for International Law, forthcoming 1983). Congressional discontent with slow action on section 301 cases has been a source of the recent surge in proposed reciprocity legislation, but a substantially more active use of this provision would run the policy risks set forth below.

So far the departures from unconditional MFN have been passive: the withholding of new concessions from a subgroup of nonreciprocal trading nations. Customs unions, the Canadian-US auto pact and the Tokyo Round NTB codes are in this category. The GSP and Caribbean Basin Initiative are also passive (withholding the benefits from ineligible countries) although their motivation is one of development assistance rather than reciprocity. The new reciprocity-retaliation approach would be an aggressive departure from unconditional MFN: new trade barriers would be erected against countries with trade practices considered nonreciprocal.

The danger of aggressive reciprocity is that foreign countries may respond in kind. Imposition of a retaliatory trade barrier may provoke the foreign country to impose counterretaliatory barriers of its own. Even if the foreign country does nothing, there will be no benefit to home-country exports, and there will probably be welfare losses to the home country from imposition of the initial trade barriers. The costs of protection include higher prices for consumers, loss of efficiency as resources are shifted to inefficient sectors, loss of competitive stimulus to technological change, and induced macroeconomic costs from the inflationary impact of rising import prices.

Higher protection abroad as the result of counterretaliation is not merely an abstract possibility. Historical experience has shown it to be a painfully real phenomenon. The most extreme case of retaliatory escalation occurred in the Great Depression. In 1930, the US Congress passed the Hawley–Smoot Act, which raised tariffs to frequently prohibitive levels.[34] After its passage by the House and before its passage by the Senate, diplomatic communications from 24 nations filled a publication of 200 pages with expressions of concern and veiled threats of retaliation. To no avail, over a thousand American economists petitioned President Herbert C. Hoover to veto the bill.

After its enactment, retaliatory actions were widespread. For example, Spain imposed prohibitive tariffs on imports of automobiles and other products and entered a preferential agreement with France. In Switzerland, shocked by the prohibitive US tariff on watches, there were mass meetings calling for a boycott of all US products. Mussolini

---

[34] The average collected tariff on dutiable items rose from 39 percent in 1923–30 to 50 percent in 1931–35. See William R. Cline, "Long-term Change in Foreign Trade Policy of the United States," in U.S. Congress, Joint Economic Committee, *Special Study on Economic Change*, vol. 9, *The International Economy: US Role in a World Market*, 96th Cong., 2d sess. (Washington: US Government Printing Office 1980), p. 188.

announced that Italy would buy no more from the United States than the United States purchased from Italy. Canada struck back at imports of 125 major products, imposing duty surcharges on items such as chemicals from the United States.[35] The round of retaliatory tariff escalation touched off by the Hawley–Smoot Act reduced world trade and played a significant role in increasing the severity of the world depression.

Episodes of trade retaliation have been rare in the postwar period, in part because policymakers had learned the lessons of the 1930s. The best known instance of retaliation in this period was the "chicken war" of 1963, when the United States increased duties on cognac and light trucks in retaliation for the restriction of imports of frozen chicken into the European Community. In 1973 there was a "cattle war" between the United States and Canada. In the face of low US prices and rising Canadian imports, Canada first protected cattle by prohibiting entry of cattle that had received a particular growth hormone; it then imposed quotas under Article XIX of GATT (safeguard against injury). The United States retaliated with quotas against Canadian cattle and meat.[36]

At the present time the atmosphere is perhaps more highly charged for a potential explosion of retaliatory measures than at any other time in the postwar period. World economic stagnation from 1980 through 1982 has been the worst since the 1930s.[37] Unemployment in Europe and the United States stands near 10 percent and is expected to continue at this level in 1983.[38] In mid-1982 the decision of the Reagan administration to block the use of US technology for the Soviet-European gas pipeline introduced a new sense of economic confrontation between the United States and Europe. And, at the same time, the announcement of high US countervailing duties against imports of European steel further heightened confrontation.

Some European spokesmen warned that the steel and Soviet pipeline issues could precipitate European retaliation.[39] An early move

---

[35] Asher Isaacs, *International Trade: Tariff and Commercial Policies* (Chicago: Richard D. Irwin, 1948), pp. 230–37.

[36] John H. Jackson, *Legal Problems of International Economic Relations* (St. Paul, Minn.: West, 1977), p. 844.

[37] Even though the 1974–75 recession was sharper, the average growth rate in industrial countries for the three years 1974–76 was 1.7 percent, compared with an expected average of 1.1 percent for 1980–82. IMF, *World Economic Outlook* (1982), p. 143.

[38] OECD *Economic Outlook* (31), July 1982, p. 4.

[39] *Washington Post*, 1 July 1982, p. A24.

by the European Community following the preliminary determination on countervailing duties in steel was to claim the right to increase duties in compensation for the US Domestic International Sales Corporation (DISC), the program deferring taxes on exports.[40] The timing of this move gave it the appearance of retaliation against the US position on steel. The EC has also reportedly threatened to retaliate against US agricultural products if US action is taken against steel.[41]

In short, the recent trading climate has been primed for a potentially explosive round of trade retaliation and counterretaliation. In this environment a new approach of aggressive reciprocity by the United States could trigger counterretaliation at least as often as it would achieve foreign liberalization.

The conditions under which aggressive reciprocity will be beneficial, and the alternative conditions causing it to leave the home and foreign countries worse off than before, can be defined more precisely. The remainder of this section develops this analysis.

The judgment about retaliation to promote reciprocity should hinge on an evaluation of domestic and international economic ("welfare") effects. Essentially, the merits or disadvantages of the strategy are similar to those of the customs union: is the net effect likely to be trade creation or trade diversion? In the case of aggressive reciprocity, the corresponding comparison is between trade creation and trade suppression (simply reduction of imports, rather than diversion from one supplier to another). And the comparison is inherently probabilistic: policymakers must evaluate the *probability* that the threat will achieve the desired opening of trade (trade creation) versus the probability that it will go unanswered and import barriers will be erected to carry out the threat. In the latter case, policymakers must consider the additional possibility that the foreign country will impose counterretaliation.

For the home country, the net expected economic benefits of the strategy of aggressive reciprocity may be conceived of as follows. The net economic benefit from the strategy *equals:*

        (a) the gains from foreign compliance with the demanded liberalization *times* the probability of foreign capitulation;

minus   (b) the economic loss from increased domestic protection from threat-enforcement *times* the probability that the foreign country will not capitulate;

---

[40] *Financial Times,* 7 July 1982, p. 18.
[41] *Washington Post,* 10 August 1982, p. A12.

plus   (c) that same probability *times* the economic benefit from
              increased export prices relative to import prices (the op-
              timum tariff effect discussed below);

minus   (d) the joint probability that the foreign country fails to
              capitulate *and* that it counterretaliates by imposing pro-
              tection of its own, *times* the economic loss resulting from
              that counterretaliation (figure 4.1).[42]

The basic economic effects for the home country are as follows.
In the first case, where the desired liberalization is achieved, there
is the economic benefit (or "welfare gain") from increased exports
as the foreign market opens. Classical static analysis ignores these
gains, but dynamic analyses of trade liberalization have focused increasingly on effects associated with investment, economies of scale,
and technological change, and to a considerable degree these effects
are related more to the export side than the import side of liberalization. A more traditional reason for welfare gain from expansion of
the export market is that the expansion of foreign demand raises the
country's export prices relative to its import prices, improving its
terms of trade (the "optimum tariff" argument).[43]

The second case, where the foreign country refuses to liberalize
its market but takes no further action, generates contradictory effects.
On the one hand, there is the economic (welfare) cost from trade
suppression. This traditional cost is essentially the additional cost that
consumers must pay for more expensive domestic production (less
the implicit transfer to domestic producers) and the economic loss
associated with diverting domestic resources from more efficient uses
to inefficient production of goods that could be bought more cheaply
abroad. Technically, the cost of production is the traditional static
welfare "triangle" of "dead weight loss" (essentially, loss of consumer
surplus and government tariff revenue uncompensated by increased
producer surplus).[44] In addition, increased protection causes dynamic

---

[42] See equation (1), in figure 4.1.

[43] Thus, Wonnacott and Wonnacott have recently explained the appeal of
customs unions over unilateral trade liberalization by the consideration of
optimum tariff gains from achieving reciprocal liberalization by the partner.
Paul Wonnacott and Ronald Wonnacott, "Is Unilateral Tariff Reduction
Preferable to a Customs Union? The Curious Case of the Missing Foreign
Tariffs," *American Economic Review*, vol. 71, no. 4 (1981), pp. 704–14.

[44] *Consumer surplus* is the excess of what the public would be willing to
pay for a product (considering that some individuals would still buy at higher
prices) over what it actually pays. *Producer surplus* is the excess of what
firms receive over the minimum they would have to receive to cover costs.

FIGURE 4.1 Factors determining whether aggressive reciprocity is effective

Factor	Influence	
P_1	Probability of foreign capitulation	Higher probability→more effective
P_2	Probability of noncapitulation by foreign country	Higher probability→less effective
P_3	Probability of foreign counter-relation, given noncapitulation	Higher probability→less effective
W_E	Economic benefits of increased exports	Greater benefit→more effective
W_M	Economic cost of increased domestic protection	Greater cost→less effective
W_{OT}	Economic benefits of increasing export price relative to import price	Larger benefit→more effective
W_{CR}	Economic cost to home country of foreign counter-retaliation	Larger cost→less effective

Note: Thus: equation (1) $w^* = p_1 W_E + p_2 [W_m + W_{OT}] + p_2 [p_3 W_{CR}]$ where w^* is the net welfare gain from the strategy of aggressive reciprocity, W_E is the welfare gain from successful opening of the foreign market, W_m is the welfare effect (loss) of increased domestic protection ($W_m > 0$), W_{OT} is the welfare gain from imposing an optimum tariff, and W_{CR} the welfare effect of foreign counterretaliation ($W_{CR} < 0$). Note that $W_{OT} + W_{CR}$ equal the net effects of an optimum tariff under foreign retaliation, in addition to other welfare losses from reduced exports included in W_{CR}. Note also that the analysis of this section uses the term "optimum tariff" as a shorthand reference to terms of trade effects (considering that the two principal economic cases for protection are the "optimum-tariff" and "infant-industry" arguments). In practice, there is no reason that the particular increase in protection chosen for implementation of aggressive reciprocity would be precisely the level of the optimum tariff (if that level could be identified).

The term p_1 is the probability that the foreign country will reduce its protection under threat as desired, p_2 is the probability that it will do nothing and the home country will impose the threatened barrier, and p_3 is the probability that in the face of the new barrier the foreign country counterretaliates with its own new protection. Either case 1 or case 2 must occur ($p_1 + p_2 = 1$); p_3 is a conditional probability that, given the decision of the partner country not to liberalize (case 2, probability p_2), that country also decides to counterretaliate.

economic welfare costs associated with loss of pressure for technological change and from macroeconomic recessionary adjustment to
increased inflation spurred by higher import prices. On the other
hand, if the home country is large enough, imposing protection may
generate benefits by depressing the home country's demand for the
good and shifting the *terms of trade* (ratio of export to import price)
in favor of the home country (*optimum tariff benefits*).[45]

It should be noted that even if an optimum tariff welfare benefit
can be obtained (before considering the impact of foreign retaliation),
this benefit may be more than offset by losses in efficiency of resource
allocation if protection is imposed on an individual sector.[46] The
traditional optimum tariff literature deals with a single import product, but once multiple products are considered, there will be efficiency
losses from protecting some and not others (because resources will
be drawn away from other sectors, where their social marginal product is higher, and devoted to the protected sector, where it would
now be lower). Some advocates of aggressive reciprocity who see it
as an opportunity for obtaining special interest protection could become much less enthusiastic if the strategy were imposed efficiently
by a uniform tariff imposed on all goods instead of being concentrated
in special sectors.

In the third case the foreign country not only refuses to liberalize
but also imposes new protection of its own, causing economic costs
to the home country. Essentially these costs amount to a reduction
of previously existing economic gains from home-country exports

---

[45] However, aggressive reciprocity would usually be applied against a single
country. For standardized commodities, such as grains, it would be unlikely
that reducing the demand for the exports of a single country would reduce
the world price of that good. Supplies from other countries would be easily
interchangeable. In this case, a terms of trade gain would be unlikely. However, trade in some manufactures (such as automobiles) tends to be based
on "differentiated products," where a single country in a sense provides a
unique product. For such products, imposing protection and reducing demand
for the country's exports could be sufficient to lower the price and yield terms
of trade benefits for the home country.

[46] Technically, the misallocation of resources is captured by the left-hand
triangle of welfare loss (excess production opportunity cost) in the standard
diagram of welfare cost from protection. See Cline, *et al.*, p. 42. Note that
the tradition of examining the optimum tariff in terms of a single, economy-
wide product has led some erroneously to apply the argument to a single
sector, such as automobiles, without considering the consequences of resource allocation inefficiency.

(analogous to the desired new benefits from still further export expansion) in addition to partial, full, or overcompensation of the optimum tariff gains the home country might have achieved in the absence of counterretaliation.

For the strategy of aggressive reciprocity to be beneficial to the home country, the expected (probability weighted) benefits from the potential gains must exceed the expected costs of the potential losses.[47]

Essentially, advocates of aggressive reciprocity implicitly assume that

(a) the probability of foreign capitulation is high (in equation [1], P_1, figure 4.1, *Note*),

(b) the gains from opening foreign markets are high (W_E),

(c) the gains from terms of trade improvement (optimum tariff protection) are high (W_{OT}),

(d) the home costs of protection are low (W_m),

(e) the probability of counterretaliation is low (P_3), and

(f) the home costs of counterretaliation are low (W_{CR}).

Once again the Japanese-based inspiration for aggressive reciprocity comes to light: advocates often suggest that Japan would find it difficult to counterretaliate because Japan imports relatively little in manufactures from the United States. This view is not firmly based, however. If all products are considered, Japan imports 77 percent as much from the United States as it exports to this country.[48] Japan could retaliate in many products. For example, despite its beef protection Japan imports 60 percent of US beef exports[49]; the Japanese government could easily reallocate its beef import quotas away from the United States to other suppliers. Other examples would include shifting from US jet aircraft to the European Airbus and from US to Brazilian soybeans.

Moreover, once legislation were in place, and a whole new trade strategy had developed, there is no guarantee that Japan would remain the only target. There would be pressure to apply aggressive

---

[47] Thus: equation (2) $P_1 W_E + P_2 W_{OT} > P_2[|(W_m + P_3 W_{CR})|]$. Note that if the country is risk averse, the ratio of expected gains to expected losses, left hand side of (2) relative to right hand side, will have to be larger for the strategy to be desirable.

[48] For 1980. IMF, *Direction of Trade Statistics* (Yearbook, 1981), p. 226.

[49] Speech by Saburo Okita, former Foreign Minister of Japan, Institute for International Economics, Washington, July 22, 1982.

reciprocity against Europe for the Common Agricultural Policy, for example. With a large trade deficit with the United States, Europe is in a good position to retaliate. Even developing countries are in a position to retaliate: 32 percent of US exports went to nonoil developing countries in 1980,[50] and it is fully conceivable that in response to new US trade barriers, erected under a policy of aggressive reciprocity, countries such as Mexico and Brazil would counterretaliate (for example, with tariff surcharges or quotas on US goods) and buy their imports from other industrial countries.

The dynamics of retaliation are set forth systematically in figure 4.2. Countries A and B make a sequence of moves in a "game." The figure summarizes the possible outcome of each move, showing the first three complete moves in the game. If the advocates of aggressive reciprocity are right, the game would end happily at stage Ia, where the foreign country eliminates the protection in question in response to the threat of A's protection. But the other outcomes show how aggressive reciprocity can escalate into more protection on both sides.

As an example of what can go wrong with the reciprocity approach, consider one of the possible sequences illustrated. Country A issues a threat to raise protection in a sector if the foreign country does not reduce its protection. Suppose the other country (B) makes no initial response (case Ib). Then home country A is compelled to follow through on its threat and impose the protection. Suppose that in the face of this action, country B then responds with a retaliatory increase in its own protection (case IIf). If the home country (A) takes no further action, both countries are left with a new, higher level of protection (case IIIm).

In the summary of all sequences of possible moves in figure 4.2, after three rounds of play there are nine ending positions (Ia, IId, IIe, IIg, IIh, IIj, IIIk, IIIm, IIIp) and two positions leading to a further round. Of the nine ending positions, only three unambiguously liberalize trade (Ia, IId, IIg). The others increase protection. Except in the case that country A's terms of trade (optimum tariff) gains outweigh its protection costs (a possibility but not necessarily likely in cases IIe and IIh), or in the case that country A has special trade elasticities that enable it to gain from imposing an optimum tariff despite foreign retaliation (possible but unlikely in case IIIm),[51]

---

[50] IMF, *Direction of Trade Statistics* (Yearbook 1981), p. 380.

[51] The special case of optimum tariff gain despite retaliation, generally considered an intellectual curiosity rather than a realistic policy option, is developed in Harry G. Johnson, *International Trade and Economic Growth* (Cambridge, Mass.: Harvard University Press, 1967). Gain despite counter-

FIGURE 4.2   Dynamics of retaliation

Country **A** *action*	Country **B** *response*		
I. Initial threat	Liberalize **a**	No change **b**	Counterthreat **c**
II. Case **Ia**:	Game ends. Foreign market liberalized. Welfare improved for A, perhaps for B.		
Case **Ib**:	Liberalize	No Change	Impose counter- protection
Impose protection	**d**	**e**	**f**
Case **Ic**:	Liberalize	No change	Impose counter- protection
Impose protection	**g**	**h**	**i**
Remove threat	* * *	**j**	* * *

III. Cases **IId, IIg**:	Game ends. Foreign market liberalized. Country **A** removes the new protection. Welfare improvement.		
Cases **IIe, IIh**:	Game ends. Increased protection in **A**. Welfare loss for both unless optimum tariff for **A** domi- nates.		
Cases **IIf, IIi**:	Remove new barrier	Maintain new barrier	Impose further barrier
Remove new barrier	**k**	* * *	* * *
Maintain new barrier	* * *	**m**	* * *
Impose further barrier	**n**	**p**	**q**

If **IIIk**,	return to *status quo ex ante*. Game ends.
If **IIIm**,	stabilize; game ends. Higher protection on both sides, welfare lower for both.
If **IIIn**,	may revert to *status quo ex ante* in fourth round.
If **IIIp**,	stabilize with higher protection in **B**, much higher protection in **A**. Game ends.
If **IIIq**,	much higher protection in both **A** and **B** with further escalation possible in round IV.

Note: undesignated cases (* * *) represent implausible responses.

or in the case of return to the status quo, country A's strategy of aggressive reciprocity backfires. In all end positions except liberalization or return to the status quo, country B is also worse off (unless its trade elasticities are peculiarly such that it gains from an optimum tariff despite retaliation). Thus, aggressive retaliation is a high risk strategy: it may achieve liberalization but may also result in higher protection and lower economic welfare for all.

An important structural feature of the risk of escalation comes from the fact that aggressive reciprocity is unilateral. It does not involve submission of a complaint to international consideration and the securing of international approval to carry out a retaliatory measure. This unilateral action seems much more likely to induce counterretaliation than would a multilaterally approved measure. Thus, in the "chicken war," the United States obtained GATT approval of compensatory retaliation. The EC did not escalate the retaliation further, but might have done so if the imprimatur of international legitimacy had not been given by GATT to the US measures.

In sum, perhaps the greatest risk of aggressive reciprocity is that it would spiral out of control in a series of retaliatory protective measures. Its unilateral nature increases this risk, as does the recent environment of trade confrontation (especially between the United States and Europe).

Sectoral Reciprocity

In addition to omnibus bills, the reciprocity proposals before the US Congress in early 1982 included bills limited to specific sectors: services, high technology, agriculture, and telecommunications, where a "mirror" bill would limit tax deductibility of broadcasting in view of a recent denial by Canada of tax deductions for border advertising on US stations.

The sectoral approach to reciprocity has some appeal and some weaknesses. Its appeal lies in its (implicit) recognition that in certain (broad) sectors national resource, factor, and technology endowments are sufficiently similar that comparative advantage may be relatively arbitrary and subject to manipulation (Appendix 4.B). If in a given sector foreign countries act strategically while the United States acts competitively, US producers in that sector may be at a

---

retaliation is usually unlikely unless the foreign country is small, in which case the initial offense would not be likely to be a major concern to the home country in the first place.

disadvantage.[52] Thus, the sectors of telecommunications, high technology, and services, where underlying conditions may make comparative advantage relatively arbitrary, are logical candidates for special action—although, again, aggressive reciprocity is a riskier and less desirable form of action than other policy alternatives (discussed below).

Agricultural products, on the other hand, are not sensible "sectors" for reciprocity. By definition an agricultural product is dominated by Ricardian resource-based trade. In sectors where trade is one-way (as in agriculture), sectoral reciprocity makes no sense. This Ricardian, specialized, interindustry trade is such that, if the sector is a major exporter, there are only small imports, if any, to retaliate against. Thus it would be incongruous to impose reciprocity on oil, chromium, soybeans, wheat, or other narrowly defined sectors in the raw materials field: a country either exports or imports such goods (they are homogeneous and product differentiation generating two-way trade is minimal). Sectoral reciprocity makes sense only where there is two-way, intraindustry trade.[53]

Even at a broader level, however, the sectoral approach to (aggressive) reciprocity has serious limitations. Because different countries specialize in different sectors, trade can be broadly reciprocal even if the concessions of one country are in one sector and those of another country are in a different sector. A crucial element in the bargaining that has led to postwar trade liberalization has been the flexibility to arrange packages that involve reciprocal liberalization in the aggregate, with swapping of concessions in different sectors. To move toward a more rigid approach of sectoral reciprocity would limit the flexibility for future liberalization. Moreover, "aggressive" threats of new protection would be open to the legitimate charge that

[52] Although government intervention or other strategic behavior is no guarantee that the favored sector will prosper. The European aircraft industry could well have been better off if it had not undertaken the government-sponsored *Concorde.* Similarly, heavy-handed government intervention has failed to establish a successful computer industry in France. John Diebold, "The Information Technology Industries: A Case Study of High Technology Trade," chapter 19, this volume.

[53] Broadening the scope to agriculture as a whole does not help much. The United States does not import agricultural products from Japan, and the minor imports of agricultural goods (for example, dairy products) from Europe are hardly sufficient to pose a convincing threat that would deal with the problem of European subsidization in third country markets, let alone bring down the CAP.

the demand was for a concession that had not been "paid for," and that in past negotiations the foreign country had already paid for liberalization in the home country in the sector in question with concessions of its own in other sectors.

The best strategy for dealing with the sectoral issues associated with arbitrary comparative advantage, while preserving the flexibility for intersectoral trade-offs necessary to broad trade liberalization, would be to develop special sector negotiations in GATT, as discussed below. It could achieve multilateral support instead of involving more risky unilateral action, and would give scope for recognition of extrasectoral concessions that country negotiators might offer (or believe had already been granted in the past).

Services and Investment

Two of the potentially most important areas for new sector negotiations are services and trade-related investment issues. These two areas have special significance for reciprocity legislation. They are both largely outside the GATT at the present time. As a result, it would be possible to adopt a strategy of "aggressive reciprocity" on services and investment without violating the unconditional MFN provision of the GATT. Also, the existing section 301 on unfair trade in the US Trade Act of 1974 does not explicitly include investment, although as amended in 1979 the act does include services.

The legal technicalities should not confuse the broader question, however: is it desirable for the United States to initiate a new regime of unilateral threat of retaliation in the name of opening foreign markets in services and in relation to investment requirements as they affect trade? All of the considerations of risk of retaliatory escalation discussed above would apply to these two areas. And while it would not violate past agreements (because the areas have been omitted from past commitments), a unilateral, aggressive reciprocity approach would be a sharp break from US policy as practiced for several decades.[54]

---

[54] However, a simple amendment of section 301 of the US Trade Act of 1974 to include investment-related trade problems, if unaccompanied by new language tending to broaden the strategy of imposing retaliatory protection (especially on narrow grounds of lack of reciprocity), might be appropriate if one believes that section 301 is desirable in the first place.

Alternative Strategies

Rather than breaking with its long tradition of unconditional MFN and risking a spiral of counterretaliatory protection from unilateral threats, the United States (and other countries) would do better to pursue some or all the following strategies for opening foreign markets.

GATT Article XXIII

This article of the GATT provides that a country has the right to seek compensation for *nullification and impairment* of past trade concessions by other countries. Tariff cuts that turn out to be thwarted by NTBs (new or previously invisible) are ideal examples of nullification or impairment of previous concessions. For example, if in high technology goods it can be demonstrated that Japan or another country is acting so as to make previous tariff cuts meaningless, the United States (and other suppliers) can initiate an Article XXIII proceeding. If the GATT rules in favor of the complaint and if the offending country makes no change, the complaining country is entitled to take compensatory actions against the country individually such as increasing tariffs on the same or other goods. This procedure permits multilateral authorization of such retaliation, minimizing the possibility that the offending country will maintain it has a basis for adopting counterretaliation.

In practice, Article XXIII has proved cumbersome, largely because other GATT members must approve the request for compensation. GATT has authorized suspension of concessions under the article only once.[55] Nevertheless, this provision of GATT represents a vehicle for dramatizing complaints about a particular trade practice, and if that practice is sufficiently objectionable to a large number of GATT members, authorization for compensation may be achieved. It would be worth an effort to revive Article XXIII, and cooperation by other members might be more forthcoming at a time when the alternative seems to be a drift toward unilateral action.[56]

---

[55] In 1952, when a complaint by the Netherlands against US restrictions on cheese imports was authorized. John H. Jackson, *Legal Problems of International Economic Relations* (1977), p. 429.

[56] The EC has recently brought an Article XXIII action against Japan. However, the complaint is so sweeping, condemning "the structure and organisation of the Japanese economy," that it is poorly suited for meaningful GATT treatment. *Financial Times*, 13 July 1982.

GATT Article XXVIII

This article of the GATT permits a country to rescind previous trade concessions, either by agreement with the principal suppliers (in which case the country is to offer compensatory liberalization in other areas), or unilaterally (in which case other GATT members are free to withdraw concessions of their own). If a concrete practice of a foreign country were objected to, the United States could raise duties (withdraw past concessions) on products of interest to the offending country, in the understanding that the country would have the right to make compensatory withdrawals of concessions. Such withdrawals (reimposition of higher tariffs) might not reduce US exports by much if the foreign country had been obstructing trade through administrative guidance or other means, thereby keeping its imports low despite past tariff cuts. This article does have its disadvantages: it spills over into the trade of other countries (as the withdrawal of concessions would be based on MFN), and it runs the risk of heightened protection on both sides. But it has the advantage of being within GATT and permitting unilateral action when multilateral support cannot be obtained for an Article XXIII action.

Negotiations on Services and Investment

Because the GATT focuses on merchandise trade, recourse to existing GATT rules is inadequate to deal with these areas. The best approach here would be to initiate negotiations for new international rules, and indeed the US administration is pursuing this approach. (Such negotiations would have to take cognizance of existing agreements such as those in the areas of civil aviation and shipping.) In the past the United States has supported international negotiations to deal with new trade problems as they arise rather than addressing them immediately with unilateral punitive action. There is no reason why the areas of services and investment should be excepted.

NTB Codes

Some of the sectoral disputes should be manageable within the existing NTB codes. For example, the conflicts on openness of government purchasing of telecommunications equipment should in principle be subject to treatment within the government procurement code.

Sectoral Negotiations

New negotiations could be pursued in the sectors of telecommunications, high technology, and any other sectors emerging as flash points in the push for an approach of aggressive reciprocity. This approach has already borne fruit in the Tokyo Round code on trade in aircraft. However, it is important in sectoral negotiations to avoid the emergence of new regimes restricting international trade. There is considerable risk that steel-sector negotiations, for example, would produce a new system of organized world quotas analogous to the Multi-Fiber Arrangement. There are better prospects for sector negotiations in the "sunrise" industries (for example, high technology) than in the "sunset" industries, because in the new sectors the problem is one of establishing rules of the game for future production and trade rather than seeking downward adjustment of existing production and employment in the face of excess capacity.

Bilateral Negotiations

To the extent that trade conflicts prompting the surge of interest in aggressive reciprocity stem from disputes with individual countries (especially Japan), a more formalized process of bilateral trade negotiations could help.

All of these alternative policy strategies would have the advantage of avoiding unilateral action, of avoiding violation of the GATT commitment to unconditional MFN, and of minimizing the risk of an outbreak of counterretaliatory trade wars.

Despite these possible alternatives to aggressive reciprocity, there should be no illusion that it will be easy to achieve the desired results. The past limitations of Article XXIII, for example, have already been mentioned. And advocates of reciprocity bills contend that without such legislation the United States will have no leverage for the various potential negotiations listed here.

In the past the leverage for trade negotiations has come from the ability to offer liberalization of the home market in exchange for liberalization abroad. As discussed above, contrary to the view of many supporters of reciprocity legislation, the United States still has considerable protection that could be reduced in exchange for foreign liberalization. An end to voluntary export restraints on automobiles could be offered to the Japanese in exchange for a list of requested liberalizations. Cuts on tariffs on imported apparel could be offered to Europe in exchange for liberalization of agricultural products. Of course, such exchanges could be painful politically on both sides; the relatively painless offers of liberalization have been largely exhausted in past negotiations.

If it is politically infeasible to liberalize the remaining areas of US protection, the fact may have to be faced that indeed the leverage for further liberalization abroad is limited. In this case the appropriate conclusion to draw is not that the United States needs a new weapon in its negotiating arsenal in the form of aggressive threats of new protection. Such threats seem likely to lead to immediate costs from higher protection at home and a serious risk of escalating trade wars, as discussed above. Instead, the appropriate conclusion is likely to be that whatever liberalization is possible must be achieved within the multilateral regimes that have been developed over several rounds of postwar negotiations, including the new codes on nontariff barriers, while seeking to develop corresponding new regimes in such emerging areas as high technology, services, and investment.

Conclusions and Policy Implications

There has been a rash of bills calling for US unilateral imposition of new protection if foreign countries do not give equal market access, comparable to that in the United States. It would be a historic mistake in US policy to adopt such legislation. It is grounded in the weak premise that the US market is much more open than the markets of other major nations. Implementation of retaliatory protection would violate not only the US commitments under the GATT but also six decades of US adherence to the principle of unconditional most-favored-nation treatment. Such action, which may be called "aggressive reciprocity" (as opposed to "passive" reciprocity whereby new concessions are not granted in the absence of reciprocal liberalization), would run a serious risk of counterretaliation, with increased protection and reduced welfare on all sides.

Advocates of the legislation have failed to take sufficient account of not only the possibility and cost of counterretaliation but also the direct domestic cost of unilateral imposition of new protection. Pursuit of open markets through more active use of GATT Articles XXIII (nullification and impairment), and XXVIII (withdrawal of concessions), and new negotiations on services and investment at the sectoral and bilateral levels, would be far preferable to adopting aggressive reciprocity.

Appendices

4.A   Selected Reciprocity Proposals

The leading general reciprocity bills are probably those proposed by Senator John C. Danforth (R-Mo.) and others (S. 2094) and by Senator John R. Heinz (R-Pa., S. 2071).[57] The Danforth bill as revised and reported favorably out of the Senate Finance Committee (on June 30, 1982) had the blessing of the administration, given certain moderating changes from its initial form. The original Danforth bill required the President to carry out annual studies that enumerate, and estimate the economic impact of, those practices by foreign countries that "deny to the United States commercial opportunities substantially equivalent to those offered by the United States." (Any analyst who has attempted to quantify NTBs knows how difficult a true assessment of this sort would be; it would probably require sample surveys in the offending country to estimate tariff-equivalents.) These practices include any in the fields of services and investment.

The initial draft of the bill required the President to "propose such actions as may be necessary to redress any imbalances," in other words, to issue a public threat to be implemented "if efforts to obtain their elimination fail." While the bill did not pose a deadline for implementing any threat, it clearly tended to tie the hands of the President, placing him in a humiliating position if he were to back down on a publicly stated threat. The bill also amended section 301 of the Trade Act of 1974, including in the definition of unfair trade the denial to the United States of commercial opportunities substantially equivalent to those offered by the United States, extending coverage to foreign investment, authorizing retaliation through government procurement and independent federal regulatory agencies, allowing Congress to initiate 301 actions, and requiring the President to announce retaliatory measures being considered. (Retaliation by restricting foreign investment is curious in that usually it is welcomed as providing a source of additional employment.)

Ironically, the original bill provided that action could be either nondiscriminatory or "solely against the products, investments, or services of the foreign country involved," yet it provided that the President "shall take into account the obligations of the United States

[57] This appendix draws upon Alfred Reifman, "Reciprocity in Foreign Trade," Issue Brief no. IB82043 (Washington: Congressional Research Service, Library of Congress, 1982), and Emilio Collado III, "Reciprocity Legislation," in addition to the underlying bills.

under any trade agreement." These two provisions are contradictory in light of the unconditional MFN set forth in Article I of the GATT, unless the authors of the bill envisioned limitations of retaliation to services or investment (not covered by GATT) and not goods, or to government procurement (which, arguably, is also not subject to Article I because of the exception given in Article III:8a).

The revised Danforth bill as reported out of committee retained most of the basic features of the original version, including the annual study of foreign trade barriers and extension of Article 301 to cover investment. The major softening of the original bill was in the elimination of the requirement that the President announce publicly in advance the options he was considering to force a change in foreign trade practices (that is, public statement of a threat).

However, the revised bill still required the President to report annually on the steps actually being taken to obtain changes in foreign practices, meaning that the procedures would still tend to build up pressure for the President to take retaliatory measures. Although the revised bill removed the language "substantially equivalent" market access from the operational section, it inserted this same language in the statement of purposes. The operational definition of "unreasonable" practices in the revised bill referred to any act that "denies fair and equitable. . . market opportunities," and the implication remained that such fairness and equity would be judged on a basis of the substantially equivalent access cited in the statement of purpose. Moreover, the revised bill removed the passage requiring that retaliatory action take into account obligations under trade agreements.

Despite the common impression that the revised bill was substantially milder than the original version, the same fundamental objections raised in this study would apply to it. It would mark the adoption of a new basic trade strategy that would be unilateral and would seek to open markets by threatening retaliation. The revised bill did add an important new dimension in that it would establish authority for new negotiations on services, foreign investment, and high technology goods; but this authority is separable from the reciprocity thrust of the bill and could be enacted independently.

The Heinz and Danforth bills are similar in revising section 301 and including investment. The Heinz bill provides additional detail on retaliatory options, such as opposing loans to the country by the World Bank and the International Monetary Fund, and provides for "mirror" legislation to impose restrictions similar to those by a foreign country. The Heinz bill emphasizes that nonreciprocal market access and nonnational treatment are grounds for US action whether or not they violate the GATT. More narrow sector-reciprocity bills have also been proposed, as noted above.

4.B Arbitrary Comparative Advantage

Much of the impetus for the new quest for reciprocity derives from the perception that in certain manufactured products (such as semiconductors) some countries are artificially achieving a comparative advantage that otherwise would lie with other countries. Analytically there does seem to be a fundamental problem that might be christened "arbitrary comparative advantage." Increasingly, trade in manufactures among industrial countries, even including the newly industrialized countries (NICs), appears to reflect an exchange of goods in which one nation could be just as likely as another, ex ante, to develop comparative advantage, and the actual outcome is in a meaningful sense arbitrary. For a range of manufactured goods, it may be argued that "comparative advantage is made, not given."

This type of trade differs from classical Ricardian trade, where comparative costs differ because (for example) one country has the climate for vineyards while another specializes in manufactures because of its abundance of skilled labor. Generally, in agricultural products and minerals the natural resource endowment prescribes an obvious national comparative advantage (although it can be thwarted by, for example, quotas to protect beet sugar from cane sugar). Similarly (though more ambiguously), Heckscher–Ohlin trade—based on different relative endowments of capital, labor, and skilled labor—involves a natural pattern of exchange whereby each country specializes in products that are intensive in the use of factors this country possesses in abundance. A third alternative trade theory focuses on technology, maintaining that the technologically leading country invents new products or techniques, exports the resulting products for a while, and is then superseded as other, less technologically advanced nations take over the product or method once it becomes routinized.

Under the theories of Ricardo and Heckscher–Ohlin, comparative advantage ought to be relatively unambiguous. The product-cycle theory is more ambiguous for comparative advantage, because it expects a temporary advantage of the leading country but at some point a transfer of specialization to technologically less sophisticated countries. A fourth theory, that of product differentiation (associated with Staffan B. Linder),[58] predicts an even more arbitrary process of comparative advantage. Different countries will produce the same range of goods but with product differentiation, and trade will tend to be intraindustry rather than interindustry. Intraindustry trade is spurred further by the desire to achieve economies of scale by spe-

---

[58] Staffan B. Linder, *An Essay on Trade and Transformation* (Stockholm, 1961).

cialization in subcategories within an industry (for example, Grubel and Lloyd).[59]

Consider modern trade in manufactures. It is largely irrelevant to the most obvious Ricardian influence of natural resources; thus, steel is not necessarily most efficiently produced where iron ore and coal are found, given modern transportation and the influence of market location. Heckscher–Ohlin trade would probably dominate labor-intensive products such as clothing, if protective regimes did not distort this trade. But for a wide range of products, the relative factor abundance is highly similar across the industrial countries (and perhaps some NICs). As for the product cycle, there is no undisputed leader in technology among the industrial countries: each can aspire to technological leadership in at least some area of manufactures, especially if government intervention occurs. Japan and even some of the NICs have successfully accomplished technological catch-up to the point where, for a range of goods, technology does not provide a determining basis for comparative advantage.

In short, for a broad range of manufactures the country allocation of comparative advantage may be relatively arbitrary, at least among the industrial countries. Intraindustry trade is the logical result of this phenomenon. In a sense, one could view the industrial-country market for a large range of goods as a vast, potentially competitive market where the country location of a particular supplier is largely irrelevant. In this context, the configuration of "comparative advantage" begins to follow more the dynamics of industrial organization (that is, competitive or noncompetitive market structure) usually associated with the closed economy rather than conventional Ricardian, Heckscher–Ohlin, or product-cycle trade. For this range of goods, the conditions of competition may take on more importance than traditional trade influences in determining production patterns. Trade may become more the outcome of strategic behavior by firms than the consequence of national factor endowments. As in domestic industrial organization, considerations such as "who gets there first" take on added importance. A national program to stimulate an industry may cause little trade concern if the country is Norway and the product is coffee or bananas; Ricardian considerations will limit any effects on competitors. National programs to develop industries raise more serious problems for international competition when the

---

[59] Herbert G. Grubel and P.J. Lloyd, *Intra-Industry Trade* (New York: John Wiley and Sons, 1975).

country is, for example, Japan or Brazil, and the product is, for example, semiconductors or light aircraft.

In these circumstances it becomes paramount that there be internationally accepted rules of the game for competition, at two levels. First, at the level of national policy, there must be uniformity in what is and what is not acceptable government practice, because governments can affect the competitive positions of their domestic firms. Other things being equal, firms from country A will be at a disadvantage if by national policy country A behaves competitively (no government intervention, except that to correct market failure) while in country B national policy is to administer trade strategically and, in particular, to favor the sector in question. (Of course, other sectors in country B may be placed at a disadvantage because intervention, to be effective, must change *relative* incentives among sectors.) Some forms of intervention may already be subject to international discipline (for example, export subsidies) but others may not (for example, special research programs, exemptions from antitrust legislation, or enactment of special product requirements in public utilities).[60] The imbalance between firms in country A and firms in the favored sector of country B is analogous to that between small, competitive firms and large, strategically behaving, oligopolistic firms (other things, such as country size, being equal). Second, at the level of the firm, international rules of the game are needed for regulating imperfect competition. There is already considerable examination of US antitrust law to determine whether it impedes effective competition by American firms against foreign firms with more leeway for coordinated behavior (for example, in the joint development of new products). Symmetry between national antitrust regulation for international trade becomes all the more important considered in the light of "arbitrary comparative advantage," because competitive dynamics assume a larger role relative to inherent country endowments.

[60] For a review of government intervention in the high technology sectors, especially in France and Japan, see John Diebold, "The Information Technology Industries: A Case Study of High Technology Trade," in chapter 19, this volume. Note that although there is currently government intervention to promote high technology industries in countries such as France and Japan, high defense expenditures have played much the same role in the United States over past decades. In this connection, it is worth mentioning that one classical argument for protection, the need to maintain certain industries for defense purposes, exerts at least some influence in government intervention to maintain the steel industry and perhaps other sectors.

In sum, the conditions of modern trade for a wide range of manufactures suggest that comparative advantage may be relatively malleable instead of rigidly predetermined by national endowments of resources and factors, and trade in this range of goods may be determined importantly by the basic conditions of competition and market organization. Strategic behavior by nations and firms influences this trade, and rules of the game are essential if some countries (and firms) are not to be artificially disadvantaged relative to others.

Aggressive reciprocity is one vehicle for addressing the need for rules of the game to govern trade in manufactures with potentially arbitrary comparative advantage. It is probably the wrong vehicle, given the risks enumerated above. But the need remains to develop rules of the game.

There is another, potentially dangerous, implication of the line of analysis developed in this appendix. To the extent that a wide group of countries has endowments of resources, factors, and technology that are broadly indistinguishable, the traditional grounds for welfare benefits from trade are eroded. After all, gains from trade accrue to both parties because of the difference between their respective relative costs of the products. With similar factor endowments, resources, and technology, these differences are not likely to be great, and neither would the losses from reduction of trade. This consideration would suggest that the welfare costs of limiting trade of this sort would not be high. But this inference is dangerous not only because it issues an open invitation to protectionist interests but also because it may overlook important economic welfare effects associated with economies of scale and competitive pressure for technological change even if the static welfare costs associated with comparative costs are limited.

CHAPTER **5**

GATT Machinery and the Tokyo Round Agreements

John H. Jackson

US Trade Representative William E. Brock stated before the US Senate Finance Committee on March 24, 1983:[1]

> Our adherence to a free trade policy requires us to strictly enforce existing trade agreements, to strengthen our domestic trade laws to make them more useful and responsive to the needs of those they protect, and seek expanded coverage of trade issues under the mutually accepted international framework of the General Agreement on Tariffs and Trade.
>
> Four principles will guide our approach to any suggested legislation:
>
> First, it must be absolutely consistent with current obligations under the GATT and other international agreements. . . .

On March 5, 1982, Arthur Dunkel, director general of GATT, stated in an address at Hamburg:[2]

> Let me go further and say that international economic policy commitments, in the form of agreed rules, have far-reaching domestic effects, indeed effects so important that they are indispensable for democratic governance. They are the element which secures the ultimate coordination and mutual compatibility of the purely domestic economic policies. They form the basis from which the government can arbitrate and secure an equitable and efficient balance between the diverse domestic interests: producers vs consumers, export industries vs import-competing industries, between particular narrowly defined industries. Last but not least, only a firm commitment to international rules makes possible

[1] Reprinted BNA International Trade Reporters US Import Weekly (ITIM), vol. 121 (March 31, 1982), p. 673.
[2] GATT Press Release no. 1312, 5 March 1982.

the all-important reconciliation, which I have already alluded to, of the necessary balance on the production side and on the financial side of the national economy.

I am still convinced that it is in the national interest of every trading nation to abide by the rules, which were accepted as valid for good times and bad, and to frame their internal policies accordingly. One of the major benefits of international disciplines is that they offer equal opportunities and require comparable sacrifices from all the countries involved in international competition. Those who believe in the open trading system must recognize and accept the need to correct those rigidities in their economic and social systems which obstruct the process of continuing adjustment on which economic growth depends. . . .

Introduction

For three-and-a-half decades, the institution of the General Agreement on Tariffs and Trade (GATT) has been the source of considerable worry among policymakers, governmental officials, and scholars.[3] Since it was never intended to be an international organization, the GATT constitutional structure is not very well thought out. That structure, such as it is, contains only the barest outlines of necessary procedures and distribution of powers. Yet somehow the GATT seems to subsist, a tribute to the improvisation and ingenuity of the diplomats and particularly, the first director general of GATT.

An international institution, such as the GATT, which purports to regulate international economic relations among countries, needs a mechanism or framework for at least three essential functions:

● discussion and exchange of views on policies and trends, including sufficient staff resources (national or international) to provide the necessary background information. (These exchanges and discussions can themselves influence the course of events as embodied in national governmental policies.)

---

[3] The interested reader may want to consult one or more of the following: Robert E. Hudec, *The GATT Legal System and World Trade Diplomacy* (New York: Praeger, 1975); John H. Jackson, *World Trade and the Law of GATT* (New York: Bobbs Merrill, 1969); Jackson, "The Crumbling Institutions of the Liberal Trade System," *Journal of World Trade Law*, vol. 12, no. 93 (March/April 1978); Jackson, "The Birth of the GATT–MTN System: A Constitutional Appraisal," *Journal of Law and Policy in International Business*, vol. 12, no. 21 (Spring 1980).

- the formulation of new rules that will keep abreast of changing international economic conditions
- a system for both formal and informal resolution of differences or disputes between nations.

The Critical Questions

In examining the GATT–Multilateral Trade Negotiations (MTN) mechanism and constitutional structure, it is necessary to bear in mind these three essential functions, and to ask how well is the existing structure of GATT and its related agreements able to support these functions. In addition, for the United States (and certain other nations), there are some other important questions. Can the United States rely on the GATT as a central instrument and focal point of international economic regulation, to the extent it has in the past, and appears willing to rely in the future? More specifically, are the United States policymakers wise in adhering to a firm commitment not to break the rules of GATT? In pursuing many US complaints against foreign government actions concerning international trade in the GATT procedures for dispute resolution? For seeking to develop new rules in the GATT context to govern areas of international economic activities which are not now adequately governed? In short, is the United States well advised in placing so many of its "eggs" in the "GATT basket?" Can the GATT as an institution cope with the problems currently facing international economic relations, and with the problems which will likely face international economic relations in the near and not-so-near future?

There is no easy way to answer the questions posed above. First of all, the masses of details bearing on these questions are not easily assembled or understood. Secondly, much of this information is kept confidential by governments, or by the GATT itself, and therefore is not readily available. Thirdly, there is a judgmental aspect to conclusions based on that information which is available and which can be understood. It is much like the difference between a glass that is half full and one that is half empty. Given the same sets of facts and details, persons with different biases or different premises can come to apparently opposite conclusions. Among the details that are available, some can support considerable worry about the capacity of the GATT system to fulfill even minimally the roles that appear to be assigned to it. On the other hand, there are other details which support a proposition that the GATT system has achieved much and shows signs of continuing to achieve much.

In this chapter, some attempt will be made to point to some of the particular aspects of the GATT–MTN constitutional and legal system, as a mechanism for achieving a variety of goals that have been mentioned above. No attempt will be made to draw a "bottom line" conclusion, however, partly because it is premature to do so in light of the revolutionary overhauling to which the GATT was submitted during the Tokyo Round negotiation. In trying to point to some of the aspects that influence the subject of this paper, it is necessary to bear in mind that the GATT–MTN institutional framework must be evaluated in the context of its total legal system. This total legal system involves not only the GATT itself, as an international instrument and institution, but an interplay between that institution and a large number of national legal systems, including constitutional and governmental structures. This is particularly important with respect to the major "players" in the GATT scene, i.e. those governments which for one reason or another seem to have a major influential role in the GATT.

"Rule Diplomacy" versus "Power Diplomacy"

In other publications[4] this author has described the distinction between two basic philosophies of methodology of international diplomacy. These can be termed "rule diplomacy" and "power diplomacy." *Rule diplomacy* is the technique of establishing international rules of behavior for governments (or other entities), and developing institutions that will ensure a certain measure of compliance with these rules. *Power diplomacy*, by way of contrast, is diplomacy that occurs generally in the absence of rules (or effective rules) and is based more on the relative positions of power of the participants (national or other entities). The dichotomy suggested is obviously somewhat oversimplified, but to a certain extent international activity (as well as a good part of national activity) can be considered to fall on a spectrum of various mixtures of rule and power diplomacy. To a certain degree, world history can be viewed as the gradual displacement of power diplomacy (including that which occurs within nations) by rule structures. The resolution of international disputes, for example, involves diplomacy based partly on reference to rules, and partly on reference to power. In a system where the rules are fairly well developed and a system of compliance is fairly effective, negotiation for settlement of a dispute will tend to occur in the context of this rule reference system. The participants in the negotiation will

---

[4] See particularly the two most recent items by Jackson, "Crumbling Institutions" and "The Birth of the GATT–MTN System."

attempt to predict what will happen if a negotiated settlement is not achieved and, if they do achieve a settlement, it is likely that that settlement result will tend to converge towards the result that would occur by compliance with the rule. Where no rules exist, or where rules exist that are not effective (because a compliance mechanism is lacking), the parties will negotiate for settlement of a dispute more in the context of their relative power positions—military power, economic power, public opinion power, and so on.

There are certain obvious advantages to a well constructed and effective rule system both at the international and national levels. In a world where the use of force is so dangerous, a rule system generally tends to diminish the value of use of force. In areas of economic affairs, rule systems may have some additional values, particularly when decision making is relatively decentralized in or among one or more of the participants. A rule system can give guidance to subordinate governmental officials, or a private enterprise decision-maker. In some cases, it is even more important that there be a rule, than that the content of the rule be "correct."

One of the essential characteristics of the GATT has been the attempt to develop a rule system for international trade and other economic relations. In this respect the GATT is not unique—other international institutions also have attempted to do this. One of the problems of current international economic affairs, is the deep division among nations and their citizens, as to the appropriate role of government (and therefore government-developed rules) in economic behavior. Another problem is that partly because of the success of some of the international economic institutions (such as the GATT and International Monetary Fund [IMF]) economic interdependence has been increasing to the extent where national sovereignty, when it comes to economic decisions, is proving frustratingly constrained. In a world where a hundred billion dollars changes hands every day through telecommunication systems unknown some decades ago, and where the monetary and fiscal policy (once considered essential domains of national sovereignty) can have a rapid effect beyond a country's borders, national government leaders find it difficult to carry out their responsibilities to their constituents, and sometimes find it easy to blame the international system for their own failures. That the rule system of international economics has not kept pace with these developments, can be generally admitted.

Overview of the Constitutional History of the GATT–MTN System

Neither the conference participants nor other readers of this chapter need elaborate instruction on the history of GATT or the seven major trade rounds of negotiation. However, a few brief reminders[5] about certain aspects of that history that bear heavily upon the GATT mechanism might be worth reviewing.

The original idea of the 1946–48 preparatory meetings was to draft a charter for an International Trade Organization (ITO) which would contain a carefully constructed institutional and constitutional system for the international regulation of many aspects of international economic behavior. The GATT itself was never intended to be an organization or institution, and indeed in its early years there was consistent and persistent denial that the GATT was an international organization (partly because the United States negotiators had been chastised by members of Congress arguing that the US president did not have the authority to accept membership in an international organization for the United States). The GATT was accepted by the United States as an executive agreement under authority delegated to the US president by the 1945 extension of the Reciprocal Trade Agreements Act. This act gave ample authority to the president to enter into the GATT, but arguably not an "organization." Many US congressmen persistently challenged that authority, and even today one sometimes hears congressional expressions of such a challenge.

At the time the GATT drafting was completed and it was to come into force (January 1, 1948), many governments still anticipated that an ITO charter would later be completed and would also come into force. For these and other constitutional reasons, national governments found it difficult to accept the GATT definitively. Consequently, the GATT as such has never come into force as an international treaty agreement. Instead, it was incorporated into the Protocol of Provisional Application (PPA) which has come into force, and remains today the underlying legal treaty structure for the GATT. The principal significance of this was the inclusion in the PPA of the clause which fostered the "grandfather right" by exempting from most of the GATT rules legislation predating the GATT.

The amending provisions of the GATT–PPA (requiring two-thirds acceptance, and then applying the new amendment only to those countries which accepted it), has proved, in the light of the great increase in GATT membership (from the original 22 to the current 78), rigid and difficult to utilize. Because in recent years major and powerful industrial countries felt the need for the development of new rules, yet were unwilling to allow a one-nation one-vote system

---

[5] See generally, Jackson, *World Trade and the Law of GATT*, chs. 2, 3, and 4.

effectively to increase the power of the large majority of GATT members which are developing countries, the major nations of GATT decided to utilize the system of developing side agreements or "codes" to embody the structure of the new rules. This effectively avoided the necessity of amending the GATT, but created certain legal constitutional problems in its own right.

The Tokyo Round of negotiations (MTN), from 1973 to 1979, was an extraordinary trade negotiation. For the first time important attention was given to nontariff barriers as well as to tariffs. The results of the Tokyo Round probably increased the jurisdictional competence (with the consequential complexity of institutional arrangements) of the GATT about fourfold or more. The following major agreements resulted from that Tokyo Round and are the subject of attention in this paper:[6]

1. Geneva (1979) protocol (tariffs)
2. Agreement on technical barriers to trade
3. Agreement on government procurement
4. Agreement on interpretation and application of Articles VI, XVI, and XXIII (countervailing duties and subsidies)
5. Arrangement regarding bovine meat
6. International dairy arrangement
7. Agreement on implementation of Article VII (customs valuation)
8. Agreement on import licensing procedures
9. Agreement on trade in civil aircraft
10. Agreement on implementation of Article VI (antidumping)
11. "Framework" agreements

National Implementation of the Tokyo Round Agreements—Legal Aspects

The GATT–MTN constitutional system cannot be understood in isolation, as a sort of island set off somewhere in the ocean of international affairs. It can only be understood in the context of its interrelationship with the national governmental systems of the contracting parties to the GATT. However, it is not possible to develop

[6] The agreements are set forth in GATT, Basic Instruments and Selected Documents, 26th Supplement (1978–79), Geneva, March 1980. (Hereinafter cited as BISD 26th Supp.)

this interrelationship for 87 countries. In the Tokyo Round negotiation, there was a tendency for the United States and European Community (EC) officials to negotiate and consult together on important issues. Sometimes the representative from Japan was present, and these three participants constituted the major "power bloc" in the GATT. This section of this chapter examines briefly some of the important issues of national implementation of the Tokyo Round Agreements in these three areas, drawing heavily on a study to be published soon written by this author and two other professors (one from Japan and one from Belgium).[7]

In broad perspective, it can be said that the United States, the EC, and Japan have implemented all of the major international agreements resulting from the Tokyo Round negotiations. However, underneath the surface of this broad statement, there are a number of very difficult legal and constitutional questions about the implementation of the Tokyo Round Agreements.

At least three important subordinate issues can be raised in the case of national implementation of the Tokyo Round Agreements. The first of these is perhaps the easiest, namely, has the nation concerned accepted, as a matter of international legal obligation, the agreement at issue? The affirmative answer to this, as to all of the Tokyo Round Agreements and with respect to the three entities mentioned (United States-EC-Japan), is established by the international acts of signing and accepting the agreements, and evidenced by the current GATT list of acceptances of the agreements. It should be noted, that the "Framework Agreements," are not international agreements, but instead are being "implemented," by virtue of a decision of the GATT contracting parties meeting in November 1979. With respect to the international obligatory nature of a nation's acceptance, it is often interesting to examine under what domestic constitutional procedure the acceptance was made, because different procedures may imply different levels of political as well as legal commitment to the international agreement.

A second important question concerning each of the international agreements with respect to the national procedures of implementa-

---

[7] The research, by John H. Jackson (United States), Jean-Victor Louis (Belgium), and Mitsuo Matsushita (Japan) will be published by the University of Michigan Press. An advance and summary version of the book has been reprinted from "Implementing the Tokyo Round: Legal Aspects of Changing Economic Rules," *Michigan Law Review*, vol. 81, no. 2 (December 1982).

tion, is the degree to which the international agreement is "directly applied" in the domestic law of the nation, a question that in US law is sometimes called the "self-executing nature." If the particular agreement is not itself directly applicable or self-executing in the domestic law of the nation concerned, is it applied through some domestic statute or regulation which "transforms" the international norms of obligation into domestic legal rules? And if neither of these cases exist, is there some reason why the international rule does not need to be applied as part of the domestic law?

A third question with respect to the national implementation, is to examine the extent of the implementing mechanisms within the nation concerned. This has at least two possible aspects, first, the question of "hierarchy of norms," which refers to the issue of whether the norms of the Tokyo Round Agreements have a higher legal status than other competing norms within the domestic legal system of the nation concerned. The second aspect of this, is the degree to which the international norms are being applied, elaborated upon, or otherwise implemented by domestic governmental regulations which have come into force.

A final question that should be asked, but cannot yet be answered in a very detailed sense, is the degree to which the national implementation of the Tokyo Round Agreements is in fact having results in changing national government, private enterprise or citizen actions with respect to international trade in a way that is consistent with the principles that underlie the Tokyo Round Agreements. This would involve a rather elaborate empirical examination of the various societies concerned, which is beyond the resources available to this author for this chapter. Some indication about an answer to this question can be seen in the international processes of dispute resolution and policy discussions occurring in the GATT–MTN system, however.

Information about these national implementing processes and their legal problems is, of course, of considerable relevance to possible future negotiations. Not only do the different processes have an influence on the negotiators and their negotiating tactics, but it could well be that there are certain asymmetries in the legal implementation of international economic negotiation results, in the various countries, which asymmetries could defeat some aspects of true reciprocity that the negotiating parties thought they were achieving, or could create certain difficulties or misunderstandings in future years of the operation of an agreement concluded internationally.

Now we will examine each of these three national systems briefly.

United States

Except for the Geneva Tariff Protocol of 1979, (which was within the president's authority to implement under the advanced delegation of such authority contained in section 101 of the Trade Act of 1974[8]) certain other tariff commitments, and the Framework Agreements (decisions of the GATT and not international agreements),[9] the United States has implemented the nine other major MTN agreements through enactment of the statute entitled the Trade Agreements Act of 1979.[10]

This statute was enacted through a novel legislative process established in section 102 of the Trade Act of 1974, by which the president was authorized to negotiate agreements on nontariff measures, notify the Congress about the content of proposed agreements 90 days before he concluded such agreements and consult on that content, and then upon conclusion of such agreements, furnish the Congress with a bill to be enacted which would approve United States' acceptance of the agreements and implement those agreements into domestic law. This so-called "fast track" procedure for the Congress to enact this legislation, built into the rules of the House and the Senate three essential points: automatic discharge from committee consideration after a certain number of days; a "closed rule," so that the bill could not be amended; and limitations on debate. The process that actually operated, almost turned the procedure on its head: during the consultation period between the executive branch and the Congress, congressional committees examined the potential agreements and potential legislative implementation of those agreements in great detail, and concluded by suggesting to the president the full text of a statute which they recommended he send to them for enactment. The president in this case sent a statutory proposal which, except for a few minor differences, was identical to the one the congressional committees recommended. This bill then was speedily enacted by the Congress with overwhelming majorities of both houses. In short, the novel procedure worked remarkably well, in this instance.[11]

Certain features of the statute are of great importance to some of the legal questions posed above. The statute and accompanying legislative history make it abundantly clear that none of the international

---

[8] *Trade Act of 1974*, PL 93–618, approved January 3, 1975, US Code, vol. 19, sec. 2101–2487.

[9] BISD 26th Supp., pp. 202, 203, 205, and 209.

[10] *US Trade Agreements Act of 1979*, PL 96–39, approved July 26, 1979, US Code, vol. 19, sec. 2501 et seq.

[11] Jackson, "The Birth of the GATT–MTN System."

agreements will, under US law, be self-executing. That is to say, none of the agreements will have "direct applicability" in the US law.

However, it can be argued, that although the agreements themselves are not part of US law, the statute which implements them (and which in many cases uses the verbatim language from the agreements), was intended to implement the international agreements and to carry out US obligations. Thus, not only the legislative history of the statute (including the presidential documents[12] submitted to the Congress, as well as the legislative history that might be available from the committee activity during the consultation between the president and the Congress), but also the preparatory work and understandings of the international agreements themselves can be utilized as interpretive material.

It is clear, however, that under normal US law, the latest in time of conflicting statutes or treaties will prevail. Thus it is possible for the US Congress and president later to enact legislation inconsistent with the international obligations of the MTN agreements, and that later legislation will prevail in US courts. This issue is not so clear in other countries, where the question of hierarchy of norms is sometimes resolved differently, with greater deference to international obligations in the domestic courts.

European Community

The legal situation with respect to approval of the MTN agreements, and the implementation of those agreements in the European Community, was the most complex of the three major negotiating partners in the Tokyo Round. Indeed, the question became a major constitutional issue within the EC, and its resolution could be a major precedent in the fascinating evolution of EC law.[13]

The basic controversy was whether the EC institutions could accept the MTN agreements on behalf of the EC, without the participation, in any direct way, of the member states. The Treaty of Rome provides that commercial agreements, and certain other agreements, can be accepted on behalf of the EC by a decision of the Council, upon recommendation of the Commission. It is the Commission officials who negotiate the international agreement, subject to the supervision of the Council. (The Council consists of representatives of each of

---

[12] Statements of Administrative Action, transmitted to the US Congress on June 19, 1979, and reprinted in House Document 96–153, part II.

[13] Based on research in progress by Professor Jean-Victor Louis, described in n. 7.

the member states, while the Commission is the executive arm, or the "international bureaucracy" of the EC.)

Certain member states strongly argued that many, if not all, of the MTN agreements must be approved as mixed agreements, by which both the community institutions and all the member states would sign and approve the agreements. Such a procedure requires that each member state take such actions as are required within the constitutional system to approve the international treaty or agreement. In most cases this would have required actions of parliaments. The EC institutions, and particularly the Commission (upon advice of its legal service), took the opposite position, that all of the agreements could be accepted on behalf of the EC by the EC institutions acting without direct participation of any of the member states. A decision of the European Court of Justice in the fall of 1979[14] came at a critical time, and implied strongly that it would support the EC Commission's approach. Solution of the problem was hurried because of the necessity of action within the time limitation imposed by the US Trade Agreements Act of 1979, (US approval was conditioned upon approval by most of its major trading partners within a certain time period). These circumstances partly forced the hand of those member states which desired a mixed agreement approach. The solution, as described by Professor Jean-Victor Louis, (Brussels University) was a decision by the EC Council that all of the agreements could be accepted for the EC by the Council, but that as to three agreements, member states would also accept. The three agreements so designated were the agreements concerning technical barriers to trade, concerning aircraft, and the tariff protocol. One of the problems with the tariff protocol was that it concerned certain products that were covered by the Treaty of Paris, European Coal and Steel Community (ECSC), in addition to products covered by the European Economic Community (EEC) Treaty. The ECSC treaty provision regarding the acceptance of international commercial agreements were slightly different from those of the EEC Treaty, and so it could have been argued that a different procedure was necessary with respect to the steel products. However the products were mingled in the same international protocol. With respect to the other two agreements: technical barriers and aircraft, the rationale for the necessity of member state participation was not entirely clear. Nevertheless, the EC accepted, upon decision of the Council, all of the MTN agreements,

---

[14] Opinion of October 4, 1979, *International Agreement on Natural Rubber* 1/78, (1979) ECR 2871.

(the 10, plus the 2 subordinate protocols, except, of course, the framework agreements which were not international agreements). In the opinion of Professor Louis, the optional acceptance by EC member states to the three MTN agreements, has virtually no legal significance in respect to community law within the EC legal order, but is in the nature of the "cosmetic" solution to a constitutional dispute.

Japan

Japan[15] has a parliamentary government, and therefore does not experience the same kind of problems that arise in the United States or the EC where there is a constant struggle for power between different branches of government. The executive in Japan is headed by the cabinet, which is drawn from the parliament and both responsive to and controlling of the ruling parliamentary party. On the other hand, Japan does have an independent judiciary, with a supreme court that has the power of judicial review, which can be utilized to override legislation which is unconstitutional, and at least arguably, likewise can override at least the domestic effect of international agreements deemed unconstitutional under the Japanese constitution. Furthermore, there is plenty of "bureaucratic" struggle between the various ministries of the Japanese government.

Treaties in Japan are entered into by decision of the cabinet, but must be approved by both houses of the Diet (the parliament). However, several different types of international agreements do not rise to the status of "treaty" in this constitutional sense. These other agreements, such as executive agreements or exchange of notes, may be entered into by decision of the cabinet alone, particularly if they merely implement a previously existing treaty, or are entered into pursuant to authority delegated to the executive in Japan by prior statute. In some cases, it is considered unnecessary for the Diet to approve an international agreement, if legislation necessarily will be introduced and approved in order to implement the treaty domestically. In general, an international treaty approved by the Diet or otherwise validly entered into by the Japanese government, is considered to be self-executing, and therefore to have direct applicability in the domestic law system, insofar as it affects individual citizen rights or obligations.

With respect to the Tokyo Round Agreement (other than the Framework Agreement) the situation in Japan has been described

[15] This is summarized by work in progress by Professor Matsushita, as described in n. 7.

by Professor Matsushita: the Japanese government signed the Geneva Protocol regarding tariffs, in July 1979, but signed the other MTN agreements in December 1979 on condition that the government would accept them definitely when the national Diet approved of them. These other agreements were formally and officially accepted in April 1980, after the requisite approval of the national Diet.

Under Japanese constitutional law, since international agreements have self-executing characteristics of Japanese law, all of the MTN agreements approved by the Diet, or accepted as executive agreements, would be invokable in domestic courts by citizens involved in litigation with the government or other parties. Although it is not quite so clear, it is also likely that foreign entities in Japan would have the right to invoke the agreements in the courts, in enforcing provisions of those agreements.

International Implementation: The GATT–MTN System

The MTN Agreements and the GATT: Integrating The Tokyo Round Results

Of the 11 major international agreements resulting from the Tokyo Round, all but 2 are basically "stand-alone" new treaties which legally can continue to exist even in the absence of GATT, at least in theory.[16] The exceptions include the Tariff Protocol, which is the traditional end product of GATT trade negotiations. (The Supplementary Tariff Protocol shares the same characteristics, and this discussion basically treats that supplementary protocol jointly with the Geneva Protocol on Tariffs.) The second exception is the group of four framework agreements. Each of the 9 other agreements is in the form of a separate treaty. It already has been noted in this paper that one of the reasons for turning to this form of concluding the results of the negotiation was the difficulty of amending GATT, and the desire of major industrial countries to avoid a negotiating posture (similar to that of the Law of the Sea Conference) where a one-nation one-vote system prevailed. By negotiating separate stand-alone treaties, it was not necessary for a minimum of two-thirds of a GATT membership to accept any agreement, and it was clear that a much smaller group of nations, such as the Organization for Economic Cooperation and

---

[16] See text agreements in BISD 26th Supp.

Development (OECD) group, could enter into an agreement and put it into effect, even over objections by other nations or groups of nations among the GATT contracting parties. One result of this approach was a degree of resentment at the end of the negotiation from the developing countries, which felt excluded from effective participation in the negotiation.[17] This resentment can be detected even on the part of negotiators from some developed countries, such as Canada, because many of the important negotiating decisions were made among the big three (US-EC-Japan). The existence of these separate stand-alone agreements posed and poses for GATT the problem of how they are to be integrated into the GATT system. The official titles of three of these agreements speak of "implementing" or "interpreting and applying" certain articles of GATT (Valuation—GATT Article VII; Antidumping—GATT Article VI; subsidies and countervailing duties—GATT Articles VI, XVI, XXIII). Many of the agreements state that they expect the GATT Secretariat to provide service to the committees and other institutions of the agreements, and several of the agreements explicitly refer to GATT dispute settlement procedures.

The first question that arises then, is whether GATT contracting parties that are not parties to one of the MTN agreements have any rights in connection with these agreements (or lose any rights in the GATT context). Concern about these matters lead the contracting parties at the November 1979 meeting (at which many of the formal acceptances of the Tokyo Round Agreements were received from national diplomats) to adopt a "decision"[18] attempting to deal with these problems. This decision stated that the "contracting parties reaffirm their intention to ensure the unity and consistency of the GATT system and to this end they shall oversee the operation of the system as a whole and take action as appropriate." The decision noted that "existing rights and benefits under the GATT of contracting parties not parties to these agreements, including those derived from Article I, are not affected by these agreements." In addition, the decision states that the various institutions of the individual MTN agreements will report regularly to the GATT contracting parties, and that the contracting parties may request additional reports on "any aspect of the various committees' or councils' work." Finally, the decision states "the contracting parties understand that interested nonsignatory contracting parties will be able to follow the proceedings

---

[17] *New York Times*, 4 July 1978, p. 30.
[18] GATT, BISD 26th Supp.

of the committees or councils in an observer capacity, and that satisfactory procedures for such participation would be worked out by the committees or councils." The discussion below of the committees or councils reveals to some extent how this objective has been realized.

If an agreement is designated as one which "implements" or "interprets" an article in GATT, at least conceptually there are some difficult legal problems about the relationship of that agreement to the GATT. Suppose the countries that have signed the separate agreement implement a provision of that agreement, which establishes a new practice or implies a new interpretation of a particular GATT clause. In theory, this new practice or interpretation would not bind GATT contracting parties which have *not* signed the new agreement, but nevertheless the new practice or interpretation is a "practice under the GATT," and can be considered or taken note of in the GATT interpretation processes. Since the new agreements tend to be more detailed and more definitive in some respects about certain ambiguities or gaps in the GATT language it seems quite likely that the practice under some of the new agreements will, over time, become de facto interpretations of the GATT itself. This phenomenon has been mentioned to this author, as one of the motivating reasons why some countries have entered and accepted certain of the MTN agreements, which they did not feel particularly attracted to. They felt they could better protect their own rights, and participate in the process of formulating the practice and interpretation of GATT rules as influenced by the MTN agreement, by becoming a member of the MTN agreement and participating in its committee or council.

Few if any of the MTN agreements state a most-favored-nation (MFN) obligation. Yet, logic as well as the November 1979 GATT contracting parties' decision, suggest that the GATT MFN clause (Article I) continues to have validity, and in most cases would require specific MTN-agreement member countries to apply uniform treatment, even on subject of that agreement, to GATT contracting parties which are not members of the specific agreement. This consideration was the basis of an argument by India against the United States, when the United States refused to apply its new injury test in US law to products from India,[19] arguing that the subsidies–countervailing duty code did not apply between India and the United States. One can expect more of this type of question to arise.

---

[19] See BNA ITIM, vol. 97 (October 7, 1981), p. 5.

One problem of integrating the MTN agreements into the GATT system is the relation of some of the specific dispute settlement procedures (that are contained in some of these agreements) to the general dispute settlement procedure of GATT. Generally, the language in the MTN agreements which specify a formal dispute settlement procedure separate from that of the GATT, specifies that a dispute between parties to the agreement relating to rights and obligations under that agreement should follow the procedures of that agreement before either party avails itself of any "rights which they have under the GATT, including recourse to Article XXIII thereof."[20] This language raises several questions. First, it raises the question whether in a dispute between two parties to an MTN agreement, once the procedure of that agreement has been exhausted, there still remains the opportunity to bring the matter to GATT (as a sort of "appeal"). Secondly, some of the MTN agreements do not include this kind of language (for example the antidumping agreement) and this raises the question of whether it can therefore be inferred that the draftsmen of the agreement intended the GATT dispute settlement procedure to coexist and be available as an option of the complaining party, for disputes involving a subject matter covered both in the GATT and in the MTN agreement. In any event, the relatively confused status of the interrelations of the various dispute settlement procedures in the MTN agreements and in GATT renders it likely that a certain amount of "forum shopping" will occur, and that procedural disputes will be a significant part of almost every complaint in the early years of the new GATT–MTN system.

One group of agreements resulting from the Tokyo Round has not been set out as a separate agreement. This is the group of texts on which consensus was reached in the "Group Framework" negotiation of the MTN,[21] relating to four subjects: More Favorable Treatment for Developing Countries, Trade Measures for Balance of Payments Purposes, Safeguard Actions for Development Purposes, and Understandings Regarding Consultation and Dispute Settlement Problems. These four texts were each accepted as a separate decision by the contracting parties at their November 1979 meeting. The texts are drafted with considerable poetic license, with a fair amount of "precatory words" which may not imply legal obligation. The understanding regarding notification, consultation, dispute settlement, and sur-

---

[20] Agreement on implementation of Article VII of the GATT, BISD 26th Supp., pp. 116, 130 (Art. XX, par. 11, of the Agreement).

[21] GATT, BISD 26th Supp.

veillance, for example, consists of a number of paragraphs which use the word "should," or the phrase "undertake, to the maximum extent possible," and appends an "Agreed Description of the Customary Practice of GATT in the Field of Dispute Settlement." The theory of at least some of the negotiators was that no innovations were being brought about by this understanding, but a careful reading of the understanding suggests that this is not entirely the case.

One of the major results of one of these decisions, that entitled "Differential and More Favorable Treatment: Reciprocity and Fuller Participation of Developing Countries," seems to have been a de facto perpetuation of the 1971 "waiver" by the contracting parties of the MFN obligation of GATT, to the extent necessary to allow Generalized Systems of Preferences (GSP). The language of this "decision" is seen by some contracting parties to make it unnecessary to renew the 1971 waiver (which was for a period of 10 years), although the language of the 1979 decision is not a model of clarity and precision on that point.

The Institutions of the New MTN Agreements

Of the 11 major subjects handled by separate agreements resulting from the MTN, 9 of these agreements provide explicitly for the establishment of a supervisory committee or council of some type.[22] Generally it is stated in the agreement that the GATT Secretariat will service these institutions. In addition, some of the agreements provide for a review such as an annual review of the implementation and operation of the agreement, or, as is the case of the Government Procurement Agreement, for further negotiations at the end of the third year from the entry into force of the agreement. Some of the agreements (such as the one on technical barriers to trade, and the one on customs valuation) established sub-bodies, such as a technical committee, to assist the supervising committee, or to be a part of the dispute-settlement process. As previously mentioned, and as discussed below, several of the agreements have explicit provisions for dispute resolution.

---

[22] Agreements in BISD 26th Supp. The 9 agreements mentioning explicitly the formation of the committee or council include all of those 11 agreements except the first and the last on that list (i.e., all except the Geneva Protocol with respect to tariffs and the so-called framework agreements).

Committees or Councils of the MTN Agreements

Under the GATT decision of November 1979, the nine committees or councils established under the MTN agreements, are supposed to report to the GATT, and be generally under the supervision of the GATT. In addition, a committee on tariff matters has been set up, to assist in the supervision of tariff protocols resulting from the Tokyo Round. This committee could probably be considered a direct committee of the GATT, since the tariff protocols are, in effect, amendments to the schedules annexed to the GATT, and thus are a form of amendment to the GATT itself. The tariff protocols do not in themselves establish committees or institutions or dispute settlement procedures.

Thus, the GATT has created, as a result of the MTN agreements, 10 new institutions which are meeting regularly. Two critical procedural questions are involved in these new committees. One is the question of voting and decision making; and the other is the question of observers.

With respect to voting, the MTN agreements are remarkably silent. They generally establish a committee, to be composed of a representative from each government that signs and accepts the agreement. In certain of the agreements (dairy and bovine meat) there was an explicit statement that the committees will act "by consensus," and presumably this means (and the language usually would reinforce this interpretation) that if any member of the committee or council formally objected to a proposal, the proposal would not be adopted. In essence it would be a requirement of a unanimity.

In other agreements (e.g., subsidies, antidumping), nothing precise is said about the decision-making process or voting. In the light of ample international practice, if an issue were forced to a head, it is likely that a one-nation one-vote procedure would be upheld, although it has been commonly stated by some contracting party representatives that "the consensus method" of decisions should prevail in these committees also.

Near the end of the Tokyo Round negotiations, there was a possibility that, from the point of view of the United States, a somewhat risky situation could occur. Since it was clear that among the parties entitled to sign and accept the agreements were each of the EC member states, plus the European Community's institutions proper (because of the special wording of the MTN agreements), it was at least theoretically possible for the Community and its member states to consist of a block of 10 (or more) representatives to the supervising committee. Thus, theoretically it would be possible for the European

Community effectively to control 10 votes in a committee which, at least, in its early years, might total only 16-to-20 members. However, due to the internal constitutional problems of the European Community in accepting and implementing the MTN agreements (described under National Implementation of the Tokyo Round Agreements—Legal Aspects above) the only signatory on behalf of the EC for all but three of the MTN agreements (tariffs, technical barriers, and aircraft) is the EC itself.[23] Consequently, this risk of the voting situation seems largely to have disappeared, at least for the present.

The question of observer status for contracting parties of the GATT which are not signatories and acceptors of the particular MTN agreement, is one that was not so easily resolved. In theory, each supervising committee of each MTN agreement, could decide for itself about extending the right to attend its meetings as an observer to contracting parties of the GATT. The GATT contracting parties decision of November 1979, however, explicitly stated the "understanding," that such observer status would be extended to all GATT contracting parties. Yet the language of the decision was not that of legal obligation. In each of the supervising committee or council meetings of the various MTN agreements, time was spent at the early meetings attempting to determine the policy to be followed on observer status.

In fact, however, achieving observer status has been something of a pyrrhic victory for GATT contracting parties which have decided not to join certain MTN codes. Although the observer is entitled to be present at the formal meeting of the supervising committee, the practice is fairly well established in GATT that prior to the formal meeting, an informal meeting is held, at which the real decisions and drafting compromises are made. Observers are not present, usually, at the "premeeting."

Most of the supervising committees and councils have now met from two to four times a year since their establishment. They have all been established since the agreement under which they operate has come into effect, i.e., in 1980, or later. Consequently, most have met five or six times.[24] Various issues have come up at these meetings.

---

[23] See, for example, GATT Document L/4915/rev. 3/Add. 8 (30 April 1982) status of acceptances, etc., as of 28 April 1982. The GATT Document Status of Acceptance shows the United Kingdom acceptance of many more of the MTN Documents, with an asterisk for a "declaration." These acceptances are on behalf of the overseas territories, particularly Hong Kong.

[24] See, for example, reports of the various committees or councils printed in BISD 27th Supp. (1979–80), Geneva, March 1981.

At the beginning, these committees were preoccupied with establishing the committee and its ground rules, establishing the rules for observers, dealing with questions of restriction of documents, formulating questionnaires for information notification regarding national activities relating to the agreement and the annual reviews of the supervising committee, dealing with questions of accession, establishing a list of persons available for dispute resolution panels, and formulating the annual report to the contracting parties.

Some of this activity continued beyond the initial meetings, but in general for the initial years of the operation of these committees, the most important work seems to have been the examination of the implementation of the MTN agreement by nations which are parties to that agreement. Thus, national parties were asked to notify the supervising committee of the exact domestic action taken in order to implement the agreement concerned. This action might be the adoption of a statute, or adoption of internal regulations, or other activity. These actions were then examined by the committee, and a number of suggestions or even informal complaints were discussed by the committee to try to improve the level of compliance and implementation of the agreement. One representative has expressed the viewpoint to this author, that this initial process went very well, that virtually all of the MTN agreements have been implemented in a good faith manner, and that there is virtually no "conscious deviation" from the constraints of the legal obligations contained in the MTN agreements, although there has been a certain amount of deviation from the requirement because of bureaucratic slowness, neglect, lack of adequate staff resources at national capitals, and the like.

Another government representative who participates in a number of these supervisory committee meetings has said to this author that one of the salutary features of the processes has been the development of a framework for ongoing discussions about the particular technical and detailed subject matter regulated under the MTN code, which framework includes the participation of various governmental experts often sent out from national capitals. As a consequence of this framework, experts from capitals of a variety of countries are regularly getting together in Geneva, and addressing the relatively detailed problems of ensuring better compliance with the obligations of the agreements. A number of small matters have been ironed out in these processes, when one country representative brings to the attention of a representative from another country a practice that the former deems dubious in the light of the MTN agreements. Much of this activity is being handled at a fairly low level, and with low visibility, and real progress can sometimes be obtained fairly efficiently and quickly on minor complaints registered by businessmen in one country to their government, which complaints then are brought up in this formal discussion framework of the supervising committee of an MTN agreement. Although this process usually does not result in the institution of a formal dispute settlement procedure, nevertheless it must be considered as a part of the overall dispute settlement facility that has developed under the MTN agreements.

Dispute Resolution Under the GATT–MTN Constitution

The United States has been an assiduous user of the GATT dispute-settlement system and procedures, and recently has initiated a number of such procedures.[25] What are the alternatives to using the GATT dispute settlement procedures? Is there adequate public understanding of those procedures and of their limitations? Have the procedures been working?

This section will necessarily be a brief overview of a rather elaborate and complex subject, upon which a separate literature already exists. This brief overview will be divided into two parts: first, a look at the GATT dispute-settlement procedures themselves; second, a look at the new procedures established in the various MTN agreements.

The GATT Dispute-Settlement Mechanisms

As mentioned in above, the GATT was not originally intended to be an international organization but has evolved into one by necessity. Its constitutional structure being weak, it is not surprising that the dispute-settlement provisions contained in the GATT are also weak, sketchy, and rather ambiguous.

The history of dispute settlement procedures in GATT[26] is the history of improvising on the extremely inadequate language of Ar-

---

[25] A full list of complaints brought in the United States under the section 301 procedure can be found (as of June 2, 1982) in BNA ITIM, Ref. File 49:0801.

[26] See Hudec, *The GATT Legal System*; Jackson, *World Trade and the Law of GATT*, ch. 8; Jackson, *Legal Problems of International Economic Relations*, cases, materials, and text (Boulder, Col.: West Publishing Company, 1977), ch. 7, sec. 5, pp. 422 et seq.; Jackson, "Dispute Settlement Techniques Between Nations Concerning Economic Relations With Special Emphasis on GATT" (paper delivered at the Sokol Colloquium, March 1982, University of Virginia, Charlottesville), to be published by the university press.

ticle XXIII, which concerns remedies for "nullification and improvement" of negotiated liberalization commitments. In the early years of GATT there were no established procedures. The contracting parties as a whole could and sometimes would examine complaints by one member against another. During this period a working party or other general committee would occasionally be set up to consider the complaints of one party against another, and report back to the contracting parties. As time went on, due partly to the leadership of Sir Eric Wyndham-White who was then executive secretary of the GATT, the concept of establishing a panel to consider the complaint of one government against another was accepted. (Individuals appointed to be members of a panel act in their own capacity, and presumably without instruction from their respective governments.)

A "restatement" of GATT dispute settlement procedures[27] was drafted during the Tokyo Round, and accepted by a decision of the contracting parties. There is a certain amount of ambiguity at almost every step of this procedure. Furthermore, there are ample opportunities for delay. Unfortunately, it is not clear what the legal results of a panel finding is. It appears that there is no *legal* obligation to carry out a panel finding, at least until the GATT contracting parties approve the panel reports, and even then there has been considerable ambiguity.

There has been only one case in GATT where, under Article XXIII an actual authorization of suspension of concessions was made (a case early in the history of GATT, brought by the Netherlands against US dairy import restriction).[28] In the "chicken war," a "compensatory withdrawal of concession" was exercised by the United States against EC member countries. This case was not an Article XXIII case, however, but was brought under different articles of the GATT which contemplate compensatory action of this type.[29]

The procedures under Article XXIII can be contrasted with certain more "automatic" responses that are authorized by other articles of GATT. For example, under Article VI of GATT a party is authorized to use antidumping duties against goods that are "dumped" and countervailing duties against goods that are subsidized. In these situations the importing country has the right to make the necessary determinations and act unilaterally (provided that it makes its findings and takes these actions in accordance with its international obligations).

---

[27] BISD 26th Supp., pp. 210, 215.
[28] Jackson, *World Trade and the Law of GATT*, p. 185 n. 22.
[29] Ibid., pp. 174–75.

Likewise, Article XIX of GATT, which is the escape clause, allows an exporting nation unilaterally to take compensatory action against another country that has excluded imports pursuant to a legitimate invocation of the escape clause criteria and procedures. There is no precondition that an international body approve these various unilateral responses. The results, in some ways, suggest that these unilateral responses, which are in effect sanctions, have been more effective in encouraging compliance with the rules of trade than the Article XXIII dispute-settlement procedures.

There is one very important aspect of the provision of Article XXIII that pervades the GATT practice and procedures of dispute settlement. When invoking Article XXIII, a GATT party must argue that benefits it expected under the GATT are being nullified or impaired. Although there is a provision for another type of invocation, in general this requirement of nullification or impairment is central to the right to invoke the GATT procedures. Unfortunately, the phrase "nullification or impairment" is exceedingly ambiguous. An early case in GATT suggested that it related to the concept of "reasonable expectations" of the other party.[30] It is explicitly recognized in the GATT practice that nullification or impairment is *not* coexistent with a *breach* of GATT obligations. A breach of a GATT obligation is neither a sufficient nor a necessary prerequisite to the invocation of Article XXIII. A breach of obligation does, however, under the practice of GATT raise a prima facie nullification or impairment.[31]

A brief look at some statistics[32] of the actual GATT practice during its 35 year history, may be helpful in getting that practice into perspective. Based on a fairly systematic (but preliminary) inventory of the disputes brought formally in GATT, mostly under Articles XXII and XXIII of GATT we have identified 159 formal dispute cases during the history of GATT. Fifty of these were brought during the 1950s, then there was somewhat of a drop during the 1960s. During the 1970s a renewal of interest in the dispute processes of GATT occurred. This interest seems to have continued, and it appears that there will be quite a large number of formal dispute cases in the GATT during the 1980s, particularly since a number of new dispute-

---

[30] Ibid., pp. 172–73.

[31] Ibid., pp. 182 et seq.

[32] Jackson, Sokol Colloquium paper. The author has been developing an inventory of GATT disputes based on his own prior writing, the book by Hudec, *The GATT Legal System*, other works, and recent interviews with and documents from government officials. This work is in progress.

settlement procedures are now available in connection with the various Tokyo Round codes.

Of the 159 cases so far inventoried, 75 percent were brought by developed countries, and 86 percent were against developed countries. It is clear that the dispute-settlement procedures are utilized mainly by the industrial nations. The United States stands out as the primary user of the procedures, being a complainant in 36 percent of the cases and a respondent in 14 percent of the cases. Thus in one-half the dispute-settlement cases in GATT, the United States is either a complainant or the respondent!

Approximately 45 percent—almost one-half of the disputes—involved agricultural products, whereas only 16 percent involved manufactured products. Since approximately 35 percent of the cases do not fall easily within a product category, only a small percentage is left for primary products. Agricultural products are clearly the predominant source of disputes within the GATT.

About one-half of the cases brought are settled or withdrawn before a panel report is issued. In nearly all of the cases in which a panel report was issued, the report was "accepted" or "adopted" by the GATT contracting parties or council and thereby approved by the GATT as a whole.

There were at least eight cases in which there has been a *refusal* to comply with the results of the dispute-settlement procedure, but as mentioned above, only one case in which an official sanction has been taken under the procedures of Article XXIII of GATT.

As is typical with most international dispute-settlement processes, only governments have direct access to the GATT dispute-settlement processes. Thus, an individual citizen or a business firm which is harmed by a foreign country's breach of a GATT obligation (such as the foreign country's imposition of import restraints which block the exports of the firm or individual), has no way to complain directly to the foreign government through the GATT. In some cases the individual or firm may be able to bring legal proceedings under the importing country's own law. In the United States, for example, this could very well occur. But normally the citizen must go to his own government and urge it to invoke the GATT procedures or otherwise bring diplomatic pressures against the foreign country. Thus, the citizen's government has control of his claim. If the citizen is out of favor with his government, he may find his government dragging its feet. Or, his government may have a different set of priorities and either trade-off the claim for other benefits, or feel indisposed to press the claim because it might affect certain other broader bilateral relationships (such as the establishment of military bases, or other political cooperation).

In the United States, citizens and their representatives in Congress have been highly critical of the alleged lack of willingness of the US government to pursue claims of breach of GATT obligations or other nullification or impairment measures against foreign governments. Congress has stepped in to try to give the citizen somewhat more access to the process. In the 1962 Trade Expansion Act the Congress, in section 252,[33] granted certain powers to the president to encourage him to use the possibility of retaliation against foreign trade practices in his negotiations with countries that took actions aggrieving American commerce and commercial interests. In the Trade Act of 1974, Congress revised this law, and reenacted it as section 301 which was designed to broaden the president's powers to take retaliatory actions, establish a procedure by which individual citizens could bring their complaints to the United States government, and encourage the US government to carry those complaints into international forums.[34] The Trade Agreements Act of 1979 revised section 301[35] so as to bring additional pressure on the US government to pursue complaints in international forums such as the GATT. Indeed, the 1979 act explicitly encourages the president to "enforce the rights of the United States under any trade agreement...."

This US law is possibly unique in that it provides a statutory right to citizens to petition their government, requires the government to respond within fixed time limits and explain its response, and encourages the government to invoke the appropriate international procedures on its citizens' behalf.

Since the Trade Act of 1974 entered into force, there have been approximately 31 formal complaints[36] to the US government under section 301, of which 26 have concerned trade in products. (International trade in services is also covered by section 301, but the GATT does not have jurisdiction over that subject, at least not yet.) The United States has been vigorous in pursuing its rights under the Article XXIII procedures of GATT. Although many section 301 complaints are settled before international procedures are actually begun, in at least 13 cases the section 301 complaint has caused the United States to engage the GATT Article XXIII procedures. In the view

---

[33] *Trade Expansion Act of 1962*, PL 87–794, 76 Stat. 872.
[34] See section 301, *Trade Act of 1974*.
[35] *Trade Agreements Act of 1979*.
[36] BNA ITIM, Ref. File 49:0801.

of some practitioners, both government and private, section 301 has been fairly effective in giving private firms and citizens some additional bargaining leverage in their efforts to obtain relief from foreign government practices detrimental to their trade. Although section 301 does not require the president to act, the procedures for the hearings, published reasons for its responses, time limits, and the like, coupled with congressional oversight have tended to make the US government pursue a number of complaints in international forums.

Dispute Settlement Under the MTN Agreements

Many of the MTN agreements contain independent and new dispute-settlement procedures which can operate totally separately from the GATT dispute-settlement procedure. Indeed, of the 11 major MTN agreements, no 2 have identical dispute-settlement procedures in them.[37] Two of the agreements contain no explicit provision with respect to dispute settlement, and presumably rely upon the GATT procedures. Two more agreements refer explicitly to the GATT dispute-settlement provisions as governing disputes on the agreements, (the Licensing Agreement and the framework understandings, the latter of which are really decisions and not agreements). Each of the 7 other agreements contain explicit provisions mentioning dispute settlement, with varying degrees of formality. The Bovine Meat Agreement (Article IV paragraph 6) only provides that "any participant may raise before the council any matter affecting this agreement...." In such a case the council will meet within 15 days to consider the matter. But at the other extreme, the Subsidies–Countervailing Duty Agreement (Articles XVII and XVIII) specifies an elaborate set of procedures, including reference to a panel, and report of the panel to the Committee on Subsidies and Countervailing Measures. The Antidumping Agreement (Article XV) also establishes a separate procedure for dispute settlement, including reference to the committee, and then to a panel. The Aircraft Products Agreement provides that the committee shall review a matter brought to it by a signatory. It also provides with respect to any dispute not covered by other instruments negotiated under the auspices of GATT, that the provisions of the GATT Articles XXII and XXIII along with the understanding relating to dispute settlement, shall be applied. The remaining three agreements: Valuation, Technical Barriers, and Gov-

---

[37] See text at BISD 26th Supp.

ernment Procurement, each contain a fairly detailed procedure for dispute settlement, following generally a pattern of consultation, then reference to the committee, then reference to a panel, and report by the panel to the committee. However, none of the three procedures is identical to any other, and each agreement contains certain specific differences in the procedure.

Some of the MTN agreements unfortunately use the nullification-impairment language of the GATT Article XXIII itself. In any event, with this plethora of different procedures, there is an increased risk of jurisdictional conflicts, forum shopping, and disputes over procedures. It is too early to tell how serious the problem will be. It is possible that after a brief period of "shakedown" there will be sufficient decisions as to procedure under each code, that procedural matters can be put in the background. It is not clear to what extent a decision as to a procedural matter under one code, will be used as quasi-precedent for the resolution of a similar issue under another code. In a few agreements, it is specified that the code procedure must be utilized by disputing parties who are both signatories to the code, before applying to the general GATT procedure. As mentioned above, it is not clear what will be the situation in those agreements which do not have such language. Neither is it clear the degree to which the "framework understanding" on dispute settlement can be utilized as a guide for procedures under any of the specific codes. Only recently (March 1982) has the first panel procedure under one of the MTN agreements been formally invoked (a dispute involving the subsidization of wheat flour by the European Community, brought by the United States in connection with the subsidies code).[38] Nevertheless, as mentioned earlier in this chapter, a number of disputes or differences have been raised formally in the various supervising committees of the MTN agreements. In a few such cases a formal complaint has been filed, and in one case there has been a ruling that the complaint could not be pursued under the procedure of that code.[39] In most cases discussions within the supervising committees with respect to matters that could give rise to a dispute about inter-

[38] See section 301 case complaint to the US government numbered 301-06, *Federal Register*, vol. 40, no. 236 (December 8, 1975), p. 57,249 and BNA ITIM, Ref. File 49:0801, ITIM, vol. 119 (March 17, 1982), p. 591.

[39] The case involved the agreement on technical barriers to trade, and whether or not such agreement applied to standards for "processes" as well as standards for the product itself. The case concerned chilling of poultry. See Report of the Committee on Technical Barriers to Trade, at BISD 27th Supp., p. 37 (GATT Document L/5068, par. 9).

pretation of the MTN agreement involved, have been discussed as general problems, and not in the context of a particular case. To a certain extent, these were interpretive problems left over from the MTN negotiations.[40]

[40] The chilling of poultry case, n. 39, is an example.

CHAPTER 6

Threats to the Multilateral System

Harald B. Malmgren

T he multilateral economic institutions created after World War II constitute a success story. They facilitated a tremendous expansion of world trade and financial flows, and a considerable liberalization of national economies. World trade grew much faster than the rate of national GNP growth for three decades—twice as fast in the 1950s and 1960s, and half again as fast in the 1970s.

Trade and international capital movements thus constituted a strong force in the growth of national economies. But this success story has also brought problems. National economies have become increasingly interactive and interdependent. The share of trade in GNP has been growing rapidly in recent years for most of the major trading nations. If one sets aside services, and compares trade to national production of goods (farm products and manufactured goods), the share of trade in national goods production has risen in the last decade even more sharply in most of the major Western industrial nations—more than doubling in the case of the United States.[1]

The Resurgence of Mercantilism

This growing interdependence and interaction of markets has broadened the sources of competition in many sectors of our national economies. It has intensified the economic pressures for structural adjustment, and not surprisingly it has also brought counterpressures

---

[1] Measurement of exports or imports relative to production activity is subject to a number of conceptual problems as well as to problems of comparability of national statistics. See the US Commerce Department series, Exports and Imports as Percent of Production of Goods, *International Economic Indicators*, with explanatory notes.

on governments to reduce the pains of adjustment and shield traditional suppliers from the strong winds of competition.

The process of national and sectoral adjustment would be far easier in a context of rapid economic growth and a high real rate of investment. But the fast growth of the 1950s and 1960s gave way to slower growth, and one major recession, in the 1970s.

At the beginning of the 1980s, the world finds itself in the third year of stagnation of world trade. In fact, in 1981 world trade declined slightly in real terms, and in 1982 this decline is continuing. Even if we exclude petroleum trade, the growth in volume of world trade has been decelerating since 1980, and has begun a real decline in 1982. Moreover, industrial production in the Western industrial countries as a group has been stagnant since 1980.

This means that the world economic pie is not growing. At the same time, for a variety of reasons (such as high levels of unemployment, economic dislocation, and foreign exchange or debt-service problems), virtually every government in the world is trying to step up exports, slow down imports, and promote expansion of domestic jobs.

With a pie that is not growing, a greater share for one can only be achieved by reducing the share of another.

Thus, the current conditions are exceptionally favorable for economic nationalism, isolationism, and protectionism. In this environment, a significant world economic contraction could easily occur, particularly because of the cumulative international effects of nationalistic policy responses.

The continued stagnation of global economic activity, with considerable downside risks, constitutes by itself a fundamental challenge to the principles and procedures of the multilateral economic system.

The shocks of the 1970s—inflation, energy prices, exchange rate volatility, emergence of new competitors, the rapid technological ascent of Japan, national political crises—were recognized early by governments as threats to multilateral cooperation. The Organization for Economic Cooperation and Development (OECD) trade standstill agreement, the courageous effort to continue the Multilateral Trade Negotiations (MTN), the further reforms of the multilateral financial system, and the emergence of Western economic summitry are examples of this high-level recognition in the mid- and late 1970s that the system was under stress. The restraint of national governments during the last decade, in the face of economic and social turbulence, is a remarkable story. That, too, is a success story.

But the political will to continue reliance on the multilateral mechanisms has nonetheless been eroding, and at the start of the 1980s we are experiencing a mood which can best be described as neo-mercantilism. Tendencies towards neomercantilism were already developing at the beginning of the last decade.[2] The current resurgence of neomercantilist thinking is fed by the tendency of each government, even at the summit level, to blame other nations for the problems experienced at home. This should not be surprising. The "politics of blame" always prevail when policies are failing. An economic or financial minister, or a party leader, is hardly likely to blame himself and confess error when his policies have proven to be inadequate or even disastrous.

The record of the period since the inception in 1975 of the Western economic summits could be interpreted as a record of national leaders blaming each other, and then meeting annually to cover up their differences with pious rhetoric, to demonstrate politically that in spite of their policy differences, they were all friends. The 1982 Versailles summit, and especially its contentious aftermath, dramatized how fragile this summit process had become.

The new mercantilism is a reflection of the frustrations and the feelings of helplessness in national governments that traditional instruments of macroeconomic policy cannot be effectively used. Slow growth and high unemployment have forced governments to assist troubled sectors. The assistance is ostensibly provided to facilitate the structural adjustment of the troubled sectors, while maintaining employment. However, the real effect of these sectoral policies has usually been to retard adjustment. I have often over the years described this process of sectoral intervention as the implementation of *adjustment resistance policies*.

More recently, fiscal austerity in virtually every nation has led governments to seek off-budget solutions. Regulations have been used to force private enterprises to alter their activities to meet social goals and at the same time to bear the costs of achieving these goals. The sprawling, incoherent, often conflicting expansion of regulations has naturally carried over to the regulation of trade flows. If a government does not wish to subsidize a sector, and at the same time is unwilling to see that sector adjust as fast as market forces might dictate, then another means to solve the problem is to limit the external sources of competition.

Because of the benefits of the broad process of liberalization that has taken place, because of the protection the General Agreement

[2] See my article, "Coming Trade Wars? (Neo-Mercantilism and Foreign Policy)," *Foreign Policy*, vol. 1, no. 1 (1970–71).

on Tariffs and Trade (GATT) provides for one's exports, and because of the fear of widespread unraveling of trade agreements, governments have been somewhat reluctant to flaunt the GATT and their own past trade agreements. Therefore, in recent years we have seen a growing, now massive process of improvisation to shield sectors and to strengthen their international competitiveness. Nontariff measures, government guidance and participation in commercial activity, performance requirements, foreign investment regulations, aggressive technological policies, and other means have been found to limit or distort competitive market forces. Many of these measures have been designed to avoid the GATT strictures, or to slip through the ambiguities in it. Many of these measures are backed by "understandings" reached between governments, or between industry associations of different nations with the acquiescence of governments.

This tendency to regulate or manage sectoral development is running into conflict with the growing global interdependence and interaction of national markets. This policy tendency is threatening the viability of the world trading rules, and of the rights and obligations so carefully developed under the GATT framework over the last 35 years.

The Erosion of the GATT System

There are many different views about what the GATT is, what it does, and what it should do, depending upon the national or professional point of perspective.

In the United States, many lawyers, government officials, and representatives of private enterprises view the GATT as a juridical system—an embodiment not only of the rule of law, but of the enforcement of law, on the international level. This is partly a reflection of the role of law in the operations of the US economy, and the role of the executive branch in regulating the economy within the framework of the Constitution and the laws written by Congress.

Viewing the GATT as a juridical system, there have been many American complaints that other nations have broken the rules. The violations are referred to GATT proceedings, but then further complaints are made that the GATT usually fails to decide who was wrong and who was right. Yet the GATT itself does not impose sanctions. The member nations of the GATT interpret the rights and obligations in a given situation, and the members may even authorize a nation to take countermeasures in the event another nation's policies have negated the value of past concessions. The GATT rules also permit certain types of unilateral countermeasures, when there is commercial dumping or official subsidization, provided that a specific degree of injury can be demonstrated.

But the GATT itself is really not a juridical system, nor is it an enforcement body.

Gardner Patterson, in his paper for this conference, defines a well-functioning international trading system as "a multilateral, nondiscriminatory one, based on negotiated general rules of behavior providing for stability and predictability."

The point on which I should like to place emphasis is that the GATT is the cumulative effect of negotiations—negotiated general rules, and specific negotiated trade concessions. The GATT is not a court. It is a system of balanced rights and obligations, together with a cumulation of trade agreements based on mutual concessions and on *national* decisions to agree, or not agree, with other nations. Reopening of past agreements tends to cause an unraveling, unless carried out on a mutual, negotiated basis. In this regard, the GATT provides for renegotiation of obligations, and procedures for restoring a mutually agreed balance of rights and obligations if a nation acts contrary to its agreements and thereby injures another party to such agreements.

The director general of the GATT, Ambassador Arthur Dunkel, recently expressed grave concern over the threats to the GATT arising from national policies.[3] He noted, first, the recent tendencies to solve sectoral problems by government intervention based on "special arrangements with protectionist effects." Noting the long history of the special treatment of textiles in world trade, he listed other sectors where intervention has recently become institutionalized: steel, shipbuilding, synthetic fibers, automobiles, agriculture. He might well have added consumer electronics, machine tools, and a number of other more narrowly defined sectors. The means of managing trade in these sectors has been through so-called self-restraint and orderly marketing agreements. These arrangements are essentially bilateral. On this, he warned: "The tendency towards bilateralism and sectoralism in trade policy is the greatest present danger both politically and economically to order and prosperity in the world economy. . . . When commercial policy is conducted on a sectoral basis, the interaction between industrial lobbies and national administrations makes an eventual return to liberal trading extremely difficult. To take away

[3] Address to Hamburg, March 5, 1982, GATT Press Release no. 1312, Geneva, March 5, 1982.

a privileged position is always more difficult than to refuse it in the first place."

In essence, the GATT system was intended to help governments avoid sectoral policies. It was meant to protect ministers from the temptation of shoring up particular sectors, by allowing them and even encouraging them to pursue the wider national interest, in the context of global rights and obligations.

The flirtation of the US administration with bilateral and sectoral reciprocity in 1981 and early 1982 has fortunately faded. When the flirtation was in full heat, it was not well known, in Congress or in the executive branch, that the long-standing US reliance on principles of nondiscrimination and global reciprocity were based on over a century of bad experience with discrimination and sectoral policies. Indeed, long before anyone thought up the outlines of the GATT or the Havana Charter, it was the US Congress itself which introduced in the Tariff Act of 1922 the authority to offer unconditional most-favored-nation (MFN) treatment. The Reciprocal Trade Agreements Act of 1934 included an unconditional MFN provision and made it a requirement of US law. (And in spite of the title of this Act, the term reciprocity cannot be found in the law itself.)

On this critical point, let me quote from Arthur Dunkel's Hamburg statement once again:

"Let me recall that in the 1920s the words "reciprocity" and "non-discrimination" (or "unconditional most-favored-nation pledge") denoted contradictions, mutually exclusive alternatives. The fact that in the GATT countries have been negotiating and contracting with each other on the basis of reciprocity is always a subjective notion which cannot be looked at in bilateral terms. It cannot be determined exactly; it can only be *agreed upon*, and such agreement is possible only among countries sharing a commitment to some higher principle which, in the case of GATT, has been, simply, the rule of law. This is what I meant by saying that strict reciprocity is technically not feasible as the sole basis for any one nation's commercial policy. One side alone cannot decide what reciprocity is."

These comments once again underline the fundamental role of *negotiation* in the functioning of the GATT.

It is sometimes now claimed that the world has changed since the GATT was drafted, and that it has become outmoded, or that its scope must be expanded to make it meaningful once again.

In this connection, a common complaint is that governments which implement trade restrictions almost always do this outside the framework of Article XIX, the so-called safeguard article. Other nations that are adversely affected by such restrictions rarely invoke their rights under Article XIX, or Article XXIII, which provides for compensatory or retaliatory actions if authorized by the GATT members. Therefore, it is claimed, the GATT has broken down, and must be repaired or replaced.

The governments that negotiated in the MTN during the 1970s considered the possibility of preparing a new code on safeguards, to bring multilateral disciplines to bear on national actions to shield troubled sectors. During those negotiations, some of the governments, particularly the European Economic Community (EEC) governments, argued that protective actions should not be taken against nations that were not the true source of market disruption. Therefore remedial action should be taken on a selective basis, only against these exporting entities and nations that were the troublemakers. This, of course, would undermine the fundamental theme of the GATT, that of nondiscrimination.

Some of the papers prepared for this conference argue, as did many governments during the last decade, that there is an urgent need for drawing up a new safeguard code, which would interpret and modify the present content of Article XIX. After all, it is said, if governments will not use the rule as it stands, then write a rule they will use.

I disagree, and believe this whole line of thinking can only further undermine the GATT and make its strictures less relevant to national policy making. To rewrite Article XIX, or stipulate exceptions to it, would simply legalize existing offending practices, and open the way for new restrictions.

It seems to me far preferable to draw nations back into the framework of Article XIX, in those case where governments feel compelled to take sectoral action. I would prefer that we take a leaf out of the book of experience that brought about dollar liberalization, and liberalization of trade after World War II.

What I propose is the establishment of an ongoing Article XIX Surveillance Committee, which would review all national trade restrictive actions (except those taken under other GATT provisions), including voluntary restraint agreements (VRAs), orderly marketing agreements (OMAs), industry-to-industry restraint agreements, and special nontariff restraints, as well as conventional Article XIX actions. This process would be based on notifications by governments implementing restrictions, on complaints of other nations that believe they are adversely affected, and on self-initiated notifications by the GATT Secretariat. To make this effective, the GATT Secretariat would be charged with maintaining an independent process of monitoring, and of initiating inquiries directed to national governments. The surveillance body would meet regularly to consider the full scope of actions and their justifications, the relation of these actions to the GATT, the implications for antitrust and competition policies of governments, and the potential impact on third parties. For each restriction a target date would be requested for its termination. Extensions of such dates would be subject to multilateral scrutiny by the full committee, not just by the countries directly affected. The procedures and economic criteria of governments that applied in each case would be reviewed. Such a surveillance body would have to review the *internal* procedures and decisions of national authorities, and gradually establish a common, codified procedure. Gradually, the economic justifications would be evaluated, so as to develop common criteria and draw national criteria closer to the concept of injury under Article XIX. In this connection, the progress in rationalization and adjustment of each protected sector might well be reviewed as well. Over time the intent of this process would be to revitalize the existing provisions of the GATT, which make a great deal of sense.

Another challenge to the effectiveness and relevance of the GATT stems from the behavior of the major players in it. The US and the EEC tend to dominate GATT proceedings, and multilateral negotiations. They like to maintain freedom of action to bring matters before the GATT, or settle between them privately, or settle their own problems with third countries without criticism of each other. They have both ignored GATT decisions, when its opinions have been uncomfortable (for example, the EEC in sugar, and the US in relation to Domestic International Sales Corporation, DISC).

Lately, the EEC and the United States have abused the GATT process by bringing poorly defined, conceptually unsound complaints. The broad Article XXIII complaint brought by the EEC against virtually the whole of Japan, Inc. and the recent spate of US agricultural subsidy complaints, based on a weak interpretation of the strictures of the Multilateral Trade Negotiations (MTN) subsidies code, are examples of this tendency to use the GATT selectively as an instrument of national or regional policy. The problem is that when such complaints fail, the governments concerned can then argue that the GATT itself has failed, and use this argument to justify unilateral action at a later date. The real problem is not the failure of the GATT, but rather that the issues addressed have simply not been fully negotiated, and there has been no agreement.

Recent decisions by the US Commerce Department on what constitutes a subsidy, in connection with European steel exports to the United States, represent a unilateral definition of subsidies, and a unilateral determination of when internal subsidies have significant trade effects. These are questions which plagued the negotiators of the MTN subsidy code in 1978–79. At that time, the negotiators could not agree, and the rules were left unclear. The GATT, not being a court, cannot decide on issues on which governments could not reach agreement. Only a *negotiated* agreement on a proper interpretation of these rules can provide a sound solution. The US government may be compelled by US law to take restrictive action on steel trade now, but it should be willing to subject its reasoning to multilateral scrutiny and negotiation later—albeit after the US has itself acted.

Indeed, this poses yet another challenge to the GATT. Since most governments are engaged in some form of subsidization, not only of exports through official credits and guarantees, but of domestic industries, a serious effort is needed to develop some agreed principles governing aids to industry. This must be based on the economic principles of public finance and focus on the *effects* of subsidies rather than on their character or form.

The fact that the two dominant trading powers often sort out their difficulties privately, and come into the GATT with convergent positions and policies that affect other nations, has undermined the confidence of these other nations in the effectiveness of the GATT system. Other nations are reluctant to disturb agreements laboriously reached between two giants, for fear of being crushed between them. Efforts to widen the "management" of the GATT activities have been made, but these have generally resulted in unduly large committees which have lost their ability to act, because of their sheer size. As a consequence, meetings outside the formal GATT framework, and even outside the city of Geneva, have become the principal means of coordinating views and negotiating solutions. The "quadrilateral meetings" between the United States, the European Community, Canada, and Japan, which began in 1981, are but one manifestation.

There are yet other challenges to the effectiveness and relevance of the GATT. Among these are the inherent conflicts between the advanced, industrial countries and the developing countries. This conflict is gradually being brought to a head by several developments. Most notable among these are the decision by the industrial countries to limit the applicability of the new MTN codes to the signatories, which contravenes GATT Article I, and the recent advocacy of a "graduation process" for the newly industrializing countries (NICs).

It is clearly in the long-term interest of the developing countries to bring their own trade and domestic economic measures into conformity with the principles of the GATT. But many of the governments of the developing nations feel this would restrict their freedom of action in pursuing their own sectoral development policies. Pre-

cisely for this reason, Mexico ultimately decided not to join the GATT
or its codes, even though Mexican representatives had participated
actively in the negotiation of the codes during the MTN.

Since the two giants seem to set the rules, and decide when they
are to be applied, and how, it is not surprising that other nations feel
uncomfortable about giving up their own freedom of action.

This is the real heart of the North–South problem in the GATT.
It is the same basic problem that exists between the Western industrial
nations themselves. The tendency of the United States and the European Common Market to pick and choose when and how to use
the GATT, and to opt for alternative venues when it suits them; the
tendency for the two giants to use their power to coerce other nations
to behave in a certain manner, outside the multilateral framework—
these are the most serious political and procedural challenges to the
viability and effectiveness of the GATT system.

The GATT, as Gardner Patterson notes,[4] is supposed to provide
stability and predictability in the behavior of governments and in the
conditions under which trade takes place. Rodney de C. Grey notes
a trend in the post-MTN period toward what he calls "contingent
protection."[5] He emphasizes in his paper the "important shift in
emphasis away from reliance on *fixed* measures or techniques of
intervention to regulate the competition between imports and domestic production toward much greater reliance on more flexible
methods of protecting the domestic producers."

The codification of permissible and prohibited measures, and the
"binding" of trade concessions, has resulted in a predictable, stable
framework of trade relations, based on very simple, objective criteria.
The recent improvisation in trade restrictions and aids to industry
has moved in the opposite direction, toward complexity of management of trade relations and toward widening the scope of administrative discretion in managing trade flows.

Again, it is the desire of governments, especially those with economic power, to maintain their freedom of action, and to pursue ad
hoc sectoral policies, that underlies the new tendencies.

Since other participants in this conference examine in detail the
specific government practices that restrict or distort trade, I shall not
attempt a laborious review here. Most of these practices are manifestations of the sectoral thrust of national economic policies discussed

---

[4] "The European Community as a Threat to the System," chapter 7, this
volume.

[5] "A Note on US Trade Practices," chapter 8, this volume.

above. I will also not dwell on the widening practices of discrimination based on regional or historical relationships. Suffice it to say that the growing scope of European Community (EC) special arrangements, including those within Europe itself, tend to reduce the effectiveness of the GATT system. The United States also has succumbed to regional temptations, with its Caribbean Basin Initiative (CBI), and other improvisations with Canada and Mexico. This, too, must be considered to weaken the GATT in the eyes of other nations (such as Brazil and the Association of South East Asian Nations [ASEAN] countries, some of which have protested the CBI proposal). The fact that GATT has not brought order to the agricultural sector has also reduced its value and relevance to a number of countries, most notably Australia and New Zealand. Again, in this case, it is the unwillingness of the EEC to bring its Common Agricultural Policy within the provisions of the GATT, and the long-standing GATT waiver for agriculture which applies to the United States, which constitute the principal source of weakness in the GATT as it applies to trade in agriculture.

It would therefore be desirable for the governments of the two giants to be less disingenuous about the failures of the GATT, and scale back their rhetoric of attack on the meaningfulness and relevance of GATT to present-day circumstances, since they together are more responsible than the other nations for the present erosion of the multilateral disciplines.

Divisions in the West

It is evident that there are profound differences among the Western industrial nations about the role of government in economic affairs, and about the political management of relations with each other and with the rest of the world. There are deep differences on how to handle East–West economic relations, and these differences in 1982 threaten to tear the fragile fabric of Western economic cooperation. There are differences over how best to handle North–South relations, and how to deal with various regions of the world (e.g., Central America, the Middle East, South Africa, and the Caribbean).

The recent tendency to link political and security objectives to the management of economic relations, particularly in the use of sanctions, is likely to generate new divisions among the Western powers. Moreover, unilateral decisions with extraterritorial application constitute a direct challenge to the concept of multilateral rules and agreements. Such tendencies replace stability and predictability in economic relations with national discretion, based on the power to coerce other nations to cooperate. The on-again, off-again use by the United States of export controls and sanctions for both national security and economic purposes in the 1970s and early 1980s has not surprisingly created an environment of doubt about the reliability of US supplies, and the availability and usefulness of US technologies.

The responses of many private enterprises will be to insulate themselves, by widening their international base. As the United States reaches into the area of technological development to carry out its national political objectives, private enterprises and other governments will tend to accelerate their efforts to develop independent capabilities. This in turn may eventually generate a backlash of technological isolationism and intensified protectionism.

This threat should not be underestimated. The pace of technological change is accelerating in the 1980s, and a widening number of countries are developing advanced technological capabilities in key sectors, with Japan the principal challenger to the present dominance of the United States in high technology.

The present major thrusts of technology, in the information revolution in the development of man-made materials to substitute for nonrenewable resources, and in biotechnology, will have profound effects on world patterns of economic growth, trade, investment, and cross-border cooperation.

Indeed, it is a widely held view in Japan and Western Europe that the 1980s will be a difficult decade of major structural adjustment, with extraordinarily high levels of unemployment to be expected. This transformation will be, in their eyes, driven by the emergence of new competitors from the developing world, by the emergence of Japan as a major competitor in the frontiers of technology, and by technology itself. These governments therefore feel that they must guide the inevitable structural transformation, and mitigate its potential for social and economic disruption to jobs, key sectors, and key regions.

This presents yet another rift, between the United States and its major trading partners, for the US government believes that governments should scale back their intervention and guidance, especially on the sectoral level. The US administration believes that the GATT and other multilateral economic institutions should be used to force governments to back away from sectoral policies that ultimately distort world trade and investment.

Macro- and Microeconomic Policies in an Interdependent World Economy

Behind all of this tension in the multilateral system is the underlying problem that governments are experiencing constraints on their sovereign powers. They are limited by their own budgetary constraints. They are limited by the growing role of international market forces within their own domestic economies. Even national monetary policy has become subject to global financial and economic forces.

Retrenchment, and a scaling back of economic interdependence, is one option. But this must inevitably cause a global economic contraction.

The other option, of learning to manage national economies in a context of international cooperation in the design and implementation of economic policies, must be a preferable course. But here again it is the major Western economic powers that refuse to cooperate with each other to the degree necessary to make multilateral economic systems work effectively.

The exchange rate and balance of payments effects of US macroeconomic policies in the early 1980s were not considered in the formulation of those policies in 1981. But their consequences included distortions of key exchange rates, especially the yen, because of the profound differences between the monetary and fiscal balance in the United States and that in other nations.

The days of autonomous, purely national economic policy making are over. Recognition of that reality will not be easy politically. Unilateral actions are the antithesis of multilateral cooperation, in a highly interdependent world economy.

This *political* challenge is the major challenge to the multilateral order. Until governments address this new reality directly, and give up their never-ending search for selective, sectoral solutions, and bilateral exceptions to multilateral agreements and procedures, the erosion of the present multilateral trading system can be expected to continue.

Gottfried Haberler

I was asked to comment on two excellent papers: one by C. Fred Bergsten and John Williamson, the other by William R. Cline. I shall concentrate on the Bergsten-Williamson paper which raises a number of questions that in my opinion require further consideration.

With the Cline paper I find myself in complete agreement. I think if offers a thorough discussion of an important subject. I therefore confine myself to the suggestion that a reference might be made to the discussions of the problem prior to the adoption of the principle of unconditional most favored nation (MFN) on the part of the United States in 1922. The history has been conveniently presented in a comprehensive report by the US Tariff Commission, *Reciprocity and Commercial Treaties* (GPO, Washington, 1918). Among the authors of the report were Jacob Viner and the first Chairman of the Commission, Frank William Taussig.*

The main theme of the Bergsten-Williamson paper is the "impact of misaligned currencies on trade protection. . . . The continued failure to link the trade and monetary aspects of international economic exchange is a major mistake."

There can be no doubt that overvalued currencies can have, and in some cases have had, a powerful protectionist impact on economic policy. But it seems to me that the authors go much too far when they say that the link between trade policy and monetary arrangements has been ignored. After all, the revised Articles of Agreement of the International Monetary Fund (IMF) which legalizes floating, provides that one of the basic obligations of IMF members is to "avoid manipulating exchange rates or the international monetary system in order to prevent effective balance of payments adjustment or to gain an unfair competitive advantage over other members" (Article IV,

---

* *Ed. note*: Chapter 4 of this volume incorporates this suggestion.

section 1) and stipulates that "the Fund shall exercise firm surveillance over the exchange rate policies of members."

It can be argued that the Fund has not succeeded in all cases in preventing serious misalignments of currencies, but it cannot be said that the impact of monetary arrangements on the real economy and on trade policy has been ignored.

The most glaring examples of misaligned exchange rates with dire protectionist consequences can be found during the period of fixed exchanges, under the gold standard and to a lesser extent under the Bretton Woods régime. The authors mention, rightly, the case of the overvaluation of the British pound in the 1920s. This put the economy under severe deflationary pressure. The resulting high unemployment was responsible for the abandonment of the gold standard in September 1931 followed in 1932 by the historic switch of Britain from the traditional free trade policy to high protection. It may be recalled that Keynes had recommended import restrictions and export bounties as an alternative to devaluation of the pound.[1] After the devaluation (which he deplored), he declared that import restrictions were no longer necessary, but it was impossible to reverse the protectionist tide.

The devaluation of the pound and later of the dollar put heavy deflationary pressure on Germany, France, and other countries whose response was to restrict imports by tariffs, quotas, and exchange controls.

The system of rigidly fixed rates caused the catastrophic depression to spread around the world, and created huge misalignments of exchange rates, thus triggering a protectionist explosion. The recognition of this fact led to the Bretton Woods reform; it also inspired the second amendment to the IMF charter which legalized floating. Therefore it cannot be said that the link between monetary arrangements and trade policy has been persistently ignored.

For twenty years or so under Bretton Woods the international monetary system worked well, because the new regulations provided for orderly exchange rate changes. But the system of the "adjustable or jumping peg" could not cope with the rising tide of world inflation, which started in the mid-1960s when the Johnson administration financed the escalating cost of the war in Vietnam and of the equally expensive Great Society programs by inflationary borrowing rather

---

[1] Keynes first recommended a uniform rate of import tariff and export subsidy. Later he dropped the uniformity principle and advocated a system of different rates for different commodities.

than by raising taxes. The first oil shock exacerbated world inflation but did not start it. Large inflation differentials developed between the United States on the one hand, and Japan, Germany, Switzerland, and some other countries on the other hand. All this forced reluctant policymakers to abandon Bretton Woods and accept a system of widespread managed floating. Floating was legalized by the second amendment of the Articles of Agreement of the IMF which went into effect in April 1976.

During the last four years or so floating has again come under widespread criticism, even from some who used to favor it, Bergsten among them. The Bergsten-Williamson paper argues that floating has not prevented persistent misalignments of exchange rates. The prime example of a malfunctioning of the exchange market under floating is the alleged overvaluation of the dollar in the last two years. But before I come to the dollar problem, I would like to make three more general remarks.

First, floating has been heavily managed. Not every alleged misalignment of exchange rates under floating can be attributed to a market failure, to "bandwagon" effects and the like; some misalignments surely were the result of faulty intervention policies by the authorities. The authors single out one such case. They say that in 1976 "Japan committed one of the most serious policy errors of the whole postwar period. . . . Japan intervened massively in the foreign exchange market to block significant strengthening of the yen. The result was a renewed undervaluation of the yen and massive Japanese surpluses in 1977–78." This policy contributed to a substantial "overvaluation of the dollar for at least two years."

The market obviously was not at fault, but it is doubtful that all the blame should be put on Japan. After the oil shock in 1974 Japan had an inflation rate of 24.4 percent (consumer prices), more than double the US rate. In Japan the inflation rate was sharply reduced over the next few years to 9.3 percent in 1976, 3.8 percent in 1978, and 3.6 percent in 1979.[2] In the United States the inflation rate was reduced to below 5 percent early in 1976 but got stuck there and climbed back to reach the two-digit level again in 1980 when the Carter administration switched macro policy prematurely from fighting inflation to expansion.

The rapidly widening inflation differential surely was the major cause of Japanese surpluses and US deficits.

---

[2] After the second oil shock the inflation rate rose again temporarily but never did return to the two-digit level.

Second, the Bergsten-Williamson paper presents a useful discussion of the concept of equilibrium exchange rates. The authors distinguish between market equilibrium, fundamental equilibrium, and current equilibrium. The market equilibrium rate is "simply" the rate which clears the markets in the absence of official interventions.

Fundamental equilibrium "is the concept in the Articles of Agreement of the IMF as interpreted in the IMF report on the exchange rate system." The authors define it as "the (real) equilibrium exchange rate . . . which is expected to generate a current surplus or deficit equal to the underlying capital flow over the cycle, given that the country is pursuing 'internal balance' as best it can and not restricting trade for balance of payments reasons." They say "this concept is what people usually have in mind when they describe rates as 'overvalued' or 'undervalued'—and it is so used throughout this paper. It relates to the real rather than the nominal exchange rate."

All this is rather vague. The authors are commendably frank about the ambiguity of the concept. "An important difference to the market equilibrium rate lies in the absence of a simple objective test of whether or not the rate is in equilibrium. At best, estimates of whether a rate is in fundamental equilibrium require judgments that in practice contain subjective elements regarding cyclical adjustment, the underlying capital flow, and trade elasticities. At worst, skeptics deny any hope of identifying the fundamental equilibrium rate."

The vagueness may be unavoidable. But I suggest that it should warn us to be extremely cautious in making categoric statements that a currency is over- or undervalued under floating. Under fixed rates it is much easier to define and to identify fundamental disequilibrium.

The third concept is "current equilibrium." "This term is intended to indicate the rate that would obtain if markets had full knowledge of all relevant facts. The current equilibrium rate will depend upon the path of interest rates (i.e., the stance of macroeconomic policy and the state of the business cycle) and, given risk aversion, on net asset positions vis-à-vis the rest of the world." This concept is even vaguer and less operational than fundamental equilibrium. But since the paper does not use it, no further comment is required.

Third, last but not least, the logical connection between misalignment of exchange rates and protectionism requires some further analysis. So far in my comments I took it for granted that the deflationary pressure and the unemployment caused by overvaluation of the currency is the trigger that unleashes protectionist reactions. This clearly was the case in all examples mentioned above, including the alleged current overvaluation of the dollar.

There exists, however, a new theory put forward in an important article by W. Max Corden[3] and espoused by the authors, which states that a misalignment of exchange rates as such, an under- or over-valuation of a currency, irrespective of whether it creates unemployment, is a form of protectionism. An undervaluation of a currency which causes a persistent export surplus,[4] constitutes protection of the traded goods sector at the expense of the nontraded goods sector. An overvaluation that causes a persistent trade deficit "protects" the nontraded goods sector at the expense of the traded goods sector. This kind of protection implies a misallocation of resources and a welfare loss, just as protection in the traditional sense of import restrictions does.

I suggest that this sort of protectionism is not much of a problem unless it causes much unemployment, for the following reason: the antagonism of the interests of export industries and import-competing industries is a reality. Import-competing industries are naturally protectionist and their protectionist efforts gain strength and support if they suffer from unemployment. The export industries on the other hand are free traders—they lobby against protection both at home and abroad and try to enlist consumer interests. It is true that exporters often clamour for export subsidies. But that is usually not much of a problem. Export subsidies are weak reeds because they are very vulnerable to countervailing duties abroad.[5]

The antagonism of traded and nontraded sectors, in contrast, lacks political reality. One never hears of an organization or lobby of the nontraded goods sector pitted against an organization of the traded goods sector.

I now come to the recent appreciation of the dollar. This was undoubtedly a depressive factor, but to call it a major cause of the recession is very misleading. In fact, appreciation of the dollar and

---

[3] W. Max Corden, "Exchange Rate Protection," in Richard N. Cooper, et al., eds., *The International Monetary System under Flexible Exchange Rates: Global, Regional, and National Essays in Honor of Robert Triffin* (Cambridge, Mass.: Ballinger, 1982).

[4] There is a problem of how to distinguish between "ordinary" capital flows that are the result of over- or undervaluation of the currency, and how the welfare judgment is altered in the case of "ordinary" capital flows. But I shall not go into these questions because they were not raised by Corden or the authors.

[5] Export subsidies become a problem in the case of "dumping" by private monopolies or nationalized industries. But dumping has little to do with exchange rate problems.

the recession were the joint effect of the same basic cause—the restrictive monetary policy that was necessary to wind down inflation. It is simply not possible to bring down an entrenched inflation without serious transitional unemployment, that is without creating a recession. Monetary restraint also produced high interest rates and strengthened confidence in the dollar.[6] The appreciation of the dollar, was also a potent anti-inflationary factor. If the dollar had *not* appreciated the Fed would have been forced to step harder on the monetary brake, and the recession would have been about the same, although the impact would have been somewhat shifted from the traded to the nontraded sector. I do not think that this shift would have been a great advantage. It would have meant, among other things, that the severely depressed construction industry would have been hit even harder by the recession.

To change the scenario, if the appreciation of the dollar had been prevented by nonsterilized interventions in the foreign exchange market, this would have undercut the anti-inflationary policy of the Fed and would have forced the Fed to step harder on the credit brake. On the other hand, there is general agreement that sterilized interventions are largely ineffective. I conclude that the recent appreciation of the dollar cannot be regarded as a major market failure.

The upshot of all this is that I have much more faith in the market than the authors have and that I am skeptical about the feasibility of an exchange rate policy along the lines sketched in the last part of the Bergsten-Williamson paper. There they seem to have forgotten what they said earlier about the vagueness of the concept of "fundamental equilibrium." Looking ex post at the movement of exchange rates, for example at the dollar-yen rate, or the dollar–Deutsche mark rate, it is tempting to say that the dollar was overvalued at a certain point and if the authorities had vigorously intervened at that time, it would have been prevented or mitigated unnecessary fluctuations, and the central bank would have made handsome profits at the same time.

Ex ante, unfortunately, it is not at all easy to interpret what is going on. This skepticism is strongly supported by the careful study by Dean Taylor, "Official Intervention in the Foreign Exchange Market, or, Bet Against the Central Bank,"[7] which shows that the official

---

[6] I am not discussing here whether and to what extent a tighter fiscal policy or possibly some sort of incomes policy could have mitigated the painful side effects of disinflation. I have expressed my views on these problems elsewhere.

[7] *Journal of Political Economy*, vol. 90, no. 2 (1982), pp. 356–68.

interventions of the central banks of Canada, France, Germany, Japan, Spain, and Switzerland in the 1970s have resulted, without exception, in large losses.

Let me repeat that I agree that a misalignment of exchange rates is a potent factor intensifying protectionist pressures, but it is not misalignment per se, but the unemployment which an overvaluation of a currency is likely to create. This does not exclude that protectionists will use an alleged misalignment of the exchange rate as an argument for protection, if the argument is offered to them by the economist.

The authors rightly emphasize the importance of US-Japan relations. But it should be kept in mind that the plight of the US automobile industry, which is probably the most important irritant in the US-Japanese trade, though exacerbated by the dollar-yen rate, has a highly significant basic structural cause. This cause has nothing to do with a possible overreaction of the dollar: the fact that despite some union concessions, wages in the US automobile industry are still at least 50 percent higher than the average wage in US manufacturing industries.

Postscript added in the proofs: What is said in my comments on the relatively minor importance of the overvaluation of the dollar and the trade deficit for the recession, is supported by the fact that in the meantime the US economy has staged a healthy recovery from the cyclical recession, despite the alleged overvaluation of the dollar and a record trade deficit.

Isaiah Frank

Professor Gottfried Haberler in his remarks, has shown us the continuity of many of the problems in international trade and has called attention to the solid progress that has been made over the years in dealing with them. I believe it was Adlai Stevenson who once said that trade policy was one field where the greatest need is for fresh clichés. Well, I can say with conviction that the papers prepared for this conference go well beyond the creation of new clichés. They include a great deal of fresh analysis and new perspectives.

It is widely accepted that we are facing a crisis today in the international trading system. The evidence abounds. Despite the successes of the post-World War II multilateral economic institutions to which Harald B. Malmgren calls attention, protectionist pressures are intensifying. Exchange rate misalignments are distorting international competitive positions and complicating trade policy. While tariffs are down, new distortions are being introduced in the form of nontariff barriers and domestic government interventions and subsidies. Trade-related performance requirements are imposing new strains on the system. Impediments to service trade are growing, and are as yet unrestrained by international rules. And the whole situation is aggravated by an overall economic environment of cyclical recession and slow growth over the longer term.

This recital is a most incomplete account of the diversity of strains in the international trading system. The range is well reflected in the papers prepared for this conference including the sectoral troubles in agriculture, autos, steel, and textiles, and the problems with a special country or regional focus on the United States, Japan, and the European Community.

From the welter of problems addressed in the papers, is it possible to identify a few central issues that lie at the basis of the current disquiet? With some trepidation I shall attempt to identify three such sets of issues.

The first, and perhaps the most fundamental, is how to reconcile domestic economic policy and management with the requirements of a smoothly functioning, efficient, and equitable international economic system. Stated another way, it is the issue defined in Richard N. Cooper's classic work[1] on the economics of interdependence: how to garner the very substantial benefits of an interdependent world economy while preserving the degree of national autonomy required for the pursuit of the legitimate goals of individual nation states.

This problem has both a macro and a micro dimension. At the macro level, the excellent paper by Bergsten and Williamson demonstrates persuasively how differences in the mix of domestic monetary and fiscal policies between Japan and the United States have contributed to the present steep undervaluation of the yen and overvaluation of the dollar. They make a strong case to the effect that periods of extreme tension in US-Japan economic relations, and that strong protectionist pressures in the United States have coincided with such situations of exchange rate misalignment.

What to do about this problem? The standard remedy, now almost an incantation, is more effective international coordination of domestic macro policies. But how is it to be accomplished? Working Party 3 of the Organization for Economic Cooperation and Development has been trying for years to achieve greater mutual compatibility among the national economic policies of countries with different domestic objectives and priorities. What lessons can be drawn from that experience?

Specifically with respect to exchange rates, the International Monetary Fund (IMF) has been assigned the major role of ensuring that countries avoid using this policy instrument to gain unfair international competitive advantage. In order for the Fund's surveillance role to be effective, it must be based on some concept of equilibrium exchange rates from which departures can be measured. One conclusion I draw from the Bergsten-Williamson discussion of this subject is that we are still far from an operational definition of equilibrium. The notion of an "underlying capital flow" to which a current account surplus or deficit should be equated is a quite subjective concept. Similarly, the assumption of "internal balance," with its employment and price implications, is hardly a matter on which precise agreement is readily attained.

---

[1] Richard N. Cooper, *The Economics of Interdependence* (New York: Columbia University Press, Council on Foreign Relations, 1968).

Apart from these conceptual problems, we must recognize an inherent asymmetry at the practical level in the IMF's conduct of its surveillance function. In the case of the developing countries, where currency overvaluation is typically the problem, the Fund can be quite effective in influencing exchange rate policy as its advice is normally given in conjunction with the extension of balance of payment credits. The occasion for such conditionality rarely arises in the case of the industrial countries so that the exercise of surveillance becomes largely hortatory. What can be done to strengthen the surveillance process as it applies to the industrial countries?

I come now to the micro dimension of the problem of reconciling national autonomy with international interdependence. It concerns the increasing tendency for governments to intervene in support of particular sectors of the national economy and the international distortions to which such intervention gives rise. There is some uncertainty and divergence in the papers by Bergsten-Cline and Hufbauer on the extent of sectoral intervention, but in both cases the data strike me as incomplete. More is involved than measures applied at the border (whether in the form of tariffs, nontariff barriers, or export subsidies) and domestic subsidies that appear explicitly in the budget. I realize, however, that such additional data—for example, on sectoral tax concessions or preferential procurement—may be exceedingly difficult to obtain and to quantify.

The implications of domestic government interventions with a sectoral bias may be more serious now for reasons nicely developed by William R. Cline in his paper on reciprocity and conditional market access.[2] In a wide range of manufacturing the allocation of production by country is arbitrary in the sense that it does not conform to Ricardian, Hecksher-Ohlin, or product-cycle principles. Neither natural resources, factor endowments, nor technological leadership is determinative. In such sectors comparative advantage is influenced by the dynamics of industrial organization but it may also be strongly affected by various forms of direct or indirect government support.

Government subsidization is generally justified on broad national interest grounds such as national security or the need to be at the technological frontier. Such externalities may be, in Professor Ed Mason's paraphrase of Samuel Johnson, the last refuge of a scoundrel. But they are regularly invoked as the basis for a wide range of government interventions at the micro level.

---

[2] Chapter 4, this volume.

Are new rules needed to contain and reconcile the international trade and investment distortions caused by domestic interventions? Gary Clyde Hufbauer's[3] paper ably addresses many of the technical issues. The subsidy code negotiated in the Tokyo Round recognizes the legitimacy of domestic subsidies but seeks to minimize their harmful external effects. Are the principles and procedures in the code adequate for this purpose? Or is there a need to move toward sectoral negotiations as suggested by Cline, citing the Tokyo Round code on aircraft?

In domestic terms, much of the debate on this issue takes the form of whether or not the US government should follow the lead of some other countries, notably Japan and France, and adopt a less ad hoc and more articulated policy of support for individual industries. But is industrial policy, defined in this way, anything but a thinly disguised form of protectionism? And how do we ultimately coordinate internationally and insure the mutual compatibility of government policies at the micro level?

A second major set of issues addressed in this conference is of particular concern to the countries of the third world. It includes safeguards against market disruption and the question of graduation from special and differential treatment for developing countries. I shall be very brief in what I say on these subjects.

The safeguard issue is skillfully analyzed in Alan Wolff's paper.[4] The basic problem is that the present General Agreement on Tariffs and Trade (GATT) rule (Article XIX) is widely ignored in practice so that no effective international discipline now governs safeguard actions. One of the main reasons is the present requirement that safeguards be applied to all imports nondiscriminatorily. However, the effort to revise the safeguard provision in the Tokyo Round by permitting the selective application of safeguards (as desired by the European Community) did not succeed. It was opposed by a number of smaller countries, and particularly by the developing countries, as an attempt to legitimize discrimination in a way that would inevitably victimize countries with weak economic bargaining power. How to resolve this dilemma is one of the main issues addressed in Wolff's paper.

The issue of graduation is growing in importance as more and more third world nations join the ranks of the newly industrializing coun-

[3] "Subsidy Issues After the Tokyo Round," chapter 10, this volume.
[4] "The Need for New GATT Rules to Govern Safeguard Actions," chapter 11, this volume.

tries and become substantial exporters of manufactured products. These countries clearly have a vital stake in a reasonably open international trading system based on agreed rules and constraints on national behavior. However, such a system is unlikely to withstand the pressures to which it is increasingly exposed when the rules apply to one group of about 20 industrial countries while all other countries, regardless of their stage or rate of development, are substantially and indefinitely free of international constraints.

Clearly, some system is needed for graduating selected countries from the second to the first group. Newly industrializing countries (NICs) should be expected progressively to relinquish differentially favorable treatment, bring their own trade and payments policies gradually into accord with regular GATT and IMF obligations, and pledge themselves to adhere to these obligations in the future. Among the principal beneficiaries of trade liberalization by the NICs would be the NICs themselves.

The third and final issue which I wish to say a few brief words is the need to strengthen the international institutions governing trade policy. This issue has both a substantive and procedural aspect.

The substantive aspect concerns the current assault on the fundamental principle of unconditional most-favored-nation (MFN) treatment and the numerous moves in the Congress to substitute for it the so-called "reciprocity" principle. The drive for reciprocity has a superficial appeal. What could be fairer than treating other countries, particularly if they are at comparable stages of development, in the same manner as they treat us? Moreover, the basic US trade legislation was called the Reciprocal Trade Agreements Act, and the results of GATT negotiations have always been justified to the Congress on the basis of reciprocal benefits to the negotiating partners.

Again, this issue is well treated in Cline's paper. Three critical elements distinguish our traditional concept of reciprocity from the present efforts to twist it toward protectionist ends. First, the traditional version was multilateral rather than bilateral. Second, the traditional version was across-the-board rather than sectoral. These two considerations mean that reciprocity has been judged in the past by the entire outcome of multilateral negotiations rather than by any concept of equivalence of results in two countries in a particular sector. Finally, the new version of reciprocity rests on aggressive retaliation through new trade barriers against nonreciprocating countries rather than the withholding of new measures of liberalization which Cline calls "passive reciprocity."

A policy of aggressive reciprocity could result in a cycle of mutual retaliation that could lead to the unraveling of the entire liberal trading system developed in the period after World War II. Fortunately, sober second thoughts seem to be taking hold, and at least for the moment the pressure may be off.

The second aspect of the institutional question concerns machinery and procedures. On this subject we have an authoritative paper by John H. Jackson which reviews the effectiveness of the implementation of the Multilateral Trade Negotiations (MTN) codes and evaluates the GATT dispute-settlement mechanisms. In the light of the limited experience thus far, Jackson withholds final judgment, but he does sound a note of cautious optimism.

I have spoken long enough, Mr. Chairman, but I would like to make one final comment. Economists are prone to impatience with matters of machinery and procedure, preferring to leave those "technicalities" to lawyers while they concentrate on more "substantive" issues. Based on such experience as I have had in the conduct of trade policy, I believe it fair to say that procedures *are* often substance. For example, in enforcing nondiscrimination in public procurement, tender procedures are the heart of the matter. Or, in ensuring against the abuse of safeguard rules, public notice and open hearings are essential if protectionist pressures are to be effectively countervailed. While some of my best friends are lawyers, I would like to see economists enter the fray and begin to exert greater day-to-day influence on the actual execution of trade policy.

Bela Balassa cast doubt on the correlation between overvaluation and protectionism, citing high protectionist pressure in the European Community (EC) in 1977 despite absence of overvaluation. He argued that there was little evidence for a ratchet effect whereby protection once implemented is not reversed despite correction of exchange rate misalignment. He especially disagreed with capital controls as a solution to yen undervaluation; on the contrary, he argued that liberalization of capital inflows (such as the floating of bonds in Japan) is essential. He endorsed Malmgren's call for greater transparency through the reporting of barriers.

Juergen B. Donges noted that the protection could be positively related to inflation rather than negatively as suggested by Bergsten and Cline. Inflationary countries such as France have tended to experience balance of payments deficits, leading to protection given reluctance to devalue. The overview paper may also understate the danger of current protection by attributing all of the slowdown in trade to slower growth in demand.

J. David Richardson emphasized that the case for free trade is not contingent on the presence of full employment, equilibrium exchange rates, and so forth. Even if these conditions are not met, it does not follow that the second-best solution is protection.

Gardner Patterson maintained that it is wrong to assume tariffs do not matter; many remain high. To Jackson's query of whether GATT is the best alternative, he responded that there is no other alternative except dangerous bilateral, closet deals. He advocated greater reliance on the process of technical findings by GATT panels on disputes, as the proper direction for change.

Åke Lindén observed that in the dispute settlement process, conciliation has not worked well to date; typically each side is unwilling to compromise before a panel finding is reached. He disagreed with Jackson that overloading of panels is a central problem, arguing instead that the European Community has used the pretext of over-loading to minimize the flow of decisions. For its part, the United States is sometimes forced by legislation (section 301, for example) to bring premature, poorly prepared cases.

PART II

The Players

Distinctive economic structural strengths and weaknesses as well as political ideologies and even cultures give the major individual players in international trade policy differing objectives, approaches, and domestic constraints on foreign commitments. In chapter 7 Gardner Patterson, formerly deputy director general of the General Agreement on Tariffs and Trade (GATT), examines the structural elements causing protectionist tendencies in the European Community (EC).[1] Rodney de C. Grey, Canada's ambassador for the Tokyo Round negotiations, reviews the protectionist practices of the United States in chapter 8, focusing on the "administered protection" of mechanisms such as antidumping and countervailing duties.

In chapter 9 Gary R. Saxonhouse of the University of Michigan explores the extent of Japanese protection by applying an econometric model of Japan's trade designed to pick up the trade-distorting influence of nontariff barriers, visible and invisible. Such indirect methods are necessary because in the realm of overt tariffs and nontariff barriers (such as quotas), it is generally agreed that Japan has low protection; nonetheless, the prevailing view is that other, indirect forms of protection make the Japanese market a highly closed one.

The developing countries are a fourth bloc at the international bargaining table. In an extensive comment presented in the discussion, Carlos Diaz-Alejandro of Yale University focuses on what the developing countries consider to be excessive demands from the North for changes in their trading practices at a time of severe debt-servicing difficulty and continuing high protection against the South in textile and apparel.

---

[1] By request, the authors of the chapters on the EC and the United States focused on the problems caused by each for the international trading system, to sharpen the analysis of trade policy problems for the 1980s. Because Japan is commonly perceived to be highly protective, the terms of reference for the Saxonhouse study on Japan called for an overall evaluation of the extent of Japanese protection.

Implicit in the review of the approaches of the major players is the fact that none of them is monolithic in policy terms; each has internal tensions. Absence of unanimity is obvious for multicountry players (EC, developing countries) but even for single countries trade policy is the net outcome of opposing domestic forces whose balance may shift from year to year. To some degree successful international trade policy may be viewed as the result of a coalition of the policy representatives of various nations acting against the pleas of special interest groups within their own countries in the knowledge that the resulting open trade régime will be best for their respective populations as a whole. Indeed, the existence of a successful international régime enhances each government's ability to refuse special-interest protection in the name of higher-level international commitments. A strong GATT and a successful process of ongoing negotiations (at least informal and bilateral if not formal multilateral rounds) therefore help create a virtuous circle of successful régime/positive player behavior/improved régime. Correspondingly, perceived erosion of the régime—a threat suggested in the Jackson and Malmgren chapters of Part I—invites a vicious circle of eroding régimes/negative player behavior/increasingly deteriorating régime. A central challenge for the 1980s is to ensure that this policy sequence is positive rather than negative, and the achievement of this goal is likely to require more concrete advances than those of the 1982 GATT ministerial meeting.

CHAPTER **7**

The European Community as a Threat to the System

Gardner Patterson

Let the purpose of this paper be clear. The assigned task was to set out the problems the European Community (EC) creates for a well-functioning international trading system, which I define to be a multilateral, nondiscriminatory one, based on negotiated general rules of behavior providing for stability and predictability. This is not, therefore, a balanced appraisal of the EC's role. Many good things can be said about the part played by the Community in world trade, but this essay does not do that. It should also be stated that this essay deals only with those policies and practices that are Community-wide.

Other chapters in this volume deal with the substantive problems that must also be touched upon here. To reduce duplication, this paper will not go into detail on the sectors of agriculture, textiles, automobiles, and steel even though these are the areas where many nations find Community policy and practice especially worrisome. Given the more detailed treatment of these matters elsewhere in this volume, I need only cite examples to illustrate the four major themes of this essay.

They are that the defensible complaints others have of Community behavior in the trade field stem in large measure from the following fundamental factors, the root causes of the EC's threat to the present trading system: the structure of the EC and its decision-making processes; the propensity of the EC to work out bilateral and sectoral deals; the EC's tolerance of, if not affection for, discriminatory practices and its frequently callous treatment of developing countries not affiliated with it; and the area's reluctance to support effective international dispute settlement procedures.

It is evident that the EC has willing partners in some of these areas and does not stand alone in others. It is also evident that difficult as changes in these policies and practices may be, changes there must be if the international trading system, which has served so well, is to survive. The alternative is drastically to alter the system.

The difficulty of bringing about changes is greatly increased by the current gloom and uncertainty. Western Europe is facing extremely difficult economic problems. Unemployment is at socially and politically dangerous levels. Inflation is rampant and deeply imbedded. Investment is low. These are not merely misfortunes of the moment but are the results of a whole series of measures taken over many years. Prominent among them are policies designed to further social and environmental goals. These took many forms—grants, subsidies, regulations, shorter work weeks, large defense expenditures—all of which it was recognized cost something in terms of economic efficiency and growth but were easily justified during the rapid growth days of the 1950s and 1960s and early 1970s. To these costs and rigidities were added the oil shocks of the last decade. In this environment, the pressure to reduce imports and to expand exports by almost any means becomes intense.

While the current economic situation in Europe bears some responsibility for those EC measures which, wittingly or not, have the effect of shifting some of the burdens of its economic problems to others, even a dramatic improvement in the internal economic situation will not automatically remove or drastically alter the basic practices and policies which are the focus of this essay.

Decision-making Structure

A well-functioning international trading system demands that the dominant players—those whose trade bulks large in the total and covers virtually the whole spectrum of products and trade techniques and practices—be able to reach decisions reasonably quickly, that their trading partners know who the decisionmakers are, and, above all, that the apparatus not be inherently biased in favor of protectionism. The EC presents major difficulties to others on all three counts.

The decision-making process is slow because of the very nature of the Community. On trade matters the Commission often takes the initiative in proposing actions or policies. This in itself takes time because a responsible Commission must ever be sensitive to the reactions of its 10 member states. But, even so, on matters of importance, *each* of the 10 members must consider its position on the matter before giving its approval. If, as one must expect, because it is inherent in the nature and diversity of the Ten, at least some of the members will find aspects of the Commission's first proposal unacceptable, then a negotiation among members and the Commission is called for. On small matters it may be that the member states' representatives in Brussels can work things out, but on important questions it has to be referred back to at least some of the capitals. Again a good bit of time is often needed because now a change in some of the elements of the earlier position are called for and it may well be that the earlier one was already the result of some delicate trade-offs within the government.

If the issue is one in which the Community is *negotiating* with another government, then this complex, back and forth process within the Ten must be repeated time and time again because the member states typically give very little freedom of maneuver to the Commission, the actual spokesman on many trade questions.[1] Moreover, the now widespread practice of requiring unanimity among the member states on all important issues all too frequently brings decision-making to a standstill.

The nature of the Community also creates difficulties for others because of the confusion and lack of knowledge by many of the respective roles of the member states and of the Commission. One perceptive writer has characterized the situation by stating that the EC is a supranational entity—represented on the institutional level by the Commission—while also retaining the character of an international entity—represented on the institutional level by the Council of Ministers and the European Council.[2] And, he notes, with much understatement, that the boundaries of their respective areas of competence are not always clear.

---

[1] In the GATT, whether it is in negotiations à la Tokyo Round or simply taking a position in a regular GATT Council meeting, it is a routine practice for the Ten to hold a "coordinating" meeting immediately prior to the GATT meeting for the purpose of giving the Commission official a final OK on what he is to do or say. And in the meeting itself, the representatives of each of the member states surround the Commission official, making certain that he does not depart in any significant way from his instructions—which, of course, the Commission official may well have influenced. Surely one of the most difficult roles any trade official anywhere has to play is that of the Community spokesman on foreign trade matters.

[2] See C. Hosoya, "Relations Between the European Communities and Japan," *Journal of Common Market Studies* (December 1979).

The Treaty of Rome gives the Commission considerable authority on trade questions. Many of the Commission officials in the relevant directorates are highly competent, energetic persons determined to maintain and strengthen the authority of the Commission. But, a fact others have to accept is that the member states have, in practice, kept considerable power in trade matters to themselves. In times past, considerable international friction has resulted from this and it seems likely to continue. Deals made and understandings reached, in good faith, between a Commission official on the one hand and officials of a third government on the other have come unstuck because one or another member state found them unacceptable, or, in its view, went beyond the Commission's authority.

This problem of with whom you should deal in the Community appears to be one the United States has finally largely solved by dealing with both the Commission and the interested member states. But this is possible only for a government with huge personnel, intelligence facilities, and financial resources. It remains a major problem for small countries, who typically simply do not have the people or breadth of experience fully to have fathomed the EC's complex functions, structure, and workings. The Japanese, despite the advantages that come with large trade, superbly competent people, and plenty of financial resources, have long been somewhat bewildered by the EC. No less a person than the chief Japanese trade negotiator during the latter stages of the Tokyo Round drew strong protests from the Commission for expressing publicly some doubts and concerns over the respective negotiating roles of the member states and the Commission.[3]

This confusion as to who is responsible becomes even more murky when resort is had to sectoral approaches to trade problems, an issue we will come back to. For a sector like steel in which most of the Ten have not too dissimilar interests, the Commission can be the locus of negotiation and decision. But, as the Japanese in particular have found, when the EC wants something done to restrain imports on electronic products, or automobiles, where EC member states' interests vary greatly, the talks have been not only between national governments, but also between representatives of the Japanese in-

---

[3] One important reason why the Japanese, along with some of the East European countries, have a strong reason for dealing directly with the member states is that the Community does not in fact have an all-inclusive common trade policy and they are subject to a series of discriminatory import restrictions applied by certain of the member states and not by others.

dustry and those from one, two, or three of the national industries in Europe as well as the Commission.

The most serious impact on the trading system growing out of the very nature of the EC and its decision-making structure, however, is that it seems to have a built-in, and serious, bias toward protectionism. This is most clearly seen in the area[4] where the EC has gone furthest in establishing a common policy: agriculture. But it is evident in other major areas as well, including textiles and apparel.

A glance at its history is needed to show that the EC's farm policies and resultant trade practices—so complained of by others—are not temporary aberrations. The Rome Treaty provides that the Common Market shall extend to trade in farm goods and that this shall be accompanied by the establishment of a "Common Agricultural Policy" (CAP) among its members. The political objective of identifying national goals with Community goals was of considerable importance in this decision, as was insistence of the French on a policy and vehicle for helping its farmers as a trade-off for benefits that German industry could expect from the removal of trade barriers within the Community. The treaty itself includes virtually no details on just what the CAP was to be—these were left to be worked out in subsequent negotiations—but it stressed that its objectives would be the noble ones of increasing productivity, insuring a "fair" standard of living for farmers, stabilizing markets, and insuring "reasonable" prices to consumers. The treaty clearly anticipates there will be need for extensive management and regulation of agricultural trade, including price controls and subsidies for both production and marketing.

Many third countries, both developed and developing, feared from the very first reading of the treaty that it permitted, and that the arrangements finally worked out would encourage, self-sufficiency or more in agriculture and so raise still higher the barriers against their farm exports to Europe and, possibly, even create surpluses that would need to be subsidized for export to third markets.

It was recognized that each of the Six (as it then was) was already, and could be expected to continue, providing all sorts of encouragement to domestic producers of farm products and would continue protecting them from imports. But, they asked, would it not be worse under the CAP because of the great potential pressure to set levels of support and protection high enough for each product to provide

---

[4] Other than the common external tariff where, contrary to the CAP and textiles, the EC doubtless has lower external tariffs than would have been the average had each member independently set its own.

a "fair" standard of living to the least efficient producer *in the whole area?*[5]

Spokesmen for the Six acknowledged that internal price systems *could* be set at levels that would encourage domestic production and displace imports, but such results were not dictated by the treaty. They pooh-poohed the worry that political pressures would operate to set levels of support and protection adequate to take care of the least-efficient producers in the whole area, thus raising barriers higher than they otherwise would have been, stating that this would not happen because that would be an inefficient use of resources and would make more difficult the Community's reaching its overriding objectives of increasing real growth. They reminded the worriers that in working out the agricultural policy account had to be taken of the fact that agriculture was only one sector of the economy. Moreover, they asserted, the Six had no intention of harming others and if they should in fact do so, that was the time to consider remedial action.

The fears others expressed then have proven all too well founded. It took nearly five years for the Community to work out the operating rules and concepts for the CAP—March 1957 through January 1962. The reaction of most third countries when they saw them was that the Community had concocted—with its "target" or "indicative" prices, the variable levy, the threshold prices, and restitution payments— about as potentially a watertight system of protection as the human mind could devise. It was acknowledged that the system did not *demand* this result. The critical issue would be how the policy developed for setting the common minimum prices.

From the very beginning the pressures have often been irresistible to set them at or near the highest level strongly desired by any one major producing country.

A good share of the reason it has worked out in this fashion is the structure of the Community decision-making process. The Commission may, and does, make proposals, but on important issues—whether their importance comes from economic or political or social sources, or some combination of these, it is the member states which decide. On agricultural issues, it is typically the national ministers of agriculture who decide, unless the matter is ratcheted up to the prime ministers. It is not to be found surprising, given the wide range of interests among farm ministers coming from such diverse agricultural regions as those bordering the North Sea and the Ionian, that a lot

---

[5] Much of this discussion took place in the GATT consideration of whether the proposed EEC fulfilled the conditions of Article XXIV.

of logrolling goes on. While a minister from a nation in which the dairy industry is important would prefer to see low-priced edible oils, and would in fact pursue a trade policy to that end were he not a member of an economic group, agreeing to high prices for edible oils may seem to him a small price for his country to pay for the support of others for a high price of dairy products. This tendency for the prices—and so levels of production, height of import barriers, and in many cases, export subsidies, to reach the highest rather than the lowest common denominator was greatly strengthened by the rule exacted by General Charles de Gaulle in 1966 giving any member state a veto over a decision of the Community on a matter of vital national importance.[6] In the field of agriculture, issues so qualified are many.

There can be no doubt that the principles, techniques, and devices developed to carry out the CAP, when combined with the decision-making process that has evolved, has diminished markets for others both in the Community itself and, via the Community's subsidy practices, in third markets as well.

The EC still has a large food deficit, but the lion's share is in tropical products and animal feed. In other sectors, most notably grains, sugar, dairy products, and beef production, under the stimulus of high prices, the Community is becoming a major exporter although it was a net importer of all these products as recently as 1974. In 1981 nearly half of all EC farm spending was (European Agricultural Guidance and Guarantee Fund payments) for export subsidies.

Although few, if any, countries have clean hands when it comes to their foreign trade policy in agriculture, the EC's policies are clearly very disruptive to an efficient world trading system. For some years now, other countries (and many in the Community) have hoped that the financial burden of the CAP would bring about reforms in it. But that still has not happened.[7] The issue of reform in the EC budget is very much in the news these days but one reads also that the French

[6] Because of the many special factors involved, it remains to be seen whether the mid-May overriding of an intended British veto of agricultural prices sets an important precedent.

[7] The Commission has recently stated that "we must have a price policy based on a narrowing of the gap between Community prices and those charged in major competitor countries," but goes on to say "we mean to support a more active export policy." It appears, however, that after the national ministers finished their work there was little if any "narrowing of the gap" for the crop year 1982–83 at least. See *Bulletin of the European Communities,* no. 6 (1981) and no. 1 (1982) and *The Economist,* 22 May 1982, p. 78.

government has let it be known that it would agree to some reforms if, inter alia the EC adopts a more "aggressive" food export policy. It is the argument of this essay that absent drastic reforms in the decision-making process, the EC's farm competitors can expect little relief.

Community policy and practice on textiles and apparel imports are similarly affected by the nature of the decision-making process. Although the US bears responsibility for initiating the import-restricting devices now known as the Multi-Fiber Arrangement, in recent years the EC has been the leader in ever more stringent application and in renewal terms.[8] The issue of trade in textiles is the subject of another chapter[9] in this volume and so it must suffice here only to point out that it is frequently alleged by participants in these negotiations that the insistence on very strict controls by two members (the United Kingdom and France) has led to a common policy considerably more restrictive than would have been the average for the Ten had each been free to set its own import barriers.

As this observer reads the available record, the Commission, if left to itself, would be considerably less trade restraining than in fact the Community is. If this is correct, then a matter of some moment is the fact that the authority of the Commission seems in recent years to have been sapped, partly by the recession but also "by the political weakness of member governments and the lack of consensus among them."[10]

Bilateral and Sectoral Deals

The second major area where Community policy and practice creates problems for many—though not all—countries and constitutes

---

[8] In the renewal of negotiations concluded in December 1981 the EC successfully insisted on means of cutting still more the dominant developing-country suppliers' level of market access, the insertion of a clause to prevent sudden surges of imports within underutilized quotas, a reduction in the earlier 6 percent a year growth rate for imports of "sensitive" products, and the suspension of certain flexibility provisions. In addition the EC stated it would still withdraw from the agreement unless "satisfactory bilateral agreements" were negotiated. See *Bulletin of the European Communities*, no. 12 (1981).

[9] Martin Wolf, "Managed Trade in Practice: Implications of the Textile Arrangements," chapter 14, this volume.

[10] Statement by Robert D. Hormats, *Current Policy*, no. 361 (Washington: US Department of State, Bureau of Public Affairs, December 16, 1981).

a potentially fatal challenge for the present multilateral trading system whose value and benefits are regularly extolled by European authorities, is its propensity to work out bilateral and sectoral deals. The Community often has willing partners in these practices. They are not mindless or capricious practices or policies. But they do create life threatening difficulties for a well-functioning international trading system.

The director general of GATT was correct when he recently stated: "The tendency toward bilateralism and sectoralism in trade policy is the greatest present danger both politically and economically to order and prosperity in the world economy. In political terms it must undermine the credibility of those in industrialized countries who champion the open trading system and commend it to the developing world. More profoundly, it endangers the very possibility of maintaining the international economic cooperation which has made possible the progress of the last 30 years: for that cooperation can only be based on multilateralism and obedience to general rules.[11]

There are many specific trade problems that are essentially bilateral or trilateral, the solution of which are of no or minimal interest to others. They sometimes have to be resolved quickly lest they spread to other substantive areas and other countries. There can be no complaint about bilateral arrangements which do not adversely affect others. But solutions reached bilaterally, especially among the giants, may also have an impact on others, and, whether justified or not, frequently lead others to suspect that the solutions may have been designed to put the burden of the solution on those not present. This can seriously poison the trading atmosphere.

The resort to bilateral negotiations by the EC and the two other giants received a great boost during the Tokyo Round. With more than four score participants, there was, as a practical matter, no choice but to restrict a great many of the negotiating sessions to a small number of those most interested in the particular issue. So long as these discussions were held in Geneva, and under the clear aegis of the GATT, it was possible—not easy but possible—to keep all others who were interested reasonably adequately informed of what was going on in the smaller groups and arrange for their interests and concerns to be fed into—taken into account though not necessarily accepted—the successive drafts. Some of the major players, most notably the Community and the United States, found this procedure

---

[11] Address by Arthur Dunkel, Hamburg, March 5, 1982, *GATT Press Release* no. 1312, Geneva, 5 March 1982.

increasingly burdensome. The substantive issues were difficult enough, they concluded, without the presence of what they sometimes referred to as "kibitzers." Anyway it was asked, did these others, while no doubt legitimately interested, have any chips on the negotiating table? Moreover, everyone agreed that unless the giants could reach accord there could be no agreement at all. As a consequence, it became the increasingly frequent practice to negotiate and reach decisions in Brussels or Washington or Tokyo.

It is an inherent characteristic of most negotiated solutions to difficult problems that the agreement finally reached by those playing an active role represents a compromise and a delicate balance of complex trade-offs. Any change after the "principals" have reached agreement among themselves needed to accommodate what all could accept as legitimate claims of the "others" can all too easily upset that balance. The consequence is that the agreed compromise is often, in effect, imposed on the others. It was this aspect of the Tokyo Round—more even I believe than the level of benefits obtained—which led the developing countries to protest the results.

These bilateral practices continued to flourish after the end of the Tokyo Round. The EC and the United States now meet frequently at high levels to discuss the whole range of issues of interest to them—and to work out solutions, where possible. Given the nature of the two economies, this often means matters of interest to many other nations as well. Beyond the periodic meetings noted in the press, there is a constant flow of people back and forth across the Atlantic. The "hot line" between certain directorates in the Commission in Brussels and the US Trade Representative's office in Washington, developed during the Tokyo Round, continues.

The Community also relies heavily on bilateral discussions with the Japanese, in Tokyo and in Brussels, and depending on the issue, sometimes in the capitals of member states. These, too, have now become institutionalized. That is, they are seen not merely as an occasional method of dealing with some particular problem that is peculiarly bilateral but rather as a method of virtually continuous discussion, negotiation, and adjustment. The EC also, to be sure, has many bilateral discussions with smaller countries and groups of them, including developing ones, but these tend to deal mainly with problems of no great interest to others and so do not undermine the multilateral system.

The multilateral trading system's past benefits are widely acclaimed. One of the more important tasks ahead if it is to continue to generate such good results, is to devise a means whereby third parties can be adequately satisfied that bilateral negotiations and arrangements, especially among the giants, do not shift burdens, broadly defined, onto others.

Even more worrisome is the fact that the Community, again a major player but not the only one, has evidenced in the current difficult times a strong tendency to approach many of its international trade problems on a sectoral basis. We see this in such major sectors as steel, autos, shipbuilding, electronics and, of course, for a long time, textiles and agriculture.

This way of handling problems, because of the usual absence of opposing interests in the debate, almost always develops in the direction of imposing import restraints of one kind or another: voluntary export restraints, orderly marketing arrangements, and the like.[12] Perhaps more serious from the point of view of the best use of the world resources (which is, we sometimes forget, the raison d'être of the multilateral trading system) is that a sectoral trade policy whose objective is to relieve the pressure of foreign competition on an industry "temporarily" in trouble is by its nature exceedingly difficult to revise, or reverse, or limit. This is because such policies are usually negotiated first between the industry and the government and then between the government and each exporting country's industry and government. A whole set of vested interests is thus created which makes reversal most difficult.

Moreover, such government involvement in helping one sector is highly contagious. In democracies, it is difficult to grant favors to one industry and refuse them to another that finds itself in trouble—perhaps in part because of the protection granted to someone else. Precedents are a powerful force here.

A sectoral approach to trade policy, attractive as it is if one suffers from a very short time horizon and a very narrow view of the national economy, often involves recourse to devices which violate the general rules that have been so laboriously negotiated. These violations are not formally protested because those who participated in the arrangement as exporters have, in effect negotiated away that right.

More important, resort to a series of discrete, separately negotiated trade policies removes this trade from the agreed general rules and thereby makes global and coherent national trade policy that much more difficult. Indeed, each such sector comes to have a trade policy

[12] The Civil Aircraft Agreement is an exception.

of its own. When this is the situation in one or more of the dominant trading groups the whole system is placed in dire straits.[13]

Discrimination

The third area in which the EC's policy and practice often make things difficult for others, especially vigorous newcomers, and pose a threat to the good functioning of the present system is its tolerance of, some would say affection for, discriminatory practices.

This is deep-seated. There is a long history here. The Community itself has been seen by some as a discriminatory arrangement in view of the incomplete nature of the union. And many of the present member states had, before the Treaty of Rome, preferential arrangements with their overseas associates of one kind or another and so find the idea congenial enough. From the outset of the Community many of these preferential arrangements were not only continued, but often extended to all of the member states, not just the previous "mother country," first by the Yaoundé and later in the Lomé Convention. Given the nature of the trade, it was the Latin American countries that suffered the most from this discriminatory treatment.[14]

The Community's discriminatory practices are not limited to trade with developing nations. One of the central issues when Japan was negotiating for accession to the GATT in the early 1950s was that of discrimination. When Japan finally acceded in 1955, four of the present members of the Community—Great Britain, France, Belgium, and Holland—invoked GATT Article XXXV. This meant the GATT, including Article I mandating nondiscrimination, was not applicable to their trade with Japan. Invocation was removed in the early 1960s, but the price Japan paid was inclusion of selective safeguards in bilateral agreements with Britain, France, and the three Benelux countries. For years now the EC has been pressing for the inclusion of a similar provision in an agreement with the Community, thus

---

[13] See Tumlir, "International Economic Order—Can the Trend Be Reversed?" *The World Economy* (London), March 1982, for an analysis of this problem.

[14] It merits noticing, parenthetically, that efforts of the Tokyo Round to fulfill the commitment by the developed states to grant "special and differential" treatment to developing countries foundered in certain important areas—especially tariffs—on the unwillingness of those countries receiving preferential treatment from the EC to share it with other developing countries.

extending the earlier agreement to all EC members. To date the Japanese have resisted this, but they have accepted various discriminatory export-restraint arrangements.

The most contentious issue in the three negotiations of Poland, Hungary, and Romania for accession to the GATT (in the late 1960s and early 1970s) was that of the discriminatory bilateral import restrictions applied by various West European countries against each of them. In none of the cases would the Community accept a firm and definite commitment to abolish these restrictions although they could not be justified under any GATT article. They did agree to their gradual reduction, but the pace of implementation has been far slower than the three socialist countries had assumed, and it is this issue that continues to be at the center of periodic, sometimes rancorous, review of the operation of these protocols of accession.

At the conclusion of the Kennedy Round the Community let it be known that it would extend the benefits of the newly negotiated antidumping code only to the signatories. Several countries believed this to be a violation of the Community's obligations under Article I of the GATT (the most-favored-nation, MFN, treatment article) and the director general of GATT issued an "opinion" (GATT rules and practice denied him the right to make a "ruling" on such matters) that the MFN rule applied. The EC then let it be further known that it did not accept this opinion. This issue came up again at the end of the Tokyo Round. The Community, this time supported by several other developed countries, made it quite clear—though not to the writer's knowledge in any formal declaration—that they intended to apply the several new nontariff barrier codes on a discriminatory basis. That is, the benefits would go only to those who sign.

This presented little difficulty to other industrial countries, which have signed the codes, but it was seen as a very serious matter by the developing countries. The director general of GATT was asked by a group of them to look into the matter. He reported that the text of the codes was not inconsistent or in conflict with the GATT. But, as all knew, the real question was whether the signatories could, in practice, apply them in a discriminatory fashion. It was not up to the GATT Secretariat to forecast how members would apply the codes. However, after extensive negotiations, the GATT Secretariat did succeed in including in the formal decision by the contracting parties, "legalizing" the results of the Tokyo Round the following statement: "The contracting parties also note that existing rights and benefits under the GATT of Contracting Parties not being parties to this agreement, including those derived from Article I, are not affected by these Agreements." So far so good, but few who have followed this matter believe this settles it. A test of the present situation will come only when one of the signatories does apply one of the codes in a clear-cut discriminatory way, a nonsignatory is harmed thereby, and a formal complaint is lodged and let run its course, that is, not settled bilaterally and out of court so to speak.

If any doubts remained about the EC's lack of enthusiasm for nondiscriminatory policies, especially vis-à-vis developing countries, they should have been dispelled by the Community's position in the Tokyo Round safeguard negotiations. There was little dissent from the conclusion that the safeguard provisions, procedures, and practices under the GATT were less than satisfactory, and the ministerial mandate for the MTN included examining the matter. The examination quickly led to the conclusion that the rules and practices could indeed be improved. Intensive, and sophisticated, negotiations took place over many many months. Considerable progress was made in defining what constitutes injury that would justify the use of safeguards; in setting forth the kind of evidence that would prove causality; in specifying the domestic procedures necessary before safeguard measures could be taken; in detailing the conditions for applying such measures: duration, degressivity, etc., and in establishing improved surveillance and dispute-management machinery. This was important progress.

But in the end the effort failed. It failed because the Community insisted that the agreement also legalize and make specific provision for the "selective" application of safeguards. That is, that discriminatory application of import restraints be permitted. The Community was not proposing that discriminatory application be the rule. They would limit selective application to "unusual and exceptional" circumstances, by which they seem to mean large and sudden *increases* in imports from a few sources. How and who was to define these were the central issues.

No subject in the entire Tokyo Round so unified the developing countries. On no other issue did they put forth such precise, carefully reasoned positions. Many objected to the proposal in principle—believing that the small and weak above all needed the protection of the general most-favored-nation obligations. They also saw it as having the effect, in operation, of creating a large constituency—those not selected for restraints—actually favoring a continuation of the selective safeguard measures, whereas a most-favored-nation application of the safeguard measure creates pressure from all countries exporting the product concerned to have the practice cease. Above all, they saw it as a blatant attempt to put on developing countries virtually the entire burden of adjustment whenever an industrial country could show that imports were the cause of injury and that there had recently been an *increase* in imports. This was because in the very nature of economic development they were often the newcomers, therefore they would be the ones who were the cause of the *increases*. But, they insisted, it was the total not just an increase that was causing injury so all exporters, including old established suppliers, should share the burden.

These countries simply did not take seriously the Community's repeated assertions that a selective approach was justified because it was "unfair" to penalize all countries just because a few were disrupting markets.

Because the EC was adamant on the issue, and because the developing countries could see important benefits coming from other parts of the text under negotiation, they finally accepted "in principle" the inclusion of some "selectivity." The conditions they then set down for its application would have made the provisions virtually unusable and so were unacceptable to the EC. At this point, time was running out for concluding the Tokyo Round and continued efforts to improve the safeguard rules were left for the future.

That future is now. New proposals in this field must deal with a long history of discriminatory practice by the Community and a strongly held belief by some of its major officials that "selectivity" is not only a well-established feature of the landscape but a necessary and proper one. Any lingering doubts about this should have been removed by the EC insistence that the late 1981 renewal of the Multi-Fiber Arrangement—which discriminates against developing-country suppliers—provide means of cutting the EC market access more severely for dominant suppliers among the developing countries than for the less competitive developing countries. Here we have discrimination compounded.

Dispute Settlement

The final item on this agenda of elemental complaints against the Community is its reluctance to support effective international dispute-settlement procedures.

No country likes to be hauled before an international body and charged with violating its obligations and commitments, which is one reason the mere existence of effective dispute settlement machinery encourages compliance. But the number and complexity of disputes is certain to increase as the number of international trading rules multiplies—and the Tokyo Round success is often measured by the number of new codes it spawned. Effective functioning of the system must, therefore, have procedures for dealing with disputes. This was foreseen in the Tokyo Round, and a good deal of effort was put into establishing, both within each code and more generally, improved procedures.

Many found the Community's position in these negotiations troublesome. It accepted the widely held view that the general system needed reform, but on four specific elements many others thought the Community's proposals—subtle and sophisticated—would have the effect of reducing the effectiveness of the apparatus, especially for smaller countries whose economic and political clout was small compared to that of the Big Three and to which therefore an efficient, fast dispute-management system was particularly important.

One debate was on the question of whether a country had a "right" to have a panel set up to consider its complaint. In the past, GATT Council action had in fact been necessary but it had never denied a request and others believe this should now be formalized. The Community took the position that the question of establishing a panel should be decided in each case by the GATT Council, arguing that while it was to be expected that the decision would be "yes" in most cases, Council action was desirable in order to stop trivial and meritless complaints. Others feared that to question the right and to require Council action would not only lengthen and delay the process to the disadvantage of the country that believed its interests had been impaired or infringed, but, given the influence the giants, especially the EC, had over other GATT Council members, they might well find their complaints not approved for panel procedures if one of the giants were the defendant in the case. (In the end the right to a panel was established.)

The question of the speed with which the process worked was a central issue in the negotiation. Because it is usually the case that the protested action continues until the dispute is settled, those, especially the smaller nations, who relied heavily on international rules and procedures to protect their interest, were anxious that any reforms have the effect of speeding up, not slowing down, the process. This was at the heart of a second debate. The Community proposed that, as a general rule, panels should have five members, while most others held out for three, which had been the typical number in the past. To some outsiders this heated discussion sounded like bureaucratic nonsense. It was not. The EC argued that for something as important as setting up an international body to sit in judgment on a sovereign nation's action, surely one needed the wisdom, experience and balance of at least five persons. To those opposed, requiring five members would not necessarily add much in the way of wisdom or balance but certainly would greatly prolong the time between the launching of a complaint and the final report of the panel. This was because experience had shown that to find persons willing and able to serve was time-consuming and five would take proportionately longer than three. Moreover, experience had also shown that scheduling meetings of the panel was a slow process because of other obligations of the members. The scheduling problem would also require much more time to solve it if five rather than three schedules had to be reconciled. Finally, the time it would take five to reach a conclusion would be increased as would the possibility of an inconclusive final report. (The final "solution" was to state that a panel should be either three or five members.)

The view that the EC was trying to weaken the process received further support when it opposed a proposal that, in the future, panel members could be either government officials, as had been the almost universal practice, or nongovernment persons. The EC argued that the GATT system was so complex, action under it so steeped in unwritten precedent, that an "outsider" would not be qualified to deal with alleged infringements. The proponents of opening up panel membership to nongovernment persons argued that widening the field of choice would speed up the selection process and that nongovernment persons would be less subject to improper pressure by either of the disputants, a not unheard of event. (Finally, it was agreed panels could have nongovernment persons on them.)

Another EC proposal others found particularly worrisome was that before finalizing its findings and recommendations, the panel be required to "discuss" them with the disputants so that, it was argued, the panel not make a serious mistake, because it had overlooked some important piece of evidence or argument, had misinterpreted the GATT, or had unwittingly ignored an important precedent. This proposal immediately ran into strong opposition on the grounds that it amounted to reopening the case after all the agreed procedures had been gone through and that it would subject the panel to intolerable pressure—especially if a large trading country or entity were involved. This proposal was, in the event, not pressed. But the fact it was brought forward, when combined with the other Community positions noted, led many to believe that the EC did in fact not want to strengthen international dispute-management systems and would, in general, prefer to handle its disputes bilaterally.

This view of things had found support since the end of the Tokyo Round by the fact that in the last two years the EC has involved the regular GATT dispute-settlement machinery only once,[15] although it is threatening, according to press reports, to bring a major case against certain of Japan's import restraints.* Much more important in raising concern over EC policy has been the record in the Australian and Brazilian complaints against the Community's system of granting export refunds on its sugar exports. In 1978, Australia complained to the GATT Council that the EC, by subsidizing its sugar exports, had contravened its GATT obligations under Article XXVI. In due course a panel was established to examine the Australian complaint. Its report, adopted by the Council in November 1979, a year later, found that the EC system did constitute a threat prejudicial to Australia's sugar trading interests.

In November 1978, another panel had been set up to examine a similar complaint by Brazil which argued that the EC system had caused or threatened serious prejudice to Brazil's interests and had nullified and impaired Brazil's benefits under the GATT. This panel, whose report was adopted by the GATT Council in November 1980, found that it could not conclude that the subsidies had resulted from the EC's having more than an equitable share of world export trade in sugar in terms of the relevant GATT article, but it did conclude that the EC system had been employed in a manner that helped depress sugar prices in the world market and that this constituted a serious prejudice to Brazilian interests.

These reports were examined at several Council meetings in 1979, 1980, and 1981, Brazil and Australia repeatedly asking the EC what action, and when, it planned to take to remove this threat and this prejudice. The EC, repeatedly pointing out that there was no evidence that its sugar policy had actually caused harm to the world sugar market, replied that it was ready to engage in further discussion and consultation. It also stated that it was considering changes in its policy and therefore it was best to wait until those changes were announced before carrying the matter further.

---

[15] The one case it has brought was against the United States with regard to the latter's import duty on vitamin B-2. It has been rumored that the Community may bring a case should the US impose countervailing or antidumping duties on European steel imports, and the press has reported the EC is considering bringing a case against a whole series of Japanese practices and policies. In contrast, the US and Canada have each brought three cases. One each has been brought by Australia, Brazil, Chile, India, New Zealand, and Hong Kong. The EC was the "defendant" in 5 of these 12 cases.

* *Ed. note*: The EC did bring a sweeping case against Japan to the GATT in mid-1982. By year-end the case had not yet been concluded.

In 1981 the EC announced to GATT members its new sugar regulations (in the meantime, let it be noted, the complained of practice continued) which it claimed fulfilled its GATT obligations. Brazil, Australia, and others challenged this, stating that the new system still constituted a major threat of injury to their exporting interests and stated they were maintaining their legal and formal complaints. There the matter rests at the time of writing, while a new GATT working group "reviews the situation".

This is a complicated case. Some of the allegations against the EC sugar policy could not be accepted by the panels, and evidence on some points is ambiguous to say the least. Nevertheless, in the commonly held view, the EC simply has not been responsive to the panels' recommendations and in the process is seriously discrediting the dispute-settlement procedures, a trend which the United States, and to a lesser degree, the EC (France, Belgium, and the Netherlands) had already pushed a long way in the infamous taxation of exports cases (Domestic International Sales Corporation and others).[16]

Conclusion

The Community's behavior creates serious problems for others and threatens an international trading system regularly extolled by European authorities. It can be traced to: the structure of the EC and its decision-making process, which is slow, hard to predict, and has a protectionist bias; the EC propensity toward bilateralism and sectoral arrangements, which ignore the global rules and endanger the very possibility of maintaining international economic cooperation; the EC's tolerance of, even affection for, discriminatory practices, which are particularly burdensome to many developing countries, the nonmarket economies, and Japan; and the Community's reluctance; to support effective international dispute-settlement procedures, which is a necessary element for a system based on general rules.

These characteristics and policies are not a consequence of the current recession and they will not disappear—although some of their manifestations may be eased—with economic recovery. They are deep

---

[16] These cases remained on the GATT agenda for nearly a decade while the practices contrary, in varying degrees and respects, to the GATT rules, were continued. In 1981 they were taken off, at least temporarily, as a result of an understanding reached by the four countries. Several other countries, however, put on the record their objections to the understanding and reserved their rights to raise the issue again.

and basic. They must be dealt with, by modifying them, by modifying the system as it is presently conceived, or both.

Finally, it needs repeating that the task assigned me was to set out the policies and practices of the EC that impinge unfavorably on others. This paper is not a balanced assessment for it makes no attempt either to cite the grievances the Community has against others or more important, to set out the ways it has contributed to the economic welfare of those outside its borders.

CHAPTER **8**

A Note on US Trade Practices

Rodney de C. Grey

The assigned purpose of this paper is to comment on US trade practices that create problems for the trade policymakers of other countries. It is assumed that there is a trade policy system, a system of trade policy relations, which can be discerned and described, which is to some extent logically coherent, and about which there is a measure of agreement, at least on broad objectives. The thesis given me was that certain US actions contradict the working rules of the system, or run counter to the objectives that the system is supposed to serve.

There is no doubt a wide measure of agreement that all major trading countries take actions or apply policies from time to time that create difficulties for other trading countries. In this paper I would like to discuss four policy areas in which problems of adjustment to imports or adjustment to the policies of others have arisen for the United States. The four areas are textiles and textile products, steel, automobiles, and subsidization of exports through the tax system such as the Domestic International Sales Corporation (DISC).

I do not want to spend any time describing these actions in conventional trade policy language and denouncing US actions. When governments of market economies decide to intervene on a discretionary and ad hoc basis in international trade, in response to pressures that seem to be intolerable in the political sense, they do so usually after considerable internal examination and enquiry, and usually they do so reluctantly, and, often, too late. On current issues it is not easy for an outsider to second-guess trade policy administrators; the outsider rarely has all the facts, and usually has fewer than the decisionmakers. We can see, from the record of General Agreement on Tariffs and Trade (GATT) dispute settlements, particularly the published findings of panels, that trade policy problems really are problems, and very often, there are no real solutions, only a process

243

of making situations tolerable. With a large measure of hindsight and with some research, we can, of course, form some judgments after decisions have been made.

I propose to deal with my assigned topic by asking a series of questions: First, what is the trade policy system which the United States has spent so much effort to create? Second, what are the features of the system that has been emerging since the Tokyo Round which are at variance with the stated objectives of the system, or which contradict the main assumptions about the system? Third, in this context, what can be concluded about United States policy reactions in the particular areas cited?

The Trade Relations System

The current system of trade relations can be viewed as being the complex of bilateral and multilateral agreements, arrangements, and interpretive notes that provide an interconnected set of rules for trade relations between states and which therefore provide part of the framework for relations between private international traders. This definition leaves to one side many agreements which govern relations between private economic actors or operators engaged in international trade but which do not involve active policy reactions by states.

In my view of the system, one can see, at one end of the structure, the multilateralized, standardized agreement: the General Agreement on Tariffs and Trade (GATT), which has replaced or serves in the place of a large number of bilateral agreements. In the immediate pre-World War II period, the key feature of these bilateral agreements was the unconditional most-favored-nation (MFN) clause. The GATT institutionalized this clause and reinforced it with the device of the multilateralized tariff "binding." Around the GATT a series of interpretative agreements and special arrangements have developed. There are the Protocols of Accession or Association for a number of countries which cannot adhere to all the GATT articles, or cannot apply the agreement to all sectors of trade. There is the Multi-Fiber Arrangement (MFA), an organized derogation from Article XIX. There are various preferential arrangements, on a regional or sector basis, some of which may not, meet the free trade area criteria of Article XXIV.

Clearly, the GATT, with all this cargo of derogation, partial rather than complete application and detailed interpretation, is the centerpiece of the system—as seen by a market economy. But there is also a range of bilateral understandings, both as between GATT signatories, and between certain GATT signatories and nonsignatories, around this central mechanism. The legal interrelations between the rights and obligations specified in the GATT and in these bilateral treaties are far from clear. There are also plurilateral agreements regarding the supply and the purchase of particular commodities. There are, too, understandings regarding the use of particular trade-regulating devices; frequently these take the form of interpretative notes to the various GATT provisions or sets of guidelines (such as the Organization for Economic Cooperation and Development, OECD, guidelines on "national treatment").

I cite these elements of the system merely to make the point that as a system it is neither well articulated nor coherent. Moreover, it looks quite different to major industrial market economy countries than it does to small countries, developing countries, the socialist countries of Eastern Europe, the USSR, or China.

This system is in part the product of a prolonged discussion, beginning in the last century, about the economic and foreign policy benefits of reducing barriers to trade on a basis of nondiscrimination. The system, as seen by the main market economies, involved some important assumptions about how, ideally, trade should take place.

- The benefits of trade are maximized if decisions to import or to export are taken by private entities responding to market forces as signaled by the movements of prices. The role of government is essentially regulatory: the formulation and enforcement of the rules necessary to maintain the freedom of markets; governments should not themselves be traders.
- Governments' main instrument of intervention to adjust price competition between imports and domestic production is the levying of a scheduled charge at the frontier.
- After that frontier levy, imports have an *unlimited* right to compete with domestic production.
- Other forms of intervention to limit the operation of the market, particularly the setting of quantitative limits on imports or exports, are acceptable only as emergency mechanisms.
- Government intervention in the market, whether by tariff or by quota, should be on the basis of nondiscrimination import or export destinations. This principle is embodied in the unconditional form of the most-favored-nation (MFN) clause.
- Other regulatory interventions by government in the market should not distinquish between foreign or domestic products in their application, other than the frontier measures specified.

All laws, regulations, and taxes, except for the tariff or the border quantitative measure, are to be applied on the same basis to imports and to domestic goods. This is the principle of "national treatment," as set out in Article III of the GATT.

This view of what the trade relations system is intended to be, this ideal toward which the system should be developing, is based on the notion that income and welfare are increased by allowing international specialization of production to take place, that encouraging the domestic production of goods that can be made more cheaply elsewhere brings the producer country's citizens only temporary benefits and long-term harm. The strength with which this view was held derived from the pre-war experience that discriminatory policies and the widespread and competitive recourse to devices for exporting unemployment, quickly made all much poorer. The GATT was premised on the conviction that all trading countries could better themselves by agreeing to a system of rights and obligations that would preclude beggar-thy-neighbor policies.

This perception of the ideal state of affairs, though a powerful motive for establishing an international system, has had some unfortunate results. Fixing our gaze on the potential gains from letting the theory of comparative advantage work, we tend to overlook some important factors in the real trading world. When governments insist on intervening in the market in a variety of ways, we should realize that they are not necessarily failing to perceive the comparative advantage, but perhaps reacting to realities that the model has assumed away.

The conventional trade model abstracts from the reality of power. It fails to take account of the central fact that there are gross differences in market power and political power as between the nation states in the system. Moreover, the trade model abstracts from the reality of private economic power; it ignores the differences in power and control of markets as between the private entities engaging in international transactions. The model also abstracts from differences in modes of production and their profound influence on market behavior. Economists have addressed all these factors as separate realities; nonetheless much of the discussion of trade policy at the public and political level seems to assume that the simplified ideal is an achievable or an existing reality.

Viewed in that perspective, many actions by the US and other governments, have to be classified as sins or backsliding. For my part, I start from the perception that developments in the real world are possibly considered attempts to deal with real problems in the complex world, not just aberrations or anomalies resulting from failures of intelligence or the wrong-headedness of politicians and advisors. Put more precisely, of course, the MFA, the import-pricing arrangements for steel, the attempts to limit automobile imports, and the particular answer to the problem of how to tax export income can be considered to deal with quite intractable problems of adjustment and adaptation to the changing economics of production, technology, and trade. None of these problems of adjustment is easily solved by a show of hands in favor of comparative advantage, however logically powerful and attractive that principle may be.

Contingent Protection

My second question was "What are the main features of the system that seem at variance with the premises of the idealized system?" One of the main characteristics of the system as it is taking shape after the Tokyo Round of Multilateral Trade Negotiations (MTN) is the impact of the attempt to "liberalize" certain of the "nontariff barriers." The term nontariff barriers is a misleading description of the complex of devices to regulate and to intervene; moreover, what has transpired should not be described as "liberalization." Rather, in the post-MTN period an important shift in emphasis has occurred away from reliance on *fixed* measures or techniques of intervention to regulate the competition between imports and domestic production and toward much greater reliance on more *flexible* methods of protecting the domestic producers. I have called the newly strengthened apparatus of intervention the *contingent protection* system.

This switch in emphasis has happened gradually. In the period of multilateralization, from Havana to the launching of the Tokyo Round, the thrust of trade policy was to organize negotiations about the conventional nineteenth century technique of intervention—the import tariffs of the negotiating countries. However, it is now evident that, as tariffs were reduced and "bound" against increase, pressure for protection against import competition, much of it arising from new sources, came to result in greater use of various contingency measures. For example, in the period immediately before and during the Kennedy Round of 1963–67, the US administration was choosing to use its antidumping provisions more and more frequently. The antidumping mechanism was, in fact, emerging as the most important component in the apparatus of contingent protection. There was particular concern about the ease with which large transnational corporations could indulge in injurious "hidden" dumping. There was concern, too, at the scope that antidumping systems allowed for harassment of legitimate trade. As a result, an attempt was made in the Kennedy Round to codify administrative procedures for the use of antidumping measures. This codification had the perverse, but not necessarily unforeseen, result that all signatories to the negotiated code thereby acquired rights to use *all* the varied procedural devices or administrative techniques that had been drafted into the code at the request of one or another negotiator. Thus each signatory could, and some did, enact antidumping provisions that could be deployed to be more restrictive of trade than the systems in effect before the negotiation.

This episode should make clear that a major result of negotiations designed to regulate the use of contingency measures, in contrast with negotiations to reduce tariffs, can be the improvment of their overall capacity to restrict trade. This sort of perverse result of negotiations— which in terms of the stated agenda, are exercises in trade liberalization—is also evident in the outcome of the negotiations on subsidies and countervailing duties and in the revision of the Antidumping Code, which were judged to be such important elements in the Tokyo Round package of trade "liberalization."

The contingency system, as a system of intervention, makes necessary a mass of detailed and subordinate legislation. The nature of the intervention requires a large bureaucratic establishment, which must be presumed to be capable of having available a detailed knowledge of a large number of transactions at any given time. Even for the most highly developed modern state, it is difficult to work this apparatus responsibly and effectively. Really substantial deployment of the contingency system, such as in the trigger price mechanism (TPM) for steel, requires that the state bureaucracy scrutinize and amass evidence about a large number of transactions at any one time, and make decisions on the consistency or inconsistency of contracts entered into outside the national jurisdiction. This means, in effect, that only a large industrial state can effectively work a contingency system. (Perhaps the test of "graduation" or "maturation" for developing countries should be their ability to legislate and operate the fully developed contingency system!) In this important sense, the contingent system is biased in favor of the large industrial countries.

In a second sense, the contingency system is power-oriented. Industries in small countries, if they are to compete on world markets, must produce in plants of optimum size; as a practical matter that will require exportation of perhaps three-quarters of the output of their plants. An antidumping action or a countervailing duty action against exports of an optimum-sized plant in a small country can be particularly damaging, simply because it affects such a large portion of the plant's output. An identical plant in a large industrial economy can dump more easily (because so much of its production may be sold in its protected domestic market) than can a plant in a smaller economy; but, an antidumping action against the plant in the larger economy will damage its profitability less. Similarly, a plant may be established in a large economy with the same subsidies as in a smaller economy, sell most of its production in the domestic market, and therefore be less exposed to countervail than the identical plant located in a smaller economy.

Thus the antidumping and countervailing duty systems, as sanctioned by Article VI of the GATT, inherently protect producers in large economies more effectively than producers in smaller economies. A modest attempt to deal with this imbalance was made in the Tokyo Round arrangements on subsidies, in that it was made clear that the injurious effects of import-replacement subsidies in larger economies on firms in smaller countries could be proceeded against in Geneva under provisions derived from Article XXIII of the GATT. However, as a form of intervention such a proceeding in Geneva is rather less effective than a countervail action under domestic law.

A similar power bias is evident in the operation of the GATT safeguard system of Article XIX, and in such various stratagems for avoiding it as "orderly marketing arrangements," " voluntary export restraints," and " industry-to-industry" understandings. The " discipline" of Article XIX is based on the threat of retaliation, or of having to pay compensation. The threat of having to pay for taking safeguard action is a meaningful brake on proposals for safeguard action when invoked by trading entities of roughly the same order of power. It is certainly credible when invoked by a large trading entity against a smaller entity. But it is far less credible if invoked by a small country—although perhaps over the years some of them have underestimated what leverage they do have.

The European Community (EC) advanced the notion during the Tokyo Round that the Article XIX arrangements should be modified by removing the obligation to apply safeguard measures on a nondiscriminatory basis. However, the assurance that Article XIX is not to be applied "selectively" is one of the few, if not the only, significant reasons for developing countries adhering to the GATT. Indeed, it is one of the principal components of the GATT system, from the point of view of any small country. Manifestly to introduce discrimination ("selectivity") into Article XIX would be to increase the element of power bias in that article.

In sum, examination of the contingency system in practice will show that the search for a system of rules designed as a partial substitute for the crude interplay of power relationships has resulted in little more than what could be called "power-oriented" rules.

The central concept in the system of contingent protection is the concept of *injury*—injury to producers, injury to an industry, injury or prejudice to the importing country. However, there is little if any economic content in this concept as it is used in the GATT. The GATT tradition (based on the Hatters' Fur case) interprets injury essentially as a matter for the government of the importing country to decide upon. The exporting country has the onus, if it does not agree with an injury determination, of proving that injury has not been caused or threatened. This is manifestly difficult to achieve. Moreover, there is no adequate apparatus of international scrutiny or surveillance. This defect in the international system has been reinforced by the fact that in importing countries, particularly in the United States, injury as a concept has been taken into domestic trade relations law primarily as a legal, not economic, concept. As a practical matter, this has tended to buttress the restrictive and protective effect of the system of contingency measures.

It is not at all clear that the developing system of contingent protection, operating in conjunction with the lower but still relevant tariffs negotiated in the Tokyo Round, will be *as a system* less restrictive or less interventionist, less trade distorting, less trade diverting, less costly, than the older system—which relied in the main on published schedules of import fees applied on an unconditional most-favored-nation basis. Moreover, we have the interventionist impact of contingent protection now—indeed, we have had it since 1975 or before, but the tariff cuts are being doled out by installments— for what they may be worth in the context of a régime of floating exchange rates.

Discriminatory Trade

In parallel with the rise of the contingent protection system as the main component in the commercial policy apparatus of the major industrial countries, there has been a whole set of decisions not to apply the unconditional MFN clause. This development is evident in two important contexts. The first is the proliferation of tariff preferential régimes, systems of tariff discrimination, many of which, of course, discriminate against goods from North America. I would assume that on any quantitative reckoning, more tariffs have been reduced on more trade over the last say, 20 years, on a *preferential* basis than on an MFN basis. The MFN principle, as a tariff bargaining rule, has been very nearly destroyed—by the EC, by the European Free Trade Association, by the developing countries as among themselves, by the United Nations Conference on Trade and Development (on behalf of the Generalized System of Tariff Preferences), even by the United States (on behalf of Canadian automotive products.) In terms of quantitative impact, these modern tariff preferences are more trade diverting, than were the older preferential arrangements that Americans for so long, so rightly opposed. I would not suggest that these modern preference arrangements should be approximated to the eighteenth century navigation acts, but surely they can be compared to the tariff preference schemes as applied in the pre-war period in the French colonial system and within the British Commonwealth after the Ottawa Conference of 1932.

The reign of unconditional MFN has also been weakened by decisions not to extend certain supplementary or interpretative GATT agreements to nonsignatories of those agreements but which are GATT members. This issue arose over the position of GATT signatories that did not adhere to the Kennedy Round Antidumping Code. At that time the EC (of Six) took the view that, as a practical political matter, the benefits of that code, particularly in terms of procedures, could not be extended to countries that would not accept the code's detailed obligations. This was an evident breach of the MFN provisions of Article I of the GATT; however, in the event, not all countries that had antidumping systems regarded it as absolutely necessary to have two antidumping systems—one for code signatories, the other for nonsignatories. Moreover, it became clear that a country might choose to sign the code, but need not itself legislate an antidumping system. The issue was raised in a more acute form by the US decision to restrict the benefits of the procurement code (after an initial period) and the subsidies-countervail code, to code signatories. The logic of the US position was made entirely clear in the course of the Tokyo Round discussions, but it is not clear whether the negotiators concerned realized the full implications for the commercial policy system of the US decision not to adhere to the unconditional MFN doctrine. It was made all the more difficult to see the GATT as a coherent arrangement and as the central component in the commercial policy system when the United States decided, very late in the day and without the necessary detailed discussions with other participants, that certain bilateral MFN treaties conveyed such completely unconditional MFN rights as to entitle the signatories to the injury test for countervail whether or not they were GATT signatories or code signatories. In any event the decisions to apply two GATT codes on a conditional basis, and not to all GATT signatories, in a sense reintroduced the conditional MFN concept into the commercial policy system.

The rise of contingent protection in parallel with the decline in tariff rates; the power bias inherent in the contingent protection system as against the tariff centered system; the extent of tariff preference arrangements; the reappearance of conditional MFN: these are now the important features of the trade relations system. They do not make a set of rules that is coherent in the sense that the ideal system centered on comparative advantage was thought to be logically coherent. Any commercial policy practitioner can add in other features of the system which evidence its disorder—for example, the nonapplication of the general rules of trade in agriculture, and the inability to devise any functionally effective framework, other than patchwork, for trade policy relations with nonmarket economy countries.

US Practices

In this chapter considerable discussion has been devoted to defining the commercial policy system, in trying to see it as it is, as a context for judging the impact on the system of US actions. There is manifestly a great difference between the system as it is and the system imagined to exist, as revealed in a number of official pronouncements from Washington.

At the beginning of the chapter, it was suggested we should discuss four US actions: restrictions on textiles and clothing, steel, automobiles, and DISC. However, in terms of the history of the GATT-centered commercial policy system, a number of European observers maintain that the first, perhaps most important, US action that damaged the integrity of the system was the waiver of GATT obligations in regard to certain US agricultural policies. When trying to evaluate this assertion, the problem, of course, arises that the US did not act in a vacuum, but in the context of other trading countries' actions, policies, and import régimes. This difficulty arises in connection with each item on our bill of particulars. Certainly the US agricultural waiver handed other countries a debating point. However, not every other country, including agricultural exporters, ran a free-market, noninterventionist agricultural policy; the United States—because it preached the GATT system—may have been a conspicuous sinner, but it was not alone. The related point, of course, is more evident now than then: that the United States might well have sought a less comprehensive release from its GATT obligations.

Textiles

The arrangements for textiles and textile products have for twenty years been central to US trade policy, as applied. The key judgment, made in launching what has become a comprehensive régime of discriminatory restrictions, was that the textile and clothing industries had to be paid not to oppose President Kennedy's proposed trade legislation. That legislative proposal, it must be recalled, pertained more to foreign policy—about emerging great power relationships— to trade-relations policy in the narrower, more utilitarian sense. Its central feature was an elaborate statistical device to help entice the United Kingdom to adhere to the Treaty of Rome, and to pay the "Romans" something tangible for permitting this to happen. This was the logic of the "dominant supplier" provision, which seems, from this distance, to have been quaint at best, dangerous and misconceived at worst—if only because it made the United Kingdom appear to be a vehicle for the American "grand design." Textile exporters were required to pay a price for this foreign policy venture: they were to surrender their Article XIX right to nondiscrimination in the use of restrictive measures, and to give up their right to insist on retaliation or compensation. The irresistible gift to the US textile industry has ensured the longevity of the textile restraint system.

In the absence of an international agreement, which provided a sort of cover or sanction for restrictions, the US textile and clothing industries would have had to seek relief under the "escape clause" of domestic legislation, and then under Article XIX. Perhaps important segments of the industry would have made a good Article XIX case. Indeed, if the situation in the various sections of the two industries met the test, as they are supposed to do, of showing at least a threat of disruption of their markets, as specified in the textile arrangement, they could well have met the less severe test of threat of serious injury required by Article XIX. What was really attractive about the textile system, as invented to clear the way for the Trade Expansion Act, was that there was no need to pay compensation or face retaliation, in the sense of Article XIX. Accepting this proposal, in return for promises of orderly sharing in the growing market for textiles and clothing (which exporters were entitled to under the GATT) was a bad bargain.

The US invention of the international textile system gravely damaged the commercial policy system developed by Cordell Hull and multilateralized at Havana and Geneva under US leadership. But that is evaluating US action by itself, in isolation and out of context. We should remember that European countries had in place a whole range of restrictions on textile and clothing imports from Japan and the developing world. Moreover, the Europeans, by and large, gave no sign that they would open their markets to absorb, in the short term, any significant portion of the supplies coming on to world markets from new centers of production. In that context, US action looks a good deal less like original sin.

The time may come when textile exporters will decide to revert to the GATT rules, to insist on their Article XIX rights and to expose themselves to the rights of others under Article XIX and Article VI, and thus to terminate what has been for them an increasingly unbalanced bargain. The question that would have to be asked is whether some sectors of the EC, US, and Canadian textile and clothing industries could not secure all the protection that they require and that the international community, in its own interest, should accord them, under the existing provisions of the GATT, particularly as amplified in the contingency system. I regard this issue, and the disorder in world agricultural trade, as more important questions, in terms of the necessary rebuilding of the international commercial policy order, than trying to invent new rules regarding traded services.

Steel

The evolution of protective action in regard to steel involves quite different considerations, although the final question is the same— why not have recourse to Article XIX for such an intractable structural problem? I regarded the US trigger price mechanism (TPM) system as too complex, too byzantine, and too bizarre a structure of intervention to erect on the flimsy foundation of the antidumping arrangements. The antidumping system was not designed to substitute for sectoral or structural adjustment policies. It was designed only to provide a remedy to deal from time to time with particular cases of price discrimination in import trade, and ideally, to be limited to those cases where predatory pricing causes meaningful and demonstrable harm to an efficiently operated industry. In the TPM we had a totally convincing example of how the system of contingent protection can be deployed by a big government with enough bureaucrats.

The collapse of the TPM and the launching of a series of antidumping and countervailing duty cases is just the second act in this theater of contingent protection. Does any other country have the administrative resources to deal with such a structural problem in such a fashion? The steel drama is not yet over, and I do not feel I have any easy answers. However, it seems that a more positive approach to structural adjustment should involve more facets of the issue than merely the subsidization of production and price discrimination in import trade. An Article XIX approach would have provided for import restrictions, where warranted, and could have been the source of a set of rules for coherent international action not inconsistent with the GATT. We may yet be driven, here in the United States and in other steel producing countries, to a more imaginative, less legalistic attack, based on the economics of adjustment, and sheltering under the rules of Article XIX, if, as is possible, the worst is yet to come for international trade in steel.*

Automobiles

The restraint applied by Japan to its exports of automobiles, after taking cognizance of the state of play in Congress, is a different matter. Here the United States is perceived to be going outside the rules for the viability of the trade relations system, to be abandoning the escape clause, to be acting in an extra legal manner, without regard to the international rules the United States did so much to put in place. This has occasioned some sanctimonious handwringing in Europe, on the theme that this noninterventionist administration is shown not to mean what it says about "free trade." This strikes me as rather odd. Japan has accepted to restrict passenger vehicles to an annual level of 11 percent of the UK market, after industry-to-industry discussions which would be illegal if ventured by the United States and Canadian industries. Japan tacitly tolerates a restriction to 3 percent of the French market, and to 2,000 vehicles a year to Italy. Part of the US problem is, of course, that Japanese vehicles are denied the market they could exploit in Western Europe. The pressure on the US market is thus greater than it would be if Europeans applied the international rules to imports from Japan. But of equal importance—the United States has managed, on this matter, to deny itself the benefit of the international rules.

The need for a restraint to be applied by Japan arises from the fact that the legal formulation of the causality requirement in the US escape clause provision is different from that in Article XIX. Without examining the precise implications of these differences, and without necessarily agreeing with the comments of certain US experts, suffice it to say that in certain circumstances application of the US escape

---

* *Ed. note*: For a discussion of the move to US quotas on European steel, subsequent to the preparation of this chapter, see chapter 1, this volume.

clause criteria could conceivably result in restrictive action by the United States that could not meet the GATT criteria. In other circumstances, application of the US criteria can result in relief being denied under the US escape clause, although an adequate GATT Article XIX case could be made. In the instance of imports of automobiles, on my reading of the International Trade Commission report, the latter case applies. The case for imposing safeguard protection would have been all the more compelling if account were taken, as it should be, in the use of Article XIX, of the impact of restrictions by other countries.

My general conclusion is, therefore, that the United States is creating a problem for itself, and getting a bad press, because the escape clause of domestic legislation is not in conformity with Article XIX. Given all the self-righteous flak the United States has taken over this issue, the United States ought to propose international discussions of what Article XIX means in regard to causality, what Article XIX should say about restrictions applied by third countries, and then bring its legislation into conformity with the international drafting.

DISC

The question of DISC raises quite a different problem. Here the question is how to make the GATT dispute-settlement mechanism work. Even the United States needs an effective dispute-settlement mechanism in the trade relations system. The problem raised by the report of the DISC panel, and indeed, the other panels composed of the same individuals that addressed the US complaints in regard to certain European tax practices, was that the reports were not adequate. The one on DISC was the most thorough, but, considering the economic importance of the issues and the complexities of the tax practice and commercial policy issues raised by the DISC system, a much more detailed analysis was warranted. That is not to say that the panel finding was incorrect.

The United States has, with some help from others, done some damage to the dispute-settlement process by delaying so long in agreeing upon the membership of the panel, by coupling the DISC complaints to their own complaints about European tax practices (which, given their relevance, should have been instigated much earlier), and then by haggling about the findings. After all, all of the negotiations in the Tokyo Round did accept the "out" for the United States in the notes to the subsidies-countervail code, and the agreement regarding export prices to controlled subsidiaries. Rather than negotiating over the panel findings for quite so long, it might have been preferable to have sought a complete set of rehearings. Surely the GATT system should provide for that eventuality.

Conclusion

These important US trade policy actions have seemed objectionable to some, have created problems for others, or have not conformed to the ideal world of some observers. I do not attach the major share of the blame for the strains and contradictions in the trade relations system to actions by the United States. The European interest in creating a preference system around the European heartland, so well described by Gardner Patterson,[1] has done more damage to the system than any policy misconceptions, misunderstandings, and miscalculations in Washington. Moreover, it is not from Europe that we are likely to get the intellectual initiatives and inventiveness, or the necessary recognition of value in a system of order that will be necessary to rebuild the system. The United States, as always, will have to provide the leadership, unlikely as this may seem at this juncture. I could go on to say what initiatives I think are necessary to restore a minimum of coherence to the system, to reduce to tolerable levels the bias in favor of the big entities, to make the system offer more real promise to developing countries, and in general to move back to nondiscrimination as central to trade policy relations between states of different power. Efforts in such directions would serve a variety of US trade policy interests and might prove of more real value, in terms of economic policy and foreign policy, than trying to extend the present incoherent and contradictory system to new sectors.

---

[1] "The European Community as a Threat to the System," chapter 7, this volume.

CHAPTER 9

The Micro- and Macroeconomics of Foreign Sales to Japan

Gary R. Saxonhouse

No lesser mind than that of Diety itself can keep up with all the subtleties and rules of Japanese import trade which are so effective in excluding American products.

—Senator Russell B. Long
Report on the Reciprocal Trade and Investment Act of 1982, page 36

I would like to take this opportunity to ask those who are engaged in public administration as well as the people in private firms who are bearing the brunt of everyday activities to be even more clear and forthcoming in taking the attitude of extending a welcoming hand to foreign manufactured goods and not discriminating against them.

—Prime Minister Zenko Suzuki
Ministry of Foreign Affairs Press Release May 28, 1982

With the exception of the high-profile treatment presently given to European competition in the American steel market, most current American concern with reciprocity in international economic relations is focused on Japan.

Barriers to Foreign Sales in Japan

It is widely believed that foreign access to the Japanese home market remains tightly controlled. This belief has such widespread credence that it may be something of a shock to discover that by the traditional indices of the international economic system foreign access to the Japanese market would have to be considered excellent.

Tariffs

In 1982, the (import-share-weighted) average level of tariffs on industrial and mining products in Japan was lower than in the United

States and for all the members of the European Economic Community (EEC). By March 1983, when Japan will have implemented virtually all the tariff cuts agreed to in the Multilateral Trade Negotiations (MTN), this average level will be no more than 2.9 percent.[1] This level, which will include some unilateral reductions beyond the rates agreed to at Geneva, will not only be lower than the levels of all other major market-oriented industrial economies, but it will also be lower than the average tariff level of any of these economies even after 1987 when all Tokyo Round agreements have been phased in. In 1987, US average tariff levels will still be 4.3 percent. Among the nine members of the European Economic Community average rates will vary from 5.2 percent to 6.9 percent.[2]

Of course, these average tariff levels are deceptively low, and the dispersion of tariffs across sectors and subsectors can make effective rates somewhat higher. Nonetheless, there is no reason to believe that Japanese patterns of dispersion will differ from those of its trading partners in such fashion as to make its average nominal rates an extremely poor index of the comparative impact of its effective rates. Similarly, and with special reference to American reciprocity concerns, these nominal tariff averages for the United States and Japan also reflect the bilateral relationship. US tariff rates on Japanese goods are higher than Japanese tariff rates on US goods.[3]

Given these low average levels it is not surprising to find that were Japan to join with its trading partners in removing its remaining tariff barriers, the impact on the Japanese trade balance would be quite small.[4] In the perspective of a prospective $19 billion bilateral surplus in trade with the United States in 1982, it is difficult to find a plausible sectoral and geographic allocation of tariff reductions which could have a significant impact on such an imbalance.

[1] Japanese government announcement of 1982 Second Round of Market Liberalization Measures, May 1982.

[2] A. V. Deardorff and R. M. Stern, "The Economic Effects of Complete Elimination of Post-Tokyo Round Tariffs on the Major Industrial and Developing Countries," chapter 20, this volume.

[3] E. Collado, "Reciprocity Legislation," in G. C. Hufbauer, ed., *US International Economic Policy, 1981: A Draft Report*, (Washington: Georgetown University Law Center, 1982). Remaining Japanese tariffs whose incidence is of interest to the United States include those on manufactured tobacco products, wood and wood products, kraft papers and paper products, electronic components, leather, and chocolate confectionary products.

[4] Deardorff and Stern, "The Economic Effects."

TABLE 9.1   NUMBER OF RESIDUAL IMPORT QUOTAS IN MAJOR
ECONOMIES

	Number of import quotas	Agricultural products	Industrial products	Discriminatory import restrictions against Japan
United States	7	1	6	—
Canada	5	4	1	—
United Kingdom	3	1	2	—
France	46	19	27	22
West Germany	4	3	1	3
Italy	8	3	5	35
Benelux	5	2	3	9
Japan	27	22	5	—

Source: Keizai kikaku chō, *Keizai hakushō*, 1981.

Nontariff Barriers

What is surprisingly true for tariff barriers is equally true for non-tariff barriers. Provided that nontariff barriers are defined exclusively as (1) import quotas, (2) approval and settlement systems, (3) customs practices, (4) application of standards, (5) government procurement policies, (6) government monopolies and pricing policies, (7) explicit trade subsidies to specific industries, (8) export incentive measures, and (9) so-called voluntary export restraint imposed on trading partners, then it is likely that Japanese nontariff barriers are no more restrictive and quite possibly, less restrictive, than those imposed by its trading partners. It is quite possible that the removal of all nontariff barriers among the world's major market-oriented economies would benefit Japan substantially more than its trading partners.

Quotas.   Japan maintains a substantial but by no means internationally unusual number of import quotas (table 9.1). Of the 27 import quotas which are maintained, 22 are directed against agricultural products and only 5 are directed against manufactures. While the agricultural quotas continue to include such long-time objects of US-Japanese economic diplomacy as beef and oranges, the manufactured products remaining under quota include nothing more exciting than coal briquettes and four types of leather products.

Customs Valuation, Standards, Testing, Government and State Monopoly Procurement, and Subsidies.   Since the onset of preparations for the Tokyo Round of Multilateral Trade Negotiations, it has been understood that import licensing procedures, customs valuation, gov-

ernment procurement practices, subsidies, and standards might be
more important than many of the traditional barriers in restricting
international trade in goods.[5] While Japan was often a target during
the negotiations meant to develop standards to govern international
behavior in these matters, after protracted diplomacy it was possible
for Japan to become a signatory to these codes. Notwithstanding the
Tokyo Round negotiations or perhaps as a byproduct, there continues
to be substantial criticism of Japanese practices in these areas. There
has been continuing criticism of

- restrictions on foreign purchases by such state trading monopolies
as the Japan Tobacco and Salt Public Corporation and the Livestock
Industry Promotion Corporation and such quasi-public corporations
as Nippon Telephone and Telegraph[6]
- idiosyncratic standards and testing requirements imposed, ostensibly for health and environmental reasons for pharmaceuticals, medical equipment, cosmetics, and for processed and unprocessed agricultural products
- Japan-specific consumer product safety requirements, particularly
for electrical products, motor vehicles, and sporting goods
- Japanese research and development subsidies for certain high technology industries and unduly generous Japanese government subsidy
of export credits.

Only in the area of valuation procedures is it generally accepted that
Japan has now responded almost fully to foreign criticism.

For the present, Japan has responded to the continuing criticism
of its practices with two very high profile trade liberalization announcements in January and May of this year.* For the most part,
these announcements flesh out Japanese compliance with MTN codes

---

[5] F. Brown and J. Whalley in "General Equilibrium Evaluation of Tariff-Cutting Proposals in the Tokyo Round and Comparisons with More Extensive Liberalization of World Trade," *Economic Journal* (December 1980), in an analysis of the impact of the removal of all pre-Tokyo Round nontariff barriers, find the global welfare gain at least double what might be gained from the removal of all tariff barriers.

[6] After protracted negotiations NTT was included in the Government Procurement Code but other state corporations such as the New Tokyo Airport Corporation, the Electric Energy Company, and the Japan Broadcasting Company remain outside these agreements.

* *Ed. note*: Further liberalization measures were announced early in 1983 upon the visit of the new Prime Minister Yasuhiro Nakasone to the United States.

already agreed to three years earlier and accelerate the implementation of steps also agreed to earlier. Nonetheless, if Japanese commitments to fully and fairly implement these steps, backed by an explicit statement by Prime Minister Suzuki, can be taken at face value, then a substantial part of the objectives of more than ten years of strenuous criticism of the character of the application of Japanese standards, health and safety legislation and even of Japanese government procurement will have been achieved. The many years of acrimonious trade relations, however, have many American observers most skeptical as to whether this will really happen.

The Removal of All Barriers. The studies that have been done on the impact of the removal of Japanese nontariff barriers such as the remaining agricultural and manufactured goods quotas, and the standards, safety evaluation testing, subsidy, and government and state monopoly procurement practices just discussed, do not suggest a quantitative impact of such magnitude as to wreak a significant change on the character of Japan's global relations or on such structural features of Japan's trade accounts as the large bilateral surplus with the United States.[7] In particular, in 1982, in the light of voluntary export restraint on Japanese automobile exports to the United States

---

[7] In a study prepared for the US Department of Labor in mid-1980, Office of Foreign Economic Research, Bureau of International Labor Affairs, US Department of Labor, *Japanese Non-Tariff Barriers: A Selective Evaluation*, it was estimated that the removal of all Japanese nontariff barriers would result in an increase in Japanese imports of little more than $2 billion in 1979 prices. Of these $2 billion in imports, $315 million would be sourced from the United States. Of this $315 million, $325 million would be from agriculture, fisheries, and food imports. These results are comparable to estimates of $650 million to $1.1 billion in increased US exports to Japan prepared by Arthur D. Little, Inc. for NIRA, a research arm of the Japanese government. Arthur D. Little, Inc., *The Japanese Non-Tariff Trade Barrier Issue: American Views and Implications for Japan-US Trade Relations* (a report prepared for the National Institute for Research Advancement). Note both the US Department of Labor and the ADL estimates purport to take account not only the impact of quotas, customs evaluation, standard and testing practices, government and state monopoly procurement, and subsidies, but also the impact of such intangibles as administrative guidance and the Japanese distribution system. In an analysis first constructed in 1978, Yujiro Hayami estimated that beef import liberalization could result in an increase in beef imports to $1 billion annually (1978 prices). Y. Hayami, "Trade Benefits to All: A Design of the Beef Import Liberalization in Japan," *American Journal of Agricultural Economics* (May 1979).

and the European Community, orderly marketing agreements (OMA) for Japanese color television sets, apparently responsible behavior of Japanese steel manufacturers under American and European trigger price mechanisms (TPM), and other voluntary export restraints, to point out only the conspicuous import barriers imposed by Japan's trading partners, the conventionally estimated $2 billion to $3 billion worth of total import restrictions do not make Japan a closed market and the $1 billion to $2 billion of lost American exports to Japan do not mean a lack of reciprocity in US-Japan economic relations. Indeed, it appears that the removal of remaining Japanese quotas and the complete liberalization of standards, safety evaluation, subsidies, testing, and government and state monopoly procurement practices at the same time that voluntary export restraints on Japanese exports to the United States might be removed would result in an increase, rather than a diminution of Japan's bilateral trade surplus with the United States.

The Impact of Previous Liberalizations

In historical perspective it should not be a surprising finding that the removal of tariff and nontariff barriers would not have much impact on US-Japanese economic relations. Already in the early 1970s, it was well understood that the Japanese trade structure was extremely distinctive by international standards.[8] The low share of manufactures in total imports, the low ratio of manufactured imports to GNP and the lack of Japanese participation in global intraindustry specialization were all being widely discussed at that time. There was a consensus on both sides of the Pacific in both official and private circles that Japanese commercial policy was a major cause of these patterns. This view was expressed in Japan in the Economic White Papers of 1970 and 1971, in articles, public statements, and widely circulated research memoranda by at least some officials at Tsusanshō (the Ministry of International Trade and Industry) and by popular articles by prominent academic economists in such influential journals as *Gendai keizai*, *Ekonomisuto*, and *Chuo koron*.[9] And there was a good deal of basic research which supported this point of view.[10]

[8] These discussions are reviewed in G. Saxonhouse, "Employment, Imports, the Yen and the Dollar," in H. Rosovsky, ed., *Discord in the Pacific* (Washington: Columbia Books, 1972).

[9] See, for example, the EPA official, T. Yamada's, "Yunyū jiyuka to bukka no sokan bunseki [Import Liberalization and the Analysis of Price Change]," *Boeki to kanzei* [Trade and Tariffs], vol. 18 (January 1970), pp. 42–57. Among

Intense domestic and international pressure led to a rapid acceleration of Japan's trade liberalization policies in the early 1970s. Between September 1970 and April 1972 the number of items restricted by quota under the General Agreement on Tariffs and Trade (GATT) fell from 90 to 33. Hand in hand with this trade liberalization came changes in the two other factors widely held at this time as major barriers to foreign access to the Japanese market. As a result of the Nixon administration's New Economic Policy, the yen began to appreciate markedly after August 1971, and there occurred a major liberalization in Japanese government policies toward foreign investment in Japan. These steps were followed in 1972 with a 20 percent across-the-board tariff cut covering 1,865 items.

Unhappily, these steep declines in average tariff levels and in the number of goods under quotas were accomplished without much perceptible impact on either US-Japan trade friction or even on the

---

popular articles, see Y. Shinkai, "Wagakuni tsusho seisaku no kihon rinen [Fundamental Doctrine of Japanese Commercial Policy]," *Gendai keizai* [Contemporary Economics], vol. 5 (June 1972), pp. 8–23; and H. Uzawa, "Nihon keizai-no kokusaiteki koritsu-tsuka chosei no shindankai o megutte [Japan's Isolation in the International System—Over the New Stage of Currency Change]," *Chuo koron* [Central Review] (February 1972), pp. 102–119.

[10] For example, a series of articles by Keio University economists Iwao Ozaki and Yoko Sazanami attempted a comprehensive comparison of West Germany and other Organization for Economic Cooperation and Development (OECD) countries and Japan's trade structure using 1965 and 1970 input-output tables which had been constructed for use with highly disaggregated international trade data. They found among many other results that by comparison with Canada, the United States, Belgium, the Netherlands, West Germany, France, Italy, and the United Kingdom, Japan imports very little in lines closely related to what it exports. Japan in 1965 and 1970 participated only in an extremely limited way in the intraindustry specialization so characteristic of trade among other advanced industrial countries. After examining other explanations, Ozaki and Sazanami conclude that Japan's different pattern was the result of the government policy of curbing imports of manufactured goods. I. Ozaki and J. Sagara, "Sangyō kōzō to boeki kōzō no henka [Changes in Industrial Structure and Trade Structure]," *Mita gakkai zasshi* [Mita Academic Magazine], vol. 65 (December 1972), pp. 38–62; Y. Sazanami, "Kōgyō seihin boeki ni tsuite no shiron [Notes on Trade in Manufactures]," *Mita gakkai zasshi*, vol. 66 (September 1973), pp. 612–43; and Y. Sazanami and N. Hamaguchi, "Sangyōnai bungyō to kokusai boeki [Intra-industry Specialization and International Trade]" *Mita gakkai zasshi*, vol. 69 (June 1976).

TABLE 9.2   SHARE OF MANUFACTURES IN TOTAL IMPORTS

Year	Percentage (index, 1973 = 100)	Year	Percentage (index, 1973 = 100)	Year	Percentage (index, 1973 = 100)
Japan					
1971	28.6 (94)	1974	23.6 (77)	1977	20.8 (68)
1972	29.6 (97)	1975	20.3 (67)	1978	24.6 (81)
1973	30.5 (100)	1976	21.5 (70)	1979	24.5 (80)
				1980	22.1 (73)
United States					
1971	66.8 (103)	1974	55.7 (86)	1977	53.2 (82)
1972	67.9 (105)	1975	53.8 (83)	1978	59.0 (91)
1973	64.8 (100)	1976	54.3 (84)	1979	55.0 (85)
				1980	54.8 (85)
United Kingdom					
1971	50.9 (91)	1974	51.5 (92)	1977	58.4 (104)
1972	54.7 (97)	1975	52.2 (93)	1978	63.9 (114)
1973	56.2 (100)	1976	54.3 (97)	1979	65.7 (117)
				1980	66.9 (119)
West Germany					
1971	58.1 (100)	1974	52.9 (91)	1977	57.0 (98)
1972	59.9 (103)	1975	55.1 (95)	1978	59.4 (103)
1973	57.9 (100)	1976	55.4 (96)	1979	57.9 (100)
				1980	58.3 (101)
France					
1971	66.3 (102)	1974	57.8 (89)	1977	58.0 (90)
1972	64.6 (100)	1975	57.3 (88)	1978	60.3 (93)
1973	64.8 (100)	1976	58.7 (91)	1979	60.2 (93)
				1980	60.9 (94)
Italy					
1971	48.5 (98)	1974	43.5 (88)	1977	45.1 (91)
1972	49.2 (100)	1975	42.1 (85)	1978	46.6 (95)
1973	49.3 (100)	1976	44.5 (90)	1979	48.1 (98)
				1980	49.7 (100)

Source: Organization for Economic Cooperation and Development, *Statistics of Foreign Trade*, various issues.

TABLE 9.3   IMPORTS OF MANUFACTURED GOODS AS A PROPORTION
OF GNP (percentage)

	1960	*1970*	*1980*
United States	1	2	5
Japan	2	2	2
West Germany	6	9	12
France	4	8	11
United Kingdom	5	9	14

Source: David R. Macdonald, "Statement," Subcommittee on Asian and Pacific Affairs, US House of Representatives.

quantitative indices used to assess the degree of market access given to foreign products. As can be seen from table 9.2 since 1973, the share of foreign manufactured products in total imports has fallen rather than risen. Indeed for no other major industrial country has this share fallen as far. The share of foreign manufactured products in total Japanese imports in 1980 was 22.4 percent. For none of the other major industrial countries in 1980 was this share less than 48 percent.

The declining share of manufactured goods in total imports does not necessarily mean that in the face of the removal of trade barriers there has been a major constriction in the access of the products of foreign manufacturers to the Japanese market. Of course, the change in this share after 1973 is in large measure the result of the change in the prices of the fuels, minerals, and agricultural products that Japan imports. When current import quantities are valued at 1970 prices, conceptual difficulties aside, the share of manufactured products in total imports today is far above what it was in the early 1970s. In 1970 prices, 1979 imports of manufactured goods are a full 50 percent larger share of total imports than they were in the early 1970s.

Changing terms of trade, by itself, however, cannot so easily explain Japan's continued low manufactured goods import share as a proportion of GNP. As seen in table 9.3, in 1970 Japanese imports of manufactured goods as a proportion of GNP were 2 percent. In 1980 this proportion remained 2 percent. During the same 10 years imports of manufactured goods as a proportion of GNP rose dramatically for all other major industrial countries.

Also, even allowing for a dramatically changing price structure, imports of manufactured goods as a proportion of GNP are well below what was optimistically projected in the early 1970s as the first widely publicized trade liberalizations were occurring. In 1972, the Japanese Economic Research Center, Japan's premier forecasting group, pub-

TABLE 9.4   THE STRUCTURE OF JAPAN'S IMPORTS, 1960–69, AND
PROJECTIONS TO 1980 (shares)

Year	Total imports	Food and Beverages (SITC 0,1)	Raw Materials (SITC 2,4)	Mineral Fuels (SITC 3)
1960	100.0	13.6	49.5	14.1
1965	100.0	19.3	36.5	19.0
1969	100.0	14.2	33.0	20.3
1980	100.0	9.0	19.2	18.8

Year	Chemicals (SITC 5)	Machinery (SITC 7)	Other (SITC 6,8)
1960	6.4	9.0	7.3
1965	5.2	9.6	9.8
1969	5.5	10.6	15.3
1980	5.8	19.0	38.1

Source: Nihon keizai kenkyū senta (Japan Economic Research Center), *Sekai no naka no nihon keizai—1980 nen (Japan in the World Economy 1980)*, 1972.

lished an extremely detailed two volume treatment discussing what these trade liberalization steps would mean for the Japanese economy. Fashionably titled, *Sekai no naka no nihon keizai-1980-nen [Japan in the World Economy in the 1980s]*, the Japan Economic Research Center study confidently projected that by 1980, manufactured imports as a share of GNP would reach 4 percent, twice the level actually achieved. Similarly, it was projected that by 1980, the share of manufactured goods in total Japanese imports would rise to European levels. As seen in table 9.4, it was projected that Japanese imports of manufactured goods as a proportion of total imports would reach 53 percent. This is 60 percent above what the share of manufactured imports was in 1980, even if all imports are valued at pre-Yom Kippur War prices.

How Can Japan's Distinctive Trade Pattern Be Explained?

From the preceding discussion it is possible to conclude not only that Japan's imports of manufactured goods are low by conventional indices, but also that past major Japanese trade liberalizations came nowhere near fulfilling expectations and did not raise the ratio of imported manufactured goods to GNP or the proportion of manufactured goods in total imports. Either preceding research incorrectly attributed Japan's distinctive trade structure to tariff and nontariff barriers, or following Senator Russell B. Long (D-La.), other policy instruments which have not been the traditional concern of international diplomacy need to be examined. Perhaps the roots of Japan's distinctive trade structure and large bilateral surplus with the United States are so fundamental as to be impervious to either public or private policy manipulation.

Towards the Harmonization of Economic Practices

Where once Japan might have been considered a pillar of the international economic system by simply maintaining nondiscriminatory tariffs, and refraining from overt quotas, the agenda for international economic harmony is now much more complicated. The past 20 years have seen an enormous increase not only in the volume of international trade, but also in its relative importance for each of the major market-oriented economies. International trade's role as a source of benefits, but also as a cause of price instability, unemployment, and structural dislocation has greatly increased over the years. The greatly increased benefits and costs of international trade have in turn greatly reinforced two seemingly self-canceling tendencies in international economic diplomacy.

The greatly increased tempo of international trade has greatly increased the number of industries seeking and getting protection from the consequences of liberal trade. At the same time that protectionist pressures have introduced new product-specific voluntary and involuntary restrictions, such complaints have also encouraged a further extension of the liberal practices of the international economic system. In the interests of bolstering a crumbling structure of legitimacy, many practices that had been an implicit and accepted part of the postwar international economic framework have been singled out and made the subject of bilateral and multilateral negotiations.

The increasing appreciation of how barriers in the international movement of capital and technology, and discriminatory domestic microeconomic policies can undermine the global benefits resulting from liberal agreements on trade in goods has meant much expanded rules of the game for participants in the international economic system. If domestic policy instruments can always be good, functional substitutes for the foreign economic policy instruments which are the traditional objects of international diplomacy, it seems that liberal domestic economic policy by all rather than just some of the major participants in the international economic system, is a necessary prerequisite for the continuing legitimacy of that system. Thus, the thrust of international economic diplomacy has already moved from tariffs to quotas and from quotas to standards, subsidies and government procurement. The agenda for international economic harmony is now demanding that much of the domestic economic affairs of participants in the international system be governed by fully competitive open bidding and contractual relationships. The history of postwar international economic diplomacy has shown that implicitly, but not yet explicitly, the increasingly difficult task of maintaining the legitimacy of the international economic system requires not just nondiscriminatory treatment of foreign goods in national markets, but also a more far-reaching harmonization of microeconomic institutions.

Japan's Illiberal Institutions

Japan's position in the international economic system as a large, rapidly growing, export-oriented, natural resource-poor market economy, has meant, as the reciprocity discussions make clear, that many of the complaints during the past two decades about the increasing costs of participation in the international economic system must name it as the culprit. A good share of the expanded agenda of international economic diplomacy, and, in particular, a good share of the interest in the harmonization of domestic economic practices in the name of transparency has been motivated by a desire to insure that the very successful, but traditionally illiberal Japanese economy is competing fairly with its trading partners.

Unfortunately, the very great success of the Japanese economy, particularly relative to American performance, has left many among the Japanese policy élites increasingly resentful of continual demands that Japan conform in increasingly intimate ways to the full liberal paridigm. Indeed, many elements of Japanese government and industry have gone to great effort to convince Japan's political and economic élites and the broader body politic in its trading partners that it is the rest of the world, and not Japan, which should be adjusting economic institutions to improve global performance. Visitors returning from Tokyo tell all who will listen that there is an alternative, if illiberal, Japanese way of conducting economic affairs and that many of Japan's trading partners' problems could be solved if only they would learn from rather than lecture Japan.

From the foreign perspective Japan's distinctive, but illiberal way of conducting economic affairs includes: (1) a major government role in formulating and facilitating an extremely high profile industrial policy; (2) special government impact on the financial system through an enormous volume of postal savings, through nonmarket forced placement of government debt, and through direct influence on the size and composition of bank loan portfolios; (3) existence of large bank-centered industrial groups and the underdevelopment of equity markets and venture capital institutions; (4) existence of very large industrial group-associated general trading companies which dominate Japan's foreign trade and important elements of Japan's distribution system; (5) presence of legislation and administrative regulation continuing to reinforce, notwithstanding great changes in recent years, Japan's highly inefficient distribution system; (6) pervasive use of cartels and an absence of continuing antitrust enforcement; (7) despite great changes recently, continuing significant limitations for Japanese households on the forms and terms under which capital assets and liabilities can be acquired; (8) treatment of Japanese labor as a fixed cost rather than as a variable cost over the course of the business cycle; (9) incomplete and delayed implementation of capital and interest rate liberalization and yen internationalization; (10) incomplete and delayed implementation of competitive bidding practices for procurement in both the public and the private sector; and (11) incomplete and delayed liberalization of service sector transactions.

For each of the 11 illiberal elements listed above, it is possible to hypothesize dynamic benefits accruing to the Japanese economy from their existence. Some of these benefits may have been important during the Japanese economy's adolescence, but may not now be important even though the market distorting institution generating them persists. In other instances, the benefits are as important today as they were in the 1950s. In still other instances, they have never been important. Regardless of benefits, past or present, each of the 11 institutions does cause major static distortions that are transmitted through Japan's international transactions to the global economy. The presumption must be that these market distortions, while clearly creating some gains as well as losses, will result in an aggregate loss of global welfare. These losses and gains may be distributed quite unevenly as between Japan and its trading partners and within these economies, as between various productive sectors, as between owners of physical and human assets, and as between consumers and producers. The only general conclusion that might be drawn from an analysis of the impact of these many market distortions is that their overseas impact almost certainly is not self-canceling, that almost certainly these impacts will not be politically neutral; and in this way, their existence will tend to undermine the legitimacy of the international economic system.

Where Does Japan's Comparative Advantage Lie?

Japanese trade structure may well be related to the Japanese economy's distinctive economic institutions. As is often suggested by foreign critics of Japan's external economic relations, perhaps only a radical change in Japan's economic institutions and attitudes will change the character of Japan's international trade structure. This is not necessarily the counsel of despair. As seen from even the recent Japanese liberalization announcements with their special emphasis on high technology and the service sector, however efficacious or otherwise this may be, the operation of almost any Japanese domestic institution is considered, at least by many in Japan's political élite, as a legitimate object of international economic discussion.

Accept that legitimate participation in the international economic system requires fully liberal domestic institutions and that Japan willingly or unwillingly succumbs to this imperative, and suppose further that all American producers of tradable goods and services immerse themselves in Japanese language and culture, how much difference would this make? Given the intangible character of many of the changes contemplated it is probably best not to attempt to assess what each liberalizing step might mean for the Japanese trade structure. Rather an alternative perspective on the trade consequences of illiberal Japanese domestic institutions can be gained by examining the evolution of Japanese comparative advantage in a cross-national empirical framework.

Economic theory does not dictate that countries' with similar per capita GNPs should have manufactured imports bear more or less the same proportion to total imports, GNP, or population. Before such comparisons among even advanced industrial economies can be made, allowance must be made for differences in natural resource endowments, distance from trading partners, and differences in the quantity and quality of labor and capital among other factors. If Japanese experience is properly normalized for Japan's capital stock, labor force, geographic position, and natural resource endowment, is there any variance left in the Japanese experience relative to that of other major industrial economies that might be explained by the existence of illiberal Japanese economic institutions?

As described in Appendix 9.A and following Hollis B. Chenery's work, it is possible to develop standards for normal export and import patterns by empirically implementing cross-nationally a version of the Hecksher–Ohlin theory of comparative advantage.[11] Unlike Chenery's

[11] Hollis B. Chenery, "Patterns of Industrial Growth," *American Economic Review*, vol. 50 (September 1960), pp. 624–54.

work and appropriate to a consideration of Japan's special position, this work involves an extensive treatment of the role of natural resources and the differing qualities of factor inputs. By drawing directly on modern production theory it is possible to obtain an explicit functional form within which the Hecksher–Ohlin framework can be implemented.[12] This general equilibrium trade framework in turn allows a multiplicative errors-in-variables specification which permits the estimation of national quality of factor-inputs differentials as a by-product of the estimation of the entire analytical framework.

Using these procedures on cross-national data for the period prior to 1973, as reported in Appendix 9.A, it is found that there is nothing abnormal about Japanese trade and industrial patterns. Japanese behavior can be explained within the framework common to most other participants in the world economy and without particular reference to distinctive Japanese policies. There is evidence that Japan does have a distinctive trade structure by comparison with other advanced industrial economies, but only because the Japanese economy's other attributes are also distinctive. No other advanced industrial economy combines such high quality labor with such poor natural resources at such a great distance from its major trading partners. It is these distinctive characteristics and not, for example, an industrial policy which the US might or might not wish to emulate which give Japan a robust comparative advantage in so many manufacturing products. It is the natural resource wealth of the United States and the natural resource poverty of Japan, far more than the real or imagined differences in the motivation of factory workers in the two countries which explains the relative Japanese success in so many manufacturing lines.

Among the 109 commodity equations actually estimated using cross-national data, in only 17 was it not possible to reject the hypothesis that sectorally specific Japanese policies were at work. The 17 commodities where statistically significant country terms indicated the tangible differential impact of such policies include:

Commodity	SITC
Maize (unmilled)	SITC 044[a]
Other cereals	SITC 045[a]
Bananas (including plantains)	SITC 051.3[a]

(Continued overleaf)

---

[12] The modern production theory made use of is described in M. D. Intriligator and D.A. Kendrick, eds., *Frontiers of Quantitative Economics*, vol. 2 (New York: Elsevier, 1974).

Commodity (Continued)	SITC
Other Fruits and Nuts	SITC 057.2[a]
Saw logs and Veneer logs—nonconifer	SITC 242.3[a]
Crude Fertilizers	SITC 27[a]
Plastic Material	SITC 58[b]
Glass	SITC 664[c]
Pearls, Precious, and Semiprecious Stones	SITC 667[a]
Aluminum	SITC 684[a]
Zinc	SITC 686[b]
Aircraft and Parts	SITC 734[d]
Footwear	SITC 85[a]
Photo and Cinema Supplies	SITC 862[b]
Medical Instruments	SITC 872[c]
Pianos and Other Musical Instruments	SITC 891.4[c]

a. Statistically significantly less than zero; fewer imports.
b. Statistically significantly less than zero; fewer exports.
c. Statistically significantly less than zero; greater exports.
d. Statistically significantly less than zero; greater imports.

While some of these products are closely associated in the public mind with Japan either as exports or imports, taken together they comprise no more than 4.9 percent of Japan's gross external trade.[13] Note also of these 17 statistically significant Japanese terms, 4 work to diminish rather than to enhance Japan's secular trade surplus. By contrast with the Japanese results, 24 Italian country terms covering 11.7 percent of Italy's trade are statistically significant. Not surprisingly, the impact of France's policies appear to have been still larger. Fully 32 country terms are statistically significant. These 32 terms account for 16.0 percent of France's foreign trade. Even less surprising are the results for the heavily regulated Korean economy. Forty-three country terms covering 28.3 percent of Korean foreign trade are statistically significant.

The above results do help to rationalize some of the failed forecasts in Japan of the future share of manufactured imports in GNP and in total imports. As was noted earlier, it was expected that the removal of formal restrictions in the early 1970s and changes in Japanese attitudes toward imports would drive manufactured imports to European levels. The results obtained here suggest that quite apart from

[13] Note it is unlikely that the sector specific additive country terms are statistically significant because the multiplicative aggregate input specific country terms (the input quality terms) are present in this analysis. Government preoccupation with a particular sector could not raise the quality of capital and labor for the economy as a whole without creating a host of statistically significant additive country terms in both the favored and unfavored sectors.

energy-induced changes in the terms of trade, the commercial policy changes and attitudinal changes of the 1970s did not bring about great changes in the Japanese commodity structure of imports because from the perspective of the policies and practices in other major industrial and Japanese trading partners, these policies involved only relatively small trade distortions.

These results should also make both US and Japanese diplomats wary of expecting too much from or promising too much for current and projected Japanese liberalization programs. Note it is also particularly difficult to argue that in the period after 1973 Japanese trade structure became somehow newly distorted by government policy or private restrictive practices and for that reason 1980's Japanese liberalization programs will yield tangible changes in trade flows when few were forthcoming from the 1970's programs.

Japan's Illiberal Institutions and US Trade Policy

If Japan's illiberal institutions cannot be shown to be unfairly tampering with Japanese comparative advantage, need US trade policy concern itself with them? It may be, however, that Japan's illiberal institutions have no special role to play in explaining distinctive Japanese trade patterns because their impact has already been embedded in the estimated parameters of the analytical framework. Japan's trading partners may have equally illiberal, if less highly publicized economic institutions of their own.[14] If this is the case, no statistically significant country terms will result, but successful reciprocal reductions of such barriers, without any special onus being placed on Japan, might improve global welfare.

More likely, public policy, in general, and trade policy, in particular, should avoid out of fear and envy, assuming too much for the illiberal institutions as might be embodied, for example, in Japanese industrial policy and Japanese science and technology policy. The empirical results just presented suggest that distinctive Japanese institutions are better thought of as substitutes rather than complements for functionally equivalent institutions that exist in the United States. In such a situation even if Japan-distinctive policies have no net effect

---

[14] For example, in Japan by comparison with the United States and the United Kingdom, the coefficient of variation in effective capital taxes across sectors and in the ratio of effective capital tax rates to effective labor rates across sectors is very low. See Appendix Table 9A.2. Implicitly or explicitly, the United States and United Kingdom use tax policy much more than does Japan to make sectoral specific allocation decisions.

on Japanese economic performance, unlike import barriers, it is not always possible to remove any single institution without having a substantial impact on the operation of the Japanese economy.

In the case of Japanese industrial policy, for example, this institution operates in some measure as a substitute for the information provided by American capital markets. Japanese industrial policy compensates for the continuing absence of full competition in the supply of capital. Large elements of discretion give the Japanese government a means through the banking system so that it can directly influence this allocation.[15] This concentration, which dates back to at least Japan's Meiji period, not only makes possible but also necessitates a government presence. Without countervailing Japanese government pressure, in the absence of market discipline and in the presence of yet another illiberal Japanese institution, the bank centered industrial group, the complicated pressures of interindustrial group politics could very well lead to large socially suboptimal allocations of resources. It is this interlocking of Japan's illiberal institutions which often makes piecemeal liberal responses to international pressure so difficult. In so many cases, the illiberal elements fit together into a grand, if implicit, design, which does allow the Japanese economy to function successfully.

Somewhat more narrowly, the Japanese government's widely discussed interfirm cooperative sponsored research programs in high technology are another element of Japanese industrial policy that can be seen as a substitute for, not a complement of, American-style practices. Unlike the American case, in Japan, training of workers and managers outside the workplace is not heavily subsidized by national and prefectural governments or by private associations. Compared to the United States, most training is provided by the firm. The widespread adoption in larger Japanese companies of permanent employment and firm experience-related wage programs means these firms can provide this training at full subsidy without tuition charge and still recoup a competitive rate of return. Inevitably, the training provided by firms, as opposed to university and research institutes, will be better suited to the firms' needs but will for that reason be narrow in scope, more task-specific and less theoretically oriented.

---

[15] This is an increasingly controversial point for many Japanese economists. See, for example, Akiyoshi Horiuchi, *Nihon no kinyu seisaku* [Financial Policy in Japan] (Tokyo, 1980), attacking this point of view and Kazumata Iwata and Koichi Hamada, *Kinyū seisaku to ginkō kōdō* [Financial Policy and Bank Behavior] (Tokyo, 1980), defending it.

Graduates of Japanese firm training programs do not have the strong professional orientation fostered by extra-firm educational institutions as in the United States.

The differing locus and auspices of training in Japan compared to the United States and the prevalence of permanent employment in Japan makes for a relatively parochial and insulated research and development (R&D) staff. The informal exchange of useful information that is a characteristic feature among American technologists is largely absent in Japan. In the absence of labor market incentives and a strong transcendent professional identity, the bases for informal cooperation do not exist in Japan. In the absence of the informal cooperation, which in the United States encourages technological diffusion even as it creates technological progress anew, it is necessary to create formal programs which encourage such interaction. Japanese government cooperative R&D programs in Very Large Scale Integration in electronic chips, in Flexible Manufacturing Systems, and in biotechnology are as much attempts to extract information from the technological leaders in Japan for the benefit of the rest of the industry as they are efforts to overcome technological bottlenecks. In this way, the Ministry of International Trade and Industry (MITI) attempts to break down the information-flow barriers created by permanent employment practices even as it pursues procompetitive policies by building up rivals to leading Japanese firms.[16]

There is no better example of how all too easy it is to assume too much for the operation of distinctive Japanese institutions without considering how functionally equivalent institutions operate elsewhere than the case of biotechnology. Through 1981 and 1982 concern has been growing in Washington regarding Japanese government research and development aid programs in biotechnology.[17] Yet such programs are trivial by comparison with $1.5 billion effectively channeled by American venture capital markets into biogenetic research and development in the period between 1979 and mid-1982. Indeed, while the Japanese government had been evaluating the industrial potential of biogenetic engineering for many years, it only initiated major programs after the very clear signal on future potential provided by American equity markets.

---

[16] See Appendix 9.B. As might be expected technological leaders in Japan usually attempt to avoid participation in such cooperative projects.

[17] Gary C. Hufbauer and Peggy Mevs, "The European Community and Japan," in G. C. Hufbauer, ed., *US International Economic Policy, 1981: A Draft Report*, pp. 11–19.

The answer to the question of what the removal of remaining trade barriers might do directly for US-Japan economic relations is: very little. Further, the preceding analysis suggests a piecemeal attempt to speed the pace of liberalizing those Japanese institutions patently inconsistent with the increasingly inclusive premises of the international economic system might disrupt the Japanese economy. Even a Japanese economy which fully institutionalizes these premises while having different economic processes, will not have a trade structure radically different from what it would have in the absence of such changes. If Japanese institutions are substitutes for, rather than complements to liberal market processes, there is no reason to expect radically different performance once the transition from one régime to another has been fully accomplished. If fully undertaken, liberalization's primary impact will be in enhancing the legitimacy of Japanese participation in the international economic system. That this will be the primary impact of liberalization should be both understood and not disparaged as an outcome by either Japanese or American policy influentials. Harmonization of Japanese institutions with foreign practice should stop the endless stream of anecdotes as to how Japanese public and private sector actors work to frustrate the import of manufactures to Japan. Such anecdotes give credence to the illusion that the structure of Japanese foreign trade is being altered by unfair public and private action and that most foreign businessmen working in Japan are continually frustrated by local institutions and practices.[18] Yet it is precisely by such anecdotes that the bodies politic of the major participants in the international economic system come to reject the global outlook which maintains the legitimacy of that painfully constructed international economic system.

Exchange Rates and Reciprocity

In the light of the current crisis in US-Japanese economic relations, the above analysis may be cold comfort. The full harmonization of microeconomic institutions can hardly happen quickly enough to provide much help in the present extremely serious situation. In light of this hard reality, what can be done in the near future?

---

[18] Note that according to a sample survey completed two years ago, the majority of businessmen working in Japan do not find the Japanese government unfairly interfering with their activity. See A. D. Little, *The Japanese Non-Tariff Trade Barrier*.

To the extent that the large, natural resource-poor Japanese economy continues to grow more rapidly than its trading partners, it is almost inevitable that this will involve the transformation of its export structure. This is turn will impose structural adjustment on Japanese trading partners and competitors. While this plainly secular process has been going on throughout the past thirty years, its tempo and the political conflict thereby engendered have been governed to a considerable degree by the workings of the international financial adjustment mechanism.[19]

Do Exchange Rates Influence the Japanese Current Account?

While trade barriers and institutional change may not have much impact on the structure of Japanese trade, is there reason to believe that changes in the yen-dollar exchange rate do have a significant impact on levels of trade flows and that such changes in levels can, to a significant degree, reduce pressure for other changes which require policy instruments not in existence? There have been times in recent years when even the efficacy of exchange rate adjustment coping with disequilibrating trade flows from Japan has been doubted. Indeed, from 1977 through the first quarter of 1979, while Japan's trading partners waited for Japan's large current account surplus to diminish, doubt was expressed as to whether in Japan's case the international adjustment mechanism could work properly. At that time, doubt was expressed as to whether appreciation of the yen was actually reflected in the foreign currency price of Japan's exports, or for that matter, in the yen price of Japan's imports. And even if such price change did occur there was doubt, on the one hand, because of the high quality of Japanese exports and, on the other, because of the alleged lack of market access for imports to Japan, that trade flows would respond in a significant way to such price changes. Such doubt was expressed in concrete ways. In the first instance, speculators drove the yen as high as ¥176:$1 in late 1978. Second, as late as the first quarter of 1979, Washington was urging Tokyo to take dramatic new steps to reduce its unacceptably large global current account surplus.

In fact, there is a massive amount of empirical work on the Japanese foreign sector and the character of the international adjustment mechanism. With perhaps a number of minor exceptions all this work

---

[19] C. Fred Bergsten, "What To Do About the US-Japan Economic Conflict," *Foreign Affairs*, vol. 60, no. 5 (Summer 1982).

suggests that a change in the price of the yen relative to other currencies will result in a substantial change in the Japanese current account balance. All the major econometric models of the Japanese economy come to this conclusion regardless of the detail or the lack of detail in their treatment of the foreign sector and its linkages with the domestic economy and abroad.[20]

Similarly, virtually all work on the price sensitivity of Japan's export demand, which is one of the building blocks of any conclusion with respect to current account balance, also finds price changes efficacious. This empirical work on export demand has been carried out at varying levels of disaggregation. Japan's export demand has been disaggregated with respect to markets and separately with respect to different goods.[21] There has also been disaggregation in some of the same models between goods and different services. None of this disaggregation changes the optimistic qualitative conclusion of the more aggregate work.

On the import side, empirical work has produced rather more diverse results. It is not uncommon for aggregate equations representing Japan's imports of goods and services not to contain any price variable at all.[22] The level of imports in such work depends solely on one or another activity variable. This means that with an appreciation of the yen such import equations would forecast a decline, not an increase, in the dollar value of imports.

Such results at the aggregate level are not surprising given the commodity structure of Japanese imports. While the commodities in the SITC Groups 0–4 are highly price elastic with respect to a particular foreign source, they are almost always price inelastic, if not entirely price insensitive, with respect to all foreign sources.

---

[20] For example, A. Amano, K. Ban, and C. Moriguchi, *A Quarterly Forecasting Model of Japan*, Kyoto Institute of Economic Research, Kyoto University Discussion Paper, no. 81, 1975, and *Short-Term Econometric Model SP-18*, Economic Research Institute, Economic Planning Agency.

[21] One of the more comprehensive elaborations of foreign markets for exports takes place in the Kyoto University Model. There are separate equations for (1) the United States and Canadian markets, (2) the EEC/EFTA, (3) Oceania and South Africa, (4) Southeast Asia, and (5) other nonsocialist economies. See A. Amano, *An Econometric Model of the Japanese Balance of Payments, 1961–70* (Kobe, Japan: Kobe University, 1975) and A. Amano, K. Ban, and C. Moriguchi, "A Quarterly Forecasting Econometric Model of Japan."

[22] See, for example, the import equation in the Japan Economic Research Center's Medium-Term Econometric Model I.

There are more diverse results in the manufactured goods SITC categories 5–9. Given that at least some of these producers are thought to be in competition with domestic suppliers, it is expected that some price-sensitive behavior might be uncovered. And this is typically, but not always the case with an econometric work on these commodity groups.[23]

Macroeconomic Policies and the Exchange Rate

If yen-dollar changes are clearly efficacious in adjusting trade flows and thereby relieving pressures for extremely difficult structural changes, why has the yen been moving seemingly perversely for almost the past two years: Exchange rates reflect the relative demands and supplies for national currencies and as such they reflect national macroeconomic policies. In the present context, with the United States pursuing a loose fiscal policy and a tight monetary policy and Japan maintaining a tightening fiscal policy and a relatively loose monetary policy, the dollar is scarce and the yen is abundant. The exchange rates reflect this and the trade accounts are forced to adjust with ensuing political conflicts which shake the foundations of the international economic system.

Clearly much of the present exchange rate related pressures faced by American import-competing industries might be eliminated if the United States were to adopt a radically different mix of monetary and fiscal policies. A smaller government budget deficit, together with an easier monetary policy by the Fed, should result in a cheaper dollar and a more expensive yen. At the same time, the responsibility for action cannot rest solely in Washington. A substantial loosening of monetary policy by the Fed during the summer of 1982 was more than overshadowed by new political uncertainties in both the South Atlantic and the Middle East and the yen-dollar rate did not move more than momentarily downward from ¥265:$1.*

---

[23] In the Kyoto University Model among eight commodity import equations only two, machinery and textile raw materials, have statistically significant price terms. More recent work by the OECD suggests that aggregate Japanese manufactured imports are extremely price sensitive. Earlier work is summarized by G. K. Taplin, "A Model of World Trade," and G. Basevi, "Commodity Trade Equations in Project LINK," in R.J. Ball, ed., *The International Linkage of National Economic Models* (Amsterdam: North-Holland Publishing Company, 1973).

* *Ed. note*: Subsequently, however, the yen did strengthen substantially, reaching the vicinity of 235 per dollar in January 1983.

Even in these uncertain times, the Japanese economy is large enough and its economic institutions are such that it does retain the capacity for influencing the external value of the yen. How should Japan make use of this capacity. Given Japan's special dependence on the international economic system, given the amount of structural adjustment that the happy increase in the Japanese standard of living, fueled by rapid economic growth, has imposed on its trading partners, and given the inflationary expectations that might be set off by the recent sharp depreciation, it is hard to imagine Japan's remaining passive. At the same time, however, political, economic, and institutional forces every bit as compelling as those faced by the Reagan administration are frustrating use of the policy instruments available. For example, with overseas export, particularly non-US, markets now heavily depressed, many sectors of the Japanese economy are welcoming yen depreciation. Earlier government surveys suggesting that many export industries could be profitable with a yen close to 200 to the dollar are now being hastily revised. It is being argued that the already very high bankruptcy rates among the heavily leveraged small and medium-scale industry will be increased by a further tightening of monetary policy. At the same time it is being suggested that, unlike the mid- and late 1970s, Japan no longer retains the large fiscal margin which could sustain the more stimulative fiscal policy required by a tighter monetary policy. Fortifying these arguments politically is the current opposition of influential elements of the Japanese banking community who oppose for different sets of reasons both tighter monetary and looser fiscal policy.

Traditionally, Japanese banks have been forced to subscribe at par to bonds covering the Japanese government deficit which are issued with yields well below market rates. Given the size of government deficits, running 30 percent to 40 percent of government expenditures in recent years, it is hardly surprising that the Japanese banking community would welcome the Liberal Democratic Party's administrative reform program aimed at substantially reducing this deficit. In a change in policy, however, the banks are also opposing alternative ways of financing these deficits. Proposals that bonds be issued directly on Japanese capital markets have been opposed by Japanese banks for fear the market-determined yield on such safe instruments would be sufficiently high as to make them an attractive alternative to deposits at the banks. This together with other opposition makes it most unlikely that the Japanese government will adopt a changed fiscal-monetary mix for reasons other than domestic recession and unemployment and that what new mix is adopted will be less radical than what is necessary to qualify as a major yen-appreciation program.

Capital Liberalization

The banking community's role in these latest policy discussions underline the continuing illiberal character of Japan's financial system. Despite substantial changes in recent years Japanese banks and the Ministry of Finance have been successful in insulating both the Japanese household from a direct relationship with potential borrowers and the Japanese firm from a direct relationship with potential lenders. These policies together with restrictions on consumer and housing finance and the interest-inelasticity of household savings in the past worked to accelerate capital accumulation in Japan by keeping the price of capital low and savings high. In the present context, unlike many of Japan's other illiberal policies, it is having a substantial disequilibrating effect on Japanese commodity and capital flows. Thus, in this case, there are reasons for commending to Japan a policy of thorough-going capital liberalization not only in the interests of enhancing the legitimacy of Japan's participation in the international economic system by removing illiberal elements but also because such a liberalization and internationalization would directly improve the system's functioning. The lack of full liberalization at home and the failure of the yen to become a fully international currency works to depress the value of the yen.

Liberalization of any financial instrument, properly speaking, has three dimensions. First, it should mean allowing the creation of the instrument. Second, the instrument should be freely available both domestically and internationally. And third, the price at which the instrument is bought and sold should be determined in the market place and not by administrative fiat. From the perspective of the range and treatment of financial instruments found in the other major industrial economies and most especially the United States, capital liberalization in Japan has been most uneven along all these dimensions.

The absence of fully competitive determination of interest rates in many segments of the Japanese capital market has left the yen-dollar exchange rate, and ultimately the US-Japanese bilateral trade account to bear much of the pressures imposed by the radically different monetary and fiscal policies being pursued by the Japanese and American governments. In a liberal environment, the very large long-term capital outflows from Japan in 1981 and 1982 seeking higher interest rates abroad, everything else being equal, should have meant higher interest rates in Japan. Within the illiberal Japanese financial system most yields have either been entirely uninfluenced or have only been weakly responsive to the impact of these outflows. This, in turn, has meant still more outflows and further depreciation of the yen than would have otherwise been the case. A liberalization of interest rates which extends beyond the relatively few instruments whose prices are market determined and which extends to all short-term government financial instruments, to national bonds and to deposit accounts would help prevent exchange rate overshooting from happening in the future.

The absence of full competition in Japanese capital markets has also meant that the financial instruments have yet to be created which will facilitate still greater international status and use of the yen. Despite the very great increase in Japan's share in total world trade in the last 25 years, the proportion of Japanese export trade which is settled in yen, while rising rapidly, is extremely low by comparison with all other major industrialized economies. Similarly, for all the enormous influx into Japan of petrodollars during 1980 and 1981, Japan's share of such financing by comparison with Europe and the United States is still remarkably low. In view of the excellent performance of the Japanese economy over the last two decades, particularly its smooth adjustment to the 1979 oil shock, and in light of the suggestion by some Japanese government officials that expansionary policies in Japan were complicated by the prospect of less than adequate future domestic savings, it is even conceivable that Japan is undercapitalized.

There is an important latent demand for the yen as a transactions medium and as a store of value, which could be realized, if a full range of sophisticated financial instruments were available. For example, the severe limitations on the ability of foreign companies and banks to issue yen-denominated securities in Tokyo, everything else being equal, has diminished the value of the yen. Note, however, that piecemeal change in the regulation of the amount and character of yen-denominated securities issued in Tokyo by foreigners may be unhelpful or even counterproductive if it simply serves as the creation of an additional means for yen to be dumped and dollars acquired. What is needed now is a quantum change in the access of foreigners to a newly sophisticated Tokyo capital market. This should result in a greatly increased demand for yen assets by both foreigners and Japanese which will in turn enhance the value of the yen relative to the dollar.

Finale

Most of the current emphasis placed on opening the domestic Japanese market to foreign product competition is misplaced. By the traditional indices of the international economic system foreign access to the Japanese market would have to be considered excellent. Indeed, when the distinctive endowments of the Japanese economy have been appropriately considered not only is foreign access good but so is foreign performance. By these standards foreign penetration of the Japanese market is equivalent to the experience of other major industrial economies. Relative to present imbalances not much can be expected from the removal of remaining explicit and implicit illiberal trade barriers. The one area where barriers do appear to have some substance is agriculture. Ironically, the liberalization of Japanese agriculture by reducing food prices and by releasing resources inefficiently used in agriculture would strengthen the competitive power of Japanese manufacturing. This would make it still more difficult for foreign manufactured products to enter Japan even as it increased Japanese manufactured exports to its hard-pressed overseas markets.

While it is unlikely to have much impact on Japan's imbalance with its trading partners, liberalization of the Japanese economy should be pursued for the sake of helping to bolster the legitimacy of the international economic system. In one important area, however, such fundamental liberalization could be an important direct aid to foreign manufacturing industries. By limiting the use of their national currency as an international medium of exchange and store of value, the Japanese are exporting less of an extremely important service than would be the case in the absence of government intervention. By restricting this export, they have implicitly encouraged the exports of other goods and services. Full Japanese capital liberalization, everything else equal, should make it easier for foreign manufacturers to compete with Japan.

Appendices
9.A   A General Equilibrium Model of Trade Structure

Too much of the discussion on the modern development of the Japanese economy stresses the special unique characteristics of Japan as explanations of this development. In turn, the aggressive Japanese business expansion pattern, the unique style of decision making, unusual business groupings, the special ways of handling the labor force, the clinging to traditional consumption patterns, the strength of the family in the context of loyalty to national symbols, the unique capacity to absorb from other cultures, have all been touted separately and collectively as a means of understanding what has happened during the last 120 years and during the last 30 years. The basic thrust of this literature is not surprising. On the one hand, many, though certainly not all, of these explanations have been developed by many of the same individuals who have helped to establish Japanese studies as a separate field of inquiry in the United States. On the other hand, many Japanese, in an effort to change the discussion of commercial disputes from low wages and unfair trade practices, have also openly promoted explanations which have emphasized the superiority of distinctively Japanese behavior and practices.

It is hardly surprising or inappropriate that either group should emphasize the gains that can be derived from cultural considerations. Understanding of the Japanese economy cannot be entirely divorced from an intimate knowledge of Japanese personality, society, and culture, but surely the situation at least in the policy context has already gone too far. In the US Congressional US-Japan Trade Task Force Report issued September 1980 it was suggested that "Japan is generally an open nation" but that "private (cultural?) barriers to trade are very serious and may account for billions of dollars in lost US export opportunity."[1] Indeed, when the areas of the economy are listed where such barriers are important they turn out to cover some 73.5 percent of total Japanese manufactured imports. Can this be true? Is Japanese behavior really so distinctive in its economic consequences?

Given this perspective, and given the desire to pose the analysis in the broadest possible context to facilitate ultimately long-term forecasting, the empirical work undertaken here uses a self-con-

---

[1] US Congress, House, Subcommittee on Trade, Committee on Ways and Means, *US-Japan Trade Report*, 96th Cong., 2d sess. (Washington: Government Printing Office, 1980).

sciously comparative analytical framework. This approach presumes that Japanese phenomena can be explained by theories which are general over time and space. It is hoped that Japanese phenomena can be explained in the context of general explanations which are relevant for all countries. The actual analytical framework used in this work is an adaptation of the Hecksher–Ohlin–Samuelson (H-O-S) theory of comparative advantage. This theory, a long-time favorite of undergraduate instructors of international trade, emphasizes that the structure and level of international trade can be explained by the distribution of inputs into the production process throughout the world's many economies. The original formulation of this model stressed the national availability of capital, labor, skills, social organization, and natural resources.

In the perspective of the 30 years since H-O-S first gained wide currency, this theory now seems a bit shopworn. Since the famous Leonteif Paradox results in 1953 numerous attempts have been made to verify the theory empirically. A review of this literature is curiously unsatisfying. The algebra of H-O-S has been worked in very great detail by a generation of pure trade economists. Strangely enough, however, testing of H-O-S makes almost no direct use of this formal framework. Often the functional forms imposed in these tests cannot be derived from H-O-S mathematics.

It is occasionally suggested that the strong assumptions necessary to the development of the formal structure of H-O-S leave little doubt about the outcome of such a test. Such an attitude seems in some respects unscientific. Theories are generally judged by their explanatory power, not by the simplicity of their assumptions. In any event, by the standards of economic research the assumptions of (1) a single, homogeneous degree of one production function for each world industry, and (2) identical worldwide preference structures, if properly understood, do not appear extreme. Rather the reluctance to test H-O-S formally arises out of the implications of this theory.

The same structure which generates the H-O-S theory of comparative advantage in a form where estimation can take place by linear methods also necessitates that prices of inputs throughout the world should be identical. At first blush this is so clearly counterintuitive as to disparage the entire analysis. Wage rates for unskilled labor are very much higher in Japan than in India. Only when it is understood that within a category such as unskilled labor, quality may vary sufficiently to account for observed international differences can the theory be rescued. This manner of rescue still creates problems for the empirical implementation of H-O-S. In order to use this framework in the context of econometric investigations, some means of assessing international differences in input quality must be established. One suspects it is this problem which is really responsible for making the empirical testing of pure trade theory so different from the testing of pure consumption or production theory. Below an approach to overcoming this roadblock is suggested. The virtue of the suggested approach is its general equilibrium nature and its relatively undemanding data requirements.

The Formal Framework

Demands. Suppose that national preferences may be summarized by a positive, continuous, nondecreasing, quasi-concave utility function.[2] Suppose further that the reciprocal, indirect utility function derived from this utility function can be approximated by the functional form

(1)
$$h(v) = \sum_{i=j}^{N}\sum_{j=i}^{N} b_{ij} v_i^{\frac{1}{2}} v_j^{\frac{1}{2}} + 2\sum_{j=i}^{N} b_{oj} v_j^{\frac{1}{2}} + b_{oo}$$

   where b_{ij} $= b_{ji}$
   and where $h \equiv$ reciprocal indirect utility function[4]
           $v \equiv$ income normalized prices.

If preferences are homothetic, i.e., the direct utility function is homogeneous, the following system of consumer demand equations can be derived from (1)

(2)
$$X_i(P_1/Y, \ldots, P_N/Y) = \frac{\sum_{j=1}^{N} b_{ij} P_i^{-\frac{1}{2}} P_j^{\frac{1}{2}} Y}{\sum_{k=1}^{N}\sum_{m=1}^{N} b_{km} P_k^{\frac{1}{2}} P_m^{\frac{1}{2}}}$$

   where $X_i = i^{\text{th}}$ good
       $P \equiv$ price
       $Y \equiv$ national income.

---

[2] For the conditions under which this is true, see Paul A. Samuelson, "Social Indifference Curves," *Quarterly Journal of Economics*, vol. 70 (February 1956) and E. Eisenberg, "Aggregation of Utility Functions," *Management Science*, vol. 7 (July 1961).

[3] h is the generalized Leontief indirect utility function and was first presented by W. E. Diewert, "Application of Duality Theory," in M. E. Intriligator and D. A. Kendrick, eds., *Frontiers of Quantitative Economics*, vol. 2 (New York: Elsevier, 1974).

[4] Ibid.

Let income be equal to the weighted sum of factors, where the weights are unit factor rewards. Substituting this into (2) we get

$$X_i \quad = G_i \sum_{s=1}^{K} W_s a_s L_s$$

$$\text{where } G_i \quad = \frac{\sum_{j=1}^{N} b_{ij} P_i^{-\frac{1}{2}} P_j^{\frac{1}{2}}}{\sum_{k=1}^{N} \sum_{m=1}^{N} b_{km} P_k^{\frac{1}{2}} P_m^{\frac{1}{2}}}$$

(3)
$$L = \text{factor of production}$$
$$W = \text{factor reward}$$
$$a = \text{quality of factor}.$$

Supply. Suppose the technology of an economy may be summarized by a variable profit function.[5] Further suppose that this profit function is approximated by

$$(4) \quad \pi(P, L) = \sum_{i=1}^{N} \sum_{j=1}^{N} \sum_{s=1}^{K} d_{is} \left(\tfrac{1}{2}P_i^2 + \tfrac{1}{2}P_j^2\right)^{\frac{1}{2}} a_s L_s + \sum_{i=1}^{N} \sum_{s=1}^{K} c_{is} P_i a_s L_s$$
$$+ \sum_{i=1}^{N} \sum_{s=1}^{K} \sum_{r=1}^{K} f_{sr} (a_s L_s)^{\frac{1}{2}} (a_r L_r)^{\frac{1}{2}} P_i$$

$$\text{where } d_{is} = d_{si}, f_{sr} = f_{rs}; d_{ii} = 0 \text{ for } i = 1, 2, \ldots, N$$

$$\text{and where } f_{ss} = 0 \text{ for } s = 1, 2, \ldots, K[6]$$

$$\text{and where } \pi \equiv \text{profit function}.$$

Using Hotelling's lemma, (4) may be differentiated with respect to

[5] The concept of a variable profit function was first suggested by Paul A. Samuelson, "Price of Factors and Goods in General Equilibrium," *Review of Economic Studies*, vol. 21 (June 1953).

[6] In what follows empirical work will proceed as if $N = K$, despite the number of inputs for which data are available being almost 100 less than the number of goods. Given the rather arbitrary aggregation and disaggregation in goods and factors in empirical work of this kind, it is appropriate to assume that the number of goods and factors are many and that included and excluded dependent and independent variables have properties such that exclusion of relevant variables does not bias parameters which are estimated.

each of the output prices to obtain a system of derived supply functions.[7]

(5)
$$X_i(P,L) = \sum_{j=1}^{N} \sum_{s=1}^{K} d_{ij} (\tfrac{1}{2}P_i^2 + \tfrac{1}{2}P_j^2)^{-\frac{1}{2}} P_i a_s L_s$$
$$+ \sum_{s=1}^{K} c_{is} a_s L_s + \sum_{s=1}^{K} \sum_{r=1}^{K} f_{sr}(a_s L_s)^{\frac{1}{2}}(a_r L_r)^{\frac{1}{2}},$$
$$i = 1, 2, \ldots, N$$
$$= \sum_{s=1}^{K} Q_{is} a_s L_s + \sum_{s=1}^{K} \sum_{r=1}^{K} f_{sr}(a_s L_s)^{\frac{1}{2}}(a_r L_r)^{\frac{1}{2}}$$
$$= \sum_{s=1}^{K} Q_{is} a_s L_s + \sum_{s=1}^{K} \sum_{r=1}^{K} f_{sr}(a_s a_r)^{\frac{1}{2}} L_s^{\frac{1}{2}} L_r^{\frac{1}{2}},$$
$$i = 1, 2, \ldots, N$$

$$\text{where } Q_{is} \equiv \sum_{j=1}^{N} d_{ij} (\tfrac{1}{2}P_i^2 + \tfrac{1}{2}P_j^2)^{-\frac{1}{2}} P_i + c_{is}.$$

Provided the much debated Law of One Price and the Factor Price Equalization Theorem hold and the price of a particular good and reward of a particular factor are everywhere the same, G_i and Q_i and w_i may be treated as constants, f_{rs} will equal zero and the remaining terms in (5) may be subtracted from (3).[8] The resulting equation explains the net trade in good X_i and is linear in parameters and variables and has a nonarbitrary functional form derived explicitly from preferences and technology.[9]

---

[7] Hotelling's lemma is discussed in W. M. Gorman, "Measuring the Quantities of Fixed Factors," in J. N. Wolfe, ed., *Value Capital and Growth* (Chicago: Aldine, 1968).

[8] Using Hotelling's lemma the second partial derivatives of the profit function with respect to factor endowments must be zero if factor price equalization is to occur. Applying Hotelling's lemma

(A1) $a_s W_s = \partial \Pi(P, L)/\partial(a_s L_s), \quad s = 1, \ldots, K$

If factor price equalization is true then

(A2) $\dfrac{\partial(a_s W_s)}{\partial(a_s L_s)} = \dfrac{\partial^2 \Pi(P,L)}{\partial(a_s L_s)^2} = 0, \quad s = 1, \ldots, K$

or from equation (4)

(A3) $\tfrac{1}{2} f_{rs}(a_s L_s)^{-\frac{1}{2}}(a_s L_s)^{-\frac{1}{2}} \left(\sum_{i=1}^{N} P_i \right) = 0.$

This, in turn, implies $f_{rs} = 0$.

[9] The Law of One Price has been hotly debated in recent years. See, in particular, the discussions in P. Isard, "The Law of One Price," *American*

(6)
$$X_i(L) = \sum_{s=1}^{K} U_{is} a_s L_s^{10}, i = 1, s, \ldots, N$$
where $U_{is} = G_{is} - Q_{is}$.

Estimation. Proposition (6) is to be estimated for N commodity groups from international cross-section data. Were it not for unknown variations in the quality of inputs across countries, estimation of (6) might proceed using ordinary least squares methods. Formally, the estimation of (6) with a_s differing across countries and unknown is a multivariate errors in a variable problem.[11] Instrumental variable methods will allow consistent estimation of the U_{is}.[12] For any given commodity cross-section a_s will not be identified. In the particular specification adopted here, however, at any given time, there are i cross-sections that contain the identical independent variables. This happy circumstance will permit consistent estimation of the a_s for

---

Economic Review, vol. 64 (December 1977); I. B. Kravis and R. E. Lipsey, "Export Prices and the Transmissions of Inflation," *American Economic Association Papers and Proceedings* (February 1977); J. D. Richardson, "Some Empirical Evidence on Commodity Arbitrage and the Law of One Price," *Journal of International Economics*, vol. 8 (May 1978). The opposing view is summarized and extended in J. A. Frenkel, "Purchasing Power Parity: Doctrinal Perspective and Evidence from the 1920s," *Journal of International Economics*, vol. 8 (May 1978). How good an approximation the Law of One Price is to reality is a most important issue for understanding the present-day workings of the international monetary mechanism. For the purposes of the econometric analysis here, how fast and in what manner domestic prices respond to exchange rate adjustment is not of critical importance. Deviations from constancy across countries of G_i and Q_{is} may be correlated with exchange rate changes, but such changes in turn may be reasonably assumed to be orthogonal to the independent variables in (6).

[10] Strictly speaking equation (6) describes trade in finished goods. For intermediate goods, the first group of terms in equation (5) which are formally identical with (6) should be used.

[11] In actual estimation an additive error term for equations will also be assumed.

[12] Following Durbin and in common with two stage least squares the approach taken here uses synthetic instrumental variables generated by examination of variables already being used and does not require the choice of new variables as instruments. This is accomplished by ordering the existing L_s according to size and using rank order as an instrument. See J. Durbin, "Errors in Variables," *Review of the International Statistical Institute*, vol. 22 (1954).

each economy.[13] These estimates of a_s can then be used to obtain new Aitken efficient estimates of U_{is}.

Proposition (6) is estimated with data taken from nine countries for 109 internationally traded commodities for the years 1959, 1962, 1964, 1967, 1969, 1971, and 1973. The nine countries include Canada, France, Germany, Italy, Japan, Korea, the Netherlands, the United Kingdom, and the United States. The seven factors treated as central to the explanation of trade flows are the directly productive capital stock, labor, educational attainment, distance, petroleum resources, iron ore resources, and arable land.[14]

Is Japan Different?   In estimating (6) using a time series of cross-sections it is assumed that with the exception of input quality and disembodied technology time trends, the preferences and technology underlying (6) do not change. Even so, because prices and wages will change over time, in (6) U_{is} will have time varying and time invariant components. The a_s will also change from cross-section to cross-section.

Each equation in (6) will also contain a set of country-specific additive dummy variables which are also assumed to be time invariant. These variables are meant to allow for those characteristics not otherwise provided for in the analysis. Such variables might reflect national policies regarding the protection and encouragement of particular industries. They might also reflect private, possibly distinctive patterns of protection. A positive, statistically significant country term for Japan for passenger motor vehicle (SITC 732.1) might well signify a *distinctively* successful policy of protection. In this case Japan would be exporting more automobiles than might be expected given the

---

[13] For example, let $a_s = 1 + a'_s$. Using instrumental variable techniques in the presence of multiplicative errors allows consistent estimation of the U_{is}. Using these estimates, for each economy an $N \times 1$ vector $[v'_i]$ of commodity equation residuals can be formed for each time period. Consistent estimates of the quality terms for each country for each time period can then be obtained from

$$\{[\hat{U}_{is}L_s]' \ [\hat{U}_{is}L_s]\}^{-1} \ \{[\hat{U}_{is}L_s]' \ [V_i]\}.$$

[14] The capital, labor, and educational attainment data are adapted from materials assembled by L. Christensen, D. Cummings, and D. Jorgensen for their study, "Economic Growth 1947–1973: An International Comparison." The trade data and the natural resource variables are adapted from data reported to the United Nations together with iron ore deposit benchmarks obtained from the US Department of Interior. The arable land data are collected from the Food and Agricultural Organization sources. Distance is measured as the average number of miles of each economy from its major trading partners weighted by the share of trade with each.

quantity and quality of its natural resources, labor force, capital, and consumption priorities. A statistically insignificant country variable in any given equation does not mean that the development of an industry necessarily conformed to liberal trade canons. If all countries with a comparative advantage in steel resorted to roughly comparable dumping practices, the country variables would be, in all likelihood, statistically insignificant. Given that this investigation is interested only in examining whether Japan's low share of imported manufactures really is evidence for distinctive Japanese behavior and practices, this limitation by no means undermines the interest of the results here. Japan's exporters and customs officials may engage in unsavory, even illegal activities, but, within the limits of this type of evidence, a statistically insignificant country term would suggest that Japanese behavior is no different from other comparably situated economies. Of course, the research being undertaken here has taken special pains to define comparably situated in a theoretically defensible fashion.

In actual estimation, relatively few of the Japanese country terms are statistically significant. In 109 commodity equations, only 17 Japanese country terms were statistically significant. The 17 commodities with such terms include:

Commodity	*SITC*
Maize (unmilled)	SITC 044[a]
Other cereals	SITC 045[a]
Bananas (including plantains)	SITC 051.3[a]
Other Fruits and Nuts	SITC 057.2[a]
Saw Logs and Veneer Logs—nonconifer	SITC 242.3[a]
Crude Fertilizers	SITC 27[a]
Plastic Material	SITC 58[b]
Glass	SITC 664[c]
Pearls, Precious and Semiprecious Stones	SITC 667[a]
Aluminum	SITC 684[a]
Zinc	SITC 686[b]
Aircraft and Parts	SITC 734[d]
Footwear	SITC 85[a]
Photo and Cinema Supplies	SITC 862[b]
Medical Instruments	SITC 872[c]
Pianos and Other Musical Instruments	SICT 891.4[c]

a. Statistically significantly less than zero; fewer imports.
b. Statistically significantly less than zero; fewer exports.
c. Statistically significantly less than zero; greater exports.
d. Statistically significantly less than zero; greater imports.

While some of these products are closely associated in the public mind with Japan either as exports or imports, taken together they comprise no more than 4.9 percent of Japan's gross external trade. Note also of these 17 statistically significant Japanese terms, 4 work to diminish rather than to enhance Japan's secular trade surplus. By contrast with the Japanese results, 24 Italian country terms covering 11.7 percent of Italy's trade are statistically significant. Not surprisingly, the impact of France's policies appear to have been still larger. Fully 32 country terms are statistically significant. These 32 terms account for 16.0 percent of France's foreign trade. Even less surprising are the results for the heavily regulated Korean economy. Forty-three country terms covering 28.3 percent of Korean foreign trade are statistically significant.[15]

These results help rationalize some of the changing expectations regarding the share of manufactures outlined earlier. In the early 1970s, consistent with Sazanami and other interpretations it was expected that the removal of formal restrictions and changes in Japanese attitudes toward imports would drive at least manufactured imports as a share of total imports to European levels. When this failed to happen and when the manufactured imports' elasticity of import demand remained constant rather than rising sharply, it was natural to assume that the grave uncertainties of a newly perceived, energy-scarce world had caused a reevaluation in the Japanese commitment to liberal commercial attitudes. The results obtained here suggest that the commercial policy changes and attitudinal changes of the 1970s did not bring great changes in the Japanese commodity structure of imports, not because of foreign cultural insensitivity to Japan, but because from the second best perspective of the policies and practices in other major industrial countries and Japanese trading partners, these policies involved only relatively small distortions. When the differing quantity and quality of Japanese labor, capital and natural resource endowments, and distance from trading partners are properly given their full allowance, the Japanese share of manufactures in total imports is comparable to European and American experiences.

The above results which question the differential direct impact of Japanese government policies on Japanese trade and industrial structure should not be understood as dismissing the role of government policy in Japan's rapid industrial evolution and postwar growth. Rather the above analysis should be seen as a decomposition between sectoral and macroeconomic explanations of rapid Japanese structural evolution. The differential influence of sectoral policies is dismissed in

---

[15] The results for Japan do not change when the investigation is carried out at a higher level of aggregation. Neither do they change when an attempt is made to assess statistical significance of the 109 country terms taken as a whole on the entire pattern of trade.

favor of a macroeconomic explanation of Japanese performance. Nothing in the above analysis suggests, for example, that the Japanese government might not have had a central role in raising the rate of aggregate capital stock growth. (*For tables, see page 298.*)

9.B Cooperative Research in Japan

That cooperation among firms in Japan does not come easily may be illustrated by the experience with research on Very Large-Scale Integration (VLSI) electronic chips. This project was initiated in 1976 as part of a continuing effort by the Japanese government to direct and promote the Japanese computer industry. The Machinery and Information Services Bureau of the Ministry of International Trade and Industry (MITI) encouraged Nippon Electric (NEC), Toshiba, Hitachi, Fujitsu, and Mitsubishi Electric (MELCO) to establish the VLSI Technology Research Association which in turn established a joint research laboratory at Kawasaki.[1] The carrot for participation in this research association over and above the usual 100 percent first year write-off of all fixed assets used in research association activities was $133 million in direct government subsidies spread out over four years.

Despite the maintenance of a joint research laboratory, which is relatively rare for a research association, each VLSI project handled within the laboratory was separately conducted by teams of researchers, each team being drawn almost entirely from a single company.[2] Each project team designed its machinery and then had it built by its own firm using a separate part of the Kawasaki laboratory. There was only irregular contact between the various project teams. Each

[1] Japanese research associations are most typically special entities for tax purposes. Firms which are members of government-authorized research associations can take a 100 percent depreciation deduction for all fixed assets used in connection with association activities. Many Japanese research associations such as the Electric Car Research Association are formed for very specific joint research and development ventures and actually have no joint laboratories. For all the seemingly generous treatment of research associations, the Ministry of Finance estimates no more than $13 million in tax revenues were lost in 1982 owing to the depreciation of assets in all Japan's research associations. Ōkurashō, *Genko sūzei tokubetsu sochi no gaiyo* (Tokyo, 1982), p. 192.

[2] There are presently about 30 research associations operating in Japan, including the Electric Car Research Association, the Nuclear Steel Making Research Association, and the Technical Research Association for Optics.

firm participating in the VLSI Research Association brought its own technology to the project and took back to its firm the further advances on company-specific information. Of the more than 1,000 patents developed by the joint laboratory at Kawasaki, only 30 were jointly held by private firms and the Japanese government.

It is highly significant that Nippon Telephone and Telegraph (NTT), a company which maintains an extremely strong technology for making electronic chips chose not to participate directly in the project teams of MITI-sponsored VLSI research association. The Ministry of Postal and Telecommunications which owns half of NTT has been able to protect it from MITI pressure.[3] NTT has been careful to keep its technical lead in many facets of integrated circuit technology by narrowly limiting the range of joint research it does with any one company at a time. In this way it has insured that no other company really understood the full state of NTT technology. Failure at the same time to participate in MITI-sponsored projects, however, has not deprived NTT of major government subsidies. In recent years, NTT has continually issued, as might be expected, government-guaranteed bonds and has had loans from resources collected by the Ministry of Postal and Telecommunications-dominated Postal Savings System.

The VLSI program is not an isolated example. Japanese government interfirm cooperative research programs with flexible manufacturing systems, fifth generation computers and in biogenetic engineering have all suffered from similar strains. With flexible manufacturing systems, Yamazaki Seikō, the firm with the most advanced technology in this area, has strenuously criticized the government-sponsored cooperative programs as aiming to research a project whose outcome would be a system less advanced than what Yamazaki Seikō was already capable of producing. Only strong pressure by the heavily leveraged Yamazaki Seikō's bank forced its participation in a project it felt would be at best of no help and at worst highly detrimental to its interests. For the fifth generation computers project, Fujitsu's position is analogous to Yamazaki Seikō in FMS. Again Fujitsu claims to have some of the technology which the government's cooperative project is seeking to research and develop.

In all likelihood, Yamazaki Seikō's and Fujitsu's claims are correct and it is equally likely that the relevant Ministry of International

---

[3] The Ministry of Postal and Telecommunications has also been able to protect NTT from MITI pressures during the epic Government Procurement Code controversy during the closing weeks of the GATT Tokyo Round negotiations.

Trade and Industry bureau chiefs are well aware of the accuracy of their claims. It may well be that seeking more leakage of proprietary information than would otherwise be the case, MITI is not unhappy if these flows are in some instances decidedly one way. It is often argued that Japanese government policy is anticompetitive in so far as market structure issues are concerned and that this is in clear contrast with the procompetitive policies continually pursued by, say, the Anti-Trust Division of the US Justice Department.

For the United States, for much of its industrial history, a giant in the world economy, a procompetitive policy could often only mean the scaling down and breaking up of its dominant firms. For Japan, however, until recently, a small element in the global economy, a domestic procompetitive policy characteristically meant insuring that no one Japanese firm exclusively locked up for itself a potentially world class industry and technology. That the motivation for such a policy often sprang from the most sordid cross-currents in inter-*zaibatsu* [industrial combines] rivalries, in no way diminishes its socially beneficial impact. On the basis of its tradition and given the reaction of many Japanese firms, it seems sensible to hypothesize that the Japanese government sponsored interfirm cooperative research programs are more programs of diffusing technology so that more Japanese firms can compete with world class technologies than they are programs pursuing advances over technological bottlenecks.

TABLE 9A.1   COUNTRY-SPECIFIC CONSTANTS BY COMMODITIES

Commodity	Japan	Italy	France	Canada	Korea
Meat and preparations	—	—	*	—	—
Dairy products and eggs	—	—	—	—	—
Fish and preparations	—	—	*	*	—
Wheat unmilled	—	*	*	—	*
Rice	—	—	—	—	—
Maize unmilled	*	*	*	—	*
Other cereals	*	—	—	—	*
Bananas and plantains	*	—	—	—	—
Other fruits and nuts	*	—	—	—	*
Tobacco and manufactures	—	*	*	—	*
Hides, skins, and furskins	—	—	—	—	*
Soya beans	—	—	—	—	*
Oil seeds, excluding soya beans	—	*	—	—	*
Crude and synthetic rubber	—	—	*	—	—
Saw-veneer logs-conifer	—	—	—	*	*
Saw-veneer logs-nonconifer	*	*	—	*	*
Shaped wood	—	—	*	—	—
Pulp and waste paper	—	*	—	—	*
All other wood-lumber and cork	—	—	—	*	*
Silk	—	—	*	—	—
Wool and animal hair	—	*	—	—	—
Cotton	—	*	—	—	—
Synthetic regenerated fibers	—	—	*	—	—
All other waste fibers	—	—	—	—	—
Crude fertilizers	*	—	—	—	*
All other fertilizers and crude materials	—	—	—	—	*
Iron ore concentrates	—	—	—	*	—
Iron and steel scrap	—	—	—	—	—
Copper ores and concentrates	—	—	—	—	—
Nickel ores and concentrates	—	*	*	—	—
Zinc ores and concentrates	—	—	—	—	—
Manganese ores and concentrates	—	*	*	—	—
All other metalliferous ores and concentrates	—	—	—	—	—
All other crude concentrates	—	—	—	—	—
Coal, coke, and briquette	—	—	—	—	*
Crude petroleum	—	—	—	—	—
Petroleum products	—	—	—	—	—
Natural gas and manufactures	—	—	—	—	—
All other minerals	—	—	—	—	—
Organic chemicals	—	—	—	—	—
Inorganic chemicals	—	—	—	—	—
Manufactured fertilizers	—	—	—	—	*
Plastic materials	*	*	*	—	*
All other chemicals	—	—	—	—	*
Leather, pressed fur	—	—	*	*	—
Rubber manufactures	—	—	*	—	*
Cork manufactures	—	—	*	—	—
Veneer plywood	*	—	—	—	*

Commodity	Germany	United Kingdom	Netherlands	$\overline{R}^2$
Meat and preparations	—	—	—	.29
Dairy products and eggs	—	—	—	.27
Fish and preparations	—	—	—	.41
Wheat unmilled	—	—	—	.43
Rice	—	—	—	.15
Maize unmilled	*	—	—	.52
Other cereals	—	—	—	.31
Bananas and plantains	—	—	—	.19
Other fruits and nuts	—	—	—	.35
Tobacco and manufactures	—	*	—	.36
Hides, skins, and furskins	—	—	—	.40
Soya beans	—	—	—	.69
Oil seeds, excluding soya beans	*	—	*	.75
Crude and synthetic rubber	—	*	—	.51
Saw-veneer logs-conifer	—	—	*	.81
Saw-veneer logs-nonconifer	—	—	*	.85
Shaped wood	—	—	—	.58
Pulp and waste paper	—	—	*	.65
All other wood-lumber and cork	—	—	*	.71
Silk	—	—	—	.13
Wool and animal hair	—	—	—	.38
Cotton	—	*	—	.24
Synthetic regenerated fibers	*	—	*	.11
All other waste fibers	*	—	—	.18
Crude fertilizers	—	—	—	.40
All other fertilizers and crude materials	—	—	—	.41
Iron ore concentrates	—	—	—	.27
Iron and steel scrap	—	—	—	.34
Copper ores and concentrates	—	—	—	.31
Nickel ores and concentrates	—	—	—	.40
Zinc ores and concentrates	—	*	—	.49
Manganese ores and concentrates	*	*	*	.67
All other metalliferous ores and concentrates	—	—	—	.42
All other crude concentrates	—	—	—	.51
Coal, coke, and briquette	*	—	—	.65
Crude petroleum	—	—	—	.85
Petroleum products	—	—	—	.84
Natural gas and manufactures	—	—	—	.82
All other minerals	—	—	—	.45
Organic chemicals	—	—	—	.69
Inorganic chemicals	—	—	—	.72
Manufactured fertilizers	—	—	—	.81
Plastic materials	*	*	*	.77
All other chemicals	*	—	—	.58
Leather, pressed fur	—	—	—	.65
Rubber manufactures	*	—	—	.52
Cork manufactures	—	—	—	.23
Veneer plywood	—	—	*	.45

TABLE 9A.1 (Continued)

Commodity	Japan	Italy	France	Canada	Korea
Paper, paperboard, and manufactures	—	—	—	*	*
Gray cotton·yarn	—	—	—	—	—
Yarn, synthetic fibers	—	—	—	—	—
Cotton, fabric, woven	—	—	—	—	—
Silk fabrics, woven	—	—	—	—	*
Wool fabric, woven	—	—	—	—	*
Cement	—	—	—	—	*
Glass	*	*	*	*	*
Glassware	—	*	*	—	—
Pearls, precious, and semiprecious stones	*	—	—	—	—
Pig iron	—	—	—	—	—
Iron and steel, primary forms	—	—	—	—	—
Iron and steel, bars and rods	—	—	—	—	—
Iron and steel, universal plates and sheets	—	—	—	—	*
Iron and steel wire, excluding wire rod	—	—	—	—	*
Iron and steel, tubes and pipes	—	—	—	—	—
All other iron and steel	—	*	*	—	*
Silver and platinum	—	*	—	—	—
Copper	—	—	*	—	*
Nickel	—	*	*	*	*
Aluminum	*	—	*	—	—
Lead	—	*	*	—	—
Zinc	*	—	*	*	—
Tin	—	—	*	—	—
All other basic manufactures	—	—	—	—	*
Aircraft engines	—	—	—	—	*
Piston engines	—	—	—	—	*
Nuclear reactors	—	—	—	—	*
All other engines	—	—	—	—	—
Agricultural machinery	—	*	—	—	*
Office machines	—	—	—	—	—
Machine tools for metal	—	—	—	—	*
Textile machinery	—	—	—	—	—
Sewing machines	—	—	*	—	—
Other clothing equipment	—	*	*	—	—
Paper mill machinery	—	—	—	*	*
Printing and binding machinery	—	—	*	—	—
Construction and mining machinery	—	—	—	—	*
Heating and cooling equipment	—	—	*	—	*
Pumps and centrifuges	—	—	—	—	—
Ball, rollers, etc., bearings	—	—	—	—	—
Electric power machinery	—	—	—	—	*
Switch gear	—	—	—	—	*
Electric distribution machinery	—	—	—	—	*
Radio	—	—	—	—	—
Television	—	—	—	—	—
Other sound equipment	—	—	—	—	—

Commodity	Germany	United Kingdom	Netherlands	$\overline{R}^2$
Paper, paperboard, and manufactures	—	—	—	.67
Gray cotton yarn	—	—	—	.28
Yarn, synthetic fibers	*	—	*	.78
Cotton, fabric, woven	—	—	—	.67
Silk fabrics, woven	—	—	—	.73
Wool fabric, woven	—	—	—	.85
Cement	—	—	—	.79
Glass	—	*	—	.91
Glassware	—	—	—	.67
Pearls, precious, and semiprecious stones	—	—	—	.62
Pig iron	—	—	—	.81
Iron and steel, primary forms	—	—	—	.87
Iron and steel, bars and rods	—	—	—	.90
Iron and steel, universal plates and sheets	—	—	—	.91
Iron and steel wire, excluding wire rod	—	—	—	.78
Iron and steel, tubes and pipes	—	—	—	.79
All other iron and steel	—	*	—	.67
Silver and platinum	—	—	—	.44
Copper	—	—	*	.57
Nickel	*	*	*	.85
Aluminum	—	—	—	.65
Lead	*	*	*	.84
Zinc	—	*	*	.85
Tin	*	—	—	.79
All other basic manufactures	—	—	—	.58
Aircraft engines	—	—	—	.80
Piston engines	—	—	—	.67
Nuclear reactors	—	—	—	.44
All other engines	—	—	—	.67
Agricultural machinery	—	—	—	.87
Office machines	—	*	—	.96
Machine tools for metal	—	—	—	.86
Textile machinery	—	—	—	.95
Sewing machines	—	—	—	.95
Other clothing equipment	—	—	—	.75
Paper mill machinery	—	*	—	.81
Printing and binding machinery	*	—	—	.58
Construction and mining machinery	—	—	—	.84
Heating and cooling equipment	—	—	—	.69
Pumps and centrifuges	—	—	—	.83
Ball, rollers, etc., bearings	—	—	—	.78
Electric power machinery	—	—	—	.90
Switch gear	—	—	—	.93
Electric distribution machinery	—	—	—	.91
Radio	—	—	—	.83
Television	—	—	—	.90
Other sound equipment	—	—	—	.84

TABLE 9A.1 (Continued)

Commodity	Japan	Italy	France	Canada	Korea
Domestic electrical equipment	—	—	—	—	—
Transistors, valves	—	—	*	—	—
Railway vehicles	—	—	—	—	—
Passenger motor vehicles	—	—	—	—	—
Lorries, trucks	—	—	—	—	—
Motor vehicle parts	—	—	—	—	—
Motorcycles	—	—	*	—	—
Aircraft and parts	*	—	—	—	*
Ships and boats	—	—	—	—	—
Clothing	—	—	—	—	—
Footwear	*	—	—	—	*
Optical equipment	—	—	*	—	—
Photographic equipment	—	*	—	—	—
Medical instruments	*	—	*	*	*
Photo, cinema supplies	*	*	—	—	*
Pianos and other musical instruments	*	—	—	—	—
Printed matter	—	*	—	—	—
Fishing, hunting, and sports equipment	—	*	—	—	—

Commodity	Germany	United Kingdom	Netherlands	$\overline{R}^2$
Domestic electrical equipment	—	—	—	.88
Transistors, valves	—	*	—	.87
Railway vehicles	—	—	—	.87
Passenger motor vehicles	—	—	—	.84
Lorries, trucks	—	—	—	.86
Motor vehicle parts	—	—	—	.87
Motorcycles	*	—	*	.90
Aircraft and parts	—	—	—	.92
Ships and boats	—	—	—	.91
Clothing	—	—	—	.87
Footwear	—	—	—	.92
Optical equipment	—	*	—	.91
Photographic equipment	—	*	—	.92
Medical instruments	—	*	—	.79
Photo, cinema supplies	—	*	*	.89
Pianos and other musical instruments	—	—	—	.91
Printed matter	—	—	—	.42
Fishing, hunting, and sports equipment	—	*	*	.64

— Statistically insignificant.
* Statistically significant at 5 percent level.

TABLE 9A.2 1973 NET TAX/SUBSIDY RATES FOR THE UNITED
STATES, JAPAN, AND UNITED KINGDOM BY SITC
SECTOR (percentage)

	United States Factor taxes		Japan Factor taxes		United Kingdom Factor taxes	
Traded goods	Capital	Labor	Capital	Labor	Capital	Labor
(1) Agriculture, forestry and fish	9.0	7.0	23.6	3.7	6.4	8.2
(310) Food, beverages, and tobacco	178.2	11.0	86.8	9.1	183.4	9.8
(321) Textiles	138.9	13.1	35.4	9.9	121.4	11.5
(322) Wearing apparel	138.9	13.1	35.4	8.1	240.2	11.1
(323) Leather products	138.9	13.1	35.4	9.4	276.5	12.8
(324) Footwear	138.9	13.1	35.4	9.4	276.5	12.8
(331) Wood products	49.6	12.5	38.4	10.5	116.6	7.9
(332) Furniture and fixtures	49.6	12.5	38.4	10.5	116.6	7.9
(341) Paper and paper products	96.8	10.3	38.4	9.6	96.9	8.7
(342) Printing and publishing	96.8	10.3	38.4	9.2	96.9	8.7
(35A) Chemicals	99.0	10.5	41.9	10.5	116.0	8.4
(35B) Petroleum and related products	19.7	8.4	41.9	11.9	230.6	12.0
(355) Rubber products	144.7	10.5	41.9	9.0	120.3	9.2
(36A) Nonmetal miscellaneous products	81.0	10.3	40.2	9.8	120.3	9.2
(362) Glass and glass products	81.0	10.3	40.2	9.8	120.3	9.2
(371) Iron and steel	81.0	10.3	37.8	11.0	6.3	9.8
(372) Nonferrous metals	81.0	10.3	34.7	11.5	6.3	9.8
(381) Metal products	81.0	10.3	45.0	9.9	6.3	9.8
(382) Nonelectrical machinery	103.5	10.5	38.9	9.6	390.2	9.0
(383) Electrical machinery	131.2	10.7	49.0	9.7	285.5	10.5
(384) Transportation equipment	86.8	9.6	44.1	9.9	282.5	8.2
(38A) Miscellaneous manufactured	86.6	10.5	43.2	9.4	144.1	9.1
Nontraded goods						
(2) Mining and quarrying	34.3	9.6	50.1	19.0	− 55.9	9.7
(4) Electricity, gas, and water	45.7	2.6	22.8	16.2	− 7.2	8.1
(5) Construction	133.3	10.4	39.3	10.7	43.9	9.2
(6) Wholesale and retail trade	112.0	10.5	29.9	8.7	275.5	9.7
(7) Transportation, storage, and communications	186.6	11.3	37.4	10.3	− 47.4	7.3
(8) Finance, insurance, and real estate	135.2	9.7	41.5	11.0	144.9	6.5
(9) Community, social, and personal services	21.2	9.6	27.9	8.5	42.9	12.9

Source: R. Stern and A. Deardorff, "The Effects of Domestic Tax Subsidies and
Import Tarriffs on the Structure of Protection in United States, United Kingdom and
Japan," in *Proceedings of Sixth Annual Conference, International Economic Study
Group* University of Sussex; Rōdōshō, Tōkei kyoku, Jōhōbu, Fukuri hassei shisetsu
to rōdō hiyō no jitai, Okurashō, *Hōjōkin benran,* Nihon ginkō, Tōkei kyoku, *Omō
kigyō keiei bunseki*; Sōrifu, Tōkei kyoku, Chōsa ku, *Kōjin kigyō chōsa nenpō.*

Carlos F. Diaz-Alejandro

T hese are times when repetition of tried and true points may be preferable to garish originality. In this spirit I will focus on the extravagant demands being made on some less developed countries (LDCs) during 1982 by industrial countries. The demands, particularly as articulated by the Reagan administration, may be summarized as follows: the newly industrializing countries (NICs) cannot expect to continue selling, much less expand their sales, in the markets of industrial countries unless the NICs reduce their own barriers to imports of commodities, services, and direct foreign investment and unless they bring their export-promotion practices in line with whatever is the fashion along the Potomac.

International trade theory emphasizes that the gains from trade to a country do not depend on "reciprocity," defined in the sense of the General Agreement on Tariffs and Trade (GATT) from its trade partners. The founding fathers of GATT were, of course, well aware that national gains could be achieved by unilateral reduction of trade barriers. Their appeal to "reciprocity" was a (then) politically clever device to enlist within each country the support of mercantilists, wanting to export more against the protectionists, wanting to import less. A terms of trade argument can be made for a reciprocal reduction of trade barriers, and for the "binding" of remaining barriers, to avoid the temptation of nationally "optimal tariffs" which could lead to trade wars. But it is doubtful that this is what the shouting about lack of NIC reciprocity is all about.

Since around the mid-1960s several important LDCs started to reorient their trade and payments policies so as to give sales abroad incentives closer to those given to domestic sales. This trend toward neutrality between "important-substitution" and export-expansion

---

* *Ed. note*: By special request, Carlos Diaz-Alejandro contributed this prepared note on North-South trade issues to the discussion of major players in the system.

typically started from situations of gross discrimination against selling abroad. The process enjoyed the enthusiastic endorsement of the World Bank, aid agencies of industrial countries, and many Northern academics.

The elimination of the bias against exports could have been achieved by the rapid abolition of import barriers and the unification of exchange rates. Most of the now-NICs, plagued by macroeconomic and balance of payments disequilibria, wisely opted instead for a package of measures including export subsidies and guidelines of various sorts, steadier and more realistic real exchange rates, plus an elimination of the most outlandish import restrictions. Foreign investors who during earlier years had received direct and indirect subsidies in their sales to the domestic market were nudged into exporting, often receiving further subsidies. (It is worth recalling that, when foreign investors sold mainly within LDCs, the prevailing Northern advice was that a good investment climate called for generous LDC subsidies to transnational enterprises.) As the new policies succeeded in expanding foreign exchange earnings, imports grew, dramatically in many cases, and barriers were further relaxed, in what appeared to be a virtuous circle.

It is moot how far import liberalization would have proceeded in the NICs had the world economy behaved in the 1970s as it did during the 1960s. What is clear is that in many NICs balance of payments difficulties caused by post-1973 exogenous shocks halted the virtuous circle, freezing complex foreign trade systems combining import restrictions and export subsidies. The variance of incentives is large and probably those systems are far from optimal from the national viewpoint, but it is doubtful that in many NICs average incentives to export now exceed those given for domestic sales. It is also clear that few, if any, NICs have been recently piling up foreign exchange reserves, or growing faster than their record for the last 20 years. Most NICs today have long shopping lists for Northern goods, plans which must be shelved due to a lack of foreign exchange. It is well known that the servicing of the NICs external debt, especially after the unexpected increase in interest rates since 1980, takes up a large share of their foreign exchange earnings, earnings which during 1982 appear to be experiencing an alarming decline. One may also note that LDCs that have drastically liberalized their import régimes, such as Chile since 1973, do not appear to have been spared Northern protectionism.

The push by the Reagan administration to open doors for services and direct foreign investments is already yielding tangible fruit in new bilateral and discriminating treaties between the United States and some LDCs with weak bargaining positions. It could be argued that if the NICs are so short of foreign exchange, they should be eager to welcome direct foreign investment and associated services. One may note, however, that direct foreign investment seldom yields in the short run substantial amounts of freely usable foreign exchange. It may bring technology, marketing networks, and even sector-specific capital goods, which may be productive in the long term, but hardly the means to service debt or pay for oil imports this year. More fundamentally, the linking of open markets for commodities with open doors for services and direct investment challenges postwar understandings regarding international economic relations.

Trade theory has focused traditionally on commodities rather than services, broadly defined to include labor and capital services. The gains from trade were demonstrated for exchanges of wine for cloth and apples for blankets, rather than for exchanges involving interest payments for workers' remittances. If reduced to algebraic symbols, one can conceive of demonstrations of the gains from trade that would obliterate the difference between apples and workers' remittances. But differences remain between commodity trade and service flows, at least those generated by foreign labor and capital. In the case of goods, transactions can be once-and-for-all affairs, involving few commitments about the future and minimizing intrusiveness between countries that like exchange but not intimacy with foreigners. Factor payments are generated by stocks of machines and people living among foreigners, a process that historically has been accompanied by asymmetrical intrusiveness and noneconomic side-effects, not all desirable either from a national or a cosmopolitan perspective. Little wonder, then, that most nations have abstained from committing themselves to free flows of capital, labor, and services, even at the height of enthusiasm for freer trade in commodities, as during the time when the GATT was created.

Reopening these issues in 1982 seems singularly bizarre and dangerous, particularly when done in an imperial style that appears to regard other countries' sovereignty and culture as nontariff barriers. Explosive issues are opened up: if Tokyo is to be made just like home for US lawyers and bankers, why not have Texas give "national treatment" to Mexican maids? Will New York City be opened up to Indian doctors and South Korean construction crews? Which services and factor flows, in short, are to be "opened up," and what principles are to be followed in those decisions? Delinkers, North and South, would receive fresh ammunition if countries were to be given an all-or-nothing choice between a closed economy and one open not just to commodity trade, but to all services and factor movements. Many countries would choose to pass up the gains from commodity trade rather than to allow foreigners to run their banking, shipping, and insurance sectors, as during pre-World War II days.

A more immediate danger exists as a consequence of the mercantilist spasm seizing industrial countries during 1982. A heavily indebted country like Brazil, to give a concrete example, is being denied the means for a smooth servicing of its external liabilities. Not only are its steel and shoe exports challenged as artificial, but also those of sun-intensive orange juice and chickens are viewed as resulting from unfair subsidies. Even sugar, which Brazil has been exporting for about four centuries, is shut out by quotas in the United States and driven out of traditional markets by (in this case) truly dumped European sugar. Eurocurrency spreads and credit availability are closely linked to the export outlook, and external recession and protectionism are not helping Brazilian efforts to roll over its debt, not to mention its search for additional finance at a reasonable cost. If both recession and Northern protectionism persist, no one should be scandalized if Brazilian voices and those from other NICs call for some form of recontracting of external obligations. Financial rules of the game should be no less flexible than those regarding trade.

In conclusion, one may emphasize that there *are* gaps and flaws in international arrangements on trade and finance as they exist circa 1982. The GATT has never overcome its birth defects, and Keynes' "lusty twins" are undergoing a difficult menopause. No "central committee" appears to be worrying about the interactions of trade and finance, as noted in the previous paragraph. The US 1982 proposals to extend the GATT into some services are misguided in timing, and substance, but at least they highlight the long-run need to reform the GATT-Bretton Woods system more along the lines of the Havana charter, an issue raised by the LDCs almost 10 years ago.

A broad reform should, inter alia, tackle the issue of how NICs and other relatively advanced LDCs should gradually be expected to accept rules applicable to the industrial countries, including the granting of preferences to the least developed countries in an unconditional most-favored-nation fashion. (Brazilian preferences just to Paraguay embody the same dangers as French preferences to Chad, or those of the United States to Jamaica.) Viewed in this broad and long-term perspective, "graduation" becomes a legitimate and important issue, both for the system as a whole and for the possible graduates. For reasons of their own national welfare, NICs will eventually want to liberalize their import régimes further, rationalize their export incentives, and also become dues-paying members of the inner club in which trade rules get written and interpreted. Other LDCs, with smaller domestic markets and weaker bargaining power, may also seek international rules yielding greater transparency and predictability in access to external markets. These smaller countries have much to gain from resisting the lure of discriminatory special trading relationships, which typically are sold to them by larger countries as being aimed at other "exotic and unfair" trading blocs, but which historically have frequently ended up limiting both the economic and political development of the smaller countries. Systemically, the gradual but complete incorporation of new Germanys and new Japans into the trading order, and the provision of a minimum of economic security for truly sovereign small countries, seem like necessary conditions for international stability. World War I and II suggest that the rationale for such conditions is more political than economic.

Yves Berthelot

T he question is not whether the European Community (EC) is more or less guilty than Japan or the United States in trade restrictions, but how to find a way out of the crisis and to what extent expansion in trade could provide a way out.

The papers presented by Patterson and Grey show clearly that in trade competition each country or group of countries tries to take advantage of the rules and to bias the system toward what the country considers its own interest. Every country is actually in favor of free trade in sectors where it has comparative advantage and for some protection in areas where it does not. It is important, as noted by Grey, that the countries nevertheless accept counterweights to this natural behavior and commit themselves to more free trade.

The actual data, as opposed to theory or a priori judgments, indicate that EC imports (without intra-EC trade) of manufactured goods exceed those of the United States and Japan and grew faster between 1968 and 1980. This first indicator shows that the EC is now more open than its main partners as confirmed by imports per capita or as a share of GNP (table 1).

For each European country taken separately, the openness is even higher because of intra-EC trade, which is around 50 percent of total trade. For textiles the results are similar. The Multi-Fiber Arrangement (MFA) did not slow down the global textile import ratio in EC countries; it led to a shift of imports from developing to industrial countries.

Saxonhouse's paper on Japan sometimes seems to be based on the hypothesis that "free trade is the best policy; because Japan is a successful country, Japan obviously has a free trade policy." In fact the paper is very interesting because it describes an efficient state intervention to improve growth and to close the gap between Japan and other developed countries. Grey also explains that inequality between countries and relative power relationships are not correctly understood in comparative advantage theory and that corrections have to be done.

More generally most of the papers, more or less explicitly, give the impression that the 1950s and 1960s were the golden age thanks to free trade policies; that increasing obstacles to trade during the 1970s partly explain the increasing economic difficulties; and that increasing trade liberalization would help the recovery of the world economy. I am not so sure.

Most of the advanced industrial countries have reached the same level of productivity, and technologies and capital circulate quickly from one country to another. In this uniformized world, comparative advantage does not clearly indicate what to export. In a slow growth period, competition appears to displace employment rather than to create new opportunities.

The priority for the medium term is to develop new markets. In the creation of new products state intervention is sometimes useful, as shown by the examples of Japan, the United States, and most European countries. It is neither inefficient nor counterproductive, as past experience demonstrates. Today, when research and development is declining and investment is low, state incentives are even more necessary. But state intervention must not be limited to the funding of research or stimulus of investments; more fundamentally, it must contribute to the adaptation of social structures. It appears,

TABLE 1   IMPORTS OF MANUFACTURES

	1968	1980
Per capita (1975 dollars)		
European Community[a]	172	454
United States	239	442
Japan	82	241
Percentage of GNP		
European Community[a]	4.2	6.7
United States	2.6	6.2
Japan	3.2	4.2
Textile products per capita (1975 dollars)		
European Community[a]	9.3	37.9
United States	15.5	24.3
Japan	2.7	15.0

Source: CHELEM, Paris.
a. Imports from outside the EC.

and Japan is a very good example, that country competitiveness does not lie in factor endowment (capital, raw material, or even skilled labor) but mainly in the capacity of society to accept and implement new technologies.

Hideo Kanemitsu

In the presence of Japan's trade surplus (over \$13 billion with the United States and over \$10 billion with European Community, EC, countries in 1981, based on Japanese data) harsh voices have been heard in this conference with many tones of accusation against Japan. Overwhelmingly, Japan is guilty with regard to market access to foreign sales, particularly of manufactured products. Furthermore, along with the categorical closedness of the Japanese market to foreign imports, an "avalanche" of Japanese exports of specific products (most recently automobiles) has been persistently a target of accusation accompanied by heavy protectionist pressures of one kind or another.

Put differently, Japan's conduct of external economic affairs and its underlying social and cultural fabric of market behaviors, taken as a whole, is a serious concern of the major industrial countries.[1] Japanese consumers, producers, and government agencies are simply reluctant to buy foreign-made products; Japanese firms have succeeded in developing and maintaining a gigantic mass-production system (typically, in steel, automobiles, ships, electrical appliance industries) with a devastatingly high tendency for export sales. Even the recent conduct of Japan's macroeconomic policy is not innocent, because the Japanese government continues a policy mix of tight fiscal and easy monetary measures which happen to be exactly the opposite direction of the US policy mix of loose fiscal and tight monetary measures. As a consequence of this policy disharmony between the United States and Japan an abnormally large interest differential

---

[1] See, for example, the EC's complaints about the Japanese trade conduct based on Article XXIII of the General Agreement on Tariffs and Trade (GATT). In this connection, see the following two chapters in an entirely opposite tone, Alan Wm. Wolff "The Need for New GATT Rules for Safeguard Actions," chapter 11, and Harald B. Malmgren, "Threats to the Multilateral System," chapter 6, both this volume.

between the two countries has caused the yen exchange rate vis-à-vis the US dollar to decline beyond the level justified by existing fundamental environment and expectations, creating tension in trade and foreign investment. In my view, most of these sweeping arguments against Japan are fundamentally of a political nature and not supported by sensible economic reasoning.[2]

Perhaps it will be all too easy to point out that Japan legally dismantled almost all the import-barrier measures such as "Buy Japanese," unlike the United States; "voluntary export restraints" have prevailed for quite some time in a substantial portion of major Japanese exports under the threat of import restrictions by the United States and EC countries; the most important objective of Japan's recent macroeconomic policy is above all to restore and maintain Japan's healthy growth, to alleviate from itself huge government deficits and from a prolonged recession which began at the time of the second oil crisis; the Japanese monetary authorities are desperately trying to support the yen exchange rate from a continuing trend of decline, against the prevailing strong forces in the worldwide foreign exchange market.

It is therefore extremely refreshing, if not totally surprising, in this context to see what Saxonhouse shows about the trade and industrial pattern of the Japanese economy in his cross-country econometric analysis, based on the best known standard model of international trade (namely, the Hecksher-Ohlin general equilibrium theory of comparative advantage). Saxonhouse shows, in essence, that, when taking fully into account relevant productive factors such as capital stock, labor quantity and quality, resource endowment of oil and iron ore, and arable land, the trade pattern of the Japanese economy is in no significant way different from other industrial countries in the free market economy world. To quote:

> No other advanced industrial economy combines such high quality of labor with such poor natural resources at such a great distance from its major partners. It is these distinctive characteristics and not, for example, an industrial policy . . . which give Japan a robust comparative advantage in so many manufacturing products.

The conclusion Saxonhouse obtains from his empirical cross-country analysis is hardly surprising and is in full conformity not only with

---

[2] See William R. Cline, "Reciprocity and Conditional Market Access," chapter 4, and Gary R. Saxonhouse, "The Micro- and Macroeconomics of Foreign Sales to Japan," chapter 9, both this volume.

rigorous economic reasoning (as the Hecksher-Ohlin theory suggests), but is also similar to the ideas of Japanese government officials and businessmen (as frequently suggested and even tentatively analyzed by various Japanese official documents). The great merit of Saxonhouse's contribution is thus not so much his conclusion about the Japanese trade idiosyncrasy, but much more distinctively his unique and quite comprehensive procedure to test the standard theory of comparative advantage with regard to Japan.

In applying this well-known theory, the international trade model Saxonhouse adopted is, strictly speaking, appropriate only for tradable final commodities, excluding the important category of traded raw materials and all the intermediate goods for production, as Saxonhouse himself notes (Appendix 9.A, n. 8). Considering that nearly 60 percent of Japanese imports belong to this intermediate category, one should exercise some caution in interpreting Saxonhouse's statistical results and the implications of these statistics.

Despite his conclusion about the Japanese trade pattern, Saxonhouse is no less keen to point out *differentia specifica* build into the Japanese economy, characterized mostly by what he calls "illiberal" institutional elements. According to Saxonhouse, there are at least 11 such "illiberal" institutional elements which are "from the foreign perspective Japan's distinctive, but illiberal way of conducting economic affairs . . . ."

Naturally most of these "illiberal" elements involve government interference into the private market economy, which we may classify broadly into the following three types:

• Industrial policy, including (1) policy guidance, (6) lack of effective antitrust policy, (10) lack of competitive procurement (Saxonhouse's numbers in parentheses);
• Financial regulation, including (2) direct government intervention in the private financial market, (7) regulation of household's capital and financial facilities, and (9) regulation of the business financial system, domestic, and foreign;
• Regulatory policy in (5) the distribution system, and (11) the service sector.

"Illiberal" elements in the Japanese private sector observed by Saxonhouse include: (3) domination of large bank-centered industrial groups in financial and capital markets, hindering, for example, the development of venture capital institutions, (4) domination of large trading company-centered groups in domestic and foreign distribution, and (8) lack of labor mobility within and among industries.

It is quite striking that 4 (2, 3, 7, 9) of the above 11 elements are closely related to the financial and capital markets of the Japanese economy, which are predominantly characterized as "illiberal" institutions.

I am not so sure whether I totally agree with Saxonhouse that each of these 11 elements is distinctively Japanese and "illiberal" in the sense that the market mechanism in general and the financial system in particular are considerably impaired.

Saxonhouse's most interesting hypothesis is that these "illiberal" institutional elements, both in the public and the private sector taken together, help to produce nothing but a typical pattern of international trade and industrial development typically observed in most of the "liberal" market-oriented economies. In Saxonhouse's own words:

> The empirical results just presented suggest that distinctive Japanese institutions are better thought of as substitutes rather than complements for functionally equivalent institutions that exist in the United States.

From this analysis, Saxonhouse speculates that "in such a situation . . . it is not always possible to remove any single institution without having a substantial impact on the operation of the Japanese economy."

To be more specific, Saxonhouse suggests that the public "illiberal" elements mentioned above (industrial policy, financial regulation, distribution and services regulatory policy) counterbalance the private "illiberal" elements (3, 4, 8). Thus, for example, Japanese industrial policy plays a countervailing role to facilitate the market mechanism in capital and labor allocation which is considerably hampered by the domination of large bank-centered industrial groups. Perhaps, under these circumstances, the lack of an effective antitrust policy may be inevitable! Saxonhouse thus concludes that "in so many cases, the illiberal elements fit together into a grand, if not implicit, design, which does allow the Japanese economy to function successfully."

The Saxonhouse hypothesis concerning Japan's "illiberal" institutions is certainly controversial and does not necessarily follow from his empirical analysis. In my view, it is neither convincing nor entirely consistent with the fact that the Japanese economy has experienced a remarkably rapid progress of liberalization and deregulation in many areas during the last two decades of high economic growth.

Saxonhouse's conclusion about the pattern of Japanese trade and industry is based on data for the period prior to 1973. The question naturally may be raised whether his conclusion and the ensuing policy recommendations are still valid for the period after 1973. I would assume there is no reason to reject the validity of his conclusion and recommendations for the present time.

In this case, however, there are difficulties concerning what Saxonhouse strongly recommends for short-run policy in connection with current international conflicts among industrial countries. Since no significant distortion has been observed in the pattern of the Japanese trade and industrial structure, Saxonhouse repeatedly suggests that changes in microeconomic policy and behavior in Japan will not induce any striking change in international trade and investment. Indeed, "a piecemeal attempt to speed the pace of liberalizing those Japanese economic institutions . . . might disrupt the Japanese economy."

Yet Saxonhouse is suddenly concerned with Japan's balance of payments disequilibrium problem and its remedies. I am not sure whether Saxonhouse's concern stems from a Japanese macroeconomic standpoint or, more likely, from a global disequilibrium point of view. In any case, Saxonhouse has failed to recognize an apparent inconsistency between his microeconomic analysis, his evaluation of Japanese trade and industry, and his macroeconomic assessment of Japan's balance of payments problem.

Without questioning seriously the nature and the cause of international conflicts facing Japan, Saxonhouse endorses a policy recommendation which is powerful enough to correct the continuing "disparity" of the yen-dollar exchange rate. According to Saxonhouse's analysis, this will be accomplished by the complete liberalization of the Japanese financial system. Only in this way can Japanese yen be transacted as a genuine international currency and eventually its exchange rate in terms of the US dollar will be appreciated up to an equilibrium level.

But Saxonhouse himself suggests, rightly or wrongly, that Japan's distinctively "illiberal" elements, predominantly found in the Japanese financial system, cannot be liberalized in a piecemeal fashion without disrupting seriously the Japanese economy as a whole. One wonders where Saxonhouse's microeconomic prescription stands in the face of his recommendation of liberalization of the Japanese financial system.

Furthermore, from the short-run policy point of view, fuller liberalization of the Japanese financial system may not be helpful at all to appreciate the yen because it will accelerate further Japan's capital export under the current conditions of interest differential between the United States and Japan. At least in the short-run Japan's further capital outflow would definitely contribute to a further decline of the yen exchange rate vis-à-vis the US dollar.

I fully agree with Saxonhouse that complete liberalization of the Japanese economic system, including the financial and capital markets, is desirable and that the Japanese yen can play an important role as an international currency in order to stabilize the world financial system. But this must be a policy objective of Japan only in the longer run.

Roberto Fendt argued that the development success stories of the past decade had been cases of outward-looking growth (Brazil, Korea, Spain) but not free trade (Argentina, Chile). He emphasized that the net margin of protection from tariffs, quotas, and export subsidies in developing countries is modest when the overvaluation of the exchange rate is discounted. He noted that the pressures from the North for graduation, latent threats of retaliation for purposes of reciprocity, and political use of trade as in the case of the Falklands conflict, were raising uncertainty for developing countries in decision making on export-oriented investments. And like Diaz-Alejandro he maintained that the debt-servicing problem not only heightened the need for continued access to northern markets but also seriously circumscribed the move for action on general trade liberalization in the near term for Brazil, Mexico, and other middle-income countries.

Wynn Godley expressed concern that the discussion had concentrated on how to liberalize the system further when high unemployment made that goal highly unrealistic. Bergsten and Williamson properly emphasize the exchange rate, and in the UK case the rate is probably overvalued by 30 percent. But it is politically infeasible to implement the incomes policy that would be necessary to carry out an effective devaluation of this magnitude. It may be necessary instead to impose protection, but on an across the board basis rather than discriminatorily across industries. C. Fred Bergsten responded that the result could be foreign retaliation, and Richard N. Cooper noted the inconsistency of imposing protection when the whole macroeconomic policy has been designed to reduce inflation.

Jagdish Bhagwati urged clarification of what it is we are asking Japan to do, and of whether the reforms are specific to Japan or apply to others. He maintained that the real problem is that Japan has grown much more rapidly than other countries, and that the resulting structural transformation causes adjustment problems for

319

the rest of the world. The undervalued yen is a red herring. He asked whether countries would react in the same way to other newcomers.

Hideo Kanemitsu argued that "Japan, Inc.," is a myth. Ministry of International Trade and Industry (MITI) guidance applied only through the 1960s. In the electrical industry, for example, there is no protection, just higher quality of Japanese goods. In agriculture Japan has the special problem that it is dependent on imports for 60 percent of its supply of food.

Yusuki Onitsuku stated that the principal exceptions to free trade in Japan are for food self-sufficiency needs and for infant-industry development in high technology. MITI expects competitive capacity within five years and does not protect uncompetitive industries. He agreed that the undervalued yen caused problems, but considered capital controls dangerous, preferring changes in the mix of monetary and fiscal policy. With respect to Japanese exchange intervention in 1976, he noted that following the oil shock Japan lost a large share of its reserves and needed to intervene to rebuild them.

Rodney de C. Grey maintained that Japan is willing to import only logs and ores from Canada, and that it structures tariffs and taxes in favor of imports of raw materials, not processed goods.

Richard N. Cooper argued that even if the estimate of increased imports from Japanese liberalization were as low as $2 billion, actual liberalization would make a great difference to the debate. He cited the deep feeling in both the private and public sectors in Japan that whatever can be produced domestically should be. It is often mid-level officials who try to stop imports.

Juergen Donges stated that Patterson need not have made his caveat: his paper presents a balanced description of European Community (EC) tendencies, which are clearly protectionist. Even internal free trade within the European Community is eroding. EC policies make no contribution to the stabilization of world grains markets, although they lead to lower grains prices for developing country importers. The second enlargement of the EC will lead to more protection to secure Spain and Portugal against competition from the newly industrialized countries.

Alan William Wolff argued that in reciprocity the real problem is Japan. Thousands of American businessmen will testify that it is difficult to sell in Japan. Japan is not open to competing goods. A company unprepared to sell proprietary technology finds that its sales disappear. The distribution system is protectionist. Japanese businesses practice buy-national preferences. They will not purchase intermediate inputs from abroad. Appreciation of the yen would affect Japan's exports but not its imports. Wolff commended Grey's paper on contingent protectionism, but noted that the alternatives may be worse, for example in the transition from countervailing duties to quotas in steel. He emphasized the need for negotiations to achieve further liberalization in services and investment to halt erosion of current openness.

Gary R. Saxonhouse, in addition to responding to other comments, emphasized in reply to Wolff that numerous surveys of businessmen had not found the type of complaints Wolff cited.

Problems from the Past

Protection in the postwar period has shifted gradually from generalized tariff barriers to nontariff barriers concentrated in a limited number of important product sectors, on the one hand, and government intervention through subsidies and other measures, on the other. Typically protection in industrial countries reflects a failure to obtain economic adjustment in certain major sectors to changing international comparative advantage. The long-term persistence of protection in some of the most important sectors indicates that this process of adjustment or maladjustment is of historical dimensions.

Despite their success in some areas, notably in cutting tariffs, past trade negotiations have failed to resolve problems of protection in several key functional and sectoral areas. In chapter 10, Gary Clyde Hufbauer reviews the unfinished business in policing government subsidies that distort trade, despite the advance made by agreement to a subsidies code in the Tokyo Round of negotiations. Broadly, US businessmen and policymakers tend to see industrial subsidies abroad as detrimental to US trade performance, often even when those subsidies are not solely directed at exports. For their part, foreigners tend to see US antidumping and countervailing duties as protective devices in their own right instead of as mechanisms for enforcing fair trade.

The single largest omission of the Tokyo Round was its failure to achieve agreement on a code regulating safeguard protection. Currently, General Agreement on Tariffs and Trade (GATT) rules on such protection are observed in the breach: for example, protection has tended to discriminate against a few suppliers and to go uncompensated, whereas GATT rules require most-favored-nation (MFN) treatment and compensation. In chapter 11 Alan Wm. Wolff, formerly deputy US special trade representative, calls for a safeguards code regulating these practices. Controversially, he favors a modified form of "selectivity" (freedom to restrict imports from selected supplying countries only), the point on which the code foundered in the Tokyo Round because of European Community (EC) insistence on it and developing-country opposition to it. And in chapter 12, J. David Richardson of the University of Wisconsin examines US programs of adjustment assistance, addressing at least one major aspect of the fundamental problem of deficient sectoral adjustment as the root of entrenched protection.

Four sector studies in Part III examine the hard core of major protection in world trade today: restrictions in agriculture, textiles and apparel, steel, and automobiles. In each area the problem is chronic failure to adjust to competition from foreign sources with greater comparative advantage: in agriculture, of Japan and the EC to supply from United States, Canada, Australia, and less developed countries (LDCs); in textiles and apparel, of the United States and EC to supply from LDCs; in steel, of the United States and EC to supply from Japan (with a strange twist that because of subsidization the US market also has faced competition from the EC); and in automobiles, of the United States and EC to supply from Japan. All four sectors have in common enormous domestic political clout because of their large labor forces (and, in the case of agriculture, additional influence for historical and districting reasons).

Dale E. Hathaway, formerly Under Secretary of the US Department of Agriculture, examines agricultural protection in chapter 13. As noted in chapter 22, the issue of EC subsidies to agricultural exports is the cause of the most recent flare-up in US-EC trade relations, at the 1982 GATT Ministerial and afterward. Martin Wolf of the Trade Policy Research Centre (London) reviews textile and apparel protection under the Multi-Fiber Arrangement (MFA) in chapter 14, emphasizing the warning that the highly protective MFA provides to policymakers against adopting supposedly temporary international régimes restricting and organizing trade. In chapter 15 Ingo Walter of New York University examines protection in steel, emphasizing the high labor cost and inefficiency of US and EC steel production and anticipating some forms of international control of steel trade—as indeed subsequently transpired in the US-EC quota arrangement (noted in chapter 1). And in chapter 16 Robert B. Cohen of New York University traces similar problems of excessive labor costs and inefficiency that, together with the overvalued dollar, have led to US protection against Japanese automobiles, a sector long considered unlikely to go protectionist because of the international dimensions of its key firms.

The central thrust of Part III is that much if not most of the problem of protection today may be found in entrenched protectionist-oriented sectors and government intervention. The trading nations must come to grips with this inheritance from the past if a credible stand is to be made either in resistance to new claims for protection by other sectors or in the more positive goal of enlargement of world trading rules to incorporate the services sector and other newly emerging areas of potential trade conflict.

CHAPTER 10

Subsidy Issues After the Tokyo Round

Gary Clyde Hufbauer

The twin sisters, subsidies and countervailing measures, played center stage in the Trade Act of 1974. They received rapt attention during the Tokyo Round. In mid-1982, they remain a lively source of trade gossip.

Introduction

Sheer intellectual curiosity explains part of the continuing fascination. But customs valuation also exhibits an intellectual dimension. Why are subsidies and countervailing measures consistently more entertaining?

Falling Water Level or Rising Reef?

One explanation is the falling water level hypothesis: as tariffs and other forms of protection decline, the remaining trade distortions have more visible effect. Subsidies are a prominent distortion; further, national differences in subsidy practices become more readily apparent as the general level of protection declines. A second explanation is the rising reef hypothesis: subsidies and surrogate practices have rapidly escalated as industrial nations have responded to rising energy prices, slow growth, and antiquated factories.

The difference between these hypotheses is more than semantic. If subsidies are an issue today mainly because the level of protection fell in the past, then subsidies may not become the dominant theme of trade policy tomorrow. The general level of protection is no longer declining; and subsidies are merely one reef among many, for ex-

327

TABLE 10.1   SUBSIDIES AS SHOWN IN NATIONAL ACCOUNTS
             STATISTICS AS A PERCENTAGE OF GROSS DOMESTIC
             PRODUCT

Country	1952	1956	1960	1964	1968	1972	1976	1980
Canada	0.41	0.39	0.81	0.85	0.87	0.83	1.73	2.34
United States	0.11	0.20	0.25	0.44	0.50	0.59	0.34	0.43
Japan	0.79	0.26	0.34	0.65	1.11	1.12	1.32	1.32
France	1.71	2.71	1.62	2.03	2.62	1.99	2.68	2.51
Germany	0.65	0.20	0.79	0.99	1.44	1.48	1.49	1.59
Italy	0.89	1.30	1.51	1.23	1.67	2.29	2.60	3.01
United Kingdom	2.68	1.76	1.93	1.56	2.06	1.82	2.78	2.32

Source: OECD, *National Accounts 1951–1980,* vol. 1, Main Aggregates, 1982.

ample, the protectionist use of technical standards and government procurement.

But if the subsidy reef is rising, the outlook suddenly changes. The escalating use of subsidies could replace tariffs as the central distortion of rational international commerce, and in time dominate other non-tariff barriers.

The rising reef hypothesis finds much support among informed observers. For example, Malmgren (1977, p. 26):

> Governments more and more are being called upon to intervene in order to shore up troubled sectors of their economies and promote sectors that are judged politically to have high potential. But as government responsibility has broadened, structural objectives have also multiplied—to the point, in recent years, that structural policies often conflict with, or undercut, international rules and the arrangements which have resulted from international bargaining.

In a simple attempt to assess the merits of the falling water level and rising reef hypotheses, tables 10.1 through 10.4 present rough indicators of the relative size of total subsidies and export subsidies.

In table 10.1, current subsidies of all description,[1] however they may be measured for national accounting purposes, are compared with GDP for the "Big Seven" countries. Three points are clear from this table. First, the general upward drift in the importance of subsidies since the early 1950s has affected every country except the United Kingdom and possibly France, two nations that had developed

---

[1] Presumably the great preponderance of subsidies shown in national accounts statistics are domestic subsidies, conferred without regard to whether the output is sold at home or abroad.

TABLE 10.2 GOVERNMENT FINANCE OF CAPITAL FORMATION AS A PERCENTAGE OF TOTAL GROSS CAPITAL FORMATION

Country	1964	1968	1972	1976	1979
Canada	16.7	18.3	16.9	13.7	12.2
United States	15.6	14.9	11.9	11.2	8.6[a]
Japan	13.9[a]	11.7	15.4	16.2	19.3
France	15.6	17.4	14.3	13.5	12.9
Germany	17.0	15.0	14.8	15.5	14.1
Italy	n/a	n/a	14.0	14.5	14.5
United Kingdom	20.9	25.4	23.8	22.2	14.1

Source: OECD, *National Accounts of OECD Countries,* vol. 2, Detailed Tables, 1981 (in particular, table 7).
a. Estimated

extensive systems of subventions by the end of World War II. Second, between 1968 and 1980, only two countries, Canada and Italy, have noticeably increased the relative degree of subsidization. Third, and perhaps most important, the United States has persistently exhibited the lowest ratio of subsidies to GDP, and unlike other countries, the United States ratio has declined since the late 1960s. The discrepancy in absolute level, together with the contrary US trend, goes far to explain US grievances with the practices of other countries.[2]

In table 10.2, government finance of capital formation is related to total gross capital formation for the period 1964 to 1979, again for the "Big Seven" countries. Government finance of capital formation generally contains some element of future subsidization, since governments seldom earn market rates of interest on their fixed assets. These data indicate that, with the notable exception of Japan, the role of government finance has generally declined since the late 1960s. However, since market interest rates rose sharply between 1968 and 1979, the implicit subsidy inherent in a given share of government capital formation may have increased dramatically, brought about *sub silentio* by the great inflation of the capital formation in the United States. Again, this discrepancy reinforces US grievances.

[2] A key theme running through the US Treasury's annual reports on *The Operation and Effect of the Domestic International Sales Corporation Legislation,* the US Export–Import Bank's annual *Report to the Congress on Export Credit Competition and the Export–Import Bank,* and commentary by academic scholars such as Mutti (1981), is that, while the United States engages in subsidy practices, it does so to a much smaller degree than other countries.

TABLE 10.3   OFFICIAL EXPORT CREDIT AUTHORIZATIONS RELATED
TO EXPORTS OF MANUFACTURED GOODS

	1973	1974	1975	1976
Official Export Credit Authorizations (million dollars) [a]				
Canada	n/a	n/a	2,048	2,171
United States	8,797	7,458	7,949	6,584
Japan	18,515	22,600	22,968	32,034
France	8,268	11,804	19,626	21,920
Germany	3,553	7,330	7,950	10,387
Italy	819	1,020	4,596	3,306
United Kingdom	5,242	14,276	9,645	10,519
Exports of Manufactured Goods (million dollars) [b]				
Canada	13,689	16,521	16,682	20,648
United States	44,740	63,544	71,023	77,297
Japan	34,741	52,499	53,167	64,576
France	26,087	33,600	40,120	43,006
Germany	60,302	78,953	79,619	90,729
Italy	18,614	24,884	29,143	31,177
United Kingdom	25,638	32,046	36,456	38,315
Official Export Credit Authorization Related to Exports of Manufactured Goods (percentage)				
Canada	n/a	n/a	12.3	10.5
United States	19.7	13.3	11.2	8.5
Japan	53.3	43.0	43.2	49.6
France	31.7	35.1	48.9	51.0
Germany	5.9	9.3	10.0	11.4
Italy	4.4	4.1	15.8	10.6
United Kingdom	20.4	44.5	26.5	27.4

Note: Official export credit authorization data are derived from information originally
collected by the Berne Union.
Sources: US Export-Import Bank, *Report to the US Congress on Export Credit Competition
and the Export-Import Bank of the United States:* biannual reports from July 1, 1974
through December 31, 1975, and annual reports dated July 1977, July 1978, and October
1980; Organization for Economic Cooperation and Development, Trade Series C.
a. In the case of Canada and the United States, authorizations represent the sum of direct
and discount loans plus insurance and guarantees. In the case of other countries, authorizations represent insurance and guarantees only, since all direct financing by those
countries is covered by insurance or guarantees. For the most part the years refer to
calendar years, but in some instances the export credit authorizations are fiscal year data.
b. Manufactured goods are defined as SITC 5, 6, 7, and 8.

Tables 10.3 and 10.4 present indicators of the most conspicuous
form of export subsidy, namely official export credits. In table 10.3,
official export credit authorizations of the Big Seven countries are
compared with exports of manufactures for the period 1973 to 1979.

	1977	1978	1979
Official Export Credit Authorizations (million dollars) [a]			
Canada	2,471	4,030	3,535
United States	5,545	7,375	9,490
Japan	33,641	31,810	39,355
France	19,145	30,660	32,155
Germany	14,515	14,960	14,505
Italy	3,053	8,705	8,020
United Kingdom	11,011	35,115	33,430
Exports of Manufactured Goods (million dollars) [b]			
Canada	23,083	27,137	30,282
United States	80,515	94,897	117,097
Japan	77,695	94,181	99,041
France	49,709	59,279	75,736
Germany	104,344	125,462	150,577
Italy	38,014	47,818	61,062
United Kingdom	46,795	57,643	70,381
Official Export Credit Authorization Related to Exports of Manufactured Goods (percentage)			
Canada	10.7	14.9	11.7
United States	6.9	7.8	8.1
Japan	43.3	33.8	39.7
France	38.5	51.7	42.5
Germany	13.9	11.9	9.6
Italy	8.0	18.2	13.1
United Kingdom	23.5	60.9	47.5

In table 10.4, the amounts of export credit financed in whole or part with official credits are compared with exports of manufactures for the period 1978 to 1980. Export credit authorization and activity levels are a better measure of overt government export promotion measures than of export credit subsidies. Of course, the better measure of export credit subsidy is the difference between interest rates actually charged for export credits and the market cost of money to governments. Throughout the 1970s and into the early 1980s, rising market interest rates, compared with rigidly low rates for officially supported export credits, implied rapidly rising subsidies per million dollars of official export credit authorization. By 1980, the annual level of interest rate subsidization had risen to $4.0 to $5.0 billion (Wallen and Duff, p. 475) compared to an amount probably under $1.0 billion in 1973.

TABLE 10.4   OFFICIAL EXPORT CREDITS RELATED TO EXPORTS OF
              MANUFACTURED GOODS

	1978	1979	1980
Exports financed by official credits (million dollars) [a]			
United States	10,358	14,508	18,594
Japan	31,885	49,046	52,798
France	18,019	20,370	21,188
Germany	14,293	14,241	15,032
United Kingdom	32,143	35,769	43,700
Exports of manufactured goods (million dollars) [b]			
United States	94,897	117,097	144,735
Japan	94,181	99,041	124,597
France	59,279	75,736	83,998
Germany	125,462	150,577	167,071
United Kingdom	57,643	61,062	86,016
Official export credit authorizations related to exports of manufactured goods (percentage)			
United States	10.9	12.4	12.8
Japan	33.9	49.5	42.4
France	30.4	26.9	25.2
Germany	11.4	9.5	9.0
United Kingdom	56.4	58.6	50.8

Sources: Export-Import Bank of the United States, Policy Analysis Staff, "Trends in Official Export Credit", May 24, 1982. Note that export activity data are derived from information originally collected by the OECD; OECD, Trade Series C.
a. In principle, these figures represent the total of exports which are accompanied (in whole or part) by some amount of official export credit finance.
b. Manufactured goods are defined as SITC 5, 6, 7, and 8.

Bearing this feature in mind, several conclusions may be drawn from the level of export promotion effort revealed in tables 10.3 and 10.4.

First, most countries exhibit a jagged profile of ups and downs in the ratio between export credit activity and manufactures exports. Only Italy and the United Kingdom seem to show a long-term upward trend in the relative magnitude of official credits. Second, during much of the 1970s, US export credit activity declined from a low base. Third, the United States, Canada, and Germany operate very much smaller programs than their industrial competitors.

All in all, conscious government policy decisions in the past decade have significantly elevated the readily observable subsidy programs in a minority of cases: Canada and Italy with respect to current subsidies as a percentage of GDP; Japan with respect to government capital formation; Italy, and the United Kingdom with respect to export credits.

More importantly, perhaps, any upward thrust in the effective level of subsidies should be attributed to the fact that, in the 1970s, inflation significantly enhanced the subsidy component of established programs. These unexpected accretions caused by inflation just might be eroded by a tide of disinflation. But it is also possible that disinflation will vanish in a flood of budget deficits, or that the pain of disinflation will prompt a noisy clamor for larger nominal subsidies.

The tables clearly illustrate why the United States feels aggrieved: its subsidy programs are consistently smaller, and in some instances trending downwards, by comparison with its major competitors. Even if disinflation erodes existing subsidies, and even if the general level of protection ceases to decline, the sense of uneven levels is likely to ensure continued if not dominant interest in subsidies and countervailing measures throughout the 1980s.

Designing a Framework of Discipline

Many observers tolerate and even welcome subsidies. In their view, subsidies are a preferred second-best solution for offsetting economic distortions that the political system cannot address directly. According to this line of thought, "irresponsible" countervailing duties need discipline, not subsidies.

Other observers greet the second-best argument with skepticism. They believe that most subsidies reflect raw political power, not rational planning. In this view most subsidies are a source of new distortions not a cure for old distortions. Accordingly, subsidies need all the discipline they can get.

The intellectual clash between these two schools has produced a system of international discipline that covers both subsidies and countervailing measures. In the process, international agreement has been sought on three issues:

• the definition of potentially troublesome subsidies
• the delineation of the trade impact required for a potentially troublesome subsidy to give international offense
• the design of effective procedures and remedies to redress offensive subsidies, but not to overcompensate for their presence.

The search for international agreement reached fever levels during the Tokyo Round. The result was a very detailed Subsidies Code.[3]

---

[3] Known formally as the Agreement on Interpretation and Application of Articles VI, XVI, and XXIII of the General Agreement on Tariffs and Trade (GATT). The code has been signed by 28 countries: Australia, Austria,

In light of this extensive effort, perhaps the time has come, say the Europeans and many others, to rely on normal implementation mechanisms to deal with remaining difficulties and to settle ambiguities. Senior Reagan administration officials, such as Deputy Treasury Secretary Robert T. McNamar and Ambassador David R. Macdonald, take the contrary view that discipline over subsidies has not yet evolved to the point of routine implementation. In their view, important work remains to be done at the negotiating level.

The General Agreement on Tariffs and Trade (GATT) Ministerial will thus be faced with the procedural question whether subsidy issues should be addressed through renewed negotiation or ongoing administration. Once the right pitch of discussions is found (a process that will determine the limits of possible achievement), attention will turn to the substantive issues.

In framing the original GATT, in subsequent amendments, and in the Tokyo Round, the international community lavished its attentions on the trade impact issue, but examined the definitional and remedial issues rather less closely. The chief result is an elaborate but not terribly satisfactory set of rules that purport to grade the requisite degree of trade impact for a potentially troublesome subsidy to qualify as an offensive subsidy. These rules, summarized and evaluated below in "The Role of Trade Impact," turn on the type of subsidy, the product subsidized, and the development status of the subsidizing country.

As a result of the Tokyo Round and the work that went before, certain hard-core export subsidies are now well defined, but the definition of domestic and export subsidies in gray cases is largely left to the case decisions of national authorities. With proper encouragement, the Subsidies Committee may come to play a constructive role in the harmonization of national definitions. Major gray areas are discussed below under "The Definitions of Domestic Subsidies."

During the Tokyo Round, only limited progress was made in the design of effective remedies. The most noteworthy achievement was the establishment of a tight timetable for panel decisions within the framework of the Subsidies Code. However, the design of remedies, apart from the familiar countervailing duty, remains an ad hoc matter. This issue is discussed below in "Effective Remedies."

Brazil, Canada, Chile, the European Community (EC, 10 members) Finland, Hong Kong, India, Japan, South Korea, New Zealand, Norway, Pakistan, Sweden, Switzerland, United States, Uruguay, and Yugoslavia. Colombia and Mexico are among the nations considering accession to the code.

The Role of Trade Impact

There are two schools of thought on the role that trade impact should play in the scheme for disciplining subsidies. One school (the "injury-only" school) is principally concerned with redressing the harm that comes from subsidized trade; the other school (the "antidistortion" school) focuses on the inefficient consequences of government intervention.

Briefly, the injury-only school believes that a country should retaliate against foreign subsidies only when those subsidies have an offensive trade impact; further, the remedy should be designed to redress the impact. By contrast, the antidistortion school believes that subsidies are a fit subject for retaliation pretty much regardless of their trade impact, but that retaliation should be precisely limited to offset the subsidy.

The Injury-Only School

The injury-only school takes the view that subsidies are a fact of modern life; that they are often used to correct preexisting market imperfections; that many subsidies are almost impossible to apportion over units of output; that exchange rate movements will offset gross differences in subsidization between countries, leaving only micro problems for specific trade remedies; and that, in any event, the principle discipline against subsidization must come from domestic political processes, not international rules. Further, if a country chooses to subsidize, and goes about its work in a regular and predictable way, and there is no measurable harm to other countries, why should its trading partners be concerned? If the subsidy distorts the economy, the subsidizing country will suffer, while its trading partners will enjoy whatever benefits flow from cheap prices on subsidized goods.

Richard N. Cooper delivered a sophisticated expression of this view (1978, p. 120):

> . . . perhaps we should not worry so much about government subsidies to economic activity—or rather government intervention of all types— as far as their effects on foreign trade are concerned, provided the interventions are introduced sufficiently gradually so that they do not impose acute adjustment costs on economic activities outside the country in question.

In a similar vein, before completion of the Tokyo Round, Barcelo (1977) called for an injury-only approach to domestic subsidies and a strict prohibition of export subsidies; after the Tokyo Round, Barcelo (1980) called for an injury-only approach to all subsidies on imports into the complaining country's market, and a strict prohibition on export subsidies to third-country markets. Ehrenhaft and Mundheim (1981) have also toyed with the injury-only approach to the domestic market.

A strong version of the injury-only approach would harmonize the requisite level of trade impact as between the US standard of relief from "fair trade" (the escape clause), namely "substantial cause of serious injury," and the US standard of relief from "unfair trade," namely "a cause or threat of material injury" or the "material retardation" of a the industry. Once these two standards were conformed, either at the higher escape clause level or the lower unfair trade level, the injury-only school would dispense with a showing of subsidization or dumping.[4] Relief would be designed to cure the injury, not to offset whatever unfair trade practice might exist. Barcelo, in his second article (1980), comes close to advocating this view.

The Antidistortion School

The guiding belief of the antidistortion school is that subsidies are bad for three reasons:

• As used in practice (if not in economic theory) subsidies generally induce world economic inefficiency and thereby diminish the gains of international exchange to all nations.
• Worse yet, a subsidy program may enable a country to "steal a march" in establishing a promising new industry (e.g., fiber optics), or "weather out" painful adjustment in an old industry (e.g., steel).
• Finally, because other countries envy the stolen march, or adjustment avoided, subsidies may provoke emulation. Emulation will bring a spiral of wasteful distortion (as in shipbuilding) or overinvestment in promising technologies (as in supersonic aircraft).

The antidistortion school concedes that some subsidies can offset preexisting market imperfections, but believes that this justification is vastly exaggerated, that any serious effort to distinguish corrective from distorting subsidies would quickly lead to an impenetrable and ultimately self-serving thicket of calculations; and that this justification is merely a cover for applying the cynical doctrine, on a national and international scale, that one bad distortion deserves another.

---

[4] It is worth pointing out that, prior to the Trade Act of 1973, the US escape clause required a connection between injurious imports and a previous trade concession. Dispensing with a showing of subsidization or dumping would be analogous to dispensing with the trade concession requirement.

Most members of the antidistortion school believe that even a very low threshold of trade impact warrants the imposition of penalties, and that the penalty should offset, as nearly as possible, the initial distortion. Trade impact is nearly irrelevant to the imposition of penalties against subsidization. In particular, subsidies that differentially favor export sales should be condemned outright. As Assistant Secretary of the Treasury (now Ambassador) David R. Macdonald once put the matter (1976):

> It is our position that the GATT should be revised to eliminate the injury test in cases of an export-titled subsidy. We analyze the export-titled subsidy as nothing more than a unilateral (negation) by one country of the legitimate tariff rate of the country to which the goods are shipped.

The Subsidies Code

Largely influenced by the antidistortion school, but mindful of the use of subsidies by the United States, Congress directed the administration to seek discipline on foreign subsidies as a central element of the Tokyo Round. This directive was reinforced by legislation that threatened to unleash the countervailing duty (CVD) statute (Marks and Malmgren 1975). In response, the Ford administration advanced a "traffic light" concept in international negotiations:[5]

• Enumerated export subsidies could be automatically and unilaterally subject to CVDs (the "red" category).
• Other subsidies, applied equally to domestic aid export goods, and having a significant trade impact, would be subject to CVDs if they cause or threaten to cause material injury (the "amber" category).
• Domestic subsidies with a minor or indirect trade effect would not be subject to CVDs (the "green" category).

The traffic light approach clearly mixes the precepts of the injury-only school and the antidistortion school. While the traffic light symbolism was rejected by the European Community (EC), much of the substance was reflected in the final text of the Subsidies Code.[6] The

---

[5] The basic themes of the traffic light approach were announced by Assistant Secretary of the Treasury (1976) David R. Macdonald. The approach was tabled in explicit form at the Geneva talks by both the Ford and Carter administrations.

[6] For excellent histories of the code and its antecedents, see Rivers and Greenwald (1979), Banerjee (1981), and Tarullo (1981).

code envisaged two tracks. Broadly speaking, a high threshold of trade impact ("material injury") would allow the *national* authorization of countervailing duties. The CVDs could not exceed the amount of subsidy per unit of exported product and preferably would be set at a lower level just sufficient to offset the trade injury. In addition, export subsidies could be penalized under a second track: a low threshold of trade impact (either a presumption of "adverse effects" or, in the case of developing countries, a showing of "adverse effects") would allow the *multilateral* authorization of compensatory measures. The compensatory measures could, in principle, take various forms, for example, countervailing duties or the withdrawal of a bound tariff.

In addition to the distinction between injurious subsidies and proscribed export subsidies, the trade impact standards in the GATT and the code vary according to whether the subsidizing country is a developed country; whether or not it is a code signatory; whether the product is a primary product; whether the complaint is brought by an industry under its national law or by a government in the GATT; and whether the adverse trade impact is located in the home market of the complaining country, in the home market of the subsidizing country, or in third-country markets.

Differentiation of the trade impact standard for domestic subsidies and developing countries is based on the argument that these subsidies are more likely to serve a corrective function than export subsidies or subsidies invoked by developed countries. Differentiation for primary products is justified by political expediency: when GATT Article XVI was drafted in 1955, US farm interests were too powerful to be disciplined; when code Article 10 was drafted in 1979, European farm interests were too powerful (Tarullo 1981). Differentiation for code signatories reflects their higher level of obligation vis-à-vis other code signatories. Differentiation according to whether the petitioner is a government or a firm is justified by the supposition that governments will balance other factors against the single-minded pursuit of redress. And differentiation by the location of impact reflects the pragmatic realities of designing effective remedies. Some of the various standards used to differentiate the degree of trade impact deserve brief comment.

Material Injury

Most celebrated, of course, is the standard of "material injury" (including the threat of material injury and material retardation of a new industry). The meaning of "material injury"has been the subject of much learned writing, revolving around the 1967 Antidumping

Code, the repudiation of that code by the Congress, the evolving standards followed by the US International Trade Commission (ITC), the 1979 Antidumping and Subsidies and Countervailing Measures Codes, and the 1979 Trade Agreements Act (Staple 1980; Ortwine 1981; Greenwald 1982).

Two clusters of factors seem to enter a ITC determination that imports are a cause of material injury or threat of material injury to an existing industry: first, the existence of material injury is predicated on declining sales, falling profits, low capacity utilization, and falling employment; second, a finding that imports are a cause of material injury rests on an absolute increase in imports; a rising market share of imports; or price undercutting or price depression by imports (Ortwine 1981).

In principle, the material injury standard applies to all national actions by GATT members against subsidized imports. But the concepts of material injury, threat of material injury, and material retardation are not blind to either the level of subsidy or the type of subsidy. Article 6 paragraph 3 of the Subsidies Code simply lists a number of factors to be given consideration and concludes: "This list is not exhaustive, nor can one or several of these factors necessarily give decisive guidance." Common sense suggests that, other things being equal, a subsidy of 25 percent is more likely to attract a finding that imports are a cause of material injury than a subsidy of 5 percent. Moreover, the code is flexible enough to allow a distinction to be drawn between a 20 percent subsidy that violates the prohibition on export subsidies and a 20 percent subsidy that arises from a domestic program. Indeed, Section 771 (7)(E)(i) of the US Trade Act of 1979 enables the ITC, on the suggestion of the Department of Commerce, to make just that distinction.

Adverse Effects

The traditional application of the "adverse effects" concept remains to be elucidated in future cases brought before the Subsidies Committee. In the meantime, it is fair to presume that adverse effects means lost sales traceable to subsidized competition, whether or not firms in the complaining country are experiencing a decline in sales, employment, or profits.

Equitable Shares and Price Undercutting

The most demanding trade impact standard in the code, inherited from Article XVI of the GATT, is the provision that subsidized agricultural exports are tolerable so long as they do not afford the subsidizing country "more than an equitable share of world trade" by comparison with a "previous representative period." Since subsidies are seldom so massive that they visibly change *world* market shares, and since the baseline concept of an "equitable share" is defined in sketchy fashion, the complaining country faces an uphill battle in establishing the requisite level of trade impact. This, of course, is a key area of tension between the European Community and the United States.

It should be noted that the Subsidies Code gave additional rigor to the equitable share standard of GATT Article XVI. Under code Article 10 paragraph 2, "displacement" of the exports of another signatory can amount to claiming more than an equitable market share; equitable shares of new markets are defined in terms of traditional patterns of supply; and previous representative period is defined in terms of the three most recent years of "normal market conditions." Moreover, the code added a new impact standard: Article 10 paragraph 3 provides that subsidies should not result in the sale of primary products at prices materially below prevailing prices.

Both to answer domestic grievances and to test the new code, the United States has brought a series of agricultural cases before the Code Committee, in particular wheat, flour, poultry, and sugar from the European Economic Community (EEC). These cases may be decisive both in giving concrete meaning to the equitable share standard and price undercutting standard.

Nullification or Impairment

The basic impact standard of GATT Article XXIII holds that no trade measure should nullify or impair another country's legitimate expectations of trade benefits flowing from the GATT. Thus, the unanticipated grant of a new subsidy on a domestic product that competes with imports of an item subject to a bound tariff, coupled with a slight but noticeable trade impact, would represent a classic case of nullification or impairment.[7] A more contemporary illustration might arise if a code signatory instituted a new subsidy program on its agricultural exports and made no effort, through internal deliberations or external consultations, to follow the injunction of code Article 8 paragraph 3 "to seek to avoid causing . . . serious prejudices to the interests of another signatory."

---

[7] This proposition is derived by extension from *The Australian Subsidy on Ammonium Sulphates,* (April 3, 1950), *Basic Instruments and Selected Documents,* vol. 2 (1952), pp. 188–96. See also Hudec (1981).

Differential Treatment of Developing Countries

The GATT has traditionally allowed developing countries special freedom in the pursuit of their commercial policies. This freedom, reflected in GATT Articles XVI, XVIII, and code Article 14, is rationalized by a generalized appeal to the infant-industry argument. In the realm of subsidies, developing-country spokesmen urge that their nations should be free to subsidize exports at least down to the world price (Balassa 1978; Kelkar 1980; OAS 1977). For example, if homemade capital goods are expensive, or if imported capital goods are subject to high tariffs, or if trade union wages are excessive, export subsidies should be permitted to eliminate these burdens, regardless of the distortion that might be visited on the world trading system.

Whatever the rationale, the code excuses developing-country signatories from the flat prohibition on export subsidies. Instead, the code requires a complaining signatory to show "adverse effects" as a prerequisite to multilateral authorization of relief.

In the US view, this higher impact standard was to be balanced by commitments of developing country signatories to phaseout or at least freeze their export subsidies. If these commitments were not followed, then other signatories could appeal to the nullification or impairment doctrine, particularly GATT Article XXIII paragraph 1 section (c), or the nationally administered material injury standard for relief.

Brazil, the first developing-country signatory to the code, agreed to phaseout an extensive range of subsidies. Thereafter, subsequent commitments from other countries descended from phaseout clauses to freeze clauses to best endeavors clauses, that is to say, from meaningful clauses to hortatory statements. One reason was that the European Community, Japan, and Canada generally viewed the export subsidies of developing countries as mere irritants to the trading system. Another reason was the US enthusiasm for a strong commitments policy weakened in 1980 when the Carter administration, searching for ways to shore up ties with Pakistan in the wake of the Afghanistan invasion, accepted a purely hortatory commitment as Pakistan's admission ticket to the code. The policy collapsed in 1981 when the Reagan administration—after a skirmish on the most-favored-nation question—acknowledged Indian membership in the code on the basis of a modest best-endeavors agreement.

The collapse of meaningful standards in the commitments process left the United States rather exposed in its bilateral negotiations with Mexico. The United States long wanted to fashion some discipline on Mexican subsidies. But the United States now finds it difficult to exact a freeze or phase-out from Mexico after best endeavors are accepted from industrially sophisticated India, particularly since Mexico is America's third largest trading partner, a large net importer of US goods and services, and suffering acute distress in its industrial sector.

Whatever the outcome of the US-Mexican negotiations, the general code standard requires complaining signatories to demonstrate "adverse effects" in the case of developing-country export subsidies. Code commitments by developing countries will affect this standard only marginally.

The Definition of Export Subsidies

The exercise of defining and limiting "export subsidies,"namely government incentive programs that differentially favor export sales by comparison with domestic sales, began in the nineteenth century. This work was inspired not by high-minded notions of comparative advantage but by the mercantile notion that subsidies might undercut "legitimate" tariffs. The most offensive practice of the time was the widespread European custom of giving excessive tax rebates for indirect taxes or duty drawbacks upon the export of merchandise. The treaty of 1862 between France and the German Zollverein was perhaps the first treaty to contain an antibounty provision; in the next 60 years some 29 bilateral commercial treaties were negotiated with similar clauses (Viner 1923, pp. 166–67).

In 1890, the United States enacted a flat rate countervailing duty to offset bounties paid on the exportation of sugar. The US statute was amended in 1897 to cover all exports and to equate the duty with the subsidy, and amended again in 1922 to cover subsidies on production (Viner, p. 169). Meanwhile, India, British South Africa, Switzerland, Spain, France, Japan, and other countries enacted similar legislation.

After World War II, the development of international standards began in earnest. These standards defined both permissible and impermissible practices. Article VI of the GATT, drafted in 1947, followed the US statutes in sanctioning the imposition of CVDs "for the purpose of offsetting any bounty or subsidy bestowed directly or indirectly, upon the manufacture, production, or export of any merchandise." Article VI defined the exemption of exported products from duties or taxes "borne by the like product" not to be a subsidy; by implication, excessive exemption is a subsidy. A note to Article VI stated that multiple currency practices could entail an export subsidy. Article XVI imposed a notification requirement as to any subsidy "which operated directly or indirectly to increase exports . . .

or to reduce imports," and provided that, if the subsidy causes "serious prejudice," the party granting the subsidy shall discuss "the possibility of limiting the subsidy."

In 1955, Article XVI paragraph 4 was endorsed by most of the developed country signatories to GATT. Signatories to this article agreed not to grant export subsidies, other than on certain primary products. While Article XVI paragraph 4 improved upon the basic Article XVI provisions, unfortunately the new article articulated a test adapted from the classic definition of dumping, namely the bilevel pricing test, as a means of identifying export subsidies. This test proved unworkable both because subsidies can be felt in forms of competition other than price competition, and because published trade and production statistics seldom enable a detailed comparison between domestic and export prices. Such data are closely held by individual companies, and GATT members have no means to compel discovery of these commercial secrets from one another.

In 1960, a Working Party Report (GATT Secretariat 1961) listed certain practices as falling within the realm of Article XVI paragraph 4 export subsidies, and implicitly downgraded the bilevel pricing test for the enumerated items. Just as the countervailing duty language of Article VI tracked the US statute, so too a number of items in the 1960 Working Party Report reflected earlier US countervailing duty decisions (Marks and Malmgren 1975).

In 1979, the Illustrative List to the Subsidies Code embellished and updated the 1960 Working Party List. Certain aspects of the 1979 Illustrative List are worth commenting upon because they are likely to attract further international discussion.

Permitted Practices: Are They Subsidies?

The evolving definition of export subsidies enumerated tainted practices, defined practices that are not export subsidies, and in some cases, identified practices that are not potentially troublesome subsidies at all. For example, the precept that the nonexcessive remission of indirect taxes is not a potentially troublesome subsidy was extended to cover value-added taxes by item (g) of the 1979 Illustrative List. The rule in item (g) represents an outgrowth of GATT Article VI and the 1960 Working Party Report, both of which in turn codified long-accepted practice that distinguished between excessive and nonexcessive tax remissions.

Unlike the nonexcessive remission of taxes, other practices that are defined by the Illustrative List not to be export subsidies are not necessarily excluded from the broader category of potentially troublesome subsidies. Four such practices are noteworthy in the Illustrative List:

• In respect of item (d), the provision of goods for use in the manufacture of exports on terms less favorable than the world market price, but still subsidized.
• In respect of item (i), the allowance of duty drawback on identical goods of domestic origin that are incorporated in exports.
• In respect of item (j), the provisions of credit guarantees or exchange risk insurance on terms inadequate, but not "manifestly" inadequate, to cover operating costs of insurance programs.
• In respect of item (k), the provision of export credits at rates below the cost of money to government, but equal to or above the interest rate norms in the Organization for Economic Cooperation and Development (OECD) Arrangement or the OECD Ships Understanding.

By common parlance each of the enumerated practices involves a subsidy. By GATT definition, none of the practices involves an export subsidy. Not all subsidies are a matter of international concern, and the question that must be decided, as cases arise, is whether the practice amounts to a potentially troublesome subsidy.

Official Export Credits

The evolution of discipline over official export credits has been ably chronicled by Wallen and Duff (1981); Moore (1981); and Czinkota (1982). Briefly, item (g) of the 1960 Working Party defined an export credit subsidy as the grant of official credit at interest rates below the cost of funds to governments. With this decision, the subsidized export credit programs of industrial countries became a fit target for GATT action.

But the slow-moving GATT mechanism was seen to be an ineffective means of redressing lost sales in third-country markets. What good would a GATT panel report achieve two years after the sale was lost? Thus, the discipline of export credit practices was consigned first to the Berne Union and then, in the 1960s and 1970s, to the OECD. Gradually a system of discipline built up that involved norms with respect to maturities, interest rates, down payments, and other dimensions, plus the positive obligation to notify derogations from those norms, and the all-important opportunity for self-help, namely the right to offer a matching export credit subsidy.[8]

---

[8] Apart from the OECD exercise, countries within the EEC agreed to limit their official export credit programs, as applied to sales *within* the Common

The Subsidies Code.   Although the OECD framework was far more effective than the GATT system, the OECD norms on interest rates were considerably more lenient than the GATT Working Party standard of "cost of money to the governments." The negotiators in the Tokyo Round thus faced the historical fact that the principal code of discipline in the sphere of export credits had been crafted within the OECD, but that the OECD norms entailed a lower substantive standard than the 1960 Working Party Report. By 1979, many countries were unwilling to condemn, as export subsidies, practices that were condoned in the OECD. The Subsidy Code draftsmen thus agreed to incorporate by reference, as a limited exemption from the "cost of money to governments" standard, both the OECD Arrangement and the OECD Understanding on Ships. The language that accomplished this objective appears in item (k) of the Illustrative List. However, the drafting of item (k) left for future resolution several important questions. For example, under what circumstances is a government applying "the interest rate provisions" of the OECD Arrangement and thus exempted, by terms of item (k), from the higher GATT standard of "cost of money to governments"?[9] As another example, when does an official export credit create a potentially troublesome subsidy, even though the credit is defined not to entail an export subsidy? Two possible standards can be envisaged: the official export credit is provided at an interest rate at or above the OECD Arrangement rate but below the cost of money to governments; or when the official export credit is provided at an interest rate at or above the cost of money to government but below the commercial rate.[10]

Market, to the provision of credit guarantees only. This agreement served to make the Common Market free of export credit subsidies provided by EEC countries. Unfortunately, the EEC has objected to an extension of this principle to all industrial-country members of the OECD Arrangement.

[9] This question arose in concrete form when the New York Metropolitan Transportation Authority (MTA) invited bids on subway cars. See *New York Times,* 19 May 1982; *Washington Post,* 29 May 1982 and 14 July 1982.

[10] In the *Ceramic Tile from Mexico* case, *Federal Register,* vol. 47, no. 90 (May 10, 1982), p. 20012, Mexico's export credit subsidy was measured by reference to the commercial rate, not the cost of money to the Mexican government. For additional detail on this case, see the US Department of Commerce Memorandum to Gary N. Horlick, Acting Assistant Secretary for Trade Administration, "Ceramic Tiles from Mexico—Final Countervailing Duty Determination," US Department of Commerce reference library, May 3, 1982.

Future Progress on Export Credit Discipline.   For the foreseeable future, the working norms for minimum export credit standards will be developed in the OECD framework rather than the GATT. At most, the GATT will play a backstop role for sectors and maturity terms not covered by the OECD Arrangement, and as a reference point for national actions against imports financed with subsidized export credits.[11]

In the fall of 1981, and again in the summer of 1982, the Reagan administration achieved major breakthroughs in bringing OECD Arrangement rates closer to market rates, and in developing sector agreements for large aircraft and nuclear power equipment sales (Czinkota 1982). If disinflation prevails, it is entirely conceivable that the subsidy element of official export credits will dramatically decline by mid-1983. In that event, the differential rate system,[12] represented in nascent form by special OECD provisions for yen lending, may spring into fuller flower, as special rates are negotiated for other low interest rate currencies such as the Swiss franc and German mark. Alternatively, the Arrangement countries may agree to denominate their export credit transactions in a single unit of account, for example, the European Currency Unit (ECU) or the Special Drawing Right (SDR) (a proposal first made by C. Fred Bergsten, October 28, 1980). The single unit of account approach would overcome the interest rate illusion problem[13] and enable each export credit agency to offer the same package of exchange risk and interest rate to potential buyers.

Tax Issues

The task of defining the permissible exemption, remission, or deferral of direct taxes on export activities has provided entertainment in GATT circles for three decades and no end of scholarly literature.

---

[11] For example, in the May 1982 meeting of the Subsidies Committee, the United States notified Export–Import Bank programs as a subsidy; this notification was a prelude to action against other countries' export credit programs.

[12] Under a full-blown differential rate system, the minimum level of export credit rates would differ from currency to currency to reflect market rates.

[13] Interest rate illusion refers to the supposed borrower indifference to a credit denominated in yen or lira, so long as the nominal interest rate is identical. Whether or not interest rate illusion exists in the minds of borrowers, the possibility that it exists creates very real competition between export credit agencies.

The basic problem is that important United States firms feel they were bested on six occasions:

- when the original GATT was drafted to permit the rebate of taxes "borne by the like product" but not direct taxes
- when the EC subsequently adopted a value-added tax (VAT) and exempted exports from taxation
- when *Zenith Radio v. United States*, 437 US 443 (1978), upheld the longstanding US administrative practice that the rebate of an indirect tax is not a subsidy under US law
- when the US Treasury Department, in the wake of the *Zenith* case, defined rebate of value-added taxes as not a subsidy, an approach that was ratified in item (g) of the 1979 Illustrative List
- when the GATT panel assigned the burden of disproving bilevel pricing and adverse effects to the United States and found the Domestic International Sales Corporation (DISC) a presumptive subsidy to the extent interest was not charged on deferred taxes
- when the GATT Panel's holding was codified as item (e) in the 1979 Illustrative List.

The language of the Illustrative List is straightforward:

(e) The full or partial exemption, emission, or deferral specifically related to exports, of direct taxes[1] or social welfare charges paid or payable by industrial or commercial enterprises.[2]

NOTES: [1] For the purpose of this Agreement; the term "direct taxes" shall mean taxes on wages, profits, interest, rents, royalties, and all other forms of income, and taxes on the ownership of real property; [2] The signatories recognize that deferral need not amount to an export subsidy where, for example, appropriate interest charges are collected. The signatories further recognize that nothing in this text prejudices the disposition by the CONTRACTING PARTIES of the specific issues raised in GATT document L/4422 (The DISC Panel Report).

Two academic commentators, Kwako (1980) and Muchow (1981) concluded, on the basis of the text of the Illustrative List and the negotiating history on the public record, that the DISC as presently constituted is an export subsidy under the terms of item (e) of the Subsidies Code. This same conclusion was in fact stated in a confidential protocol to the Subsidies Code. The protocol was later renounced by Ambassador Reubin Askew, but when it comes to the tax systems of other countries, the United States has no doubt that the exemption, remission, or deferral of direct taxes constitutes a subsidy under US CVD law.[14] Since US CVD decisions have exerted considerable influence on the evolution of GATT standards, those decisions would seem to have more than passing bearing on the definition of an export subsidy.

Against this background, US Trade Representative (USTR) General Counsel Donald DeKieffer has stated flatly that DISC is not a subsidy.[15] According to this extraordinary doctrine, the reference point for measuring an export subsidy is the territorial tax system. If DISC provides a lesser tax benefit than a territorial tax system, then DISC is simply not a subsidy at all.

This "functional equivalent" doctrine, if extended to other export subsidies, would have far-reaching consequences.[16] For example, the limits on the rebate of indirect taxes in cascade-type systems could be avoided under the rationale that the rebate was in fact no greater than what would be allowed under a VAT system. Or the refund of social security taxes on an exported product could be justified as the "functional equivalent" of another country's VAT exemption. Or, to take a devastating extension of the argument, countries such as Brazil and Mexico might justify a whole range of subsidies as the "functional equivalent" of an exchange rate devaluation.

The "functional equivalent" doctrine might be admissible if the purpose of GATT discipline was to strike an overall balance on subsidies provided by different national systems. But that has not been the GATT approach for three good reasons:

• In the grander assignment of instruments to targets, the goal of overall balance has been assigned to flexible exchange rate movements
• Precise measurement of each country's use of permitted practices is quite difficult
• An overall balance approach could well stimulate a race to the bottom, contrary to the purpose of the GATT and the code.

The outcome of the DISC dispute remains in doubt. The United States could conform DISC to the GATT standard, with little re-

---

[14] See, for example, *Certain Electronic Products from Japan, Federal Register*, vol. 40, no. 25 (February 5, 1975), p. 5378; *Certain Scissors and Shears from Brazil, Federal Register*, vol. 42, no. 29 (February 11, 1977), p. 8634; *Ceramic Tile from Mexico, Federal Register*, vol. 47, no. 90 (May 10, 1982), p. 20012.

[15] Bureau of National Affairs, *Daily Tax Report,* May 6, 1982, p. G-1.

[16] The "functional equivalent" argument was considered and rejected by the DISC panel. GATT Doc. L/4422, November 2, 1976.

duction in tax benefits to US exporters, simply by exempting from tax the foreign source portion of export earnings, and taxing at normal rates the domestic source portion.[17] This obvious surgical cure is resisted by many business groups for fear of the unknown: if Congress concerns itself with DISC, it might slash away at DISC as it did in the Tax Reform Act of 1976.

Meanwhile, Canada has asked the United States to notify DISC as a subsidy under Article 7 of the code, and the EEC continues to pursue its Article XXIII remedies. At any time, Canada or Europe could choose to countervail against DISC, and apply a material injury test interpreted in light of a breach of international agreements. More likely, however, the EEC and Canada will keep the DISC issue alive to quell excessive US enthusiasm against *their* subsidies. Quite possibly, the main consequence of continued US refusal to conform the DISC to the code will be a weakening of the overall US drive to limit subsidies through multilateral discipline.

Performance Requirements and Associated Incentives as an Export Subsidy

The most familiar performance requirements are local value-added requirements, local ownership requirements, and export requirements. Such performance requirements clearly intrude on management discretion; firms accept that intrusion mainly because it is accompanied by inducements—for example, permission to establish operations in an attractive market or eligibility for fiscal incentives. These requirements and inducements raise assorted GATT issues (Fontheim 1981). In particular, export performance requirements raise the question: Under what conditions does the linkage of a performance requirement and an inducement amount to an export subsidy?

The historical process of defining export subsidies has progressed through three stages. In the first stage, the focus was on cash payments from government, typified by excessive duty drawbacks. Later, the focus was enlarged to cover the exemption from tax obligations, in other words, the absence of a rightful cash payment to government. Still later, the focus was broadened to cover the government provision of services at bargain prices, for example, export credits or rail facilities. The time may now be at hand to expand the concept of export subsidies to cover the provision of licensing rights conditioned on

[17] This approach would require the enunciation of reasonable safe-harbor rules for distinguishing between foreign source and domestic source income.

export performance, such as the right of establishment, or the right to apply for fiscal incentives, even though a charge is not normally made for such rights.

This conceptual extension may require extensive international negotiation. In the negotiating process, many countries are likely to raise the defense that export performance requirements and associated incentives are simply a practical way to offset the inordinate preference of multinational enterprises to buy within the corporate group and to divide markets regardless of comparative advantage. In short, many nations may be unwilling to accept greater discipline on government actions so long as large multinational enterprises are allowed to operate free of public scrutiny. These objections may postpone widespread agreement that export performance requirements and associated inducements properly belong on the list of prohibited export subsidies. But in instances where "direct subsidies . . . contingent upon export performance" are paid to the firm, these practices may nevertheless be condemned by the Subsidies Committee under item (a) of the 1979 Illustrative List. When no such "direct subsidies" are paid (which is probably the more common situation), any condemnation by the Subsidies Committee will almost certainly require a demonstration of bilevel pricing. Indeed, condemnation may be avoided altogether on the argument that the grant of licensing privileges does not entail a "charge on the public account" (to use the phrase of item (2) of the 1979 Illustrative List). Nevertheless, national authorities may well take action against the more egregious export performance measures, even if they do not involve direct subsidies, when the exports result in "material injury."

The Definition of Domestic Subsidies

In the negotiation of the Subsidies Code, it was widely believed that defining a potentially troublesome subsidy was not nearly as important as defining the requisite trade impact. This view is overly complacent for two reasons. First, it is evident that the calculated amount of subsidy will influence the determination of whether material injury exists by reason of subsidized imports. If an industry is injured, or threatened with injury, or retarded, it is easier to link that injury or threat or retardation with imports subsidized to the extent of 30 percent than to the extent of 10 percent. Second, once the requisite trade impact is found, the extent of the remedy can extend (and some would say should extend) up to the amount of the subsidy.

Therefore, an important issue for the international trading system is to define potentially troublesome subsidies. Obviously, the class of potentially troublesome subsidies includes, but is much broader than, export subsidies. But which practices, out of the vast range of government intervention measures, qualify as potentially troublesome subsidies?

Polar Positions

Two extreme positions on this question have been articulated and rejected.[18] One position is that any government interference with an idealized free market economy must be regarded as a subsidy. This position was urged in the Treasury Department brief in the famous *Downs v. United States* case, 187 US 496 (1903), record at 236, quoted in Brown, 1977, p. 1238[19]:

> . . . any special favor, benefit, advantage, or inducement conferred by the government, even if it is given as a release from the burden and is not a direct charge on the Treasury, is fairly included in the idea and meaning of an indirect bounty.

Malmgren proposed a modern restatement of the comprehensive definition of a subsidy (1977, p. 22):

> For working purposes, a subsidy might therefore be considered to be any government action which causes a firm's, or a particular industry's, total net private costs of production to be below the level of costs that would have been incurred in the course of producing the same level of output in the absence of government action.

The other extreme position is that only export subsidies are troublesome to the international order. Indeed, prior to 1973, the administrative practice of the US Treasury reflected this view (Marks and Malmgren 1975, pp. 348–49; Tarullo 1981, pp. 25–27). More recently, the narrow view has broadened to include preferential sub-

---

[18] Ethnocentricity tempts some observers to define, as potentially troublesome subsidies, all forms of intervention not practiced by their own governments. This approach is almost too crass to be taken seriously.

[19] A celebrated line of *dicta* in *Downs v. United States,* 187 US 496, 515 (1903), seemed to endorse to broad interpretation: "When a tax is imposed on all sugar produced, but is remitted upon all sugar exported, then by whatever process, or in whatever manner, or under whatever name it is disguised, it is a bounty upon exportation." This endorsement was undercut by *Zenith Radio v. United States,* 437 US 443 (1978).

sidies that result in selectively favorable treatment for particular firms
or industries.

US law began shifting towards the modern form of the narrow view
in the celebrated *Michelin* case[20] in which a Canadian regional assistance program was defined as a countervailable subsidy. The transition from the narrow export subsidy view was easier in this case
because 75 percent of the output was shipped to the United States.
In the *Float Glass* cases, *Federal Register*, vol. 40, no. 10 (January
15, 1975), p. 2718, a "rule of reason" was enunciated: regional subsidies that were merely designed to offset local disadvantages, or were
provided to firms with limited exports, or were of *de minimis* extent,
were not countervailed because they did not create a "trade distortion."

After a certain amount of hostile comment from the courts and
the US Congress,[21] the "rule of reason" approach was narrowed to
emphasize the particularity of subsidies. In code Article 11 paragraph
3, reference is made to "subsidies granted with the aim of giving an
advantage to certain industries." The "particularity" concept serves
as Ockham's razor to eliminate a wide range of government programs
from the sphere of international concern. For example, general subsidies for rail or electric service, manpower training programs, uniform tax credits, and similar broadbrush measures should not qualify
as potentially troublesome subsidies. Nevertheless, there are still a
number of gray areas, for example, upstream subsidies, equity in
public enterprises, and research and development.

Upstream Subsidies

Under what circumstances should an "upstream subsidy"—namely
a subsidy on an input purchased by the exporting industry—be regarded as a potentially troublesome subsidy subject to remedial action

---

[20] *X-Radial Belted Tires from Canada, Federal Register*, vol. 38, no. 4
(January 8, 1973), p. 1018.

[21] Congress disavowed the regional offset calculations in the Trade Act of
1979; see S. Rep. no. 249, 96th Cong., 1st sess. (1979), p. 45. With respect
to pre-1979 US law, the Court of Customs and Patent Appeals struck down
the Treasury's "trade distortions" test in *ASG Industries, Inc. v. United States,*
610 F2d 770 (CCPA 1980), reversing 467 F. Supp. 1187 (Cust. Ct. 1979).
Thus in the *Ceramic Tile from Mexico* case, *Federal Register*, vol 47, no. 90
(May 10, 1982), p. 20012, a regional subsidy, CEPROFI, was countervailed
even though exports of the industry were modest. However, since an export
purpose was not shown, the CEPROFI was prorated over the entire production of the benefited firms.

once it causes the requisite level of trade impact? The broad view is that any upstream subsidy qualifies. The more restrictive view is that an upstream subsidy is potentially troublesome only when it operates to benefit a particular industry; and it results in the provision of inputs at a cheaper price than the price on world markets. The clash between the broad and restrictive views became particularly lively in the context of countervailing duty cases brought against European steel. In the preliminary decision, *Federal Register*, vol 47, no. 117 (June 17, 1982), p. 26299, the Department of Commerce upheld the restrictive view. Subsidies on the production of European coking coal production were not imputed to the production of steel since they did not result in a lower than world price of coal and thus conferred no benefit on the steel industry.[22]

Equity or Loans to State-owned Enterprises

The characterization of equity and loans to state-owned enterprises has emerged, in the recent steel cases, as a leading issue in the definition of domestic subsidies. The antidistortion school is quick to point out that equity ownership and loans by the state open up vistas of potential subsidization opaque both to the taxpaying public and to foreign competitors, involving outright coverage of operating losses, cross-subsidization among products, and informal targeting of the export market (Walters and Monsen 1979).

In its preliminary decision in the European steel cases, *Federal Register*, vol 47, no. 117 (June 17, 1982), p. 26299, the Department of Commerce took the position that equity contributions do not entail a per se subsidy unless the government purchases shares at higher than prevailing market prices, in those cases where a private market exists for the shares. In other cases, government equity was held to entail a subsidy only to the extent subsequent earnings were less than the average return on equity investment for the country as a whole.

Further, the amount of subsidy would in no event exceed an amount that would be calculated if an outright grant had been given instead of the purchase of equity. In the same decision, the Department of Commerce announced a policy of allocating "large" outright grants in equal nominal installments (including interest at the national average rate on corporate debt) over the useful life of equipment.

---

[22] See also US Department of Commerce memorandum to Gary N. Horlick, Deputy Assistant Secretary, "Certain Steel Products from Belgium," June 10, 1982, especially Appendix B.

In the case of loans and loan guarantees, the Department of Commerce distinguishes between creditworthy and uncreditworthy companies. Government loans at market interest rates and guarantees to a creditworthy company simply do not entail a subsidy. Loans to an uncreditworthy company are regarded as the equivalent of a contribution of equity and the annual amount of subsidy is calculated in the same manner as for an equity contribution, with the same limitation not to exceed the grant equivalent of the original loan.

Research and Development Subsidies

The emerging standard seems to hold that government assistance at the product development phase counts as a potentially troublesome subsidy, but that government support of basic research, or government support by way of generally favorable tax treatment for research and development (R&D), are not potentially troublesome. Thus, in the lead case, *Liquid Optic Level Sensing Systems* from Canada, *Federal Register*, vol. 44, no. 5 (January 8, 1979), p. 1728, the US Treasury Department found a subsidy because the Canadian R&D grant was awarded after the patent had been granted.

The "basic" versus "applied" distinction fits naturally into customary R&D labels. But in practice, these are the wrong labels for defining an unfair trade practice, not only because it is hard to demarcate "basic" from "applied" research, but more importantly because what counts in the industrial setting is whether the government *concentrates* its R&D effort on particular industries, and whether it *delays*, even temporarily, the dissemination of the R&D findings to foreign firms. US biogenetic and semiconductor firms do not much care about the basic or applied nature of R&D financed by the Japanese government. They are more concerned with the massive targeting of those industries for government assistance and the fact that the research results are only slowly disseminated outside of Japan. In the future, such targeted assistance may come to be viewed as a potentially troublesome subsidy. This, in fact, is the position taken by the Department of Commerce in its preliminary determination in the European steel cases, *Federal Register*, vol. 47, no. 117 (June 17, 1982), p. 26299.

Effective Remedies

While a great deal of effort was lavished in the Tokyo Round on defining the appropriate level of trade impact required to designate a subsidy an offensive subsidy, and some attention was paid to defining export subsidies, very little attention was paid to the design of effective remedies. Ideally, remedial measures would serve several functions: redress the adverse trade impact; offset the distortion; avoid harm to innocent parties; prompt the subsidizing country to alter its policies; avert an escalating spiral of retaliation; and not require the complaining country to spend public monies. Few, if any, remedies meet all criteria. The design of effective remedies is further complicated since they must address the impact of subsidies in three quite different settings:

- in the domestic market of the complaining country
- in the domestic market of the subsidizing country
- in a third-country market.

The countervailing duty, when applied to the home market of the complaining country, under procedures that lead to its acquiescence by the subsidizing country, comes fairly close to meeting the criteria for an ideal remedy. But even the CVD does not necessarily redress the adverse trade impact (it may overcompensate or undercompensate), nor does the CVD necessarily induce the foreign country to abandon its practices.

More importantly, the CVD does not address trade impacts in the home market of the subsidizing country or in third-country markets. These cases are largely left to the design of ad hoc responses, either multilaterally or on a national basis (for example under section 301 of the US Trade Act of 1974). The problem with ad hoc remedies is that they take time and negotiation to craft. The uncertain application of an uncertain remedy has little deterrent value.

Countervailing Subsidies

One candidate for wider and more automatic application is a countervailing subsidy. This is the remedy now used in the export credit area, under the label of matching. Unfortunately, a countervailing subsidy imposes heavy budget costs on the complaining country. Moreover, in the short run it compounds the initial distortion. Finally, if applied to the home market of the subsidizing country, a countervailing subsidy runs a real danger of prompting escalation. Some of these defects of the countervailing subsidy might be mitigated. For example, the budget costs could be defrayed with monies raised by imposing, with prior authorization from the Subsidies Committee or the GATT, a low-rate duty on all imports from the subsidizing country. The prior authorization procedure would enhance the acceptability of the measure and might even lead to a withdrawal of the initial subsidy.

Remedial Action in Third-Country Markets

The practical problems in agricultural trade largely arise in third-country markets. One possibility is to institute proceedings in third-country markets, a recommendation offered by Barcelo (1980). GATT provides a basis for such proceedings in Articles VI:6(b) and (c):

> (b) The CONTRACTING PARTIES may . . . permit a contracting party to levy an antidumping or countervailing duty on the importation of any product for the purpose of offsetting dumping or subsidization which causes or threatens material injury to an industry in the territory of another contracting party exporting the product concerned to the territory of the importing contracting party. . . .
>
> (c) In exceptional circumstances, however, where delay might cause damage which would be difficult to repair, a contracting party may levy a countervailing duty for the purpose referred to in subparagraph (b) of this paragraph without the prior approval of the CONTRACTING PARTIES; *Provided* that such action shall be reported immediately to the CONTRACTING PARTIES and that the countervailing duty shall be withdrawn promptly if the CONTRACTING PARTIES disapprove.

Selected signatories could build on Article VI paragraph 6(c) and allow one another ready access to their administrative proceedings "in exceptional cases." The onus would fall on the subsidizing country to persuade the contracting parties to disallow the action. The "threat of material injury" analysis applied to these cases could be defined to focus on market-specific issues, by contrast with the "equitable share of world trade" analysis called for in the code.

The practical difficulty with this solution is that the few countries that keep their agricultural markets open generally do so because they are delighted with lower prices. But even these countries may have some third-country markets that they want to insulate from unfair trade practices. Thus, it might be possible to craft a limited agreement that covered both selected agricultural commodities and possibly some industrial products. For example, Switzerland might be willing to let American firms have access to its administrative remedies with respect to poultry in exchange for access to US remedies on watches.

Is the Remedy Adequate?

The code encourages, and US law permits, the settlement of subsidy cases by an undertaking that removes the injury. Presumably no exporter will agree to an undertaking that has a more restrictive impact than a CVD calculated to offset the subsidy. Thus, with the concurrence of the domestic industry, the extent of injury sets a potential ceiling on remedies. But some observers are concerned that injury does not set a floor. These observers have the following scenario in mind: an R&D grant could lead to the creation of a mighty enterprise. Any remedy against the initial grant, when apportioned over units of output, will not address the possibility that, because of its head start, the enterprise was able to grow by earning very high profits on its initial sales and then, thanks to "learning curve" effects, continued to earn high profits while progressively cutting its price one step ahead of the competition.

At bottom, of course, this is the infant-industry argument applied to high technology fields. The success of many enterprises turns on small events—the genius of a single individual (Henry Ford), or the good fortune of a single patent (the Haloid Company, later Xerox). As a matter of principle, how can the infant-industry argument be invoked to justify unusual protection against successful R&D subsidies yet not be invoked when other fortuitous factors give some other enterprise a head start?

The potential US riposte to this criticism, of course, is that other countries *do* invoke infant industry protection in high technology areas—through government procurement practices (France with computers, Japan with telecommunications), licensing restrictions, (Brazil with minicomputers), and technical standards (Japan with drugs). Only the United States does not apply infant-industry principles to high technology; and, at least in instances where other countries subsidize research, this oversight should be redressed.

The answer to the riposte is that countervailing measures are ill-suited to serve the more ambitious goal of protecting infant, high technology industries. After all, many Japanese firms have led the way in new fields without extensive government support, for example automobiles and consumer electronics. If the United States is genuinely concerned about its leadership in emerging new industries, it should develop its own specific programs to support those industries rather than rely on the accidental emergence of a countervailing duty case.

Agenda for Trade Policy

Out of this morass of detail, what guiding precepts can GATT members rely upon for their work at the Ministerial and thereafter?

The main precept seems to be that the powerful quest for harmonization of international trade practices—the long search for an elusive "level playing field"—cannot be ignored. Either GATT deliberations point the way toward harmonization at lower levels, by restraining subsidies, or disadvantaged countries will, on their own initiative, harmonize at higher levels, by introducing new subsidies.

If Europe, Canada, and Japan do not agree to greater discipline over their subsidies, the United States is likely to answer in kind, when the next turn of the domestic wheel favors a more liberal approach toward government spending. From the perspective of 1990, DISC may come to be seen as merely the first installment on the long US campaign to "get even." Indeed, the tepid approach of all nations towards the GATT Ministerial makes it rather more likely that nations will "harmonize up" than "harmonize down."* But the health of the international system would be better served if GATT negotiations could point the way toward tighter discipline. Toward this end, three broad suggestions can be offered.

First, the time is at hand to conform the trade impact standard applied to agricultural subsidies with the lower trade impact standard applied to other goods. At most, the complaining party should be required to demonstrate bilevel pricing (the GATT Article XVI paragraph 4 standard), but the respondent might be permitted to demonstrate that its subsidies have no adverse effects.

Second, a major effort should be undertaken to define potentially troublesome domestic subsidies. This program could parallel the 1960 Working Party Report and the 1979 Illustrative List that sought to define export subsidies. In the course of this work, circumstances should be defined in which subsidies are not troublesome because they genuinely offset, in the least offensive manner, sector-specific distortions.

Finally, effective remedies must be found for subsidization that affects third-country markets. The most promising approach would involve an agreement, within the framework of GATT Article VI, that signatories open their regular administrative proceedings to foreign petitioners who are wrongfully deprived of export markets; failing that remedy, the injured party could offer countervailing subsidies financed (with multilateral approval) by a low rate tariff imposed on all its imports from the subsidizing country.

Ed. note: In any event, the November 1982 GATT Ministerial took no new actions in the area of subsidies.

References

(*Note*: This is a general list of current references; not all are cited in the text.)

Balassa, Bela. "The New Protectionism and the International Economy." *Journal of World Trade Law* 12 (1978) 409–36.

Banerjee, Sumitra. "The Antidumping and Subsidy Codes and the Trade Agreements Act of 1979." Unpublished manuscript. Washington: Georgetown University Law School, 1981.

Barcelo, John J., III. "Subsidies and Countervailing Duties—Analysis and a Proposal." *Law and Policy in International Business* 9 (1977) 779–853.

———. "Subsidies, Countervailing Duties and Anti-Dumping after the Tokyo Round." *Cornell International Law Journal* 13 (Summer 1980) 257–88.

Bergsten, C. Fred. "Toward Fairer International Trade: The New Subsidy/Countervailing Duty Code." Address before the Symposia Society of America, US Treasury Department, Washington, March 7, 1979.

———. "A Framework for Trade Policy in the 1980s: The New Subsidy/Countervailing Duty Code." Address before the American Society of International Law, US Treasury Department, Washington, April 26, 1979.

———. "The International Monetary System in the 1980s." Address to the Center for International Business of Dallas, US Treasury Department, Washington, October 28, 1980.

Brown, Craig M. "Bounty or Grant: A Call for Redefinition in Light of the Zenith Decision." *Law and Policy in International Business* 9 (1977) 1229–1257.

Bryan, Greyson. *Taxing Unfair International Trade Practices*. Mass.: Lexington Books, 1980.

Carlson, G. N., G. C. Hufbauer, and M. B. Krauss. "Destination Principle Border Tax Adjustments for the Corporate Income and Social Security Taxes: An Analysis of Sectoral Effects." Proceedings of the 69th Annual Conference, National Tax Association—Tax Institute of America, 1976.

Cline, William R. "Exports of Manufactures from Developing Countries: Performance and Prospects for Market Access." Unpublished manuscript. Washington: Brookings Institution, February 1982.

Cohen, Richard A. "The Trade Agreements Act of 1979: Executive Agreements, Subsidies, and Countervailing Duties." *Texas International Law Journal* 15 (1980) 96–115.

Cooper, Richard N. "US Policies and Practices on Subsidies in International Trade." In *International Trade and Industrial Policies*, ed. Steven J. Warnecke. New York: Holmes & Meier, 1978.

Czinkota, Michael. "The Export-Import Bank." In Gary Clyde Hufbauer, ed., *U.S. International Economic Policy 1981: A Draft Report*. Washington: International Law Institute, 1982.

Dally, Lester. "The Impact of Export Subsidies on International Trade." *New Zealand Law Journal* (November 1981) 490–94.

Evans, John W. "Subsidies and Countervailing Duties in the GATT: Present Law and Future Prospects." *International Trade Law Journal* 3 (Fall 1977) 211–45.

Fontheim, Claude G. B., and R. Michael Gadbaw. "Trade Related Performance Requirements under the GATT–MTN System and US Domestic Law." *Law and Policy in International Business* 14 (1982) pp. 129–30.

General Agreement on Tariffs and Trade. *Basic Instruments and Selected Documents*, ninth supplement. "Declaration Giving Effect to the Provisions of Article XVI(4) of the GATT." Geneva, 19 September 1960. GATT: Geneva, 1961, pp. 186–87.

————. *Agreement on Interpretation and Application of Articles VI, XVI, and XXIII of the General Agreement on Tariffs and Trade.* GATT: Geneva, 1979.

Greenwald, John D. "Material Injury." *Federal Bar News and Journal* 29 (January 1982) 38.

Grey, Rodney de C. "Some Notes on Subsidies and the International Rules." June 1981. *Interface III.* Washington: International Law Institute, forthcoming 1983.

Hudec, Robert E. "Regulation of Domestic Subsidies under the MTN Subsidies Code." June 1981. *Interface III.* Washington: International Law Institute, forthcoming 1983.

Hufbauer, Gary Clyde, and Joanna Shelton-Erb. "The International Discipline of Subsidies and Countermeasures." Unpublished manuscript. Washington: Institute for International Economics, 1983.

Kelkar, Vijay Laxman. "Export Subsidy: Theory and Practice." *Economic and Political Weekly* 15 (June 7, 1980).

————. "GATT, Export Subsidies and Developing Countries." *World Trade Law* 14 (July–August 1980) 368–73.

Kwakow, Thomas. "Tax Incentives for Exports, Permissible and Prescribed: An Analysis of the Corporate Income Tax Implications of the MTA, Subsidies Code," 12 *Law and Policy in International Business*, 1980.

Macdonald, David R. "Annual Report on International Unfair Trade Practices." Address to the International Trade Club of Chicago, US Treasury Department, Washington, March 11, 1976.

Malmgren, Harald B. *International Order for Public Subsidies.* London: Trade Policy Research Centre, 1977.

Marcuss, Stanley J. "Subsidies—Like the Poor—Shall Always Be With Us: And Like Poverty Itself, Harder and Harder to Define and Cure." June 1981. *Interface III.* Washington: International Law Institute, forthcoming 1983.

Marks, Matthew J., and Harald B. Malmgren. "Negotiating Nontariff Distortions to Trade." *Law and Policy in International Business* 7 (1975) 327.

Moore, John L., Jr. "Export Credit Arrangements: Background and Rationale." July 1981. *Interpretation and Implementation of International Agreements.* Washington: American Society of International Law, forthcoming 1983.

Muchow, Dan. "Export Incentives: United States DISC Legislation as an Invalid Subsidy Under the GATT Provisions." *Washburn Law Journal* 20 (Spring 1981) 535–56.

Mundheim, Robert H., and Peter D. Ehrenhaft. "What is a 'Subsidy'?" June 1981. *Interface III.* Washington: International Law Institute, forthcoming 1983.

Mutti, John. *Taxes, Subsidies and Competitiveness Internationally.* Washington: National Planning Association, Committee on Changing International Realities, January 1982.

Organization of American States (OAS). "GATT Rules and US Law Regarding Export Subsidies and Countervailing Duties." (Report prepared by Tracy Murray.) OEA/Ser. H/XIII. Washington: OAS, September 12, 1977.

Ortwine, Bruce A. "Injury Determinations Under United States Antidumping Laws Before and After the Trade Agreements Act of 1979." *Rutgers Law Review* 33 (Summer 1981) 1076.

Pestieau, Caroline. *Subsidies and Countervailing Duties: The Negotiating Issues.* Report to the Canadian Economic Policy Committee. Quebec: C. D. Howe Research Institute, 1976.

Rivers, Richard R., and John D. Greenwald. "The Negotiation of a Code on Subsidies and Countervailing Measures: Bridging Fundamental Policy Differences." *Law and Policy in International Business* 11 (1979).

Staple, Peter D. "Implementing 'Tokyo Round' Commitments: The New Injury Standard in Antidumping and Countervailing Duty Laws." *Stanford Law Review* 32 (July 1980) 1183–1209.

Tarullo, Daniel K. "The MTN Subsidies Code: Agreement without Consensus." October 1981. *Interpretation and Implementation of International Economic Agreements*. Washington: American Society of International Law, forthcoming 1983.

Verrill, Charles Owen, Jr. "State-Owned Enterprises and the Countervailing Duty Law: Where, Oh, Where, to Draw the Line." June 1981. *Interface III*. Washington: International Law Institute, forthcoming 1983.

Wallen, Axel, and John M. Duff, Jr. "The Outlook for Official Export Credits." In *The International Framework for Money and Banking in the 1980s*, ed. Gary Clyde Hufbauer. Washington: International Law Institute, 1981.

Walters, Kenneth D., and R. Joseph Monsen. "State-Owned Business Abroad: New Competitive Threat." *Harvard Business Review* 57 (March–April 1979) 160–70.

Warnecke, Stephen J., ed. *International Trade and Industrial Policies*. New York: Holmes & Meier, 1978.

Weaver, Kathleen T. "Subsidies and Countervailing Duties Under the Trade Act of 1979." *NC Journal International Law and Commercial Regulations* 5 (Summer 1980) 533–45.

CHAPTER 11

Need for New GATT Rules To Govern Safeguard Actions

Alan Wm. Wolff

> *The real danger to the GATT is not that a trade war will break out, but that the major signatories to the GATT will simply pretend that the General Agreement is not there,. . . .This would effectively end the GATT.*
> —Arthur Dunkel
> Director General of the GATT[1]

This is not a paper about conferring new freedom on signatories to the General Agreement on Tariffs and Trade (GATT) to enable them further to restrict trade. This freedom they have in fact already obtained. The purpose of this paper is to examine ways in which the effectiveness of the GATT's rules can be increased in order to place additional contraints on national behavior when protectionist actions are being contemplated.

One does not have to take too dismal a view of future growth in the Western economies to conclude that the urge for nations to restrict trade will continue to increase. In part this is a product of the GATT's success. The GATT has eliminated the general incidence of protection at the border; at least for the industrialized Western countries. The first decades of reconstruction after the war saw the dismantling of most quantitative restrictions. Seven rounds of tariff negotiations will have reduced the average industrial tariff of the European Community (EC), Japan, and the United States to around 4 percent when the Tokyo Round concessions are fully implemented in 1987. However, this very openness means that national economies are increasingly affected by international trade flows.

The impact in every trading country of economic change in *other* countries is increasing, accelerated in part by rapid advances in tech-

---

[1] Speaking in Washington, DC, at the National Press Club, July 15, 1982.

363

nology in many sectors as well as by the economic development of newly industrializing countries (NICs). Adjustment to change without resort to trade restrictions can more easily be accommodated in a period of high economic growth. In the presence of continued high unemployment, due to recession and to adjustment to sweeping shifts in industrial structures, the desire or need to slow the pace of at least some changes—those transmitted by international competition—will increase.

During this conference, ample evidence has been presented of the increasing disregard of the GATT's provisions by the contracting parties to the agreement. To avoid anarchy, it is essential that a common understanding be reached concerning the conditions which warrant the imposition of trade restrictions, as well as agreement as to how the restrictions will be applied (for example, to all countries or only to some), their duration, the procedures through which they will be imposed and reviewed, and the form that these trade measures should take. There can be no question but that there is an urgent need for reform if confidence is to be restored in the GATT and trade is to be subject to agreed rules of appropriate behavior.

An important requirement of any contractural agreement, if it is to endure, is that there be sufficient flexibility in its terms so that as circumstances change, the agreement can accommodate those changes. In this respect, the GATT is deficient, and therefore, at risk.

For several decades there has been widespread recognition among the GATT contracting parties that the safeguard provisions are not functioning. For the better part of the last 10 years, there has been a concerted effort to remedy this defect, with no success. Another effort—perhaps the last—is being undertaken in the context of the GATT Ministerial meeting scheduled for November 1982.* This paper is intended to address in broad terms several of the problems caused by the current shortcomings in the GATT escape clause, and to argue that to continue to allow world trade to be subjected to a patchwork of ad hoc restrictions not governed by agreed international rules or procedures threatens to erode severely the current relatively open world trading system—a system which can be credited with much of the worldwide prosperity created after World War II.

---

* *Ed. note*: For a discussion of the outcome of the GATT Ministerial, including its call for completion of a safeguards code within one year, see chapter 22, this volume.

Introduction

The explicit rules that are considered the foundation of the GATT are well known: the granting of nondiscriminatory (most-favored-nation, MFN) treatment for goods of other contracting parties at the border, and according national treatment to imported goods once they enter into internal commerce. Less apparent, but even more fundamental, are a number of basic expectations of major trading countries signatory to the GATT which, although inherent in the agreement, are less explicit. These are mutuality of benefits, reciprocity of obligations, and increasingly, an expectation that other major contracting parties will seek to minimize barriers to trade, even if they are not obligated to do so.

Central to the functioning of the GATT is the existence of reciprocity—generally in the form of fulfillment of the expectation that the agreement will be adhered to by other signatories. While there are dispute-settlement procedures to remedy one party's nullifying or impairing the benefits accruing to another, this is not enough. For the agreement to endure as an effective body of international rules, departures from its terms must be limited.

Violations of the GATT's safeguard rules have, however, been widespread. This is extremely serious for a number of reasons. It frustrates the GATT's basic purpose; namely, the prevention of the imposition of unauthorized trade restrictions. Of equal or greater importance than the adverse effects on trade of these restrictions is the damage caused to the international trading system itself by the very fact that the rules are ceasing to have application. This circumstance must be of broader concern than just to GATT lawyers, who are in any event very few in number.

Regrettably, governments do not generally behave with respect to trade as liberal economists would wish. In each country, there is a political imperative toward mercantilism. It is not good will toward others or enlightened self-interest that must be relied upon to curb destructive trade-distorting behavior. In the first instance, conduct must be governed by agreed rules—by the rule of law. The existence of social and economic organization depends upon adherence to agreed norms of behavior. In the case of safeguard actions, the agreed norm is ignored more often than it is applied.

No signatory would dissent from the GATT's central objective—to reduce restrictions on international trade flows to the minimum possible. The question for the next round of GATT negotiations is how best this principle can be achieved. A major cause of excessive restrictions being put into place is the absence of a working set of international safeguard rules. It is not a question of orderliness versus principle. Currently, in the imposition of safeguards, there is neither.

To remedy this, this paper proposes a series of procedural reforms that will assure that *all* national safeguard actions are notified to the GATT, reviewed, and regulated. It also examines a secondary question. That is whether the substantive rule of the GATT's safeguard clause—that restrictions be applied to all suppliers, rather than solely to the ones that are causing injury—can be usefully modified.

To some, the suggestion of departure from the most-favored-nation rule in the case of safeguard actions is seen as an unconscionable abandonment of principle. This may result in part from confusion of the MFN rule, which is a tool to achieve an end—maximum trade liberalization (and for that matter, orderliness)—with an end in itself. The discussion should center not on the morality of applying rules other than the MFN rule, but on the practical effects of doing so.

Individual judgments differ sharply on whether GATT Article XIX in its current form, requiring the use of MFN measures only, still has a significant inhibiting effect on the resort to illegitimate measures, sufficient to warrant its preservation unchanged. There is also disagreement over whether amending the existing rule to allow selective action would not result in an opening of the floodgates to such actions, or whether, conversely, officially acknowledging the existence of these measures might lead to effective regulation of their use.

Disagreement on this issue prevented a conclusion being reached to the Tokyo Round safeguards negotiations. While it would be hoped that the procedural reforms endorsed in this paper could be agreed upon in any event, it may well be impossible to reach international agreement on these issues without resolving the question of whether selective safeguard actions will be permitted. It is this negotiating reality that forces an examination of the merits of amending the current rules to allow selective safeguard actions.

The Place of the Escape Clause in the GATT

The GATT is designed to reduce or eliminate those government-induced distortions of trade that were most prevalent at the GATT's inception in 1997—quantitative restrictions (prohibited by GATT Article XI) and tariffs (bound at negotiated levels under Article II). In addition, the GATT provides a general injunction that signatories shall not discriminate against foreign goods through customs measures (the most-favored-nation requirement of Article I) or internal taxation and regulation (the national treatment requirement of Article

III). In 1955, a prohibition was added on the use of export subsidies by developed countries.

This would, however, have been too rigid a framework to serve as a realistic trade régime, and much of the rest of the GATT's text and practice concerns exceptions to these rules. Several of these classes of exceptions are very extensive. For example, much of the world's agricultural trade is treated, however erroneously, as outside of the GATT rules. Equal in prominence is the exclusion of developing countries from a substantial part of the coverage of the GATT's obligations.[2] Less well understood, but also of importance, is the fundamental inapplicability of the GATT's concepts to nonmarket economies and to sectors of market economies in which market forces are not allowed to operate freely.

Coexistent with these gaping holes in the fabric of the GATT are relatively smaller, more tailored exceptions—for customs unions and free trade areas (Article XXIV), balance of payments adjustment measures (Article XII), measures to counter dumping or subsidization (Article VI), renegotiation of concessions (Article XXVIII), national security (Article XXI), government purchasing (Article XVII), suspension and waiver of obligations (Articles XXIII and XXV), and restrictions for public health, safety or welfare (Article XX).

None of these provisions affords sufficient scope and flexibility for governments generally to restrict imports so as to remedy serious injury to their industries. Except for the important separate régime provided for textiles under the Multi-Fiber Arrangement (MFA), if a trade restriction is to find sanction in the GATT at all, it must be within Article XIX, the escape clause.

In every trade agreement, there is an escape clause—a provision allowing for suspension of the rules to prevent or remedy serious injury due to imports. While participants in a symposium may indulge themselves in condemning "protectionism,"[3] it must be remembered

---

[2] See Article XVIII and Part IV of the GATT, generally.

[3] As a reference point for use in the construction of a trading system, some common concepts are needed. In the GATT and US law, there is no stigma attached to the appropriate invocation of the escape clause, and therefore the labeling of safeguard measures (or countervailing or antidumping measures) as "protectionist," a pejorative term, is unwarranted. A more useful terminology would be to label "protectionist" those measures which thwart rather than promote adjustment. Not every grant of protection is in these terms "protectionist" just as interventions in foreign exchange markets can be appropriate if they iron out short-term disturbances and inappropriate if they attempt to alter market-dictated, longer-run equilibrium rates.

that, but for the permitting of some exceptions to trade liberalization commitments to permit the granting of import relief, the prevailing general régime of liberal trade would not exist. In US law the president *must* grant relief from imports which cause injury *unless* he finds it *"not in the US national interest"* to do so. In a very real sense, it is thus the exception that proves the rule.

To qualify for "Emergency Action on Imports of Particular Products" (the title of Article XIX), a product must (1) as a result of (a) unforeseen developments and (b) the effect of GATT obligations (including tariff concessions), (2) be imported (a) in such increased quantities, and (b) under such conditions, (3) as to cause or threaten serious injury (4) to domestic producers of like or competitive products (an industry), in the territory of the contracting party affected. If this set of criteria is satisfied (as a practical matter, a standard to be met solely in the judgment of the importing country), that country may (1) withdraw or modify the concession on the product (that is, usually, increase the tariff), or (2) suspend the relevant obligation (that is, usually, impose a quota), (3) to the extent and for such time as may be necessary to prevent or remedy such injury. Whenever possible ("unless delay would cause damage which it would be difficult to repair"), advance consultation with exporting countries is required.

It is contemplated that the countries immediately involved will attempt to reach agreement on the proposed measure. One subject of discussion is usually the "compensation" that may be offered by the country taking the safeguard action. As the GATT is based on a balance of concessions through which countries commit to an agreed level of openness of market access, the balance can be restored by the importing country through its offering of additional access for other products of the exporting country. In this way, it compensates for the restrictions being imposed.

The concept of compensation is only implicit in the GATT, however. Article XIX spells out only what happens in the event that no agreement is reached between the countries involved. In that case, the importing country is free to impose the restrictions, and the exporting country is free to retaliate or, more accurately, itself to restore the balance of concessions by imposing such additional import restrictions on the trade of the country taking the escape clause action as will serve to compensate itself for the loss of market access for its exports. In GATT terms, it is free to suspend "the application to the trade of the Contracting Party taking such action of . . . substantially equivalent concessions or other obligations under . . . [the GATT]

. . . the suspension of which the contracting parties do not disapprove."

Experience under GATT Article XIX

Article XIX provides a straightforward, reasonably clear-cut rule, which would apparently offer wide scope for safeguard actions. With no need for the approval of any international organization, and with only an obligation to consult the exporting country (or countries), a contracting party is completely free to restrict imports if, by and large in its own view, the rather general criteria of Article XIX are met. Why, then, is there an abundance of restrictions currently in effect, and relatively few instances where the countries imposing these measures have cited the GATT escape clause as authority for their action?

In many cases, this absence of justification under Article XIX can be attributed, as noted above, to the fact that large categories of trade are regarded by many to be largely GATT exempt—such as trade in agricultural products and the import régimes of developing countries. But even if an examination is confined to trade in industrial products imported by industrial countries, GATT Article XIX is rarely invoked, other than by the United States, Canada, and Australia. And even in the case of these three countries, there are very significant departures from resort to Article XIX as justification for the restrictions which are imposed.

The American Experience

Some of these departures have been solely a matter of form, and it is questionable whether they should be an issue for broad international concern. In 1975, the United States specialty steel industry was found by an independent agency, the US International Trade Commission (USITC), to be suffering serious injury caused by imports. Under the import relief provisions of US law, the president negotiated an orderly marketing agreement (OMA) with Japan, the principal supplier, and established a series of other import quotas, some for individual countries (Sweden and Canada) and some for groups of countries (such as the member states of the European Communities) and an "all other" basket category for the smaller suppliers (such as Korea, Finland, Argentina, Mexico). The OMA had no explicit GATT sanction, while the quotas based on recent historical shipments were consistent with GATT Article XIII (requiring nondiscriminatory treatment). Was the OMA, which technically violated Japan's GATT obligation not to impose quantitative restrictions on its exports, in some way inferior to the GATT-based basket category quotas?

The OMA was in fact orderly in its trade effects. Being the product of a negotiation, it took into account Japan's export interests, providing for some flexibility in shipments between product categories, and some carryover of unused amounts. It provided what businessmen need most when a government intervenes in trade—certainty—a clear expectation of what would occur.

Life in the basket category was far less comfortable, and was compared by some to swimming in a pool filled with piranha. From the exporter's (or importer's) point of view, customs entry was accomplished with all of the orderliness of an Oklahoma landrush. Entries were taken on a first-come, first-served basis. No one supplier was apt to know what others were shipping, and thus, whether the quota would fill prior to arrival of his or her own merchandise.

The next use of orderly marketing agreements by the United States involved another "basic" industry. In 1976, the USITC found that imports of leather footwear were causing serious injury to the domestic American shoe industry. In 1977, the president determined to provide relief. Taiwan and Korea had doubled their combined shipments to the United States over a two-year period. Italian and Brazilian shoes, however, had begun to lose favor in the US market. Footwear shipments from the European Community as a whole had steadily declined year after year, and the average unit value of European shoe imports was well above the pricing of Taiwanese and Korean footwear. The Argentine shoe industry had fallen prey to the general chaos of the Argentine economy and had ceased to be an important factor in the US market.

The US domestic industry asked for the imposition of a global quota, allocated by country and by product, an approach well within the rules of GATT Article XIX. Several liberal economists in the administration suggested that if any relief were granted, it should take the form of a single global quota, with the chaos of that régime relieved somewhat by a system of auctioning import quotas.

The president decided instead to utilize his authority under the Trade Act of 1974 to seek to negotiate formal bilateral orderly marketing agreements with the two largest, and on the basis of the facts, arguably the most disruptive suppliers, Taiwan and Korea. These agreements were successfully negotiated and lasted for four years.

This footwear import relief was in some respects not entirely discriminatory. Each agreement contained an "equity" clause under which the exporting country could ask for consultation with the United States if there were large increases in imports from other countries.

The United States might then agree to take appropriate remedial (restrictive) action against imports from third countries. There was quickly some diversion of US demand to other sources of supply, most notably Hong Kong (involving a scheme to avoid the Taiwanese export restrictions). Hong Kong agreed to require licensing of its exports.

The result of the shoe decision was not illiberal from the viewpoint of preserving, to the maximum extent possible under the circumstances, the flow of international trade. The action was, however, a greater departure from the nondiscriminatory nature of Article XIX than the specialty steel régime. While this was criticized by the US liberal trade community, curiously, so was any contemplated additional shoe agreement, even though it would have made the original action less discriminatory.

The escape clause investigation with respect to color televisions presented an even clearer case of a distinguishable source of injurious import competition. Japan had average exports to the United States of 1.1 million color television sets in each of the five years 1971–75. In 1976, there was, in the words of then Japanese Prime Minister Fukuda, "a torrential downpour" of Japanese television sets on the American market, amounting to 2.9 million sets. In early 1977, the ITC found that serious injury had been caused. Since the commission does not identify separate sources of injury in escape clause cases (other than in a case involving solely the products of a nonmarket economy), it found that imports (in general) were causing the injury, and recommended the imposition of restrictions against products from all suppliers.

The president chose instead to negotiate an orderly marketing agreement with a single supplier, Japan. There was some immediate movement of production to other supplying countries including Canada and Mexico, and eventually an even more significant shift by Japanese producers to invest in US production facilities. Eventually orderly marketing agreements were required with Taiwan and Korea, in order to honor the "equity" commitment made to Japan, and to preserve the effectiveness of the relief.

Before the agreement with Japan expired in June 1980, Japanese shipments had fallen well below the levels provided for in the agreement, which by then no longer had a restrictive effect. The agreements with Taiwan and Korea expired in mid-1982.

The fourth example of a US escape clause case which resulted in a negotiated settlement moved United States practice furthest from the pattern envisaged in GATT Article XIX. In the middle of 1980, an import relief petition was filed with the USITC with respect to imported automobiles. Imports from Japan had been steadily increasing since early 1979, when the shah of Iran fell and the fear of gasoline shortages and energy price increases changed American buying habits back once again to smaller, more fuel efficient cars. These cars were supplied mostly by Japan. The fact that larger cars made by American producers were no longer attractive in the US market was compounded by the serious recession to which the United States had succumbed. Automobiles, the only capital good other than housing that most families purchase, sold in ever decreasing quantities.

Japanese market share as a percentage of total sales rose above 22 percent, but Japan's share of the small car market remained constant. This was due to the fact that it was the larger cars that had stopped selling, and the larger cars were made in Detroit. Higher interest rates and higher sticker prices which applied to all cars affected imports less because imported cars generally found greater favor among white collar workers, who were as a group less affected by the recession.

By November, the US International Trade Commission dismissed the case on the grounds that recession and (in the view of some Commissioners) a shift in consumer preference to more fuel efficient cars, were more important than imports as causes of serious injury to the domestic automobile industry.[4] Despite this finding, in March 1981, the US administration procured a formal export restraint from the Japanese government for a period of two to three years, with the first year's shipments restricted to 1.68 million cars.

In five years, from the specialty steel case to the auto case, the United States had moved from escape clause-justified import relief, to a negotiated settlement in the form of a voluntary restraint agreement (VRA)[5] in the face of rejection of relief pursuant to established statutory procedures. Ironically, this auto deal was concluded by an administration deeply committed philosophically to the complete absence of government intervention in trade. In fact, the very lack of formality of this trade measure stemmed in large part from an unwillingness of the administration to admit to itself that it was actively negotiating export restraints with the Japanese government. Nevertheless, the negotiation was an active one, to the point of not only

---

[4] This weighing of causes is a requirement of US domestic law that has no explicit parallel in GATT Article XIX.

[5] A VRA differs from an OMA in that in a VRA the importing country does not apply restrictions to enforce the agreement. It relies solely on export restraint.

working out the numerical limits but also reviewing the details of the domestic authority to be used by the Japanese government in imposing export restrictions.

The European Example

The countries of Europe began their GATT membership with the widespread imposition of quantitative restrictions, deemed necessary in the early years of postwar reconstruction. The phase out of these restrictions has been one of the important accomplishments of the GATT. Since that period, according to GATT records, of the 95 instances where Article XIX was invoked between 1947 and mid-1978, the member states of the European Community—the world's largest trading entity—have accounted for only 9 cases, and half of these occurred before 1965.

The early actions appear to have been solely national, as opposed to Community actions: Germany, coal, 1958– ; France, pig iron, 1969–70; Italy, pig iron, 1964–70; France, horse meat, 1968–71; Germany, oil, 1964– . Over time the Commission has assumed a greater role, as the administration of the EC implies action by the Community rather than by individual member states. Thus, it was the Community that terminated the pig iron actions, disinvoking Article XIX. A tariff increase on raw silk imports was put into place in 1970 by the EC for Italy, as was import licensing of tape recorders into Italy in 1973 (lasting only eight months). In 1977, the EC applied import quotas *from Korea only* for imports destined *for the United Kingdom only.* In 1978, the EC notified suspension of import licenses for preserved cultivated mushrooms.

This list of Article XIX notifications is interesting principally because it would appear to indicate that everything else could have been imported freely into the Common Market and its individual member states throughout the three decades following 1947. This was not the case, however. A variety of other restrictions were applied. For example, the number of Japanese automobiles allowed into the Italian market has for some years been restricted to 3,000 per year. For France the limit has been 3 percent of the market, and for the United Kingdom, Japanese imports have not been allowed to exceed 11 percent of new automobile registrations.

None of these actions were notified under GATT Article XIX or under any other GATT provision. Nor were there notifications of the series of bilateral restraint agreements governing imports of steel mill products—agreements entered into by the EC in the last half of the 1970s with principal supplying countries pursuant to the Simonet and Davignon Plans. From time to time other examples of restrictions, such as those with respect to Japanese electronics products, have surfaced in the press.

Thus, while the United States has only just again begun to wander outside the strict confines of GATT Article XIX,[6] the countries of Europe have maintained over the years a significant number of restrictions with only sporadic invocation of Article XIX. In the last few years, EC invocation of Article XIX has increased, but there does not appear to have been any corresponding decline in GATT extralegal restrictions.

Japan

The GATT's 30 year list of 95 Article XIX actions does not contain a single entry for Japan. This is not evidence that Japan has never resorted to import restrictive measures. It was not until 1969, shortly after Japan's application to the Organization for Economic Cooperation and Development (OECD), through which it committed itself to open its economy, that the Japanese government ceased to ration foreign exchange and thus regulate trade through the budget control of the Ministry of International Trade and Industry (MITI).[7] Ever thereafter, however, the Japanese market has proved to be import-resistant in the view of its major trading partners.

While Article XIX has not been invoked, antirecession cartels for textiles, steel, nonferrous metals, rubber, shipbuilding, and chemicals have been used both to restructure the domestic Japanese industry and effectively to block imports. Less formal restrictions have been encountered repeatedly in Japan by foreign businessmen, most recently documented in a study prepared on the Japanese semiconductor market.[8] In many product areas, import penetration has proven exceptionally difficult, originally due to high tariff levels, subsequently because of nontariff barriers (such as standards and customs valuation), and perhaps most importantly because of the way the

[6] The United States engaged in a number of bilateral negotiations designed to impose trade restrictions much earlier in its history (in the 1930s), and led the way toward bilateral textile agreements, first for cotton and then for other fabrics.

[7] Chalmers Johnson, *MITI and the Japanese Miracle* (Stanford, Calif.: Stanford University Press, 1982), p. 253.

[8] "International Competition in Advanced Industrial Sectors: Trade and Development in the Semiconductor Industry," Joint Economic Committee Print, February 1982.

Japanese market is organized (whether by cartel, the close interrelationship of firms in a sector, or due to difficulties encountered in the distribution system).

This import imperviousness has been recognized publicly by the Japanese government as recently as the last week of May 1982, in its most recent announcement of trade liberalization measures. It is equally evident in the frustration of other trading countries, indicated in 1982 alone by a Taiwanese import ban on a thousand different Japanese consumer products, a GATT Article XXIII case brought by the European Community against Japan for having a closed market, and the consideration of legislation by the US Congress to redress the lack of "reciprocity" in international trade relations, primarily with Japan.

In these circumstances, resort by Japan to the escape clause does not seem to have been a necessary tool for its management of import competition problems.

There are a number of reasons for lack of adherence to the GATT's escape clause rules. The agriculture ministries of all countries, and the industrial and planning ministries of the developing countries opted out of the system at an early stage. Countries like Japan, which have had more of a state-guided economy, have had other means at their disposal to deal with potentially injurious import competition. But beyond this, why the reluctance of all but Australia (33 Article XIX actions through mid-1978), the United States (21 cases), and Canada (15 cases) to utilize Article XIX?[9]

Perhaps part of the answer is to be found in an examination of the legal systems of the three countries which account for three-quarters of the cases notified through mid-1978. These systems place a particularly high value on the rights of individuals to contest actions of their national governments as well as to influence the policy-making process. This strong emphasis on individual rights is buttressed by elaborate curbs on the powers of the national executive authorities, stemming from the fact that they are federal governments. The United Kingdom and the continental European nations are far more used to having the commerce powers of their central governments largely unfettered. Add to this their greater degree of socialism—there would

---

[9] A more recent GATT report for a later period provides a somewhat different picture of the statistical breakdown of countries invoking GATT Article XIX. In the period 1971–81 Australia still led with 16 cases. Canada claimed 13. The EEC accounted for 13 (3 for mushroom embargoes, 3 for fish embargoes). The US is credited with 10 actions.

appear to be far less public concern in these countries over a close collaboration between the state and industry—and the path is cleared for negotiated agreements between governments and between industries to channel, however informally, the flow of trade for the benefit of a domestic industry. Therefore, other than in the case of Australia, the United States, and Canada, formal trade measures, which are highly visible as departures from international obligations, could be avoided.

What is Wrong with the Current GATT Rules?

One is struck by the simplicity of GATT Article XIX. The criteria and procedures for its invocation are simple and few. There is no involvement of the GATT as an organization either through requiring GATT approval or even monitoring of trade actions, unless an adversely affected party brings the matter to the attention of the GATT Council (which Korea did briefly with respect to EC restrictions on televisions in 1978). It is perhaps this very lack of procedure that constitutes the main defect of Article XIX. The lack of involvement by an international body encourages the practice of leaving the regulation of trade solely to negotiation (or unilateral action and reaction, if any) between the parties most directly concerned—the importing and exporting countries. Informal arrangements or accommodations are in reality subject to no rules, and are limited only to what the exporting country will agree to, or will tolerate.

There are also impediments to the application of Article XIX which are incorporated into the provisions of the Article itself, however. The first of these is the fact that GATT Article XIX is written so that safeguard actions taken pursuant to its terms are to apply to all imports from all sources under the MFN principle.[10]

It is a significant impediment to the imposition of formal import restrictions that they must apply to all sources of supply. This is true for a number of reasons. Across-the-board import restrictions generally affect many countries, each of which may oppose the action and under Article XIX has a right to retaliate, or may need to be offered compensation. Complex discussions may have to be held with

---

[10] This position has been attacked by the EEC, and even flouted by it in the case of Korean TV imports into the United Kingdom. Nevertheless, a review of the drafting history of the GATT, and subsequent practice and GATT discussions, indicate clearly that safeguard actions must be nondiscriminatory under the current GATT rules.

a number of supplying countries. The compensation bill can be expensive.

There is also the problem of appearances. Few governments, if any, wish to appear protectionist (although they do wish to be credited by the protected domestic industry with having acted). A government's across-the-board restriction will often seem to its own people to be anticonsumer in nature. It appears restrictive to limit all foreign supplies of a product. On the other hand, export restraint exercised by one or a few principal suppliers (whether or not pursuant to a formal intergovernmental agreement) can take on a character of the foreign government engaging in an appreciated act of solicitude for a domestic industry which has come upon hard times.

The avoidance of unilateral restrictive action also can avoid foreign policy costs, in that the result is agreed to (even though perhaps under duress). There are no unpleasant surprises for the exporting country. The measures are the result of negotiation. They may even be, and often are, moderated by the negotiation process to take into account the trade interests of the exporting country. Even the unpleasantness of publicly notifying the restrictions to the GATT can be avoided.

Thus, by using negotiated restraint as a substitute for an Article XIX escape clause action, a government can wrap itself in a cloak of pragmatism. It just appears to be managing its problems. It may even be able to do so without public review at any stage—either in terms of domestic public procedures in which consumer costs and foreign policy concerns (as well as other export interests) would be heard and weighed, or internationally, where a multilateral forum might be able to examine the action. The quieter the transaction, the less likely that affected parties at home or abroad will be able to affect the result. In short, government bureaucracies generally prefer maximum freedom of action with minimum accountability, and departing from GATT Article XIX can help confer this freedom upon them.

There also may be a special factor with respect to the European Community which causes the EC Commission to prefer more informal means of handling problems of import competition. With a common commercial policy, it is the Community as a whole which in theory should act against imports. However, if a single member state has an import problem, it is difficult to get the Ten to agree to protect the one through a formal change in the common external tariff, or through formal quantitative restrictions. Moreover, it is not entirely clear that only the Community as a whole, and not individual member states, has access to Article XIX. A pragmatic, informal solution avoids these questions. For example, representatives of the UK automobile industry now sit down each calendar quarter with their opposite numbers in the Japanese industry to work out the level of UK imports. They seek to ensure that the Japanese producers do not obtain more than an 11 percent share of new car registrations in Great Britain. This informal procedure is certainly widely known, and is tolerated by the Community. These voluntary export restraints (VERs) need raise neither troublesome jurisdictional issues nor more fundamental constitutional questions for the Community.

Another reason for the avoidance of use of Article XIX is the right given to exporting countries to retaliate (even though this can possibly be avoided through payment of compensation). In international trade relations, as in personal relations, virtue (in this case notification under GATT Article XIX), at least in the short term, appears to be its own reward. For a country to notify a restriction is to make it vulnerable to retribution. This is illustrated by the Canadian action against imports of US beef in 1976.

The United States had banned the use of a hormone called diethylstilbestrol (DES) in cattle feed, and the Canadian government had followed suit. Unfortunately, the US Food and Drug Administration's ban was voided by the US courts because applicable domestic procedures had not been followed in its imposition. Consequently, Canada embargoed further imports of US beef, and would not allow any reasonable certification procedure to be worked out to permit entry of imports of DES-free beef. The US government believed that the Canadian action was in reality imposed as a safeguard action rather than as a valid health restriction.

Due to the curious manner in which the GATT deals with this kind of situation, the absence of a Canadian notification under Article XIX left the United States with no automatic GATT right of reaction. The US government's options were either to itself declare the Canadian action an Article XIX action (for which there was no GATT precedent), and then to invoke the retaliatory provisions of the article to compensate itself; or it could bring a GATT Article XXIII case (a complaint for nullification and impairment of trade agreement benefits) against Canada. This latter route is time-consuming and uncertain in result. It has never led to a grant of authority to retaliate which in fact was then utilized. The United States was thus without the right to impose immediately GATT-consistent sanctions against Canada as leverage to obtain a more reasonable Canadian trade policy.

The Canadians themselves, for whatever reason (one would hope that it was virtue—governments generally in fact do not like to violate their international obligations), solved the problem eventually by notifying the beef import action under Article XIX. The United States promptly retaliated (without seeking compensation) by limiting meat imports from Canada. Within a matter of months, an agreement was worked out to restore two-way trade in beef between the two countries.

The principle of retaliation or compensation clearly worked in this instance. While no complete record of compensation and retaliation exists, GATT records for the period 1947–78 indicate that compensation was paid in 17 cases. Retaliation was imposed only four times, and in one case was threatened but not imposed when the import restriction was modified. From this record one can assume that the compensation issue is another ground for the reluctance of countries to invoke Article XIX formally.

Should There Be Reform?

There is disagreement internationally as to whether or not GATT Article XIX should be modified so that it will be more likely to be applied by the GATT contracting parties. The balance of international opinion is, however, tipping toward acknowledging that new international safeguard rules are needed.

Those who oppose reform do so not because they feel that the current rules work, but because they believe that new, more realistic rules will only encourage greater use of import restrictions. They seem to regard Article XIX as at least having the force of moral suasion—as a standard to be aspired to. They also feel that is conduct is truly egregious, there is always the possibility of bringing a country into the GATT to answer a complaint for its wholly illegal conduct.

This argument could be summed up as follows—a strict rule little adhered to is to be preferred to a less stringent rule which might actually govern national conduct. The same argument was heard for many years in connection with the proposed reform of GATT Article XII. Article XII, governing the imposition of trade restrictions for balance of payments purposes, allows countries to utilize only one kind of import measure—quantitative restrictions. Major developed countries (Canada, France, the United Kingdom, and the United States) had in recent years employed import surcharges instead. They did so for a variety of reasons: surcharges are less disruptive or distortive of trade; they require less bureaucracy; and they can be put into place quickly. The United States imposed an import surcharge in 1971. This measure was promptly condemned by the GATT as clearly illegal. The US retort was that it could have imposed GATT-lawful measures which would have caused far more damage to the trading interests of others. The GATT rule against surcharges no longer stood as a significant inhibition to resort to this form of balance of payments measure.

No change was made in the rules for another eight years. The fear prevailed that to legalize other trade measures would encourage their use. In the Tokyo Round of trade negotiations, a compromise was struck. The participants in the GATT framework negotiations noted that restrictive measures other than quantitative restrictions had been used for balance of payments purposes, and they agreed that henceforth the procedures and requirements set forth in GATT Article XII (and of a new Declaration on Measures taken for Balance of Payments Purposes) should apply to all restrictive import measures taken for balance of payments purposes.

As with the Canadian beef case and previously in balance of payments cases, countries acting completely outside the GATT rules had had complete freedom from review and multilateral consultation. In the future, the Balance of Payments Declaration held, this would no longer be permitted. The presence or absence of international review would no longer be a matter subject to the control of the country imposing import restrictions, to be avoided by breaking the GATT's rules completely rather than only partially.

A Central Issue for Negotiation—Selectivity

In international discussions regarding reform of the GATT, the most contentious issue is whether "selectivity" should be allowed in taking a safeguard action. Selectivity is the term used to describe acting against imports from one or a few supplying countries, rather than, as presently required, restricting imports from all sources.

Selective actions must be allowed if the GATT rules are to govern conduct as it actually exists now or will exist in the foreseeable future. This is necessary not only to recognize reality—selective measures have become a more important form of import relief than nondiscriminatory, MFN actions—but because selective actions can be more reasonable than MFN actions as trade restrictive actions. Failure to amend the GATT rules is hardly likely to result in countries abandoning selective action.

The negotiating imperative for a new safeguards code—that selective actions be permitted but regulated—is not blunted by the fact that Article XIX actions can presently be selective in effect even though they are nondiscriminatory in form. Just as a tariff concession must in principle apply to all countries equally but can sometimes be written to apply to products from only one source (cheese made from milk of cows which graze not below 10,000 meters in the summer and not above 2,000 meters in the winter), import restrictions imposed as safeguard measures can and do try to target disruptive goods. This is accomplished by price-breaks (for example, restrictions only against low-cost footwear), exclusions of certain products (stainless steel strip for the manufacture of razor blades), or otherwise by product description.

A similar result can often be achieved by imposition of a quantitative restriction, allocated by country, with quantities set on a recent historical base. Imports that cause injury will generally be seen to have increased rapidly in a very recent period (despite the minority view holding that different classes of imports of the same product are indistinguishable in their effects for this purpose). Taking as a base the most recent three years for which statistics are available (a common standard under GATT Article XIII), and allocating proportionate shares to countries on the basis of their respective shares in that period, often has the effect of most sharply curtailing exports from countries whose shipments have advanced rapidly in the most recent past.

This degree of selectivity afforded by Article XIX as it currently exists is obviously not deemed sufficient by major contracting parties. Thus, for example, when the United States considered the form of import restrictions that it would impose on footwear, the European Community insisted that its products were not the problem and should not be covered by the US action. The EC maintained that import controls that excluded high value footwear would not adequately assure that Italy would not be adversely affected. Even a quota based on historical shares was deemed unacceptable, although this would not have been likely to have resulted in any curtailment of Italian shoe shipments to the United States, which had been declining. The Common Market clearly regarded any restrictions against its shoe exports, regardless of their effect, as unwarranted. A number of American policymakers were very sensitive to the fact that US agricultural (and other) exports to the Community could be at risk if US import restrictions covered Community exports, even purely as a matter of form. Selective actions against Taiwanese and Korean products were imposed.

The central question of past and future negotiations for a new international safeguards arrangement is whether, in permitting selective import restrictions, adequate controls can be established to regulate the use of selective measures. One obvious form of control is to make selective action subject to the agreement of any exporting country that is directly involved. This has the advantage of recognizing current forms of selective action (the OMAs, VRAs, and VERs) in the GATT framework. It also preserves the pragmatic, consensual nature of the GATT.

This is not to say, however, that permitting the imposition of selective safeguards primarily on the condition that the agreement of the exporting country is obtained is without any drawbacks. Many smaller exporting countries would regard a rule of this kind as an invitation to extortion of consent, threats of severe import restrictions being the duress applied. Nor would some importing countries and competing suppliers necessarily deem this an adequate system. There would always be cases where the exporting country whose products were clearly the principal cause of the injury might refuse completely to agree to the safeguard action, or find itself unable politically to do so, resulting in unwarranted MFN restriction on all suppliers, or in the inability of an importing country to impose needed import relief. Moreover, there will be occasions, the European Community's negotiators have argued, when safeguard actions must be taken very quickly because large quantities of a product are in transit, threatening to cause further injury to an already seriously injured industry. (We have not had much experience with this problem in the United States, perhaps due to our geography compared with that of Europe.)

Consensual trade restrictions, where they are successful from an importing country's point of view, still suffer from a serious drawback from the point of view of the world trading community in general, unless they are notified to the GATT and are made subject to common rules (which is not now the case); the interests of other parties affected by the distortions of trade created by an orderly marketing agreement are unlikely to be taken into account at all. Governments are left the freedom by agreement to opt out of the rules of the international trading system and create their own trade régimes. In effect, this is what the Common Market did with Japan, Sweden, Spain, and others in steel trade in the 1970s. The American steel industry, arguing that through trade diversion the United States had a direct interest in the redirection of world steel trade resulting from the efforts of the Community's negotiators, tried unsuccessfully to obtain redress from the US government. This would have been the subject of an interesting GATT dispute, had it not been for the fact that the US administration deemed the case to be mooted by the institution of the US steel trigger price mechanism (TPM).

Whether or not selective action is expressly permitted in a new safeguard code, it is clear that further controls on the use of this form of safeguard action must be established. Two general means that suggest themselves are the establishment of specific objective criteria which must be satisfied before selective action may be taken, and multilateral surveillance and review of every restrictive measure, selective or otherwise.

Objective criteria should specify the circumstances in which selective action is appropriate, with the intent of ensuring that the one, few, or several countries against which action is taken, are clearly the cause of the problem. The criteria would have to be satisfied even if the exporting country agreed to the application of the restriction. These factual preconditions (beyond general requirements in the code including the serious injury criterion which would have to be satisfied in all cases) could require that:

- The supplying countries involved have increased their market shares absolutely, or relative to domestic production in the importing country, (some may have increased their shares while others may have stable shares but are nevertheless contributing to the injury)
- The products of these countries differ in terms of quantities, prices, or kind, from other imports which are not being restricted, so that these products can be reasonably determined to be the cause of serious injury, or threat thereof
- Exclusion of other countries' exports from restrictions is not inequitable (other imports must be nondisruptive, noninjurious in effect)
- If a substantial advantage in terms of acquisition of market share is being conferred on other countries' exports which are not subjected to restrictions, an "equity" provision will allow a country that is restricting its exports to seek and obtain redress by: having the restriction made nondiscriminatory (MFN), putting additional suppliers under restraint, or liberalizing the restrictions vis-à-vis the supplier under restraint in order to eliminate the inequity.

GATT negotiating proposals in the Tokyo Round negotiations contained a number of other criteria that would have rendered selective action far less accessible: agreement of the exporting country would have been required (except as noted below); selective action could have been taken against no more than two or three countries; a very sharp and substantial increase of imports over a short period of time from only one, two, or three countries would have had to be present; a rapid increase in market share would have had to have occurred; a substantial portion of total imports would have to have been covered by any restrictions; *unusual* and *exceptional* unforeseen circumstances would have to have been clearly established; other imports could not have been regarded as a significant factor; and no imports could have been discriminated against because of low price. Under this régime, if agreement between the parties involved could not be reached, the safeguards code committee could approve the action, provided that it met the above criteria. However, in critical circumstances, provisional action by the importing country would be possible after 10 days of trying to reach an agreement. This unilateral action could last no longer than 45 days.

The need for establishing enforceable objective criteria for selective action is demonstrable, as is the need for mandatory international review to establish that the criteria have been met. The criteria of previous negotiating proposals noted above, however, taken together, can be considered to be excessively restrictive.

Why should action solely against low-priced sources of supply be prohibited? High-cost (and -priced) suppliers are less likely to be causing injury. In the case of the US footwear import relief action, Bally shoes from Switzerland and cowboy boots costing over $100 a pair from Mexico were manifestly not a significant part of the problem.

Why should selective actions be acceptable if they are highly discriminatory—covering 1, 2, or 3 producers—but unacceptable if they cover 8 out of 12 producers, when it can objectively be established that the other 4 suppliers excluded from the restrictions are not contributing substantially to the serious injury?

Why must the import penetration be excessively sharp, and circumstances be "unusually and exceptionally unforeseen"? Article XIX already requires that unforeseen developments must cause serious injury to a domestic industry. Sharp or dull, if the import-caused injury is mortal, or nearly so, these are not logical criteria for choosing between selective and nondiscriminatory restrictions.

Countries shipping in an orderly fashion—the older, larger, established suppliers as well as the new entrants who have no appreciable market share, should, under a new system, be eligible to have their trade unaffected by import restrictions if they are not a significant cause of the problem. Arguably, in a new safeguards system, selective action should not be discouraged and relegated to the highly unusual case *if* equitable treatment can be assured to those suppliers subjected to selective restrictions and promiscuity in the use of this form of restriction can be prevented.

The content of earlier negotiating proposals has been outlined above, along with some of the problems posed by the limitations that would be placed upon the use of selective safeguards. One is struck by the fact that the proposed limitations appear to be less related to making sure that selectivity is used only when appropriate than to an objective of assuring that such actions are rare relative to actions covering imports from all sources. This wariness of selectivity should properly be reserved for any code provision allowing the unilateral imposition of selective measures. Indeed, the most delicate balance to be struck in the negotiations is the extent, if at all, to which a selective safeguard measure may be imposed *without* the consent of the exporting country.

The requirement for consent, although not an absolutely reliable firebreak against the proliferation of restrictions, is regarded by many governments as indispensable to protecting them against unreasonable demands for export restraint. One can only dispense with this inhibiting factor if other conditions are imposed that assure that these selective measures would be used only where appropriate. One means of obtaining this assurance would be to require that international approval in some form be obtained with respect to nonconsensual import relief—for example, in the form of a finding by a standing GATT panel that objective, substantive, and procedural criteria had been met. The international approval should be automatic, however, if objective criteria are met. This process should not be in the hands of a political body (the GATT Council, or a committee of national representatives) which would be susceptible to influence by either the party requesting relief of by the party for which export restrictions are proposed. To give assurance that prompt action could be taken by an importing country, where there were exceptionally acute circumstances (where delay would cause serious injury that would be difficult to repair), unilateral action by the importing country could be allowed if

• it filed a statement with the panel outlining the satisfaction of procedural steps and the substantive conditions required for the imposition of selective relief
• the panel did not disapprove the action within a short period of time (30 days)
• the exporting country, after notification, did not object to the action.

The exporting country would have a right to object at any time during the period that restrictions were in effect. If it did so, the panel would be required to approve or disapprove the continuation of the selective action within 60 days. Disapproval would result in the importing country's being required to terminate action, make it nondiscriminatory, or face collective sanctions by the contracting parties.

If an action were approved over the objection of the exporting country, reasonable compensation (in the judgment of the exporting country) would have to be offered. The exporting country's right to compensate itself (i.e., impose equivalent restrictions on the goods of the importing country) would remain unimpaired. The most difficult case posed is where the action is disapproved by the panel and the importing country nevertheless imposes unilateral selective measures (rather than taking nondiscriminatory action). In this circumstance, some form of sanction for noncompliance could be required by GATT Council decision (see below).

Building Confidence in a New System

The major open question about a new system will concern its fairness.

Multilateral Review

Can adequate international review provisions be established to assure equitable treatment? For multilateral procedures to be effective, they must be known to be unavoidable. Multilateral review should be automatic, whether or not a country notifies a restriction. There should be an aggressive GATT Secretariat effort (supported by the contracting parties) to seek out all restraints, selective or otherwise. Fortunately, governments can hardly ever resist taking credit for providing protection to their domestic industries. Therefore, little more than a review of press clippings is required in order to gain information about government-approved safeguards.

Information on safeguard actions should be put promptly before an independent GATT panel for initial review. In the absence of a presentation by an importing country of its justification for its action, the panel would determine, based on the best available evidence, the nature of the restriction and the degree of noncompliance with the new rules. All actions would have to be justified, and reviewed periodically throughout their duration.

Sanctions for Noncompliance

Self-help is still the best device for preservation of rights in the international trading system. This means that the right to self-compensate—to restore the preexisting balance of concessions—must not be abrogated or diluted. The fact that the importing country complies with all criteria and procedures should not deprive a country of regaining the level of concessions it bargained for in past negotiations.

Other sanctions are also needed, and creative thought should be given to the problem of inducing compliance. One method—a presumption that allegations are accurate if a party fails to defend its actions—has been mentioned above. There are other possibilities—allowing greater retaliation for unjustified action, or requiring compensation, either equal to or in some cases greater in trade coverage than the import restriction.

Another area worth exploring is creation of stronger linkages between the GATT and the International Monetary Fund (IMF) and the World Bank. A country acting in extraordinarily serious violation of the multilateral economic system's rules (in this case, the trade rules) could be ruled to have impaired its creditworthiness with the Fund and the Bank. Not even a developed country in heavy surplus would gladly accept qualification of its lines of credit at the IMF. Sanctions would, of course, have to be proportional to the degree of offense, and would require a policy level decision by the institutions concerned.

There must be costs for acting outside commonly agreed upon rules. Without the imposition of sanctions, the trend towards cynical disregard of the GATT's requirements will only increase.

Coverage

The system must be all-inclusive. If a trade restriction exists, whether notified or not, it must be justified. There could be an automatic exclusion, however, for restrictions adequately covered by other codes (for example, countervailing duties, antidumping, standards requirements, government procurement). Orderly marketing agreements, voluntary restraint agreements, voluntary export restraints, interindustry agreements, and any other form of government-sanctioned trade restriction, including toleration of cartels, must be subject to a comprehensive safeguards system, notified and reviewed.

Other Requirements

There is a rather extensive list of other desiderata for elements to be included in a new code: criteria for the injury standard; criteria for a standard of causation; limits on duration; progressive liberalization of restrictions; requirement of an adjustment plan; domestic public procedures; requirement for early consultation; conditions for "emergency action"; remedies for trade diversion; dispute-settlement procedures; surveillance procedures; rules governing export restraints of all forms; special rules for developing countries; and, transitional rules for preexisting measures.

These are in addition to the elements of a new code described above. Of the elements listed, three deserve special mention: the need for domestic public procedures; plans for adjustment; and standards of causation.

Public procedures not only give notice to interested parties, but also give governments a chance to hear all sides of a question and make an informed judgment prior to acting. Consultation with governments of exporting countries is not an adequate substitute for information supplied by the trade and the industry involved. This is an area where there will be great resistance to change on the part of many governments. It is extraordinarily inconvenient and time consuming to try to make fully informed judgments. However, if governments can afford personnel to run complex import restricting régimes, they can devote some resources to allowing interested parties to be heard and to present their views. It would create a healthy check against protectionist forces.

Plans for adjustment should also be made part of a new safeguards system. A delicate balance is required here. Adjustment may well mean an orderly transfer of resources out of a domestic industry rather than "revitalization" to make it internationally competitive. This is a politically sensitive area, and one deep within what is rightly considered a preserve for national sovereignty. However, other countries (exporters) are carrying part of the burden of this adjustment, and they should have some assurance that the protection will not be permanent or excessive, unless a renegotiation of concessions takes place. The details of the plan need not all be revealed, but a government should have some notion about what adjustment it can foster, rather than simply fobbing the problem off onto others abroad.

Lastly, general standards of causation could be included in a new code. There are almost always a variety of causes of injury to a domestic industry. These include changes in costs, relative efficiency, aggregate demand (recession) and consumer preference. While no international weighing of causes should substitute for a nation's reasonable judgment on this question, the restrictions applied to trade should bear a proportional relation to the degree of injury caused by imports, and not by other causes. Conversely, the fact that recession or other factors are temporarily dominant as the principal causes of an industry's problems should not prevent a government from imposing some degree of restriction of imports to counter the injury attributable to imports. A period of recession should not confer on other countries a license for accelerating injurious market penetration.

Fair and Unfair Import Competition

The escape clause is designed for broad import problems which are not necessarily unfair. The absence of a need to prove the existence of unfair acts is essential to the nature of a general escape clause, and this should remain as it is now. Yet there is no special remedy in the GATT when the injury to another country's industry is, in effect, intentionally inflicted. This may occur where a country marshalls its national resources to gain market share in a particular sector, heedless of short-term returns. Likewise, the maintainance, as opposed to the creation of, excess capacity in an industrial sector can cause distortions of trade that can injure the more mature industries. The GATT does not deal adequately with these forms of aberrant behavior.

A new international safeguards code should address these questions. One way to deal with harm "intentionally" caused by national policies would be to employ a lesser injury standard, such as "material" injury, rather than "serious" injury or a standard of "serious prejudice." Remedies could include recommendations to governments to ameliorate or offset their policies that cause industry-wide trade distortions, and a freer hand on the part of importing countries to take defensive measures.

The Interests of Trading Nations in a New Code

Any attempt to provide new proposals concerning a GATT safeguards code[11] must be based on an understanding of the use of safeguard measures in the international trading system. According to GATT records, from 1971 to 1981 Article XIX has been invoked 61 times by 11 countries and the EC. All these countries were developed countries (if Spain is included in this category), with 85 percent of the escape clause actions accounted for by Australia, Canada, the EC, and the United States. Almost all the actions were taken with respect to the products of developing countries (primarily the newly industrializing countries) and Japan.

It is principally the safeguard actions which are not recorded—those currently outside the GATT rules—on which attention must

---

[11] For a well-written and valuable contribution to this subject, see John M. Leddy, et al., *A New Safeguards Code: Report of the Atlantic Trade Council's Advisory Trade Panel* (Washington: Atlantic Trade Council, November 1981).

be focused. The GATT Secretariat is currently compiling an inventory of these voluntary export restraints, orderly marketing agreements, and similar safeguard measures. So far 63 cases have been identified where these "other" safeguard measures have been used since 1978 or were still in effect during this period, compared with only 19 actions notified under Article XIX.

Again, the use of these arrangements was initiated by developed countries (including Austria and Spain) and these measures were directed almost exclusively at exports from the developing countries and Japan. The types of products involved included automobiles, footwear, color TV receivers, steel, leather garments, motorcycles, and many types of agricultural products. Although the data are incomplete, the EC appears to be the major user of these types of measures.

These non-GATT safeguard measures appear to be replacing more traditional Article XIX measures. The ratio of measures identified as being imposed outside the GATT framework exceeds by a factor of three to one those actions within the system. The ratio is in fact far greater in that, there being no obligation to notify the taking of the extralegal measures, presumably not all are known. Moreover, it is the largest industrial safeguard measures, in terms of trade coverage—such as autos, steel, electronics—which are unreported and unregulated.

The empirical evidence available, though incomplete and lacking quantitative dimensions, indicates that a wholesale circumvention of Article XIX is in progress. This should be a compelling reason for the major participants in the international trading system to agree in November at the GATT Ministerial to initiate a new negotiation on a safeguards code. Otherwise this kind of interference with trade will continue and expand unchecked, undermining existing GATT obligations and the health of the trading system these rules protect. Thus, the need for a safeguards code goes beyond the narrow interests of those countries most directly affected by these measures.

Given the use of escape clause actions cited above, the developing countries should be strongly interested in reforming Article XIX. They should wish to tighten up the procedures for Article XIX actions by setting forth more specific time limits for escape clause actions, more precise definitions of domestic injury and market disruption, and by covering similar safeguard actions now taken outside of the GATT. The developing countries, generally, however, fear legitimizing new forms of restrictions. Japan has taken a similar position.

The EC has argued strongly for flexibility in remedying import injury, including the unilateral use of selective measures. The United

States has argued for a comprehensive system which provides greater procedural controls over safeguards, including perhaps selective measures, but is still very concerned about the latter question.

The basis for a negotiated compromise exists. If, as Henry Kissinger was fond of saying, world security interests are indivisible, in a sense so too are interests in the maintenance of a sound and liberal international trading system. In this regard there should be no disagreement among the EC and its member states, other developed countries including the United States, and the developing countries.

It is said that the newly industrializing countries are coming into the front door of the GATT, just as the mature, developed countries are leaving by the rear door. We should pause before we informally take our leave from the GATT, and instead restore it to a central role in maintaining an open international trading framework. The issue is not "selectivity" versus "nondiscrimination." It is whether we will have a GATT that applies to world trade versus one that increasingly does not.

To be successful, GATT must apply not only to all trade measures, but to all countries, even if somewhat differentially because of differences in levels of development. There can be no free riders nor can there be mature participants who consider themselves to be above the rules. The increasingly widespread contempt for the GATT's rules must be converted to respect.

This cannot be accomplished by our insisting that the GATT must remain pure, and therefore, irrelevant, as its signatories engage in increasingly unregulated trade-restricting activities. The erosion of the GATT system must be reversed and confidence in it restored. Substantial progress can be made toward this goal through a major good-faith effort at creating a rigorous, pragmatic new international safeguards code which is in fact applicable to world trade.

CHAPTER 12

Worker Adjustment to US International Trade: Programs and Prospects

J. David Richardson

Two charges were given for this paper. The first charge was to reflect on US experience with trade adjustment assistance (TAA), especially its adjustment aspects, in light of the recent trimming and impending scuttling of the program. The second charge was to assess the international sources of sectoral employment growth and displacement in the 1980s, reflecting on the roles of the robotics revolution and demographic change in shaping the trends.

Much has been written on the first topic. Broad analyses of recent US experience with trade adjustment assistance include Corson, et al. (1979), Wolf (1979), Bayard and Orr (1979), Richardson (1980), Jacobson (1980), US General Accounting Office (1980), Miller and Van Erden (1981), and Aho and Bayard (1980a, 1980b, 1981). The papers by Aho and Bayard contain many sound suggestions for improving the design of trade adjustment assistance. The Wolf monograph seems to be the most recent treatment of US adjustment assistance as a species of adjustment programs in all developed countries. More technical analyses of the labor market consequences of US and Canadian trade adjustment assistance include Jenkins, et al. (1978), Corson, et al. (1979), Jacobson (1980), Glenday, et al. (1980), and Cropper and Jacobson (1982).

These are hardly exhaustive bibliographies on the first topic. In light of the number of citations even without exhaustiveness, an effort is made below to say what seem to be new things about trade adjustment assistance, and to repeat the old only when necessary. An effort is also made to provoke (gently), since trade adjustment assistance seems recently to elicit an unwarranted intellectual ennui in the United States, born perhaps out of fatalistic consignment of the program to the 1983 budget knife.

Less has been written on the second topic. Gray, Pugel, and Walter (1982) and Personick (1981) are excellent places to start. An effort is made below to push beyond their work. Sectoral US employment trends in the 1970s are classified and decomposed in a unique way. The aim is to infer as much as possible from them regarding *future* employment trends and their international determinants. Some broader observations are also included on demographics, robotics, and labor mobility, especially as they affect the linkage between United States sectoral employment and international competitive forces.

US Trade Adjustment Assistance and the "Market" for Labor Adjustment

It has become commonplace in recent discussions of US trade adjustment assistance to speak of its tripartite goals: equity, efficiency, and political efficacy.[1] Equity describes the goal of compensating those who are deserving and have been injured by a government trade policy undertaken in the name of society's general welfare. Efficiency describes the goal of promoting intersectoral adjustment of productive resources in directions indicated by international market forces. And political efficacy describes the goal of "bribing" or "buying off" the coalitions of agents with credible political power that could block the desirable trade policy and resource adjustment.[2]

US Trade Adjustment Assistance

With these goals in mind, US trade adjustment assistance since the early 1970s is often thought to have been tolerably successful at providing compensation for injury and in response to political threats, but quite unsuccessful at facilitating adjustment. With respect to equity, TAA payments to workers generally exceeded unemployment insurance payments and lasted longer, although they were highly uncertain

---

[1] The particular language to describe the goals is Aho's and Bayard's (1980a, 1980b, 1981). See also Richardson (1980).

[2] "Policy" is always taken quite broadly to include preservation of the status quo, a passive option that could be blocked by coalitions of protectionists lobbying politically for increased trade barriers.

in their timing and lumpiness.[3] Initially there seemed general agreement that TAA recipients were deserving—poorer, older, less educated, and more typically minority status. With respect to political efficacy, several "successes" are cited. The interpretation of eligibility requirements was loosened considerably in the early 1970s to offset growing political support for the protectionist Burke-Hartke legislation. Eligibility was then broadened formally in the Trade Act of 1974 as a sweetener to gain political support for American initiative in the "Tokyo Round." And US administrations opted for TAA rather than new import barriers in a number of import-relief cases from 1974 through 1980, thereby defusing political support for the protectionist alternatives (Aho and Bayard 1981, pp. 40–3) provide a useful summary).

But was US trade adjustment assistance really ineffective at facilitating adjustment? It seems wise not to answer too hastily. And if the answer is yes, then that is not necessarily an indictment of the program. It is well documented that trade-displaced workers took very little advantage of "adjustment services." But very little money or productive resources were spent offering them (Aho and Bayard 1981, p. 35). So nothing ventured, nothing gained—or lost, either. And if the "market for labor adjustment" worked tolerably well for the United States in the 1970s, a question examined below, then it is perhaps just as well that in practical administration of the TAA program, adjustment provisions were unused.[4] Whether the "market for US labor adjustment" can continue to work well in the 1980s, however, is quite another question. Some general and international aspects of that question are analyzed in the second part of this paper.

From the perspective of equity, efficiency, and political efficacy, some of the reasons are clear for the recent near demise of the US TAA program. The program could continue to function as long as it served two of its three masters adequately. But toward the late 1970s, equity seemed to many commentators to be increasingly sacrificed on the altar of political efficacy—expediency was the pejorative synonym. Increasing numbers of TAA recipients turned out to be only

---

[3] See Aho and Bayard (1981, pp. 31–36) who summarize and compare the relevant studies. Cropper and Jacobson (1982) reveal evidence that suggests even the possibility of overcompensation.

[4] Provision of adjustment services was the responsibility of Comprehensive Employment and Training Act personnel whose orientation and experience was toward the problems of young, inexperienced, and disadvantaged workers. See also Aho and Bayard (1980a, pp. 368–69).

temporarily displaced—more than half in a survey of 1975–76 experience (Corson, et al. 1979). Increasing numbers turned out to be relatively high-wage steel and autoworkers. Neither temporarily displaced nor high-wage workers seemed compellingly deserving victims of injury. And when President Jimmy Carter nearly quadrupled the TAA budget to compensate US autoworkers just before the 1980 election, the move seemed altogether too close to Democratic party patronage and devoid of equity.[5] It seemed inevitable in the aftermath of President Ronald Reagan's election victory that a program which had begun to live by the sword of political expediency would die by the sword of political expediency.

In retrospect, what appeared to be a weakness of US TAA—its impossible charge to be "all things to all men"—had perhaps been a strength, and quite consistent with the political notion of checks and balances. Tendencies for US TAA to become more generous in its compensation were checked by political efficacy and the trenchant observation that the more generous the equity-based assistance, the less adjustment incentives remained. Tendencies for US TAA to become a species of patronage were checked by the perceived inequity of the drift and its obviously perverse adjustment implications.

From this point of view it may be desirable for any new US TAA program to continue to serve a tripartite constituency of goals. The alternative of having narrow programs aimed separately at trade-related compensation, adjustment, and political lubrication runs the risk of quickly becoming vested and entrenched, both in Washington and in the expectations of trade-competitive firms and workers.

The alternative of having no trade adjustment assistance runs the risk of neglecting valid reasons for such a categorical program. First, trade-competitive workers and firms can be argued to face greater unanticipated sectoral shocks than others, information is generally more mobile (cheaper to acquire and convey) within a nation than across national boundaries.[6] Trade adjustment assistance can help

---

[5] Aho and Bayard (1980a, p. 364) and (1981, pp. 41–42) provide factual details. The fiscal year 1980 benefits of roughly $1.63 billion were six times larger than the previously largest benefits paid in fiscal 1979.

[6] See Grossman and Richardson (1982, pp. 20–22) for an expansion of these observations. The reason is straightforward. Except for those largest multinational corporations with operating roots in virtually all important economic centers, firms and other economic institutions will generally find it optimal to acquire less information about foreign markets and government policy than about domestic equivalents. (Presumably they proceed in such a way that an extra dollar spent on information-gathering would reap results

agents adjust to and weather the mistakes that go with greater uncertainty in international trade.[7] Second, categorical trade adjustment
assistance is one of the most direct ways of responding to a properly
disenfranchised but nevertheless important constituency: foreign exporters and governments, especially of developing countries, who are
concerned about the predictability of access to the US market (Aho
and Bayard 1980a, pp. 364–5).

It is of course tempting to recommend that any new TAA program
serve its "adjustment master" better. But that recommendation pre-
supposes first that the historical TAA program had little favorable
effect on US labor adjustment, and second, that markets provide
inadequate adjustment incentives so that they must be supplemented
by government programs. We will touch on a few aspects regarding
the first issue here, and a few regarding the second in the next subsection.

Was TAA really devoid of adjustment stimuli? One of the less
appreciated favorable impacts of the US program on labor market
adjustment was its signaling dimension. If it did nothing else, TAA
certification signaled to employers and workers that a plant or firm
was under important competitive pressure from imports. And it did
this on the face of it without significantly impeding any sympathetic
adjustment signals from the market itself.[8] The TAA program caused

---

of the same marginal value for information abroad as at home.) The result
is that economic agents will generally be better able to anticipate and forecast
domestic events than foreign events; they will be better able to take advantage
of those that are favorable, and to insure against those that are unfavorable.
Or conversely, economic agents will be regretfully or happily surprised more
often from recurring foreign fluctuations than from recurring domestic fluctuations. The variance of unexpected business shocks should be larger the
more dependent a sector is on exports or the more competitive it is with
imports.

[7] This argument for a categorical trade adjustment assistance program puts
a high payoff on credible governmental provision of information and signals.
Especially on the import side of trade for the United States it also suggests
the possible wisdom of a self-financing insurance/loan system where favorable
unexpected surprises are presumed to provide the revenue for firms and
workers in tradables sectors to pay the premiums that tide them over unfavorable unexpected surprises (Grossman and Richardson 1982, p. 26). See
also the *Wall Street Journal*, 7 April 1982, p. 27 for a fledgling private job
insurance program along these lines.

[8] The word "significantly" is important because research by Kathy Utgoff
at the Public Research Institute of the Center for Naval Analyses suggests
that TAA compensation, which was neither taxed nor experience-rated (un-

no significant change in product prices or factor costs—or, more exactly, less change than protectionist import barriers would have caused. Layoffs continued. Competitive pressures from imports continued. Market signals to adjust were left largely intact. From this point of view, TAA certification provided both symptomatic relief (equity-based compensation) and a strong diagnostic signal that the patient was sick, leaving it to the patient to take the requisite preventive medicine of responding to the market.[9]

TAA certification may thus have encouraged a desirable sort of "leading adjustment"—in the direction of cautious reserve for workers contemplating commitments and firms contemplating investments in import sensitive sectors. "Leading adjustment" has the virtue of being controlled by *expected* wages, prices, costs, and profits, all of which are flexible, thereby contributing to market clearing and minimizing adjustment distortions such as unemployment and excess capacity.

TAA may also stimulate desirable adjustment by discouraging inefficient adjustment. If the alternative to TAA's preservation of adjustment signals is protection, then the adjustment result is perverse. Prices, wages, and profits all move in a direction to defer adjustment, encouraging additional workers and larger firms, and increasing the size of equitable compensation claims if in the future protection is abandoned. For example, it seems arguable that more, not less, TAA compensation was paid to US garment workers, shoeworkers, and steelworkers in the 1970s because those sectors benefited from increasing US protection during that time.

The Market as an Adjustment Mechanism

Of course, yet another alternative with significant support these days is *no* government adjustment policy and *no* protection either. The US Trade Representative William E. Brock put it this way:

---

like unemployment insurance), increased the labor supply in industries with high incidence of TAA certification; lowered wages in such industries; increased layoffs in such industries; and increased "job attachment" in such industries.

[9] And TAA may have provided more. A highly tentative but intriguing possibility uncovered by Richardson (1980, p. 52) is that although TAA compensation (being more generous than unemployment insurance) increased a recipient's first spell of unemployment, it reduced the incidence and duration of subsequent spells. It thereby seemed to increase the "effi-

Adjustment assistance . . . [does not of itself] effectuate adjustment. It is US policy to place primary reliance on market forces to facilitate adjustment in affected industries. . . .

A better solution to the problems associated with shifts in competitiveness is to promote positive adjustment of economies by permitting market forces to operate.[10]

Ambassador Brock's use of the words "positive adjustment" to describe market forces is a thinly veiled reminder that they *are* a viable alternative to the ponderously dirigiste "positive adjustment policies" promulgated by the secretariat, committees, and consultative bodies of the Organization for Economic Cooperation and Development (OECD 1979).

But just how effective then is the "market for labor adjustment"? Does it succeed reasonably well or fail? Do government adjustment programs succeed better or fail worse? Aho and Bayard (1980a, pp. 367–71) provide a useful introduction to these questions in the context of US trade adjustment assistance. Their litany of problems with market adjustment is familiar, but worth repeating; imperfect information, uncertainty, incomplete factor mobility, wage-price rigidities, and insufficient access to the capital market to finance the human capital investments that are the concomitants of adjustment. One reason that the litany is worth repeating emerges in what follows: some of the entries on it are reflections of social attitudes and institutions that are not immediately under the influence of economic considerations. These attitudes and institutions may exact a high and initially hidden economic cost if they impede the ability of the market to administer adjustment adequately.

Only one cautionary note needs to be added to the litany of problems. Even with the problems, US markets for labor adjustment have probably worked fairly well until now. Furthermore, market forces will always be sufficient to generate acceptable labor adjustment if there is an adequately large margin of workers, even a minority, *with* adequate information, confidence, ambition, acceptance of risk (observe how these personal attitudes are the counterparts to the ap-

---

ciency" of job search. The first job taken after separation seemed to be a "better match" for the worker, perhaps because of more generous TAA compensation.

[10] Opening statement to the Joint Oversight Hearing of the Senate Committee on Finance and the Senate Committee on Banking, Housing, and Urban Affairs, July 8, 1981, quoted at greater length by Gray, Pugel, and Walter (1982, end of chapter 3).

parently impersonal forces labeled uncertainty, incomplete factor mobility, and wage-price rigidities), and access to the capital market.
Only the margin matters. Characteristics, histories, and personalities
of the average worker do not.[11]

With that note of caution in mind, there are two potential problems
in leaving the adjustment goal of the US TAA program to be achieved
in the market. The first is that the international fluctuations that will
be experienced in the 1980s may be so much larger than those of
recent history that they will "overwhelm" the margin of workers who
can and will adjust to market signals. It may then be desirable for
policy to mediate the adjustment to the extent that the market cannot.

The second potential problem is that US attitudes and institutions
may change in such a way that the margin is narrowed, and even
historically moderate fluctuations cannot be accommodated by market adjustment. Attitudinal and institutional sclerosis seems arguably
the "European disease." [Blackhurst et al. (1977, pp. 44–52) pro-
vocatively entitle one section "Protection and the Refusal to Adjust."] There are signs that Canada has caught it, and that the United
States has been exposed. Even in today's Congress, there is fundamental and regressive questioning of market reliance in US international economic transactions, with surprising support for a "negotiated" world trade structure that would administratively constrain
and channel global market forces (Richardson 1982b, point 60). And
Congress may be faithfully representing a shift in social attitudes and
institutions that aggravates market distortions and shrinks the margin
of workers who can and will adjust. Attitudinal and institutional shifts
may include:

• a decline in intellectual curiosity and increasing satisfaction with
shallow and indulgent education, such that uncertainty and specu-
lation displaces information and reasoned judgment
• increasing expansion of "rights" at the expense of privileges, positions, and property that are contingent on performance, such that
perceived entitlement to a particular job at a particular salary level
in a particular community precludes all but a semblance of mobility
and rigidifies wages, work conditions, and promotion paths
• higher real interest rates, crowding out, and credit limitations relating to wealth inequality, all of which constrict the availability of

---

[11] Dore (1980) provides some engaging profiles of the easy adjustment
undergone by firms and workers on the "margin" of adjustment to international competitive forces.

capital-market resources not only for conventional physical investment but for human investments in retraining and relocating as well.

Each of these shifts intensifies the distortions that impede the market adjustment mechanism—imperfect information, uncertainty, incomplete factor mobility, wage-price rigidity, and insufficient capital-market access. If little can be done about these fundamental shifts in the short run, then it may be desirable to have short-run policies that reexpand the margin of workers who can and do adjust, policies that implement efficient and effective incentives to do so. It is anomalous that the social shifts so frequently decried in conservative diagnoses also undermine the conservative prescription for relief. Recourse to the market alone for labor adjustment may be ineffective without complementary government adjustment programs.

Some Reflections on US Sectoral Employment Trends in the 1980s

International economic dimensions of future trends in US sectoral employment and labor mobility will be sampled in this section. Strictly domestic dimensions of such trends will be introduced when useful for perspective and symmetry. But this is by no means an exhaustive consideration of this complicated subject. More comprehensive treatments are Gray, Pugel, and Walter (1982) and the August 1981 issue of the US Department of Labor's *Monthly Labor Review* (the "projections issue").

Some General Observations

Let me begin with some general observations. First, US demographic trends may be much more favorable to productivity growth and saving in the 1980s than they were in the 1970s (for example, Freund 1982). The size of the US population between the ages of 15 and 24 will shrink dramatically in the 1980s, more dramatically than it rose in the 1970s. And the size of the US population over 65 will grow less rapidly. To the extent that US trade-related employment problems have been aggravated by low US savings rates and productivity growth during the 1970s, they will be ameliorated by improvement in these areas during the 1980s.

Second, technological change associated with the "robotics revolution" may have less significant effects on employment trends than it would first appear.[12] Increased recourse to the use of robots in production—or any other technological change for that matter—affects long-run production, employment, and trade only if it is adopted *unevenly* across industries or nations. A technological innovation that affected all industries comparably and was applied globally would not alter any sector's equilibrium employment in any nation. No relative prices would change. No relative wages would change. Changes in nominal wage and price levels would be accommodated by changes in exchange rates and money stocks. Therefore demonstrating unevenness of robotic innovations is the key to proving their dramatic implications for future employment. And at least two characteristics suggest that robotic innovations will be on the contrary more *evenly* applied across industries and nations than technological changes of the past.

• Robots have considerable potential for use in agriculture as well as manufacturing, and even perhaps in services since certain labor-intensive monitoring, retrieving, sorting, and counting functions can be performed robotically.
• To the extent that modern technology increasingly "belongs" to multinational and not strictly national firms, it is more likely to be applied simultaneously in a number of global locations where the innovating leader (a firm, not a nation) has affiliates.[13]

Third, adjustment needs to robotics innovation may be readily identifiable by both labor and management, and susceptible to advance planning, precautionary negotiation, and contingent contracting in the same way as wages and work rules. Adjustment needs to trade policy innovations, by contrast, or to innovations in competitive foreign capacity, are not so readily identifiable by either labor or management.[14] Thus the case for some unique government adjustment policy toward robotics seems weak in comparison to more familiar government adjustment policies that deal with the international trade ramifications of robotics.

Fourth, if manufacturing becomes automated at a disproportionately rapid rate compared to agriculture and services, then the importance of national security in competitive manufacturing advantage

---

[12] Other reasons for this observation, besides those given in this subsection, are outlined in the second half of this section.

[13] See Richardson (1982b, point 42) for a slight elaboration.

[14] Information-theoretic reasons for this are referred to briefly above on pp. 6–7.

may increase, and the importance of labor costs may diminish (relatively). The global location of industrial employment may be increasingly determined by political stability, military vulnerability, and national philosophy toward ownership.

Fifth, US intersectoral labor mobility may decline in coming years due to the increasing importance of interindustry trade, creating "complementarity" between imports and domestic production (Branson 1980, Krugman 1980, Richardson 1982a).[15] Skills, technology, and equipment promise to differ more radically between import-competing industries and the rest of the US economy than in the past, when US trade was more heavily of an intraindustry variety. Ebbs and flows of US competitiveness may cause structural/transitional unemployment and excess capacity to be correspondingly larger than in the past. Offsetting these tendencies, however, may be increasing incidence of intra*firm* yet intersectoral labor mobility due to corporate conglomeration trends. Several recent contract renegotiations seem to have indirectly encouraged intersectoral mobility by bargaining aggressively for job security within multisector firms.

Sixth, US interoccupational mobility may decline in coming years to the extent that US capital formation remains sluggish. Shifting occupations almost inevitably involves some retraining or reeducation, both of which are investments in human capital. If real costs of borrowing remain high, and if the return on human investment continues to be low due to recession and sluggish growth, then retraining and reeducation will be discouraged. Protracted unemployment will be encouraged, nursed by the hope of a "lucky break" that would restore the payoff to already accumulated human capital, and by the despair of any better alternative.

Seventh, US interregional labor mobility may increase in coming years to the extent that: changing trade patterns increase the share of skilled, service, and white-collar workers in the US employment mix; labor markets for such occupations are more national in scope; such workers are more willing to change location than less skilled or blue-collar workers.[16] Offsetting international economic forces is any

---

[15] Shifts toward interindustry trade patterns seem less characteristic of Europe and Japan. According to a recent study by Fieleke (1981), Britain and Japan seem in the recent past to have enjoyed roughly the same degree of intersectoral labor mobility as the United States.

[16] Gray, Pugel, and Walter (1982, chapter 3 and table 3.14) summarize US Department of Labor data that show only minor dispersion among regional unemployment rates for white-collar and service workers, but considerable dispersion among regional unemployment rates for blue-collar workers.

continuation of the extraordinary growth in household secondary workers who are virtually immobile geographically.

Finally, all three kinds of mobility may decline due to the otherwise favorable demographic changes described above. As younger workers fall and older workers rise as a proportion of the labor force, the "average worker" will likely have greater identity with and attachment to a traditional sector, occupation, and location. Cumulated on-the-job and on-the-spot training will further solidify this immobility. With a labor force that is more clay and less putty than in the 1970s, the United States will be even less able than it was then to shift workers among sectors, occupations, and regions.

An Empirical Examination

Tables 12.1 to 12.4 record retrospective trends in employment for the 53 US manufacturing sectors with the largest employment in the 4-digit input-output classification. These 53 sectors account for roughly half of US manufacturing employment. The tables are organized and decomposed in a unique way designed to make them suggestive of prospective employment trends in the 1980s.[17]

The average annual percentage growth in employment from 1972 through 1979 is the upper left entry for each sector. "Employment" denotes total employment, not just production workers.

Just below each trend in employment is the average annual percentage growth in "income to 'capital,'" defined in a convenient but admittedly simple way. Income to "capital" is sectoral value-added less employee compensation. (Employee compensation measures earnings of all employees, inclusive of bargained and legally mandated benefits.)

Retrospective trends in income to "capital" are an arguably useful indicator of prospective trends in employment. Industrial income outside of employee compensation is the principal source of funds for capital formation in the United States. Indeed aggregate US "business savings" are three to four times as large as "personal savings." At a sectoral level, familiar capital-market imperfections make internally generated earnings an important source of funds for expansion, and for many firms the marginal source. Cross-sectoral differences in growth rates of "capital" income can thus be important

---

[17] Exhaustive projections of sectoral employment trends for the 1980s at this level of detail can be found in Personick (1981) but without the interpretative classification and decomposition on which this section concentrates.

TABLE 12.1 LARGE[a] US MANUFACTURING SECTORS WITH *BELOW* AVERAGE[b] GROWTH OF *BOTH* EMPLOYMENT AND INCOME TO "CAPITAL,"[c] 1972–79

		Decomposition of employment trend[d]			
Input-output sector	*Real output component*	*Output price component*	*Inter-mediate input component*	*"Wage" component*	*Labor productivity component*
Average across 284 sectors					
Average percentage growth in					
• employment	1.55				
• income to "capital"	11.22	2.84	8.15	−.67	−7.98	−.80
1301 Complete Guided Missiles					
Average percentage growth in					
• employment	−1.77				
• income to "capital"	10.47	−.21	8.01	−.13	−8.11	−1.33
1401 Meat Products					
Average percentage growth in					
• employment	.43				
• income to "capital"	10.38	2.15	7.45	−.41	−7.85	−.92
1418 Bakery Products (Bread, Cake, Cookies and Crackers, Related Products)					
Average percentage growth in					
• employment	−.20				
• income to "capital"	9.25	−1.06	9.69	.05	−8.30	−.57
1601 Broadwoven Fabric Mills and Fabric Finishing Plants					
Average percentage growth in					
• employment	−1.15				
• income to "capital"	8.48	.44	7.95	−.69	−8.33	−.52
1603 Yarn Mills and Finishing of Textiles, N.E.C.					
Average percentage growth in					
• employment	−2.27				
• income to "capital"	6.86	−.28	5.88	.55	−7.91	−.51
1804 Apparel Made From Purchased Material					
Average percentage growth in					
• employment	−.64				
• income to "capital"	7.61	.05	5.85	.66	−6.42	−.77

TABLE 12.1 (Continued)

Input-output sector	Decomposition of employment trend[d]				
	Real output component	Output price component	Inter-mediate input component	"Wage" component	Labor productivity component
2201 Wood Household Furniture (Includes Wood TV and Radio Cabinets)					
Average percentage growth in					
• employment	− .21				
• income to "capital"	6.19	− .38	7.51	− .39	− 7.34	.39
2500 Paperboard Containers and Boxes					
Average percentage growth in					
• employment	− .97				
• income to "capital"	5.37	1.77	7.93	− 2.92	− 8.61	.86
2603 Book Printing and Publishing					
Average percentage growth in					
• employment	1.39				
• income to "capital"	10.57	2.34	7.58	− .25	− 6.82	− 1.46
3201 Tires and Inner Tubes					
Average percentage growth in					
• employment	− .58				
• income to "capital"	2.92	− 1.72	8.96	− 1.92	− 8.13	2.23
3402 Footwear Except Rubber					
Average percentage growth in					
• employment	− 3.44				
• income to "capital"	4.88	− 3.60	8.12	− .79	− 6.36	− .81
3501 Glass and Glass Products, Except Containers					
Average percentage growth in					
• employment	1.13				
• income to "capital"	6.38	2.81	6.54	− 1.47	− 8.19	1.44
3701 Blast Furnaces and Basic Steel Products					
Average percentage growth in					
• employment	− .22				
• income to "capital"	10.32	1.28	10.92	− 1.76	− 10.73	.07

	Decomposition of employment trend[d]				
Input-output sector	Real output component	Output price component	Inter-mediate input component	"Wage" component	Labor productivity component
4004 Fabricated Structural Metal					
Average percentage growth in					
• employment	.63				
• income to "capital"	9.37	− .89	10.00	− .55	− 7.48	− .46
4102 Metal Stamping					
Average percentage growth in					
• employment	1.43				
• income to "capital"	10.39	1.33	9.21	− .84	− 7.90	− .37
4203 Hardware, N.E.C.					
Average percentage growth in					
• employment	1.02				
• income to "capital"	7.28	1.39	7.95	− 1.03	− 8.16	.86
5203 Refrigeration and Heating Equipment					
Average percentage growth in					
• employment	− .19				
• income to "capital"	7.00	2.08	5.77	− .57	− 7.78	.30
5903 Motor Vehicles and Parts					
Average percentage growth in					
• employment	1.25				
• income to "capital"	6.86	2.68	7.50	− 1.39	− 9.10	1.54

Source: Robert E. Baldwin, Rachel McCulloch, J. David Richardson, and Andre Sapir, *US Policies in Response to Growing International Trade Competitiveness. Final Phase I Report. Industry Detail Supplement,* Report on NSF Grant PRA-8116448, University of Wisconsin Center for Research on U.S. Trade Competitiveness, April 15, 1982.
a. Measured by employment. Tables 12.1 through 12.4 include all 4-digit US input-output industries with 1979 employment greater than 100,000 workers.
b. Weighted average across 284 4-digit US input-output industries; weights *equal* number of employees.
c. Income to "capital" is defined as value added *less* employee compensation.
d. See Appendix 12.A for details and interpretation of decomposition.

TABLE 12.2   LARGE[a] US MANUFACTURING SECTORS WITH *ABOVE*
AVERAGE[b] GROWTH OF *BOTH* EMPLOYMENT AND
INCOME TO "CAPITAL."[c] 1972–79

	Decomposition of employment trend[d]				
Input-output sector	*Real output component*	*Output price component*	*Intermediate input component*	*"Wage" component*	*Labor productivity component*
Average Across 284 Sectors					
Average percentage growth in					
• employment	1.55				
• income to "capital"	11.22	2.84	8.15	−.67	−7.98	−.80
2005 Millwork and Wood Kitchen Cabinets					
Average percentage growth in					
• employment	2.44				
• income to "capital"	12.72	.88	9.85	.23	−7.35	−1.17
3204 Miscellaneous Plastics Products					
Average percentage growth in					
• employment	4.87				
• income to "capital"	12.56	5.52	8.80	−1.83	−7.52	−.09
3702 Iron and Steel Foundries					
Average percentage growth in					
• employment	1.57				
• income to "capital"	12.91	1.20	11.24	−1.28	−8.93	−.67
4006 Fabricated Plate Work (Boiler Shops)					
Average percentage growth in					
• employment	4.93				
• income to "capital"	15.99	5.05	9.26	.39	−8.77	−1.01
4101 Screw Machine Products and Bolts, Nuts, Rivets, and Washers					
Average percentage growth in					
• employment	2.68				
• income to "capital"	12.02	3.33	8.04	.32	−7.63	−.73
4204 Coating, Engraving, and Allied Services					
Average percentage growth in					
• employment	3.11				
• income to "capital"	14.31	7.18	6.64	−1.73	−7.38	−1.60

	Decomposition of employment trend[d]				
Input-output sector	Real output compo- nent	Output price compo- nent	Inter- mediate input compo- nent	"Wage" compo- nent	Labor produc- tivity compo- nent

4208 Pipe, Valves, and Pipe Fittings

Average percentage growth in
- employment
- income to "capital"

	4.22				
	15.66	3.64	10.44	−.23	−8.05	−1.59

4302 Internal Combustion Engines, N.E.C.

Average percentage growth in
- employment
- income to "capital"

	5.27				
	14.05	7.11	8.79	−1.70	−9.04	.12

4400 Farm Machinery, Lawn and Garden Equipment

Average percentage growth in
- employment
- income to "capital"

	3.94				
	15.15	7.19	7.41	−.80	−8.57	−1.28

4501 Construction Machinery and Equipment

Average percentage growth in
- employment
- income to "capital"

	3.85				
	14.27	3.79	20.27	−.75	−8.46	−.91

4703 Special Dies and Tools and Machine Tools Accessories

Average percentage growth in
- employment
- income to "capital"

	3.36				
	13.61	3.29	9.07	−.60	−7.34	−1.06

4901 Pumps and Compressors

Average percentage growth in
- employment
- income to "capital"

	4.46				
	16.81	5.70	9.03	.14	−8.69	−1.73

5000 Machine Shop Products

Average percentage growth in
- employment
- income to "capital"

	6.30				
	15.09	3.58	10.59	−.01	−7.27	−.58

5101 Computing and Related Machines

Average percentage growth in
- employment
- income to "capital"

	7.99				
	19.82	16.82	−.19	.74	−6.93	−2.46

TABLE 12.2 (Continued)

Input-output sector	Decomposition of employment trend[d]				
	Real output component	Output price component	Inter-mediate input component	"Wage" component	Labor product-ivity component
5304 Motors and Generators					
Average percentage growth in					
• employment	2.44				
• income to "capital"	12.69	2.89	8.95	−.46	−7.99	−.95
5604 Radio and TV Communication Equipment					
Average percentage growth in					
• employment	2.73				
• income to "capital"	15.42	6.05	4.87	.93	−7.28	−1.83
5702 Semiconductors and Related Devices					
Average percentage growth in					
• employment	5.45				
• income to "capital"	21.30	18.47	−2.51	.76	−7.55	−3.72
5703 Electronic Components, N.E.C.					
Average percentage growth in					
• employment	5.81				
• income to "capital"	22.13	7.47	6.51	.68	−7.81	−1.03
6001 Aircraft					
Average percentage growth in					
• employment	2.36				
• income to "capital"	15.92	5.05	8.41	−.98	−8.13	−1.98
6002 Aircraft and Missile Engines and Engine Parts					
Average percentage growth in					
• employment	3.20				
• income to "capital"	20.10	3.26	9.92	1.22	−8.37	−2.83
6101 Ship Building and Repairing					
Average percentage growth in					
• employment	2.40				
• income to "capital"	18.44	3.67	8.59	.47	−9.14	−1.19
6202 Mechanical Measuring Devices					
Average percentage growth in					
• employment	5.86				
• income to "capital"	18.66	8.97	5.64	.23	−6.75	−2.23

Note: The notes and sources are identical with those in table 12.1.

TABLE 12.3 LARGE[a] US MANUFACTURING SECTORS WITH *ABOVE* AVERAGE[b] GROWTH OF EMPLOYMENT AND *BELOW* AVERAGE GROWTH OF INCOME TO "CAPITAL,"[c] 1972–79

| Input-output sector | *Decomposition of employment trend*[d] | | | | |
	Real output component	Output price component	Inter-mediate input component	"Wage" component	Labor productivity component
Average across 284 sectors					
Average percentage growth in					
• employment	1.55				
• income to "capital"	11.22	2.84	8.15	−.67	−7.98	−.80
2002 Sawmills and Planing Mills, General					
Average percentage growth in					
• employment	1.56				
• income to "capital"	9.44	.03	10.96	−1.18	−8.60	.36
2407 Converted Paper, Products, N.E.C., Except Containers and Boxes					
Average percentage growth in					
• employment	2.58				
• income to "capital"	8.86	2.73	9.07	−2.42	−7.36	.55
2601 Newspapers					
Average percentage growth in					
• employment	1.83				
• income to "capital"	10.23	.73	8.88	−.68	−6.04	−1.07
2605 Commercial Printing (Includes Lithographic Platemaking and Services)					
Average percentage growth in					
• employment	2.52				
• income to "capital"	10.74	2.72	7.71	−.81	−6.42	−.68
2901 Drugs					
Average percentage growth in					
• employment	3.25				
• income to "capital"	8.65	5.17	5.80	−1.61	−7.92	1.81

Note: The notes and sources are identical with those in table 12.1.

TABLE 12.4   LARGE[a] US MANUFACTURING SECTORS WITH *BELOW* AVERAGE[b] GROWTH OF EMPLOYMENT AND *ABOVE* AVERAGE GROWTH OF INCOME TO "CAPITAL,"[c] 1972–79

	Decomposition of employment trend[d]				
Input-output sector	*Real output component*	*Output price component*	*Intermediate input component*	*"Wage" component*	*Labor productivity component*
Average across 284 sectors					
Average percentage growth in					
• employment	1.55				
• income to "capital"	11.22	2.84	8.15	−.67	−7.98 −.80
1422 Bottled and Canned Soft Drinks					
Average percentage growth in					
• employment	−.25				
• income to "capital"	12.43	3.49	8.40	−.99	−9.23 −1.94
2402 Paper Mills, Except Building Paper					
Average percentage growth in					
• employment	.19				
• income to "capital"	16.99	4.38	9.09	−.13	−9.62 −3.53
2701 Industrial Inorganic and Organic Chemicals					
Average percentage growth in					
• employment	1.42				
• income to "capital"	15.03	2.74	13.37	−2.29	−9.61 −2.79
3101 Petroleum Refining and Miscellaneous Products of Petroleum and Coal					
Average percentage growth in					
• employment	1.50				
• income to "capital"	27.91	4.84	19.16	.36	−9.84 −13.02
3203 Reclaimed Rubber and Miscellaneous Rubber Products					
Average percentage growth in					
• employment	.91				
• income to "capital"	12.56	1.62	7.66	−.83	−7.79 .25
5603 Telephone and Telegraph Apparatus					
Average percentage growth in					
• employment	1.08				
• income to "capital"	12.02	4.86	7.40	−1.68	−8.44 −1.06

Note: The notes and sources are identical with those in table 12.1.

indicators of cross-sectoral differences in future investment, future competitive advantage in global markets, and future employment growth.[18]

The 53 large sectors are divided twice and regrouped into the four tables. The 24 sectors that had slower-than-average employment growth appear in tables 12.1 and 12.4. The 29 sectors that had faster-than-average employment growth appear in tables 12.2 and 12.3. The standard for "average" growth in employment is the weighted average of employment growth rates across 284 four-digit manufacturing sectors, not just the 53 largest that are described in the tables.

The 24 sectors with slower-than-average employment growth were divided and regrouped once more. Eighteen had slower-than-average growth in income to "capital" as well, and appear in table 12.1. Six had faster-than-average earnings growth and appear in table 12.4. In light of the important role that growth in "capital" income plays in sectoral capital formation, the sectors appearing in table 12.1 probably face bleaker employment prospects in the 1980s than those in table 12.4.

A similar subdivision of the 29 sectors with rapid employment growth in the 1970s reveals most to have had correspondingly rapid growth in income to "capital" (22 in table 12.2), and comparatively few to have had slow earnings growth (7 in table 12.3). Because of the more optimistic outlook for investment in table 12.2 sectors than in table 12.3 sectors, the former seem more likely candidates for continuing to enjoy favorable employment trends in the 1980s than the latter.

Indeed it seems sensible to think of the sectors in table 12.2, with only a few exceptions, as those where the United States is likely to have the most enduring comparative advantage. Sectors in table 12.3 are, by contrast, potential "transition sectors" where the US may be "losing" comparative advantage. For these table 12.3 sectors, employment growth in the 1980s may slacken or even slip to slower-than-average. Casual reflection seems to confirm this characterization—especially reflection on the growing international competitive pressures confronting labor involved in sawmills, drugs, aircraft components, and photographic equipment.

Sectors in table 12.1 are correspondingly those with the strongest US claims to comparative disadvantage. And even though earnings trends are above average in all table 12.4 sectors, they are notably so only for Petroleum Refining, Chemicals, and Paper Mills. Of these,

---

[18] See, for example, Kotlikoff, Leamer, and Sachs (1981, p. 15).

only the latter two seem potentially on the transitional edge of comparative disadvantage.

The tables also confirm the familiar link between US comparative advantage and technological leadership. To the extent that there is any positive correlation between the technological intensity of a sector's production and its two-digit input-output identification, employment declines are concentrated in "low tech" sectors and employment growth in "high tech" sectors. The average two-digit input-output prefix for table 12.1's declining sectors is 30. For table 12.2's growing sectors it is 48. And for table 12.3's and table 12.4's "transition" sectors it is 35 and 31, respectively.

It is also worth elaborating on an international economic reason why there were more large US sectors with above-average rates of employment growth in the 1970s (29) than with below-average rates (24).[19] The corresponding regularity is that small US manufacturing sectors in the 1970s had below-average rates of employment growth. This pattern is exactly what should have been expected from the rapid growth in the orientation of US production toward international trade in the 1970s. Such "internationalization" should cause increasing specialization of production toward sectors in which the United States has comparative advantage—sectors that would already be large because of that comparative advantage—and shrinkage of sectors in which the United States has comparative disadvantage—sectors that would already be small because of that comparative disadvantage.

"Internationalization" in the 1970s should also have caused increasing intrasectoral specialization due to scale economies and learning-by-doing. Tables 12.1 to 12.3 contain suggestions of this as well. Part of the two-digit primary iron and steel group is among the slow-growing sectors of table 12.1 (3701, Blast Furnaces and Basic Steel Products), part among the fast-growing sectors of table 12.2 (3702, Iron and Steel Foundries). A similar split of a two-digit group occurs for heating, plumbing, and fabricated structural metal products.[20]

Similar patterns of employment growth based on increasing intersectoral and intrasectoral specialization are unlikely in the 1980s. They are unlikely because growth rates of world trade have declined precipitously and fallen in many instances below domestic growth

---

[19] The two largest sectoral employers are, however, found among the slow-growing sectors of table 12.1: Apparel Made from Purchased Material (1804) and Motor Vehicles and Parts (5903).

[20] Table 12.1 includes 4004, Fabricated Structural Steel; Table 12.2 includes 4006, Fabricated Plate Work (Boiler Shops).

rates. Protectionist caution makes improbable a renewed rush toward further internationalization. Equally improbable, therefore, are the concomitant sectoral shifts that make large sectors and their work forces larger, and small sectors and their work forces smaller. The correspondents to tables 12.1 to 12.4 for the 1980s would almost surely reveal many table 12.3 sectors and even a few table 12.2 sectors to have slipped into tables 12.1 or 12.4, with sub-par or even negative growth in employment. Prime candidates for slippage from table 12.2 into tables 12.1 or 12.4 in the 1980s—based on how close they were even in the 1970s to critical classificatory boundaries—are: 2005, Millwork and Wood Kitchen Cabinets; 3702, Iron and Steel Foundries; 5304, Motors and Generators; and 6001, Aircraft. Indeed, day-to-day US business commentary has noted the increased international competitive pressure on many of these sectors. It also suggests perhaps the addition of 4400, Farm Machinery, Lawn and Garden Equipment, and 5702, Semiconductors and Related Devices, despite their buoyant 1970s growth in employment and "capital" income.

In each of the four tables there are five additional entries to the right of the average percentage growth rate of employment for each sector. These five figures represent an exhaustive decomposition of the trend in employment growth that is described in detail in Appendix 12.A. The way that international forces affect each of the five elements is also described there. To illustrate the use of the decomposition, the "real output component" can be interpreted as the contribution made by sectoral output growth to sectoral employment growth. More technically, it is an estimate of the rate that sectoral employment would have grown if none of the other contributors had changed—if there had been no inflation, of either prices or wages, no change in the input mix between intermediate and primary factors, and no change in labor productivity (productivity in producing value added). Each of the other components can be interpreted similarly, as the contributions to sectoral employment growth of trends in: output price, substitution in production of intermediate goods for labor, "wages" (actually employee compensation, a negative contributor to employment trends), and labor productivity. international forces shape each, as outlined in Appendix 12.A.

The "labor productivity" component for each sector is interesting in its own right. It is *not*, however, an estimate of the trend in average sectoral labor productivity. It is instead an estimate of the trend in the *ratio of marginal to average* labor productivity, as the appendix shows in detail.

As such, the "labor productivity component" is especially useful in addressing the troublesome question of how technological change affects employment. Conventional approaches to answering this question often rest on average labor productivity. Some studies, for example, illustrate how employment trends attributable to average labor productivity seem to dominate employment trends due to international competitiveness.[21]

There is a mistake that is all too easy to make in absorbing such studies. It is to infer that technological change that improves average labor productivity must be employment-destroying. That is a mistake because it ignores *marginal* labor productivity. No workers will be displaced, for example, if technological change is neutral, raising the productivity of extra (marginal) workers by exactly the proportion that it raises the (average) productivity of existing workers. And technological change may even be employment-creating if it raises marginal labor productivity more than average.

The issue of whether future automation or robotation will displace workers hangs importantly on the "labor productivity component" recorded in tables 12.1 to 12.4. If that component is negative, it suggests that technological change induces labor-"capital" substitution that shrinks employment, because the marginal productivity of extra workers grows less rapidly than the average productivity of existing workers. If the labor productivity component is positive, it suggests that technological change induces labor-"capital" substitution that stimulates employment, because the marginal productivity of extra workers grows more rapidly than the average productivity of existing workers. Without indicators such as provided by the labor productivity component, commentary on the impact of automation or robotation is all the more speculative. And contradictory positions based on considerations of self-interest should not be surprising:

> Unions fear members will lose jobs to automatons. . . . the international Union of Electrical Workers and the Machinists meet with General Electric and Westinghouse Electric officials. The unions warn the concerns that advance notice and retraining for workers affected by robots will be a serious issue in 1982 bargaining talks. . . .
>
> But General Electric, whose 120 robots perform boring or hazardous jobs, says the resulting higher productivity "increases jobs."[22]

The labor productivity component may also be revealing as an indicator of future sectoral employment trends, along with the trend

[21] For example, Saxonhouse (1972a, 1972b), Frank and Levinson (1977, pp. 27–33), Krueger (1980), Wolter (1980), and Yonezawa (1982), critiqued by Grossman (1980) in the same way as follows, as well as in other ways.

[22] *Wall Street Journal*, 17 February 1981, p. 1.

in "capital" income. To the extent that future technological change springs from and builds on current and recent innovations, it can be expected to retain much of its employment "bias." Labor-saving technological change will breed more labor saving technological change and exert a drag on future sectoral employment growth. Labor-engaging technological change will breed more labor-engaging technological change and encourage future sectoral employment growth. It is notable from tables 12.1 to 12.4, however, that this determinant of employment growth is much less important quantitatively than output growth and wage-price trends. And it is probably less important as a determinant of future employment growth than future capital formation that is reflected in trends in current income to "capital."

Productivity and technological change may become a more important source of sluggish US employment growth in the future, however. It seems likely that despite slower "internationalization" in the 1980s the US production mix and comparative advantage will continue to shift slowly away from table 12.1 sectors and toward table 12.2 sectors, with table 12.3 and 12.4 sectors being somewhere in between. US manufacturing in the aggregate will begin to reflect less of the characteristics of table 12.1 sectors and more of the characteristics of table 12.2 sectors. One such characteristic that is striking is that only 4 out of 18 table 12.1 sectors had a below-average labor productivity component to its employment growth, whereas 17 out of 22 table 12.2 sectors did.[23] Even more striking is that while only 10 out of 18 table 12.1 sectors revealed productivity trends that displaced workers (i.e., negative labor productivity components), 21 out of 22 table 12.2 sectors revealed this. Hence to the extent that table 12.2 sectors grow at the expense of table 12.1 sectors, "technological displacement" may become a more and more important feature of employment trends.

It is curious that the largest incidence of employment-generating technological change took place in the sectors where employment is declining most rapidly. No compelling explanation springs into mind or print.

---

[23] The average labor productivity component across all US manufacturing was -0.80, suggesting that technological change and labor-"capital" substitution during the 1970s was on balance labor-saving, causing aggregate manufacturing employment to grow by almost 1 percent per year *less* than if technological change had been neutral.

Summary and Recommendations

A large number of changes have been examined in this paper for what they suggest about US labor adjustment to international trade. The changes have been attitudinal, institutional, demographic, technological, economic, and political. When weighed together, they appear to imply a moderate increase in trade adjustment problems for US labor in the 1980s. Furthermore, new protectionist measures would aggravate labor adjustment problems still further. These measures are well within the realm of probability.

For these reasons and others given in the paper, it seems wise to consider seriously a successor to the US TAA program of the 1970s. A sensible trade adjustment program for the 1980s might put more weight on adjustment and less on compensation than historical TAA programs. To be evaluated in accomplishing this goal are: extension of existing US employment subsidy programs to workers certified as having been permanently (not temporarily) displaced by trade; self-financing and voluntary loan/insurance programs for the same kind of worker to underwrite retraining and reeducating; and *conditional* extensions of unemployment benefits beyond normal for trade-displaced workers—conditional, for example, on employed workers and firms bearing some sizable portion of the extra financial burden through negotiated "cost-sharing." This last innovation would hold down government outlays directly and indirectly as well, since employed workers and their firms would be charged a share of any largesse toward the unemployed. In addition, a new trade adjustment program should avoid clear shortcomings in the administration, eligibility, and design of past TAA programs. Aho and Bayard (1980b, pp. 21–28) make helpful suggestions along these lines.

An alternative, of course, is to let all US trade adjustment and assistance programs die a natural death. This alternative seems distinctly inferior. The paper outlines reasons why reliance on markets alone for labor adjustment may be riskier and less successful in the 1980s than in the 1970s. it also discusses the important role that a trade adjustment program serves in assuring foreign countries of open and fair access to US markets. This in turn pressures them to maintain open and fair access for US products. Finally, trade-related employment problems will not go away even if trade adjustment programs do, and could likely become worse. To abolish such programs is hence an open invitation to accelerate alternatives that are much more sinister and inscrutable in dealing with the admittedly serious employment problems that trade can create. Such alternatives include tax breaks, loan guarantees, hidden subsidies, orderly marketing agreements, concessionary export financing, and abuse of safeguard mechanisms. All of these are influenced importantly by employment considerations. But they usually generate costly and undesirable by-products, far more costly and undesirable than the labor-market policies that deal directly (albeit imperfectly) with trade-related employment problems.

Appendix
12.A   A Decomposition and Interpretation of Trends in
Employment Growth

The growth rate in employment during any time period can be separated into five components: (i) a part due to growth in domestically produced real output; (ii) a part due to growth in revenues through rising prices of domestic output (with any negative effects on revenues through reduced demand for real output being captured in component (i)); (iii) a part due to any substitution of primary inputs for intermediate inputs, or vice versa; (iv) a part due to wage fluctuations; and (v) a part due to trends in labor productivity, including among other things trends in substitution between labor and other primary inputs. In short-run analysis of employment trends, (iii) through (v) can generally be ignored as being very small relative to (i) and (ii).

Tables 12.1 to 12.3 of the text calculate all five elements for a sample of US input-output sectors over the period 1972–79. The exact calculations performed are sketched below, and are robust in the sense that they rest for the most part on very general and unobjectionable (weak) assumptions. They assume maximizing but not necessarily competitive behavior on the part of producers and workers. No agent is a price taker; each has some measure of market power. Firms as sellers choose from among price-quantity combinations measured along a product demand schedule. And firms as employers choose from among positively related wage-employment combinations that are either negotiated with factor suppliers and reflected in contractual overtime arrangements, work rules, and profit sharing, or else dictated to the firm by positively-sloped sector-specific factor supply. The calculations assume that the elasticities of product demand and wage-employment responsiveness have no significant trend relative to other variables. That is, if these elasticities do grow or shrink over time, their trends are taken to be quantitatively small relative to trends in (i) through (v), and are ignored. The productivity component (v) is calculated residually after all the other components are removed from employment trends.

Under these very general and familiar regularities, additional employment continues for as long as the extra revenue earned from the product attributed to it exceeds the extra costs associated with it. Such costs are of course of two kinds. One is the cost of the additional workers themselves. The other is the cost of paying workers more per unit when employment is buoyant. When the extra revenue (marginal revenue product) falls to the point where it is just equal to the extra labor cost (marginal labor cost), extraordinary creation of new jobs ceases. Equilibrium or trend employment is measurable as the value of employment for which equality between extra (marginal) revenues and extra (marginal) costs hold.

This equality can be expressed algebraically as

$$
(1) \qquad w\left(1 + \frac{1}{\omega}\right) = p_V\left(1 - \frac{1}{\gamma}\right)\left(\frac{V}{L}\right)\varepsilon;
$$

where w is a vector of wages for various types of labor services; ω is a vector of elasticities of the schedules relating wages to employment; p_V is the "price" of "real" value-added; γ is the elasticity of "demand" for real value-added; V is "real" value-added; L is a vector of various types of labor services; ε is a vector of real value-added elasticities with respect to various types of labor services, also interpretable as a vector of ratios of marginal to average productivities of labor (see equation (4) and discussion below); and (V/L) is therefore quite simply a vector of marginal products for various types of labor.

Multiplying and dividing the right-hand side of (1) by the value of a sector's shipments (pO) yields:

$$
(2) \qquad w\left(1 + \frac{1}{\omega}\right) = \left(1 - \frac{1}{\gamma}\right)\left(\frac{pOF\varepsilon}{L}\right);
$$

where p is the price of a sector's output, O is its quantity, and F is the ratio of value-added (not real value-added) to the value of shipments $(p_V V/pO)$.

To establish a decomposition of trends in employment, equation (2) can be differentiated with respect to time and expressed in proportional terms. It seems likely that the elasticities of product demand and wage-employment responsiveness will have no significant trend relative to other variables. That is, even if these elasticities do grow or shrink over time, their trends will be quantitatively small relative to trends in p, O, F, W, and ε. They can thus be ignored and the time-differentiated version of (2) becomes

$$(3) \qquad \hat{L} = \hat{O} + \hat{p} + \hat{F} - \hat{w} + \hat{\varepsilon};$$

where "hats" over a variable denote proportional rates of change over time ($\hat{Z} = (dZ/dt)/Z$).

Equation (3) can be described as a "dynamic decomposition" of trends in employment. Rates of growth in employment over time can be attributed to rates of growth of output, prices, wages (negatively), substitution of labor for intermediate inputs, and labor productivity.

The component of employment trends attributable to labor productivity ($\hat{\varepsilon}$) is especially suggestive. ε is defined in equation (1) as the ratio of the marginal product of an additional worker to the average product of all workers (both "products" being of course real value-added):

$$(4) \qquad \varepsilon = \frac{(\partial V/\partial L)}{(V/L)}.$$

Thus trends over time in ε measure the numerical difference between trends over time in labor's marginal product and trends over time in labor's average product. Given values for $\hat{O}$, $\hat{p}$, $\hat{F}$, and $\hat{w}$ growth in labor's marginal product with no change in its average product causes sectoral employment to grow. Given the same values, by contrast, growth in labor's average product with no change in its marginal product causes sectoral employment to shrink.

A familiar controversy in studies of sectoral technological change is whether it is "labor-saving" (employment-discouraging), "labor-absorbing" (employment-encouraging), or "neutral." A central aspect of the controversy is whether technological change causes labor's marginal product to grow slower, faster, or at the same rate as labor's average product. The decomposition described above provides an empirical means of answering that question. Data on $\hat{L}$, $\hat{O}$, $\hat{p}$, $\hat{F}$, and $\hat{w}$ can be used to estimate $\hat{\varepsilon}$ residually. ($\hat{\varepsilon} = \hat{L} - \hat{O} - \hat{p} - \hat{F} + \hat{w}$). Positive values of $\hat{\varepsilon}$ suggest that the primary factor substitution caused by technological change has been on balance employment-generating over the period of measurement. Negative values of $\hat{\varepsilon}$ suggest that the primary factor substitution caused by technological change has been on balance labor-displacing over the period of measurement.

There are other impacts of technological change on employment, of course, besides those taking place through primary factor substitution ($\hat{\varepsilon}$). Other impacts of technological change on employment take place through output effects, output price effects, or substitution between intermediate and primary factors. These are all reflected in the measured values of $\hat{O}$, $\hat{p}$, and $\hat{F}$. Therefore a thorough study of the impact of technological change on employment would attempt to segregate technology's impact on $\hat{O}$, $\hat{p}$, and $\hat{F}$ from other impacts on them. Yet so much popular attention is focused just on the substitution between "men and machines"—witness the intuition underlying Luddite-like concerns over automation, robotation, and technological unemployment—that measures of $\hat{\varepsilon}$ aimed at capturing only that influence are quite useful.

In the decomposition described above, international competition affects employment trends indirectly. International competition most immediately affects trends in a sector's output and prices, and thereby employment trajectories for the sector. Methods for distilling the international competitive portion of sectoral output trends have been developed by Robert E. Baldwin in Baldwin, et al. (1982).

International influences other than directly competitive products affect employment as well. Some of these are reflected in other trends. Tables 12.1 to 12.3 in the text, for example, suggest a trend toward greater dollar expenditure by producers on intermediate inputs at the expense of employment, presumably because of "shocks" to oil and raw materials prices during the 1970s [reflected in components (iii)]. Another potential influence stems from any direct pressure that international forces have on wage demands [reflected in component (iv)]. Imports, for example, have clearly played some role in the rebargaining of existing labor contracts in the US auto industry.

References

Aho, C. Michael, and Thomas O. Bayard. 1980a. "American Trade Adjustment Assistance After Five Years." *The World Economy* 3 (November 1980):359–76.

———. 1980b. "Trade Adjustment Assistance Pro and Con: A Scope Paper." November. Processed.

———. 1981. "Costs and Benefits of Trade Adjustment Assistance." Presented at the Western Economic Association meeting, July 2. Processed.

Baldwin, Robert E.; Rachel McCulloch; J. David Richardson; and Andre Sapir. 1982. *US Policies in Response to Growing International Trade Competitiveness, Final Phase I Report.* Report to the National Science Foundation from the University of Wisconsin Center for Research on US Trade Competitiveness, April 15.

Bayard, Thomas O., and James A. Orr. 1979. "Transitional Equity and Efficiency: An Analysis of US Trade Adjustment Assistance Policies." Paper presented at the American Economic Association meeting, December.

Bhagwati, Jagdish N., ed. 1982. *Import Competition and Response.* Chicago: University of Chicago Press.

Blackhurst, Richard; Nicolas Marian; and Jan Tumlir. 1977. *Trade Liberalization, Protectionism, and Independence*. GATT Studies in International Trade, no. 5. Geneva: General Agreement on Tariffs and Trade, November.

Branson, William H. 1980. "Trends in United States International Trade and Investment Since World War II." In *The American Economy in Transition*, ed. Martin Feldstein. Chicago: University of Chicago Press, 1982.

Cline, William R. 1982. "Trade Policy in the Eighties." Washington: Institute for International Economics, February 8. Processed.

Corson, Walter; Walter Nicholson; J. David Richardson; and Andrea Vayda. 1979. *Final Report: Survey of Trade Adjustment Assistance Recipients*. Report to the Office of Foreign Economic Affairs, Bureau of International Labor Affairs, US Department of Labor. Mathematica Policy Research, Inc., December.

Cropper, Maureen, and Louis Jacobson. 1982. "The Earnings and Compensation of Workers Receiving Trade Adjustment Assistance." CRC 459, February 11. Washington: Public Research Institute, Center for Naval Analyses.

Dore, Ronald P. 1980. "Adjustment in Process: A Lancashire Town." In Bhagwati. 1982. *Import Competition and Response*.

Fieleke, Norman S. 1981. "Productivity and Labor Mobility in Japan, the United Kingdom and the United States." *New England Economic Review* (November/December): 27–36.

Frank, Charles R., Jr., with the assistance of Stephanie Levinson. 1977. *Foreign Trade and Domestic Aid*. Washington: Brookings Institution.

Freund, William C. 1982. "The Looming Impact of Population Changes." *Wall Street Journal*, 6 April 1982.

Glenday, Graham; Glenn P. Jenkins; and John C. Evans. 1980. *Worker Adjustment to Liberalized Trade: Costs and Assistance Policies*, World Bank Staff Working Paper, no. 426. Washington: World Bank, October.

Gray, H. Peter; Thomas A. Pugel; and Ingo Walter. 1982. *Employment, Trade, and North–South Cooperation, United States Study*. February 15. Processed.

Grossman, Gene M. 1980. "On Measuring the Employment Effects of Import Competition." In Bhagwati. 1982. *Import Competition and Response*.

Grossman, Gene M., and J. David Richardson 1982. "Issues and Options for US Trade Policy in the 1980s: Some Research Perspectives." *Research Progress Report*. Cambridge, Mass.: National Bureau of Economic Research.

Jacobson, Louis. 1980. "The Earnings and Compensation of Workers Receiving Trade Adjustment Assistance." (PRI) 80–10. Public Research Institute, Center for Naval Analyses, February 12.

Jenkins, Glenn P.; Graham Glenday; John C. Evans; and Claude Montmarquette. 1978. *Trade Adjustment Assistance: The Costs of Adjustment and Policy Proposals*. Report to the Economic Analysis Branch, Department of Industry Trade and Commerce (Canada), Econanalysis, Inc., June.

Kotlikoff, Laurence, J.; Edward E. Leamer; and Jeffrey Sachs. 1981. "The International Economics of Transitional Growth." National Bureau of Economic Research (NBER) Working Paper, no. 773. Cambridge, Mass.: NBER, September.

Krueger, Anne O. 1980. "Protectionist Pressures, Imports, and Employment in the United States." *Scandinavian Journal of Economics* (May 1980): 133–46.

Krugman, Paul R. 1980. "Trade in Differential Products and the Political Economy of Trade Liberalization." In Bhagwati. 1982. *Import Competition and Response*.

Miller, Michael J., and James D. Van Erden. 1981. "The Increase in Trade Adjustment Assistance Benefits Program and Policy Implications of the Auto Recession." Paper presented at the Western Economic Association meeting, July 5.

Organization for Economic Cooperation and Development (OECD). 1979. *The Case for Positive Adjustment Policies, A Compendium of OECD Documents*, 1978/79. Paris: OECD, June.

Personick, Valerie A. 1981. "The Outlook for Industry Output and Employment Through 1990." *Monthly Labor Review* 104 (August): 28–41.

Richardson, J, David. 1980. "Trade Adjustment Assistance Under the US Trade Act of 1974: An Analytical Examination and Worker Survey." National Bureau of Economic Research Working Paper, no. 556. Cambridge, Mass.: NBER, September. In Bhagwati. 1982. *Import Competition and Response.*

———. 1982a. "Issues, Options, and Insights for US Trade Policy." February. Processed.

———. 1982b. "Further Issues, Options, and Insights for US Trade Policy." March. Processed.

Saxonhouse, Gary R. 1972a. "Employment, Imports, the Yen, and the Dollar." In *Discord in the Pacific*, ed. Henry Rosovsky. Washington: Columbia Books.

———. 1972b. "The Textile Confrontation." In *Pacific Partnership: United States-Japanese Trade*, ed. Jerome Cohen. Lexington, Mass.: D. C. Heath.

US General Accounting Office (GAO). 1980. *Restricting Trade Act Benefits to Import-Affected Workers Who Cannot Find a Job Can Save Millions*. Report to the Congress by the Comptroller General of the United States. Washington: GAO.

Wolf, Martin. 1979. *Adjustment Policies and Problems in Developed Countries*. World Bank Staff Working Paper, no. 349. Washington: World Bank.

Wolter, Frank. 1980. "Restructuring for Import Competition from Developing Countries, II: The Case of the Federal Republic of Germany." *Journal of Policy Modelling* 2, no. 2.

Yonezawa, Yoshie. 1982. "Trade Friction and Employment Adjustment: An Empirical Study." July. Processed.

Robert E. Baldwin

Each of the papers by Hufbauer, Wolff, and Richardson makes a significant contribution toward the better understanding and clarification of the specific policy issues with which they are concerned. They are especially notable for the degree of expertise that each author demonstrates concerning his topic and for their appreciation of the complexities of the policies issues they discuss. Moreover, each comes out with a strong policy recommendation.

Wolff develops a powerful case for "selectivity" in the application of safeguard actions; Hufbauer urges that the upcoming ministerial meeting of the General Agreement on Tariffs and Trade point the way toward restraining subsidies at lower levels of modifying the trade impact standard for agricultural subsidies, by defining more specifically what is or is not a potentially troublesome domestic subsidy, by defining export subsidies in gray areas, and by finding an effective remedy for subsidies that affect third countries. Richardson argues that the US trade adjustment assistance program, though nearly defunct at the present time, deserves to be revived for the 1980s, especially in view of the protectionist alternatives.

In commenting upon these policy recommendations one immediately faces—as the authors do themselves—the question as to what the goal or objective is that we are trying to seek. More specifically, what is the community of international policymakers trying to achieve with a safeguards code or code on subsidies? Similarly, what are domestic policymakers trying to accomplish with a trade adjustment assistance program?

From an exclusively economic viewpoint one would say that the main purpose of such sets of rules and policies is—or at least should be—to promote the efficient allocation of resources within and among countries. Leaving aside the question of what should be, we know that in fact those who are usually most closely involved in formulating and modifying trade policies, as well as the political constituencies to which they are responding, do not place much weight upon attaining the marginal welfare gains that economists talk about and measure when, for example, tariffs are reduced 50 percent across the board. This may be because policymakers recognize that the traditional static economic welfare gains associated with such a tariff cut are small—the static welfare gains from the Tokyo Round are, for example, estimated at less than 0.1 percent of world GNP. Or it might be because they are not subjected to political pressures for liberalization from important interest groups that can significantly affect their political future. For whatever reason, we would probably all agree that the attainment of the resulting static welfare gains was not a significant motivating force behind the Tokyo Round of trade negotiations. Moreover, as one examines the history of US trade liberalization as well as the history of the GATT, it appears that achieving the gains in economic welfare resulting from the marginal economic changes associated with most trade policy actions played only a minor role as a motivation behind the policies.

All three papers of this session are also based on the view that the purpose of the policy changes they recommend is much more than simply the associated changes in economic welfare. Alan Wolff seeks a rigorous but pragmatic new international safeguard code that will help to restore confidence in the central rules of the GATT system. He is concerned that the widespread flouting of the GATT safeguard rules will, in the face of the likely greater adjustment pressures of the future, lead to anarchy in international economic relations. More specifically, Wolff like Cordell Hull and his colleagues who shaped modern US trade policy and played an important role in formulating the rules of the GATT, is afraid that we might lose not the marginal benefits from trade but the very large intramarginal economic benefits that stem from reasonably unimpeded international exchange. The large losses that were incurred in the 1930s through competitive devaluations and retaliatory tariff increases are presumably what he has in mind. Moreover, like most of us, he probably is also concerned about the consequences of such an economic environment for political stability and world peace.

Hufbauer adopts the same general viewpoint. He speaks of the need to define "potentially troublesome subsidies" as well as the need "to redress offensive subsidies, but not to overcompensate for them." More specifically, he first presents data showing that, although there may not be a significant upward trend in the degree of subsidization, the level of subsidization in the United States is considerably lower than in Europe, Japan, and Canada. He then argues that, as international competitive pressures continue to build up, the United States is likely to increase its degree of subsidization on equity grounds.

However, in doing so, it may set off a spiral of subsidization that results in discrete and significant economic losses to all.

Richardson, too, stresses the other goals behind trade adjustment assistance besides resource-allocation efficiency, namely equity and political efficacy. Like the others, he sees the United States being faced with increasing competitive pressures in the 1980s and on equity as well as efficiency grounds rejects the use of the market as the sole adjustment mechanism. Trade adjustment assistance may not achieve ideal resource allocation but the economic costs from the likely increased protectionism in the absence of such a program are, in Richardson's view, likely to be considerable.

Thus, among the three authors and among most, though by no means all, who are actively concerned with trade policy issues, there seems to be general agreement that the intended purpose on the part of policymakers of such measures as a safeguard or subsidies code is to manage international economic disputes in a manner that at least maintains the major economic and political benefits that stem from a reasonably open trading system. Their purpose is not to eliminate all trade distortions, as the antidistortion school described by Hufbauer would maintain, but to resolve in a mutually satisfactory manner those disputes that if not settled could lead to actions that seriously erode the basic benefits from trade. In other words, the codes and other rules are not for fine tuning but for keeping a reasonable degree of order in the world economy. The same applies to the goals of such domestic policies as adjustment assistance programs. The intended aim of those who frame the policies is to obtain some, though not perfect, adjustment without touching off other policies that are very costly in economic terms.

A recognition and acceptance of these goals still leaves, however, considerable room for differences in views concerning the best way to achieve them. A case in point is the recommendation that we deal with our problems in the safeguards area by accepting the principle of selectivity. Alan Wolff presents a very effective case in favor of selectivity. But I would argue that implementing selectivity involves greater risks of leading to major economic costs to the world economy than a continuation of the present, admittedly unsatisfactory state of affairs. I am particularly concerned about its effect on the economic and political policies of the developing countries. As Wolff notes, many of these countries are already being badly discriminated against under the current practice of going outside of the GATT with voluntary export restraints and orderly marketing agreements. Yet the less developed countries (LDCs) are in general also very much opposed to selectivity. They believe that discrimination against them will be much worse with selectivity, despite various rules designed to limit its use. And I think they are right.

But even if they are not correct in this assumption, the LDCs perceive selectivity as another powerful weapon that will be used by the industrial countries to undermine their economic and political growth. And it is perceptions of unfriendly actions that matter in international relations. They are likely to react by practicing selectivity among themselves and against the industrial countries, by increasing the degree of their export subsidization of some products, and most importantly by pursuing more vigorously than ever their import-substituting policies.

The developing countries are becoming more important to the United States and other industrial countries not only as sources of imported manufactured goods but as export markets for our manufactures, especially capital goods. Now is the time to encourage these nations to reduce the many trade barriers they impose. Such a step will benefit their own economies most of all but also will help us. To introduce selectivity will turn them inward and encourage them to discriminate.

I am also fearful of the ability of governments in the industrial countries to withstand domestic political pressures to introduce selective import controls in a manner that unduly favors particular domestic sectors. I see an even greater ability than we have now for large, well organized industries to obtain protection whereas small sectors that are faced with equally serious import problems fail to secure import relief.

Still another danger, I think, is that selective import controls will be used for foreign policy purposes that are unrelated to economic injury to domestic industries.

Finally, I think that most selective import controls do not achieve their stated purpose except for a time period that is too short to permit significant adjustment in the affected domestic sector. We are all familiar with the problem of transhipments through third countries. But even if this does not occur, there is an incentive for shipments from the country discriminated against to increase to third markets and for third market exports to increase to the country practicing the discrimination. One ends up—as in the textile case—by having to impose more and more quotas in a selective fashion. Workers and management in the injured industry tend to think they have been treated badly by their own governments, third countries resent the trade diversion to their markets, and the country discriminated against still is offended even if the economic costs to it are modest.

Of course, it is much easier to find arguments against discrimination than it is to come up with alternative suggestions to deal with the problems that Alan Wolff is concerned about. As I said, I would prefer no action at all to accepting selectivity. One might argue, however, that what the ministerial meeting should aim at is a reaffirmation of the rules and procedures of Article XIX of the GATT. Yet I do not think this is realistic, given the very bad economic conditions in many countries and their fears of severe import competition in the future. A more realistic goal might be simply agreement to permit the GATT Secretarial to undertake a study of the extent of the current and likely future import-injury problem in the industrial nations that would include a survey of the extent to which actions outside of Article XIX have been taken. During the study, which could last two years, the members might also agree not to take safeguard actions outside of Article XIX or at least to notify the GATT of any such actions. But it may well be unrealistic to expect even agreement of this kind.

Another possible action that would help to improve the current situation is to undertake some of the actions with respect to subsidies that Gary Hufbauer recommends. I think his recommendations with respect to domestic subsidies are especially important. Part—though by no means all—of the reason for the import-injury problems that some countries face is the targeting by other countries of very significant increases in exports in particular industries. And these planned increases often involve some form of government subsidization. It may be that without these subsidies we would not get many of the very rapid increases in imports that cause serious injury to domestic industries. If they could be brought under control or if countervailing actions were taken against them, we might be able to mitigate the problem to a considerable extent without having to change basic GATT rules.

Unrelated to the safeguards issues, another recommendation I would like to see in Hufbauer's list is one aimed at improving the dispute-settlement procedure in this code, as well as the others. The points John Jackson makes about the existing arrangements are, I think, very compelling and I do not see the small industrial countries or the LDCs ever having much faith in the fairness of the GATT without the kind of changes he recommends.

One other point I would like to make about subsidies is that we should strive to change the perception that if a country takes countervailing action in response to a new or increased subsidy the country is somehow guilty of starting a trade war rather than trying to maintain the international economic order by carrying out the procedures of the GATT. Clearly, we can help to change the current perception by bringing—as the US administration is apparently doing—more and more of our subsidy cases to the GATT. However, as Harald Malmgren stressed, we must make sure we have solid cases.

I have few comments to make about David Richardson's paper, since I agree with his policy suggestions about adjustment assistance and also very much like his analysis decomposing output trends in the 1970s. One point about which I would like to hear a comment from him or someone else is the feasibility of providing a wage subsidy to producers in expanding sectors if they hire displaced workers from an industry suffering serious import-related injury. On the surface it seems to be an appealing ideal but, to my knowledge, has not been tried. Is this suggestion a nonstarter politically? Or, if not, are there important economic problems associated with its implementation?

Leonard Weiss agreed with Wolff on the need to discipline safeguards. He suggested a possible compromise on the issue of selectivity, whereby the normal procedure would require nondiscrimination, but selectivity would be allowed under exceptional circumstances and with tighter rules. He maintained that the 1979 decision by the General Agreement on Tariffs and Trade (GATT) signatories meant they had not lost most-favored-nation (MFN) rights with respect to the new codes on nontariff barriers.

Bela Balassa stated that it is not true that the United States refrains from infant-industry subsidies; it supports research and development in the defense and space industries, for example. On selectivity, he argued that a new safeguards code would not introduce selectivity—as Baldwin maintained—but that selectivity already existed. The key issue on safeguards is ensuring that they are temporary.

William R. Cline noted that for safeguards a central issue was whether the present departure of the EC from legitimate GATT practice exercises some restraint through the stigma of noncompliance, and correspondingly whether the legitimization of such practices (even with more discipline) might not do more harm than good. On countervailing duties and antidumping measures, he pointed out that it is necessary to address the basic issue of whether these measures are protective devices or merely instruments for enforcement of fair trade.

Richard N. Cooper contended that there was no evidence supporting Richardson's assessment that the pace of change has accelerated. Wolff had outlined why the European Community (EC) did not use GATT Article XIX, but would introduction of selectivity change matters? The result could be the worst of both worlds, with legitimization of discriminatory protection without meaningful curtailment of its use. He noted that by Hufbauer's criteria, military research and development could be potentially troublesome subsidies; he questioned whether trade rules should be extended to this

431

level of issues. Ever greater refinement moves in the wrong direction. To Cline he replied that countervailing duties and antidumping need not be protective, but as defined in US law antidumping is unquestionably protective in effect. Its concept of constructed cost includes a normal rate of return on capital; on this basis almost all US firms would fail to survive an antidumping test during recessions.

Martin Wolf argued that MFN treatment is at the core of GATT, and that it would further erode GATT to legalize its abandonment. The key question is whether a safeguards code with selectivity would actually reduce or increase discriminatory and protective behavior; it could increase such behavior by legitimization.

Åke Lindén agreed that MFN is central to GATT, noting that departures are controlled by GATT. With respect to MFN application of the Tokyo Round codes, however, he stated that despite the November 1979 decision of the GATT signatories, the EC still argues that the benefits of the antidumping and subsidy codes apply only to signatories of the codes. The most important loopholes in the subsidies code now are those concerning agricultural trade and domestic subsidies. On GATT notification, for example with respect to safeguard measures, the problem is that many countries do not want GATT to monitor their activity.

Rodney de C. Grey felt that once developing countries expend their bargaining chips on safeguards by accepting selectivity, they will have no leverage to get application of GATT Article XIX. Yet a code with selectivity still would not secure Article XIX treatment. As for GATT surveillance, it would never be possible as long as the EC opposes it.

W. M. Corden proposed the following program. All quota restrictions and voluntary export restraints would be abolished. Any safeguards would be absolutely temporary. As for subsidies, it is impossible to prevent countries from using them, but they have an automatic discipline because of their cost. The Tokyo Round followed an enlightened approach by attacking those subsidies that most distort trade.

Gary Hufbauer argued that countervailing duties are definitely not protective devices. Even antidumping measures are not protective in practice. The hypothetical profit calculations cited by Cooper have rarely been used and are not a major problem. It is necessary to push ahead with the definition of troublesome subsidies; even military subsidies should be so classified if they are targeted to a particular industry.

Alan Wolff mused that the discussion here had demonstrated why there had been no agreement on safeguards in Geneva. In reply to the question of the inhibiting effect of GATT violation on EC practices, he drew an analogy with the prohibition of liquor: because it was not observed, the law became useless. It is better to licence the practice and control it.

CHAPTER 13

Agricultural Trade Policy for the 1980s

Dale E. Hathaway

It is probably small consolation to those concerned about the trends in international trade to point out that many of the issues arising in trade in manufactured goods are issues that have plagued agricultural trade since the founding of the General Agreement on Tariffs and Trade (GATT). However, despite these problems, trade in agricultural products has been rising at a reasonably healthy pace over the past two decades, and these agricultural trade problems have not yet brought out an all-out trade war, although the prospect is never completely absent.

In order to deal with trade policy issues in the 1980s, one must first look at some of the unique features of agricultural trade and recent developments that have changed the nature of international agricultural trade. Second, a review of the "old problems" plaguing agricultural trade is in order, namely those caused by domestic agricultural programs in the developed industrial countries. Third, new problems and issues which are often variations or extensions of past issues must be examined.

Finally from this background, one can attempt to deal with both new and old issues, the institutions that have attempted to deal with them and why they have failed.

A Review

At the outset it is useful to review briefly the nature of agricultural trade which for many reasons differs markedly from trade in either manufactured goods or services.

While trade in foodstuffs may be one of the oldest forms of trade, it has not until recent years had a significant effect on total food consumption in the world. Apart from a few city-states most nations have had and still have an amazingly high self-sufficiency in foodstuffs, because of a variety of factors, including conscious national policies.

Over the last three decades world food consumption per capita has increased, but it has been unequally distributed because it is heavily dependent upon income growth. Starting in the late 1960s and through the decade of the 1970s a higher proportion of the world's increase in food consumption was based on trade than had been the historical trend. During the 1970s world trade in agricultural products grew at a compound rate of over 6 percent per year, or almost three times the rate of growth in production and consumption. US agricultural exports over that period grew at a compound rate of almost 9 percent.

Another fact about agricultural trade is surprising. Despite the great advances in processing and packaging the bulk of the trade in agricultural products is in raw or semiprocessed commodities. Thus, the largest trade is in grains, oilseeds, raw cotton, sugar, and similar products. There is of course, considerable trade in meats and poultry, but generally in semiprocessed form.

Thus, the United States, which has the world's most sophisticated agricultural processing industry finds itself in the same position as developing countries in agricultural trade, i.e., as a supplier of agricultural raw material, albeit the world's largest supplier. In 1980 for instance, something over three-quarters of US agricultural exports were raw commodities.

However, despite the healthy growth in per capita food consumption and in trade in agriculture during the 1970s, agricultural products as a proportion of world trade fell steadily over the decade.

In order to get a more accurate picture of trends in agricultural trade during the recent decades, one must look at several of the major commodities separately: wheat, coarse grains, sugar, soybeans, cotton, and meat and animal products.

Trends in Agricultural Trade in Major Commodities

Wheat and Course Grains

As one looks at the data on world trade in these wheat and coarse grains two factors sharply distinguish them from many other internationally traded commodities and have significant implications for the future of the grain trade.

The first is the major expansion in the level of trade in both wheat and coarse grains over the last four decades. World trade in wheat, for instance, during the period immediately prior to World War II averaged less than 17 million metric tons per year. In the immediate post–World War II period, trade in wheat increased by about one-third, with most of that increase occurring after the 1950s.

Starting with the 1960s, there have been substantial increases in world wheat trade. Using 1960 as the base year, we now find that the average world trade in wheat in the last three years is more than double that of the early 1960s. To briefly summarize, world wheat trade approximately doubled from the late 1930s until about 1960. Since that time, in less than two decades there has been another doubling of wheat trade and, it should be noted, current record levels of wheat trade have been maintained despite concurrent new world records in food-grain output.

The rate of increase in world coarse grain trade has been even more rapid than world wheat trade. Prior to World War II, coarse grain trade was somewhat below wheat trade, at about 15 million metric tons per year. Immediately after the war and continuing through the 1950s, there was an appreciable growth in coarse grain trade, unlike the growth in wheat trade. Starting, however, in the 1960s and continuing almost without interruption a veritable explosion has occurred in coarse grain trade which is now approximately six times the pre–World War II level and more than three times the 1960 level.

The second important element relating to world trade in grains is not only its growth, but the change in who exports and who imports. In the case of wheat prior to World War II, the developed market economies accounted for 60 percent of the exports and for two-thirds of the imports. In other words, prior to World War II over half of world wheat exports originated in developed market economies, namely North America and Australia. Importers were mostly the developed market economies. After World War II this situation drastically altered. The trend is clear and there is no indication that it is changing. Throughout the postwar period and continuing to the present time the proportion of exports furnished by developed market economies has grown steadily; they now provide over 90 percent of total world wheat exports. Conversely, whereas the proportion of imports from developed market economies has dropped from three-quarters to one-quarter of total wheat trade, the developing countries now account for half or more of all wheat imports and the centrally planned economies account for a quarter of all wheat imports.

For coarse grains, the trend in market shares has both some parallels with wheat and some important differences. Prior to World War

II developing market economies exported nearly 60 percent of all coarse grains entering the world markets. The centrally planned economies provided another 20 percent. Thus, the developed market economies provided less than 20 percent of world coarse grain exports 40 years ago. At that time the major importers, in fact virtually the only importers, were the developed market economies which imported 85 percent of all coarse grains entering world markets. In the prewar period, the developing market economies accounted for only 2 percent of the coarse grain imports while the centrally planned economies accounted for about one-eighth of the imports.

In the post–World War II period, a new trade pattern has evolved steadily and consistently. The developed market economies,namely North America and Australia, increasingly have come to dominate exports of coarse grains to the point where they now account for more than 80 percent of the exports of coarse grains entering world markets. This has been accompanied, as might be expected, by a steady decline in the proportion of exports from both centrally planned and developing countries.

A marked shift in the import pattern for coarse grains has also occurred. During the post–World War II period the advanced or developed market economies show a steady and continuing decline in the proportion of coarse grain imports, and Japan is removed from these statistics, the decline would be even more apparent. Concurrently, the developing market economies and the centrally planned economies have increased their imports of coarse grains.

To summarize the changing trade patterns for these two major grains, we have seen the developed market economies rapidly become the major source of exports while the developing market economies and the centrally planned economies have become the significant grain importers during the postwar period.

Soybeans

Another major traded agricultural commodity is soybeans and soybean products. As in the case of wheat and coarse grains, world trade in soybeans has grown tremendously. Prior to World War II, soybean exports were dominated by China, a developing country, and the developed market economies were the major importers. Since World War II there has been a sharp change in exporters, but the importers have only recently begun to change. Since World War II the advanced market economies, namely the United States, have held a dominant position in world soybean exports, while Brazil and Argentina have replaced China as the only other exporters of consequence. The de-

veloped market economies, however, are still largely the importers
(in fact over 80 percent). However, the centrally planned economies
have been importing significantly more soybeans since about 1960.

Wool and Cotton

Wool and cotton are two commodities in which world trade patterns
have been different from those for grains. The differences are significant in several ways. For wool, the data indicate that the level of
world trade in wool in the mid-1970s was not markedly higher than
prior to World War II or in the immediate postwar period. Indeed,
it appears in some periods during the 1970s the average level of world
trade was lower than during the late 1930s. Not only has world wool
trade not expanded; there has not been a sharp change in the patterns
of world trade. Prior to World War II the trade was dominated by
the developed market economies both on the export and import side.
This pattern has continued, the only change has been a decline in
developing country exports and their share of world trade; therefore,
again the developed market economies now provide an increasing
percentage of world exports (about 90 percent). The wool imports
of both the developing market economies and the centrally planned
economies appear to be rising in a somewhat irregular pattern while
the import share of the developed market economies is trending
downward.

World cotton trade shows many similarities with world wool trade
and some dissimilarities. As in the case of wool, world cotton trade
has not expanded rapidly since World War II as have grains and
soybeans. Indeed, the level of trade in the 1970s was not markedly
higher than the level achieved in 1960. There have, however, been
some significant shifts in the trade patterns for cotton.

Cotton is one agricultural commodity where the advanced market
economies have steadily and consistently lost export market shares,
mostly to the centrally planned economies. The developing countries,
which still provide slightly over half of the world cotton exports, have
maintained their market share at the same levels they enjoyed immediately prior to and after World War II.

There also have been significant shifts in world imports of cotton.
Whereas developed market economies constituted over three-quarters of import markets during the late 1930s through 1950, they now
import only half of the world's cotton. At the same time, the developing market economies have increased their cotton imports to nearly
a quarter of all the cotton traded at the present time. Centrally planned
economies have now increased their import share to more than a

quarter of all world trade. Thus, for cotton both the export and import shares of the advanced market economies in world trade have declined mostly because of the export expansion of centrally planned economies and the imports of both the developing countries and centrally planned economies.

Meat and Animal Products

Trade in meat follows the pattern of the other foodstuffs. It has expanded rapidly since just after World War II and especially so since 1960, but the rate is slower than for grains or soybeans. As in other foodstuffs, however, it is the expansion of exports from developed market economies that has been most rapid, while developing countries and centrally planned economy exporters have lost export market shares.

One would expect the meat imports would go in large part to developed market economies, and this is the case. It is worth noting, however, that the growth rate in meat imports is much faster in both developing and centrally planned economies. The two groups now import about one-fifth of meat traded on world markets.

Sugar

Sugar is another commodity that did not experience a substantial expansion in world trade between the late 1930s and the mid-1950s. Since that time, however, there has been a slow but steady expansion in world trade. By the late 1970s, world trade in sugar was 50 percent higher than two decades earlier. Again, a substantial shift has occurred in the sources of both exports and imports. Here again the advanced market economies have increased their share in world export markets. The developing market economies, which have always dominated sugar exports, have experienced a decline in the world export market share, while the centrally planned economies appear to have maintained an irregular but approximately stable share of world trade over a long period of time.

World sugar imports also have shifted. Between the late 1930s and 1950, the developed market economies imported 80 percent of the raw sugar traded. This share has now fallen to only slightly more than half of all imports. The share imported by developing market economies has grown moderately but not significantly and still fluctuates around one-fifth of world sugar imports. The major change has been in the centrally planned economies that have rapidly increased their sugar imports over the last two decades.

Implications of Commodity Trade Trends

Can one generalize from this brief review of commodity trade patterns? Some generalization can be made and certain implications can be drawn.

First, the major growth in agricultural commodity trade has occurred in basic foodstuffs, and the growth rates have been highest for products associated with increased production and consumption of meat and poultry, i.e., coarse grains and soybeans. The growth rate for products for which there are close substitutes, namely fibers, have shown modest or no growth in trade.

Second, with the exception of cotton, the export shares of the developing countries have declined and those of the developed market economies have risen.

Third, with the exception of wool, the developing countries and/ or the centrally planned economies are becoming increasingly significant importers. In the case of wheat, these two groups of countries account for a combined total of three-fourths of the imports and for about half of world imports of cotton and sugar. In coarse grains, these two groups of countries account for 40 percent of all imports and for a fifth of all world soybean imports.

This brief review suggests some of the important differences between agricultural trade and nonagricultural trade. In commodity trade which dominates agricultural trade, the number of exporters is declining and there is increasing dominance of the developed market economies, often termed the "industrialized" countries, on the export side. On the importing side, the importance of the developed market economies is declining with the major growth in consumption and, therefore, trade occurring in the centrally planned economies and developing countries. These trends are at the heart of many of the trade problems in agriculture.

There are two sets of problems in agricultural trade: old problems and new problems. Most of the current attention and controversy is centered on the old problems, yet the new problems may be more important in terms of their impact upon world resource use, economic adjustment, and domestic political problems for a number of countries. Some of the new issues cause the old problems to appear worse than they are, and because no one knows how to focus on these new issues, countries concentrate on the old ones.

Old Problems Revisited

In every market economy in the world there is a major public investment in agricultural research, credit, education, and other related factors. The United States has been the leader and the prototype in this regard. Further, in almost every market economy there is a varying web of government intervention in domestic agricultural markets via price supports, purchase programs, marketing orders, health and sanitary restrictions, to give a few examples. Many of these go back a half century or more and many are explicitly or implicitly embodied in GATT. There is not space nor is it particularly useful to trace the historical web of economic and political circumstances that led to government investment and intervention in the agricultural sector. For our purposes it suffices merely to say governmental intervention in agriculture exists in market economies and is likely to continue to exist, a judgment confirmed by the fact that even this most conservative and market-oriented of any US administration in recent memory has made no fundamental change in domestic farm programs and has in several ways intervened in markets more than at any time in a decade.

This immense web of domestic agricultural policies influences domestic production and consumption of farm products in almost every country, albeit probably less than many critics claim.[1] They lead moreover, to border restrictions (quotas, levies, tariffs, and outright bans) in order to protect domestic prices and producers' incomes from foreign competitors. And, where domestic production exceeds consumption, they lead to export subsidies, export credit competition, multiple (cut-rate) export pricing in the guise of aid, and export pricing below domestic pricing, which would be called dumping in nonagricultural circles.

Agricultural trade is further complicated by the price and product interrelations between agricultural products. Flour is related to wheat prices, chickens to feed grain prices, and so on. Thus, a flour or chicken subsidy or tariff is predicated, not on the milling or broiler-producing industry, but on the different domestic policies relative to basic products, much as natural gas prices are related to chemical and fiber prices and thus to fair trade.

---

[1] Economists tend to forget their own estimates of very low price elasticities for food products and of farm prices as a small portion of retail prices of food. Moreover, economists ignore the strong effect of custom and tradition on food consumption and tend to blame different consumption levels on government-induced internal price pattern.

In centrally planned economies and in many developing countries the role of the government in agricultural commodity trade is absolute. There often is some kind of monopoly state buying and selling agency which maintains internal price levels via purchases and sales. In these situations governmental intervention at the border is even more pervasive since imports and exports are controlled by centralized government agencies.

All of this is very obvious to anyone familiar with agricultural trade. It also is obvious that these domestic policies are a result of political and economic pressures in developed market economies and state economic planning in centrally planned economies. GATT never has been able to deal with this national root cause of international agricultural trade problems.

The relationship of domestic agricultural programs to trade was recognized in both the Kennedy and Tokyo Rounds of trade negotiations, but no appreciable progress has been made in dealing with the relationship and the issues it raises. There was a Committee II on agriculture in 1958 and an agricultural committee following the Kennedy Round, and the famous "Cathedral" initiated by the late Finn Gundelach in the Tokyo Round. The latter seems headed, as did the earlier attempt, into the obscurity of the memories of a few skeptical professionals. All were attempts to deal with the issues of domestic programs effects upon trade and none has done so effectively.

There are two problems in discussing the domestic policies of respective nations. One is institutional. The Organization for Economic Cooperation and Development (OECD) says that it, not GATT, is the forum where national economic policies are discussed by member nations. Some GATT members say that national policies are outside GATT's purview. The United Nations Conference on Trade and Development (UNCTAD) would be happy to discuss them but it would not make any difference. Many institutions think such issues fall within their purview and simultaneously avoid discussing them seriously. The second problem is that no sovereign country is willing to put its domestic food and fiber policy forward as a candidate for outside negotiation and determination. At the present time it would be political suicide for the European Community (EC), Japan, or the United States to do so, yet it is the domestic agricultural policies of these trading partners that are the root cause of the continuing agricultural trade problems that threaten to erupt into a major trade war. It is worth noting that the democratic nations are the least able to put their domestic policies on the block, for it is only in democracies that interest groups are allowed to flourish and protect their various economic interests through overt political action.

Agricultural trade is an area in which the world has sought perfect solutions and ended up with third-best solutions. As a practical matter, perhaps one should start over by facing reality and start searching for serious second-best solutions. The reality is that most countries have and will continue to have domestic agricultural programs which distort trade from the theoretical norm by some unmeasurable amount. But different programs distort different variables. Some encourage high-cost output, some reduce internal consumption, some encourage substitutes in use and in trade, and some intrude directly into third-country markets. There is no way to deal with trade issues raised by domestic agricultural programs until there is some kind of international agreement about which policy instruments may be used by participating nations to achieve their domestic agricultural objectives.

There has never been serious discussion, let alone agreement, on any of the underlying domestic policy issues involved. Is there general agreement that a nation has a right for economic, political, or other reasons to engage in income transfers to its farm population? Does it have the right, as do Japan, the EC, and the United States, to name a few, to achieve this income transfer by setting internal prices higher for some products than world traded prices, even though these higher prices may reduce consumption of the product involved? If internal pricing is not acceptable as a practice, what are acceptable ways to achieve and maintain the desired internal prices?

There is intense international controversy regarding export subsidies in agricultural trade,* but oddly enough, what constitutes an export subsidy is not well defined. Everyone agrees that the EC's export restitution program is a subsidy, but what about target price payments for export crops that the United States employs, special export credit programs, or national programs which guarantee pro-

---

* *Ed. note*: For a discussion of the flare-up in the US-EC controversy over agricultural subsidies in the GATT Ministerial and thereafter, see chapter 22.

ducers a high fixed price for wheat consumed domestically, regardless of international market prices, such as Canada uses?

The problem of the GATT approach to domestic agricultural policies is that it has concentrated on matters of degree and not on matters of the effects of basic policy instruments. Thus, the subsidy code concentrates on the degree of market share and not on what constitutes it, and on subsidy but not on whether or not some kinds of agricultural subsidies are more or less disruptive in world trade. Agricultural commodity trade is notoriously unstable because of fluctuating supplies and, thus, issues of degree of interference in trade by various national programs is difficult to determine at best and invariably leads to contention without resolution.

There appear to be no realistic prospects that agricultural programs will fade away in the developed market economies as they have long been embodied in the economic and political structure of most countries. As long as this is true, arguments over the degree of trade distortion will be fruitless. Therefore, even though the outcome is likely to be less than satisfactory, the only feasible approach would seem to be a return to a discussion of basics, i.e., a discussion and possible modification and limit on the use of certain policy instruments.

If there are to be GATT rules for agricultural trade that work, there have to be agreed-upon rules for all domestic programs relating to agriculture, not just tariffs, quotas, and direct export subsidies.

Even if such agreements were reached, they would cover a portion of agricultural trade which is declining with the passage of time. But, the change in world import markets is changing the nature of the trade problems and the sources of instability, even though the rhetoric has not changed.

New Trade Issues

Outside the socialist countries agriculture is generally held up as the classical model of competition. Little notice has been given to the nationalization and or centralization of the exporting and importing function for agricultural products, especially the basic commodities, and what this does to trade.

On the selling side, are the Canadian and Australian Wheat Boards and numerous governmental agencies which sell sugar, palm oil, cotton, rice, peanuts, etc., in world trade. On the buying side, governmental agencies are legion, ranging from the Japanese Food Agency to Compañía Nacional de Subsistencias Populares (CONASUPO) in Mexico. Such agencies are universal in socialist countries.

It is hard to imagine a set of conditions that violate the basic concepts underlying free trade more than these centralized selling and buying agencies. However, reaction to the activities of centralized agencies vary. The United States rails against the EC direct subsidies which allow them to sell grain to Brazil and hardly blinks when the Canadian Wheat Board makes a sale to Brazil or Mexico. The US even sells butter to the New Zealand Dairy Marketing Board so they in turn can sell into world trade without "breaking" world prices. Exportkleb (USSR buying agency) switched from buying 60 percent of its grains from the United States (surely an artificial level) to 30 percent (an equally artificial level).

None of these buying and selling agencies need to violate GATT because GATT rules are irrelevant. Who needs tariffs and import quotas when a central buying agency can say "sorry, we are not importing this year"? Who needs export subsidies when your export prices are only known to individual buyers, each of whom may have separate prices, credit arrangements, and so on?

Oddly enough, it is in industrial trade where this issue has arisen, not in agriculture. There is the famous Polish golf cart case and the nationalized telecommunications problem in industry, but the fraction of world trade in industrial products involved in direct government-controlled purchases is a fraction of the proportion of agricultural trade affected by such purchases.

Economists talk about the fact that trade barriers are a way of isolating one's economy from economic adjustments. This, of course, makes others bear a greater burden. But very little is made of the fact that centralized buying and selling agencies do exactly the same thing and do it in less transparent ways.

There can be no doubt that the combined actions of these government buying and selling agencies increase instability in that portion of international agricultural trade which moves through markets. This instability exacerbates the "old problems" in market economies which have become the major exporters of agricultural products. One example is the current US-EC controversy over export subsidies on grains and related products. As mentioned earlier, the big growth in imports of these items has been in the centrally planned and developing countries economies. As a result of various economic difficulties both groups have slowed their import rate and basic agricultural commodity prices have declined appreciably in the face of high world output. At the same time the Canadian and Australian Wheat Boards have continued to expand exports instead of building stocks. The United States has reacted by blaming its current export problems on EC export subsidies without recognizing the immense effects of state buying and selling practices on the current situation.

It is amazing that these agencies and their effects on world trade have received so little attention, both in theory and in practice of agricultural trade policy. This is probably so because the idea of a network of state-trading systems is so outside the concepts of GATT founders that it never arises as an issue. Whatever the case, while there is a well-documented list of trade distortions, and charges and countercharges about how national agricultural policies distort trade, there are none about how these state-trading organizations similarly distort trade. Certainly, these agencies cannot be omitted from a discussion of the real issues.

However, if changes in national agricultural policy are difficult to discuss, certainly any suggestions that the methods whereby food imports and exports are procured or sold is likely to be an even more thorny issue. It probably ranks second only to military procurement in terms of political sensitivity. Moreover, inasmuch as it is a part of the basic economic system in socialist economies, which are large participants in international agricultural trade, it is an issue which is not open to discussion with these countries. Therefore, in an attempt to be evenhanded, one cannot attack the friendly market economies that have government buying or selling entities (such as Japan, Australia, Mexico, or New Zealand) without recognizing that socialist country agencies have the same effect.

This growing set of institutions and their practices violate GATT principles and are more restrictive than tariffs, quotas, and other finely honed trade barriers can ever be. This is true because above all the day-to-day trading practices of these entities are never transparent. They make a mockery of the concepts of equal access, most-favored-nation status, and most other precepts or general conditions laid down for "open" trade. In fact, US interests attack other governments for maintaining high prices which reduce consumption of US exports, while accepting food rationing or total absence from US products in a country with centralized buying authorities as a matter of understandable economic management. However, many agribusiness and commodity groups in the United States do not attack or criticize these centralized buying and selling agencies.

But the problem is more than inconsistency; the real problem is the effect of these centralized systems on trade. Some have argued that the way in which trade is conducted is not important as long as the outcome is acceptable. I would argue, however, that the outcome is not the only serious consideration. Increasing trade distortions put great pressure on the few relatively open trading systems which still exist, such as the United States.

Another growing feature of agricultural trade is the long-term agreement (LTA). These bilateral supply-purchase agreements became popular in the 1970s as some countries became concerned about short supplies of grains and oilseeds. Such agreements were pioneered by centralized selling agencies as the wheat boards in the 1950s and 1960s, and are especially liked by the buying agencies of the centrally planned economies. The United States became heavily involved in LTAs in the mid-1970s with the Russian grains agreement, the Japanese understanding, and several others.

The long-term agreements have one common feature and otherwise have widely varied terms. The common feature is a commitment by the importer to a minimum purchase amount and by the exporter to provide at least that amount. In the case of the US agreements the products were unpriced and no credit or other terms were attached. Other countries' LTAs probably have been somewhat more complex than were the US agreements, and thus even further violate the precepts of free trade.

It is difficult to evaluate how much such agreements distort trade, however exporting competitors believe the effects are substantial. Canadian, Australian, and Argentine competitors felt that the US-USSR agreement gave the United States an unfair advantage in a market which they had first developed. However, since they have seen the US share of the Soviet business drop by half since the 1980 embargo despite the agreement, they now may be less impressed. In any case, Argentina and Canada have now signed LTAs with the Soviets. More recently, the EC has announced a policy of LTAs as a part of a Common Export Policy, a move which was attacked by the United States, despite US participation in such agreements under both Republican and Democratic administrations.

It is probably useful to examine the varying reasons for the popularity of LTAs. In the case of the exporting country, the driving force for LTAs is market share, a belief that an LTA will insure a larger proportion of a country's import market than would be the case without the LTA. Whether that belief is justified is another question, but in some cases it probably is.

On the importing side, the desirability of the LTAs seems linked to supply security. In other words, LTAs are ways for importing countries to avoid adjusting to trade shortfalls if they occur.

If these perceptions are correct, then LTAs are in fact designed precisely to avoid the adjustments in trade which might occur in a freely operating world market. In such a theoretical market, year-to-year changes in supply would be shared by trading nations. In the real world exporting nations attempt to isolate themselves from the effects of excess supplies and importers from sharing the adversities of short supplies. As a result, the economic shock transmitted by changes in supply are forced onto a smaller and smaller "free" market, exacerbating the instability in that market, and of course, putting a higher incentive upon developing trade restrictions to avoid market instabilities.

Based upon my knowledge, there has never been a discussion in GATT of long-term agreements and their effects. Since such agreements are limited in duration and thus expire, it is an example of an issue that could be dealt with before too many national policies regarding LTAs are established and before too many domestic political constituencies are built around them, making their alteration or abandonment impossible.

A serious GATT discussion of LTAs could conclude that they were consistent with GATT principles; however, a more likely outcome would be the development of agreed-upon rules about what such trade agreements could contain, rather than either an outright ban or endorsement of LTAs.

A related issue which periodically causes charges of unfair competition in agricultural trade is the granting of credit for agricultural exports. This concept was pioneered by the United States with its famous PL-480 and Commodity Credit Corporation (CCC) credit programs. And, as with most competitive trade practices, it was an idea which caught on and has become hard to control. Despite whatever else can be said about US agricultural export credit programs, they are totally transparent. The same cannot be said about deferred payments, credit programs of state trading organizations, and other credit arrangements now common in agricultural trade. Further complicating the problem is the ambivalent use of credit in international trade. On one day a country will urge all their allies to grant favorable credit terms to an ally or favored nation, and on the next day it will suspend credit and urge others to do likewise to nations in disfavor. Thus, credit, including agricultural export credit, has become a foreign policy tool of some importance, and therefore the likelihood of controlling its use under rules related to its trade effects seems difficult, at best.

This raises an even more complicated agricultural trade problem, the linkage between agricultural trade and foreign policy. GATT has rules for emergency action on imports under specified economic conditions and similar rules on exports. There are no rules related to foreign policy restrictions on either imports and exports, nor are such rules likely to be established. However, interesting and significant trade dislocation issues are involved in trade restrictions linked to foreign policy issues.

A case in point is the US grain embargo in 1980 in response to the Soviet invasion of Afghanistan. The important question in that action, which never became an open issue, was the extent to which the nations participating in the embargo had an obligation to prevent the embargoed products from moving into other countries' markets and seriously disrupting them. In that specific case the US government took extraordinary action to isolate an equivalent amount of US grains from world markets via price supports and purchase.

Simultaneously, for domestic political reasons, the United States was forced to announce aggressive export expansion programs in other markets involving government credit, food aid, and LTAs with Mexico and China. It is not clear that these had any real effect on exports beyond what would have occurred without such aids. Even so, other grain-exporting countries were never satisfied that they did not suffer market loss, and thus were significantly displeased by the US action following the embargo.

A parallel problem seems likely regarding the recent Common Market action to ban Argentine imports as a result of the British-Argentine dispute over the Falklands. What rights do other countries have to protect their import markets against the sudden surge of Argentine products shut out of the EC and how can they do so without taking a position in a foreign policy dispute?

There probably are no answers to these questions, but in recent years the use of economic sanctions as a foreign policy tool have become common. Such actions are potentially very disruptive to agricultural commodity trade and may lead to other reactions which put additional pressures on the system.

This issue is compounded by the state-trading agencies. They are always subject to foreign policy considerations and can change buying or selling patterns without notice or announcement in ways which can only be seen after the fact and can never even be documented.

Food Security as a Trade Issue

The sharp run-up of food grain and oilseed prices in the early 1970s coupled with the soybean shock created by the US export embargo in 1974 brought the ever present issue of food security to the fore again in the mid-1970s.

Food security was not a new issue, for it underlies much of the agricultural policy structure of the traditional food-deficit nations. Increased self-sufficiency was a stated objective of European policy both within and outside the EC, mostly as an aftermath of the World War II and postwar experience. The same kind of experience underlies Japanese rice policy which maintains internal rice prices at three times world levels in order to maintain self-sufficiency in rice cultivated under high-cost conditions.

What the 1970s did was to add a new group of countries to those traditionally concerned about food security. These were the middle-income, and in some cases low-income, developing countries whose dependence upon imported grains and oilseeds had grown rapidly since the 1960s. When the tight markets of the 1970s appeared there was a sudden rush to the idea of some kind of world food security program of buffer stocks in basic grains and oilseeds.

Americans, who have lived their lives in a country which is a chronic producer of agricultural exports and where obesity is more of a problem than malnutrition, clearly do not understand the psychological strength of the food security issue. The United States tends to ignore the fact that food shortages can cause governments to fall, whereas it is hard to discover where a similar shortage of other consumer goods has the same effect.

This heightened interest in food security happened to converge with the EC mandate for commodity agreements as part of the Tokyo Round of trade negotiations. Because the interested countries (and major trading nations) were not all members of GATT participants concurred that the negotiation of such an agreement would be conducted under UNCTAD rather than GATT sponsorship.

The commodity agreement approach was an attempt to leapfrog most of the old and new problems of agricultural trade through all encompassing commodity agreements for the major traded products. The theory was that such commodity agreements which stabilized prices, insured adequate supplies, and provided access to markets, would cause domestic programs to become less important and to be less of an impediment to agricultural trade.

It became obvious during the negotiation for a wheat agreement in 1978–79, that the major obstacles to negotiation and operation of a wheat agreement were the wide differences in national programs and systems and the unwillingness of governments to alter national programs to make international agreements function. Perhaps the most classic example is the sugar agreement. Both EC and US domestic programs have in different ways operated to make the international agreement ineffective even though they played key roles in its negotiation.

In retrospect, during the wheat negotiations the varying and sometimes conflicting objectives of participating countries prohibited them from reaching any agreement. On the one hand the EC objective was a series of commodity agreements to serve as a framework within which national agricultural policies could be maintained and rationalized. The other four exporters (United States, Canada, Australia, and Argentina) were interested in price and trade stabilization agreements which would force the rest of the world to share the costs of adjustment related to building stocks in periods of surplus and reducing consumption in years of shortages. Middle-income and rich importing nations were interested in supply assurance without assuming the costs of adjustment, and the poor importing countries' objectives were supply assurance, protection against price increases, and increased food aid.

Achieving any one of these goals in an international negotiation would have been a major task: to achieve all of them proved impossible. That is not surprising for they are mutually inconsistent in part. Thus after 60 weeks of negotiation the effort was abandoned.

Above and beyond the fact that international commodity agreements collide with national programs, there is another fact which makes commodity agreements unlikely to succeed: fluctuating exchange rates. One only has to look at the "green currency" problems besetting the EC common agricultural policy to see the implications of commodity agreements on a global scale. If it is politically impossible for most countries to negotiate issues concerning their national agricultural policies, can one imagine the consequences of tying domestic farm prices of one country to the policies of central bankers in another country. Therefore while there may be a certain intellectual appeal for international commodity agreements as a way of solving agricultural trade problems, it is not a practical approach that offers a serious solution. The same political pressures that create national programs will almost certainly resist the changes in domestic programs that are necessary to make international agreements work.

Since the wheat negotiations in 1978–79, progress has been made on two issues. Food aid programs were strengthened under the Food Aid Convention of the International Wheat Agreement. Second, the Food Financing Facility of the International Monetary Fund (IMF) has been established to deal with low-income countries' balance of payments problems arising from sharp increases in food import costs.

What is still required is an international system that will share the costs of carrying stocks from good crop years to lean years, and it is unlikely that such a system can be developed either within or outside GATT. Perhaps the best possibility is a system in which the big five exporters coordinate their individual production, stocking, and destocking policies in a way that would provide year-to-year stability and adequate growth in supplies. Such an informal system was being discussed by the exporters in the late 1970s, but now discussions seem to have ceased. Presently, the United States is using government programs to reduce production and is accumulating stocks while the Canadian and Australian governments are encouraging expanded production. At a time when two of the major participants in world grain markets, the United States and the EC, are fighting over old problems in agriculture, it hardly seems likely that they will find ways to solve this relatively new one.

Summing Up

Agricultural trade has never conformed to the rules of trade which underlay GATT. The original deviations were largely the result of domestic farm programs in the developed countries. Now, however, the patterns of trade are moving even farther from the liberal trade concept by the increasing trading role of countries that use central buying and selling agencies to market or import agricultural commodities. Lately LTAs have been developed which move even farther from GATT concepts.

World markets for agricultural commodities have always been volatile because of the inelasticity of demand for food products and the uncontrollable effects of weather on crop output. This volatility appears to be increasing in recent years as the result of the various devices used by trading nations to isolate their domestic food-price system from the world economy.

Most of what GATT does relating to agricultural trade fails to touch the real issues in agricultural trade because the real issues are deeply embedded institutional issues which member states consider politically untouchable. Conversely, if a sufficient number of member nations considered the agricultural trade system unsatisfactory it could be reformed. The prospects for such reform seem dim, and thus agricultural trade issues are likely to be an irritant for the foreseeable future.

CHAPTER **14**

Managed Trade in Practice: Implications of the Textile Arrangements

Martin Wolf

The Arrangement Regarding International Trade in Textiles, commonly known as the Multi-Fiber Arrangement (MFA), is the apotheosis of the concept of managed trade. Over time the system of restraints on exports from poor countries by commodity, source, and destination has become increasingly restrictive and complex. In the European Community (EC) alone there are as many as three thousand distinct quotas, leaving aside the many more flows on which there is surveillance. Such a system did not leap fully armed from the head of a trade negotiator; it evolved over a period of twenty years.[1] Indeed, it is difficult to imagine that such a system could have been consciously designed.

© 1982. Trade Policy Research Centre, London. By permission. Martin Wolf is director of studies at the Trade Policy Research Centre, based in London. The views expressed are his own and do not necessarily reflect those of members of the Council and staff of the Centre. Parts of the paper draw on Martin Wolf, Hans H. Glismann, Joseph Pelzman, and Dean Spinanger, Costs of Protecting Jobs in Textiles and Clothing, *Thames Essay* No. 38 (London: Trade Policy Research Centre, 1983).

[1] For a history of the origin and evolution of the textile arrangements, see Kenneth W. Dam, *The GATT Law and International Economic Organization* (Chicago and London: University of Chicago Press, 1970), chapter 17, and Donald B. Keesing and Martin Wolf, *Textile Quotas against Developing Countries*, Thames Essay, no. 23 (London: Trade Policy Research Centre, 1980), chapters 2 and 3. For a recent review of the issues, see Gerard Curzon, José de la Torré, Juergen B. Donges, Alastair I. MacBean, Jean Waelbroeck, and Wolf, *MFA Forever? Future of the Arrangement for Trade in Textiles*, International Issues, no. 5 (London: Trade Policy Research Centre, 1981), which contains an annotated bibliography.

455

Why does the evolution of the MFA matter? For the industrial countries, more than just the direct economic costs of protection are involved. The question is whether the status accorded to these industries can remain exceptional. For the developing countries, textiles and clothing are not only important in themselves, accounting for almost 30 percent of manufactured exports and providing for most countries the first step on the ladder of export-oriented industrialization, but their treatment is also seen as a harbinger of things to come. What will happen in other industries if more and more developing countries attempt to pursue the path of outward-looking development recommended by many economists? At the same time, many developing countries are being faced with the question of whether they can expect open markets if they do not grant them in return.

In terms of what are now called North–South relations, the MFA in its present form represents the harsh reality as opposed to the rhetoric accompanying the demands for a "new international economic order." What is that reality? It is that those who succeeded by market-oriented development and laud the idea of an open international system do not wish their words to be taken too literally by developing countries.

At present, after more than twenty years of being treated as exceptions to the internationally agreed rules on trade embodied in the General Agreement on Tariffs and Trade (GATT), the textiles and clothing industries of many of the industrial countries, including those of the United States and the EC, demand a still more exceptional status. They suggest that their share of the domestic market of the industrial countries should be guaranteed against the competition of poor countries, and the governments of major countries appear to have granted this request. What is involved in this important case is abandonment of the principle of comparative advantage. If generalized to other industries, the progressive increase in international specialization that characterized the dynamic period from 1950 to 1973 would cease. Yet in spite of these radical implications it appears that the demand is being met, but without the discussion of its wider consequences that is clearly required.

This study surveys the principal issues raised by the evolution of the MFA. These are: its history; the significance of the threat to which the MFA is a response; the effects of the MFA on levels and patterns of trade; the costs of the protection afforded by the MFA, set against the purported benefits of adjustment postponed; the present status and future prospects of the MFA; and the lessons of the MFA. Most of these issues can only be dealt with briefly and many questions will be ignored altogether. In particular, other forms of protection, especially the tariff, will not be discussed, even thouqh high tariffs are an important part of the protection afforded to textiles and clothing in many developed countries.

History of the MFA

The ancestor of the MFA was the Short-Term Arrangement on cotton textiles (STA) of 1961, which led almost at once to the Long-Term Arrangement Regarding International Trade in Cotton Textiles (LTA) of 1962. The main protagonist of the LTA was the United States, the dominant economic power at that time and the main force behind the liberalization of international trade through multilateral negotiations under the auspices of the GATT.

The United States' reasons for bringing such an arrangement into being are instructive. There were five main factors, which *mutatis mutandis* have remained constant to the present day. The first was a desire to avoid new legislation authorizing import restrictions. The second was the perceived need for President John F. Kennedy to reward the textile industry for its electoral support in 1960 and to ensure its acquiescence in the Kennedy Round of multilateral trade negotiations. The third was the desire to bring about "burden sharing," as it has since been called, namely, to persuade other industrial countries (above all Western Europe at that time) to take more imports from developing countries. The fourth was to put the cloak of international respectability over what was clearly a violation of the principle of nondiscrimination upon which the GATT system had been based. The fifth was a desire to ensure a degree of accommodation to the emerging comparative advantage of the developing countries with the ultimate promise of adjustment and a return to unrestricted trade. All of these objectives were obviously not compatible and the contradictions have survived to this day.

In succeeding years many changes took place in the industry and exports from developing countries grew rapidly. Indeed, in certain respects the LTA worked quite well. New suppliers were treated fairly generously and many products were exempted from restrictions. Moreover, as Japanese exports of cotton textiles declined, other exporters could fill Japan's place. At the same time, since the major change in the industry was the switch to man-made fibers, and this change was also the basis for the success of developing countries in the export of clothing, strong pressures built up to widen the scope of the system.

In the early 1970s the United States reached agreement with its major suppliers on the control of exports of textiles and textile products made of man-made fibers and wool. These restrictions were clearly not justified within the framework of the LTA and for that reason the United States pushed for an international arrangement, a successor to the LTA, which would cover textiles and textile products of cotton, wool, and man made fibers. The US initiative was successful and the MFA, which was the product of its efforts, went into effect on January 1, 1974.

The reasons for the MFA were very similar to those for the LTA, and the text of the MFA accordingly embodied the same fundamental confusions. The difference, however, was that the United States was willing to make concessions in return for the legitimization of restrictions on a wider range of textile products than had been authorized by the LTA. The statement of objectives is, therefore, full of noble rhetoric, emphasizing that the objectives were "the expansion of trade, the reduction of barriers to such trade and the progressive liberalization of world trade in textile products, while at the same time ensuring the orderly and equitable development of this trade and avoidance of disruptive effects in individual markets . . . ." Another "principal aim . . . shall be to further economic and social development of developing countries . . . ." Consequently, the minimum growth rates for quotas, the "flexibility" provisions, and the rules, procedures, and implementing arrangements were all more favorable than were the corresponding aspects of the LTA. Perhaps the most important provisions were that increases in quotas past the first year should not be less than 6 percent per year, except in "exceptional cases," and the establishment of the Textiles Surveillance Body (TSB).

The MFA was signed just before the recession of 1974–75, which decisively changed the environment in which it operated. The combination of rising protectionist pressure, especially in Western Europe, and the ready availability of an internationally sanctioned instrument, the MFA, led to major alterations in its operation when it came up for renewal in 1977. The main problem was that, while the United States had already reached restrictive bilateral agreements with its main suppliers, the EC had failed to secure a common position or to negotiate quickly enough with its principal suppliers. As a result, the United States was little affected by increased imports, while the Community was much more heavily affected. Moreover, productivity growth in both textiles and clothing was higher in the Community than in the United States, and, consequently, job losses in the former were substantially greater. In this situation it was easy to blame the decline in employment on the growth of imports. The Community resolved to tighten up dramatically on imports from "low-cost" countries, largely at the instigation of France and the United Kingdom, and became for the first time in this lengthy history the leader in turning the protectionist screw.

The negotiations of 1977 were remarkable for a number of important innovations, especially the attempt to impose global ceilings on aggregate imports from "low-cost" suppliers of certain sensitive products under the doctrine of "cumulative market disruption." This doctrine violated the bilateralism implicit in the MFA and its obvious corollary that action could be taken against a supplier only if its individual exports were the source of identifiable injury. Moreover, for sensitive products both the base for determining quotas and the growth rates permitted were clearly in violation of MFA norms. In sum, the renegotiation of the MFA in 1977, in which the European Community was the leader but other industrial countries soon followed, changed the characteristics of the arrangement in fundamental ways.

Before considering the present status of the MFA, it will be useful to consider the nature of the threat with which the MFA is intended to deal, and the experience under it.

Threat of Developing Countries' Exports

The basis of developing countries' comparative advantage is indicated in table 14.1, which also reveals the importance of these industries to developed countries. The textile and, especially, the clothing industries are labor-intensive. In 1976, the share of the textile industry in industrial countries' manufacturing output was 40 percent less than its share in employment. For clothing the share of output was only 50 percent of the share of employment. Value added per man in these industries was about half that in manufacturing as a whole, a prime indicator of vulnerability to competition from poorer countries.[2] This very labor intensity was a reason for political importance of these two industries. Although the two industries together

---

[2] Value added per man is a useful indicator of the physical and human capital intensity of a particular activity. Indeed, in a classic work on the comparative advantage of developing countries, Lary used exactly this measure. See Hal B. Lary, *Imports of Manufactures from Less Developed Countries* (New York: Columbia University Press for the National Bureau of Economic Research, 1968).

TABLE 14.1   SHARES OF TEXTILES AND CLOTHING IN
             MANUFACTURING OUTPUT AND EMPLOYMENT IN
             INDUSTRIAL COUNTRIES (percentage)

	Textiles			
	1963		1976	
	Output	Employment	Output	Employment
European Community	6.7	9.9	4.2	6.5
Japan	9.0	14.3	5.7	9.4
United States	3.8	6.3	3.5	5.9
All industrial countries	5.3	9.8	4.2	7.2

Note: The industrial countries are the members of the Organization for Economic Co-operation and Development (OECD). Output is value added.
Source: Yearbook of Industrial Statistics, United Nations, New York, annual.

accounted for only about 2 percent of GNP, they accounted for as much as 9 percent of total employment in the industrial countries.[3] They are, therefore, both vulnerable and visible.

Despite the apparent comparative advantage of developing countries, import penetration continues to be fairly modest. Table 14.2 shows that in 1979 imports from developing countries took 9.6 percent of the developed countries' total market for clothing and textiles combined. The clothing categories are, as might be expected, those in which import penetration has been growing most rapidly. By 1979 import penetration by developing countries had reached 14.1 percent in industrial countries' markets. In certain categories, knitted apparel, for example, penetration was higher. Indeed, on a still more disaggregated basis penetration can be higher still.[4]

Table 14.3 puts the whole issue of the threat further in perspective. Table 14.3 shows that trade was modest in relation to output for the large economies. Individual members of the European Community have high ratios of trade to output, but this is largely because of trade among themselves. In all, trade can have had only a modest effect on the textile and clothing output of the United States and European Community as a whole, although this is not true at the country level

[3] As might be expected, these industries are much more important in the developing countries, accounting for close to 30 percent of factory employment and 15 percent of manufacturing output. See Keesing and Wolf, *Textile Quotas against Developing Countries*, p. 1.

[4] Ibid., p. 88.

	Clothing			
	1963		*1976*	
	Output	*Employment*	*Output*	*Employment*
European Community	4.0	5.9	2.6	4.7
Japan	1.3	2.8	1.8	4.3
United States	3.6	7.0	2.8	6.3
All industrial countries	3.6	5.6	2.6	5.1

in the latter, (especially in the cases of Italy, which had a large surplus, and of West Germany and the Netherlands, which had large deficits).

While the developing countries generally have substantial surpluses in relation to output, their magnitude is small in relation to the output of industrial countries. Brazil, Hong Kong, India, South Korea, and Taiwan together had gross output in 1976 equal to about 40 percent

TABLE 14.2 SHARES OF IMPORTS FROM DEVELOPING COUNTRIES IN THE INDUSTRIAL COUNTRIES' APPARENT CONSUMPTION OF TEXTILES AND TEXTILE PRODUCTS, 1970–79

		Developing-country market penetration		
ISIC Code		*1979 (percentage)*	*Growth rate 1970–79 (percentage)*	*Total apparent consumption (billion dollars)*
32	Clothing, textiles and leather	9.6	14.8	n.a
3211-1	Cotton fabrics	10.7	8.3	12.3
3211-7	Fibers for textile use	13.8	3.4	5.2
3214-1	Knotted carpets	29.2	4.4	3.1
3215	Cordage, rope and twine	13.1	7.0	1.8
3220	Wearing apparel	14.1	17.6	84.0
3220-2	Women's, girls' and infants' outerwear	10.5	22.8	30.0
3220-3	Underwear	16.9	14.2	11.9
3220-4	Leather apparel	38.7	17.7	4.0
3220-5	Headgear	12.7	19.0	0.9
3220-6	Knitted apparel	36.5	10.7	7.0

Source: Helen Hughes and Jean Waelbroeck, "Can Developing-country Exports Keep Growing in the 1980s?" *The World Economy* (June 1981), tables 2 and 3.

TABLE 14.3   A COMPARISON OF OUTPUT OF TEXTILES AND CLOTHING
IN INDUSTRIAL AND DEVELOPING COUNTRIES, 1977

	Value added *(billion US dollars)*	*Gross output* *(billion US dollars)*
Developed countries		
United States	36.73	82.80
European Community (1976)	29.47	68.10
West Germany (1976)	8.58	18.78
France	6.97	16.87
United Kingdom	6.11	15.15
Italy	5.97	13.46
Belgium/Luxembourg (1976)	1.61	4.03
Netherlands (1976)	0.91	3.00
Japan	14.57	36.95
Canada	2.88	6.51
Australia	1.46	3.28
Sweden	0.73	1.43
Austria	0.87	2.34
Finland	0.61	1.29
Intermediate countries		
Spain (1976)	2.00	4.68
Yugoslavia	1.54	4.29
South Africa	n.a.	1.42
Greece (1975)	0.71	1.95
Portugal	0.59	1.56
Developing countries		
Brazil (1974)	2.83	7.58
Hong Kong (1976)	1.83	5.03
South Korea	2.10	6.12
India (1976)	1.42	6.16
Taiwan (1976)	n.a.	4.28
Turkey	1.24	3.22

Sources: Yearbook of Industrial Statistics, United Nations, New York, 1978, vol. 1; *Yearbook of International Trade Statistics,* United Nations, New York, 1979, vol. 1; *International Financial Statistics Yearbook,* International Monetary Fund, Washington, 1979.

of that of the United States or of the European Community and their combined gross exports were only about 15 percent of US or EC output.

At the same time, the range of developing countries' comparative advantage is quite restricted. In 1978 they accounted for only 42 percent of market economies' clothing exports and 22 percent of textiles. In general, developing countries did best in the most labor

	Exports as percentage of gross output	Imports as percentage of gross output
Developed countries		
United States	3	7
European Community (1976)	30	32
West Germany (1976)	28	41
France	22	22
United Kingdom	20	22
Italy	38	12
Belgium/Luxembourg (1976)	70	58
Netherlands (1976)	69	101
Japan	11	5
Canada	4	25
Australia	1	31
Sweden	33	110
Austria	41	54
Finland	38	35
Intermediate countries		
Spain (1976)	10	6
Yugoslavia	10	6
South Africa	4	20
Greece (1975)	26	7
Portugal	34	9
Developing countries		
Brazil (1974)	6	2
Hong Kong (1976)	74	30
South Korea	52	6
India (1976)	17	—
Taiwan (1976)	59	4
Turkey	10	2

intensive and technologically simple parts of textiles and clothing, while industrial countries dominated exports of knitted fabrics, man-made fiber yarns and fabrics, carpets (other than knotted), coated textiles, textile machinery, and man-made fibers. In these products industrial countries did not only have an overwhelming share of exports but enjoyed surpluses as well.[5] Thus, the dividing line of com-

[5] Information is from the *Yearbook of International Trade Statistics*, vol. 2 (New York: United Nations, 1979).

TABLE 14.4   IMPORTS INTO THE UNITED STATES OF TEXTILE PRODUCTS, BY SOURCE, 1971–81 (million equivalent square yards)

Year	Apparel	Other textiles	Total	Origin of total imports — Hong Kong, Taiwan, South Korea
1971	2,098	3,853	5,951	1,762
1972	2,226	4,010	6,236	1,810
1973	2,090	3,035	5,125	1,523
1974	1,937	2,473	4,410	1,475
1975	2,077	1,751	3,828	1,599
1976	2,428	2,560	4,987	2,040
1977	2,466	2,511	4,977	1,978
1978	2,905	2,834	5,739	2,247
1979[b]	2,671	1,968	4,639	1,927
1980	2,884	2,000	4,884	2,210
1981	3,136	2,626	5,762	2,460
Annual growth rates				
1971–81	4.1	−3.8	−0.3	3.4
1971–76	3.0	−7.9	−3.5	3.0
1976–81	5.3	0.5	2.9	3.8
Percentage share				
1971	35.2	64.8	100.0	29.6
1976	48.7	51.3	100.0	40.9
1981	54.4	45.6	100.0	42.7

n.s.   Not significant.
Note: Errors are due to rounding.
Source: The History and Current Status of the Multifibre Arrangement, 1978 (Washington: International Trade Commission, 1978); *The Multifibre Arrangement, 1973 to 1980* (Washington: International Trade Commission, 1981); and *US Imports of Textile and Apparel Products Under the Multifibre Arrangement, 1976 to 1981* (Washington: International Trade Commission, 1982).
a. Defined here as Asia and Africa (except Israel and South Africa).
b. For 1979 the figure for total imports is below the sum of imports by origin by 9 million equivalent square yards. The reason for this discrepancy is not explained.

parative advantage goes through the textile category, with clothing, cotton and jute textiles, and knotted carpets on the developing countries' side and synthetic and woolen textiles, knitted fabrics, and everything else in the industrial countries' side. Moreover, since both industrial and developing countries protected industries most strongly those sectors where they had a comparative disadvantage, the pattern of that comparative advantage without protection would probably be

	Origin of total imports				
Year	Latin America	Other developing countries[a]	Japan	China	Europe and others
1971	293	383	1,691	0.2	1,822
1972	369	559	1,249	11	2,238
1973	453	635	813	33	1,668
1974	422	571	861	84	998
1975	362	432	536	141	758
1976	457	696	747	894	894
1977	418	552	943	91	995
1978	605	776	853	201	1,058
1979[b]	516	812	492	231	670
1980	461	820	461	325	608
1981	543	993	503	562	702
Annual growth rates					
1971–81	6.4	10.0	−11.4	100+	−9.1
1971–76	9.3	12.7	−15.1	100+	−13.3
1976–81	3.5	7.4	−7.6	29.7	−4.7
Percentage share					
1971	4.9	6.4	28.4	n.s.	30.6
1976	9.2	14.0	15.0	3.1	17.9
1981	9.4	17.2	8.7	9.8	12.2

as revealed but be still more marked on both sides of the dividing line.

What would be the consequence of the abolition of the restraints under the MFA? This issue was analyzed quantitatively in the book, *Textile Quotas against Developing Countries*, already cited.[6] The conclusion was that while output of textiles and clothing might rise by 5 percent between 1980 and 1990, employment could fall by 33 percent. (Indeed, employment would fall somewhat under any assumptions about the trade régime.) In terms of jobs lost, these figures imply a decline of 1.65 million employees in textiles and clothing in the United

[6] Keesing and Wolf, *Textile Quotas against Developing Countries*, pp. 133–40. The assumed growth of consumption and productivity in that analysis is probably too high, but the errors cancel each other out.

States and the European Community together, which is less than 1 percent of their total labor forces.

Effect on Trade of Restrictions Under the MFA

Turning to the effects of the MFA, it is important to note first that protection appears to achieve what it is supposed to, namely a reduction in the growth of imports from restricted suppliers. Tables 14.4 and 14.5 show for the United States and the European Community the growth of imports in terms of the quantities that the bilateral agreements under the MFA attempt to control. What can be seen is how slowly restricted imports have grown, especially since 1976, which was used as the starting point for many bilateral agreements under the second MFA.

The United States has had relatively tight restrictions since the early 1970s. In square yard equivalent (SYE) imports were lower in 1981 than 1971. The composition changed as well, from textiles toward apparel and from imports from industrial countries toward imports from developing countries. Both of these structural changes continued thoughout the decade. Imports from Hong Kong, South Korea, and Taiwan experienced marked ups and downs, while their growth over the whole decade was a little over 3 percent a year; imports from other developing countries generally grew more rapidly than those from Hong Kong, South Korea, and Taiwan, while imports from China grew exceptionally rapidly. In all, the United States was able to curb import growth very successfully.

The European Community made a serious effort to control imports only after 1976, as is clear from table 14.5. Thereafter, unlike the United States not only did total EC imports grow at a modest rate but imports into the Community from countries covered by MFA restrictions grew more slowly than those from both industrial countries and countries under preferential agreements. Thus, total EC imports grew in metric tons at a compound rate of 2.1 percent a year between 1976 and 1981, while imports from countries with bilateral agreements grew at only 0.9 percent, imports from industrial countries at a compound rate of 3.9 percent a year, and imports from "preferential countries" (including Greece) at 9.6 percent. Between 1976 and 1980 (the latter a peak year) total imports into the Community grew at 4.9 percent a year but imports from all "low-cost" suppliers at 2.9 percent. Of the latter, Hong Kong, South Korea, India, and Brazil achieved only 1.2 percent growth a year, while other restricted "low-cost" suppliers (excluding "preferential countries") enjoyed

TABLE 14.5   EUROPEAN COMMUNITY IMPORTS OF MFA PRODUCTS,
1973–81 (thousand metric tons)

| Year | Industrial countries | "Low cost" countries | | | Total |
		Countries with agreements	Preferential countries[a]	Total	
1973	254	n.a.	n.a.	572	826
1974	334	n.a.	n.a.	752	1,086
1975	306	n.a.	n.a.	855	1,161
1976	356	651	n.a.	1,093	1,449
1977	332	598	301	1,001	1,333
1978	354	598	366	1,072	1,426
1979	472	697	421	1,225	1,697
1980	526	709	396	1,227	1,753
1981[bc]	436(431)	687(680)	324(434)	1,073(1,176)	1,509(1,607)
Annual average growth rates (percentage)					
1973–81	6.8	n.a.	n.a.	9.4	8.7
1973–76	11.9	n.a.	n.a.	24.1	20.6
1976–81[d]	3.9	0.9	9.6[e]	1.5	2.1
Percentage share					
1973	30.8	n.a.	n.a.	69.2	100.0
1976	24.6	44.9	n.a.	75.4	100.0
1981[f]	26.8	42.3	27.0	73.2	100.0

n.a.   Not available.
Sources: The European Community's Textile Trade, Europe Information No. 44/81 (Brussels: Commission of the European Communities, 1981) and unpublished data from the Commission of the European Communities.
a. Includes ACP countries.
b. In 1981 Greece was included in the Community. Thus its exports to the Community, previously included under 'Preferential Countries' were excluded from Community imports in 1981, while its imports from outside the Community were included in Community imports. In 1981 Greece's exports to its Community partners were MT 111.9 thousand, up from MT 105.7 thousand in 1980. Its imports from outside the Community were MT 5.5 thousand from industrial countries, MT 7.1 thousand from countries with agreements, MT 1.5 thousand from 'preferential countries', MT 8.9 thousand from all 'low cost' countries, and MT 14.4 thousand from all extra-Community sources. The results of treating Greece as if it were still outside the Community are shown in parentheses for 1981. It is these figures that are comparable with those for the previous years.
c. In 1981 import figures were not collected consistently for the United Kingdom because of industrial action by civil servants. Figures for United Kingdom have been estimated.
d. Growth rates for 1976–1981 were computed with Greece treated as being outside the Community, in order to preserve consistency.
e. For 1977 to 1981.
f. Excludes Greece from the Community.

TABLE 14.6   COMPETING SUPPLIERS' CHANGING SHARES IN THE
IMPORTS OF THE INDUSTRIAL COUNTRIES OF WESTERN
EUROPE AND NORTH AMERICA, 1963–80 (percentage)

	Clothing					
	1963	*1973*	*1976*	*1978*	*1979*	*1980*
Developing countries	19	31	40	38	37	39
Southern Europe	3	8	8	8	9	9
Centrally planned countries	1	5	5	5	5	6
Japan	9	3	2	1	1	1
Other developed countries	68	53	45	48	48	46
World	100	100	100	100	100	100

Note: Errors are due to rounding.
Source: International Trade, 1978/79 and 1980/81, (Geneva: GATT Secretariat, 1979 and
1981), tables A7 and A8.

slightly greater growth of 3.4 percent a year.[7] Meanwhile imports
from other industrial countries actually grew at 10.3 percent a year
between 1976 and 1980, before falling sharply between 1980 and 1981.

There is a noteworthy difference between the experience of the
European Community and the United States as far as the buoyancy
of imports from industrial countries is concerned. The reason appears
to be the higher general tariff protection of textile and clothing in
the United States and the growing comparative disadvantage of a
number of important European countries in textiles and clothing vis-
à-vis other industrial countries.

The effect of the restrictions imposed by the industrial countries
has been to create a marked break in the emerging pattern of trade
with developing countries. Table 14.6 illuminates this point. In textiles
the share of developing countries in industrial countries' markets has
changed not at all in the last two decades. In clothing, however, their
share of the imports into Western Europe and North America rose
from 19 percent in 1963 to a peak of 40 percent in 1976. Thereafter,
however, their share actually fell and even in 1980 had not returned
to the 1976 level.

Table 14.6 suggests that diversion of trade may have occurred.
Since the restrictions under the MFA are discriminatory, purchases
are diverted toward the most competitive unrestricted producer, who

[7] These data are from *The European Community's Textile Trade*, EEC
Information, no. 44/81 (Brussels: Commission of the European Communities,
April 1981), p. 6.

	Textiles					
	1963	1973	1976	1978	1979	1980
Developing countries	15	13	15	14	14	15
Southern Europe	3	5	5	5	6	5
Centrally planned countries	2	3	4	3	3	4
Japan	7	3	3	3	2	3
Other developed countries	73	76	73	75	76	73
World	100	100	100	100	100	100

is as likely to be located in another country as in the importing country itself. Italy seems to have been the major beneficiary of trade diversion in the European Community, while the United States has also benefited, especially under the second MFA.

Detailed information on developments in the late 1970s in the European Community further illuminates the issue of diversion. Those developments show how the quantities of imports of the five clothing items classified by the Community as most "sensitive" to imports from poor countries changed between 1978 and 1980. The really remarkable development was the growth of imports from the United States, especially of knitwear (categories 4 and 5). In category 4 (T-shirts) imports from both the United States and Portugal exceeded those from Hong Kong, South Korea, and Taiwan in 1980, while in category 5 (jerseys) imports from the United States were not far behind those from Hong Kong and Korea and were ahead of those from Taiwan. Moreover, while imports from the United States soared, those from the restricted developing countries generally stagnated.[8]

The main sources of extra-Community imports of textiles and clothing in 1980, ranked by value, were Hong Kong, followed by the United States, Switzerland, Austria, Greece, South Korea, India, Portugal, Yugoslavia, and Taiwan, in that order. Thus, not only were some of the most important suppliers not restricted but, more striking still, while rich countries like the United States, Italy, or Switzerland faced no restrictions in industrial-country markets, developing coun-

[8] These data are from the Commission of the European Community and were published in *The European Community, the Consumer, and the Multi-Fiber Arrangement*, BEUC 91.81 rev. 1 (Brussels: Bureau Européen des Unions de Consommateurs, 1981), table 2.

tries with negligible exports by comparison, like Sri Lanka or Thailand, did. In these circumstances diversion of imports from poorer to richer countries is probable.

It has occasionally, but wrongly, been suggested that because of upgrading of quality, even the tight quantitative restrictions of the later 1970s have not seriously limited the ability of developing countries to expand the purchasing power of their textile and clothing exports, which is, after all, what exports are for. A simple way of obtaining evidence on this point is to deflate the value of developing countries' exports of textiles and clothing to the industrial countries by the unit value index of the latter's exports of manufactures to developing countries.[9] The resulting numbers show the change in the purchasing power of developing-country textile and clothing exports in terms of other manufactured goods.

On this basis, the purchasing power of developing countries' textile exports to industrial countries rose by 12.8 percent between 1976 and 1980 (a compound rate of 3.1 percent a year), of their clothing exports by 19.0 percent (a compound rate of 4.5 percent a year), and of both together by 17.2 percent (a compound rate of 4.0 percent). When set against the physical quantities of exports to the United States and the European Community shown in tables 14.4 and 14.5, these numbers suggest that the purchasing power of textile and clothing exports has risen a little more rapidly than physical volume, but that this growth was nevertheless modest after 1976.

It is useful to stress the contrast between the period 1976–80 and the period 1970–76. (Use of 1976 as the dividing point is justified because this was the last year in which the last large open market, the European Community, remained so.) In the earlier period 1970–76 the purchasing power of developing countries' textile exports to industrial countries rose by 61 percent (a compound rate of 8.2 percent a year), of clothing exports by 184 percent (a compound rate of

---

[9] Data on developing countries' exports of textiles and clothing to industrial countries are from *International Trade* (Geneva: GATT Secretariat, annual). Countries of South Europe are excluded from the developing countries. Industrial countries include the European Community (excluding Greece), European Free Trade Association (EFTA) (excluding Portugal), the United States, Canada, and Japan. The deflator used is the unit value series of manufactured exports on a c.i.f. basis from developed to developing countries, which has been taken from unpublished World Bank sources and is based on UN data. Export data for Hong Kong and South Korea are from *Yearbook of International Trade Statistics* (New York: United Nations, 1979 and 1980).

19 percent) and of both together by 131 percent (a compound rate of 15 percent). The fall in the growth rate of the purchasing power of total textile and clothing exports to industrial countries, from 15 percent for 1970–76 to 4 percent for 1976–80, suggests a profound adverse change in the trading environment.

The conclusion that upgrading did not offset the effects of quantitive controls in the later 1970s is confirmed by the experience of two major exporters, Hong Kong and South Korea. Using the same deflator as above, the purchasing power of the former's exports of textiles and clothing rose by just 13.9 percent between 1976 and 1980 while the latter's rose by 15.6 percent. The corresponding compound rates of growth are only 3.3 and 3.7 percent per year.

Costs of Protection and Adjustment

The simplest evidence on the effects on prices of quantitative restrictions under the MFA is provided by the premiums paid on transfer of quota rights among firms in the exporting countries. The existence of such "quota premiums" is not only proof that the restrictions are binding, but also provides evidence of the difference between the costs of production in the exporting countries and import prices in the industrial countries, and thus evidence of the prices that might rule under unrestricted trade.[10]

---

[10] The most important defect of the quota premium as a measure of the price-raising effects of export-restraint agreements is that the supply price of the restrained exporters is unlikely to be constant, irrespective of demand. Thus, prices would not fall by the full extent of the premium if the restraint were to be abolished. The argument that the quota premium is an inadequate indicator of the scarcity created by the restriction, because only a small proportion of quota rights is actually traded, is invalid. If the firms who receive the quota rights hold on to them, this must be because the value of those rights to the firms is at least as great as their market price. This means that they can sell their goods at a markup over marginal production cost at least equal to the market value of the quota rights which they need to effect the exports. Otherwise, they would make more money by reducing exports and selling quota rights. If future access to quota rights depends on current use, however, the above argument holds only over the long term. It is then possible for a profit-maximizing firm to hold on to quota rights even though in the short term more money can be made by selling them and reducing exports. In this case quota premiums show the long-run rather than the short-run effect on prices.

There is a certain limited amount of evidence on quota premiums. It appears that they are significant only for exports from Hong Kong, South Korea, and Taiwan, which indicates that the restrictions are not binding on most of the other exporters. In Hong Kong firms are allowed to transfer quotas to one another. According to an editorial in *Textile Asia*, published in Hong Kong, on the transfer the transferor obtains considerable profit, say 15–25 percent of the export value, although the price fluctuates widely with changes in demand and supply for the particular item.[11] A related piece of evidence consists of the quota premiums reported by the United Kingdom's Consumer Association. It found that in March 1979 the (fluctuating) quota premiums charged to British buyers in Hong Kong averaged $2.31 (American dollars) for a pair of jeans, $1.24 for a woman's blouse, $1.16 for a man's or boy's shirt, and $0.98 for the average knitwear item.[12]

Some detailed information has been collected by Glenn Jenkins of the Institute for International Development at Harvard University on Canada's imports from Hong Kong, South Korea, and Taiwan (table 14.7). The table shows both how high the protection for a large range of garments appears to be, as well as the extremely important role played by the quantitative restrictions. Their effect is clearly not marginal: in many cases the addition of the quotas has an effect on prices equal to that of the tariffs.

The most thorough study of the effects of quotas is that by Jenkins. Table 14.8 summarizes the main results of his analysis. He estimates that the total cost to consumers of tariffs and quotas was Canadian $467.4 million in 1979, of which Canadian $269.1 million was accounted for by the tariffs alone. Of the total, more than half was a direct transfer to the producers from consumers. Economic losses to Canada were Canadian $107.5 million from tariffs and quotas together, but only Canadian $20.9 million from the tariffs. Indeed, the main lesson of the analysis is not merely the large transfers from consumers—Canadian $100 per family of four—and large economic losses—Canadian $25 per family—but the extraordinary economic

---

For a discussion of the actual procedures for internal transfer of quotas in developing countries, see Keesing and Wolf, *Textile Quotas against Developing Countries*, pp. 125–28.

[11] *Textile Asia* (April 1976), p. 11.

[12] *The Price of Protection: A Study of the Effect of Import Controls on the Cost of Imported Clothing* (London: Consumers Association, 1979), p. 16.

TABLE 14.7   THE PROTECTIVE EFFECTS OF TARIFFS AND QUOTAS
ON CANADA'S IMPORTS FROM HONG KONG, SOUTH
KOREA, AND TAIWAN, 1979 (percentage)

Garment category	Total protective rates[a]	Tariff protection (without quotas)	Effect of quotas
Outerwear	60	26	34
Structured suits, blazers	43	25	18
Shirts with tailored collars	74	20	54
Blouses and shirts	34	24	10
Sweaters, pullovers, cardigans	33	23	10
T-shirts, sweatshirts	41	20	21
Trousers, slacks (men's and boy's)	33	22	11
Trousers, slacks (women's and girls')	34	23	11
Overalls, coveralls	37	16	21
Dresses and skirts	32	24	8
Underwear	41	12	28
Shorts	37	19	18
Pyjamas, sleepwear	24	22	2
Foundation garments	31	24	7
Swimwear	35	20	15
Overcoats, topcoats and rainwear	38	25	13

Source: Glenn P. Jenkins, *Costs and Consequences of the New Protectionism: the Case of Canada's Clothing Sector* (Ottawa: The North South Institute, 1980), tables 2 and 5. By permission.
a. Duty plus quota premium over net landed cost.

inefficiency of the bilateral quotas. Thus, while the tariffs transferred Canadian $269.1 million and led to economic losses of Canadian $20.9 million, the quotas transferred an additional Canadian $198.3 million at an economic cost of Canadian $86.5 million. Thus, for every Canadian $1 taken from consumers by the bilateral quotas, 21 cents went to the exporting countries, 23 cents were wasted via economic inefficiency, and only 56 cents went to the Canadian beneficiaries.

One important cost of protection, on which there is a little evidence, is the distribution of its costs across income classes. Jenkins, in particular, estimates that for households with income of less than Canadian $10,000 the costs of tariffs and quotas per household in Canada in 1979 was Canadian $86.06; for households with incomes between Canadian $10,000 and Canadian $20,000 the cost was Canadian $78.09; for households with incomes between Canadian $20,000 and Canadian $30,000 the cost was Canadian $122.21; and for households with

TABLE 14.8   COSTS OF QUOTA AND TARIFF PROTECTION OF
CLOTHING IN CANADA, 1979 (million Canadian dollars)

	Tariffs alone	Tariff plus quota	Addition of bilateral quotas
Transfers within Canada	248.2	359.9	111.8
Tariff revenue	105.1	92.8	− 12.3
Addition to producer profit	143.1	267.1	124.1
Losses to Canada	20.9	107.5	86.5
Transfer to foreign producer	—	41.1	41.1
Waste of resources in production	14.7	45.7	31.0
Loss in standard of living from reduced consumption	6.2	20.7	14.4
Total cost to consumers	269.1	467.4	198.3

Notes: The analysis assumes a price elasticity of domestic demand of -0.5 and of supply of 1.0. Foreign supply elasticities are assumed to be infinite, as is indeed plausible for a relatively small country like Canada.
Source: Jenkins, *Costs and Consequences of the New Protectionism,* table 6.

incomes Canadian $30,000 and over the cost was Canadian $182.61.[13] The distribution of these costs per household is much more equal than that of income. Thus, for the consumers in the lowest income group, the tax is no less than 1.3 percent of income, while for those in the highest group it is only 0.4 percent of income. The reason for this discrepancy is that in Canada lower income groups spend a higher proportion of their income on clothing.

Turning to the workers affected actually or potentially by imports, table 14.9 confirms that employees in these industries, especially in clothing tend to be predominantly female and low paid. More than 80 percent of clothing workers in the major developed countries are women. It is necessary, however, to keep in perspective the adjustment to employment imposed by imports and bear in mind the primary role of productivity growth. In the European Community between 1973 and 1979, a 7 percent rise in clothing consumption turned into a 2 percent decline in output, because of changes in the trade

---

[13] Glenn P. Jenkins, *Costs and Consequences of the New Protectionism: The Case of Canada's Clothing Sector* (Ottawa: The North–South Institute, 1980), pp. 42–44.

TABLE 14.9 EMPLOYMENT AND WAGE CHARACTERISTICS OF
TEXTILES AND CLOTHING INDUSTRIES IN INDUSTRIAL
COUNTRIES, 1977 (percentage)

	Textiles		Clothing	
	Female share in employment	Relative hourly earnings[a]	Female share in employment	Relative hourly earnings[a]
France	55.0	83.6	82.6	76.5
Germany	51.0[b]	82.6	82.0[b]	74.3
Japan	67.1	n.a.	83.4	n.a.
United Kingdom	47.8	86.5	81.3	65.6
United States	46.6	69.9	80.9	63.7

n.a. Not available.
Source: Textile Industry in OECD Countries (Paris: OECD Secretariat, annual) and
'Wages and Total Labour Costs for Workers, International Survey 1967–1977' (Stockholm Swedish Employers' Confederation, 1979).
a. The average hourly earnings in manufacturing are set at 100.
b. These data are for 1975.

balance. At the same time, the 2 percent decline in output yielded a
21.5 percent decline in employment because of soaring productivity.[14]

What costs do displaced workers face? It should be emphasized
that costs to workers directly affected are considered here, both because they are the source of political pressure and because the overall
economic costs imposed by job displacement are a controversial theoretical and empirical question beyond the scope of the present discussion.

Relevant data have been collected for Canada and the United
States. The central issue is how the experience of unemployment and
changes in wages determines the overall losses or gains of those who
were laid off. For Canada data on job losses have been analyzed for
the Sherbrooke region of Quebec, where a high proportion of the
layoffs occurred in textiles and clothing.[15] From this analysis emerge
a few points, which seem to be generally valid of the industrial countries: first, women experienced much larger gross and net earnings

[14] Data on consumption, production, employment, and productivity in the
European Community are from *The European Community's Textile Trade*,
Appendices A and B.

[15] See Graham Glenday, Jenkins, and John C. Evans, *Worker Adjustment
to Liberal Trade: Costs and Assistance Policies*, World Bank Staff Working
Paper, no. 926 (Washington: World Bank, 1980), tables 3, 4, 9, and 10.

losses than men, both because of greater difficulty in obtaining a new job and the greater likelihood of wage reductions between the initial and subsequent jobs. At the same time, it is clear that these losses occurred partly because the women were more willing to drop out of the labor force: they placed a higher premium on not working than men. Second, in certain cases workers were actually better off after leaving their jobs than before, especially when taxes and government benefits were taken into account. This was particularly true of the men in this sample. Third, the government's benefits seemed to be effective in making up for most of the earning losses at least in the case of relatively low-paying activities like textiles and clothing manufacture. This last finding is likely to be true of most of the industrial societies, especially the welfare states of northern Europe.

It is useful to look also at some wider data for Canada. A report of the Canadian government on a Labor Force Tracking Survey suggests that the private income loss (after taxes and government benefits) over three years to a worker, who lost a job in a textile plant cutback, was only Canadian $2,100.[16]

The earning losses of apparel workers, unfortunately not differentiated by sex, has been estimated for the United States.[17] The distinction made in the study is between those who were permanently separated from their employers and those who were not. The former group experienced large average losses ($10,800 on a present value basis over three years), only half of which was made up by unemployment compensation and trade adjustment assistance. The latter group experienced negligible losses. For the purposes of examining the effects of trade liberalization or cheaper imports, it seems to be the former group that is relevant. Although significant, the private losses of separated workers, after government transfers, amounted to only about $2,000 a year per worker for the three years.

The private costs of worker adjustment can be set against the social costs of the protection that postpones that adjustment. For Canada

[16] See *A Report of the Labor Force Tracking Project/Costs of Labor Adjustments Study* (Ottawa: Department of Industry, Trade, and Commerce, Government of Canada, 1979), p. 35.

[17] See Walter Corson, Walter Nicholson, David Richardson, and Andrea Vayda, *Final Report: Survey of Trade Adjustment Assistance Recipients*, report prepared by Mathematica Policy Research for the Office of Foreign Economic Affairs (Washington: US Department of Labor, 1979; processed), table VI.5.

the study by Jenkins, already cited, analyzes the cost per job saved.[18] Using values of labor input per unit of output he estimates that in 1979 Canadian tariffs saved 7,458 man-years of employment and the quotas, 6,016 man-years of employment. The annual consumer cost of the tariff per man-year of employment preserved was Canadian $36,035 and of the quotas, Canadian $32,959. More to the point, the deadweight annual economic loss per man-year of employment preserved was Canadian $2,804 for the tariffs and Canadian $14,386 for the quotas.

At the same time, the highest estimate of the gross earning losses of laid-off workers in Sherbrooke, excluding all government transfer payments to the affected workers, was Canadian $14,153 over five years for a 25-year old single woman (under the Labor Force Tracking Survey).[19] Thus, the *annual* economic cost of the quotas per man-year of employment preserved exceeded the highest estimate of the *present value* of the gross costs of the displacement of one worker over five years.

On a present value basis the economic cost of the quotas, if maintained forever, (with a 3 percent growth of the market and a 7 percent discount rate) would be about Canadian $360,000 per man-year of employment preserved. For tariffs the corresponding figure would be Canadian $70,000. At the same time, the highest private cost of job loss would have a present value of less than Canadian $5,000 after government transfers.[20] Thus given the government's other benefits, a social cost of Canadian $360,000 would be borne, if the bilateral restrictions were maintained indefinitely, in order to save workers who would otherwise lose their jobs from a private loss of at most Canadian $5,000 each. In other words, for every cent that a worker who would otherwise lose his job is better off, society as a whole is 72 cents worse off as a result of a permanent policy of quantitative restrictions.

Present Status and Future of the MFA

Despite its economic irrationality, the MFA goes rolling on. On December 22, 1981, a protocol extending the MFA for four-and-a-

[18] See Jenkins, *Costs and Consequences of the New Protectionism*, table 7.

[19] See Glenday, Jenkins, and Evans, *Worker Adjustment to Liberal Trade*, table 3.

[20] Ibid., table 9.

half years was agreed in Geneva. What are the main characteristics of this renewal? The text is, as always, silent on practical ways of reaching the long-run goal of ending these costly and disruptive restrictions. The text is also vaguely and ambiguously worded. Thus, while the infamous words of the previous protocol on "jointly agreed reasonable departures" no longer appear, which can only be an improvement, it is not obvious that any practices justified under that clause will be outlawed.

There are several important new openings for more restrictive measures:

• A decline in the rate of growth of per capita consumption in textiles and clothing in importing countries is referred to as "an element which may be relevant to the recurrence or exacerbation of a situation of market disruption." This reflects the view that domestic industries are entitled to a certain market share with import growth related to market growth (paragraph 4).

• So-called dominant suppliers are obligated to find and contribute "to mutually acceptable solutions to particular problems relative to particularly large restraint levels" (paragraph 6). This compromise text arose from a European Community proposal for a specific provision permitting such restraint levels to be adapted (i.e., cutback). No such provision is included in the protocol. The importing countries could, however, be expected to claim that permission for cutbacks is implicit, notwithstanding the express contrary provisions of the MFA.

• The minimum flexibility provisions of the MFA can be violated: in agreement with so-called dominant suppliers, where a growth rate lower than the norm of 6 percent growth has been justified (paragraph 9); and in agreements made by countries claiming that their minimum viable production is threatened (paragraph 11). In both cases, "any mutually acceptable arrangements" with regard to flexibility may be agreed.

• Bilateral agreements can include an "antisurge" mechanism to limit full utilization of previously underutilized restraint levels. As Hong Kong and South Korea fill their quotas, it is clear that this mechanism is likely to affect other developing country suppliers more (paragraph 10).

There is also some language implying greater discipline on the importers:

• A Subcommittee of the Textile Committee on adjustment will be established, replacing the previous Working Group (paragraph 15).

- There is a commitment to provide relevant specific information on market disruption, when it is used as a justification for restriction, and to review the supposed market disruption periodically (paragraph 8).
- Mention is made (in paragraph 12) of small suppliers and new entrants and the text is full of things that "should" normally not be done to them, like imposing restraints (clause a), preventing them from obtaining "commercial quantities of imports" (clause b), restraining their cotton exports, which should be given "special consideration" (clause c), or exploiting the provisions relating to the "exceptional circumstances" in which growth rates of less than 6 percent are permitted (clause d).
- Developing countries restricted under the antisurge mechanism will be entitled to compensation elsewhere (paragraph 10).

The result of these negotiations was a permissive MFA from the point of view of importers who wish to restrict growth, and one that certainly embodies no procedure for its termination.[21] The implications of MFA III became clear, however, only in the course of the negotiations over the bilateral agreements which are authorized by Article 4 of the MFA. These negotiations took place during 1982 under a threat by the European Community to withdraw from the MFA if it did not get what it wanted. Fortunately (or unfortunately, depending on one's point of view) the Community was sufficiently content with what it obtained to stay inside the MFA framework.

Because of strong and reasonably well-coordinated resistance by the exporting countries, the importers failed to get all that they demanded in the bilateral negotiations. Indeed, the agreements that were finally made do not appear to be as restrictive as the pronouncements of 1981 and 1982 had led one to fear. Nevertheless, they are highly restrictive—probably more so even than those in effect under the second MFA. The difference between the negotiations of 1977 and those of 1981 and 1982 was that in the former year the change in the degree of restrictiveness was considerable, while in the latter case it was far more modest. Unfortunately, however, the general movement is still in the same direction.

The United States has had extremely effective constraints on all textile imports from "low-cost" suppliers since the early 1970s, (although it has recently had difficulties in reaching an agreement on

---

[21] For a thorough discussion of the provisions of the third MFA, see Bhagirath L. Das, "The GATT Multi-Fiber Arrangement," *Journal of World Trade Law* (March–April 1983), pp. 95–105.

the control of imports from China). Moreover, during the life of MFA II, repenting of its relative liberalism (compared to the European Community) in 1977, the United States repeatedly renegotiated its agreements with its major suppliers in a more restrictive direction.

It is impossible to discuss all twenty or so of the new US agreements, (which is unfortunate since they all tend to have special features but is inevitable for the same reason). Nevertheless, that with Hong Kong is sufficiently revealing (and important). This agreement was ratified in June 1982 and runs from January 1982 to the end of December 1987 (the first year superseding the final year of the previous 1977 agreement). Restraints were imposed on some twenty-six categories which account for about 60 percent of Hong Kong's exports to the United States. The base levels for 1982 were 1981 trade, which meant a cutback from the previously agreed 1982 restraint level of about 2.5 percent. Growth rates were set at either 0.5 or 1.5 percent a year, but with 18 of the 26 categories at the lower rate.[22] Any unrestrained categories can be put under restraint following consultation.

On balance, the agreement with Hong Kong imposes very low growth on items in which Hong Kong has shown a marked comparative advantage. Moreover, the agreement appears to make Hong Kong's right to take advantage of the flexibility provisions of the MFA subject to consultations. It does not include an "antisurge" mechanism, however, (although the removal of restrictions on a number of categories with the option of imposing fresh restraints in the future may turn out to have the same effect).

The European Community has reached agreement with 25 countries under MFA III, as well as imposed unilateral limits on exports from Taiwan and obtained a separate agreement with Yugoslavia. The Community has also reached informal agreement on the control of exports from associate countries, other than Turkey, with which it has had difficulties. Like the United States, it now appears to be having difficulty in reaching a new agreement with China.

The Community's MFA agreements, which run until the end of 1986, are similar to those under MFA II but with growth rates in the more sensitive categories about 1 percent a year lower than under

---

[22] For purposes of comparison, in the agreement with the Republic of Korea of December 1982, there are 32 categories with specified restrained levels. Growth rates are between 0 and 6 percent but in 18 cases the growth rates are 0.6 percent or less. Thus here too many growth rates have been set at very low levels.

the previous agreements. This means, in effect, that the growth rates are between 0.2 and 0.5 percent a year on Group I categories (the most sensitive) and between 1.5 and 2.5 percent a year on Group II (the next most sensitive). Growth rates on other categories, where under restraint, are mostly between 4 and 5 percent. To indicate coverage: in the agreement with Hong Kong, restraints levels have been agreed on 60 product categories, but there would be fewer restraints in agreements with other exporters.

In the case of the so-called dominant suppliers (Hong Kong, the Republic of Korea, and Macao) the Community wanted cutbacks of 10 percent on restraint levels for the most sensitive clothing categories but in the end settled for cutbacks of 6 to 8 percent. It should be noted that these cutbacks, when combined with the flexibility provisions, generally do not entail a reduction in actual trade in the sensitive categories. Partly for this reason, the Community wanted to impose severe restraints on the use of the flexibility provisions of the MFA but had to settle for smaller reductions in what the MFA mandates (in Annex 14.B) than it desired. While being restrictive with the dominant suppliers, the Community offered step jumps in base levels for some of the smaller suppliers and argues that it was its treatment of the former that made the latter possible.

Apart from tighter control on growth and reductions in base levels for certain suppliers the Community introduced (or attempted to introduce) four new elements in its bilateral agreements: a provision for outward processing; an antisurge mechanism; a revised and generally more liberal "basket extractor" mechanism; and summary penalties on circumvention. In the event, none of these new elements appear to have made any significant difference to the situation existing under MFA II. One potentially important innovation, however, is the authorization for members of the Association of South East Asian Nations (ASEAN) to exchange quotas among themselves.

In sum, MFA III and the bilateral agreements reached under it can be seen as another small turn of the protectionist screw.

Lessons of the MFA

The MFA and its predecessors offer two important general lessons for those interested in commercial policy.

The first lesson is that a sectoral system of discriminatory protection tends to develop in the direction of greater restrictiveness. This follows from the political process that motivates its design. Most of the significant producers are directly satisfied or indirectly bought off:

domestic producers by protection; exporters from powerful countries by exemption from protection and by the protection against some of their competitors; and exporters from competitive restricted suppliers by the ability to enjoy the fruits of the cartelization that export restraints permit. Those most damaged—consumers, other industries in the protecting countries, and potentially competitive exporters—either do not notice what is going on or are politically weak. They are, therefore, barely taken into account. Moreover, in many countries the particular sectoral actions are taken without public discussion or even visibility.

The second lesson is that authorization of a system of selective safeguards tends to increase the resort to such measures. At the same time, the various restrictions on the right to exploit this privilege tend to erode. In other words, it is impossible in the long run to limit abuse of even tightly restricted permission to abuse a basic obligation like nondiscrimination. Each deviation is a precedent for the next until one reaches a stage like the present in textiles: a system based rather on coercion than on universally acceptable, economically sensible rules.

In the light of this experience, the MFA can serve a purpose for those responsible for developing either a GATT code on safeguards or commercial policy for vulnerable industries. Like the wreck of a ship on concealed rocks, it is a warning to the unwary.

CHAPTER 15

Structural Adjustment and Trade Policy in the International Steel Industry

Ingo Walter

Increasingly, questions of international trade policy have been shifting from broad issues, such as general tariff levels and behavioral codes for nontariff distortions, to problems of structural adjustment at the level of individual industries. Few have been as intensely scrutinized, or subject to more acrimonious debate and intergovernmental dispute, as has the steel sector. Here is a basic building block of the modern industrial state—a highly capital-intensive, regionally concentrated, technologically variegated industry, vital to the national defense, with powerful input linkages to many other sectors. Here, too, is an industry beset with intractable problems, ranging from monopoly unionism, pollution controls, and plant obsolescence to direct and indirect government intervention, lethargic management, and highly cyclical demand.

Exposed to the international competitive environment, these industry attributes and problems combine to create a highly charged set of trade policy issues. Long-term shifts in competitive advantage within the industry run up against serious structural adjustment difficulties. Short-term demand variations encourage beggar-thy-neighbor tactics on the part of firms and governments alike. Unprecedented exchange rate movements alter competitive conditions facing enterprises with severely limited capacities for absorbing shocks. Direct government ownership of steel firms in market economies and penetration by suppliers in centrally planned economies raise questions about appropriate competitive behavior. And the need to deal with short-term problems gives ample opportunity to introduce long-term competitive distortions.

This chapter traces the evolution of the international steel industry during the past several decades, with specific reference to competitive relationships and policy responses. The dynamics of structural adjustment are related to the politics of sectoral protection. The policy analysis that follows focuses on prospective global scenarios for the industry, and the prospects for maintaining the predominance of economically driven—as against politically driven—outcomes.

The Evolving Saga of International Steel

There are four principal characters in the international steel story: the United States, the European Community, Japan, and a geographically dispersed collection of the more advanced developing countries, with supporting roles played by Canada, South Africa, Spain, and certain East European countries. The broad sweep of the main story line—focused on long-term shifts in competitive advantage at the industry level—generates a number of subplots, which differ widely among countries and regions.

The United States

The global preeminence of the American steel industry lasted for over seventy years, based on the existence of a large domestic and export market, international technological leadership, low-cost raw materials, plentiful skilled labor, capital adequacy, and significant economies of scale. That era ended in the late 1950s, when the industry gradually began to lose its international competitive position. This occurred for a number of reasons.

First, and perhaps most important, has been the key role of monopoly labor, linked to the oligopolistic structure of the industry itself. In the 1950s, average hourly earnings in the industry were only slightly above the average for all US manufacturing employment. As indicated in table 15.1, by 1967 they stood at 128 percent of the manufacturing average. By 1975 they had reached 148 percent, and by 1980 had increased still further, to 163 percent. The gap actually declined from 1961 to 1970, but widened rapidly thereafter. Meantime, total hourly employment costs (wages and fringe benefits) rose even faster, from $4.00 in 1961 to $18.45 in 1980. Steelworker compensation also outpaced by far the consumer price index.

There are obviously a variety of reasons why labor compensation in an industry might differ substantially from the national manufacturing average. But it may not be unreasonable to suggest that management's resistance to extraordinary wage demands on the part of

TABLE 15.1 STEELWORKER COMPENSATION TRENDS, 1961–81

Year	Steel industry, average hourly earnings (dollars/ hour)	(1961 = 100)	All manufacturing average hourly earnings (dollars/ hour)	(1961 = 100)	Steelworker relative average hourly earnings [(1)/(2)]	Consumer Price Index (1961 = 100)	Steel, average hours worked divided by average hours paid
1961	3.20	100.0	2.32	100.0	1.38	100.0	.95
1962	3.29	102.8	2.39	103.0	1.38	101.1	.94
1963	3.36	105.0	2.46	106.0	1.37	102.3	.94
1964	3.41	106.6	2.53	109.1	1.35	103.7	.93
1965	3.46	108.1	2.61	112.5	1.33	105.5	.92
1966	3.58	111.9	1.72	117.2	1.32	108.5	.94
1967	3.62	113.1	2.83	122.0	1.28	111.6	.92
1968	3.82	119.4	3.01	129.7	1.27	116.3	.92
1969	4.09	127.8	3.19	137.5	1.28	122.5	.94
1970	4.22	131.9	3.36	144.8	1.26	129.8	.92
1971	4.57	142.8	3.57	153.9	1.28	135.4	.91
1972	5.15	106.9	3.81	164.2	1.35	139.8	.91
1973	5.56	173.8	4.07	175.4	1.37	148.5	.93
1974	6.38	199.4	4.40	189.7	1.45	164.8	.91
1975	7.11	222.2	4.81	207.3	1.48	179.9	.89
1976	7.86	245.6	5.19	223.7	1.51	190.3	.91
1977	8.67	270.9	5.63	242.7	1.54	202.6	.91
1978	9.70	303.1	6.17	265.9	1.57	218.0	.90
1979	10.77	336.6	6.69	288.4	1.61	243.0	.91
1980	11.84	370.0	7.22	311.2	1.63	275.7	.91

Sources: American Iron and Steel Institute, *Annual Statistical Reports*, 1980. Bureau of Labor Statistics, *Monthly Labor Review*, April 1981.

the United Steelworkers of America (USW) reinforced by a no-strike pledge in 1974—was weakened by the assumption that the associated costs could simply be passed through to consumers via a tightly knit industry pricing structure. It is this assumption whose validity was progressively eroded by intermaterial substitution and import competition.

Value added per production worker failed to keep pace with wage rates in the US steel industry during these years. In 1960 this figure stood at 121 percent of the national manufacturing average; by 1980 it had declined to 103 percent. As an international comparison, labor productivity in the US steel industry, as measured by physical output (tonnages) per man year increased 27 percent during 1970–80 compared with about 85 percent in Japan; at the end of that period absolute labor productivity in the two countries was roughly the same (Walter and Jones 1981). As against its major international competitors, unit labor costs in the US steel industry rose (1964 = 100) to

321 in 1980 (223 for all manufacturing), compared with 220 in Japan (218), with 197 in West Germany (215), with 341 in France (281), and with 691 in the United Kingdom (528), (Kreinin 1982).

Additional labor problems in the US steel industry have included stiff resistance by the union to changes in work rules and crew sizes, seniority requirements that have prevented assignment of the most skilled workers to particular tasks, poor worker training programs, sloppy attitudes about quality, high levels of absenteeism and labor turnover, and confrontational industrial relations at the plant level.

As noted, the extraordinary rise in labor costs appears to have been passed through to domestic purchasers by virtue of the oligopolistic competitive structure of the industry. The evidence in this respect has been reviewed repeatedly in recent years. For example, in 1980 submission to the US International Trade Commission (USITC), the US Department of Justice indicated that "since the 1930s the conduct of domestic steel producers has been characterized by oligopoly and administered prices that have been relatively inflexible downward" (Department of Justice 1980, p. 6). The Council on Wage and Price Stability likewise argued that price rigidity is the pattern of domestic steel producer behavior and suggested that, unlike other metals, these prices have been insensitive to changes in market demand. Indeed, when world prices of steel fell in 1969–70 and again in 1974–75, the council reported that "US domestic prices remained comparatively stable, which opened a large gap between US and imported steel prices" (COWPS 1977, p. 20).

Relatively stable prices established as a makeup over costs are the hallmark of oligopoly, and this seems an accurate description of an industry in which the seven major steel producers accounted for about 85 percent of domestic output in 1981. At least part of the explanation of how this industrial structure emerged can be found in the economies of scale that exist in the basic steelmaking process, resulting in higher prices and smaller outputs than would exist under more competitive conditions. The relatively low level of profitability in this industry seems to suggest that the majority of these gains did in fact accrue to labor, with adoption of a fairly rigid cost-plus administered pricing rule by all domestic suppliers eroding management's resistance to extraordinary wage claims.

Second, the nature, availability, and cost of technology in the industry has changed dramatically over the years. Steelmaking today involves very little truly proprietary technology. Production techniques are relatively standardized, and innovations can be purchased internationally in the open market on a competitive basis, either from some of the more advanced steel firms or from contract engineering concerns. Innovation tends to come at the margin—in the form of process improvements such as computer-controlled production-equipment—and is usually widely available. Nevertheless, US firms have been slow to upgrade their plants to world technical standards in the production process—such areas as continuous casting, direct reduction, and advances in basic oxygen steelmaking, as well as production-control equipment. While the US industry has been rather innovative in product improvements such as dual-phase, microalloyed, and coated steels, the traditional US technological edge is long gone with respect to basic carbon steel as well as certain specialty and stainless product lines.

Third, capital investment in the industry has been inadequate both quantitatively and, in terms of embodied technology, qualitatively as well. The industry has consistently had difficulty attracting debt and equity capital for major investments in steelmaking (as opposed to corporate diversification) due to unimpressive and erratic earnings in the steel business generally. The result is an average age of capital stock which significantly exceeds that prevailing in competitor countries. Moreover, with a few exceptions most capital investment has gone into "rounding out" of capacity in existing plants, rather than "greenfield" plants. This has produced an average level of in-plant efficiency, attributable to design, layout, and equipment quality factors that has lagged significantly behind the foreign competition (Kawahito 1981).

Fourth, government enforcement of environmental and worker health and safety standards has seriously affected US steelmakers, who are engaged in an inherently dirty and dangerous business (Walter 1975). Estimates are that expenditures for such purposes during the 1970s absorbed about 17 percent of total capital investment in the industry (American Iron and Steel Institute 1980). Comparable environmental and health and safety requirements have confronted steel industries abroad as well, including Japan. But in some cases they have lagged well behind the United States. In others, a significant part of the costs were borne by government, and in no case were the measures imposed on the industry by regulators in such an abrupt, incoherent and confrontational manner as in the United States.

Fifth, unlike most other countries, the US government has been only indirectly involved in business decisions affecting the steel sector at the level of the firm. It has, however, played an important part in setting prices and wages in the industry as a whole, beginning with the Truman administration's threats to nationalize all steel firms in 1952 and the Kennedy administration's jawboning on prices in the early 1960s, continuing through various wage-price guideline schemes

TABLE 15.2   THE US STEEL MARKET AND IMPORT COMPETITION, 1960–80
(thousand net tons and percentage)

	Shipments by American steel producers	Exports	Imports	Apparent consumption
1960	71,147	2,977	3,359	71,531
1961	66,126	1,990	3,263	67,299
1962	70,552	2,013	4,100	72,639
1963	75,552	2,224	5,446	78,777
1964	84,945	3,442	6,440	87,943
1965	92,666	2,496	10,383	100,553
1966	89,995	1,724	10,753	99,024
1967	83,897	1,685	11,455	93,667
1968	91,856	2,170	17,960	107,646
1969	93,877	5,229	14,034	102,682
1970	90,798	7,062	13,364	97,100
1971	87,038	2,827	18,304	102,515
1972	91,805	2,873	17,681	106,613
1973	111,430	4,052	15,150	122,528
1974	109,472	5,833	15,970	119,609
1975	79,957	2,953	12,012	89,016
1976	89,447	2,654	14,285	101,078
1977	91,147	2,003	19,307	108,451
1978	97,935	2,422	21,135	116,648
1979	100,262	2,818	17,518	114,962
1980	83,853	4,101	15,491	95,243

Source: American Iron and Steel Institute, Washington, *Statistical Report*, various issues.
a. Nine European Community countries.

affecting all industries in the 1970s. In addition, there have been severe legal constraints on the ability of firms to undertake cost-saving mergers and joint ventures, yet with little government effort to curb the monopoly power of organized labor. Taken together, these external factors may well have contributed to profit levels chronically inadequate to finance capital expansion and modernization. The US steel sector thus suffered the negative aspects of government meddling in economic decisions without having the benefits of access to the public purse available to its competitors abroad.

On the positive side, steel is an energy intensive industry, and is heavily dependent on coal, oil, natural gas, and electric power, both directly and indirectly in the process of manufacture. The rise in world energy costs since 1973, and in particular the dramatic jump in 1979, is well known. The US government, using price controls, allocation schemes and related measures, for a long time failed to allow these

	Imports as percentage of apparent consumption	Japan (percentage)		European[a] Community (percentage)		All others (percentage)	
1960	4.7	596	17.9	2,080	62.4	777	19.7
1961	4.7	597	18.9	2,117	66.9	451	14.2
1962	5.6	1,072	26.1	2,337	57.0	692	16.9
1963	6.9	1,808	33.2	2,596	47.6	1,048	19.2
1964	7.3	2,446	38.0	2,870	44.6	1,123	17.4
1965	10.3	4,418	42.5	4,911	47.3	1,054	10.2
1966	10.9	4,851	45.1	4,589	42.7	991	9.2
1967	1.2	4,468	41.6	5,660	52.6	625	5.8
1968	16.7	7,294	40.6	8,400	46.8	2,266	12.6
1969	13.7	6,253	44.6	6,093	43.4	1,689	12.0
1970	13.8	5,935	44.4	5,397	40.4	2,032	15.2
1971	17.9	6,908	37.7	8,513	46.5	2,882	15.7
1972	16.6	6,440	36.4	7,779	48.1	2,728	15.4
1973	12.4	5,637	37.2	6,510	43.0	3,003	19.8
1974	13.4	6,159	38.6	6,424	40.2	3,387	21.2
1975	13.5	5,844	48.6	4,123	34.3	2,046	17.0
1976	14.1	7,984	55.9	3,188	22.3	3,113	21.8
1977	17.8	7,820	40.5	6,833	35.4	4,654	24.1
1978	18.1	6,487	30.7	7,463	35.3	7,185	34.0
1979	15.2	6,336	36.2	5,405	30.8	5,777	33.0
1980	16.3	6,005	38.8	3,887	25.1	5,599	36.1

cost increases to have their full impact on domestic industry or consumers. Throughout most of the 1970s, US energy costs remained far below those in the rest of the world, and only at the end of the decade did they begin to rise as a result of gradual decontrol. This was made possible, of course, by the considerable degree of US energy self-sufficiency in relation to Western Europe and Japan, and by the political unacceptability in the 1970s of dramatic energy cost increases and their potential effects on domestic income distribution. One could thus argue that US steel manufacturers benefited significantly in the international competitive environment from this particular energy policy. Their energy costs, while rising, were kept far below those of their European and Japanese rivals, whose competitiveness was duly eroded.

The global oil price increase additionally affected foreign steel suppliers because of its impact on transport costs. These costs tend to follow global energy prices, while domestic transport costs—in addition to being lower on average—were kept in check by controlled domestic energy prices. On the other hand, dramatic reductions in bulk transport costs have favored certain steelmakers abroad, both in the effective cost of raw materials imports and in the cost of shipping finished steel to major markets, including the United States.

Finally, the professional management that has run the US steel industry over the years can only be judged as poor. Oligopoly conditions bred managerial lethargy. Minimal consideration was, for a long time, given to future global competitive conditions in the industry and how best to meet them. Innovations, even when developed at home, were slow to be recognized and often first applied abroad. Little though was devoted at the corporate level to adaptability, diversification, or foreign investment activity. Marginal domestic and export markets were neglected, often to be captured by imports. Foot dragging was the general response to growing environmental and health and safety challenges. Successful product innovation was frequently the result of market inroads of other materials, such as glass, aluminum, plastics, and paper, rather than in internal drive to advance the state of the art. And the condition of management-labor relations in the industry was a perennial cause for concern.

The results of these developments on trade flows are not difficult to identify. Whereas US steel imports remained under 5 percent of apparent consumption in the 1950s, a 116-day strike in 1959 for the first time demonstrated the viability of imported steel for many domestic customers. During most of the 1960–82 period, prices of US integrated suppliers lay significantly above those of Japanese and European suppliers—20 percent and 30 percent, respectively, in 1981— subject to exchange rate movements and other sources of price volatility, although the differential was generally much smaller or absent entirely in the case of nonintegrated suppliers (Dirlam and Mueller 1982). From 4 percent of apparent consumption in 1960, steel imports rose to 16.7 percent in 1968 and a high of 18.1 percent in 1978, as depicted in table 15.2. The data also illustrate the dramatically growing role of "other" suppliers (particularly Canada and certain developing countries) in the 1970s.

While the share of imports in US apparent consumption rose steadily from 1973 to 1978, the share accounted for by the European Community fell from 43.0 percent to 35.3 percent, and further to 25.1 percent in 1980. In contrast, over the 1973–78 period the share accounted for by Canadian imports rose from 7.2 to 11.2 percent and that from other suppliers, such as Taiwan and Korea, from 12.6 to 22.8 percent. Thus, during the latter part of the 1970s the traditional sources of imports were losing ground to new suppliers.

Apart from price advantages, foreign suppliers in some cases are able to provide better quality than domestic mills and, as they gained market foothold, better services as well—especially in often neglected smaller regional markets. But the real problem for US suppliers centered on the price-suppression effects of imports, which rendered it impossible to make posted prices stick and led to widespread discounting and profit erosion.

Trade Policy Response

Deepening import penetration under the conditions in which the US steel industry has found itself in the past 20 years naturally led to intensified protection-seeking behavior, in 1967 for the first time forging an alliance between major firms in the industry and the United Steelworkers on trade policy matters.

In 1968, American steelmakers were able to obtain protection through voluntary export restraints (VERs) on carbon steel negotiated by the State Department with Japanese and European suppliers, having presented a credible threat to alternatively ram quota legislation through Congress. The VERs provided for import limits of 5.75 million tons each in 1969, with permissible increases of 5 percent in 1970 and 1971. They were later extended to the end of 1974, at which time they were abolished under conditions of extremely strong domestic steel demand—and needled by an antitrust suit filed on behalf of steel users by Consumers Union.

In 1976 a depressed domestic steel market, coupled with a new surge of (mostly Japanese) imports, allegedly dumped in the American market, moved American steel firms to seek more airtight forms of protection. Relief was first sought through a petition filed with the Office of the Special Trade Representative by the American Iron and Steel Institute, and then through individual antidumping suits filed with the Treasury Department. The Gilmore Steel Corporation filed the first of these in February 1977, followed by the United States Steel Corporation in September—both against Japanese suppliers— and over a dozen others by the end of the year. These effectively swamped Treasury's ability to cope with the time-consuming and complex dumping investigations. In February 1978, following a report by an interagency task force, the Carter administration introduced a more systematic protection device, the trigger price mechanism (TPM).

Ostensibly an antidumping and not a protectionist measure, the TPM established "fair value" import reference prices constructed on the basis of estimated Japanese production costs, profit margins, and expenses. Imports entering below these reference prices were presumed to be dumped (sold at less than fair value—LTFV) and were then subjected to "fast-track" antidumping investigations. The dubious nature of the fair-value estimates and the impact of the trigger device itself through increased risk faced by shippers and importers deterred low-priced steel imports in general. Especially the Japanese import share dropped dramatically from 1977 to 1978. It has been estimated that the TPM caused import prices in the United States to rise by about 10 percent in 1979 (Crandall 1981).

Throughout this period, an argument developed at the public policy level regarding the benefits and costs of steel protection with respect to the interests of the nation as a whole. One study, for example, concluded that possible lost earnings of steelworkers declared redundant or placed on short-time, together with possible losses incurred by shareholders, that could have resulted from removing all restrictions on steel imports over the period 1969–73 would have been more than offset by the gains to steel consumers (Jondrow 1978). Other studies come to similar conclusions (FTC 1977; Crandall 1981).

However, the TPM did not succeed in stilling protectionist sentiment among US steelmakers for long. Because of the imperfect substitutability between imported and domestically produced steel, the TPM caused *average* domestic steel prices to rise by only about 1 percent in 1979 (Crandall 1981). The TPM procedure also gave high-cost European steel suppliers a virtual license to dump in the US market, leading to inflated European import shares at the expense of Japan. Together with a reversal of the upward movement of the Japanese yen, ending a series of quarterly upward trigger price adjustments, this prompted the United States Steel Corporation to file a massive antidumping suit against European Community (EC) suppliers in March of 1980. In retaliation, the Carter administration immediately suspended the TPM, established at the outset as an alternative to antidumping action. Imports from Europe dropped precipitously under the new threat, especially in view of a preliminary finding of material injury by the USITC. In an accord between the government and the steel industry, stimulated in part by threats of European retaliation, the TPM was reinstated in October 1980—with significantly (12 percent) higher trigger prices as well as special provisions for quantitative import restrictions in the event of future import "surges," accelerated depreciation on the industry's capital equipment, and pollution control relief for the domestic steel firms. US Steel thereupon abandoned the suit.

The revitalized TPM notwithstanding, imports once again began to rise steadily during 1981 (to over 19.9 million tons, or about 23 percent of US steel sales), especially from Europe and Canada, influenced in part by a strengthened dollar on foreign exchange markets. This prompted some European suppliers to begin selling steel in the United States below trigger prices on the presumption that they could withstand TPM scrutiny, and indeed the Reagan administration proposed lowering trigger prices for certain steel products entering Great Lakes ports. Both Canadian and European suppliers sought "preclearance" of their prices to insure them against antidumping investigations under the TPM.

Once again, with the domestic industry operating at about 60 percent of capacity, at least 10 major plants closed, and with employment down from 403,000 in 1970 to 285,000 in 1981, threats of suits aimed at alleged subsidization of the industry in Western Europe and certain other countries emerged. Fearing yet another collapse of the TPM, the government itself filed suit against suppliers of a range of carbon steel products in Canada, France, Belgium, Romania, Brazil, Spain, and South Africa, and at the same time desperately tried to convince suppliers to cut back their shipments and increase prices to the US market. The European defense rested primarily on the exchange rate issue, massive imports of oil-country goods in short supply in the United States, and semi-finished slab imports bought by the American steel industry itself, indicating a notable lack of sympathy for the US position.

There followed in December 1981 and January 1982 a preliminary USITC finding of material injury in the government's favor, signs of some progress in coming to terms with the Europeans on voluntary monitoring of quantities and prices on steel shipped to the US market, and direct intervention by President Reagan with the US industry. Nevertheless, in early February 1982 the seven largest US steel firms filed 110 charges of unfair trading practices (3 million pages of documentation) against 41 competitive suppliers of nine steel products in 11 countries including Belgium, France, Italy, Luxembourg, the Netherlands, Spain, Romania, United Kingdom, West Germany, South Africa, and Brazil. Those deemed to warrant investigation covered about $2 billion worth of trade, or about 20 percent of total US carbon steel imports in 1981. With carbon steel selling in the United States for about $500 per ton, the allegations included European sales as much as $300 below production cost ($533 in the case of Britain). Once more, the TPM was suspended in retaliation—a suspension that left the door open for sizable preemptive purchases by US importers.

Among the US industry's complaints this time around was that European suppliers were shipping via dummy third parties to evade the TPM, thereby ignoring implicit agreement on the part of the Europeans to comply with the trigger prices. In some cases, importers owned or controlled by European steel suppliers apparently brought steel in at the trigger price and subsequently sold it at a lower price—with the parent organizations covering the losses. Alternatively, an affiliated buyer offshore might have obtained the steel at a price well below the trigger, and then sold to an affiliated US distributor at the trigger, booking the profits offshore (Dirlam and Mueller 1982).

By the middle of 1982, US domestic steel shipments had dropped to their lowest levels since 1970, with the industry operating at only 43 percent of rated capacity (down from 77 percent in 1981) and massive losses (up to $55 per ton) encountered by all of the major firms. One supplier, McLouth Steel, filed for bankruptcy and was ordered to cease all steelmaking operations. Capital spending and plant maintenance budgets were cut back sharply, nonsteel assets sold, white collar staff reduced, nonunion salaries and benefits slashed, and major steelmaking facilities closed—some permanently. The industry also asked the United Steelworkers to renegotiate their basic labor agreement, in particular to eliminate the open-ended cost of living adjustments, and institute work-rule changes and cut crew sizes, and reduce expensive health care benefits. All of this appeared to signal a very substantial de facto structural adjustment and slimming down of the US carbon steel industry driven by the severe recession in demand as well as by imports.

Besides the apparent view that the TPM represented an unreliable instrument in affording acceptable levels of protection, the US steel industry seemed set on applying massive pressure on the administration to negotiate voluntary export restraints with the Europeans, as had been done a year earlier with Japan in the case of automobiles.

Among the European rejoinders appeared the $6.4 billion purchase of Marathon Oil Company by US Steel, allegedly prima facie evidence against serious injury. Rumblings of retaliation centered on soybeans, textiles, electronics, and other manufactures, together with possible withdrawal of European support for new US trade initiatives on agriculture and services.

By late February of 1982, the USITC had eliminated all but 38 of the complaints. These covered imports of carbon steel plate, sheet strip, and structurals from Britain, France, West Germany, Italy, Belgium, the Netherlands, Luxembourg, Romania, and Brazil accounting for about 90 percent of 1981 steel imports from these countries by volume and 85 percent by value. In April 1982 a section 301 investigation was started by the Special Trade Representative of stainless and alloy tool steel imports from Austria, Britain, France, Italy, and Sweden, following allegations of "massive" subsidization leveled by the domestic industry and the United Steelworkers. Finally, in early May 1982, the industry's complaints were extended with the filing by US Steel of subsidy complaints against South Korea, France, Italy, Brazil, and West Germany on welded pipe, which had been in acutely short supply only a year earlier. This action, along with additional complaints by US Steel against South Korea on plate and sheet, completed the coverage of allegations against every major foreign supplier and every major product category, with the notable exception of Japan.[1]

Amid this rapidly unfolding series of events, therefore, the American steel industry and its political allies had hardened their protectionist position. At the end of 1981, American steel prices lay about 20 percent above the domestic prices of the most efficient international supplier (Japan) and 8 percent above the least efficient one (Britain), leading to imports of 1.96 million tons in the first quarter of 1982, or roughly 26 percent of apparent domestic consumption. The combination of high US production costs, unfavorable exchange rate movements, and questionable competitive practices on the part of foreign suppliers—coupled to a serious recession in domestic steel demand—had deeply scarred the structure of steel pricing as well as capacity utilization. Spot prices in early 1982 averaged about $200 per ton below list prices. Even major contract buyers, such as General Motors, announced that steel purchases would henceforth be open to competitive bidding, thereby further eroding traditional price discipline.

As the steel battle strained trade relations particularly between the United States and the EC, imports from Japan remained surprisingly stable, apparently as a result of an informal understanding reached with the Carter administration on a 6 million ton ceiling, which in fact held firm after 1978. The existence of such an understanding was, however, strongly denied by all sides.

As the US complaints wound their way through USITC injury and Commerce Department subsidy investigations, intensive efforts were underway with the EC to seek a compromise solution. US negotiators, in close consultation with domestic steel interests, offered the Europeans a 4 to 4.5 percent share of the American market, while the

---

[1] The US specialty steel industry was likewise active in seeking protection. The broadest antisubsidy case in its history was filed in autumn 1981, charging Austria, France, Italy, Sweden, and UK suppliers, followed by charges in February 1982 against Spain and in April 1982 against West Germany, alleging dumping. The ITC issued a preliminary affirmative material injury ruling in April 1982 in the latter two cases.

EC wanted 6 to 6.5 percent—with exclusion of steel tubes and pipes from any agreement. Throughout, the US government appeared most reluctant to negotiate quotas that would reduce the domestic industry's incentives to pursue adjustment. However, they did propose a pricing formula that would set quota imports close to US domestic prices and require the EC Commission to monitor shipments both by product and by country of origin. Meantime, the domestic industry was arguing that quantitative limits on EC shipments would have to be matched by similar limits on non-EC suppliers.

In June 1982, the Commerce Department issued a preliminary ruling in favor of the subsidy complaints against West Germany, Italy, Britain, Belgium, the Netherlands, Luxembourg, France, Brazil, and South Africa, involving 1981 imports of 3.9 million tons valued at $1.4 billion, or 20 percent of all US steel imports and 4 percent of the total US market. Imports from these sources were subject to an immediate posting of bond equal to the estimated weighted-average subsidies of 20 to 25 percent (falling between one-half percent and 40 percent) to be forfeited in the event of a final subsidy determination in August 1982. A final determination of material injury in October 1982 would then lead to the imposition of permanent, retroactive import duties. Specific alleged subsidy ranges included 20 to 30 percent for France, up to 18 percent for Italy, up to 21 percent for Belgium, and minimal amounts for Germany and the Netherlands. Concurrently, 18 cases of alleged steel dumping were being investigated. And, shortly after the affirmative subsidy finding by the Department of Commerce, a USITC preliminary finding of material injury was announced on the May 1982 complaints regarding hot-rolled sheet, galvanized sheet, and welded carbon pipe from South Korea, and pipe and tube products from Brazil, France, and West Germany.

EC responses included development of a list of products exported by the United States allegedly benefiting from subsidies, a challenge to the legality of the US action under the General Agreement on Tariffs and Trade (GATT), and discussion in the Organization for Economic Cooperation and Development (OECD) Steel Committee. Spokesmen also pointed to violation of the Versailles Summit commitment to continued trade liberalization and to the increased difficulties the EC would have in restructuring its own steel sector. Of particular concern appeared to be the strict US definition of subsidies, including support for company housing and state participation in the industry itself in terms of its impact on the firms' cost of capital. Similarly, EC subsidies designed to *reduce* capacity and redeploy labor were included in the US calculation. At the same time, differences of view emerged *among* EC steel suppliers regarding the possibility of negotiated quotas because of the differential incidence of alleged subsidies and the implications of quantitative limits on exports to the United States for the intra-EC market.

What the American steel industry really appeared to be after was quantitative import limits as the only "reliable" protection device,* to replace what seemed to be regarded as an overly flexible and poorly enforced TPM. With the Japanese already behaving "responsibly," this strongly suggested a de facto Orderly Marketing Agreement (OMA) negotiated with the Europeans covering carbon steel products, and subsequent extension to specialty steel items and even to fabricated steel if the effective protection of fabrication becomes eroded (Kirkland 1982). Thus, despite affirmative subsidy and injury findings, and the promise of more to come, the US industry remained set on quantitative limits in part because of the likelihood of continued relatively free access to the US market for producers in West Germany, the Netherlands, Canada, South Korea, Taiwan, Mexico, and Brazil. Only by maneuvering the government into a politically untenable position vis-à-vis its trading partners using a concerted attack on allegedly unfair trade practices could such a result come about in a political environment ideologically committed to the market economy.

The European Community

While competition for the US steel market has increasingly centered on political rather than economic factors, conditions in the European steel industry have involved far greater intervention on the part of government. Large-scale nationalization of steel firms has occurred in Britain, France, Italy, and Belgium, some dating back to the years immediately following World War II. Massive investments in steel modernization have been financed out of government grants and concessionary credits, adding enormously to productive capacity. However, European governments have often refused to permit obsolescent plants to be shut down, in order to safeguard depressed regions, thereby allowing productive capacity to expand well beyond any reasonable projection of demand. Operating losses among major steel suppliers in Europe have reached epic proportions, with mainly

---

* *Ed. note*: This is precisely what they subsequently obtained. For a discussion of the outcome of the US-EC conflict over antidumping and countervailing duties on steel, see the discussion on steel in chapter 1, this volume.

the German steel firms and small, efficient minimill operators in northern Italy able to produce without massive government subsidy. Aggressive price cutting from time to time marked the European steel producers' attempts to raise rates of capacity utilization.

Late in 1975, the EC Commission announced minimum voluntary reference prices for certain steel products, preceded by a VER agreement negotiated with major Japanese steel suppliers in Mexico City that successfully rolled back Japan's exports by 25.5 percent from 1975 to 1976 (Bradford 1977). Some of these shipments were undoubtedly diverted to the US market in 1976 and 1977. In addition, the Commission set out to gear EC steel production increasingly to export markets, specifically to the United States. However, conditions facing producers in the EC steel market did not improve very much as a result of continued cutthroat pricing by European steel firms, and the EC's "forward program" was thus quickly judged a failure.

In October 1976 a crisis cartel, Eurofer, was created to set and enforce minimum prices for steel reinforcing bars and reference prices for six other product categories. EC producers were forbidden to align their own prices to those of imported steel. Import monitoring and mandatory licensing were introduced, as was a set of uniform antidumping procedures, representing a clear signal that undercutting the established minimum price levels would meet with stern action on the part of Community authorities.

New EC reference prices for steel were instituted on a mandatory basis in May 1977 under the Davignon Plan and seemed to stick reasonably well. However, they had to be protected against erosion by imports, and this was done beginning in December 1977 by means of the "basis price system" (BPS). Announced shortly after the US TPM, the BPS set "fair value" import prices based on estimated Japanese costs for all carbon steel products. Imports below BPS prices met with an immediate assessment of antidumping duties, an official antidumping investigation, and an offer to withdraw these measures if the affected suppliers would agree to negotiate VERs with the Community.

VERs were in fact very quickly negotiated with Austria, Finland, Norway, Sweden, Portugal, and Switzerland, subsequently also by Japan, South Africa, Czechoslovakia, and Spain after preliminary BPS fines had been levied against them. Only after final determination of BPS fines did Hungary, Romania, Australia, Poland, and South Korea also conclude VERs with the Community. The BPS/ VER system, coupled to a tightened dirigiste régime for EC steel, thus sought to deliver a comprehensive governmental "solution" to problems created in large measure by governments themselves.

Yet, because of market pressures and the complexity of steel pricing, actual compliance with EC price dictates was not always forthcoming. By the summer of 1980, the failure of minimum prices to hold up in the face of continued crisis conditions caused the Commission to abandon them completely. In their place, more drastic intervention in the form of mandatory production quotas was introduced in October 1980 under Article 58 of the EC coal and steel treaty and extended in June 1982. The controls were largely adhered to, with the resulting higher prices improving especially the German steel firms' income statements—25 percent of EC steel output was removed from mandatory control and placed under voluntary control in June 1981. Nevertheless, imports from noncontrolled suppliers (especially Brazil and Mexico), price cutting by northern Italian minimill operators, and US import restrictions hit a number of EC suppliers particularly hard and continued to put pressure on the Community régime by threatening to destroy internal price discipline. All of this threatened the 1981 EC commitment to phase out all subsidies to the steel, engineering, and textiles industries by 1985.

Nevertheless, crisis conditions have in fact caused some movement toward restructuring the EC steel industry. Some capacity in older plants has indeed been shut down and the work force reduced commensurately—but not without serious social unrest in heavily impacted areas of Belgium, France, and Germany. In addition, there have been a number of moves toward rationalizing production among existing suppliers.

For example, a 1981 agreement between two major German steel producers, Hoesch and Krupp, to coordinate production is indicative of one form of industry response that reflects EC goals. The two firms were jointly to decide who produces what and where, exchange customer lists, and market each other's products. By complementing the product and process strengths of its partner, each hoped to form a competitive yet smaller entity a proposal replaced later by a new proposal for full merger. Hoesch itself had already been involved with a Dutch steelmaker, Hoogovens, in the Estel partnership, which lost $245 million in 1980 and which had to be broken up in order to ultimately permit a full merger between it and Krupp's steelmaking operation into a new venture called Ruhrstahl. Krupp is to produce some steel on the Rhine, Hoesch concentrating on finished products, with a reduction in the combined work force from 65,000 in 1980 to 45,000 in 1985. Carrying out the plan will involve tapping into German federal and state government allocations of perhaps $1 billion for steel industry restructuring to cover two-thirds of the cost, with the remainder coming from private investors and banks. For the Community as a whole, government aid to the steel industry amounting to $1.4 billion was approved by the Commission in January 1982.

Japan

While the United States and the EC steel industries and their respective governments struggle with unique sets of problems, Japan has remained by far the world's most capable steel supplier, with a major part of its industry concentrated in large-scale, modern, linear-layout, energy-efficient integrated mills, usually located adjacent to deepwater port facilities with easy access to imported raw materials and export shipping.

As noted earlier, Japanese unit labor costs remain well below those in the United States (and Europe), and this advantage is reinforced by high worker motivation and performance. Technically, Japanese mills incorporate the most recent advances in automated, computerized production processes, plant layout based on indigenous innovation, and careful technology monitoring around the world. Unlike the US industry's growth phase in the 1940s and 1950s, the period of major Japanese steel plant construction occurred after such technological developments as bulk carriers, basic oxygen furnaces, continuous casters, and computer process control had been developed. This, plus exceedingly high-leverage financial structures of firms in the industry, favorable tax and antitrust policies, financing of plant construction before the capital-cost spurt of the 1970s, and elimination of historical disadvantages in raw-material cost and availability, all help to account for Japan's preeminent position in international steel markets.

These competitive advantages are perhaps best illustrated by comparative data. Table 15.3 lists major Japanese steel plants in existence during the mid-1970s, when their international competitive advantage was nearing maturity, showing the respective completion dates and projected capacity levels. Most came on stream in the 1960s when capital costs were moderate and the principal postwar steelmaking innovations had been proven out. With plant economics dependent in part upon blast furnace size, table 15.4 indicates the global dominance of Japanese steelmakers in this respect during the late 1970s, with over half of all furnaces over two million tons capacity either installed or under construction in 1977. Table 15.5 shows the placement of Japanese facilities among deepwater world-scale steel plants in 1982, with 10 of 16 such facilities located there—the Burns Harbor,

TABLE 15.3 MAJOR JAPANESE STEEL PLANTS

Company	Name of plant	Date of first operation	1973 output	Projected capacity
			(million metric tons)	
Nippon	Kimitsu	1965	9.0	14.0
	Yawata	1959	9.8	12.0
	Sakai	1961	4.4	4.3
	Nagoya	1958	6.2	7.3
	Oita	1971	3.5	12.0
NKK	Fukayama	1965	11.8	16.0
Kawasaki	Chiba	1952	6.1	6.5
	Mizushima	1961	7.9	10.0
Sumitomo	Wakayama	1960	7.2	9.5
	Kashima	1967	5.2	15.0
Kobe	Kogogawa	1968	4.4	10.0
Total			75.5	116.6

Source: Individual companies.

Indiana plant of Bethlehem Steel being the sole American representative.

Besides in-plant efficiency and highly competitive labor costs, a traditional source of disadvantage faced by Japanese mills, raw materials transport costs declined sharply during the 1960s. Table 15.6 shows such costs dropping by over 50 percent during the decade ended in 1973 to a level equal with those of US Great Lakes mills and only half of those faced by mills in the Pittsburgh area. The well-known leveraged capital structure of major Japanese steel suppliers can be seen in table 15.7, with an average of 91 percent of new capital coming

TABLE 15.4 WORLD'S LARGEST BLAST FURNACES, 1977

Country	Number of furnaces over two million tons capacity	
	Operating	Under construction
Japan	25	9
USSR	9	5
European Community	7	6
United States	0	3
Other	0	5
Poland	0	1
Brazil	0	3
Austria	0	1

Source: Individual companies.

TABLE 15.5 DEEPWATER WORLD-SCALE STEEL PLANTS,
EARLY 1980s

Plant	Country	Projected capacity (million metric tons)
Fukayama	Japan	16
Kashima	Japan	15
Kimitsu	Japan	14
Yawata	Japan	12
Oita	Japan	12
Chiba	Japan	10
Kagagawa	Japan	10
Mizushima	Japan	10
Fos	France	10
Taranto	Italy	10
Wakayama	Japan	9
Dunkirk	France	8
Nagoya	Japan	8
Hoogovens	Netherlands	6
Tubarao	Brazil	6
Pohang	Korea	6
Burns Harbor	United States	6

Note: Excludes USSR.
Source: Individual companies.

TABLE 15.6 TRANSPORT COSTS OF JAPANESE IRON ORE[a]

	Constant (1973) dollars per ton
1964	8.00
1965	7.12
1966	6.20
1967	5.36
1968	4.87
1969	4.45
1970	4.52
1971	3.93
1972	3.45
1973	3.50
Upper Minnesota to Chicago (Great Lakes), 1973	3.50
Upper Minnesota to Pittsburgh, 1973	6.50

a. Average, all mills and mines.

TABLE 15.7 THE FINANCING OF INVESTMENT BY MAJOR JAPANESE
STEEL COMPANIES, 1966–72 (percentage)

Cash sources for financing	
Debt	91.0
Retained earnings	1.1
New equity	7.9
Asset growth per year	23.6
Average return on assets, 1966–72	1.8
Average return on equity, 1966–72	20.0

Source: Annual reports and balance sheets of the major steel companies.

from debt. Extraordinary leverage permitted an average return on assets of 1.8 percent to be translated into average return on equity of 20 percent.

Domestically, price discipline among the major Japanese steel suppliers appears to be extremely tight, and market shares consequently highly stable. The five largest producers Nippon Steel, Nippon Kokan, Kawasaki Steel, Sumitomo Metal, and Kobe Steel share about 70 percent of the domestic market between them. While no official cartel exists, it is probably not by chance that, for example, Nippon Steel has held a precise 41.3 percent share of the output of the top five each year since 1976, or that the production shares of each of the others has been completely unchanged as well over the same period (*Economist* 1982). Voluntary quarterly production guidelines are published by Ministry of International Trade and Industry (MITI). Executives from each of the top five meet weekly to discuss matters of mutual interest. Each has similar raw materials costs (jointly negotiated with overseas suppliers), as well as similar levels of plant efficiency, and distributes mainly through the large trading companies.

Nevertheless, imports into Japan have grown from 108,000 tons in 1975 to 1.4 million tons in 1981, with significant penetration from the new South Korean Pohang mill (built by the Japanese themselves) and China Steel Corporation in Taiwan. This, plus a growing market share in certain product categories on the part of domestic minimills, is beginning to introduce an element of competition at the margin which may eventually alter the industry's domestic competitive conduct.

Despite their underlying international competitive strength and tightly organized domestic market, Japanese steel firms have periodically been accused of being heavily subsidized and engaging in cyclical dumping. The latter involves less-than-fair-value export sales during recessions in order to avoid the domestic worker layoffs that are anathema in the Japanese industrial system, and to help contribute to heavy debt service costs. There is some evidence that LTFV sales did occur in 1976 and may in part explain the runup in Japan's exports to the United States in that year. However, they probably involved only a few product groups and did not extend beyond a few months (Kawahito 1981). And most studies come to the conclusion that subsidization of Japanese steel exports has in fact been negligible (Federal Trade Commission 1977). But it is hard to deny that the public policy environment and institutional capital market factors that guarantee Japanese steel firms capital adequacy have backstopped the industry's highly successful export drive, with exports as a percentage of output rising from 27 percent in 1966 to 44 percent in 1976.

During the 1981–82 steel import battle in the United States, major Japanese steel firms evidenced an interest in direct investments in the US industry—a defensive motivation very similar to earlier reactions by Japanese auto manufacturers to US protectionist pressures. While not triggered specifically by US protection moves, Japanese suppliers apparently felt that they would be caught in the wringer of any general move to establish import quotas or voluntary export restraints as a "solution" to the domestic industry's troubles. Kobe Steel, for example, apparently held joint-venture talks with Wheeling–Pittsburgh Steel on a seamless pipe mill, and acquisition negotiations with McLouth Steel.

In the 1980s, the Japanese integrated steel producers are aiming increasingly at the high value-added end of the production spectrum. They have already cut back plans for future carbon steel production capacity in the light of prospective adverse global market developments, focusing more on higher-valued steels and steel products, and reducing the industry's overall role in the national economy. In part, this may be due to the recognition that the days when large productivity gains from new plants using the latest technology lie mainly in the past, and that international competitive advantage in the industry is probably already shifting elsewhere. It may also be due to the fact that steel demand is likely to expand only slowly in the decades ahead, making the industry itself a poor bet as an agent of national economic growth. Moreover, the industry is increasingly selling steel-making technology and turnkey plants to countries such as China, Taiwan, Brazil, and even to steel firms in the United States and Europe. Indeed, there are few major steel firms today that do not have some sort of technology cooperation agreements with at least one of the Japanese majors.

Emerging Suppliers

The final set of players in the international steel game are the more advanced developing countries. Some, such as India, have been active in steel for a long time with decidedly mixed success. However, it is the newer entrants in South Korea, Taiwan, and Spain as well as Mexico, Venezuela, and Brazil that are making increasing market inroads. The reasons for this are very similar to the factors underlying the Japanese competitiveness of the 1970s—new mills, state-of-the-art technologies, optimal plant siting, good labor quality, and low transport costs and wages. The latter seem unbeatable in the foreseeable future. It has been estimated that new mills in Taiwan or South Korea, for example, could undercut an identical US mill by almost 20 percent in delivered prices of major steel product categories in principal American markets (Crandall 1981).

As an example of Brazil's steelmaking potential is the new $3 billion Tubarao plant, just north of Rio de Janeiro, capable of adding 3 million tons to that country's 1981 installed capacity of 17 million tons, and to possibly double its 1981 exports of 2.45 million tons. A joint venture of the state-owned steel holding company Siderbras (51 percent), Kawasaki Steel of Japan, and Finsider of Italy (49 percent), the facility benefits from very low labor and iron ore costs and the latest Japanese technology, but suffers from high interest charges on $6 billion of external borrowing. The latter will bias production to export markets, including significant sales of steel slabs to Japan.

Moreover, it is generally in the earlier stages of the development process that economic growth tends to be relatively steel-intensive as compared with the later stages, when growth often shifts from heavy industry and infrastructure to light manufacturing and services. Therefore, one would expect the only really buoyant demand for steel to reside in the developing countries themselves during the 1980s and beyond. If several of these countries also have an emerging competitive advantage in steel, these relatively high-growth markets ought to be supplied partly from intra-LDC trade and partly from Japan. In addition, LDC suppliers will be able to undertake increasing exports to the United States, Japan, and Western Europe. However, a number of LDCs have themselves pursued highly protectionist steel-import policies and subsidization on infant-industry grounds.

Appendix tables 15A.1–3 present comparative data on a number of competitive variables, focusing on scale economies, technological performance, and environmental aspects, for the principal steel players in the late 1970.

Structural Adjustment and the Politics of Protection

Competitive shifts in the world steel industry, as the foregoing discussion is intended to show, have been and will continue to be dramatic, due in part to market forces and in part to direct government intervention in the industry for essentially political and sometimes ideological reasons. Industry-specific characteristics have made it difficult for the steel sector to adjust and this, when combined with managerial inertia, government ownership in some countries, and the *expectation* of protection, have produced adjustment scenarios that seriously depart from market dictates.

The arguments for protection in the steel sector have been inherently powerful (Walter and Jones 1982). When combined with the regional and national significance of the industry, this has generated political influence sufficient to overcome countervailing interests and ideological commitments to liberal trade to generate widespread protection. The vehicles of choice have been VERs, minimum import prices, and subsidies, resulting in substantial trade deflection and suppression, reactions on the part of other countries, adverse impacts on steel-using industries, consumer welfare effects, and the like.

Why did the steel industry obtain protection where other industries have not? In general, the ease of adjustment is a central element in determining the motivation of firms in an industry to seek protection. The private cost of adapting to structural change reflects the industry's inflexibility in response to competitive shocks. High fixed costs resulting, for example, from the capital intensity of an industry or long-term contracts for inputs, increase the difficulties of adjustment. Inflexibility of wages and work rules creates rigidity on the labor side, with the sometimes politically difficult alternative of layoffs. The specificity of factors to the production process may preclude their easy transfer to alternate uses, and the specialized nature of the production process itself may prevent firms from moving into different lines of activity.

Moreover, the specific nature of firms' operations and the structure of the production process also provide a measure of its adaptability to change. For example, to the extent that the manufacturing process can be disaggregated into intermediate goods and firms are vertically integrated, the possibility exists to transfer component operations to geographic areas where more cost-effective production methods or lower factor costs can be exploited. Thus, multinational companies can absorb at least part of the effects of shifting competitive advantage by reaping its benefits and are frequently absent among those pleading the case for protection in the political arena (Gladwin and Walter 1980). This has certainly not been true of the steel industry.

The greater the inflexibility of response along one or more of these lines, the higher the expected private cost of adjustment and the more reluctant the firm or industry will be to accept the consequences of its shifting competitive position. This is amply demonstrated in the steel sector. Management and shareholders who face the prospect of writing down the value of a firm's capital are joined in political co-alitions by workers who have acquired a vested interest in the main-tenance of the industry since (at international prices) their wages may well be excessive.

Receptivity to such a call for sectoral protection at the policy-making level depends on an often subtle formation of public and official attitudes based on both the economic and political dimensions of the contemporary environment—not only macroeconomic condi-tions that may create a bias against imports, but also associated po-litical circumstances that foster xenophobia, isolationism, social ma-laise, as well as an ideological belief in free markets and trade (Walter and Jones 1981). The focus, however, has to be on the efficacy of individual currents of political influence on final policy decisions re-garding specific industries. The size and regional concentration of an industry, coupled to logrolling and political compromise may, for example, point to potentially strong power and impact. The lobbying organizations maintained by the industry, as well as support from the relevant trade unions, reinforce its power to affect policy decisions.

In order to obtain protection, however, these elements of political influence must find resonance within the national policy-making struc-ture. The authorities must ultimately perceive the fate of the industry, for example, as being politically sensitive with respect to the achieve-ment of certain high-priority national goals, such as employment, regional balance, or the national defense. Elected or appointed of-ficials may, in addition, associate a commitment to these goals with their own personal or collective fortunes, and there may exist a gen-uinely interventionist ideology among policymakers who inherently distrust the market or fear its consequences (Walter and Jones 1981). Intervention may even be institutionalized in the form of national industrial commissions or planning bureaus, in which case protec-tionism may be able to find ready acceptance within the bureaucratic structure—the "low road" to protection via administrative and tech-nical action rather than the "high road" via political decisions (Finger et al. 1980). The degree of interaction that is achieved between the industry's own influence and the government's receptivity to its pleas will determine the power of protectionist sentiment in the national policy-making process.

Opposition to protectionist thrusts at the sectoral level arises in part as a reaction to its adverse potential welfare effects and in part (as noted) as an imbedded social belief in the advantages of free and open markets. In practice, the first category of opposition may well be limited to any user industries that will be directly hit by the increased price or reduced availability of the protected goods. Of course, all industries and consumers who reap the benefits of trade in general are potential opponents of protection thrusts at the industry level. In the steel case, user industries have been remarkably silent as have, with one or two exceptions, consumer advocates. Ultimately, it is often a conscious public commitment to liberal trade that stands largely alone against sectorally oriented protectionist pressures, reinforced, to be sure, by the fear of retaliation from abroad.

There are, finally, elements in national competition law and international trade agreements that restrict the types of protection that can ultimately be adopted. As the steel example shows, these tend to divert protectionist sentiment toward certain other—often more subtle—measures, especially nontariff barriers. Ironically, restrictions imposed on unilateral changes in tariffs under the GATT have effectively closed what is one of the least onerous valves for protectionist pressure, and have contributed to the development of alternative tools for sectoral protection that may be significantly more damaging to society at large.

Superimposing such general aspects of the politics of protection on the unique characteristics of the steel industry, it is not difficult to explain its extraordinary adeptness in obtaining shielding from imports in national political environments. Basically, the interaction of the industry's political impact with the perceptions of policymakers has created enormous influence. In the United States, the size and visibility of the industry translate quickly into the potential of large-scale worker layoffs, media headlines and political pressures, which have strengthened the voice of the "Steel Caucus" protectionist constituency in Congress and the steelmakers' industrial lobby. In the EC, on the other hand, the higher propensity of governments to intervene directly in industry difficulties has transformed the political power of the steel sector into the vested interest of an established industrial policy apparatus.

The perceived link between steel and the national well-being is no less important in determining the industry's influence. The alleged strategic value of steel to national defense, although perhaps exaggerated by industry claims—and almost never couched in intellectually defensible terms of the requirement to maintain an excessively large steel industry as an "insurance premium" to be added to the cost of national defense—still carries considerable persuasive power with policymakers. And steelmaking is surrounded by a mystique which seems to be deeply rooted in the consciousness of industrial society. Because it is so closely associated with the heyday of economic growth, there is a widespread belief that further growth cannot occur without "Big Steel." As the very symbol of industrial strength, the prospect of steel's decline or contraction has apparently excited a certain fear of economic impotence.

Accordingly, the steel industry has shown a singular ability to penetrate governmental institutions and achieve a telling impact on public policy. This has created among governments a high propensity to shield the industry, strong enough to override the general reluctance to implement protectionist actions and long-standing constraints against taking such action based on overall welfare effects, the impact on steel-using industries, international commitments and the possibility of foreign retaliation. Governments have gone to great lengths to assure the proper legal and political frameworks within which the sectoral protection of steel can be realized.

Prognosis

The world steel business finds itself in an unprecedented state of flux, with shifting competitive advantage and trade patterns among traditional suppliers, newly emerging export-oriented LDC mills, relatively stagnant demand, and stiff competition from other materials— all pointing to substantial market-driven structural adjustment in virtually every country involved in the industry. The picture is complicated by the cyclical nature of steel demand, sector-specific and geographically relatively immobile factors of production, direct, and indirect government involvement, highly variegated national competitive structures, and significant medium-term exchange rate movements. There is also the strategic (externality) aspects of the industry, with respect to both the national defense and national development goals. Such considerations raise questions whether the free market basically *will* be allowed to determine where steel is produced for the global market, and some of them raise questions whether it *should* be allowed to do so. These issues can be divided into long-term and short-term components.

Long-Term Aspects

Despite all of the problems described here, global structural adjustment has proceeded apace. An economist on the moon looking down on the evolution of steel production and consumption patterns on earth would find cause for substantial optimism. The fact is that the location of global steel production and patterns of trade *have* been changing—despite sometimes significant and prolonged deviations—according to the dictates of comparative advantage. The dynamic picture seems far more positive than the static one.

Various studies suggest that long-term international competitive advantage in the steel products is shifting to a select group of developing countries (Crandall 1981; Walter 1979). These are able to purchase raw materials at the lowest possible world market prices, benefit from predominantly ocean (as opposed to inland) transport costs, will continue to have significantly lower labor costs than even Japan, and are constructing "greenfield" plants embodying the most modern technologies available, with capital borrowed at highly competitive rates in the Euromarkets. This should lead to a gradual reallocation of world steel production over the coming decades. A number of such countries, including Taiwan, China, South Korea, Brazil, and Mexico have the characteristics of significant future steel suppliers in the international marketplace. Production conditions are shifting in their favor, much as Japan developed a major competitive advantage in the 1960s. However, the shift will not be as dramatic, mainly because of supply-related bottlenecks which, in some of these countries, will take time to overcome.

Meantime, basic steelmaking in the advanced industrial countries would certainly continue to survive, albeit in slimmed down form, with integrated production concentrated in the most efficient mills. In the United States, for example, perhaps 20 percent of existing capacity would eventually be shut down and most of the remaining integrated mills concentrated in the Great Lakes area. At the same time, a larger share of basic steel production would be captured by the minimills—currently about 60 plants owned by 45 firms. These are nonintegrated electric furnace mills using ferrous scrap to produce primarily structural steel. They are generally nonunion, flexible, low-cost, efficient plants able to undersell both the domestic integrated suppliers and imports in their respective region markets. In 1980, minimills accounted for about 15 percent of US capacity, expected to expand to 25 to 30 percent by the latter part of the decade. Return on equity for these firms in 1980 averaged 14 percent, twice that of the integrated firms. It is expected that the availability of 153 million tons of scrap in the United States annually, together with technical innovations permitting them to widen their product lines, will play a role in further strengthening this segment of the US steel industry (Office of Technology Assessment 1981).

A leaner, more efficient and combative integrated sector should, in combination with the nonintegrated sector, be able to exploit locational and supply-reliability advantages sufficient to offset sizable cost disadvantages vis-à-vis even the most competitive imports in many of the traditional major steel markets in Western Europe, North America, and Japan. Competitive positioning should be strengthened by increasing downstream concentration of production in specialty steels, high technology applications, high value-added metalworking, and similar leading-edge activities. Certainly such a restructured steel sector should be of sufficient size to handle defense needs and throw off related external benefits, without special governmental measures, in most OECD countries.

A purely market-driven world steel industry in, say, the year 2000 would thus show major quantitative and qualitative production and trade-flow shifts, both in the OECD countries and in the LDCs, reflecting both regional demand developments and the evolution of competitive advantage. Is such a long-term market-driven solution politically feasible?

Broadly, the answer is probably positive, and ongoing restructuring in Western Europe, Japan, and the United States shows encouraging signs of following long-term market dictates. This does not mean that restructuring can be accomplished smoothly or quickly, so that significant deviations from such a market-determined adjustment path will appear from time to time, often for prolonged periods. Neither does it mean that the end result will be fully market-determined, given that certain firms may not play according to free-market rules in nationalized steel industries, that some LDC steel sectors will be promoted as prestige objects or as positive-externalities generators, and that the behavior of the steel sector in centrally planned economies in any case will tend to contribute long-term deviations from pure market-driven solutions. But it is possible to take comfort in the view that, as long as a very significant part of the industry is playing by market rules, those who deviate will be saddled with costs that in the end will be viewed as prohibitive against a free-market benchmark.

Short-Term Aspects

In the short term, the world steel industry will continue to be subject to severe shocks in the face of a limited capacity for dealing with them. The traditional source of these shocks is to be found in demand volatility, leading to production instability significantly greater than cyclical movements in broad economic aggregates. Capacity utilization fluctuates wildly and, if labor comes to be regarded as a fixed cost as well, no reasonable capital cushion can be expected to absorb such shocks. This clearly puts pressure on "deep pocket" government intervention during cyclical downturns, and raises questions about the respective roles of shareholders and taxpayers in management control. It also puts pressure on the use of exports as cyclical buffers in order to transmit shocks abroad. And it puts pressure on steel firms to diversify horizontally in order to gain greater stability in the expected stream of returns facing shareholders, and to secure the cash flows needed for longer-term competitive operations.

Given the cyclical nature of the industry and normal risk aversion on the part of shareholders and managers, horizontal diversification may be inevitable and perhaps even desirable if the two other options, cyclical dumping and increased government intervention, are to be avoided. Cyclical dumping will lead to trade policy responses which—though perhaps legitimate in the short term—may in fact prove to be lasting and ultimately thwart the long-term interplay of market forces. Direct government involvement in the industry, as has been amply demonstrated in the steel sector, has much the same effects.

A second source of cyclical shocks is exchange rates. For example, during a one-year period ended in October 1981 the Belgian franc depreciated fully 37 percent against the US dollar. It would have been surprising indeed if this had no effect on the competitiveness of Belgian steel suppliers in the American market, yet the resulting import "surge" brought a strong protectionist response. An industry with massive in-place capital facilities and a sector-specific labor force is naturally going to be highly sensitive to real and nominal exchange rates. This sensitivity is heightened by the industry's lack of multi-nationalization, which could absorb exchange rate shocks within the firm—at least from a profit-and-loss standpoint. Medium term exchange rate volatility of the type experienced in recent years, which originates largely in the macromonetary sphere, clearly poses the danger of attempts at sectoral "insulation" through offsetting trade policy measures which, once again, may well become permanent. Problems with administration of the TPM in the face of movements in the dollar-yen rate are yet another way in which exchange rate movements can complicate a sectorally oriented trade policy. No solution has appeared thus far to address this problem.

The industry has also been vulnerable to shocks arising out of abrupt shifts in environmental and worker health and safety policies.

Such measures may be applied abruptly or inconsistently, both over time and across countries, thereby leading to international competitive strains. Moreover, some countries have approached these problems by regulations or charge strategies, while others have relied more heavily on public sector subsidies, thus further influencing sectoral competitiveness internationally. The industry's unusual sensitivity ("dirty and dangerous") to such issues as periodically raised demands for compensatory protection from steel imports produced under less stringent conditions abroad.

The problem is that short-term shocks to the industry, whether emanating from macroeconomic swings, exchange rate changes, or other sources, all give rise to demands for protection or other forms of government involvement which may outlast by far the underlying cause. Hence short-term considerations in this particular industry can and do lead all too easily to essentially permanent distortions of international competitive conditions.

Policy Initiatives

This chapter has traced long-term steel industry developments in the United States, Western Europe, Japan, and the developing countries over almost three decades, focusing on the evolution of competitiveness, trade, and government intervention. Protection-seeking as against adjustment-seeking behavior by the steel industry has been assessed within the framework of national political contexts. A set of long-term and short-term prognoses for the industry have been offered. How can we distill the policy lessons from what has happened and what can we conclude, in a normative sense, about the evolution of policy in the years ahead?

First, there are the dangerous political dynamics of sectoral protection—international accommodations on industry-level trade policy by a club of "concerned parties," in the absence of antagonistic trade interests and their countervailing power—probably inherently biased toward "solutions" of a fundamentally protectionist nature (Walter 1979).

Second, governments do not get very high marks for adapting their short-term policy responses to the particular long-term needs of the steel industry according to market criteria. Protection has been accorded, pointing to some sort of eventual international market-sharing arrangement for the industry. Politics threatens to replace economics as the main determinant of the structure of global production in the industry.

Third, questionable competitive behavior by some important suppliers have probably played a catalytic role in accelerating developments toward protection and organization of international markets. This places a premium on the operation of the subsidies code negotiated during the Tokyo Round and an enforcement of antidumping regulations in cases of predatory and cyclical dumping without using them as permanent protectionist devices.

Fourth, the steel case points to the growing inflexibility in labor force use that appears to be taking hold in many industrial countries. Intended to provide a greater measure of equity for factors of production affected by import competition and structural change, there is the danger that such rigidities will evolve into a kind of economic sclerosis—a hardening of the economic arteries—which will at once misallocate resources, slow economic growth, and lead to even greater future pressures for protection. New ways need to be found to deliver affirmative adjustment and retain the necessary degree of flexibility in national economic structures.

Fifth, judging from the steel case, it may well be that companies that are multinational in their operations and diversified in production tend to adapt more readily, and are less likely to plead for protection, than companies that are not. This issue is clearly related to the prospects for intrafirm adjustment versus the need for adjustment via factor markets. The efficiency and growth benefits of affirmative adjustment clearly exist, but the equity aspects related to the impacted factors of production need to be considered as well. At least in the steel industry, the solution of this problem remains obscure. Until it is addressed, protection will continue to be accorded by political routes and structural adjustment to economic change impeded.

In our discussion, we have dealt almost entirely with trade and adjustment problems faced by large, integrated firms in the basic carbon steel industry. It should be emphasized that the story is rather different in the stainless, alloy, and tool steel segments of the industry, where product differentiation, quality control, and product application to specific user requirements render product innovation and applications technology far more important. This is the part of the product spectrum into which productive resources in the developed countries' steel industries should increasingly be redeployed. The story is also quite different in the nonintegrated part of the carbon steel business, where minimill operators in countries like Italy, Japan, Britain, and the United States face quite different production and market conditions from the integrated majors, and appear to have a positive future even in the advanced industrial countries.

It would appear now that some sort of international rules of the game specifically addressed to the basic steel industry are essentially inevitable, this despite the evident dangers involved. The nature of the industry, its political clout, and the foreseeable recurrence of short-term crises may, indeed, make such an arrangement superior to the heretofore totally uncoordinated approach to the problems of the industry. Whatever such a mechanism turns out to be, it is critical that it adhere as nearly as possible to market-driven solutions.

Components of such a market-oriented world steel arrangement might include: a strong up-front commitment to competitively governed adjustment and liberal trade via a strong institutional link to the GATT; full integration into such an arrangement of the nontariff barriers (NTB) codes, particularly the subsidies code, agreed during the Tokyo Round of multilateral trade negotiations; an institutionalized "surge" mechanism, related to specific safeguard arrangements for the steel industry, involving rigorous tests that distinguish short-term factors from underlying shifts in competitiveness, using statutory self-destructing, time-limited import charges—*not* quantitative restrictions; a commitment by all parties to affirmative adjustment to change in world steel industry competitive patterns, including plant phase-outs, encouraged corporate diversification and multinationalization, joint production facilities where scale economies can be realized, and incentive packages for attracting replacement industries into declining steel regions; vigilance against anticompetitive practices on the part of both firms and organized labor; and measures to encourage moves in the industrial countries up the value-added ladder within the steel sector and into allied activities complementary to steel.

The question "Should a GATT capability exist to deal with sector-specific problems?" such as those described in this study of the global carbon steel industry is answered here in the affirmative with the greatest reluctance and with a profound lack of sympathy for the cast of characters in the global steel story. The problems and the protectionist fallout that describe contemporary behavior in steel are neither transitory nor destined to end with worldwide economic recovery and a return to reasonable medium-term exchange rate stability. In this, as in other highly capitalized industries with limited short-term adjustment capability, they will return time and again. And the danger is that the virus of sectoral protection will spread quickly and irreversibly to the entire liberal trading system that has been so painstakingly constructed over the years.

The issue is thus one of *damage-control*. We have a choice among two alternatives: to rely on the traditional set of general trading rules with sectoral problems attacked in direct violation of the spirit or letter of those rules, unilaterally, by countries facing intactable sectoral problems finding a high level of resonance in domestic politics; or to establish a set of agreed principles that conform in large measure to these more general rules but are capable of defusing specific sectoral problems with the least damage to the system as a whole. At this point it seems reasonable to opt for the latter, and to propose a sectoral capability in the GATT that combines high levels of transparency with careful attention to due process and dispute settlement, based on strictly time-limited, self-destructing import charges. The intent is to produce the smallest possible deviation from a market-driven adjustment scenario at the sectoral level, and at the same time to contain effectively the protectionist virus so that broad-based trade liberalization can continue to make progress.

Such an approach involves a number of dangers, but it may well hold greater promise of long-term efficient and equitable outcomes than either uncoordinated unilateral measures or other, less transparent sectoral initiatives.

References

American Iron and Steel Institute (AISI). *Steel at the Crossroads: The American Steel Industry in the 1980s.* Washington: AISI, 1980.

Anderson, R. G., and M. E. Kreinin. "Labour Costs in the American Auto and Steel Industries." *The World Economy* (June 1981).

Aylen, Joanathan. "Plant Size and Efficiency in the Steel Industry: An International Comparison." Salford, U.K.: University of Salford, September 1981. Processed.

Bradford, Charles. *Japanese Steel Industry: A Comparison with its American Counterparts.* New York: Merrill Lynch, 1977.

Council on Wage and Price Stability (COWPS). *Report to the President on Prices and Costs in the United States Steel Industry.* Washington: COWPS, 1977.

Crandall, Robert W. "Steel Imports: Dumping or Competition." *Regulation* (July/August 1980).

————. *The US Steel Industry in Recurrent Crisis.* Washington: Brookings Institution, 1981.

Department of Justice. Submission to the International Trade Commission. Washington, 1980. Processed.

Dirlam, Joel B., and Hans Mueller. "Import Restraints and Reindustrialization: The Case of the US Steel Industry." Kingston, R.I.: University of Rhode Island, 1982. Processed.

Driscoll, D. *Steel and the European Community: The Protection Issue.* Washington: Congressional Research Service, 1980.

Federal Trade Commission (FTC). *The US Steel Industry and Its International Rivals.* Washington: FTC, 1977.

Finger, J. Michael. "The United States Trigger Price Mechanism for Steel Imports." Washington: World Bank, 1981. Processed.

Finger, J. Michael; H. K. Hall; and D. R. Nelson. "The Political Economy of Administered Protection." Washington: Office of Trade Research, US Treasury Department, 1980. Processed.

General Accounting Office (GAO). *Administration of the Steel Trigger Price Mechanism*. Washington: GAO, 1980.

————. *New Strategy Required for Aiding Distressed Steel Industry*. Washington: GAO, 1981.

Gladwin, Thomas N., and Ingo Walter. *Multinationals Under Fire: Lessons in the Management of Conflict*. New York: Wiley, 1980.

Jondrow, J.; E. Levine; L. Jacobson; A. Katz; and D. O'Neill. *Removing Restrictions on Imports of Steel*. Arlington, Va: Center for Naval Analyses, 1975.

Jones, Kent A. "Forgetfulness of Things Past: Europe and the Steel Cartel." *The World Economy* (May 1979).

————. *The Political Economy of Voluntary Restraint and the Incidence of Trade Diversion in Steel Import Markets*. Unpublished dissertation. Geneva: Graduate Institute of International Studies, University of Geneva, 1981.

Kawahito, Kujoshi. "Japanese Steel in the American Market, Conflict and Causes." *The World Economy* (September 1981).

————. *The Japanese Steel Industry*. New York: Praeger, 1972.

Kirkland, Richard I., Jr. "Steel's Subtle Bid for Quotas." *Fortune*, 8 February 1982.

Kreinin, Mordechai E. "United States' Comparative Advantage in Motor Vehicles and Steel." In *Michigan's Fiscal and Economic Structure*, ed. Harvey E. Brazer and Deborah S. Laren. Ann Arbor, Mich.: University of Michigan Press, 1982.

Mueller, Hans. "The Competitiveness of the US Steel Industry After the New Trigger Price Mechanism." Murfreesboro, Tenn.: Middle Tennessee State University, 1981. Processed.

————. "Distortion Resulting from Sectoral Solutions to Problems in the US Steel Market." Murfreesboro, Tenn.: Middle Tennessee State University, 1981. Processed.

Office of Technology Assessment (OTA). *Technology and Steel Industry Competitiveness*. Washington: Congressional OTA, US Congress, 1981.

————. *US Industrial Competitiveness: A Comparison of Steel, Electronics and Automobiles*. Washington: Congressional OTA, US Congress, 1981.

Plant, Robert. *Industries in Trouble*. Geneva: International Labor Organization, 1981.

Pugel, Thomas A., and Ingo Walter. "Firm and Industry Determinants of Trade Policy Behavior." New York: New York University, 1981. Processed.

Putnam, Hayes, and Bartlett, Inc. *Economics of International Steel Trade*. Washington: American Iron and Steel Institute, 1978.

————. *The Economic Implications of Foreign Steel Pricing Practices*. Washington: American Iron and Steel Institute, 1978.

Walter, Ingo. *International Economics of Pollution*. London: Macmillan, 1975.

————. "Protection of Industries in Trouble: The Case of Iron and Steel." *The World Economy* (May 1979).

Walter, Ingo, and Kaj Areskoug. *International Economics*, 3d ed. New York: Wiley, 1981.

Walter, Ingo, and Kent A. Jones. "The Battle over Protectionism: How Industry Adjusts to Competitive Shocks." *Journal of Business Strategy* (Fall 1981).

————. "Politics, Economics, and the International Steel Industry." Institution of Electrical Engineers (UK) *Proceedings*. Stevenage, Herts.: Institute of Electrical Engineers, 1982.

Walters, Robert S. "The US Steel and Automobile Industries: Patterns in Domestic Economic and Foreign Trade Policies." Pittsburgh: University of Pittsburgh, 1981. Processed.

Statistical Appendix

TABLE 15A.1 COMPARATIVE STEEL INDUSTRY OPERATING ECONOMICS

	United States	Japan	West Germany	United Kingdom	France	Year
Comparative dollar costs vs home-currency costs (percentage)	100	37	37	26	30	1981
Share of fixed costs in total mill costs (percentage)	22	36	32	35	38	1981
Hourly employment cost per worker (US dollars)	23.00	10.75	13.25	9.00	13.00	1982(II)
Manhours per ton shipped (90 percent operating rate)	8.5	6.9	8.3	11.0	10.0	1982(II)
(actual operating rate)	9.1	9.0	10.6	14.0	11.1	1982(II)
Material costs per ton shipped (US dollars)	330	291	275	388	286	1981
Financial costs per ton shipped (US dollars)	44	102	56	76	91	1981
Pretax costs per ton shipped (US dollars)	610	475	490	560	490	1982(II)
Pretax profit per ton shipped (US dollars)	−30	−25	−50	−100	−50	1982(II)
			All European Community			
Debt (billion US dollars)	8.5	25.0	24.3			1980
Equity (billion US dollars)	16.4	4.7	14.8			1980

Notes: 1982 figures are estimates for the second quarter. Comparative dollar versus home-currency costs can be used to assess exchange rate changes on pricing and costs.
Source: Peter F. Marcus, Comparative Circumstances of Major Steel Mills in the United States, European Community and Japan (New York: Paine Webber Mitchell Hutchins, Inc., April 29, 1982).

TABLE 15A.2   PLANT AND EQUIPMENT ECONOMIES OF SCALE, 1979

		United States	EC total	Germany	Japan	Canada
Plants	Capacity of the largest 5 plants (million net tons maximum raw steel output)	36	52	34	68	—
	Capacity of the largest 10 plants (million net tons maximum raw steel output)	59	83	—	112	—
	Number of plants with raw steel capacity > 6 million net tons	4	8	2	12	1
Blast furnaces	Number of blast furnaces with an inner volume > 70,629 cubic feet (2,000 cubic meters)	4	19	8	39	1
Steelshops	Number of oxygen converters 220 net tons or larger[a] (charge weight)	31	39	16	32	5
	Average annual capacity of oxygen steelshops (million net tons)	2.1	2.8	3.6	3.5	2.5
	Capacity-weighted average converter size[a]	225	240	239	218	174
High technology continuous casting	Slab casters a. Number of machines[a]	19	43	20	39	3
	b. Weighted strand area inch²[a]	860	877	896	978	576
	Bloom casters a. Number of machines[a]	4	19	6	19	4
	b. Average strand area inch²[a]	300	330	410	346	302

		United States	EC total	Germany	Japan	Canada
Hot wide strip mills	Number of mills					
	a. Fully continuous	23	11	2	9	—
	b. Semicontinuous	14	14	4	8	3
	Average rated annual capacity (million net tons)	2.3	3.1	3.6	3.5	1.3
Plate mills	Number of mills (only heavy and medium reversing, except two and three high)	18	34	10	16	3
	Average total annual capacity (million net tons)	.67	.62	73	1.68	.55

Source: Mueller 1981b. Taken from Institute for Iron and Steel Studies, *Commentary*, (April–May 1978) and maps (with plant capacity and location data) on "The Steel Industry of Western Europe" and "The Steel Industry of Canada and the United States;" *Metal Bulletin; Iron and Steelworks of the World*, 1978; Japan Iron and Steel Federation, *Japan Steel Bulletin* (June 1979); and Aylen (1981).
a. *Note:* 1977 data.

TABLE 15A.3 SOME INDICATORS OF TECHNOLOGICAL PERFORMANCE, 1979

	United States	Total EC av.	Germany	Japan	Canada
Blast furnaces (smelting)					
Adoption of the bell-less system[a] (percentage; best practice = 100 percent)	0.5	9	8	8	14
Fuel rate (coke and fuel oil only[b]; best practice = 0.460–0.480)	0.596	0.538	0.540	0.466	0.546
Steelshops (melting)					
Total output (million net tons)	136.3	155.2	50.7	123.2	17.7
Output in oxygen converters (million net tons)	83.3	110.2	38.6	94.2	10.0
Output in electric furnaces (million net tons)	33.9	35.6	7.1	29.0	4.0
Output with obsolete methods (million net tons)	19.2	9.3	5.0	—	3.6
Adoption of modern melting processes (percentage; best practice = 100 percent)	86.0	94.0	90.1	100.0	79.5
Continuous casting					
Output (million net tons)	22.7	47.4	17.9	64.1	3.5
Adoption rate (percentage; best practice = 70–80 percent)[c]	16.7	30.9	39.0	53.0	19.9

	United States	Total EC av.	Germany	Japan	Canada
Yield, or the amount of finished steel obtained per ton of raw steel produced (percentage, adjusted for differences in product mix)	72	77	75	84	75
Energy use, per ton of finished steel (million BTU)[b,d]	29.98	24.9	25.1	20.43	24.8
Scrap ratios (percentage)	51.5	43.8	58.3	31.9	47.4

Source: Mueller 1981b. Taken from American Iron and Steel Institute, *Annual Statistical Report*; 1980; *Steel at the Crossroads*, January 1980; Japan Iron and Steel Federation, TeKKo ToKei NenKan International Iron and Steel Institute, *A Handbook of World Steel Statistics*, 1978; *World Steel in Figures*, 1980; Office of Technology Assessment, *Technology and Steel Industry Competitiveness*, 1980; Aylen, 1981.

Notes:

a. 1977 data.

b. United States 1979; other data, 1978.

c. Certain products, such as very large plates, can only be produced via the conventional ingot route.

d. The greater the use of scrap, the lower should be the total energy use of a steel industry.

TABLE 15A.4   COMPARISON OF AMBIENT AIR QUALITY STANDARDS

Pollutant	Averaging time	Japan	United States
SO$_2$	Annual	(0.017)PPM[a]	0.03PPM
	24-hour	0.04PPM	0.14PPM
	1-hour	0.1PPM	—
NO$_2$	Annual	(0.02–0.03)PPM[a]	0.05PPM
	24-hour	0.04–0.06PPM	—
Photochemical oxidants	1-hour	0.06PPM	0.12PPM
Hydrocarbons (non-methane)	3-hour	—	0.24PPM
CO	24-hour	10PPM	—
	8-hour	20PPM	9PPM
	1-hour	—	35PPM
Particulates	Annual	—	75ug/M^3
	24-hour	100ug/M^3	260ug/M^3
	1-hour	200ug/M^3	—

— Negligible.
Source: Mueller 1981b, from a paper presented by A. Mukaida, Nippon Steel Corporation, at a meeting of the International Iron and Steel Institute, Tokyo, May 19, 1980.
a. Not stipulated but calculated from other averaging time values.

Pollutant	West Germany	Italy	France
SO$_2$	0.05PPM	—	—
	0.14PPM	0.13PPM	0.35PPM
	—	—	(0.29PPM)
NO$_2$	0.05PPM	—	—
	0.15PPM	0.1PPM	—
Photochemical oxidants			
Hydrocarbons (non-methane)			
CO			
Particulates	—	—	
	100ug/M^3	300ug/M^3	—
	200ug/M^3		

CHAPTER 16

The Prospects for Trade and Protectionism in the Auto Industry

Robert B. Cohen

Faced with stiff competition at home from Japanese small cars and challenges in important foreign markets from European and Japanese car manufacturers, General Motors (GM) and Ford have responded with massive shifts in product lines and international investment, with new labor-management approaches and cost-cutting efforts (outsourcing, just-in-time parts delivery, automation, and greater exploitation of economies of scale), and with "world cars" and efforts to liberalize costly government regulations.

Traditional economic theories of comparative advantage teach us that capital-intensive, high-skill industries should be most competitive when based in nations such as the United States. Foreign firms in countries with lower labor and capital costs, however, are aware that such competitive advantages can be overcome. The Japanese provide one of the best lessons in shifting comparative advantage through a highly scientific application of new technology, well-planned marketing forays, significant reorganization of production that improves cost and quality, inexpensive financing, and government support. Auto production has begun to shift to low-cost production centers, especially for smaller cars and a number of auto parts (engines, transmissions). In order to survive, US firms are moving abroad, choosing to utilize Japanese production to supply entire lines of subcompact cars (GM) or investing significant amounts in Brazilian and Mexican plants to build engines for US cars (Ford and GM). In the latter case, government subsidies are often responsible for making a newly industrializing country (NIC) a low-cost producer, but US firms are also attracted by the need to obtain a long-term strategic base for production that will serve emerging markets in both Latin America and the Pacific Basin.

The problem with such adaptation to structural change in the automobile sector is that while it demonstrates that multinationals can adapt to a transformed industrial environment better than nationally oriented firms, it also brings about more serious consequences. The offshore sourcing of small cars in sizable amounts and of parts and components will bring with it a substantial rise in the US trade deficit in automobiles by 1984, conservatively estimated at $2.5 billion to $3.0 billion for GM's small cars and at least $3.0 billion worth of engines and transaxles.[1] Given existing estimates that the auto-trade deficit with Japan will reach $25 billion by 1985[2]—assuming import share remains at about the 1981 level of 27.2 percent and total domestic production recovers to close to 10 million cars—this additional trade deficit could well have severe consequences for the economy.

If GM and Ford increase outsourcing, there may be far greater pressure for strong protectionist measures unless a program is developed to place autoworkers and displaced employees from parts suppliers in new industries. If, as some observers believe, Japanese imports go as high as 45 percent of the US market by 1984 after voluntary export restraints (VERs) are removed,[3] the nation may well find itself faced with sizable protectionist sentiment from the Northeast and Midcentral states and possibly from some Sunbelt states.

In addition, since offshore sourcing of parts and components is directly tied to the establishment of a future network of facilities to serve the newly industrializing countries by Ford and GM,[4] parts

---

[1] These estimates are based on projected values of $5,000 for each of the 500,000 Suzuki cars to be imported and $1,000 for each engine (2.5 million to 3 million) and $300 for each transaxle (1.7 million). Estimates for amounts of the latter two items come from John O'Donnell, "Restructuring of the Auto Industry and the Impact on Employment" (Cambridge, Mass.: US Transportation System Center, February 1982), and from Robert B. Cohen, "International Market Positions, International Investment Strategies, and Domestic Reorganization Plans of the US Automakers" (MIT Future of the Automobile Program, International Policy Forum, May 16–20, 1982, Hakone, Japan).

[2] This estimate has been derived from government analyses, primarily those done with a model developed for the Council of Economic Advisers.

[3] James Harbour is one expert who is convinced that once export restraints are removed the Japanese will take as much as they can get of the US market. He cites the 45 percent figure as one that is not unrealistic.

[4] I have explained this evolution in Cohen, "International Market Positions, International Investment Strategies, and Domestic Reorganization Plans of the US Automakers," and will summarize it below.

imports are likely to grow considerably over the next few years. Although parts suppliers have been less involved in the politics of protectionism, they, too, will most likely shift a large share of their production to many offshore centers to support the development of integrated production networks to serve specific continents or sub-global regions.

The policy debate in the auto sector revolves around a number of complicated issues concerning factors that determine competitiveness and how or whether they should be affected by government policy. Previous approaches have been inclined to let the market provide solutions. However, present trends suggest that multinational automakers, acting in a logical way to respond to a structural adjustment problem, may not only raise protectionist sentiment but also rekindle concerns about whether government should control foreign investment.

Status of Auto Protection

Auto trade policy in the industrial nations has been framed primarily as a response to increased competition from the Japanese. At the same time, however, it is important to realize that a number of other factors have played important roles in determining government positions affecting the industry. Certainly the overall economic decline in Organization for Economic Cooperation and Development (OECD) nations and high interest rates have reduced auto sales dramatically. But the major debate has been over whether these factors or imports have been responsible for the decline.

While the Carter administration resisted protectionist demands, President Reagan obtained a Japanese agreement to impose VERs limiting exports to 1.68 million passenger cars in early 1981. This followed the disastrous domestic auto sales of 1980. (The US VER excludes light trucks, a growing part of the exports of Toyota and Nissan.)

Auto producers in the United States were not alone in seeking trade barriers. Domestic auto producers in Belgium and the Netherlands also pressed for such barriers as Japanese penetration increased. Automakers elsewhere in Europe were concerned that the 10.9 percent European Economic Community (EEC) tariff would prove ineffective against Japanese exports. They felt that they would lose exports to Japanese competition and face increasingly strong pressure from Japanese imports.

Japanese recognition that some self-restraint in exports was in their own long-term interest helped sustain the opposition to new trade barriers. The EEC nations set up a formal monitoring program for Japanese auto imports, but left it to individual nations to reach bilateral accords with the Japanese. In 1981, new limitations were imposed by informal agreements with the Japanese to limit the *growth* of sales to West Germany to 10 percent per year and to limit sales to Belgium and the Netherlands. Strong existing restraints in the United Kingdom (10 percent share), Italy (2,200 units), and France (3 percent share) were enforced more vigorously. The strong trade dependency of some European nations (West Germany exports 53 percent of its auto production) fueled the pressure to cap the Japanese export surge.[5] European nations, with high unemployment rates, also feared the impact of declining employment in autos on their supplier industries (for a summary of trade barriers see table 16.1).

Although the Japanese government had originally indicated its intention to increase the VER by 16.5 percent for 1982, it agreed to maintain the VER at 1.68 million units because of the continued sluggishness of US auto sales in 1982. While the May 1981 agreement setting up the VER announced that the Japanese government would monitor auto exports to the US between April 1983 and March 1984, it leaves the Japanese with the power to determine if any export restraints are necessary. It also allows the Japanese to decide how exports would be restrained. The VER and export monitoring will not be extended beyond March 31, 1984.

In a move designed to respond to the US government's demands for greater access to Japanese markets, the Japanese government eliminated tariffs on 38 auto parts categories in April 1981. At the present time, the US Department of Commerce is monitoring the results of missions to sell auto parts to Japanese firms.[6]

The most notable previous attempt by US auto interests to restrain Japanese imports had proven unsuccessful, though it did achieve some of its ends in the VER. This was the International Trade Commission's evaluation of the complaint brought by the United Automobile Workers of America (UAW), on June 12, 1980, and later by Ford, that passenger cars, trucks, and chassis for trucks were being imported into the United States in such increased quantities as to be a substantial cause of injury to the domestic industry. In a split decision, three to two, the commissioners agreed with the findings of their staff

---

[5] US Department of Transportation, *The US Automobile Industry, 1981*, [DOT-P-10-82-01] (Washington: Office of the Secretary of Transportation, May 1982), pp. 16–17.

[6] Ibid., p. 5.

that "the maximum potential loss to US producers resulting from declining consumption was greater in the period January 1979–June 1980 than that resulting from increasing import penetration."[7]

Although this initial attempt failed, continued import pressure on the US market, together with little improvement in auto sales during late 1980 and early 1981 and the precarious financial status of the large US automakers—between 1978 and 1981 the Big Four auto manufacturers (GM, Ford, Chrysler, and American Motors Corporation) had a cumulative shortfall of $23 billion and the working capital of the Big Three fell from $12.3 billion to just $1.8 billion[8]— led to the first calls for some limit to imports, Ford initially recommending a quota of 1 million Japanese cars.[9] GM's chairman at the time, Thomas Murphy, had suggested some type of gentlemen's agreement with Japan.[10] This position had been advocated by Chrysler's chairman for a long time. After substantial infighting, the Reagan administration adopted this approach as a means to buy some time for US producers to revamp their product mix.[11]

One response to trade conflict with Japan more generally has been a spate of proposed bills for restrictions to ensure reciprocity. The most controversial piece of legislation concerning the auto industry is the recent bill introduced by Congressman Richard Ottinger that would impose "local content" requirements on firms selling at least 500,000 cars in the United States. Under this UAW-backed proposal, firms selling this many cars would have to add at least 90 percent of

[7] US International Trade Commission, *Certain Motor Vehicles and Certain Chassis and Bodies Therefor*, [USITC Publication 1110] (Washington: December 1980), p. A-9. One problem with this analysis was that it assumed that consumption and the ratio of imports to consumption change independently. Because US car lines differed substantially from Japanese, this would not be true. In fact, the substantial decline in US auto consumption during this period largely affected purchases of larger vehicles and meant that imports that were concentrated among subcompacts and compacts would increase relative to consumption, as the staff discussion notes. For the data presented by the staff in reaching its conclusion, see Appendix table A-1.

[8] US Department of Transportation, *US Automobile Industry, 1981*, pp. 20–22.

[9] "Detroit Seeks Help in 'Dear Ron' Letter," *Industry Week*, vol. 208, no. 6 (March 23, 1981), pp. 28–31.

[10] Dan Corditz, "Can America Win? Trade War," *Texas Business Executive*, vol. 6, no. 2 (Fall–Winter 1980), pp. 10, 12–13.

[11] Daniel D. Cook, "Reagan is Riding to Detroit's Rescue," *Industry Week*, vol. 209, no. 1 (April 6, 1981), pp. 19–21.

TABLE 16.1   TRADE BARRIERS, MAJOR AUTO PRODUCING NATIONS

Trade barrier	United States	Japan	West Germany	France
Tariff	3%[a]	None	10.9% EEC tariff	10.9% EEC tariff
Local content	None: but see note 2 under Nontariff barriers	None	None	None
Quantitative restrictions	None	None	None	Imports of Japanese cars limited to 3% of market
Value-added tax	None	None	13%	33.3%
Nontariff barriers	(1) Strict safety, emission and fuel economy standards (2) Fuel economy standards, embodied in Energy Policy and Conservation Act of 1975, differentiate between North American-made (75% or more value added in United States) and foreign-made vehicle in computing corporate average fuel economy	(1) Strict emission control standards (2) Difficult compliance procedures (3) Complex distribution system (4) 15–20% commodity tax on *all* cars, varying with size and weight (5) High dealer margins on luxury (United States) cars	(1) Safety and emission standards (2) Graduated motor vehicle tax based on horsepower	(1) Emission standards (2) Cars must be certified to be roadworthy (primarily to restrict Japanese imports)

Trade barrier	United Kingdom	Italy	Brazil	Mexico	Argentina	Korea
Tariff	10.9% EEC tariff	10.9% EEC tariff	Imports of autos prohibited; 250% rate on other motor vehicles	Range from 35% to 100% ad valorem	85% cars, to be lowered to 75% in 1981 55% on CU's, to go down to 45% in 1982	Auto imports banned in principle. Rates: 150% on autos and parts
Local content	None	None	Individually determined; if company makes positive contribution to balance of payments, more imports permitted	70% for passenger cars, 80% for trucks—both to rise 5% in 1981	Range from 96% to 75% depending on weight— will be lowered in next 2 yrs	Range from 60–95% for most cars assembled and produced
Quantitative restrictions	Imports of Japanese cars limited to about 10% of the market	1980 quota for Japanese cars: 2,200 vehicles	Quantity of imports affected by amount of exports— tax incentives for export	Import licenses required for most automotive products	Import licenses are being eliminated	Depending on "supply and demand" situation import licenses may be granted
Value-added tax	15%	18–35%	Varies from 11–14%, depending on region— may be reduced if the firm exports a certain value of output	10%—but producers of export goods are eligible for a refund of taxes paid in all stages of production	16%	13% gasoline VAT: 10%

(*continued overleaf*)

TABLE 16.1 (Continued)

Trade barrier	United Kingdom	Italy	Brazil	Mexico	Argentina	Korea
Nontariff barriers	Surtax of 5% on all vehicles	(1) Strict enforcement of "vehicle construction requirements"	(1) Usage tax of 3.5% on cars (2) Foreign exchange tax, 25% (3) Minimum payment terms above 180 days (4) Other severe restrictions	(1) Safety and emission standards (2) Excise tax on gas	Imports subject to other changes including a 1.5% "additional charge," a 3% consular fee, a 4% tax on ocean or river freight, and a sales tax	(1) Excise tax on gas, 180% (2) Registration tax, 5% (3) Defense surtax, 20% of registration tax

EEC European Economic Community.
Note: Value-added taxes (VAT) and so-called nontariff barriers noted here allegedly distort or limit trade, but are not necessarily discriminatory under the General Agreement on Tariffs and Trade.
Source: Business International, Survey of World Automobile Restrictions. Reprinted in US Department of Transportation. Partially revised.
a. This table refers to passenger automobiles only, and therefore the recent reclassification of cab chassis as light trucks, with the resulting 25% tariff rate is not shown. However, the import of the 25% traffic is highest on imported light trucks which are thought to be used primarily as passenger vehicles.

their products' value in North America (defined as Canada and the United States) by 1985. The expectation is that this requirement would force Toyota, Nissan (Datsun), and Honda to start substantial manufacturing operations in the United States and to cut back sharply on exports. Volkswagen (VW) would also be unable to continue to import the Audis and Porsches that make up a lucrative part of its product line.[12]

The UAW has estimated that such legislation would save over 800,000 US jobs at auto and parts producers. The Council of Eco-

[12] Richard I. Kirkland, Jr., "War of Words," *Fortune* (April 5, 1982), p. 39.

nomic Advisers (CEA) has argued that cutting off Japanese imports might actually reduce employment because of the closing of dealerships that sell Japanese cars. Other government estimates suggest that the job gain is likely to be between 110,000 and 200,000, with some offset because of reductions in foreign car dealerships and distribution. In addition, these last estimates suggest there would be a .3 percent increase in the consumer price index resulting from a 10 percent increase in car prices. Besides these changes, inadequate consideration has been given to the income effects and "second round" effects of decreases in foreign demand for US auto products, mainly for intermediate goods used to produce engines or cars overseas. There might also be countervailing duties imposed on US exports in retaliation for the imposition of local content regulations. This might include not only Japan but also several European nations (France, Italy, England, West Germany).

European auto producers have also been quite concerned about protectionism. On the beneficial side, restrictions provide a way to protect the all-important domestic markets.[13] However, they might also limit European auto firms' abilities to export parts and components and to maintain and expand cooperative ventures that have been organized to develop more advanced engines and to refine other technological improvements.

Structural Trends in World Production and Trade

There has been a dramatic international growth of new centers of auto production since the early 1960s. In part, this was due to the recovery and rapid growth of automakers in Europe and Japan. There was also a less well-appreciated relocation of production to Spain, Brazil, Mexico, Poland, and South Africa, the five nations that account for the major growth in the other category in figure 16.1, in order of their current importance. After 1970, however, the share of world production in the United States, Canada, and in Europe declined, while the Japanese share continued to grow.

There was also a sizable growth in production and assembly of cars in the developing nations. Although only a few nations had sizable amounts of production, such as Spain, Brazil, and Mexico (see table 16.2), the entire group accounted for almost 10 percent of world

[13] On the domestic orientation of European automakers, see R. D. Hocking, "Trade in Motor Cars Between the Major European Producers," *Economic Journal*, vol. 90, no. 359 (September 1980), p. 504.

Figure 16.1   *Shares of world production, selected countries*

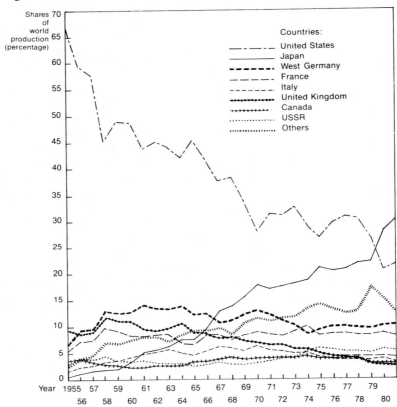

Source: R. Cole and R. Hervey, "Internationalization of the Auto Industry: A Background and Introduction."

production by 1975. Much of this growth was due to investments by multinational firms.[14]

Besides the well-recognized geographical dispersion of the industry, several other important structural changes occurred during the post-World War II years. Changes that occurred throughout the period included: moves by government to promote the development of export-oriented auto industries in both developed and developing

[14] Henk Kox and Arno van der Kruys, "The Passenger Car Industry: Tendencies of Relocation of Production to Peripheral Countries," Occasional Paper no. 11 (Tilburg, Netherlands: Development Research Institute, Tilburg University, 1981), p. 8.

Robert B. Cohen

TABLE 16.2 PRODUCTION AND ASSEMBLY OF CARS (ISIC 3843–07),
PERIPHERAL COUNTRIES, SELECTED YEARS
(× 1,000 units)

Country	1960	1965	1970	1975	1977
Europe
Spain	40	160	455	702	1,028
Portugal	—	33	56	43	33
Africa
Morocco[a]	—	5	20	24	21
South Africa	87	128	195	206	132
Asia
Turkey	—	—	5	75	58
Iran[a]	—	4	32	87	102
India	25	35	45	31	48
Malaysia (West)	—	—	21	39	53
Philippines	3	7	8	28	34
Indonesia	2	—	9	34	n.a.
South Korea	—	—	13	18	44
Latin America
Brazil	57	114	255	554	463
Argentina	50	135	169	185	168
Mexico	25	67	137	254	193
Venezuela	7	41	48	92	n.a.
Chile	2	6	21	5	10
Columbia	—	—	8	23	28

— Negligible.
n.a. Not available.
Source: UN Statistics from H. Kox and A. van der Kruys, "The Passenger Car Industry:
Tendencies of Relocation of Production to Peripheral Countries."
a. 1976 instead of 1977.

nations; and the use of less costly foreign centers for the production of cars or major components (engines, transmissions). Important structural changes that became widespread after the Iranian crisis of 1979 were: the shift of the US market to compacts and subcompact cars; the move to "downsize" cars; the development of "world cars"; international investment strategies that resulted in networks of facilities to serve entire regions; and cooperative arrangements for production.

On the trade side, the most apparent change was the rise of Japanese firms to a position as the largest exporters in the world. However, the decline of car producers in Western Europe from a position of net exporters towards a position of net importers has also been striking.

The structural changes in the auto sector resulting from higher prices were most evident in the US auto market. The share of compact cars grew from 39 to 66 percent between 1972 and 1980, while full-sized cars declined from 39 to 14 percent. These changes occurred while Japanese producers maintained a share of about 40 percent of the US compact car market.[15] These changes were part of the move to "downsize" US cars, that is, to reduce their weight, as a first step toward improving vehicle fuel economy. This enabled automakers to achieve 20 percent weight reduction by using new sheet metal for the body, shifting to a V–6 engine from a V–8, using smaller and lighter components (rear axles, suspension parts, and radiators), and an all new frame. While these were primarily design changes, they required new tooling or retooling, and a changeover of engine lines, typically costing $500 million per car line. In this phase the basic US rear-wheel design philosophy was maintained.[16]

The next three phases represented a change in components, based on the shift to front-wheel drive, major materials substitutions and redesign of the car, and the use of new technologies. In the first, some major changes were the use of a unitized body design; elimination of the frame and the rear axle; and replacement of the drive shaft and transmission by the transaxle. Second, for the car of the 1980s, materials substitutions are to be based on the use of new alloys and the development of techniques to use these materials. Third, even greater fuel economy is being sought by the development of new engines, advanced fuel management and engine electronics, and chassis and body refinements to improve aerodynamics and reduce weight.[17]

Many of these structural changes also allowed automobile firms to exploit economies of scale much more readily than before. Where a major subcomponent, such as an engine, might have previously been

---

[15] US Congress, "Current Problems of the US Automobile Industry and Policies to Address Them," staff working paper (Washington: Congressional Budget Office, Natural Resources and Commerce Division, July 1980), pp. 11, 14.

[16] John P. O'Donnell, George Byron, and Mike O'Connell, "Identifying Automobile Changes in Facilities and Capital Equipment and Assessing Community and Employment Impacts," [DOT-TSC-OST-81-3] (Washington: US Department of Transportation, Office of the Secretary of Transportation, May 1981), pp. 6–7.

[17] Ibid., pp. 8–15.

Figure 16.2   Motor vehicle exports, selected countries

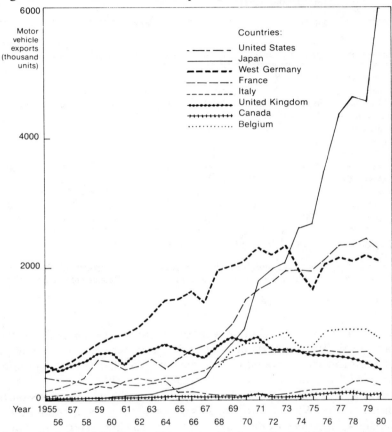

Source: R. Cole and R. Hervey, "Internationalization of the Auto Industry: A Background and Introduction."

produced at a level of 200,000 to 300,000, economies of scale were now thought to extend to a level of one million or more. These developments were very much linked to the development of a world car.[18]

In trade, Japan emerged as the dominant auto exporting nation during the 1970s, although France also showed strong growth (see figure 16.2). Japanese exports not only grew in the US market, but

[18] Robert B. Cohen, "Brave New World of the Global Car," *Challenge*, vol. 24, no. 2 (May–June 1981), pp. 28–35.

TABLE 16.3   WORLD TRADE IN CARS, 1979
             (thousand units)

Exports by	North America	West Europe	Japan	Latin America	COMECON	Rest of world	Import total
Exports to							
North America	n.a.	700	1,500	0	0	0	2,200
Western Europe	50	n.a.	600	0	200	0	850
Japan	0	0	n.a.	0	0	0	0
Latin America	100	100	100	n.a.	0	0	300
COMECON	0	0	0	0	n.a.	0	0
Rest of world	50	700	800	0	100	n.a.	1,700[a]
Export total	200	1,500	3,000	0	300	0	5,000[a]

COMECON Council for Mutual Economic Assistance.
n.a. Not applicable.
Sources: Eurofinance, *European Car Industry Report*, no. 4, 1980, p. 31; R. Cole and R. Hervey, "Internationalization of the Auto Industry: A Background and Introduction."
a. Totals fail to sum in the original.

also rose from 2.0 percent of West European markets in 1970 to 10.4 percent in 1980. Exports outside of Western Europe as a percentage of West European production dropped over much of the same period, from 17.1 percent in 1970 to 11.9 percent in 1979.[19]

Table 16.3 illustrates the level of auto trade between various parts of the world. While half of Japan's exports are to the United States, Japanese exports to other markets were growing faster than North American sales; the rates were 11.6 percent for North America, 30.9 percent for Southeast Asia, and 24.7 percent in Europe.[20]

Another trend after 1965 was the growth of trade in automotive parts, engines, and bodies. Table 16.4 provides data on this trade for the United States. Overall, the table shows that between 1970 and 1979, US exports of parts grew faster than imports. Table 16.4 also

[19]   Robert E. Cole and Richard Hervey, "Internationalization of the Auto Industry: A Background and Introduction" (Ann Arbor: University of Michigan, Center for Japanese Studies, March 5, 1982; processed), p. 4.

[20]   Industrial Bank of Japan, "Motor Vehicles," *Japanese Finance and Industry: Quarterly Survey* (July–September 1981), pp. 1–21 cited in Cole and Hervey, *Internationalization of the Auto Industry*, p. 9.

TABLE 16.4   US IMPORTS AND EXPORTS OF AUTOMOTIVE PARTS,
ENGINES, AND BODIES, 1965–79
(million dollars)

Year	Total, all areas	UK	EEC-6[a]	Total, Western Europe	Canada	Latin America	Japan
Imports							
1965	193.2	17.6	50.3	71.6	112.8	.7	6.9
1970	1,464.3	38.7	158.5	207.4	1,079.9	19.3	151.6
1975	3,235.4	72.8	324.5	433.3	2,033.1	207.3	528.1
1976	5,146.1	72.4	389.5	506.4	3,007.9	291.6	1,221.7
1979	6,964.9	210.8	1,058.6	1,337.2	3,748.8	568.7	1,084.4
Exports							
1965	867.4	17.6	32.2	71.3	621.8	115.5	3.5
1970	2,236.5	32.1	74.4	148.9	1,601.5	274.5	17.0
1975	4,993.0	56.0	160.1	314.0	3,521.2	648.3	34.9
1976	5,908.0	73.0	211.0	397.0	4,280.7	668.0	53.4
1979	8,445.6	165.1	376.3	667.0	5,316.6	1,530.4	286.8

Source: US Department of Commerce, Bureau of Economic Analysis, Balance of Payments Division, Special Tabulations for the Congressional Budget Office Study of the Auto Industry.
a. Belgium, France, Germany, Italy, Luxembourg, Netherlands.

illustrates that, while Canada accounted for much of the growth of trade in these parts with the United States, trade with Latin America and Europe was becoming more important during the late 1970s. A similar trend occurred in Europe, with intra-European and East-West trade in parts increasing rapidly.[21]

International Dimensions of the Response by Auto Firms

A major factor promoting change in world production and trade has been the internationalization of the auto industry, defined as the establishment of overseas affiliates for the production of intermediate and final products.

[21] On this trend, see B. Kortus and W. Kaczorowski, "Polish Industry Forges External Links," in F. E. I. Hamilton and G. J. R. Linge, eds., *Spatial Analysis, Industry and Industrial Environment*, vol. 2, International Industrial Systems (Chichester, England: John Wiley & Sons, 1981), pp. 119–54.

Due to the emergence of world-scale competitors that have eroded their domestic dominance, US automakers have taken new risks to assure their future survival and to catch up to their competitors. This response is also a result of the shift of auto demand to smaller cars that can be built from a similar design throughout the world. It reflects the need to build cars much more cheaply if US auto producers are to stay price competitive.

Foremost in the minds of US auto executives is how to achieve a significant position as a producer in the key markets of the future in the United States, Europe, and the Pacific Basin that will assure the long-term survival of their firms—what I call "strategic positioning." Previously, firms had focused largely on home markets and on the exploitation of oligopolistic advantages in the large foreign markets. But the center of growth is shifting to the developing nations and with the changes mentioned above, regional, rather than local, markets become the key.

International Market Positions and Investment Strategies

To respond to the rising international competitiveness of foreign automakers Ford and GM have explored several investment alternatives. First, to establish key positions in strategic markets, they have had to invest sizable amounts in key production centers over the last few years or face substantially higher costs in trying to enter them later. This is essentially the case documented by F. T. Knickerbocker for entry into foreign markets by US firms during the 1960, but with a slightly different twist. By using their bargaining power in a sophisticated way with host governments, US auto firms may be able to limit the number of "follow the leader" entrants described by Knickerbocker and to outflank their foreign competitors.[22] Second, the export incentives and subsidies available from foreign nations make production in nations where "greenfield" plants are highly subsidized much cheaper than in traditional centers. Thus, Ford and GM can begin to regain part of the cost disadvantages in competing with the Japanese by obtaining major components and subassemblies from plants in such nations. Such incentives also reduce the amount of capital that must be invested in developing nations and provide US auto firms with greater flexibility in the use of their investment funds. Third, US automakers have begun to achieve substantial cost

---

[22] F. T. Knickerbocker, *Oligopolistic Reaction and the Multinational Enterprise* (Boston: Harvard University Press, 1973).

TABLE 16.5   INVESTMENT BY FORD AND GM, BY REGION
(billion dollars)

Region	Ford investments 1976–80	Ford investments 1981–83	GM investments 1979–82
Continental Europe	.725	1.3	5.6[a]
United Kingdom	2.0	4.9	.230
Latin and Central America	.535[b]	1.4[c]	.915
Australia	.475	.080	.510[d]
Far East	.300	.055	>.300
Canada	—	—	3.0

— Not available.
Sources: Carol MacLennan, "GM Investment/Capital Spending Program," Department of Transportation, NHTSA, processed, April 17, 1981. J.K. Richardson, "Ford Expansion/Investment Information," Department of Transportation, NHTSA, processed, February 2, 1982.
a. Includes $3.4 billion in West Germany for OPEL.
b. 1974–79.
c. 1980–84.
d. 1979–83.

reductions by demanding wage and workplace concessions from unions in the United States.

International Market Positions.   Recent investments by Ford and GM indicate where they have decided to situate their future production (table 16.5). Each company is making half or more of its capital expenditures over the next few years in Europe, largely in its key subsidiary—Ford UK for Ford and Opel for GM. The importance of subsidized investment in lower-wage areas of the world is clearly evident. Ford has received substantial subsidies for its new investments in the United Kingdom and tax benefits from Brazil and Mexico. GM will utilize sizable government subsidies from Austria and Spain, in addition to tax concessions in Mexico and Brazil.[23] Plans for new investment in key production centers for the Asia-Pacific region appear to have increased substantially over the last few years.

[23] Many of the data cited in this discussion come from compilations of recent investment plans prepared by Carol MacLennan and James K. Richardson at the US Department of Transportation's NHTSA. See Carol MacLennan, "GM Investment/Capital Spending Program," April 17, 1981, processed, and J. K. Richardson, "Ford Expansion/Investment Information," February 2, 1982, processed.

Several examples illustrate the regional, rather than national, focus of these new investments. Ford's regional strategy in Asia and the Pacific is built around selling Laser models. These are assembled in plants in New Zealand and five other plants from knocked-down parts of the "Familia," a front-wheel-drive subcompact produced by Toyo Kogyo (Mazda) in which Ford holds 25 percent interest.[24] In the case of GM, J–car engine sourcing has been integrated regionally and worldwide. Engines from Australia are to be shipped to Japan and the United States, Australia, and Brazil will also supply J–car engines for the new Opel plant in Kaiserslautern, West Germany.[25]

Ford has faced special problems in achieving a market position in Scandinavia where imports are relatively unrestricted[26] and price competition rather important. Ford traditionally sourced cars from its European operations for sale to Scandinavian nations, but has recently switched this strategy to include more cars produced in Brazil. Although Ford succeeded in achieving its desired 14 percent share in Norway in the late 1970s, its market share in most Scandinavian nations has dropped precipitously since the end of 1979. In contrast with Ford, the total Japanese shares in a number of these nations grew rapidly, rising from 16.5 percent, 21.9 percent, and 28.3 percent in Denmark, Norway, and Finland, respectively, to 35.2 percent, 38.7 percent, and 43.3 percent between 1976 and September 1980. (These composite shares include Toyota, Nissan, Mazda, and Honda.) The most rapid increase occurred during 1980, a period when the Japanese cars enjoyed a substantial price advantage over Ford's offerings (table 16.6).

Ford's loss of market share in these traditional export markets was proportional to the size of its price disadvantage. It now faces Japanese competitors who sold nearly one of every two new cars in these markets during 1980 with the realization that it does not have the ability to adjust prices to meet local competition.

Since these markets are not restricted, one solution is to market cars produced in less developed nations where labor and materials

[24] "Toyota-Ford Collaboration Proposal," *Oriental Economist* (September 1980), p. 8.
[25] MacLennan, "GM Spending Program," and figures from the International Metalworkers Report on GM.
[26] US International Trade Commission, *Certain Motor Vehicles*, pp. A-108–A-109.

TABLE 16.6   EUROPEAN AUTOMOTIVE OPERATIONS, JAPANESE CAR
PRICE POSITION

Country	Model	Price	Ford (over) Japanese (percentage)
Denmark	Fiesta L 1.1	$11,809	(27.7)
	Toyota Starlet	9,246	
	Escort Base	$12,813	(38.5)
	Mazda 323	9,249	
Finland	Escort Base	$10,712	(12.5)
	Datsun Cherry	9,522	
	Taunus I 1.6	$14,060	(11.7)
	Toyota Carina	12,592	
Norway	Escort Special	$11,390	(2.5)
	Toyota Corolla	11,115	
	Taunus I. 1.6	$13,978	(13.1)
	Mazda 626	12,359	
Sweden	Fiesta GI	$ 8,107	(3.0)
	Datsun Cherry	7,870	
	Escort L. 1.6	$ 8,917	(11.5)
	Mazda 323	7,998	

Source: Ford of Europe, Body and Assembly Operations, "1980 Controller's Office
Review Meeting," December 18, 1980.

costs are much lower than in Western Europe.[27] Indeed, one of Ford's
responses has been to market Brazilian Escorts in these markets.[28]
Thus, global sourcing of cars becomes a viable alternative in markets
where imports are not restricted and price competitiveness can be
achieved by low-cost auto production.

Overseas Sourcing of Engines.   Table 16.7 indicates the vast changes
that have occurred in foreign sourcing since the late 1970s. Only a

[27] Labor and materials costs are usually lower than in Western Europe,
but the subsidies that firms receive under Brazil's export promotion plan
most likely cause the biggest difference in overall production costs.
[28] Ford of Europe, "Product Letter on the Brazilian Escort," internal
memorandum (January 1981).

TABLE 16.7   ENGINES TO BE OUTSOURCED BY US AUTOMAKERS,
MODEL YEAR 1983

	Brazil	*Mexico*	*Canada*	*Japan*	*France*
Ford	4-cyl. 2.3L 700,000ª	4-cyl. 2.2L 200,000 6-cyl. (?)	6-cyl. 3.8L 300,000	4-cyl. Diesel 160,000	
GM	4-cyl. 1.8L OHC 200,000	4-, 6-, and 8- cyl. 25,000 6-cyl. 450,000	V-8 4.4L 125,000 V-8 5.0L 110,000	4-cyl. 1.6L Diesel 60,000	
Chrysler		4-cyl. 2.2L 350,000	4- & 6-cyl. (?)	4-cyl. 2.2L 4-cyl. 2.6L 150,000	4-cyl. 1.6L 150,000 Turbodiesel 1.7L 100,000
VW	4-cyl. (?)	4-cyl. 350,000	n.a.	n.a.	
AMC		Renault of Mexico 200,000			
Total	900,000	1,575,000	535,000	370,000	250,000

n.a. Not applicable.
Sources: Various Articles in trade journals, including *Ward's Auto Reports, Ward's Engine Update, Automotive News, American Metal Markets, Iron Age*, and *Jobber and Warehouse Executive*
a. Includes an unknown amount from the United Kingdom.

few years ago, sourcing was limited to Chrysler's purchases of less than 100,000 L–6 and V–8 engines from its Mexican subsidiary, and Ford's 50,000 2.3 liter L–4 engines from Ford do Brazil. These imports were insignificant when compared to total domestic production.[29]

By the fall of 1983, however, the situation will change dramatically. One-third to one-half of the engines in cars produced in the United States will be purchased abroad, some three million engines, with

[29] US Department of Transportation, *The US Automobile Industry*, [The Goldschmidt Report] (Washington: Office of the Secretary of Transportation, 1980), p. 56.

another half million being imported from Canada. Why the rapid shift? First, because automakers are seeking ways to reduce the costs of major subassemblies, they have resorted to sourcing from overseas firms with excess capacity or to establishing engine plants in foreign subsidiaries where export subsidies or tax concessions make production quite profitable.[30] (Engines account for one-sixth of the price of a small car's material costs according to figures from Rath and Strong.) Overseas production also lowers costs because it reduces tooling and fixed costs.[31]

To achieve integrated international sourcing, US auto firms are often not concerned about whether foreign investment can be justified solely on economic grounds. Rather, they want to know whether they and their parts suppliers can benefit from export incentives and from tax reductions that are linked to export volumes. In the case of Ford's recent decision to locate an engine plant in Mexico, government policies that reduced the overall cost of building the plant made the difference between producing in Japan, the United States, or Mexico (table 16.8). Indeed, as William Johnston has argued, without the benefits provided by the Mexican government, it would have made little sense "for Ford management to accept the risks of longer supply lines, less assured Mexican government policies, and the inevitable criticism from US politicians and union leaders."[32]

Thus, lower labor costs are not the primary factor leading automakers to move facilities such as engine plants abroad. This is particularly true since labor is not a very important element in the production of the major subassemblies currently being moved abroad, such as engines. In Japan, engines require only 3.5 hours or $40 of labor each, or less than 5 percent of total costs and as Johnston has noted, capital—research and development, design, engineering, and tooling—is the most important factor for optimal production.[33]

All of this is not meant as a criticism of the policies of nations such as Brazil and Mexico. Rather, it suggests that there is a need for the establishment of international rules to govern what might be "fair" subsidies for developing nations to offer to international firms to set

[30] William B. Johnston, "Relocating Automobile Production to the Developing World: The Multinational View," MIT Future of the Automobile Program, June 1981.
[31] See the figures published in "Why Detroit Can't Cut Prices," *Business Week* (March 1, 1982), pp. 110–111.
[32] Johnston, "Relocating Automobile Production," p. 14.
[33] Ibid., p. 16.

TABLE 16.8 FORD ENGINE SOURCING ALTERNATIVES

	Purchase Japan	*Build United States*	*Build Mexico (Peugeot)*	
Total investment (million dollars)	469	1,074	834	
United States[a]	228	833	228	
Mexico[b]	241	241	606	
			Ex benefits	With benefits[c]
Landed cost (c.i.f. Detroit, dollars per engine) (4)	1,233	1,235	1,221	821
Gas	998	1,062	1,078	738
Diesel	1,665	1,556	1,487	975
Average annual profit, (compared to purchase Japan) (million dollars)	—	7	32	227
Time-adjusted rate of return (percentage)	—	1	5	29

Source: Office of Senator Howard Metzenbaum (not confirmed or denied by Ford)
a. US investment needs for all options include $228 million of engineering, design, and vehicle modifications.
b. Mexico investment needs for Japan and US options include $241 million for small Mexican engine plant.
c. Mexican export incentives include rights to increase imports into Mexico (which increase Ford earnings by $.37 per dollar), and tax reductions equal to 8 percent of export volume.
d. Weighted Average of 65 percent gas and 35 percent diesel.

up "infant industries." Without such accords between industrial nations and newly industrializing ones, subsidies are likely to continue to contribute to the continued migration of important parts plants to the newly industrialized countries.

Integrated Regional Networks.   Ford's integration of motor vehicle manufacturing in Western Europe took advantage of the formation of the EEC and the abolition of intra-EEC tariffs on industrial goods in 1968. Since any factory in the EEC has access to the entire market, plants can be established in nearly any nation to serve operations in the others, subject to transportation cost constraints. Ford integrated its operations in the 1960s to spread investment (largely because its British subsidiary was prone to labor unrest), to avoid labor shortages near existing plants, to spread the high costs of new model development, and to take advantage of the market opportunities in the EEC—Britain was not yet a member.

As integration has proceeded, plant assembly has become more specialized and larger model runs have been achieved. With the introduction of the Fiesta in 1976, new and complex patterns of sourcing emerged, linking together distant plants. Carburetors and distributors from Belfast and transaxles from Bordeaux were linked to assembly plants in Britain, Germany, and Spain.[34]

Coproduction Arrangements. The growth of the East European auto industry has been based upon "coproduction agreements, licenses, buy-back arrangements, and some minority equity participation"[35] rather than on investments by multinational firms. Technology is purchased from firms in the West and the projects are usually directly linked to countertrade.

Fiat has been the most active in arranging operations in East Europe. It has granted three licenses in Poland, Romania, and the USSR that account for the production of 920,000 vehicles, or almost three-fourths of the annual production under license in these nations. The remainder is accounted for by Renault, Citroen, and VW. GM has licensed truck rear-axle assembly in Hungary since 1975, while Ford has subcontracted starter-motor production to Yugoslavia since 1979.

Export arrangements are usually tied into the technology transfer agreements for production in Eastern Europe. These so-called industrial cooperation agreements account for over 80 percent of East-West trade in auto products.[36]

Summary

The extent of the international expansion of firms depends upon several considerations. First, how much flexibility can firms gain in dealing with labor at home. Firms can demand substantial cost reductions to meet competition from abroad and rationalize their domestic investments along cost/benefit lines, that is, can a component be purchased more cheaply from an outside supplier or overseas, is

---

[34] Gerald T. Bloomfield, "The Changing Spatial Organization of Multinational Corporations in the World Automotive Industry," in F. E. I. Hamilton and G. J. R. Linge, eds., *Spatial Analysis*, p. 382.

[35] United Nations Center on Transnational Corporations, *Transnational Corporations in the International Auto Industry*, restricted draft (New York: United Nations, April 1982), pp. 113–118.

[36] Ibid., pp. 113, 116.

there a way to spinoff plants and achieve major cost reductions, and can productivity be enhanced by stricter regulations and a broader definition of job content?

Second, firms can use their bargaining power to gain economic advantages through political means. By investing in less developed nations, US automakers can take advantage of the host government's ability to restrict the number of local producers and to offer export incentives. By limiting the number of entrants host governments assure investing firms a higher than normal level of profit. The restrictions provide a limited number of firms with a base to serve an emerging *regional* market (for the Pacific Basin, Mexico, Brazil, Australia, and possibly the Philippines).[37]

Third, automakers will try to obtain substantial cost advantages by developing new cars and devising new ways to produce them. How sizable gains from automation will be remains unclear.

Ford, GM, and a number of other large automakers have now adopted a strategy of "strategic positioning." By selecting the right locations for production facilities in specific *regions* of the world rather than specific *nations*, they assure that integrated production can be achieved by linking together facilities within each region. The extensive investments major automakers have made in developing nations is a good indication that in the future these countries will be a major site for competition among the world's largest auto firms. They also suggest that market distortions due to host-government subsidies will continue to be important determinants of investment.

US Competitiveness

One of the great dilemmas facing students of the auto industry is to explain why US firms lost their competitiveness in the world's auto industry. Economists face a unique situation, because the auto sector is traditionally assumed to be an industry that is well-suited to compete from an industrial nation such as the United States, being capital-intensive and skill-intensive, and requiring numerous technologically advanced inputs.

---

[37] The argument I make here concerning the need for "strategic positioning" to serve emerging regional markets is further corroborated by the case of Ford's 1972 investment in Spain. In that case, an export subsidy from the Spanish government substantially lowered the costs of producing Escorts in Valencia compared to the costs of producing in existing European plants.

The usual list of problems used to explain the declining competitiveness of US firms will be examined here—an isolated, profitable domestic market dominated by a few large producers; high labor costs and low productivity; poor strategic planning by management; lags in technological innovation. However, it is interesting to begin from the opposite extreme and examine the reasons for the growing competitiveness of Japanese firms.

According to Kōichi Shimokawa, the factors that resulted in significant improvements in Japan's international competitive position and productivity in the face of the trials caused by the oil crisis of 1973 were both internal (micro) and external (macro). On the macro level, Shimokawa cites four factors:

- the support given to the auto industry by the government and banks, especially in establishing mass-production systems in the early 1960s and bringing about the reorganization of the industry
- the late development of Japan's auto industry, enabling its firms to acquire the latest and most advanced technology developed by others, and to develop up-to-date production facilities
- the competitive domestic market in Japan that fostered the introduction of new facilities and technology, and promoted the development of better quality control systems and other control techniques
- the constantly improved techniques used by producers of basic material inputs (steel, rubber, aluminum castings, and glass) and parts producers.

Among the micro factors Shimokawa cites are: the excellent industrial relations that depend largely on company unions and promote contributions by workers to improvements in the quality of production; the strong cohesion between parts producers and automakers; and the introduction of industrial robots and other labor-saving devices; Japanese-style management techniques, characterized by quality circles; and concerted efforts by management and labor to achieve technological breakthroughs.[38]

In addition, Shimokawa acknowledges the key role of the policy adopted by the Ministry of International Trade and Industry (MITI) in 1955 that was designed to promote the growth of the auto industry as a strategic industry. The measures taken by MITI included preferential access to foreign exchange to purchase patents and import advanced production facilities, tax incentives, preferential treatment

---

[38] Kōichi Shimokawa, "Automobiles—Groping for Coexistence Rather Than International Rivalry," *Japan Quarterly* (1982).

in depreciating plants and equipment, encouragement of the technological improvement of small- and medium-sized parts manufacturers. As a result, supporting industries, such as casting, metal fabricating, and machining eliminated their technological backwardness. Again in 1965, although a MITI move to promote mergers to strengthen the industry in the face of growing foreign competition failed, the two major automakers, Toyota and Nissan, formed their own groups that accounted for 60 percent of Japan's market.[39]

Management Insularity

A number of the innovations that facilitated Japan's increase in competitiveness were certainly available to managers in US firms. The introduction of automation, the extra attention paid to quality control, and the importance attached to technological innovation in Japan could have been matched by US firms. However, US firms were quite profitable throughout the 1960s and early 1970s, although some major problems of product management were quite well-known to those at GM. One also gets the impression from observers that top management was quite reluctant to recognize trends, such as the move to small cars, that were apparent in sales charts from 1965 on, but contrary to GM's traditional approach.[40]

In addition, plant visits suggest that in some areas little new investment has occurred since the 1950s. Stamping machines are often 30 years old and lack more up-to-date tracks that permit rapid die changeovers. Working conditions are often little better than in the 1930s, with noise, fumes, and oil spills commonplace. One rarely sees much contact between workers and supervisors. After a series of plant visits, it is not difficult to understand why there is such antagonism between workers and GM management.

Cost Disadvantages

According to most studies, Japanese manufacturers enjoy a substantial cost advantage over US producers in the subcompact range. There are various estimates of the gap, with Harbour and Associates citing a net Japanese cost advantage of $1,718 (table 16.9). The overall cost advantage results from the Japanese supplier network as well as

---

[39] Ibid.

[40] Patrick Wright, *On a Clear Day You Can See General Motors* (Grosse Pointe, Mich.: Wright Enterprises, 1979), especially ch. 7, "Big Problems at Chevrolet," and ch. 12, "Pushing Small Cars in a Big Car Company."

TABLE 16.9 SUMMARY OF JAPANESE PRODUCTION COST ADVANTAGE FOR A TYPICAL SUBCOMPACT CAR (1973 dollars)

Technology	73	*Subtotal*	73
Management systems and techniques[a]			
Quality control systems	329		
Manpower			
Scrap			
Warranty savings			
Just-in-time production	550		
Smaller plants			
Plant complexes			
Fewer people			
Utility savings			
Interest savings			
In-bound freight savings			
Material handling engineering	41		
Other productivity improvements	478		
Quality circles			
Job classification		*Subtotal*	1,398
Union management relations			
Absenteeism (unscheduled)			
(United States 6–8 percent vs Japan, 2 percent)	81		
Relief systems and allowances	89		
Union representatives	12	*Subtotal*	182
Wage and fringe rates	550		
(Total hours Japan × difference in weighted average wage rate)		*Subtotal*	550
Total manufacturing cost advantage		*TOTAL*	2,203
Japanese ocean freight, duty, and port cost			(485)
Net Japanese landed cost advantage		*NET*	1,718

Source: "Analysis of Japanese Landed Cost Advantage for the Manufacture of Sub-Compact Cars." © 1982, Harbour and Associates, Inc., Berkley, Mich., reprinted by permission; US Department of Transportation, Office of the Secretary of Transportation, *The US Automobile Industry 1981.*

a. Chapter 3, *Japanese Landed Cost Advantage*, pp. 76 to 83 for a description of these techniques.

TABLE 16.10   COMPARISON OF US-JAPAN PER UNIT LABOR COST:
CAR MIX[a] ($1 = ¥ 215)

	Production labor hours	Dollar cost per hour (including fringe)	Total dollar cost per unit
United States			
Assemblers	110[b]	20	2,200
Components	30[c]	12[d]	360
		18.28	
Total	140	(weighted)	2,560
Japan			
Assemblers	40[e]	12[f]	480[g]
Components	50[h]	7[i]	350
		9.22	
Total	90	(weighted)	830
		Difference =	1,730

Sources: Japan labor: Ministry of Labor (MOL) survey, MITI survey, Japan Automotive Manufacturer's Association (JAMA) survey, Japan Auto Parts Industries Association (JAPIA) survey, and individual company reports. US labor: Bureau of Labor
Statistics (BLS) survey, company reports. Japan labor cost: individual company reports
(including Japanese language financial reports showing labor break-out); MOL survey;
annual survey by Japan's auto union; MOF quarterly finance survey; BLS; Ministry
of Foreign Affairs ("Wages in Japan"). US Labor Cost: individual company reports;
BLS data; state-specific employment surveys. M. Anderson, "Retrenchment and Reconstruction in the US Auto Industry."
a. Includes assemblers and components; excludes raw materials. Excludes heavy trucks
in United States; includes light trucks and *clerical* workers in Japan to compensate for
any possible subcontract production labor.
b. On recent years' car and light truck mix: GM shows 140 to 170 hours without
clerical workers, 180 to 200 + with clerical; Ford shows 95 to 125 hours without clerical,
135 to 160 + with clerical.
c. Probably low: BLS SIC-code aggregation plus Bureau of Census data suggest peripheral industries, excluding materials, could add as many as 60 hours to main producers on car and truck mix.
d. BLS "All manufacturing" about $1 lower; but auto suppliers tend to skew higher.
Also note supplier hours probably low; therefore possible difference not significant.
e. Toyota 33 hours (1981), Nissan 44 hours (1980) (including clerical); 1979 MITI
Labor survey plus JAMA production = 40 hours/unit average for assembler including
clerical.
f. Toyota reports $10 (1980), $10.80 (1981); union survey in Japan says $9.00 to $9.50
(1980).
g. Toyota shows $350 (1981), Nissan shows $341 (1979).
h. JAIPA survey says 58 hours (1980) *including* clerical, *36 hours* excluding clerical;
some of this labor goes to aftermarket parts and motorcycles.
i. BLS suggests $7 to $8 for Japan auto industry, including assemblers, $5 to $6.50
for all manufacturing in Japan.

the prime manufacturers, with many of the differences related to
labor costs. The advantage not only restricts the pricing options of
US auto firms, but also provides Japanese manufacturers with handsome profits.

Several factors cause the large difference in labor costs. One is the significant differences in the *number of hours* it takes to build a vehicle (table 16.10). Another factor is the difference in wages per hour. A third is the fact that labor content—which was roughly similar in Japan and the United States in the late 1960s at about 150 hours per vehicle—has improved steadily in Japan but remained static in the United States. In 1980 there was still 150 hours of labor in each US car, but only about half as much in Japanese cars. A fourth factor is that real labor costs in the United States increased against production efficiency trends. Fifth, social systems also allowed the labor costs (including all benefits and subsidies) to remain significantly lower in Japan than in the United States.[41]

Another source of the labor cost disparity is the fact that the proportion of labor content hours contributed by lower-paid supplier labor is greater in Japan than in the United States (table 16.10). The Japanese auto assemblers' extended coordination over suppliers through the group structure of the auto-producing entities may be responsible for this disparity.

According to Anderson's calculations, even if Japanese firms had to pay US wage rates and benefits, they would still have a cost advantage because of the difference in labor content. The labor differential is large and derives from a number of different factors, all of which need to be addressed to reduce the present cost disadvantage.[42]

Automakers and some economists argue that regulation contributed substantially to the decline of competitiveness among US auto firms. They find that such investments imposed substantial new costs on automakers and did not contribute to improved innovation or technological change. Others counter this argument, holding that federal regulation stimulates innovation in an industry that has been slow to innovate.[43]

[41] Martin Anderson, "Retrenchment and Reconstruction in the US Auto Industry: Labor Management, and International Implications," MIT Future of the Automobile Program, pp. 5–6.

[42] Ibid., p. 7.

[43] See Lawrence J. White, "Automobile Emissions Control Policy—Success Story or Wrongheaded Regulation?" and Joan Claybrook, "Concluding Remarks: Regulation and Innovation in the Automobile Industry," in W. J. Abernathy and D. H. Ginsburg, eds., *Proceeding on the Workshops on Technological Change in the US Automobile Industry, October 1977 through April 1978 and the Symposium on Technology, Government and the Automotive Future, October 19–20, 1978*, [DOT-TSC-NHTSA-79-33] (Washington: US Department of Transportation, NHTSA, 1979).

Exchange Rate Influences

With the yen at near 250 to the dollar in June 1982, it is argued that if the exchange rate were 170 yen to the dollar there would be a dramatic improvement in US competitiveness. Daniel Citrin has shown that although Japanese firms were able to limit some of the effects of yen appreciation in the past by lowering their yen-based export prices (in part, as a result of greater productivity and lower wage rates), their relative export price did rise significantly in the late 1970s.[44] According to Frank Vargo, the US Commerce Department's Assistant Secretary for Europe, a 25 percent increase in the value of the yen would probably permit Ford and GM to enter the small-car market more aggressively. Thus, a change in exchange rates could have a substantial impact on auto prices and, therefore, on the sales of imports, particularly those from Japan.

But US automakers face several difficulties in taking advantage of exchange rate shifts. First, the US dollar has been appreciating, rather than depreciating in value. Research by Alan V. Deardorff and Robert M. Stern using a disaggregated trade model has shown that the transportation equipment sector will have the largest increase in imports of any sector because of actual exchange rate shifts during the second quarter of 1980 and the second quarter of 1981. Four quarters after the exchange rate change occurred, imports are expected to grow by nearly $4 billion.[45] Second, Japanese automakers have significantly improved the quality and image of their cars by adding more accessories to them. This has enhanced their nonprice competitiveness. Third, recent Commerce Department data suggest that Japanese firms are loading more options onto their cars to obtain as much dollar value in sales as possible from each car imported under the new voluntary export restraints. This creates a problem for US automakers, since it entices Japanese automakers to compete in the medium- and luxury-car markets, the very areas where US automakers obtain their greatest profits.

---

[44] Daniel Citrin, "Dynamic Adjustment of Japanese Exports to Exchange Rate Fluctuations for Selected Industries," unpublished Ph.D. dissertation (Ann Arbor: University of Michigan, 1982).

[45] Alan V. Deardorff and Robert M. Stern, "The Sectoral Impact of the Recent Appreciation of the US Dollar" (Ann Arbor: Department of Economics and Institute of Public Policy Studies, University of Michigan, April 1, 1982; processed), p. 28.

As consumer loyalty in those larger car markets that are less price elastic is lost, price increases on imports may result in less improvement in the sales of larger US cars. This may also be true of small- and medium-sized cars—note consumers' perceptions that Japanese cars are far more durable and less troublesome than US cars of the same size. As a result, even sizable exchange rate adjustments may not cause a substantial improvement in the competitiveness of US autos.

Summary

The reasons for the decline of the competitiveness of US auto firms are numerous and it is difficult to identify a single dominant factor. While exchange rates are thought to be important, they appear to be less of a problem than the market-oriented strategy of Japanese firms and the Japanese government, the labor cost advantages, and the inability of US firms to innovate in product design and production. Another factor that has contributed to the decline but is difficult to measure is the perception of consumers that Japanese cars are better made than US ones.[46]

Recent events suggest that there have been significant shifts in strategy by some of the multinational firms in the industry. These changes have resulted in firms paying much greater attention to total costs and to systemwide, rather than division-level benefits.[47] In addition, firms appear to be more amenable to flexible schemes of production. The emerging interest in confederations of autonomous partners, such as the one involving GM, Isuzu, Suzuki, and Toyota is quite strong.[48]

These new forms of behavior indicate that some major adjustments are taking place to address the problem of declining competitiveness. A major unknown is whether the substantial investment by GM and Ford in new plant and equipment—largely in the United States—can turn the industry around.

[46] US International Trade Commission, *Certain Motor Vehicles*, pp. A-65–A-66.

[47] Robert E. Krapfel, Jr., John T. Mentzer, and Rex R. Williams, "International Logistics Management at General Motors: Philosophy and Practice," *International Journal of Physical Distribution and Materials Management* (United Kingdom), vol. 11, no. 5–6 (1981), pp. 12–20.

[48] Peter F. Drucker, "The Shape of Industry to Come," *Industry Week*, vol. 212, no. 1 (January 11, 1982), pp. 54–59.

From this discussion of the problems that have led to the declining competitiveness of the US auto industry it should be apparent that even if the vehicle market in the United States expands considerably, US auto firms must change their past practices. In addition, as the US auto public's preference has shifted to small cars, the domestic market has become highly attractive to European firms, adding another competitive group to the powerful Japanese. US auto firms will also be subjected to growing competition for the lucrative, top-of-the-line market that was formerly their own domain.

The Future: Protectionism, Bilateral Agreements, Export Restraints, or Free Trade?

The international linkages of the auto industry that have been described here, and the tendency for United States and West European auto firms to respond to competition by investing abroad or obtaining major parts or car lines from abroad should argue against any restraints on trade. However, the major multinationals in this sector are only now beginning to recognize the extent of the crisis they face and the drain that the resources needed to reorient their product lines has imposed on their balance sheets. There is little working capital left at GM or Ford, though few have raised any alarms over this sorry state of affairs.

Nonetheless, the financial crisis of these large multinationals and the likelihood that their financial situation will not improve greatly over the next two years creates enormous pressures for protectionism. There is a strong inclination in the general public to give these firms some breathing room, particularly when so many jobs are tied to their continued existence. Any surge in imports after Japanese VERs are removed would only trigger a further outcry for some kind of protectionist response, be it a tariff, quota, or a local content requirement. The major US automobile firms have not united in pressing for such a response, but if their attempts to reposition their product lines fail, they have a tremendous amount of influence that could be exerted in Washington, especially since the automobile industry has a reach that permeates the US economy in both a sectoral and geographic sense.

What might stem such a response? Certainly a rapid recovery of the industry would do so, and such a recovery might be facilitated by an increase in the value of the yen. However, I think these two events are unlikely to occur. Rather, a protectionist response might be blocked by the emerging struggle for markets in newly industrializing nations. The move into such markets—what I have described as "strategic positioning"—requires extensive lines of supply between parent firms and their subsidiaries and between major subsidiaries and new entities in key markets. Success in these new markets requires that there be no disruption of supply or substantial increase in the price of intermediate goods and that there not be any barriers to shipping major subassemblies to industrial nations.

With the growth of cooperative agreements between firms such as GM, Isuzu, Suzuki, and Toyota, that is, sourcing of entire car lines from Japan or other centers where production costs are lower than in the United States, another powerful factor is added that is likely to limit the private sector's desire for a protectionist solution. It is more likely that both the US and West European firms will seek to arrange more cooperative ventures with Japanese auto producers, and in a political sense this would also be highly beneficial to the Japanese.

The problem in the move to foreign markets for sourcing and with the growth of cooperative agreements is that they reduce the number of auto-related jobs in the United States and create more of an imbalance in the trade accounts. The public response to substantial new unemployment could be significant. Any further worsening in the auto trade balance would probably contribute to demands for some type of protectionist response. I see this aspect of the adjustment by US multinationals as the most perplexing policy issue for the future, because we have been conditioned to think of trade problems as a nation-to-nation issue. What happens when GM or Ford is importing their own cars in sizable numbers from Japan, Mexico, or Brazil?

Thus, I see little likelihood that the trade policy issues in this sector will become less complicated in the future. Because of the internationalization of the industry and the extensive patterns of sourcing from abroad, I think that an Multi-Fiber Arrangement (MFA)-type of agreement with bilateral arrangements between trading partners is unlikely. In addition, given the desire by many governments to strengthen their auto sectors, further market distortions—subsidization of new investment or of export sales, for example—are likely to occur and the propensity to follow beggar-thy-neighbor policies when trade earnings are increasing will be great.

If US firms do not pull out of the stagnant situation that they are now in, there will be far more overseas sourcing and more cooperative arrangements to purchase cars (and important components) from low-cost producers. This movement of capital away from the United States, if it is sizable and creates substantial unemployment, could trigger a strong protectionist response. Such a response could reopen issues, such as whether a national policy is needed to control the flow of capital, that proved to be quite contentious when first raised in the late 1960s.

References

Abernathy, W. J., and D. H. Ginsberg, eds. *Proceedings of the Workshops on Technological Change in the US Automobile Industry, October 1977 through April 1978 and the Symposium on Technology, Government and the Automotive Future, October 19–20, 1978.* [DOT-TSC-NHTSA-79-33.] Washington: US Department of Transportation, National Highway Traffic Safety Administration (NHTSA), 1979.

Anderson, Martin. "Retrenchment and Reconstruction in the US Auto Industry: Labor Management, and International Implications." MIT Future of the Automobile Program, International Policy Forum, May 16–20, 1982, Hakone, Japan, pp. 5–6.

Bloomfield, Gerald T. "The Changing Spatial Organization of Multinational Corporations in the World Automotive Industry." In *Spatial Analysis, Industry and the Industrial Environment*, ed. F.E.I .Hamilton and G.J.R. Linge. Vol. 2, International Industrial Systems. Chichester, England: John Wiley & Sons, 1981, pp. 357–94.

Citrin, Daniel. "Dynamic Adjustment of Japanese Exports to Exchange Rate Fluctuations for Selected Industries." Unpublished Ph.D. dissertation in economics. Ann Arbor: University of Michigan, 1982.

Cohen, Robert B. "Brave New World of the Global Car." *Challenge*, vol. 24, no. 2 (May–June 1981), pp. 28–35.

———. "International Market Positions, International Investment Strategies, and Domestic Reorganization Plans of the US Automakers." MIT Future of the Automobile Program, International Policy Forum, May 16–20, 1982, Hakone, Japan.

Cole, Robert E., and Richard Hervey. "Internationalization of the Auto Industry: A Background and Introduction." Working Paper Series, no. 1, from Joint US-Japanese Automobile Study. Ann Arbor: Center for Japanese Studies, University of Michigan, March 5, 1982.

Cook, Daniel D. "Reagan is Riding to Detroit's Rescue." *Industry Week*, vol. 209, no.1 (April 6 1981), pp. 19–21.

Corditz, Dan. "Can America Win? Trade War." *Texas Business Executive*, vol. 6, no. 2 (Fall-Winter 1980), pp. 10, 12–13.

Deardorff, Alan V., and Robert M. Stern. "The Sectoral Impact of the Recent Appreciation of the US Dollar." Ann Arbor: Department of Economics and Institute of Public Policy Studies, University of Michigan, April 1, 1982. Processed.

"Detroit Seeks Help in 'Dear Ron' Letter." *Industry Week*, vol. 208, no. 6 (March 23, 1981), pp. 28–31.

Drucker, Peter F. "The Shape of Industry to Come." *Industry Week*, vol. 212, no. 1 (January 11, 1982), pp. 54–59.

Ford of Europe. "Product Letter on the Brazilian Escort." Internal memorandum, January 1981.

Hocking, R. D. "Trade in Motor Cars Between the Major European Producers." *Economic Journal*, vol. 90, no. 359 (September 1980), p. 504.

Industrial Bank of Japan. "Motor Vehicles." *Japanese Finance and Industry: Quarterly Survey* (July–September 1981), pp. 1–21.

Johnston, William B. "Relocating Automobile Production to the Developing World: The Multinational View." MIT Future of the Automobile Program, May 1982.

Kirkland, Richard I., Jr. "War of Words." *Fortune* (April 5, 1982), pp. 35–39.

Knickerbocker, F. T. *Oligopolistic Reaction and the Multinational Enterprise.* Boston: Harvard University Press, 1973.

Kortus, B., and W. Kaczorowski. "Polish Industry Forges External Links." In *Spatial Analysis, Industry and Industrial Environment*, ed. F. E. I. Hamilton and G. J. R. Linge. Vol. 2, International Industrial Systems. Chichester, England: John Wiley & Sons, 1981, pp. 119–154.

Kox, Henk, and Arno van der Kruys. "The Passenger Car Industry: Tendencies of Relocation of Production to Peripheral Countries." Occasional Paper no. 11. Tilburg, Netherlands: Development Research Institute, Tilburg University, 1981.

Krapfel, Robert E., Jr., and John T. Mentzer, and Rex. R. Williams. "International Logistics Management at General Motors: Philosophy and Practice." *International Journal of Physical Distribution and Materials Management* (United Kingdom), vol. 11, no. 5–6, 1981, pp. 12–20.

MacLennan, Carol. "GM Investment/Capital Spending Program." Washington: US Department of Transportation, National Highway Transportation and Safety Administration, April 17, 1981. Processed.

O'Donnell, John. "Restructuring of the Auto Industry and the Impact on Employment." Cambridge, Mass.: US Transportation System Center, February 1982.

O'Donnell, John P., and George Byron, and Mike O'Connell. "Identifying Automotive Changes in Facilities and Capital Equipment and Assessing Community and Employment Impacts." [DOT-TSC-OST-81-3.] Washington: US Department of Transportation, Office of the Secretary of Transportation, May 1981.

Richardson, J. K. "Ford Expansion/Investment Information." Washington: US Department of Transportation, National Highway Transportation and Safety Administration, February 2, 1982. Processed.

Shimokawa, Kōichi. "Automobiles—Groping for Coexistence Rather than International Rivalry." *Japan Quarterly* (1982).

"Toyota-Ford Collaboration Proposal." *Oriental Economist* (September 1980), p. 8.

United Nations. *Transnational Corporations in the International Auto Industry.* Restricted draft. New York: Center on Transnational Corporations, April 1982.

US Congress. "Current Problems of the US Automobile Industry and Policies to Address Them." Staff working paper. Washington: Congressional Budget Office, National Resources and Commerce Division, July 1980.

US Department of Transportation. *The US Automobile Industry*, [The Goldschmidt Report]. Washington: Office of the Secretary of Transportation, 1980.

———. *The US Automobile Industry, 1981.* [DOT-P-10-82-01.] Washington: Office of the Secretary of Transportation, May 1982.

US International Trade Commission. *Certain Motor Vehicles and Certain Chassis and Bodies Therefor.* [USITC Publication 1110.] Washington: December 1980.

"Why Detroit Can't Cut Prices." *Business Week* (March 1, 1982), pp. 110–111.

Wright, J. Patrick. *On a Clear Day You Can See General Motors.* Grosse Pointe, Mich.: Wright Enterprises, 1979.

Statistical Appendix

TABLE 16A.1   US AUTO AND TRUCK INDUSTRY: DOMESTIC
SHIPMENTS, APPARENT CONSUMPTION, AND
ESTIMATED EFFECTS OF DECLINE IN CONSUMPTION

Item and period	(A) US producers' domestic shipments (thousand units)	(B) Apparent consumption (thousand units)	(C) Ratio of imports to consumption
Passenger automobiles and light trucks			
January–June 1979	5,870.5	7,750.7	.242
July–December 1979	3,999.1	5,719.7	.301
January–June 1980	3,687.8	5,746.4	.358
Total	13,557.4	19,216.8	—
Passenger automobiles			
January–June 1979	4,369.8	5,807.7	.247
July–December 1979	3,148.4	4,507.6	.301
January–June 1980	3,099.9	4,731.7	.345
Total	10,618.1	15,047.0	—
Light trucks			
January–June 1979	1,500.7	1,943.0	.227
July–December 1979	850.7	1,212.1	.299
January–June 1980	587.9	1,014.7	.421
Total	2,939.3	4,169.8	—

— Not applicable.
Source: Compiled from data submitted in response to questionnaires of the US International Trade Commission and from official statistics of the US Department of Commerce.
a. US producers' shipments, holding ratio of imports to consumption constant at January–June 1979 level $(1.00 - C_{j-J79}) \times B$.   b. Maximum loss to US producers resulting from increasing share of imports $(D - A)$.   c. US producers' shipments holding consumption constant at January–June 1979 level $(1.00 - C) \times B_{j-J79}$.   d. Maximum loss to US producers resulting from decreasing consumption $(F - A)$.

Item and period	(D) US producers' shipments, hypothetical[a] (thousand units)	(E) Implied loss to producers[b] (thousand units)	(F) US producers' shipments, hypothetical[c] (thousand units)	(G) Implied loss to producers[d] (thousand units)
Passenger automobiles and light trucks				
January–June 1979	5,870.5	0	5,870.5	0
July–December 1979	4,335.5	336.4	5,417.7	1,418.6
January–June 1980	4,355.8	668.0	4,975.9	1,288.1
Total	1,004.4	16,264.1	2,706.7	
Passenger automobiles				
January-June 1979	4,369.8	0	4,369.8	0
July-December 1979	3,394.2	245.8	4,059.6	911.2
January–June 1980	3,563.0	463.1	3,804.0	704.1
Total	11,327.0	708.9	12,233.4	1,615.3
Light trucks				
January–June 1979	1,500.7	0	1,500.7	0
July–December 1979	937.0	86.3	1,326.0	511.3
January–June 1980	784.4	196.5	1,215.0	537.1
Total	3,222.1	282.8	3,987.7	1,048.4

Juergen B. Donges

I find myself much in agreement with the diagnosis given in the interesting and stimulating sector papers. They provide valuable confirmation on the results of empirical research on the international competitiveness of West German industries, undertaken at the Kiel Institute in recent years. Whatever the peculiarities of the industries concerned, their competitive position is being challenged by newcomers in world trade (mainly Japan and the newly industrializing countries, NICs) which are carefully exploiting their comparative advantage. Changes in comparative advantage are nothing exceptional; they go on all the time, and they are not unique to agriculture, textiles, steel, or automobiles. However, they often tend to cause major sectoral, or even macroeconomic problems, and provoke protectionist sentiments, particularly when industries fail to acknowledge that competition is in the nature of market-oriented economies. Indeed, the three industry papers attribute a great amount of the actual troubles of these industries to the observed resistance to adjusting to the changing international division of labor.

As often happens in in-depth analyses of single sectors, the authors could not always resist the temptation to identify the well-being or the problems of particular activities with the well-being or the problems of the economy as a whole; or to stress the "uniqueness" of the industry under consideration; or to focus the discussion of trade effects in terms of harm, not of mutual benefit as we once were taught (Martin Wolf, to be sure, could resist this temptation). I am deliberately not going to discuss the details in these papers, mainly for two reasons: one is that we would need at least one session for each industry to do justice to the rich analysis presented; the other is that sector-by-sector studies, valuable as they are, must not cloud the basic issue. The basic issue is protection and its implications, and it may be useful to focus the discussion on this issue.

From the analysis in the papers, it is safe to conclude that protective devices, however, imaginative, do not serve the intended purpose

565

(incidentally, the value-added tax, which European countries impose on imports, is not a protective measure, as Robert B. Cohen assumes). Depending on the device used, the artificially created scarcity rent accrues to different parties. But competitive imports go on rising fast, the reason being, as Martin Wolf and Ingo Walter show, trade diversion toward (still) unrestricted suppliers as well as the capability of restricted foreign exporters to upgrade into higher valued products or to sell via third parties.

At the same time, such devices do not, contrary to what advocates of industry-specific protection usually claim, lead domestic (ailing) firms to adjust to import competition more easily. If anything, "breathing spaces" reduce the incentive to adjust efficiently, so that firms adhering to a mere survival-by-protection strategy normally run into serious difficulties; uncompetitive jobs are definitively lost. The unassisted (dynamic) sectors in the economy are inevitably taxed via distorted factor and input prices as well as currency overvaluation.

Even more, industry-specific protection tends to become permanent in practice, although originally it always was intended to be temporary (Martin Wolf mentioned rightly the Multi-Fiber Arrangement, Ingo Walter could have mentioned the so-called structural crisis cartel agreements within the European Community (EC) under the various Davignon Plans). Therefore, I am very skeptical about proposals to legitimize selective safeguards, even if formally restricted to a limited time period.

Unfortunately, the story does not end here. Once a government has set the political precedent for special support, it will proliferate across sectors (e.g., protection granted to producers of steel can lead to demands for extending protection to the automobile industry which is a user of steel). This proliferation ultimately reflects the propensity with which a country tries to export the adjustment burden as it emerges, although it originates at home to a large extent (as the papers show). As each of the major trading nations behave in a similar manner industry-specific protection cannot but escalate into international political tensions—a really high price for so few benefits.

It is in the light of these conclusions that I suggest focusing attention not so much on whether a particular industry has this or that special problem but rather on the fact that our economies are facing a general adjustment problem. General problems call for general solutions. In this context I would have preferred the authors to have discussed whether or not a major shift in overall public policies is required. I think it is, in particular with regard to strengthening the mechanism of relative prices to signal changes in comparative advantage and also with an aim to encouraging, directly and indirectly, savings, research, skill acquisition, the willingness to work and to take risks, and productive investment in plant and equipment. After all, empirical evidence abounds, and the sector papers before us confirm, that the roots of the problem in the United States and the European Community are to be sought on the supply side: what is at stake is the promotion of economic efficiency. Thus efficient adjustment becomes a prerequisite for the recovery of particular industries and the economy as a whole (not the other way around, as some national accounting exercises seem to suggest). If we do not get this message through to politicians and bureaucrats, and to the business community and trade unions as well, I see little chance for the restoration of a viable international trade order, to which all sectors, including agriculture, conform.

All the papers end with a pessimistic view regarding the prospects that the market mechanism may replace government control as the major determinant of sector-specific adjustment. It is difficult to disprove this view, although the runaway budget deficits in most Organization for Economic Cooperation and Development countries might force governments at least to reconsider their countless subsidy programs, including industry-specific "adjustment" assistance, which in practice is maintenance assistance.

But what the authors emphasize by implication is the fact that the interaction between the profit-maximizing behavior of sectoral interest groups and the vote-maximizing behavior of policymakers (let alone the aligning behavior of bureaucrats) in a representative democracy has pushed policies toward sectoralism in the internal market and bilateralism in international trade. The four sector studies reveal a disquieting historical trend: agriculture was the first major sector allowed to derogate from the rules of the General Agreement on Tariffs and Trade, the textiles and clothing industry followed in a much more elaborate way, more recently the steel industry has gotten its turn, and the automobile industry could be the next case. Are we inevitably on the path toward corporatism?

Stanley Nehmer

T he papers prepared by the outstanding group of people assembled at this meeting are impressive in the scope and depth of their analyses, if not, in some cases, their conclusions. I will attempt to add a perspective different from the one permeating so many of these studies. I will first make some comments on the question of protectionism and then discuss some of the papers at this session.

In recent testimony before the Senate Finance Committee on the issue of reciprocity, the US Chamber of Commerce—which certainly cannot be accused of being a protectionist organization—stated quite correctly: "For international trade policy to be an effective instrument of national will, it must be publicly supportable, it must be implemented in an even-handed fashion, and it must be administered in a manner consistent with trade statutes both in letter and in spirit. The alternative is an erosion of public support and an eventual change in policy." I might add that providing import relief in accordance with the trade statutes, when the criteria for such action are met, enhances the credibility of a liberal trade policy. It is only when there is no "safety valve" in operation that protectionist pressures will bring down such trade policy.

In agriculture, steel, or textiles, we are dealing with concrete trade issues. They are also concrete political issues, and they also interface with serious economic issues facing our country. These realities will preclude the executive branch from securing authority for any new trade initiatives until at least the most serious of the sectoral problems can be solved. On Capitol Hill, GATT is not God.

In reading several of the papers, I get the distinct impression that protectionism in the United States is being conjured up, like Merlin's demons. But how protectionist is the United States when exports of some key products have grown substantially, both absolutely and in relation to the US market, particularly over the last several years?

Let us look at the record of imports of some of the key sectors over the last several years.

• *Textiles and apparel.* In 1974, the first year of the Multi-Fiber Arrangement, the United States imported 4.4 billion square yards equivalent of cotton, wool, and man-made fiber textiles and apparel. In 1981 our imports were almost 5.8 billion square yards equivalent. Imports in 1981 increased by 18 percent over the preceding year.

• *Nonrubber footwear.* While the two Orderly Marketing Agreements with Korea and Taiwan were in effect, from mid-1977 to mid-1981, imports were fairly stable with a peak of 405 million pairs in 1979 as new starters and Italy increased their exports to the United States. With the termination of the import relief by President Reagan a year ago, imports began to creep up. In the first four months of 1982, imports of nonrubber footwear were 22 percent higher than in the same period a year earlier. Import penetration rose a full 10 percentage points from 50 percent to 60 percent.

• *Color TVs.* Despite the continuation of the Orderly Marketing Agreements with Korea and Taiwan up to the end of June 1982, imports of color TVs rose 54 percent in 1981 above the 1980 level.

• *Steel.* Imports of carbon steel mill products rose 26 percent in 1981 above the 1980 level and slowed down in the first four months of 1982 to 6 percent growth over the same period of 1981. In the case of specialty steel (that is, stainless and alloy tool steel) the growth has been even more dramatic. Specialty steel imports in 1981 rose 27.4 percent above the 1980 level, and in the first four months of 1982 rose 49.6 percent above the level of the same period of 1981.

Let us look at the record of that "protectionist" device called the "escape clause," sections 201–203 of the Trade Act of 1974. How protectionist has the "escape clause" been? There have been 45 cases completed under this statute since the 1974 legislation went into effect. The US International Trade Commission (USITC) had affirmative findings of injury from imports, or a tie vote, in 26 cases. The president in office has seen fit to deliver import relief in only 9 of these 26 cases. Of these 9 industries which received import relief, only 4 will retain import relief at the end of this month. In not a single one of the 9 cases of import relief did the president adopt the import relief recommended by the USITC. The poor track record of cases under the "escape clause" has resulted in no new cases under this statute. I might point out also that the present administration has taken great pride in being able to say that it extended import relief recently for the clothespin industry, with a few hundred workers. This is the same administration that refused to extend import relief for the nonrubber footwear industry a year ago, an industry with 120,000 or so workers, about half the number of workers in this industry only a dozen years ago.

Have so-called "protectionist" measures affected the prices consumers have had to pay for these products? The answer is negative, certainly when compared to the overall consumer price index. Over the last five years (1977–81) we find the following: CPI less food up 51.7 percent; apparel less footwear, up 15.5 percent; footwear, up 27.7 percent; televisions, up 3.5 percent.

This is not the record of a protectionist trade policy. It is a record of a trade policy that is inconsistent with the spirit if not the letter of the trade statutes as Congress passed them, and certainly inconsistent with the promises made to Congress, industry, and labor. I should like to interject here an important point regarding the role of retailers in all of this. No one should be misled that the retailer gives the consumer the benefit of lower prices for imports. It has been clearly established and acknowledged by retailers that they take a much higher markup on imported products than they do on domestic products. That in itself is a major reason why imports of consumer goods have grown.

I should now like to concentrate on the papers by Ingo Walter and Martin Wolf in the remainder of my remarks. Three key issues arise on matters of trade policy in these papers. First, is an international agreement an effective way of resolving serious industry sectoral import-export issues? Second, in the case of an existing international agreement—the Multi Fiber Arrangement (MFA)—what are the policy implications regarding jobs that may be lost if the agreement is terminated? Third, how should trade policy deal with problems faced by technologically advanced industries as a result of serious import competition made possible by foreign government subsidies?

On the first issue, I was struck by an interesting divergence in conclusion between Walter and Wolf. Walter suggests in his concluding paragraphs that "some sort of international rules of the game specifically addressed to the steel industry are essentially inevitable . . . ." He suggests that such an arrangement would be superior to the heretofore uncoordinated approach to the problems of the steel industry. He outlines the components of a world steel arrangement. He concludes that such an approach involves a number of dangers, but may hold greater promise of long-term efficient and equitable outcomes than uncoordinated unilateral measures or other sectoral initiatives.

Martin Wolf, on the other hand, has seriously criticized the MFA. He concludes with two lessons that the MFA offers us. The first is that a sectoral system of discriminatory protection can only develop in the direction of greater restrictiveness. The second lesson, he says, is that authorization of a system of selected safeguards will only increase the resort to such measures.

I believe Walter is the more correct of the two. When a difficult international trade problem develops in a politically sensitive industry, where actions are taken or may be taken unilaterally to protect jobs and investment, international rules are certainly far better than unilateral action. Indeed this concept is fundamental to the MFA itself, since most import limitations under the MFA have been the result of bilateral agreements operating within the guidelines of the internationally negotiated MFA.

There are three principles basic to the MFA and, indeed, its predecessor arrangements.

First, the alternative to the MFA is not a free market. The alternative to the MFA is unilateral action by importing countries. Second, negotiations to limit imports under the MFA's bilateral agreements have never hinged on principle, but rather on the numbers, that is the levels of restraint. Exporting countries have never refused to enter into a bilateral agreement, so long as the agreement provided adequate access to the markets of importing countries. Third, exporting countries have as much stake in the continuation of the MFA as do the importing countries.

These three points may concern Martin Wolf very much. They are the antithesis of what he does not like in the MFA. But they are the facts of life. They have been so for many years and will continue to be so for many more.

This brings me to the second issue. Wolf clearly would be happier if the MFA was abolished. Drawing on the 1980 essay which he coauthored, *Textile Quotas Against Developing Countries*, he points out that employment could fall by 33 percent between 1980 and 1990 in the absence of the MFA. This implies, he says, a decline of 1.65 million jobs in textiles and apparel in the United States and the European Community, which is about 1 percent of the total labor force, a decline which he believes "would hardly be noticed."

I guess this tossing around of figures of 1.65 million human beings losing their jobs is quite fundamental to Wolf's thesis. Who are the workers in textiles and apparel? The workers in these industries in the United States are predominantly women, they are often over 50 years of age, they often have no more than an elementary school education, they are predominantly minorities, and, in apparel manufacturing, they are predominantly in urban, inner-city areas or single-industry rural towns. These workers cannot easily shift to other employment. They cannot pick up and move to Seattle to assemble aircraft. Essentially the labor force in this industry is immobile. Thus, the unemployed worker in textiles and apparel most often becomes a worker without a job indefinitely.

Wolf estimates that employment could fall by 33 percent between 1980 and 1990. For workers who are difficult to reemploy, a loss of some 700,000 to 800,000 textile and apparel jobs in the United States would be a disaster. What happens to these workers? Wolf suggests that certain workers in Canada were actually better off after leaving their jobs than before and that the government's benefits seemed to be effective in making up for most of the earnings' losses. Wolf would be referring to adjustment assistance measures insofar as the United States is concerned. First put into US legislation in 1962 and made more effective in the Trade Act of 1974, unfortunately adjustment assistance for workers and firms today is essentially a thing of the past. There was a tacit agreement when the Trade Act of 1974 was going through Congress that the labor movement would accept reduced domestic trade barriers in return for help in retaining and relocating workers unemployed as a consequence of increased imports. That covenant has now been broken and adjustment assistance is not available to help the 700,000 or so workers who Wolf suggests will be unemployed in the absence of the MFA. Incidentally in my judgment there is no way now to reverse the process; labor will not bite again.

Parenthetically I should point out that 700,000 to 800,000 jobs lost in textiles and apparel means an additional 350,000 to 400,000 or so additional jobs lost in other sectors of the economy which are dependent on textiles and apparel.

What about the economic and social costs to the local community and to the nation as a whole when 700,000 to 800,000 workers in a single industrial complex lose their jobs? On the economic side we should compute the lost tax revenues to the local, state, and federal governments, unemployment compensation and family assistance payments, and lost income to the economy.

Wolf says that the social costs imposed by job displacement are a controversial theoretical and empirical question, beyond the scope of the present discussion. Maybe so, Wolf, but the need to avoid those unnamed social (as well as economic) costs is why there is an MFA and why there will not be a 33 percent decline in employment.

Finally, on the third issue: Ingo Walter's prognosis suggests that "competitive positioning (for the steel industry) should be strengthened by downstream concentration of production in specialty steels . . . ." This statement perhaps best underlines the dilemma faced today by some American industries adversely affected by imports and by a trade policy that promises much and performs little. Most of Walter's excellent paper is really talking about carbon steel. Aside from earlier references to the "escape clause" import relief in effect for the US specialty steel industry from mid-1976 to February 1980, this is really his only reference to the smaller but much more technologically advanced brother of the carbon steel industry.

The dilemma for the US specialty steel industry arises from the fact that it is probably the most technologically advanced specialty steel industry in the world. The industry has invested heavily in leading-edge technologies. Its expenditures for research and development have been substantial. Its productivity has continually advanced. Yet the industry is under siege today from imports, largely from Europe. The competition from Europe is not from companies which are more efficient than those in the United States, but mostly from subsidized or government-owned steel companies which would not be in business today in the United States where they must operate under the discipline of profit. Without these subsidies, Europe would not be competitive in the United States specialty steel market. With these European subsidies, the US industry cannot compete.

The US specialty steel industry has already seen several plants close, the industry as a whole is now in a net loss position, and worker layoffs are equal to a fourth of the job force. Its future lies in the effective implementation of our unfair trade statutes, particularly section 301 and the countervailing duty law.

The dilemma for US trade policy rests in the fact that the administration pledged last July that it would effectively implement these statutes. If it does, our European friends will cry "protectionism." If it does not, a technologically advanced, capital-intensive American industry will gradually wither away.

I, for one, cannot join the call against "protectionism" in these circumstances. I hope the readers of this volume will bear these thoughts in mind.

DISCUSSION, SESSION 4

A negotiated settlement is not always better than letting a conflict run its course, *C. Fred Bergsten* suggested, because of the tendency to devise illiberal régimes. He expressed special concern about the most recent protectionist development, in automobiles. Unlike steel, textiles, and more traditional products under protection, multinational companies dominate automobiles, and most analysts had assumed that their commitment to an international orientation would rule out protection. With respect to textiles he asked why it would not make sense to require that firms in this sector go through the same hurdles to receive protection that are expected for other industries (for example, demonstration of injury). More generally he considered it unlikely that the forces of protection could be resisted in the absence of an adjustment assistance program and recommended that a new program be more directly oriented toward labor adjustment.

Gary Clyde Hufbauer supported his earlier proposal to convert nontariff barriers to tariffs. This reform would deprive the system of present rents. These rents could instead be used to promote adjustment by allocating the tariff revenues to adjustment programs that would compensate both workers and firms.

Yves Berthelot observed that we must expect new sector agreements regulating trade because the share of imports is so high. And such agreements can be a good thing; they can be used by the government in negotiations with unions and firms, to say that the government is already doing something for them. In agriculture, any agreement would have to be supported by the farmers, and the small farmers are politically dominant.

Gardner Patterson emphasized that one of the worst aspects of the Multi-Fiber Arrangement (MFA) was that the established exporters like it because it protects their market shares against newcomers. The MFA is contrary to adjustment; many workers have been attracted

574

into the textile-apparel sector since the MFA began, and in a meaningful sense they are now in the sector because of the MFA.

Richard N. Cooper cautioned that in examining individual sectors it was necessary not to lose sight of the general economic environment. The steel and automobile sectors are overwhelmingly influenced by the fact that there is a severe recession. These are highly capitalized industries affected by recession. With respect to Nehmer's emphasis on female employment in textiles, Cooper cited the widespread replacement of female workers by mechanization in the life insurance industry in the 1950s, and asked whether it would have been better to suppress that technological innovation. He compared new trade sources such as Hong Kong and Korea to technical innovations that enable us to use our resources more efficiently.

Martin Wolf replied to Stanley Nehmer that a large body of research shows that workers do find alternative jobs when displaced by imports, and that their losses are modest.

William R. Cline remarked that the thrust of the sector papers was pessimism for open trade. They implied that nothing can be done on agriculture; that nothing can be done on textiles and apparel except perhaps reshuffling quotas to lesser developed countries; that in steel the system is inevitably moving toward a quota régime; and that in automobiles potential job losses are so severe that the risk of continued or intensified protection is great. He suggested, however, that it might be overly pessimistic to generalize these inferences. He noted that these sectors all have large employment forces and therefore unusually strong political clout. He also concluded that experience shows it is wise to stay away from sector arrangements administering trade, because they tend to entrench protection. In addition, the record suggests that it is better to avoid new trade legislation where possible—for example, in authorizing new negotiations—because typically a high price must be paid to protectionist interests to secure their acquiescence in the legislation.

PART IV

New Issues in the 1980s

As technology and the structure of international production and business organization change, new trade problems emerge. Technological change in sectors such as the information industry have opened up new possibilities in trade, such as the international electronic transmission of data. Change in business organization toward the spread of the multinational corporation has raised new issues such as the use of investment performance requirements to meet trade and other goals. As a nation with an abundance of skilled manpower and an advanced technological base, the United States may be in a position to establish comparative advantage in new services trade, and indeed may need to do so given erosion of more traditional comparative advantage in trade over a range of manufactures.

In addition, some of the most controversial trade issues concern the fostering of new industries at the frontier of high technology. There is little consensus on the rules of the game in this field concerning what is essentially industrial policy. One country's industrial policy favoring the development of sophisticated new industries may have the effect of preempting markets that, with less government intervention, would more naturally become the province of specialization by other countries. In a sense, the question of high technology industrial policy is equivalent to the question of whether any nation acknowledgedly at the vanguard of development and technology has the right to resort to "infant-industry" protection to stimulate new industries. Unlike the traditional case whereby infant-industry protection is necessary only because other countries already have a competitive edge over the country in question but with a period of temporary intervention the country could become competitive, preemptive infant-industry protection among peer nations tends to give unfair advantage to the country so intervening. And yet any set of international rules in this area would be counterproductive if its effect were to discourage the general level of technological development worldwide, considering that technical change is usually an area of underinvestment because of the externalities it generates that cannot be captured privately.

This range of issues faces trade policymakers as they look forward to the 1980s and beyond, adding to the unresolved trade issues from the past. Because it takes years of preparation to develop the informational base for any such area before new negotiations are possible, the time is ripe for concentrated attention to these issues. In chapter 17 William Diebold, Jr., and Helena Stalson of the Council on Foreign Relations examine the possible expansion of the General Agreement on Tariffs and Trade (and other vehicles) for liberalization of trade in services, an area that has largely been omitted from past progress on liberalizing international trade. The United States in particular has stressed new régimes for open trade in the services sector, in part because of the belief that the area is a natural one for US comparative advantage. A. E. Safarian of the University of Toronto explores trade-related investment issues in chapter 18. As in the case of services, there exists no "GATT for investment," and increasingly both the industrial countries as well as newly industrialized countries such as Brazil and Mexico have sought to influence their trade by introducing incentives and performance requirements for investment by multinational corporations.

In chapter 19 John Diebold of the Diebold Group examines trade in the information industry as a case study in high technology trade. His study raises broader questions that concern the appropriate approach to industrial policy domestically as well as internationally.

The final new issues examined in this volume are the the logical culmination of the oldest staple of trade negotiations: tariff reduction to the point of elimination. Even though tariffs are now low on average, some remain high, and their escalation by degree of processing means that the effective protection as value added can still be high in many cases, especially for processed forms of goods that at present the developing countries export chiefly as raw materials. Moreover, in the Tokyo Round tariff liberalization proved to be a useful focal point for negotiations even though the more significant area of new negotiations was on nontariff barriers. In chapter 20, Alan Deardorff and Robert Stern of the University of Michigan apply their general equilibrium model of world trade to examine the potential effects of complete tariff elimination.

CHAPTER 17

Negotiating Issues in International Services Transactions

William Diebold, Jr., and Helena Stalson

Severation years ago the United States took the initiative in urging international discussion of the activities of service industries that operate beyond the borders of their home countries. We write in advance of the General Agreement on Tariffs and Trade (GATT) Ministerial meeting of November 1982 but assume that it will carry this process forward.[1] Even so, active negotiations for multilateral arrangements governing services are not likely to begin seriously for a year or two and will then probably go on for a long time. Meanwhile there is a need for extensive explorations of possible goals and methods. As yet, there is little common ground in these matters, politically or intellectually. Complex problems arise that are not well understood. Although there have been some well-prepared discussions and careful reports on the need for international understandings on trade and investment in services, it is still not clear how the benefits from one set of actions or another would be distributed.

The purpose of this chapter is to clarify some major issues by setting forth a range of possible objectives of international negotiations and commenting on the kinds of national interests and measures that will have to be taken into consideration. It suggests possibilities more than it proposes programs. It is cast in general terms and does not examine the details of international service transactions, the current restrictions on them, or the limited international agreements that

---

[1] For a discussion of the outcome of the GATT Ministerial, which addressed the services issue in a modest way by calling for two-year studies by individual nations with the results to be coordinated by GATT and other international entities, see chapter 22, this volume.

exist. Although it sees an important place for bilateral negotiations, it is not a tactical manual for American policy or legislation. The authors are not lawyers or specialists in services. They are economists with particular concern for international economic cooperation and the trading system.[2]

What are Service Transactions?

Few generalizations about services are valid for all of them. A service economy is frequently regarded as characteristic of the "post-industrial" society, but it turns out that the service sectors of developing economies are often very large, sometimes as a result of tourism or the export of labor. Moreover, services in all societies are frequently associated with the production and distribution of goods, and that is true of international transactions as well.

Statistics about services are bad for different reasons and in different ways; there are problems both in measurement and concept. The same service is likely to be recorded differently if it is carried on within a manufacturing firm or contracted for outside. Moreover, the boundaries are shifting. While some manufacturing firms have been abandoning in-house service operations in favor of contracts with independent suppliers, others have diversified by buying outside service firms that are expected to contribute to their cash flow and help to offset fluctuations in their earnings from manufacturing. Hence, although the total supply of services may not have changed, the way they are recorded complicates the measurement problem. The increasing level of employment that makes the service sector the biggest

---

[2] We have been interested in services for many years. During that time we have accumulated far more obligations for help than can be acknowledged here. Of particular value in recent years have been two discussion groups on services at the Council on Foreign Relations organized by Helena Stalson and chaired, respectively, by William N. Walker and Matthew Nimetz. Our understanding of many of the issues dealt with here owes much to Ronald K. Shelp, who stimulated the discussion of services in the Council's 1980s Project with papers that eventually became his pioneering book *Beyond Industrialization*. We are also grateful to Geza Feketekuty for help over a period of years. None of these people has any responsibility for what we say in this chapter, which they have not seen. That is equally true of the members of US Trade Representative's (USTR) Services Policy Advisory Committee on which William Diebold sits. We are grateful for the comments made by readers of the first version of this paper at the conference and otherwise and have taken account of them in making revisions.

in the US economy adds together people of extraordinarily high skills and productivity in finance and consulting with the employees of cleaning firms and fast-food stores. There are activities that are confined to limited localities and others that can be provided any place in the world. Government and education are major service industries in all countries.

Useful statistics are even harder to come by when one tries to measure the flow of services across national borders. The US balance of payments figures for services have traditionally included dividends and interest earned on foreign investments as well as receipts from exports of US services. Official figures for what are generally thought of as services proper ranged from $35 billion to $45 billion for 1980. Private estimates for services exports put the total at about $60 billion, and this figure would be significantly higher if receipts from sales of services by US firms established within foreign markets were added to exports. These receipts would be larger than the balance of payments investment returns, which represent income after deduction of taxes, not the value—comparable to an export—of the total foreign payment.[3]

In spite of the confusion there is no doubt that there is "something there" and that, although it would be hazardous to attempt to discern trends in service transactions, whatever measurement is used shows a rapid increase in the flow of services internationally. That is to say, there are significant international transactions in a range of activities that have to be called services, such as insurance, accounting, consulting, design, and advertising. There are transportation, communications, and banking, each of which is in some respects a special case, as well as mixed activities, such as motion pictures, art, and music, in which physical objects may move but the true value added lies in the services they record or embody. Legal, educational, and health services can be provided internationally as well as domestically and so can common or skilled labor.

---

[3] Even the most generous estimate of US services provided to foreigners cannot take account of the total contribution of services. All goods include an element of services performed domestically or abroad. For example, a growing fraction of the cost of an automobile is spent on the services of a programmer for the numeric control data. Goods and services are also combined in another—consecutive—sense. Japan buys oil rigs from the United States (an American export of goods), then leases them to US clients (an American import of services) at low interest rates. A US engineering company designs a building abroad and then arranges for installation of American equipment in it.

For present purposes we have not thought it necessary to provide either a strict definition of services or a full list of activities, although negotiators will need to identify precisely what kinds of activities are covered by negotiations or international agreements.[4] In what follows we try to generalize when possible and illustrate specific issues by referring to individual sectors.

One premise of the American initiative on services is that these activities have been neglected in US legislation and international arrangements. This is broadly true but there are some exceptions. The Trade Act of 1974 gave the president authority to negotiate on services and to respond to US complaints about unfair practices by foreign service industries or foreign governments. That negotiating authority has never been used and only five cases of unfair practices have been presented. Although the Export-Import Bank is authorized to facilitate any export transaction, in practice the only services it finances are those that accompany delivery of equipment.

Legislation permitting deferral of taxes to Domestic International Sales Corporations (DISCs) covers only a few services, chiefly engineering and architectural work on construction projects. Unlike most US agencies, the Overseas Private Investment Corporation provides significant export assistance to service industries. And one of the chief beneficiaries of the Webb-Pomerene Act's authority for the formation of export associations has been the US motion picture industry. This industry is the only service specifically included in GATT rules; for the most part, the articles of the agreement refer to merchandise trade, although a few could be interpreted to include services. Of the GATT codes negotiated in the Tokyo Round, the government procurement code includes services provided they are incidental to the delivery of tangible products.

The Organization for Economic Cooperation and Development's (OECD's) Codes of Liberalization of Current Invisible Operations and of Capital Movements were intended to liberalize trade and investment in services as well as goods, but their vulnerability to reservations and exceptions has left little opportunity for significant

---

[4] Legislation before the Senate in 1982 defined services as "economic outputs which are not tangible goods or structures, and they include, but are not limited to, transportation, communications, retail and wholesale trade, advertising, construction, design and engineering, utilities, finance, insurance, real estate, professional services, entertainment, and tourism, as well as the overseas investments which are necessary for the export and sale of these services.".

reductions in services barriers. Ronald K. Shelp concludes that the two codes "tend to treat the symptoms rather than the malady. They focus on transactions and thus often miss the root of the problem."[5] The OECD has established committees to deal with various service issues—maritime transport, telecommunications, insurance, tourism, financial markets—that have grappled, with varying degrees of success, with the problems of harmonizing and liberalizing national regulations. The work on maritime liberalization has been the most successful; at a recent meeting the OECD ministers urged all the committees to examine new ways of removing unjustified barriers. A 1976 declaration on international investment and multinational enterprises committed the OECD members to accord national treatment to foreign enterprises in services as well as in other sectors, but so far the promise has been greater than the reality.

Under the aegis of United Nations Conference on Trade and Development (UNCTAD) a Committee on Invisibles and Financing Related to Trade has made studies and issued reports on insurance and tourism, but the major work of UNCTAD in services has been done by its Committee on Shipping. Long before UNCTAD was organized, shipping, aviation, and communications were subject to a variety of international rules and agreements that have quite effectively regulated certain aspects of these industries' activities, while leaving large areas open to bureaucratic as well as legislative discrimination against foreign competitors.

The question of including banking in any effort to negotiate an international services agreement is debatable and there is no unanimity on the matter among the interested parties. On the one hand are the characteristics peculiar to banking, such as its close links with monetary policy and credit control, existing laws and practices in each country regulating foreign as well as domestic banks, highly developed consultative and cooperative arrangements among central bankers, and the active discussion of international cooperation in bank supervision. All these argue for treating banking separately from other services. On the other hand, banks carry on a wide range of activities that go well beyond traditional banking and a large number of non-banks compete directly with them in these activities and carry on functions that closely resemble or substitute for banking. This argues for the need to include at least certain aspects of banks' activities in service negotiations as does the fact that international adherence to general principles about services (access to markets, national treat-

[5] Shelp, *Beyond Industrialization* (New York: Praeger, 1981), p. 131.

ment, most-favored-nation, MFN, treatment, reciprocity) would have implications for banking. Another factor in the situation is that quite different parts of national bureaucracies are likely to be concerned with banking and other services. This is true of other activities as well (transportation, communications) but is perhaps of special importance in banking where it is hard to imagine central banks and finance ministries turning over significant negotiating or supervisory power regarding banking to people whose main concern is trade.

As will become apparent, one of the problems of setting objectives and selecting policy instruments is to know exactly what will be understood if one tries to deal with "services" in general. We can only hope that readers will agree that the fuzziness of the treatment is warranted by the fuzziness of the subject matter. As Aristotle said, "the man of education will seek exactness so far in each subject as the nature of the thing admits. . . ."[6]

The Objectives of International Negotiations

Whatever definition of services one uses and whatever confidence one reposes in one set of statistics or another, it seems obvious that there is an international phenomenon worth paying attention to. International trade in goods and investment in their production have long occupied the attention of economists and others, along with the international flow of funds. A great deal less attention has been given to transactions in services, and in only some of them have the effects of government restrictions and regulations been examined. Consequently, there are two kinds of problems in the field of services. First, there is a need for description and analysis, to understand what is going on and how important it is. Second, there has to be a discussion of what policies governments can best follow for stated purposes, acting singly or together. Into the latter category fall those problems which international service businesses feel they encounter as the result of government activities.

What are some of the barriers that Americans face when they go abroad? Many barriers are specific to certain industries or imposed by certain countries. Others, more general, include a widespread use of government procurement policies that give preferential treatment to local service firms and taxes and personnel restrictions that discriminate against foreign firms. Many barriers are administrative, and

[6] D. P. Chase, trans., *Ethics* (New York: Everyman's Library, Dutton, 1931), p. 3.

the outsider encounters informal procedures that frequently cannot be identified as restrictive or discriminatory but that effectively limit his opportunity to provide his service. Many are more formal: banks are restricted in their ability to accept deposits; an insurance firm is permitted to sell only certain policies; an airline may face serious restrictions on its landing rights or minor frustrations in delays in baggage handling; accountants may be required to belong to a local professional association but find it almost impossible to gain admittance; motion picture producers are subject to quotas based on a ratio of foreign to local films that may be shown; data processing firms may be denied licenses for computer time sharing unless the processing is done locally.

The evidence of an increasing flow of US services to other countries does not in itself suggest that there has been an accompanying increase in foreign barriers. But the experience of American firms trying to increase their market shares abroad has tended to support the charge that, as the competition grew, restrictions were put in place to contain it. To determine the kind of international arrangements on barriers to services that would be desirable from the US point of view, one has to look at the place of services in the international economy and consider the interests and attitudes of other countries. Only by doing that can one formulate specific approaches that have a realistic chance of removing barriers to international business in services.

The American initiatives already taken implicitly recognize this; they call for international acceptance of the idea that trade in services as well as goods should be liberalized and look toward international agreements to that effect. Such agreements can obviously not be reached unless they are seen to be in the interest of other countries as well as of the United States. Therefore, American proposals should take account of those interests and aim at creating a broad multilateral system (or at least something that can develop into that sort of a system). In other words, the approach is analogous to that of the United States to international trade in goods when GATT was originally set up.

There are also major differences between that situation and the present one. The spirit of the times is different. The need to build a new system of international economic cooperation is not as obvious. The position of the United States in the world economy has changed. The mutual interest of almost all countries in the reduction of barriers to trade in goods had been informed by a century of theory and the still vivid lessons of the beggar-my-neighbor policies of the Depression.

Today, there is not nearly as much agreement on the gains to be had from the liberalization of trade in services or on who the beneficiaries would be. For example, two commonly heard European reactions to the American initiatives are "This may be a good idea but the Americans haven't figured out what should be done about it" and "If the Americans are so strong for this, they must expect major gains and we had better be careful." The lack of understanding of the economics of international services and doubts as to who will gain from different kinds of action are basic factors in the situation which have to be taken into account in discussing the objectives of negotiations. Fortunately, a good bit of exploration is already under way by economists, research institutes, international organizations, and some governments. By the time real negotiations begin in GATT, we should know a great deal more than we do now about many of the questions raised in this chapter.

For the present we have to be content with some basic assumptions. Three are crucial to what follows:

• There are gains that can be shared by most countries from reducing existing restrictions on international trade and investment in services and limiting the imposition of new ones.
• The United States is well placed to take advantage of such action and there is a national interest in pursuing liberalization (going beyond the interests of American firms in the service industries).
• The correct approach is to seek international agreements in these matters. As it is likely to take some years before firm agreements can be worked out, there will also have to be bilateral negotiations at least about particular issues and perhaps about general principles and approaches.

We cannot give much attention to these possibilities but call attention to three points. First, in bilateral negotiations American officials and firms should seek treatment as much in accordance as possible with the multilateral agreements it is hoped will be reached later on. Second, to press bilateral negotiations may accelerate the process of multilateral negotiations, especially by making the governments and industries of other countries aware of their interests in broader understandings. Third, the relative simplicity of bilateral methods should not be allowed to obscure the American interest in multilateral arrangements. Other countries too will follow this route and it is not to be taken for granted that the bargaining power of other service-exporting countries will always be inferior to that of the United States. A myriad of bilateral understandings is not likely to produce a very desirable international régime.

Much of the American discussion has focused on applying to services the kinds of arrangements that have worked well in trade in goods. There are also analogies with investment—where there is nothing comparable to GATT—that will come up as we proceed. That "liberalization," a key word in these discussions, means the reduction of barriers to services is clear, but that does not tell us very much. The liberalization of merchandise trade is not total, after all, and was never meant to be. There will always be some tacit proviso to a government's general endorsement of liberalization in services; the problem of making it explicit is probably the single most important task that is faced by anyone trying to think through these problems.

One must be concerned with two elements, the kinds of barriers and their incidence. It may be possible to ban certain kinds of barriers entirely but there will be others that will have to be agreed to as exceptions to liberalization for one reason or another (GATT is full of these barriers to trade in goods). When barriers are not altogether banned, the concern will be how restrictive they are. It will take time to dismantle existing restrictions.[7] A central issue will be to determine the amount of liberalization that is needed to ensure an acceptable flow of services and the kinds of bargains that must be struck to achieve it.

In its treatment of goods GATT proscribes quotas (except in certain circumstances) and some other kinds of barriers, but it does not rule out tariffs or say anything about justified or unjustified protection, or the height of tariffs. It simply creates a mechanism through which the member countries can bargain for the removal of tariffs to their mutual advantage. To what extent are the barriers to trade in services[8] comparable to tariffs in the sense of being taxes on foreign services that do not apply equally to domestic sellers or producers of these services? Licenses and other fees that fall particularly on foreigners could be treated like tariffs, but it is our impression that while these may be of some importance they are not the largest part of the

[7] There can be little doubt that the late Andrew Shonfield was right when he said, in 1969, that "any future negotiations on a world-wide scale involving the services sector . . . will surely be of a complexity and *longueur* at least as great as the Kennedy Round. . . ." There may well not be a "services round" but rather a range of quite varied negotiations extending over a period of time. Charles P. Kindleberger and Andrew Shonfield, eds., *North American and Western European Economic Policies* (New York: Macmillan, 1971), p. 534.

[8] We will use this term for convenience, although "transactions in services" is broader and at the same time more exact.

problem. In addition to the common complaint of US service firms that they are denied the right of establishment abroad, the difficulties of doing business, once established, center on onerous licensing and certification requirements, limitations on the range of services that may be offered to the public, restrictions on employee nationality and foreign equity, and discrimination in government contracts in favor of national firms.

It is likely, therefore, that the process of bargaining is going to be a good deal more like negotiations about nontariff barriers to trade in goods than to the earlier rounds of tariff reduction. Hence it is useful to think in terms of the process by which the codes were negotiated in the Tokyo Round and how they will be applied. This means that bargaining will take place in two ways. First, there will be the negotiations about the rules exceptions, and related matters which will be influenced by how people think their practices will be affected. Subsequently, there will be bargaining about the interpretation and application of the rules, and the kinds of negotiations involved in, for example, the efforts to settle an issue before using the dispute settlement procedure (or allowing it to go to completion), to interpret the findings of a panel, or to provide adequate compensation.

The codes are a combination of agreed rules with regard to certain kinds of practices (or their prohibition) and a rather elaborate set of arrangements whereby other practices (such as subsidies) are treated as sometimes legitimate and sometimes illegitimate depending on a variety of circumstances. Another possibility is something analogous to the government procurement code in which rules are reasonably clear but apply to agreed sets of transactions. Thus there is already a procedure for limiting the treatment of "services" generally. Needless to say, there are very wide gray areas between these two concepts and much of the grayness will stem from disagreements as to how much regulation is needed for the protection of consumers, the stability of the economy, and national autonomy and other goals.

When the problem is one of reaching international agreements about industries that are regulated in most countries, there are two possible approaches. One is to aim at bringing about as much harmony or standardization as possible in the national regulations. The implied premises would be that there were fairly common objectives for most national regulation and that some uniformity would facilitate international transactions.[9] The alternative approach is to assume that

---

[9] An example is provided by the OECD guidelines on transborder data flows, which set out principles to which national legislation should conform.

countries will be quite diverse in the ways they regulate each service and that the aim of an international effort should be to limit the resulting distortion of international service activities and the unfair distribution of burdens. Since there are bound to be differences of judgment about distortion and equity, it is likely that consultative and dispute-settlement arrangements would play a prominent part in this kind of activity.

We return now to a consideration of several other possible objectives of international negotiations. A basic principle of GATT is nondiscrimination. There is no doubt that it will appear desirable and reasonable to many people that the same principle should apply to international trade in services. However, equal treatment in trade is not the same as equal treatment in investment, and there is at least a strong similarity between some service transactions and the activities of foreign direct investors. Thus we come immediately to questions not only of most-favored-nation treatment but of national treatment (and of some kinds of discrimination between domestic and foreign companies that coexist with the general rules).

Foreign discrimination in one form or another is one of the main complaints of American service industries. Undoubtedly, American companies would like national treatment when they set up operations abroad. When they are selling services across national boundaries they would presumably want most-favored-nation treatment plus the same kind of national treatment that GATT provides for goods. In some countries, domestic service firms have certain obligations that a foreigner might hope to escape; then he would have better than national treatment, as foreign banks have had in the United States. It seems unlikely that so privileged a position would often be agreed to formally, but it might arise if governments both accepted national treatment and agreed to refrain from imposing certain kinds of burdens on international transactions.

Among the issues that need fuller exploration are the implications of MFN and national treatment in services, on the one hand for companies and on the other for the aims of regulating governments.

USA-Business and Industry Advisory Council (BIAC) Committee on International Information Flows, *The OECD Guidelines Governing the Protection of Privacy and Transborder Flows of Personal Data: Implications for US Business* (New York: By the author, January 1982). This approach should not be translated into the proposition that there cannot be liberalization until all national legislation is uniform or "harmonized." That view—which had advocates in Europe not only before the creation of the Common Market but before the Benelux agreement was accepted—leads to an impasse.

For example, the aim of creating domestic service activities might be met by restricting imports but giving foreign investors national treatment, but a policy of insuring that essential services are controlled by nationals would rule out national treatment. In manufacturing, even where formal national treatment for foreigners exists there is often a certain amount of de facto preference given to domestically owned firms in such matters as government procurement. How wide a margin would be regarded as tolerable in services? It must also be recognized that national treatment is compatible with requirements regarding the amount of foreign equity that is allowed, nationals on boards of directors, and a number of other issues (some of which are in controversy).

The analogy with investment emphasizes that to an important degree what is involved is the right of establishment and how it is provided. Often the principle of the right to establish is not in dispute, but the procedures for getting permission are slow or otherwise unsatisfactory. Sometimes licensing authorities have great discretion and need not explain refusals. Barriers of this sort present quite different problems from those of national policies that simply deny foreign companies the right of establishment, as happens in banking and insurance in some countries.

Most of the time the basic issue seems to be how much the right of establishment is circumscribed by restrictions and regulations on the operation of the foreign-owned company. In the European Community (EC), much of the discussion of the right of establishment concerns the provision of personal services and the acceptance of immigrants (or foreign visitors) in the professions. These items were not generally thought about in the initial US discussions of the liberalization of services, but have now taken their place on the agenda. Some effort will have to be made to decide whether these kinds of activities are to be distinguished from other services or whether what is agreed on as reasonable treatment for bankers, insurance people, and advertisers should also apply to doctors, lawyers, and psychologists.

Reciprocity

Well before the new burst of enthusiasm for "reciprocity" in American trade policy, the idea had a good deal of support in American service industries as a proper objective for international negotiations. While some people and recent bills in Congress use this elusive term broadly to cover the exchange of benefits in different fields, it more often is taken to mean, "I will treat your industry the way you treat mine" (meaning the same industry). Reciprocity has been a lively issue in banking and there are divisions of opinion among American bankers as to the extent to which it is wise to try to insist on such provisions.

While the general idea of reciprocity has much attraction and there is no question that a sense of reciprocal advantage is a necessary basis for any government to participate in international negotiations and adhere to international agreements, there are some awkward points to be taken into account. Reciprocity based on bilateral understandings about the treatment of industries is incompatible with unconditional MFN. It is compatible with a kind of conditional MFN extended to many countries whenever the conditions of reciprocity are satisfied. It provides a means of exchanging national treatment. Should reciprocity become a central theme in negotiations about services, there would almost certainly be some spillover to goods and to negotiations about investment. Nevertheless, in principle, a rule of reciprocity in services could exist side by side with MFN in trade.

There is, however, another dimension to reciprocity—its retaliatory form—that has to be taken into account. Americans complain that the US market is relatively open while the markets of other countries are more regulated. To the extent that this is correct, it follows that if foreign governments are not prepared to treat American companies the way the US government treats foreign companies, then reciprocity will require the imposition of restrictions in the United States to match those abroad. Whether this is a sensible arrangement that will give either economic gains or true bargaining power to the United States is not something that can be settled in the abstract.[10]

A second set of complications arises whenever service industries in the United States are regulated by the states, as is true of insurance and some banking. The federal government is not then in a position

---

[10] The formula that leaps to mind is the delegation of discretionary power to impose restrictions in some circumstances. Caution is in order, however, since, when the government has this power, it is vulnerable to protectionist pressure to use it. The idea of using this power for bargaining purposes may be sound in some circumstances, but it also has to be borne in mind, as Henry Wallich remarked in connection with banking reciprocity, that "the benefits to the United States of buying foreign goods and foreign banking services are what they are, whether there is reciprocity or not." "Perspectives on Foreign Banking in the United States," (remarks at a conference on foreign banking in the United States, Washington, March 1, 1982), p. 7. The question of who gains and who pays for restrictions in services in the United States requires some study.

to provide reciprocity to foreigners, and therefore the definition of the objective would have to be qualified. It is recognized in the OECD code on invisibles that its provisions do not apply to activities under the jurisdiction of American states or Canadian provinces. The legal questions as to what kinds of obligations could be undertaken by the federal government (or assumed by the states) are beyond our competence.

The US Trade Representative (USTR) has begun consultations with state governments, but it will undoubtedly be unclear for some time how the divided jurisdiction will affect the ability of the United States to reach comprehensive agreements with other governments. In banking, substantial changes are under way that are breaking down some of the barriers to interstate banking; the reach of federal regulatory power may expand correspondingly. In insurance, it is worth asking what trade-offs would appeal to the American insurance industry if, in order to enable the US government to improve access to foreign insurance markets on a reciprocal basis, it were necessary to shift some domestic regulatory powers from the states to the federal government.

A third set of complications arises from an economic rather than a legal approach. Can it make sense to treat as "reciprocal" access to the large American market and the market of a small foreign country? If Americans say they will not worry about that, there will surely be some foreign arguments that it is in fact not reciprocal to open one's market to a strong American industry when the indigenous industry is too weak to take advantage of the nominally reciprocal access that is provided to the American market. Whether this is a valid argument depends largely on what is to be said about the reasonableness or unreasonableness of any kind of protection based either on the development of an indigenous industry (infant industry) or the need for some degree of national control. We return to these problems later. If one country lacks the industry in question, is it to be given reciprocity by concessions in another field?

Finally, an emphasis on reciprocity is exposed to the risk that one country may change the rules of the game for very good reasons that have nothing to do with foreign business. For example, the decontrol of the US trucking industry made it easier for Canadian firms to compete in the American market. There was no change in Canadian practice where regulation is by provinces and municipalities.[11] When

---

[11] New investment or changes in foreign ownership have to be passed on by the Foreign Investment Review Agency but the emphasis here is on trucking rights.

new American trucking firms sought permission to operate in Canada, they were sometimes refused. Some of the resistance came from established firms (many of them American). The Canadian government denied there was any discrimination against foreigners. If the denials were simply the result of a regulatory approach, should either Canada or the United States change its basic trucking policy for the sake of reciprocity?

The episode is a reminder of another problem with which the United States will have to deal in negotiating international agreements on services. Much service regulation in the United States is by quasi-independent bodies operating under statutes that give them a good bit of discretion in dealing with foreign applicants for licenses. Unless there are legal changes or new cooperative arrangements, conflicts can arise between the activity of these regulatory bodies and the international arrangements being negotiated.

More General Approaches

The difficulty of seeing just what various principles would mean if applied to services should not lead us to forget that it is not yet fully accepted that international transactions in services ought to be subject to some general set of rules and principles, as merchandise trade is (though investment is not). So the question poses itself. Could a step be taken toward recognizing the general principle while leaving its application to different cases and circumstances to be worked out over time? "Our long-term objective," said Ambassador Brock, "is to negotiate a services code in the GATT that will incorporate a set of general rules and principles that govern trade in all service industries. Additionally, they would establish mechanisms for discussing issues and solving disputes following procedures already established by the GATT."[12] That is for the long term and seems to require a

---

[12] Statement before the Subcommittee on Investigation and Oversight of the House Committee on Public Works and Transportation, April 12, 1982. Ambassador Brock has suggested that the standards code "could be easily expanded to include services." The idea of a general code does not preclude "sector-specific agreements dealing with market access and related issues" which Ambassador Brock has also said should be explored. (Testimony before the Subcommittee on Trade of the Senate Finance Committee, May 14, 1982.) No statements at this stage of the discussion ought to be interpreted as defining precisely the proposals the United States will make in GATT when negotiations begin.

resolution of most of the issues already touched on and others we shall come to later. Are there any shortcuts?

Suppose one were to start by trying to see how far existing GATT rules and principles could be applied to services. One approach would be to argue that a large number of services are inextricably linked with the trade in goods that GATT already deals with. This applies not only to transportation, distribution, and advertising but also insurance and, in addition, servicing—an exact but narrower sense of the word which is extremely important in some activities but not in others. There cannot be an extensive trade in goods without an extensive trade in these services. The value of the goods depends on certain kinds of services and is reduced (or the price increased) if they are restricted, taxed, or absent. It then becomes reasonable to say that the logic that applies to trade liberalization should apply to the provision of these ancillary services.[13] Thus, the interesting possibility arises of arguing that some restrictions on services are already forbidden by international agreement because they nullify or impair tariff reductions made under GATT.

A second approach would go further. It would say that in general (*ceteris paribus*, *mutatis mutandis*) the same principles that apply to international trade in goods should apply to international trade in services. A practice that would violate GATT if it applied to goods should be regarded as a violation when it applies to services unless there was a good reason to the contrary. In practice that "good reason" might be the unwillingness of a government to accept that rule in a specific case. Then it would have to explain its reasoning and enter into negotiations with other governments that felt damaged. The dispute-settlement procedure would become one of the means of interpreting the general commitment and of adapting GATT to services.

The limits and defects of this approach are clear. It says nothing about the range of investment-like issues that are not covered by GATT and are important to services. The application of the GATT principles would not affect the height of barriers that were not ruled out in principle. The impact on some countries would be much greater than on others and that would increase the tendency to find excuses

---

[13] This reasoning does not apply to all the activities of the service providers; for example, insurance companies and banks do more than handle goods and their other activities might perfectly well be subjected to a different set of rules from those that might be necessary to protect the liberalization of trade in goods.

to avoid carrying out the obligations (but a longer period of adaptation could be allowed to those with difficulties). There would be instances in which it could correctly be argued that the economic effect of applying the rules to services was quite different from that of applying them to goods. Still, the approach would mark a major gain from the present stituation and make the basic question: "Why not apply the GATT rule?"

In one respect, the approach looks like simple reason. If a country is not permitted to use exchange controls to limit the transfer of proceeds from goods sales and returns on investments, why should it be permitted to discriminate against services as is done in some cases? The principle ought not to be limited to GATT commitments. But in GATT there is also a precedent that is not very encouraging. The one service industry specifically included in GATT is motion pictures. They are subject to regular GATT rules except that governments are permitted to establish screen quotas for the showing of domestically made films. However, subsidies and other practices are used to provide further support for domestic production, sometimes in apparent violation of GATT, efforts to widen the scope of the provisions and to cover films shown on television have been resisted on cultural and political grounds.[14] The way satellite transmission, video cassettes, and other technological developments have outrun past efforts to make rules about films and television illustrates a set of problems of great importance to discussions of transborder data flows, a matter into which we cannot enter in this paper.

If these two approaches to the application of GATT principles seem too ambitious, one could imagine starting with a simple international recognition of the principle built into American legislation since 1974 that complaints about unfair trade in services should be as legitimate as complaints about unfair trade in goods. That could lead to the use of the GATT dispute-settlement procedure. This seems a rather minimal step but it should be recalled that we are considering here measures that might be taken before there is agreement on some fairly

---

[14] Television films as well as those shown in theaters are covered by the OECD code on invisibles, but extensive reservations reduce the effect of these provisions. Canada, for example, has excluded its film industry from the code. Other Canadian examples of "cultural" protectionism concern the tax treatment of advertising by Canadian firms in American media and the elimination of advertising in American broadcasts on Canadian cable television. These matters are discussed in Janice L. Murray, ed., *Canadian Cultural Nationalism* (New York: New York University Press for the Canadian Institute of International Affairs and the Council on Foreign Relations, 1977).

fundamental matters and that might help to fill gaps piecemeal. To a degree one could build on the GATT codes as well as the basic agreement itself.

There are other variations of these general approaches. Space does not permit spelling them all out here. Several are mentioned in the penultimate section of this paper where the question is also raised as to what might be undertaken in OECD or other organizations. There is, however, still another way to get at the problem.

As it will take some time to work out acceptable principles for liberalization or fair trade in services—or whatever goal is agreed on—one should try to find ways to prevent further deterioration. A truce on the imposition of new barriers to services would be a very substantial achievement and not something that is unreasonable to ask for. It is unlikely, however, that an overall truce would be acceptable to very many countries since any run-of-the-mill bureaucrat can think of all sorts of exceptional circumstances in which the government's hands should not be tied. Therefore there would have to be escape clauses and exceptions (national security for one, which seems to count heavily in discussions of the transmission of data across borders). But again some sort of step in this direction would not be implausible. In fact, simply the need to argue about the justification for the escape clauses (and later consultations about their use) could help significantly in clarifying objectives and views of various countries about different services, something that is badly needed in the present state of our knowledge.

Commitments to avoid, or at least limit, the imposition of new restrictions could have special importance for some services that are not yet closely regulated in many countries. The practice of protection may not be as widespread in services as it was in goods trade when GATT was established; technological and other changes are creating new kinds of activities that may escape restriction because vested interests are not yet established. It has to be recognized, however, that the prospect of some kind of rules will itself stimulate some countries to put regulations in place in advance.

While this section on objectives has not come to a clear conclusion as to which would be most desirable, perhaps enough has been said to show why the clear-cut objectives frequently set out in the United States are unlikely to be widely accepted and that some objectives are in fact not as clear-cut as is generally thought.

The following section discusses some of the problems that arise with regard both to national policies toward services and to the general economics of the situation. These have a bearing on why countries might do one thing rather than another or which goals should be pushed for intensively and which can be thought of as secondary.

Conditions and Questions

It is difficult to speak with assurance about some of the conditions that shape negotiating issues without a better knowledge than seems to exist of the economics of service industries. There we again face the central problem of generalization versus differentiation among services. For present purposes we shall assume that in the absence of evidence to the contrary the reasoning that explains the gains or losses from liberalizing or restricting trade and investment in goods is applicable to services as well.

One assumes, therefore, that a country has a comparative advantage in some services compared to others (and compared to the production of goods) in the basic sense that it can do some things more cheaply and efficiently than it can do other things. When it comes to international comparisons, it is less clear how one might know in advance what competitive advantages one country had over another. Old-fashioned factor proportions analysis seems less likely to be the guide than ideas about human capital.

Product-cycle may have some bearing, although the international mobility of human capital suggests that in many service industries one is talking about activities in which a relatively small number of highly skilled people supervise a less skilled body of workers. Learning curves are very important so it may be in the common interest of foreign owners and host countries to bring in foreigners to start with and then train local people. Comparative advantage may shift quickly within a country and competitive advantage more rapidly from one nation to another.

The economics of services may well differ from sector to sector. The necessary stimuli may come only at a late stage of development; established producers may have great competitive advantages; the economics of near-global operation may be enormous. In these cases, there would seem to be an argument for some infant-industry protection but there may also be instances in which its cost is very high because of the amount of capital needed to become competitive and the lack of confidence of lenders and investors in untried enterprises.

Economies of scale pose interesting questions since it seems quite clear that many services are highly labor-intensive and involve something like face-to-face relations whereas in others financial considerations, communications, the pooling of knowledge, and, probably, corporate strategy mean that a concentration of high talent in a few places may well serve world markets more efficiently than if there were dispersal. The technologies for data processing and dissemination seem to create great possibilities for economies of scale in the information industries. Whether on balance they make for increased competition or greater concentration of control is not clear, and this balance should be a matter of basic concern for national and international policy.

All of the familiar questions about multinational corporations and international trade and investment seem to apply to quite a few services. For example, multinational firms are able to adjust to trade barriers and investment regulation more easily than national corporations. Do they almost by definition deal in markets of a size that make for greater efficiency than firms that work in only one country? Would individual governments find it more advantageous to deal separately with individual multinational enterprises (MNE) without international rules than to have to conform to a code in these matters?[15]

When it comes to noneconomic values one tends to think in national terms. Here national security is one dominant element but it is not well understood. This is in some respects a different factor in small, weak countries from what it is in large and middle-sized ones. Autonomy, however, is likely to seem a more homogeneous value until one runs into the familiar contradiction that there is a trade-off between doing things by one's self with limited national capacity and joining with others in pooling of interests (interdependence) that can greatly enhance the ability to meet needs though at some loss of autonomy. Also to be taken into consideration are the kinds of mixed motives that lie behind many national industrial policies: long- and short-run economic and political considerations, ideas about achieving economic security through diversity in domestic production, and the view that certain functions have to be performed within the national boundaries. If there are certain activities a country wishes to nurture, it will argue in infant-industry terms no matter how developed its economy is. How legitimate is this approach?

Concepts of security and political interests in services seem to be very prominent; they are also much neglected in American discussions of what can reasonably be asked of other countries. Once one accepts the idea of a "security" interest of some sort, it becomes very difficult to define the kind of exception to liberalized treatment of services

---

[15] This has almost certainly been the case in matters of investment and may go far to explain why there is no GATT for investment.

that this should justify and how it should be applied. This is apparent in trade where GATT and other instruments virtually leave the matter to national self-definition and it is only by a combination of tradition, plausibility, and worry about retaliation that resort to the exception is kept within bounds. This may well prove to be true of services too, but until we find this out it seems likely that the more sharply the security interest can be defined the better the chance of its not becoming an escape clause. A failure to acknowledge a security interest where it exists will lead either to no agreement at all or to one that will be widely breached.

This matter is particularly important in communications services where national security and personal security in a variety of forms, including privacy, have been advanced in favor of restrictions on international freedom of business communications. Presumably something like this reasoning applies to transportation both in terms of the control of air fields and air traffic within one's jurisdiction and in traditional matters with regard to ports. The extension of the security argument to shipping, as is done in the United States, shows how easily the line between commercial and security interests becomes blurred. Control over the banking system is thought of largely in economic terms but foreign domination of banking could be seen as a threat to security in the broader sense. Some governments are concerned about the accumulation of capital by big foreign insurers.

It is only a step further to ask whether a certain degree of self-sufficiency in all major services is equally requisite. Another question arises in government procurement and investment regulation, whether a foreign-owned but domestically incorporated, financially liable and technically capable installation should be treated as national or foreign. Finally, political calculations have to be made, particularly in a large economy where the proportion of any service industry operating internationally is small and the interests of the firms that are national in scope may not extend to multilateral agreements on liberalization.

American Restrictions

It is not just foreign countries that will be making these arguments. One of the most basic requirements for entering into negotiations is to be altogether clear about the pattern of American policies and practices toward service industries, the way these may be regarded by foreign governments or service industries, and the extent to which the United States is prepared to modify its practices as a result either of bargaining or to conform to a set of international rules. The general picture of the United States as a relatively open market in services when compared with many foreign countries is undoubtedly correct.

A certain number of American restrictions, however, might well be called into question by other countries. Perhaps the most obvious is the requirement of American ownership of domestic radio and telegraph communications. This is presumably based on the general security consideration mentioned above. If so, is there any serious ground for our removing it? If not, can we expect other countries to do differently? Is the boundary between the communications that have to be reserved for nationals and those which are essential for the conduct of international business all that clear? Unless communications as such are to be put in a special category because of their relevance to security, who is to contradict another country that puts some other sort of activity on the same footing?

Most of the recent discussion of services has focused on the restrictions of other countries that limit American exports and investment. It would be useful to have a better catalog than we can provide of American protection in this field or of the points at which it might arise. The shipping laws are an obvious example. In banking the interest in American opportunities to expand abroad held down the resistance to foreign competition at home.

Part of the interest in reciprocity seems to be traceable to worry about the possible expansion of foreign services in the American market. Some of the proposed services legislation would apply countervailing and antidumping laws to services. It is hard to quarrel with this in principle but one wonders what the practical results would be, given the rather unsatisfactory record of that legislation in dealing with goods. Is there a serious problem?[16] Much government procurement discriminates against foreigners. How open to foreign contractors is the American construction industry? In some fields the immigration and visa laws have a central place in limiting what foreigners can do in the United States. The link between goods and services is emphasized by foreign accusations that certification procedures nominally based on airline safety in fact discriminate against foreign aircraft.

The US ability to make international agreements about services also depends on congressional-executive understandings, which might well be shaped by other considerations than the merits of the case.

---

[16] Complaints about foreign subsidies damaging American service industries often refer to competition in third markets, as in the construction industries, and these are not reached by countervailing duties.

Indeed it seems quite clear that services generally is a field where, as in many nontariff matters concerning goods, a continuing process of action or at least consent by Congress is essential to effective operation. Whether the intricate processes by which new cooperative arrangements can be worked out and made effective are in any significant way different in services from those in goods is not at all clear. Different committees of Congress, different parts of the executive branch, and different economic and political constituencies are involved. It cannot be assumed that their approaches to international service issues will be similar to those established in American foreign trade policy.

Two final points about the US position need to be mentioned. There is an asymmetry between the United States and the rest of the world with regard to the degree of restriction on services in the domestic market and at the frontiers, then the analogy with the history of tariff bargaining is called into question. In that earlier case there was no question that the United States was itself one of the major centers of restriction and therefore had a great deal to offer and bargain with. If this condition does not exist in services, some thought needs to be given to what the United States can expect to achieve in the bargaining process and what it has to offer. Here again the link with reciprocity is obvious.

The other point is that it is not at all obvious that negotiations about services should be concerned only with services. In past trade bargaining, countries have often sought concessions on different products from those on which they gave them. No doubt package deals will find their place in bargaining about services, but there is no reason to expect them to be confined to services. Indeed, if it is true, as is often said, that the decline in American competitiveness in many branches of manufacturing is offset by a gain in competitiveness in many services (plainly not all), then the United States should be especially interested in bargains that reduce foreign restrictions on services and may have to offer easier access to domestic markets for some products in return. That there are then problems to be faced comparable to those which in the past have led to accusations of "selling out" farmers for manufacturers or vice versa is obvious. The rise in interest in sectoral reciprocity (first legislated in 1974) is not unconnected with this matter.

Types of Agreements

Without having resolved the many uncertainties we have raised and without having yet reached a clear set of conclusions except to the effect that there is a problem that ought to be dealt with, we now simply list with comment a number of different concrete arrangements that one might propose as the basis for international negotiations. As will become apparent, some of these are mutually exclusive but quite a few of them represent a range of steps, or in some cases different approaches, which could with a certain degree of ingenuity be fitted together over time. Some of these possibilities have already been mentioned but are repeated here to help focus discussions.

Applying GATT

(1) There would be much greater international understanding than now exists if a significant number of countries made a joint declaration that the principles of GATT were to apply to services as well as goods.

(2) Could the nullification and impairment approach suggested earlier be used?

(3) The statement suggested above might be made about various of the GATT codes, notably those regarding subsidies and public procurement. This would cover at least some of the practices being complained of and would establish a complaint and disputes settlements procedure for certain activities.

(4) It also would be worth trying to make any new initiative in GATT, such as that concerning performance requirements, apply to services from the beginning.

New Codes

New codes could be established:
(1) a code for services
(2) codes for individual services or groups of services
(3) a code for codes.
Here the analogy is with the commodity agreements chapter of the International Trade Organization (ITO). It laid down standards that any commodity agreement would have to meet, such as representation of consumers and transparency. To approach the question of services codes in this way would permit flexibility in dealing with the different characteristics of various service industries while at the same time assuring some standards as to principles and procedure.

An Armistice

(1) As suggested earlier, there could be a pledge to impose no new barriers to international transactions in services for a given period of time or while negotiations were proceeding.

(2) The OECD pledge not to deal with current economic problems by measures that would damage others is phrased to apply to all current account transactions, not just trade. Would there be any value in reaffirming the pledge's application to services?

A Complaints Procedure

(1) How much could be accomplished if, without trying to work out detailed rules and standards, governments announced that they would accept the right of others to complain about impediments to transactions in services and that they would talk about the matter? This pledge could be made multilateral and a complaints center established in GATT.

(2) As part of the preparation for negotiations the GATT Secretariat would presumably collect from member countries their complaints about other countries' services barriers and make an orderly catalog of these (as was done with nontariff trade barriers (NTBs) before the Tokyo Round. Could this accumulation be used as an agenda for conferences and consultation to deal with certain industries or problems without waiting for a general negotiation? Would it be useful to work out model agreements of some sort?

A Distinct Role for the OECD

(1) Could the OECD codes about invisibles and investment be used to deal with the problems of services more effectively than in the past? Is the main problem one of interpretation, amendment, or enforcement?

(2) Would further and extended consultations or studies in the OECD on the problems of services be particularly useful?

(3) Should the aim be to draw up some kind of a model agreement in the OECD even if it finally had to be negotiated elsewhere? Might this pertain to bilateral agreements?

(4) To what extent are the problems of impediments to services to be thought of as OECD questions, either in the sense that the biggest problems concern relations among the industrial countries or that by and large the industrial countries have common interests vis-à-vis third countries, especially those in the third world, or that the chances of drawing up any kind of code or understanding are much better in the OECD group than on a broader basis?

Other International Arrangements

(1) While the debate on the existing code for shipping cannot, as a practical matter, be extracted from UNCTAD, other service ques-

tions should not be introduced into that forum; they are not inherently North-South issues. For example, Brazil and Korea have construction and engineering industries with international markets. They can be damaged by barriers, discrimination, and subsidies to their competitors.

(2) The idea of a "GATT for services" should also be rejected in favor of relating the existing GATT to services.

(3) Regional understandings on services—for example, in the European Community and the Andean Pact Group—need more attention than we have given them. It may be, as Andrew Shonfield once suggested, that regional blocs will be pacesetters in the liberalization of services because they will find it easier "to develop new techniques of compromise amongst themselves" than "might be done on a universal scale." The other side of the issue is that these compromises "will pay little heed to the economic interests of nations outside" and, as in trade matters, intensify discrimination while improving relations inside the group.[17]

Bilateral Agreements

(1) Should an effort be made to lay down standards for bilateral agreements covering services? These could state objectives, establish standards, and guard the interests of third countries against discrimination. They would sanction the idea of piecemeal approaches that would be faster than reaching broad multilateral agreement.

(2) Should the emphasis be procedural so that any bilateral agreements could be either reviewed more broadly or brought into some sort of relation to one another, even if only by a procedure in which a third party could complain about damage done to its interest.

(3) Whether formal agreements are reached or not there will certainly be bilateral negotiations about particular complaints concerning services. These may result in various forms of understanding which ought to be published and perhaps formally registered. A major aim should be to find ways to prevent the accumulation of bilateral understandings or negotiations from impeding the development of multilateral agreements or the acceptance of general principles. So far as possible, bilateral agreements should be used to improve the chances of reaching multilateral agreements.

Would it be better for the United States to pursue a primarily bilateral approach to the services issues and let multilateralization

---

[17] Kindleberger and Shonfield, eds., *Economic Policies* (New York: Macmillan, 1971), p. 534.

take place later on? The case for this would depend at least in part on the possibility that some countries are willing to make more "progressive" agreements than could possibly be accepted multilaterally (and for which they would not accept multilateral undertakings except on a reciprocal basis) or that at a minimum bilateral agreements are likely to be better than the kinds of unilateral actions that would probably be taken in the absence of an international approach to the services issue.

Conclusions

In spite of all our caveats and the ignorance we have underlined about both the economics of services and the way many of the industries operate, we have reached certain broad conclusions. They are put forward as reasonable proposals but are not tested for feasibility, acceptability in the United States or abroad, or the prospects of getting them through Congress. They also do not deal with the question of what the United States should do if its initiatives were to meet with negative responses in much of the rest of the world.

The American initiative to explore the possibilities of liberalization[18] of trade and investment in services is sound. Building on what has already been done, the United States should move towards a more explicit definition of objectives and methods. The aim should be to arrive at multilateral agreements covering as wide a range of international services transactions as possible. American interests will be served best by trying to work out cooperative arrangements and for that Americans must be sensitive to the interests and attitudes of other countries.

The list of foreign barriers already compiled by USTR should be used to stimulate foreign complaints about the United States. As these come in, the US government, industry, and independent scholars should study them to determine the costs and benefits to the United States of continuing these practices or changing them (in return for comparable measures by other countries). The political feasibility of various courses will have to be tested; sensible public debate on these matters will require not only a great deal more information than is generally available about the services industries but extensive study and analysis of their operations at home and abroad.

---

[18] We use this term as shorthand subject to the questions raised in the chapter about its precise meaning.

It seems inevitable that differences among service industries will require different kinds of agreements and that for political and economic reasons choices will have to be made about priorities among them. The political and diplomatic consequences of this differentiation should be anticipated and allowed for in working out an American strategy.

All this will take time. Meanwhile, the United States should push for some multilateral agreements on "services" generally. These will be mainly statements of principle which can be invoked to guide work on separate industries and called into play in dealing with cases that come up before agreements are reached. The aim should be acceptance, insofar as possible, of the idea that existing GATT commitments and codes should apply to services as well as trade in goods. There should be a strong emphasis on nondiscriminatory treatment which should be understood as meaning most-favored-nation treatment for trade and national treatment for investment. An effort should be made to codify the conditions in which the many inevitable exceptions to the latter are made. As in goods trade, there should be a presumption that there are economic gains from liberalization and that the reasons and costs of not liberalizing should be made as clear as possible.

While all this is going on, the United States will have to negotiate bilaterally about particular foreign practices. The remedies sought and the agreements made in connection with them should, so far as possible, be compatible with the kinds of multilateral agreements that are being sought, in spirit as well as particulars. This does not preclude the use of these negotiations to obtain advantages for American industries that are not yet guaranteed to others; that may hasten the process of broader agreement.

As in any bargaining process, some reciprocity in the exchange of commitments is unavoidable. However, the United States should not adopt a narrow interpretation of reciprocity (as embodied in much recent discussion) as the dominant characteristic of what it seeks in services. There may be times when retaliation against foreign restrictive practices in services will be the best course and when some degree of reciprocity will be a reasonable formula for arranging the mutual removal of restrictions, but it should be an aim of foreign economic policy to keep these cases to a minimum and then to test in a tough-minded way the costs and benefits of such a course for the general national interest of the United States.

As in goods trade, a certain number of countries are likely to be of exceptional importance in reaching agreements on services. We do not know just who they are; they will probably be different for different services, but it is safe to assume that Japan, some EC members, probably some other European countries, and very likely Canada will be among them. On some matters, however, and certainly when general principles are in question, some or many developing countries will also be important.

It should be an American objective to keep services issues, both in general and so far as possible in regard to particular services and practices, from being treated as items on the North–South agenda. Care must be taken to use the OECD for what it can contribute without implying any exclusion. It may well be necessary to deal with certain services in specialized agencies—for example, shipping, aviation, and telecommunications—but, unless there is a compelling reason to do that, the emphasis should be on lodging most services agreements in GATT whether they concern general principles or detailed practices for which codes are developed.

The United States should not let the pursuit of the liberalization of services and reaching agreements in this new field—important as they are—divert attention and energies from work on trade in goods, investment in the production of goods, and other measures of international economic cooperation. If the GATT codes were to become dead letters before they were truly tested, that would imperil the entire cooperative system to which services should be added.

CHAPTER 18

Trade-Related Investment Issues

A. E. Safarian

Government policies toward foreign direct investment and multinational enterprises have displayed a great deal of ambivalence in most countries. Such policies encompass measures both to attract and to regulate such activities with the emphasis on each aspect differing by country and over time.

A decade ago various writers drew attention to the potential damage to the international economic system and its participants from the fiscal competition with regulation involved in this process. They also pointed to the need for international policy instruments to deal with the problems involved (Bergsten 1974, Goldberg and Kindleberger 1970, Safarian and Bell 1973). The apparent spread of such measures in recent years of high unemployment, and the effects on investment and foreign trade in particular, have led to renewed calls for bilateral or international agreements. The US government has been particularly active in seeking such agreements.

This chapter will outline the evidence on the extent of such measures, the effects on investment and trade, and possible policy approaches. It is clear that the measures involved may distort trade. Governments bid very large sums in order to influence the location or relocation of investment, with consequent trade effects. They also set many regulations with similar effects, including quite specific export targets or import limits. How far they affect trade, given the other influences on it, is a more complex question. The reasons for the measures and their characteristics are also important in considering possible international constraints on them.

The particular topics that interest us are fiscal incentives, performance requirements, exceptions to national (that is, nondiscriminatory)

The author is grateful to the Social Sciences and Humanities Research Council of Canada for financial assistance in support of this study.

treatment, and sectoral restrictions that are directed to multinational enterprises (MNEs), and that distort trade. There are two preliminary points to note about these topics.

First, there is a serious problem of measurement involved here, or even of simple description. Many of the measures have a poorly defined basis in law or judicial interpretation, reflecting administrative processes with varying degrees of explicitness all the way to quite informal understandings. In addition, many governments, in reporting these measures, are inclined to put the most general or least restrictive interpretation on their measures, especially in what they see as possible bargaining or review situations with other countries in various organizations. Companies in turn are sometimes reluctant to report on such measures, even confidentially, partly because they hesitate to appear critical of the wielders of regulatory and fiscal power. For these and other reasons there are substantial discrepancies in published sources. What are often opaque measures at best are also often opaquely reported.

The second point is that these particular measures are often part of a larger set aimed at providing a fiscal, monetary, and regulatory framework for multinational companies. These have been outlined, somewhat tersely, in a variety of sources (for example, Safarian 1978; OECD 1978, 1979; US Commerce 1978; UN 1978; Price Waterhouse in US Senate 1982). Our immediate task in this chapter is to consider foreign-trade issues flowing from policies towards foreign direct investment and MNEs in particular. However, it is impossible to limit the topic completely in that way. Some of the more general policies towards MNEs impact on trade. And investment policies that do not discriminate between domestically and foreign-owned firms may distort trade. In addition, little emphasis is given to trade in such service industries as banking and shipping (chapter 17, this volume).

Most of the emphasis in this chapter is given to the industrial countries, both for reasons of space and my greater familiarity with conditions there. Some reference to the experience of developing countries is necessary, however, since the incidence of such measures is very large in many of them.

Performance Requirements

In the process of regulating MNEs, whether systematically or ad hoc, generally or sectorally, governments have developed a wide range of devices and attempted to achieve many objectives. The most explicit policy is the designation of sectors closed to foreign direct investment. Many countries have more or less formal notification or review mechanisms on establishment and often on subsequent merger as well. These sometimes apply also to entry into sectors other than the original one. Finally, there are a variety of often ill-defined exceptions to national treatment after entry, that is, government discrimination against foreign-owned companies in access to finance, fiscal measures, and regulation, not to mention some purely private understandings that have the same effect.

The performance requirements involved cover a wide range of measures. Some are clearly trade-related, notably those setting minimum export or maximum import targets or the equivalent in domestic value added or the effects on the balance of payments. Others could well affect investment or trade at one or more removes and given certain assumptions, for example, requirements for technology transfer, maintenance of jobs, and various financial requirements.

Such performance requirements, especially when directly related to trade, tend to shift production and related investment and jobs from other countries. A requirement that exports be a given percentage of production or a minimum volume has the same effect as an export subsidy, since it raises exports beyond what they would otherwise be. With resources fully employed in the countries concerned, one could argue, with some exceptions, that what occurs is a decline in efficiency of resource use rather than direct employment effects as such. In a world of unemployed resources, international shifts are more likely to happen. Imitation and retaliation may add negative employment and efficiency effects. As for limits on imports or minimum requirements for value added, these are equivalent to various types of quotas.

All of this assumes, first, that the performance requirements are not simply what the firms would have done in any case but, since they wish to gain entry or to get an incentive, they have had to make them explicit; and, secondly, where the commitments made by firms go beyond this, that they are in fact honored by firms or enforced by governments (see below).

The most comprehensive study of incentives and of performance requirements is based on the 1977 benchmark survey of US direct investment abroad (US Commerce October 1981). An average 14 percent of the entire population of 23,641 US nonbank affiliates of nonbank parents reported they were subject to one or more performance requirements. Specifically, five such requirements were involved: 2 percent reported a minimum export requirement; 3 percent a maximum import limit; 3 percent a minimum local content requirement; 8 percent a local labor requirement; and 6 percent had to limit

TABLE 18.1   INCIDENCE OF PERFORMANCE REQUIREMENTS, BY TYPE
AND AREA

Number of affiliates reporting	At least one requirement		Minimum export amount		Minimum import limit	
	Number	(per-centage[a])	Number	(per-centage[a])	Number	(per-centage[a])
23,641	3,240	(14)	356	(2)	582	(3)

Number subject to performance requirements imposed upon
foreign-owned[b] companies only

			132	(37)	121	(21)

Developed country

15,603	1,008	(6)	130	(1)	169	(1)

Number subject to performance requirements imposed upon
foreign-owned[b] companies only

			54	(42)	28	(17)

Developing country

7,627	2,217	(29)	226	(3)	(D)	

Number subject to performance requirements imposed upon
foreign-owned[b] companies only

			78	(35)	(D)	

(D) Data suppressed to avoid disclosure.
Source: Calculations based on data from: *US Direct Investment Abroad, 1977*, US Department of Commerce, Bureau of Economic Analysis, International Investment Division; and a special tabulation of data, gathered through the BE-10 Benchmark Survey of US Direct Investment Abroad-1977, provided by the International Investment Division. Reproduced from US Commerce (October 1981).
a. Of reporting affiliates.
b. BEA questionnaire did not specify definition of "foreign-owned," but it is assumed to represent equity of 10 percent or more.

the parent's equity in the affiliate. The incidence of these particular requirements was far greater for the developing countries (notably Latin America) at 29 percent, than for the more developed countries at 6 percent. It will be noted from table 18.1 that 37 percent of these requirements were for foreign-owned firms only.

This is a welcome pioneering census, the only one of its kind, but for present purposes the results must be interpreted with caution. It is not simply a matter of the date, 1977, and the possibility that such requirements have grown since then. Even if the study was for 1982, a census of the entire stock of companies which have gone abroad

Minimum local content		Minimum local labor requirement		Limit on US parent's equity in affiliate	
Number	(per-centage[a])	Number	(per-centage[a])	Number	(per-centage[a])
593	(3)	1,885	(8)	1,349	(6)
145	(24)	529	(28)		
154	(1)	493	(3)	374	(2)
42	(27)	120	(24)		
(D)		1,384	(2)	968	(13)
(D)		(D)			

over many decades necessarily diminishes the incidence in recent years of requirements of the kinds we are discussing. There are two conditions in which such requirements are likely to be necessary. One is when a firm enters a country for the first time, or, having entered earlier, expands by way of merger. In some countries, entry into a new line of production, however done, would also be a matter for review. So long as the firm expands in its traditional lines, and especially if it avoids mergers, it will typically escape such review mechanisms. The other condition is when it agrees to a performance requirement in return for fiscal incentives of various kinds.

The Commerce study does not address these issues directly. We do not know, for example, how many of the firms which have gone abroad in recent years, or had mergers in recent years, were subject to such requirements. Dating of the firms' investments will perhaps permit such estimates to be derived from the Commerce study. Equally important, the Commerce question on performance requirements asks if government requires the particular performances noted "as a condition for the affiliate operating in the country" (US Commerce, April 1981, p. 475). While this would cover the point just noted, provided it was dated as suggested, it does not address the widespread practice of requiring performance as a condition of receiving incentives, as distinct from operating in the country.

These data, therefore, appear to considerably underestimate the recent incidence of these requirements. Other evidence is not nearly as carefully compiled, but worth noting to give further evidence of the possible dimensions. We can note, first, some generalized attempts to describe these requirements, concentrating again on those most directly related to trade. A US Commerce study (1978) describes a wide variety of incentives and performance requirements for foreign direct investment, of which five or six are clearly trade-related and frequent.

Studies by the Organization for Economic Cooperation and Development (OECD) (1979) of member government policies with regard to direct investment, both inward and outward, bear frequent references to criteria for approval such as foreign exchange effects, export increases, and use of local inputs and employment effects, not to mention broader terms regarding national benefit which encompass these. The OECD's published studies are rather general, but a major effort has been underway in recent years to increase the degree of specificity and transparency involved in reporting such policies. The Labor–Industry Coalition for International Trade (LICIT) (Wolff 1981) has integrated material from a variety of sources to try to get an overview of the subject. One of its major conclusions is that all but 2 of the top 20 recipients of direct investments, which include many developed countries, have performance requirements which limit imports or expand exports.

When one passes from attempts to generalize, which suffer from the uneven availability of data and the problems of interpreting these, the situation moves into sharper relief. The incidence of performance measures is particularly heavy, as one would expect, in industries where foreign-owned firms are most heavily represented, such as electrical, transportation equipment, chemicals, nonelectrical machinery, and primary industries such as mining and petroleum. The automobile industry has been one of the prime targets for such measures, both in terms of incentives to attract major projects and in terms of local content and export regulations to attempt to capture nationally as much of the various demands as possible. This has been and continues to be the case for many developing and developed countries; a common pattern in this industry is to begin with import restrictions and local content rules, then to encourage and perhaps set export requirements to achieve scale economies. Some countries have tariffs which fall as an inducement to and reward for increased exports. But methods such as these go well beyond automobiles. Brazil has been particularly active in setting export goals more generally, related in part to permission to locate there or expand a direct investment, but many other countries are actively attempting similar programs.

Turning to the evidence by country, the Foreign Investment Review Agency in Canada (FIRA) has attracted considerable attention in the past few years. The agency was established to improve the net economic benefit to Canada from inward direct investment. One of its criteria, however, and a critical one in some industries, relates to increased Canadian ownership and participation rather than conventional economic benefits. Proposals involving benefits are not mandatory but they obviously enhance the likelihood of approval. The undertakings given are both general in nature and quite specific. They are also legally binding. While no prosecutions have been made to date, that they can be made poses a very different set of sanctions compared to the situation in some other such agencies.

For present purposes the most relevant point is the undertakings made as part of the process of securing entry or approval for a merger, particularly those which could directly affect trade. FIRA, like its Australian counterpart and unlike most other such agencies, publishes each year the principal factors used, that is, benefits received in assessing each application. These are the expected effects of the proposals as indicated by the firms and assessed by FIRA. Except for a number of important cases, we do not know the specific details of undertakings. In the former more qualitative sense, about one-third of the applications indicate "additional exports" and closer to two-thirds indicate expected benefits by way of "increased resource processing or use of Canadian parts and services."

A reading of the available cases suggests many of these "undertakings" made by the firms in support of their proposals are very general statements of intentions to which they could be held with difficulty, if at all. Others are hedged by conditions, such as purchases from Canadian manufacturers "subject to availability, competitive prices, quality and suitability" which suggest a best-efforts approach, at most. Nevertheless, it is also not difficult to find unqualified and quite specific undertakings in international trade, both in the more important cases where details are made public and from other sources.

FIRA is worth noting if only because it is an unusual form of review mechanism among the more developed countries. The formality of the review process, the fact that detailed undertakings are given, the administrative complexities of a process where all cases go to cabinet for ultimate approval and where the relevant province(s) must be consulted first, and the height of the rejection rate at the point of formal application—these are unmatched in the developed countries (Safarian 1978; Schultz et al. 1980).[1]

In the Australian agency, for example, there is much clearer emphasis on one or two objectives, notably Australian participation in ownership and the clarification of taxation questions. Other economic benefits are claimed, including some that are trade-related, but there is much less emphasis than in Canada on securing detailed lists of undertakings except for the major resource projects.

Nevertheless, one must add that FIRA appears to have drawn more than its due share of criticism on some of these points. In part this is because it rests on a comparatively well-defined law, and is thus required to live with a more explicit process and to be more open about it than most of the equivalent institutions in the developed countries. In some West European countries, for example, interdepartmental committees, foreign exchange regulations, and other devices permit, usually on a less systematic and more flexible basis, conditional approval of entry or merger. The conditions are almost always related to the effect on the balance of payments, investment, and employment, including the creation or maintenance of exports, and the encouragement of import substitution. Conditions on technological transfer may also be involved, both to assure access to it and, in the case of a merger, to attempt to limit its export. A particularly interesting variant is practiced in Norway where access to valuable concessions in oil is linked in part to the success with which foreign investors can give Norwegian industry technical access and markets abroad. Finally, many of the developing countries attempt investment screening, both to determine investment eligibility and for the award of incentives. Foreign trade criteria figure prominently in the criteria used (UN 1978, pp. 36–37, 47–48).

Many countries have been turning their attention to outward direct investment. None of the major exporters of such capital, to my knowl-

---

[1] This section deals only with review mechanisms on entry and merger, not other areas of policy on foreign investment such as the number of closed sectors or the issue of national treatment. Review mechanisms are described in the sources noted above and in various reports by *Business International*, among other sources.

edge, has a well-developed system of reviewing this at the present time, comparable to some of those on the inward side. One key problem has been that of judging the timing of the investment from different viewpoints: firms will argue they must go abroad now because of market, supply, or regulatory requirements, but especially if they fear entry into that market by other investors, while governments, conscious of the need for more jobs in the short run, often prefer that firms continue exporting for a longer period.

Despite this and other problems, some attempts are being made to review outward direct investment. Sometimes these are for purposes associated closely with exchange control, or as a check on transfer pricing. Sometimes, however, the objectives are similar to those noted in this chapter. Broad criteria, such as the effects on domestic employment, trade, and the balance of payments will be considered, and companies may be asked to consider options more favorable from the government's viewpoint, with suitable fiscal and other persuasion applied. The emphasis on export promotion as a condition of approval is particularly notable in countries' official statements (OECD 1979, part II). In some countries the authorities are more precise: the company may have to agree not to import certain products from its affiliate or joint venture partner abroad, for example. This area deserves more study since it is likely to grow in importance as governments become more informed on the choices available to them and as the number of important home countries increases.

National Treatment and Closed Sectors

A question quickly arises: how far to pursue the trade-related issues when one is considering investment. Some of the sources noted earlier raise a much larger set of questions about the treatment of foreign direct investment, issues which affect trade directly in some cases and indirectly in others. There is a question of how far some of these issues should be put on the agenda for trade policy.

These policies can be conveniently grouped, for our purposes, under the headings of national treatment and closed sectors.

In the first, exceptions to national treatment involve situations in which government discriminates among established firms by nationality of ownership.[2] The problem is evident right from the point where

---

[2] In the OECD Declaration on International Investment and Multinational Enterprises, national treatment is "treatment under their laws, regulations

the extent of any establishment rights of the firm are defined. Governments have generally agreed, for example, in the OECD instruments, that review of a new entrant to a country by way of new investment or merger will not constitute an exception to national treatment. Many are careful to retain also their right to review *subsequent* expansion of the foreign-owned firm by merger (and not just for reasons of competition policy) and, in some cases, any expansion into new product lines as well. For the established firm which is foreign-owned a long list of exceptions to national treatment is involved (OECD 1978; Business 1982). They range over a wide area taxes, government aids and subsidies, access to local finance, government purchases and contracts, some aspects of investment by established companies, and regulatory practices.

This leads on to the issue of sectors which are partly or wholly closed to foreign-owned firms. Many sectors are closed by law, especially those deemed closely related to government policy (defense, some financial sectors, basic transportation) or culture (media). In many countries, natural resources, including agriculture, fall in whole or part into closed sectors. Few of the developed countries include as such "key" sectors the manufacturing industries where multinationals tend to concentrate, perhaps in part because efficient substitutes are somewhat harder to develop there than elsewhere (OECD 1978; UN 1978, 1980). Another long list of industries, partly overlapping, is closed to private investment generally, including foreign direct investment, because of public monopolies or extensive public ownership (*Economist* 1978). These points are additional to the situations, notably in many developing countries, where direct investors can proceed only after agreeing to take a minority equity position in the subsidiary.

These areas deserve a close look partly because exceptions from liberalization have been made in them, judging by the limited examination allowed by problems of transparency and partly because the temptations are significant for governments to use these areas as channels for trade restriction. The European Economic Community (EEC) permits exceptions based on public order and essential security interests, provided these are not used to develop arbitrary discrimination or as disguised trade restrictions. The qualifications do not appear in OECD instruments. Moreover, in the Multilateral Trade Negotiations (MTN), the agreement on government purchasing ap-

---

and administrative practices, consistent with international law and no less favorable than that accorded in like situations to domestic enterprises."

plies only to the listed government entities, in effect generally excluding entities in power generation, transportation, and telecommunications. Subnational governments are excluded from this agreement. In the OECD code, government-sanctioned monopolies, both public and private, are exempted.

The incentives to favor discriminatory trade and foreign investment policies in these areas hardly need elaboration. Governments are not likely to develop public firms as instruments of domestic policies and then permit imports to erode their most secure market (Vernon 1979, p. 11). The establishment of a sector that is closed to foreign-owned firms is not a matter of interest only to the country concerned. If foreign-owned firms already exist in the sector and are allowed to remain, the question of national treatment arises. Trade policy is also likely to be involved where government purchases are directed to that sector, and at times, only to the resident-owned firms in it. Some governments, such as France and Finland, reserve the right to such selective procurement by nationality of firm on a broad front, and a number of others more selectively (OECD 1978, pp. 14, 61–62): (My interviews suggest this significantly understates the number of countries involved.) If the firms in such closed sectors establish subsidiaries abroad, other countries may raise questions such as reciprocity and possible export subsidization.

These complex and sensitive areas involve important issues other than trade policy. In part they should be left to institutions which deal with the treatment of foreign direct investment and multinational companies, as distinct from trade discrimination. They cannot be left entirely to such institutions which, as presently organized, can only take limited action against them. The fact is that these areas offer large and tempting exceptions to the GATT both in their treatment of international investment and the distinction between private and public firms. So long as the emphasis is on trade distortion, and particularly those aspects which are fairly direct, they should be included in attempts to strengthen those agreements.

Incentives

Subsidies to investment have become both varied and extremely complex in recent years as a response to many forces, such as the renewed desires to modify regional imbalances, long-run industrial adjustment, employment maintenance, an attempt to capture new growth sectors, small business development, and environmental controls. Many such incentives are given automatically to all firms meeting clearly stated criteria; others are tailored to specific situations.

Two points make these incentives of interest for present purposes. First, they can be used by states specifically to attract international investment. Second, conditions attached to the subsidies can have trade effects similar to the performance requirements noted earlier. This is particularly likely to be the case for subsidies tailored to a specific and important project, where the problem of transparency often becomes acute. The overlap between incentives of various kinds and performance requirements is well illustrated by the following quotation:

> These performance requirements generally occur in combination with other government policies that limit imports of similar products into the host country. Such import limiting policies might include high—often prohibitive—tariffs, various types of tax and other non-tariff barriers that discriminate against imports, limitations on foreign exchange available for imports, or other forms of restrictions such as quotas. In order to stimulate domestic production of the import-limited product, tariff concessions which often reduce or waive the high rates imposed on selected imports are given to firms that make the desired investments in local production. Other industrial policies may provide for tax rebates applicable variously to local sales, or to export sales of items produced in the host country, or to the investment required to accomplish local production. Additional forms of industrial policy may include modifications or waiver of limitations on foreign ownership, more liberal terms for remittance of dividends, concessionary credit facilities, duty free importations of machinery and equipment, etc. Moreover, many of these national policies can be informal or shaped to fit the circumstances of individual investment programs approved by the host government.[3]

This statement, it may be added, is for a manufacturing industry. It is not difficult to find equally elaborate requirement-incentive systems in natural resources industries. Table 18.2 reproduced from the survey by US Commerce for 1977, shows that 26 percent of the total stock of US firms abroad had received at least one such incentive. There was little variation in this overall average between the more developed and less developed countries as a whole, but substantial variation by country and industry. More detailed evidence on incen-

---

[3] Statement of the Motor Vehicle Manufacturers Association of the United States, Inc., to the US Congress, Senate, Subcommittee on International Economic Policy of the Committee on Foreign Relations, *US Policy Toward International Investment*, Hearing, 97th Cong., 1st sess. (Washington: US Government Printing Office, 1982), p. 588.

tives related to foreign direct investment is available from various sources, such as the 1978 study by US Commerce. The OECD also has under way a major study on the subject. A study by the United Nations notes a number of developing countries in which incentive schemes are based on a specific contribution to exports (UN 1978, pp. 47–48). LICIT has brought together a number of specific examples from a variety of sources (Wolff in US Senate 1982).

Such measures, when applied to international investment, can have trade effects which are analogous to those for performance requirements. Insofar as they shift investment between countries, notably in those relatively mobile industries where technological change makes more global sourcing possible, the effect is to shift employment and other benefits from countries less willing or able to subsidize such investment. When the incentive involved is a major element in the decision to invest, there is also a significant risk that the infant may not become a healthy adult, but may require further support with continuing trade consequences. When firms learn to "subsidy shop" the problem is compounded. Other countries are likely to be tempted to match the offers, with the result that any reallocation of investment is less likely, but public subsidies for investment are higher all around. Indeed, they may end up transferring revenues to both firms and the home country treasuries (Bergsten and Hormats' presentations in US Senate, especially pp. 14–15, and 232–33).

Subsidies to investment serve many purposes, as already noted, many of which certainly cannot be labeled as uneconomic or even trade distorting. The focus of concern here is those subsidies that are directed to international investment, do distort trade, and thus impose costs on other countries. Here we run into a number of problems which will have to be clarified, specifically, how far investment subsidies are directed to international investment and how far the firms do respond to them by shifting investment from locations they would otherwise utilize. If the answer in both cases was clearly negative or at least not significantly positive, the effects of such policies on investment allocation would be of less concern, although the effects on tax misallocation would remain. (It is recognized that subsidies to domestic investment can distort international trade.)

At the present time, the answer would appear to be anything but clear. The study summarized in table 18.2 notes that 26 percent of US affiliates abroad in 1977 had received at least one incentive via tax and tariff concessions, subsidies, and other forms of incentives. In each of the four types noted, about one-fifth of the firms replied positively to the question whether "to the best of your knowledge, the incentive or the requirement applies only to foreign owned com-

TABLE 18.2   INCIDENCE OF INCENTIVES, BY TYPE AND AREA

Number of affiliates reporting	At least one incentive		Tax concessions	
	Number	(percentage[a])	Number	(percentage[a])
23,641	6,041	(26)	4,686	(20)
Number receiving incentives available to foreign-owned[b] companies only				
			1,001	(21)
Developed country				
15,603[c]	3,922	25	2,986	19
Number receiving incentives available to foreign-owned[b] companies only				
			585	20
Developing country				
7,627	2,081	27	1,664	22
Number receiving incentives available to foreign-owned[b] companies only				
			403	24

Source: Calculations based on data from: *US Direct Investment Abroad, 1977,* US Department of Commerce, Bureau of Economic Analysis, International Investment Division; and a special tabulation of data gathered through the BE-10 Benchmark Survey of US Direct Investment Abroad, 1977, provided by the International Investment Division. Reproduced from US Commerce (October 1981).
a. Of reporting affiliates.
b. BEA questionnaire did not specify definition of "foreign-owned," but it is assumed to represent equity of 10 percent or more.
c. 66 percent of all affiliates in developed countries.

panies" (US Commerce April 1981, p. 475). It is difficult to find corroboration of such a high proportion of incentives directed only to international investment. The OECD studies suggest some sectoral differentiation in a few countries, but most countries give such incentives without distinction by ownership (OECD 1978, pp. 10–13).[4]

In the general case, the Commerce finding may mean that the incentives were tailored to the needs of the firm under discretionary procedures, as distinct from those available more or less automatically, but not that they would be unavailable to firms owned nationally if they were prepared to undertake similar types of investments. Some countries, such as Ireland and Belgium, have had the needs of in-

[4] That is also the conclusion emerging from interviews I have underway with government and company officials in some developed countries.

Tariff concessions		Subsidies		Other incentives	
Number	(percentage[a])	Number	(percentage[a])	Number	(percentage[a])
1,926	(8)	2,053	(9)	1,195	(5)
382	(20)	389	(19)	191	(16)
840	(5)	1,691	(11)	807	(5)
130	(16)	337	(20)	125	(16)
1,086	(14)	359	(5)	382	(5)
252	(23)	52	(15)	63	(17)

ternational companies very much in mind when establishing their incentive schemes, but that does not mean they are not available in the main to nationally owned firms also. More precise studies may well show that incentive schemes in recent years in some particularly mobile industries are indeed largely geared to the international side, especially if one takes into account, as one should, government attempts to persuade their own multinationals to invest at home and not just the effect of incentives on foreign companies.

The other question is also hard to answer. Investment abroad is obviously a response to many forces—market and growth, actual and potential competition, supply and cost questions, government policies and attitudes to business generally, including political risks and, minimizing exchange rate risks. How important are incentives in this set of determinants? Much of the evidence suggests they are not of great importance, although that finding is qualified in significant ways.

One study found firms were unwilling to undertake investments heavily dependent on incentives for acceptable rates of return (Reuber et al., 1973). Another study tested the influence of a number of policy instruments in manufacturing investment in three sets of developing countries that were classified by their general attractiveness to investment. It found that tax incentives failed to attract foreign investment in manufacturing; the most that could be said is that they are sometimes necessary for competitive tax reasons but certainly not sufficient to attract investment (Root and Ahmed 1978).

The Business and Industry Advisory Committee (BIAC) to the OECD concludes from a qualitative analysis that, with regard to the basic decision to invest internationally, incentive programs have very little influence. Incentives may play a role, depending on the type of program involved, in the choice of a location, or the timing of the investment. Even such a role may depend on the alternative locations' being roughly comparable, however. Some OECD countries are reported to offer incentives which are as much as 25 percent to 50 percent of the value of new plant, although it is not known what this would amount to in relation to projected net returns (Business 1982). Other studies could be cited to the same effect, generally undertaken some years ago before the economic climate made both firms and governments more sensitive to these issues.

It would be tempting to leave the question of international action on incentives to one side, at least until some recent and fairly precise estimates on decision making by sectors are available. There is also a fiscal restraint on such incentives by way of tax revenue forgone. There are two difficulties at least with such an approach. One is that it does not address the issue of tax loss or reallocation to the extent that competitive subsidization schemes exist in some sectors. The other is that such incentives, as noted, are often tied up with quite specific performance requirements that are trade related. To leave investment incentives aside entirely could leave a potentially large loophole for trade distortion in some sectors, one that would hurt fiscally weak states most.

A better approach might be to concentrate on investment incentives that are related to specific measures of trade performance by firms, thus tying in with the latter, and which can be demonstrated to damage trading partners. This is the approach taken for trade flows in the MTN code on subsidies and countervailing duties, which recognizes a variety of subsidies other than export subsidies, does not attempt to restrict them despite some external effects, but concentrates instead on direct export subsidies. No doubt in either case the limits involved will have to be clarified, but that is inevitable in complex economic issues.

Monitoring Processes

The effectiveness of performance requirements and incentives, and their effects on trade, depend in good part on the extent to which the undertakings given by firms are met and enforced. Some are relatively easily monitored and fairly strictly enforced: financial effects on the balance of payments fall into this category, if there is an exchange control or authorization system, and so may such matters as ownership of the firm and nationality of officers. If financial incentives are involved, and especially if geared to performance effects, the likelihood of enforcement is high. But even here, although public fiscal accountability is involved, one must be careful not to infer too much. Governments often give grants over relatively short periods of a few years (in some cases fully in the first year) which can involve problems in assuring undertakings given by firms are met and enforced.

Some of the undertakings of most interest to us are not so easily enforced. For example, FIRA has a relatively ambitious objective in terms of the variety of criteria of benefit it uses for assessment and the details of the undertakings involved. The undertakings, once set out and accepted in a letter from the minister, are legally binding. As noted earlier, many of the "undertakings" are no more than the general statements in company proposals indicating what they hope to achieve if conditions warrant. It is true that FIRA uses these to assess benefits, but it could hardly hold companies to them if circumstances change. Thus an intention to export is a conditional statement which any number of unforeseen (and arguable) developments can change. FIRA does monitor commitments, of course, especially those which can be measured in the companies' accounts-investment and jobs, for example, and certainly attempts also to seek explanations if more specific commitments of other kinds are not met. That is a long way, however, from meeting or enforcing the detailed list of benefits in the proposals. Only once, to my knowledge, has FIRA sought a court injunction, while in some other cases it has required, without resort to court procedures, a reordering and stricter adherence to specific commitments.

I do not wish here to understate the effects of such agencies. By actual denial of entry or merger, or the possibility of such denial, they can play a large role in shaping investment plans. Moreover, in some of the more important cases the requirements are specific and closely watched. Brazil has adopted such a policy on exports so far as intended direct investors in many industries, both natural resource and manufactures, are concerned. Some of the European countries with review agencies have concentrated on relatively few requirements and measurable shorter-term effects, such as on investment or employment. Nevertheless, the trade-related performance requirements and some of those on technology transfer are among the more difficult to monitor. Many governments in the developed countries rely not on detailed monitoring systems in such cases but rather on limited follow-through and the knowledge that the firms involved will take into account that they will be dealing with government often again. What this amounts to in practice is difficult to say.

To summarize, one of the important areas for research in this entire subject is the extent to which firms by relevant industry groups do respond to incentives in fact, and how far both associated and un-related performance requirements are monitored. Fortunately, a re-search study under way for the World Bank promises some testable results on these points.[5] Meanwhile there is enough evidence on problems in this area, and a potential for far more difficulty if more countries decide that greater efforts at emulation and retaliation are the best ways to handle these problems, to suggest that policy issues must be addressed soon.

Why the Policies Exist

It is useful to begin by asking briefly why the policies noted above exist and also by looking at how various institutions are tackling related issues. Countries have adapted these policies on trade and investment, and the sometimes closely related policies on foreign ownership of industry, for a wide set of reasons. The policies may reflect a view that MNEs create special performance problems from a national viewpoint which require special measures, in the present context, for example, problems arising from export limitations or excessive import reliance by subsidiaries. They may reflect an attempt to capture nationally more of the net gains possible from such en-terprises, by measures that may get around the GATT provisions on trade restrictions. Investment incentives, often with trade effects, are particularly likely in a period of high unemployment and of renewed demands for regional development. Long-run adjustment problems, in part in response to the spread of technology through MNEs, have led to enormous challenges both in adjusting to declining sectors and attempting to capture some of the growing ones. And such policies reflect often a preference for nationally controlled corporations, be-cause of close links to the state in some cases as well as a more general desire in some countries for a larger public sector.

---

[5] A study is being prepared on foreign direct investment incentives and controls for the International Finance Corporation, by a team directed by Professor Stephen Guisinger of the University of Texas (Dallas).

We shall not try here to separate and evaluate the strands of non-economic motives and of various types of market failure which are often assumed in discussion of these topics. What is important to add is the reasons why the particular policy approaches noted above have been adopted, with their frequent emphasis on discretionary and opaque approaches. For regulation often fails to achieve its welfare objectives, and often for the same reasons, such as transaction costs and free riders, that limit welfare results in private markets. The literature on public decision making in general and regulation in particular suggests that many of the outcomes, far from approaching general welfare norms, tend rather to maximize rents and other returns for particular private and public groups, and particularly to reflect short-run vote maximization.

Contrary to the views in some groups, including US government circles, foreign ownership and the industrial performance of MNEs are still very much of concern in a number of developed countries, despite temporary modification of emphasis on such issues in the desire to attract investment. Not far below the surface, moreover, are very different viewpoints on the virtues of free markets as distinct from more direct intervention or more public ownership.

The central point for our purposes is that governments which adopt very different approaches to issues such as these have to reconcile the foreign trade and investment aspects so as not to damage their trading and investing partners and the international system which they claim to support and from which they benefit. If such reconciliation is not attempted, emulation and retaliation mean that positive national and international outcomes are less likely, and inefficient resource use and a higher public subsidy for investment are more likely.

At the same time, there is no need to attempt to reconcile quite different *internal* policy objectives and approaches, much as one may have reservations about some of them, provided that they respect their international obligations and do not use measures which export their problems. A similar point can be made with regard to national policies on foreign direct investment and multinational companies. Such policies clearly overlap with trade policy, as noted above, and to that extent should be constrained in the same way and for similar reasons. But they go far beyond trade policy to other issues on which it is going to be much more complicated to get agreed and enforceable policies. They should be pursued simultaneously given not only the overlap with trade issues but the weakness of many multinational policies on multinational investment, but progress is likely to be slower than for the trade-related aspects.

It is instructive to review briefly the experience of two organizations that have worked on elements of the problems noted here. The Treaty of Rome provides in Article 92 that aid given through state resources is incompatible with the Common Market to the extent that trade between member states is affected. A number of exceptions are allowed, such as for regional development, to promote a project of common European interest, or to remedy a serious disturbance in a state. The Commission has attempted to set rules which limit the amount of investment incentives allowed in these and other circumstances and has authority, subject to appeal, to reject arrangements proposed by particular countries which are inconsistent with the Common Market. It has undertaken intensive country-by-country reviews to determine which types of subsidies are consistent with its rules. At the moment, a broad set of French measures to aid investment and industry are under review.

Even in a community that is comparatively integrated, and where income transfers have been to states with fewer development options, such an approach has experienced serious difficulties. Transparency has been a serious problem. It is often impossible to know at the time just how large a subsidy is involved in a complex package of tax, expenditure, and regulatory items, and it may well be too late to do much about it once the investment is in place. The attempt to get equality of treatment in this regard for private and public undertakings has been particularly difficult. A Commission Directive on this has been challenged by the United Kingdom, France, and Italy before the Court of Justice of the European Communities (Commission 1980). While it is true that Community control of national subsidy plans has been limited, it has been suggested that the policies involved are more rational and consistent in economic terms because of the need to justify them (Warnecke 1978).

One of the important aspects is that in the EEC private companies can go to the European Court—or, more likely, threaten to do so—in order to challenge national policies, as well as having the opportunity to press their case before Community organizations during the consideration of policies. A bargaining situation is likely to be more common than court tests in many of the complex issues of interest here. Despite the opposition of its Community partners and a court decision against it in 1969, France insisted it had the right to review takeovers of French firms from Community countries. Since 1980, France has agreed that, at least in principle and subject to some standard exceptions, takeover of French firms from Community sources will be more or less automatically approved after they are reported to the French authorities. France has insisted that such attempts by

Community firms whose parents are outside the Community will still be subject to review.

Turning to the OECD, the key instruments for our purposes are the Code of Liberalization of Capital Movements, covering transactions between residents and nonresidents and including a commitment to liberalize policy on direct investment, and the Declaration and Decisions on International Investment and Multinational Enterprises. All but three members have acceded to the former instrument. The Declaration and Decisions cover performance guidelines for multinational enterprises, provide for notification of exceptions to national treatment, and call for review and consultations on incentives and disincentives to direct investment.

These instruments are important in that they provide for ongoing notification of policies and procedures, various types of review and consultation, and pressure by partners either to liberalize policies or to justify restrictive approaches. Business and labor groups are involved in the organizations. In recent years the OECD has been quite active in a number of matters of considerable interest to the present topic, such as improved reporting and discussion on incentives, national treatment, and review mechanisms for direct investments.

The OECD approach presents several problems. Developing countries, where the policies discussed earlier are most prevalent, are not generally involved. Sanctions are weak. Important areas of activity appear to be excluded from the instruments, at least in part, including some aspects of the right to establishment in a country, a number of regulated or public sectors (including, but going beyond, issues of public order and security), and investments that would be deemed by the member to be exceptionally detrimental to its local industry or national economy.

Recognizing the possibility of significant divergence from the objectives of the Code and Declaration through these routes, the OECD has been defining these areas more precisely and assuring better reporting and more consultation on them. However, transparency also remains an important problem here. One sometimes has the impression in all such sources that there is a negative correlation between the actual degree of restrictiveness and the degree to which the governments involved are prepared to report it.

Policy Approaches

For international policy to be effective in this area, at least the following points should be considered. Transparency is the key to much of the rest. Consideration might be given to notification by governments of each other's policies, a method used in the approach to nontariff barriers in the most recent General Agreement on Tariffs and Trade (GATT) negotiations. State corporations should be included, both because they are becoming more prominent as multinationals and because there could be a substantial deviation from the provisions of any treaty or code otherwise. While important constitutional and political questions are raised by this, it is difficult to see how subnational governments can be excluded without substantial damage to any such agreement.[6] Those developing countries which are included should be asked to consider explicit transition rules, so that at some predesignated stage they would begin to bring their policies into line with those of developed countries if they wished to continue to benefit from the organization involved. Finally, and most important, governments are likely to agree to policies in these areas, which limit their fiscal and regulatory options, only if they are direct in terms of trade distortion and demonstrably damaging in terms of the interest of others. There is scope for consideration of wider issues in terms of policy on MNEs more generally. If early action on trade and investment distortion is desired, as I believe it is, then a more limited approach is more likely to get results.

Let us turn, finally, to policy approaches, which are not necessarily mutually exclusive except in the case of the first approach. That approach would be to do nothing beyond what is already being done: emphasis on the OECD instruments and, with less certainty, certain aspects of any agreed UN codes at a later stage. The logic of so doing is that there are budgetary limits to incentives and that countries that develop excessive performance requirements may limit their access to direct investment. The policies will, in this view, tend to be self-limiting, but they may take a good deal of time and occur very unevenly by country. Moreover, at least some of the reasons for such

---

[6] Many of the policies discussed earlier which may distort trade or investment have their counterparts within federal systems, reflecting a similar, though usually less severe, conflict between the requirements of an economic union and the use of independent fiscal and regulatory powers by subnational governments. These can have an impact on foreign, as well as domestic, trade and investment. See Safarian (1980) for examples from Canada. Limitations on foreign direct investment (sometimes on all out-of-state firms, whether US or foreign) by· US states are detailed in Waldmann (1980). The OECD instruments require that a central government in a federation use its best efforts with its subnational governments, while GATT includes the latter in its subsidy code but not in the code on government purchases.

policies, which were noted earlier, point to spread rather than decline in their numbers. In such circumstances, some governments may not be prepared to accept the costs they see imposed on their economies or particular groups in them.

A number of unilateral options are available to such governments. One is to find ways, consistent with international commitments, to encourage private or public actions that would impose costs on host governments or derive compensation for injured parties in home countries. Possible approaches in this regard are discussed in a paper by Gary Clyde Hufbauer (US Senate 1982, pp. 143–59). Bergsten, while preferring other methods, has noted the possibilities under certain circumstances of a US response by way of emulation and retaliation (US Senate 1982, pp. 1–18).

Various bills for "reciprocity" now before the US Congress would also achieve, if passed, similar types of effects. Such unilateral approaches could conceivably expedite serious negotiations on the issues in this paper, but they could also lead to similar responses with results that might be highly damaging to international economic relations.[7] It would be unrealistic not to take account of such possibilities if other approaches are not followed. It is ironic to observe that one of the arguments used to press the establishment of FIRA in Canada in the early 1970s was the attempt by the United States and other countries to correct their balance of payments situations by direct intervention in the activities of multinational companies.

Bilateral approaches have also been proposed, specifically, investment protection treaties of the kind developed successfully by several European countries. Bilateral treaties are most likely to succeed on technical matters where the issues are quite specific, as with taxation, and where the interests of the two states are similar on the matters involved. They are worth pursuing for a number of items not covered in this paper. In two countries with as much economic spillover as Canada and the United States, and with different approaches to industrial policies, there may be a useful role also for some types of bilateral institutions which undertake a variety of technical functions. No doubt bilateral discussions in general will continue to play an important role in resolving, defusing, or clarifying a number of

---

[7] Legal action under actual or proposed legislation is not necessarily the same thing as emulation and retaliation. My concern with a substantial emphasis on the former arises from some doubts about how far judicial processes can help resolve complex economic conflicts of the kinds involved here. (Fawcett 1977.)

issues. But a largely bilateral approach to issues of the kind noted here suffers from a serious problem when considering relations between countries such as Canada and the United States—the fact that international issues are more important to the former than the latter, and that the overall leverage each can bring to bear through linkage with other issues is far greater for the United States than for Canada. In circumstances where the two countries have quite different views on, for example, the role of public ownership and government intervention, the inevitable appearance will be that of the more powerful partner attempting to impose its views on the less. One can argue that the record of wins and losses does not support such a view (Leyton-Brown 1974). That is certainly not the public perception in Canada, and, in any case, I am not sure how good a guide historical experience would be for an issue on which both governments have strong views.

In multinational institutions, such issues are at least dispersed to a degree. And, whatever bilateral approaches may develop, eventually the multilateral aspects of the issues discussed here will have to be tackled if the principle of most-favored-nation treatment is not to be severely damaged. In two institutions—GATT and the OECD—there is already sufficient community of interest in other respects to permit an approach to such questions. Let us consider what might be done first in terms of the existing accords in these institutions and then in terms of any extension of them.

In terms of existing accords, GATT offers the best means to tackle performance requirements and investment incentives that are directly related to trade. It has been suggested that some types of performance requirements that are related to trade can be challenged under various articles, specifically those on national treatment (Article III), subsidies (Article XVI), and state-trading enterprises (Article XVII) (US Senate 1972, submission by LICIT, p. 38). Just how far such challenges are likely to succeed remains to be tested. Criteria for determining trade distortion and investment relocation are not going to be easy to define in this context. Some experts believe even some of the quota-like requirements, such as minimum local content or value-added requirements, may not be effectively challenged in GATT if they are done through an investment regulation rather than an import quota (Bergsten, US Senate, 1982, p. 5). One problem is that a number of important countries, such as Mexico, are not members of GATT. The United States and Canada are currently in a dispute before GATT on the operations of FIRA, so that some clarification may appear on this issue. Sanctions are available in GATT and also in related national legislation, as noted above when discussing unilateral measures.

The OECD instruments have the advantage of a wider range of issues. This could be important if a broader approach is taken, that is, if stronger policies toward both trade-related investment issues and the treatment of the MNEs are pursued simultaneously. The relation between them would argue for such an approach. The advantages and limitations of the OECD approach were noted earlier. Unless more effective methods are found to bring pressure to bear on seriously offending members, however, it is unlikely that the OECD alone can lead to significant constraints in the near future on the use of the more important national policies noted in this chapter.

If such approaches fail to deal effectively with the problem noted, as they well might, an extension would involve a section in GATT which explicitly applies to a defined set of trade-related investment policies. A first step might be to ask governments to register detailed information, secured partly from private sources, regarding one another's procedures and based on an agreed set of these. This would be followed by agreement on what should be eliminated and by when, accompanied by a prohibition on any new such measures.

Despite the problems involved, such an approach seems the most straightforward, assuming the GATT rules are considered not applicable or too narrowly so. It concentrates on trade aspects without getting tied up in the short run with the more complex issues surrounding MNEs. It would include in the discussions a number of developing countries in the GATT, with consideration of the circumstances under which the more developed among them would be expected to accede to this aspect of the agreement. It complements the work already done on nontariff barriers, which some of the measures considered here strongly resemble. It addresses the issue which international constraints on trade restrictions do not address: once the investment has been made, attempts to challenge the resulting trade flows because of performance and incentive policies are much harder for governments and others to accept.

Yet, many governments will limit dearly, if at all, their powers to influence investment, especially in an economic climate as dismal as the present. The strongest case for action is specific trade-related performance requirements, with secondarily but often associated, those investment incentives that depend on specific trade performance. These are so close to what is now explicit on trade flows in the GATT that it is difficult to see how the latter can survive without such additional interpretation or extension. All else can be considered in other settings or subsequently.

This chapter does not address a number of issues about MNEs which many would see as complementary (Bergsten, et al., ch. 13). A number of countries, both developed and developing, have reservations about aspects of MNE operations and their treatment in such areas as industrial relations, competitive practices, expropriation and dispute settlement, taxation, and technology transfer, areas of activity which have been prominent in such forums as the EEC, OECD, and UN. Moreover, the chapter has underemphasized the discussion of trade-related measures in the developing countries where they are more frequent. Whether and how far such measures are more justifiable in some other countries, in terms of the fewer policy options available and the stage of development, is something that cannot be prejudged here.

What can be urged is that the more developed countries are not in much of a position to make recommendations to the rest of the world until they have given a far better example of their own discipline in these respects. Most of all, the policies noted in this paper are in part a response to massive failure at the macroeconomic level with all of its attendant tragedy. I do not propose that we wait for full employment and sustained growth before tackling these problems, since they are longer term in part and since failure to tackle them could complicate the resolution of the macro problems. But a more concerted attack on the latter may well be necessary as an important aspect of countries' willingness to collaborate in avoiding exporting their problems by micro and trade related measures.

References

Bergsten, C. Fred. "Coming Investment Wars?" *Foreign Affairs*, vol. 53 (October 1974), pp. 135–52.

Bergsten, C. Fred, Thomas Horst, and Theodore H. Moran. *American Multinationals and American Interests*. Washington: Brookings Institution, 1978, p. 20.

Business and Industry Advisory Committee (BIAC) to OECD. "Relationship of Incentives and Disincentives to International Investment Decisions." 1981. Processed.

———. "Statement on National Treatment." 1982. Processed and preliminary.

Commission Directive, 25 June 1980. On the transparency of financial relations between member states and public undertakings. *Official Journal of European Communities*, no. L 195, pp. 35–37 and C 273, pp. 5–8.

Economist. "The State in the Market." 30 December 1978.

Fawcett, James. *International Economic Conflicts: Prevention and Resolution*. London: Europa Publications, 1977.

Goldberg, P. M., and C. P. Kindleberger. "Toward a GATT for Investment: A Proposal for Supervision of the International Corporation." *Law and Policy in International Business*, vol. 2–2 (Summer 1970), pp. 295–325.

Leyton-Brown, David. "The Multinational Enterprise and Conflict in Canadian-American Relations." *International Organization* (Autumn 1974), pp. 733–54.

Organization for Economic Cooperation and Development (OECD). *National Treatment for Foreign-Controlled Enterprises Established in OECD Member Countries.* 1978.

————. *International Direct Investment: Policies, Procedures and Practices in OECD Member Countries.* 1979.

Reuber, G., et al. *Private Foreign Investment in Development.* Oxford: Clarendon Press, 1973.

Root, F. R., and A. A. Ahmed. "The Influence of Policy Instruments on Manufacturing Direct Foreign Investment in Developing Countries." *Journal of International Business Studies* (Winter 1978), pp. 81–93.

Safarian, A. E. "Ten Markets or One? Regional Barriers to Economic Activity in Canada." Toronto: Ontario Economic Council, 1980.

————. "Policy on Multinational Enterprises in Developed Countries." *Canadian Journal of Economics* (November 1978), pp. 641–55.

Safarian, A. E., and Joel Bell. "Issues Raised by National Control of the Multinational Corporation." *Columbia Journal of World Business* (Winter 1973), pp. 7–18.

Schultz, R., et al. "The Cabinet as a Regulatory Body: The Case of the Foreign Investment Review Act." Working Paper, no. 6. Ottawa: Economic Council of Canada, 1980.

United Nations. *National Legislation and Regulations Relating to Transnational Corporations*, and *Supplement*. New York: 1978, 1980.

US Congress, Senate, Subcommittee on International Economic Policy of the Committee on Foreign Relations. *US Policy Toward International Investment.* Hearings held on July 30, September 28, and October 28, 1981. 97th Cong., 1st sess. Washington: US Government Printing Office, 1982. Items cited in the text of this chapter include statements or evidence by C. Fred Bergsten, pp. 1–26; Alan W. Wolff on behalf of the Labor-Industry Coalition for International Trade (LICIT), pp. 27–83; Gary C. Hufbauer, pp. 143–59; Robert D. Hormats, pp. 224–39; a study by Price Waterhouse and Company on Investment Policies in Seventy-Three Countries, pp. 258–587; and a statement by the Motor Vehicle Manufacturers Association of the United States, pp. 588–600.

US Department of Commerce, Bureau of Economic Analysis. *US Direct Investment Abroad, 1977* (April 1981).

————. International Trade Administration. *Summary of Foreign Investment Policies* (October 1978).

————. Office of International Investment. *The Use of Investment Incentives and Performance Requirements by Foreign Governments* (October 1981).

Vernon, R. "International Aspects of State-Owned Enterprises." *Journal of International Business* (Winter 1979).

Waldmann, Raymond J. *Direct Investment and Development in the US.* Washington: Transnational Investment Ltd., 1980.

Warnecke, S. J., ed. *International Trade and Industrial Policies.* London: Macmillan, 1978.

CHAPTER 19

The Information Technology Industries: A Case Study of High Technology Trade

John Diebold

The information technology sector is a cluster of industries whose products and services provide for the original entry of information and its subsequent processing or treatment, indexing, description and classification, storage and retrieval as well as its transport and communication. Its services component includes communications, data processing bureaus, information or data base providers, financial services, electronic publishing, and programming services. Its manufacturing component includes computer equipment, communications equipment, office equipment, and semiconductor devices. The manufacturing sector is technology-driven in that the cost of equivalent functional performance has been declining at a rate of 20 percent or more per year.

Information technology is a large and rapidly growing high technology industry with direct impact on office as well as factory productivity. Moreover, information technology is unique in its pervasiveness for it is incorporated in, and is changing the competitive basis of, a wide range of industries from auto to consumer appliances to heavy machinery. It is having a dramatic impact on services such as banking and publishing.

In addition to being a prime industrial policy example of a "sunrise" industry (with so much industrial policy literature addressing the problems of "sunset" industries), information technology industry has dynamics that pose a variety of international economic problems:

• the disparity between the rate of change of the technology and the nature of its impact on other industries on the one hand and the rate

639

of change of pertinent public policies, both nationally and internationally, on the other
• the difficulty each nation faces in determining what is in its national interest vis-à-vis information technology, and how to achieve these interests domestically, let alone what it should and can do about the international aspects of these problems
• the complexity of the sector's development, and the economic importance of its many interrelationships with virtually all other aspects of society, which make the development of effective policy-coordinating mechanisms exceptionally difficult on national, let alone international levels
• the major negative effects that the policies a less developed country (LDC) pursues toward it (in particular those to insure a domestically viable information equipment industry) can have on virtually all other national industries because of the sector's impact on international competitiveness.

National industrial policies toward this increasingly key industry vary widely. In the United States the basically *laissez faire* approach has been overlaid with a complex vestige of old regulations and attitudes that begin to put at risk the country's leading position in this evolving industry. This situation results from the disparity between the rapid pace of scientific/technological development and the slow pace of the US public policy process and the fact that what started as a brand new computer industry is converging with a highly regulated communications industry. This situation contrasts with the recognition of the seminal importance of information technology among several other major countries. Most of these countries have shown little ability to translate this vision and considerable technological brilliance into a strong economic position (France is an example in the European Community, EC) while one country is well on its way toward capitalizing on those developments (Japan).

The international economic issues raised by the information industries are of considerable interest for they are in many ways an ideal example of the policy problems of *sunrise* versus the *sunset* industries. For example:

• A harsh but not inaccurate caricature of the current US view has it that Nippon Telephone and Telegraph Company offers to buy telephone poles from the United States in return for a license from AT&T which in turn assists Japanese suppliers to sell advanced electronic equipment in the United States.
• Japanese regulations prevented the importation of US-manufactured integrated units containing more than 200 circuits per chip (circa

1974) until a date that coincided with Japanese semiconductor manufacturers' developing the capability of producing competitive products.
• To be fair, AT&T in 1981 chose Western Electric over a lower bid by Fujitsu for a major fiber-optics telephone trunking system in what had been advertised as a completely open competitive procurement.

In other words, the information technology industry provides almost daily examples of international economic problems. The question is whether these problems are new or unique and therefore whether they require particular attention or policy mechanisms.

The choice of the information industry as the focus of this paper is consistent with the recent statement by the Japanese Ministry of International Trade and Industry (MITI) that we are examining what is probably the key determinant of international economic competitiveness during the remaining years of this century. National success in dealing with this new industry requires a national perception of this new industry, coherent national industrial policies, and successful resolution of the relevant international economic issues.

The Role of the Information Technology Industries

For purposes of describing the information industries we would include: the semiconductor industry, including the manufacturing of components, subsystems, and test equipment; the computer and peripheral equipment and systems industry; the telecommunications equipment and systems industry; the office equipment and systems industry; information processing services; telecommunications services; electronic publishing services; and programming services for computers and electronic systems.

In their primary role as direct contributors to the economy, these information industries represent, in their own right, a major contribution to the US economy. The value of domestic US shipments or revenues of these industries amounted to approximately $171 billion in 1981. In other countries the contribution of information is generally proportionately smaller.[1]

In addition to the actual revenues, the export component of these revenues must be considered. This export component is substantial and amounted to approximately $17 billion in 1981 for the United States. If the service components are excluded, this represents 20

[1] US Department of Commerce figures.

percent of the value of US domestic equipment shipments. The $8.8 billion positive balance of trade of the information industries represented a very strong contribution to the US economy in 1981.[2]

The already pervasive diffusion of information technology into every home is indicated by the growth in installed "active element groups." An active element group is that electronic technology necessary for one bit of logic or one bit of memory. Eight bits are required to identify or store one alphanumeric character. The average home in the United States utilized 700 active element groups (AEGs) in 1970, increasing to 7,000 AEGs in 1980. The pace will increase in the 1980s, and the average US residence is forecasted to have several hundred thousand AEGs in the late 1980s.[3] This suggests that every home in the United States will be a consumer of the electronic information industry. This follows the trends of other industries where the initial applications are industrial but then become pervasive throughout society.

The sustained growth of the information industries is predicated on the continued increase in functional capability of semiconductor chips and on the declining costs per function. The increasingly efficient information technology will have more indirect impact on international competitiveness as the incorporation of increasingly powerful miniature computers into consumer and industrial products—from autos and sewing machines to video games—will determine the salability of these products on world markets.

In addition to this large direct economic contribution, important secondary and tertiary benefits arise from the development and application of the information industries that permeate the nation's economy. These secondary benefits underline the importance of the information industries, for the computer and communications necessarily must precede their inclusion in industrial equipment and processes and consumer goods. Secondary effects of the information industries are pervasive and very important. Unfortunately we are not aware of any studies which quantify these secondary effects of the information industries on national economies and they are treated anecdotally. Porat has attempted to indicate the growth of employment in the information industries in the United States and has suggested that half of the working force is engaged in information-intensive tasks.[4]

[2] Ibid.

[3] The Diebold Group, Inc.

[4] Marc V. Porat, *The Information Economy,* Report 27, vol. 1 (Stanford, Calif.: Stanford University, Institute for Communication Research,

These secondary effects from information technology include: the development of entire new industries; improved operations of existing industries; the development of new and expanded services.

To cite several information technology examples which have a broad impact on the public, note first the growth of international communications, which, utilizing satellites, permits live television transmission and improved and lower cost voice and data communications. These improved and lower cost communications provide substantial benefits to the economy and society.

Another example with international implications is the development of worldwide computerized airline reservation systems providing instantaneous confirmations. A third example is the availability of remote, automatic-teller stations that permit individual banking and other transactions after hours.

Among industrial users the process industries, such as steel, chemicals, and petroleum have been improved by feedback control systems incorporating electronic instruments and microcomputers. Now it is the turn of the discrete manufacturing industries to incorporate microcomputer-based robots and controls to improve quality and reduce costs. In consumer goods, automobiles, voice-alerting functions, "smart" appliances, voice response systems, calculators, digital watches, and PAC-MAN are all manifestations of the incorporation of electronics.

There is also a belief in certain countries that information technology in its "automation phase" can displace workers rather than create employment. These concerns are best articulated in those European countries with a strong labor participation in government. There are and will be dislocations in certain industries and opportunities in others with the possibility of local labor force stresses. The alternative of not participating in information technology advances leads to noncompetitiveness and/or dependency on governmental subsidies.

The list of secondary impacts could be expanded to great lengths. A significant consideration is that the *information industries are central to the economic development and important to the personal development of our society.* Successful application of information industry products and services to other industries provides the basis for improved competitiveness of those industries. This improved com-

---

August 1976), p. 189, quoted in OTA, *Computer-Based National Information Systems,* September.

petitiveness of existing industries and development of new industries are the most important secondary effects.

Tertiary effects arising from the information industry developments have and will continue to have worldwide consequences. These consequences include improved and expanded computer literacy, which will enable large numbers of people to have direct access and to participate in the information-processing evolution. Another important tertiary effect is that the availability and lower costs of communication will stimulate individual and group economic, intellectual, and cultural activities, all of which have an impact on the economic and political fabric. From the longer-range perspective, the feedback from these tertiary effects may well prove to be the most enduring.

Structural conditions work to the disadvantage of the US information industry when in competition with the Japanese. Venture capital markets in the United States encourage formation of a number of small specialized companies, often with a narrow product range. Conversely, MITI provides funds to the large integrated Japanese firms where no single product is vital to the ultimate profitability. These integrated Japanese companies (both vendors and semiconductor suppliers) can use the strategy of lower prices to enter markets. As an example, a large integrated Japanese electronics firm was recently found by the US International Trade Commission (USITC) to have dumped its Klystron and traveling wave tubes, used in satellite communications, in the US market. These Japanese electronic tubes were priced far below what the two small American suppliers could charge and below what the Japanese firm charged at home. But in the meantime, the Japanese firm had won the principal procurement from the Communications Satellite Corporation (COMSAT), and the survival of the two small US firms is in question.

Similarly, in the semiconductor industry US firms have as their principal business the sale of semiconductor components and systems, while the Japanese digital semiconductor industry consists of large integrated firms. The Japanese firms have demonstrated in the past that they will use low prices to gain market entry. This pricing approach has been used in the 16KD RAM and the 64KD RAM products and is currently under review by the appropriate US agencies.

National Information Industry Policies: United States, Japan, and France

A new set of industrial and trade policy conditions will arise as we find industrial nations actively promoting their "sunrise" or emerging industries and the developing countries seek access to these industries. Birth, growth, and decline of industries is a cause of international tensions. Up to now, most of these international tensions arose from the attempt to arrest the decline of industries. A further qualitative set of trade issues arise when it is recognized that the grouping of high technology industries chosen as our case example, the "information industries," are regarded as the driving force; they propel the postindustrial society into the knowledge-intensive society.

Information has several unique attributes. In contrast with the finite nature of material resources, the value of information increases as it is used. Information is not depleted although it may become obsolete. Information is a basic factor of productive activity comparable with labor, capital, energy, or raw materials. The considerations of information transport, information access, and information processing form the basis for the information technology industries.

National industrial and public policy has played a stimulating role in the competitiveness of information industries in various countries. Japan and France have already committed themselves to such nationally overseen information industry programs. As would be expected, particular national policies have varied according to national philosophy and goals as well as market and other economic conditions. Nonetheless, most information industries policies have been characterized by attempts to provide R&D funds and to protect domestic industries against competition in general and foreign competition in particular through protectionist procurement policies, restriction of foreign investment and other more subtle nontariff barriers. Countries have typically attempted to promote their industries via massive direct and indirect subsidies, including tax provisions and preferential loan treatment.

As might be expected, the results have been mixed. The lack of success in the development of state-supported information industries suggests the limits of state intervention in industries that form an integral part of an international marketplace; that are characterized by rapid change; and whose scope is not limited to a single sector in the economy.

The Importance of a Long-Term Outlook and Market Orientation

Countries with a long-term outlook and well-established mechanism for public policy in the high technology industries sector have had numerous advantages. The information industries is a good example of just where such factors are really important.

Japan is the most effective in implementing national information policies as a component of industrial policy. As a result of well-directed industrial policies toward certain knowledge-intensive industrial and consumer markets based on a careful assessment of its industrial comparative advantage, Japan has emerged as one of the world leaders in information industries. Unlike the United States, which has allowed market forces to dictate the direction of investment, the Japanese government has selected industries, allocated tasks and promoted national champions or "winners" in consultation with industry and the banks ("administrative guidance"). Close attention is given to product gaps or weaknesses in the international marketplace that do or may be made to correspond to the Japanese comparative advantage.

However, such priorities and allocation of tasks are not necessarily sufficient. Although the French have had an "overarching" vision of the central role of information technology in the economy, French firms and the French government have consistently failed to translate technological advances to the competitive marketplace, despite their considerable technical and industrial expertise. The heavy hand of the French state and the lack of dynamism in the French market have limited the advance of the French information industries. The much discussed "gap" between French and American industries—now Japanese, too—has not been technological. Rather it relates to dependence on government orders, particularly communications and military, attitudes of distaste toward the competitive marketplace, a lack of entrepreneurial attitudes in the electronic industry, and dependence on foreign sources for advanced semiconductors.

Technological Change Outstrips Public Policy

As a result of vast technical changes since World War II in the United States and most other countries, public policy has not kept pace with technology. The continuation of antediluvian regulations and outmoded policy frameworks in traditional areas and the absence of policy guidance in new areas have been major roadblocks to the emergence of information technology and the information industries. Furthermore, the complexity of information-based societies has led to certain issue clusters, which have not been appropriately addressed in national policies; national policies still focus on compartmentalized issues. The Japanese have in some cases addressed these issue clusters, but other countries have not.

The inhibiting role played by inappropriate public policy has been the most apparent in the telecommunications industry for different reasons in the United States and Western Europe. Modern technology has blurred traditional distinctions on which current national communications policies are based. The merging of communications and computer industries has raised numerous regulatory questions concerning competition versus "natural" monopolies, local versus regional, national, and international interests, social goals of privacy versus economic efficiency, and national security objectives versus efficiency and local interests.

In the United States, industries that were once analytically placed in either a regulated or nonregulated environment because of existing technological possibilities and public interests have become competitors as a result of the complex and rapidly evolving changes in the structure of the information industries.

These technological changes have made current policy approaches obsolete in most countries. In the United States, communications regulations are still based primarily on the separation of the computer and communications industries, although there have been some piecemeal changes recently with AT&T's settlement and dismissal of IBM's antitrust cases. The 1934 Communications Act, although much modified by the Federal Communications Commission (FCC), placed monopoly and national interests ahead of competitive and local interests. As a result, decisions in the United States have been fragmentary, inappropriate, and limiting.

In Europe and Japan, government-owned communications authorities continue to control communications services and investment. Competition is limited by protectionist procurement policies, subsidies, and other barriers. The rationale is to provide a reliable infrastructure for national security, commercial, and consumer interests. Yet communications costs are high and service is often unreliable. Nevertheless, in response to the new technological developments, most governments have merely widened their protectionist scope to incorporate the technologies in traditional terms, not recognizing the competitive issues involved and their possible economic benefits.

Policy approaches of governments continue to be within a strictly national framework, despite the truly international character of the information industries. Increasing numbers of international joint ventures, particularly between the Japanese and the European and now Japanese and American firms, indicate limits of policies directed toward "national" industries. Despite importance of technology transfer through these arrangements, foreign investment is frequently regulated and limited. Competition in these industries is still considered basically in domestic terms, although important competitive issues are usually between firms from different countries. In the United

States, antitrust policy is still considered in terms of domestic competition. Relevant markets and market shares continue to be defined
in purely domestic terms. In Japan and Europe, although some joint
ventures are blessed and encouraged for international competitive
reasons, competitive policies frequently restrict the participation of
foreign companies, especially American, in those domestic markets.
For example, France refused Digital Equipment the permit to establish a factory for minicomputers near Grenoble.

Political and Social Goals Often Undermine Technical and Economic Goals

There has frequently been confusion between political and social
goals, on one hand, and technical and economic goals in the promotion of these industries on the other. Confusion often occurs because of the general importance of the information industries for
countries, as a source of world economic and political power as well
as the legitimacy of social goals, such as protection of privacy and
national security objectives. Technological independence, which
combines technical and political components, has been a common
goal of governments at all economic levels. Generally, the extent of
"independence" has been ill-conceived in relation to a country's resource endowment. As a result, political objectives have undermined
technical objectives. National interests of countries should be examined more closely, with the goal of obtaining the best technology
available, rather than building a national industry for political reasons.

Public Policy for High Technology in the United States

It is time to raise the question of US national industrial policy for
high technology. The complete disarray of public policy in the United
States has had a negative impact on international competitiveness of
US high technology industries, particularly information technology.
Lack of a coherent national policy plus certain structural constraints
of the industry serve to erode the US industrial leadership.

A most damning indictment arose in June 1982, from the Office
of Technology Assessment, which is in itself a high technology "watch
dog" for Congress. The OTA report cites the erosion of US leadership
in the civil space launch and satellite industry and attributes this to
a lack of clear and consistent sustained national and industrial objectives by the executive and legislative branches of the federal government. Conversely, the European Space Agency and also the Japanese have developed national plans, supported by their respective

governments and communications authorities. International trade policies form an important subset to these national policies.

The market-oriented economy based on relatively free competition has stood the United States in good stead and its industrial leadership has prospered. However, the US leadership must recognize that increasingly in the high technology "sunrise" industries it is faced with international competition backed by coherent national policies. Competition in international high technology is not pure competition and is strongly tainted by government intervention and support. The United States is obliged to strengthen its high technology industries seeking world markets while maintaining its competitive, capitalistic structure.

US international trade policy is a morass of dispersed responsibilities lodged with the departments of Defense (DOD), Commerce, Justice, and the United States Trade Representative (USTR), National Aeronautics and Space Administration (NASA), the Federal Communications Commission (FCC), the Office of Technology Assessment in Congress, and other entities.

The Inter-Agency Committee on International Communications and Information Policy, established on July 10, 1981, is a belated and insufficient attempt to coordinate US responses to international bodies and international issues.

Clearly the result is that the United States technology outpaces policy. The most glaring example is the FCC's attempts to come to grips with the convergence of telecommunications and computers. After several decree years of deliberations, the FCC issued the so-called Computer Inquiry I; this was immediately recognized as obsolete and inappropriate in attempting to separate telecommunications and computers. The FCC attempted again with Computer Inquiry II. At least the FCC is consistent in its technical approach, but the process has become bogged down in adversarial and judicial proceedings. In turn these FCC problems arose out of the 1956 DOD-AT&T consent decree, which restricted AT&T to regulated communications businesses. Siemens in Germany, Compagnie Générale Eléctricité and Thomson-CSF in France, Philips in the Netherlands, General Electric Company Limited in the United Kingdom, and Hitachi, Fujitsu, and Nippon Electric all have been active for years in implementing the equipment convergence of computers and communications. AT&T was restricted as to what products and business its subsidiary Western Electric could enter. The question of a regulated common carrier possibly subsidizing its equipment is a unique situation and does not appear to be the case for Western Electric.

So not only does the United States lack coherent national information industrial policies and related international trade policies, but we have a situation where a regulatory agency, FCC, has great difficulty effectively relating to the restrictions imposed by the Department of Justice.

France

The Giscard régime recognized that *télématique* [telecommunications and teleprocessing] and *bureautique* [office systems] were important to French internal development and export sales. In 1974 the French government forced the sale of the IT&T (US) and Ericsson (Swedish) telecommunications subsidiaries to Thomson-CSF and CGE, thus completing the French control of the telecommunications industry. Only the fact that IBM and Texas Instruments were too important to the French economy and both had very strong management kept the French from gaining direct control of the computer and the semiconductor industry in their country.

The French télématique product strategy (not based on market research) was to oblige the postal, telephone, and telegraph ministry (PTT) to purchase large quantities of new communications terminals so as to achieve a low price and thus permit even larger export sales. Although the plans for the PTT proved to be overly-ambitious, Matra and Thompson-CSF have developed low-cost work stations which incorporate a telephone, television screen, and local intelligence. These work stations have been ordered in the United States in substantial quantities by Tymshare and GTE, respectively, who resell them to end users. French suppliers may be 12 to 18 months ahead of their principal American competitors; however, the two-step distribution is costly. If the two French companies shipped 25,000 terminals per year the revenues would be approximately $10 million, which is modest in comparison with the French negative balance of trade in information products.

The same Giscard program also helped French industry to develop low-cost digital facsimile equipment. This too is being sold in the United States and despite the two-step distribution appears to be an attractive device with several years of sales life; it will contribute only modestly to the French balance of trade.

Both terminal and facsimile equipment illustrate that French industry can be competitive in product design and manufacturing cost. These are not the problems. The government contracts have been superimposed on existing French industry without making this industry the focal point of a sustained and scientific, engineering, and export marketing program for the basic information sector.

The Mitterrand government has indicated that it considers high technology so important that it was considered a separate agenda point at the economic summit at Versailles. The principal French thrust announced to date is a World Center for Microcomputers and Human Resources with the stated purpose of carrying the benefits to the Third World. This French effort is funded at $20 million in 1982 and far exceeds in funding any comparable laboratory in the United States. The French have recruited many of the best-known researchers, including leading Americans, for their center.

The Diebold Group's view is that the price of personal computers will decline so rapidly in the next five years that there is little that the French center will contribute to that development. US and Japanese firms will provide low-cost personal computation to large numbers of consumers and even the developing countries.

The caliber and specialities of the research staff recruited by the French suggest that advanced and esoteric applications will be studied. What is not clear at this time is how this center is coupled to French industry and how effective this coupling will be. Now that the French electronics industry has been nationalized, will they develop the marketing infrastructure that is essential to domestic and export sales of information products? With the exception of CII-HB, the French industrial electronics companies have limited experience selling to large numbers of small users.

Japanese and French policies remain profoundly different despite the fact that both countries have publicly announced that the information industries are the key to their national industrial policy.

Japan

National industrial policy formulation has been ingrained in the Japanese government since the Meiji restoration. The Japanese, coordinated by MITI, have created a "vision of the 1980s" which is based on commercial exploitation, domestic and export, of the knowledge-intensive industries.

The distinguishing feature of all the Japanese "visions" is that they harness all development, product planning, marketing, and financing programs to clear commercial objectives. These plans have been drawn up in a concerted set of meetings with government, university, industry, and banking representatives who together forge an industry consensus.

The most recent MITI "vision" differs from previous plans in that
it places emphasis on the "R" in R&D. The Japanese excel in product
design, manufacturing, and quality control. Now they intend to be
competitors in research, a more problematical task.

Through a series of MITI-sponsored meetings the critical events
are identified and direct funding and other forms of financial assistance are provided. The MITI funding is substantial and the programs
are funded over a three- or four-year period. Apart from development
funding, modest Japanese assistance programs are comprised of a
multitude of financial benefits or allowances which in aggregate make
commercial success more possible.

Examples of Current and Proposed Information
Industries Development Policies

International trade policies of the individual country have usually
been centered on the support of declining industries. Much recent
effort has gone into international trade negotiation on the imports of
European or Japanese steel into the US market. These trade issues
are exacerbated in economic recessions such as we are encountering
today.

The Diebold Group would consider it more productive for the
national and international focus in international trade and public
policy to concentrate at least as much effort on the emerging, or
"sunrise," industries. These "sunrise" industries are often based on
high technology.

We can identify several national high technology programs which
have been successful and which have contributed to international
economic development. Perhaps the most successful initiative was
the US Communications Satellite Act of 1962.

This uniquely American initiative for structuring an advanced technology business led subsequently to an international consortium for
satellite communications. Comsat blended the launch vehicle (rocket)
expertise with the communications system expertise, both of which
were developed for defense or space agency purposes, with a private
management structure. Technological innovations have continued in
the past twenty years and will continue for the foreseeable future.
Satellite communications will eventually have their dramatic impact
on communications in developing countries. Yet despite the pioneering efforts of the United States in satellites, the previously mentioned
OTA report is very critical of the US present lack of clear national-
commercial objectives in civilian space progress.

Another successful national implementation has been the Japanese integrated circuit project. The Japanese government agencies led by MITI and the finance ministry have provided the "administrative" guidance, massive financial support, and protection where necessary to foster the development of the computer industry and the very large scale integration (VLSI) program for the semiconductor industry.

Through MITI the Japanese government has recently launched its vision of a "fifth generation" computer development program which will endure through the 1980s. This is a very ambitious goal for it would incorporate artificial intelligence as well as the most advanced technology. Although the program is firmly under Japanese control, they have welcomed foreign participation. The British Department of Industry is, to say the least, intrigued. US firms are observing with interest.

The United States has demonstrated that when government leadership has decided on a major program requiring advanced technology it can successfully mobilize immense resources. The audacious Apollo "Man-on-the-Moon" program was a major technological and political success. The material benefits to the world community are still, for the most part, indirect, and the medium-term direct benefits are probably not commensurate with the project cost.

Given the immense technology and management resources resident in the United States the question arises, can the United States identify programs or projects vital to its economy and society which are of national magnitude and importance? Such national projects should be possible in the energy industry, biogenetics and health industry, and the information industry just to mention the most obvious. Step one could be the identification of a short list of such vital projects. Given the fact that projects of national or worldwide importance can be identified, the question then arises as to what mechanism does the United States have for national prioritization, coordination, and implementation.

The Comsat experience is very appealing to the United States. The Congress mandated an enteprise to implement satellite communications. Comsat is now very successful, continues world technological leadership, and is increasingly involved in competitive and profitable ventures. The cost to the taxpayer has been nominal and the entire world has benefited. Comsat was unique in that it brought together two industries, one of which was completely dependent on the US government for its development.

Could the United States or other industrial countries replicate the Comsat experience in other industries? To answer this question obviously requires expert analysis in each of those industries.

In the United States step two would be the analysis of these projects and industries to develop in each a "Comsat-like" approach that would be congenial to private industry, yet limit the cost to the taxpayer. This concept is at best a considered approach to projects of vital national interest. These projects are not the equivalent of a coherent national program, but they could be effective, and would represent the best that the United States could accomplish in peacetime given the present national economic and political ethos.

International Diffusion of Technology and Its Impact
on Domestic Industrial Policies

In developing public policies for the information industry, we must recognize the increasing internationalization of this industry. This internationalization with its attendant diffusion of technology will require shared research and development and in some situations, joint manufacturing and joint marketing and services. Both American and Japanese firms have recognized the difficulty of penetrating each other's industrial markets and therefore there is an increasing trend towards marketing and services arrangements. These arrangements are not symmetrical, for the United States exports technology while Japan exports products.

We would expect that technology developments will continue to outpace the evolution of public policies and regulatory agencies. Even the most responsive US government agencies would be handicapped by the litigious nature of the adversary position in a quasi-legal environment. The best work of the FCC staff and commission is often thwarted by the atmosphere in which it must operate. Semiconductor industry structure suggests some need for shared research which the Department of Justice has recognized since 1980 as beneficial.

In the United States, the annual R&D effort from all sources is about $80 billion.[5] Private industry provides over 50 percent of R&D funds with the federal government funding most of the remainder. The DOD funds approximately one-third of the total or $25 billion. A small fraction of this is seed money for fundamental and basic research. Most of the funding is for the ad hoc development of military-specific products. Contrary to what most European experts believe the US defense and space programs provide only occasional *direct benefits* to industry. This is demonstrated by a recent analysis

---

[5] Organization for Economic Cooperation and Development, "Technical Change and Economic Policy," Paris, 1980.

TABLE 19.1 PERCENTAGE ALLOCATION OF GOVERNMENT-FUNDED R&D, BY OBJECTIVES, 1975

Country	Advancement of knowledge	Military	Civilian industry[a]	Other[b]
United States	3.9	49.8	21.3	25.0
Japan	55.8	2.2	20.0	22.0
France	25.3	29.5	25.8	19.4
West Germany	51.0	11.1	22.3	15.6
United Kingdom	21.4	48.9	26.8	2.9

Source: Technical Change and Economic Policy (Paris: Organization for Economic Cooperation and Development, 1980), p. 37.
a. Civilian industry includes space.
b. Includes health, agriculture, and environmental protection.

by the Organization for Economic Cooperation and Development (OECD) summarized in table 19.1.

These military objectives often place rigid design specifications that are not appropriate for commercial products. In almost every instance the R&D effort proved product feasibility but several important steps remained prior to the adaptation of the design to successful commercial products.

The direct fallout of commercial products from the Department of Defense or the National Aeronautics and Space Administration (NASA) has been limited. There are few such direct examples as Boeing basing its original 707 jet aircraft design on the Air Force KC135 refueling tanker.

The indirect contributions from Department of Defense or NASA projects have been substantial including digital computer designs, digital communications devices, and medical electronics. Indirect fallout requires that the individual company decide to develop a specific product for the commercial market, and these specifications are usually different from the military product.

Forecasting the evolution of the commercialization of scientific breakthroughs is a hazardous activity. For example, few if any, foresaw the parallel development of laser optics and semiconductor materials developments that led to the development of the semiconductor lasers and semiconductor detectors. These electro-optical devices will have a profound impact on future telecommunications and information processing systems.

However, the most poignant contrast of US government support of industry as contrasted with Japanese programs is evident in the key semiconductor industry. The Department of Defense has its Very

High Speed Integrated Circuit (VHSIC) program and the Japanese had their Very Large Scale Integrated Circuit (VLSIC) program. The DOD VHSIC program was directed toward the development of very high speed electronic circuits that would operate in the difficult military environmental conditions. In this $314-million program, many small contracts for a few million dollars each were spread among a number of US semiconductor firms with considerable emphasis on developing "second sources" or multiple suppliers. Several of the principal US firms chose not to participate in the VHSIC program. In contrast, the VLSIC program of the Japanese is directed toward commercial applications and $300 million is divided among a small number of large integrated Japanese firms that have competent R&D and are funded for both the heavy capital costs and for the aggressive pricing strategy in market entry—which is characteristic of the integrated Japanese electronic firms.

A second example is the DOD requirement for a high-tensile strength fiber optics cable for use in missile programs. The acknowledged world leader in fiber optics is Corning. Japanese firms, however, seem willing to make development efforts in order to gain market share. This fiber-optics example interposes several critical issues—national security, reciprocity of market entry, long-term US industrial interests, US employment, all of which should be weighed before a decision is made. At present we have the DOD's immediate position plus what narrow political pressures can be brought to bear by the US industry as the determinants of national policy in a critical technology. The US does not have an adequate mechanism, apart from ad hoc DOD or executive judgments, to deal with such issues.

Action Issues

Public Policies for the High Technology Information
Industry in the United States

In democratic countries effective national public policies must have substantial support from the opinion makers and the informed public. In the United States it is therefore necessary to raise the recognition level of the importance of the high technology industries to the economic success and personal enrichment in the knowledge-intensive postindustrial society.

Given the present high-decibel level of discussion regarding deregulation of communications and the AT&T settlement, in the United States it is unlikely that the respective industries comprising the information industry can come to some agreement with regard to the technology implications for the future. It may be essential to appoint a blue-ribbon panel of the highest quality to develop positions that would reflect a general consensus of the business opportunities and social enrichment that should be the twin objectives of the US industrial policy. There is always the danger in creating such a panel that technical developments could continue to outpace the panel's understanding and comprehension.

We have previously discussed the "Comsat model." A necessary early step is the examination of the operative conditions of both the "Comsat model" and the Japanese MITI-industry relationship in order to ascertain what is most appropriate for the United States. The "Comsat-MITI" analysis would be most useful in formulating possible mechanisms for US policy.

An Example of a High Technology National Project

As an example of a project of national importance that could be structured along "Comsat-MITI" lines we have chosen portable personal communications equipment capability that would enable connections to local, national, and international networks. A portable personal communications project, while representing formidable technical problems, is not dominated by major systems engineering tasks. The magnitude of the project lies more in the development of receiver sensitivity. Transmitter power would be limited by health and technical considerations. One may question why the government should become involved when major electronics firms are aware of both the challenge and the opportunity. Such a project is politically attractive, for demonstrable progress should be possible while the ultimate usefulness has almost universal appeal.

Such a program should be outlined by the best telecommunications talent in the United States. The critical research paths should be identified and funded to a modest degree at universities or other nonprofit institutions. The results should be made available on a royalty basis to US industry. Collaborative research by private industry could well be an alternate to some or all of government funding. Once beyond the difficult research phase, the project should become market driven. This proposed American approach is dependent on identifying the key research tasks and, at the most, providing research seed money.

This personal portable (mobile) communications project is cited despite the fact that almost all foreign telecommunications authorities are state owned and are not necessarily market driven. French telecom authorities are notorious for favoring their local equipment suppliers. The US public policy would have objectives of encouraging substantial export revenues for domestic suppliers while recognizing that the individual foreign telecom authorities will probably utilize their monopoly position in negotiating with multiple American suppliers. The US industry will, in effect, confront foreign government cartels and monopolies.

Public Policy Issues: United States

Can US leadership in the information sector be sustained by traditional responses to the broad front of other purposeful government-directed efforts to challenge that leadership? The uncoordinated, pluralistic, market-driven US business environment has served US information industries well in the past. Has it become inappropriate for the new competitive conditions of the 1980s and beyond? Government policies that were created during one era in the United States are being applied in another. Technological change, competitive and economic shifts, and the increased role of governments in industrial policies for the information sector may well render the US approach inadequate. US policies are often contradictory and generally inappropriate. But what is the alternative? How far can a coordinating mechanism go without loss of the dynamism and innovation that have served the United States so well in the past?

The United States would derive the greatest advantages from promoting its strongest feature, its market-driven economy, rather than adopting forms that are alien to it. Because of the structure and attitudes of the US business, and political communities that encourage confrontation rather than cooperation, a policy modeled completely on the Japanese system would clearly be inappropriate.

Nonetheless, there is currently a need in the United States for coordinated public policy in the information sector based on the appreciation of the central importance of the information sector for the future of the entire economy. The central policy issues include the following:

Appropriate and Consistent Regulations for New Technology Development. Technological development has made existing regulatory guidelines and structures inappropriate in numerous ways. As a result, policy has been formulated piecemeal. For example, the settlement between the Justice Department and AT&T has changed Bell from a telephone company to an information company. Recent technological changes have led to many questions, but few answers:

• How should interests in competition be balanced against the need for regulation, particularly given new changes in technology which mean that computers and telecommunications industries and services are virtually indistinguishable?

• Is the theory of natural monopoly in communications still relevant under current technological conditions?

• How can the government resolve its interest in regulating the communications industry with its other interest in encouraging the competitive aspects of the industry? For example, the Department of Defense opposed the breaking up of AT&T on national security grounds, while Justice Department and FCC decisions concerning the industry have emphasized competition.

• How should local needs be balanced with regional, national, or international needs?

• Will the new communications industries be regulated? If so, which jurisdiction will have the primary regulatory powers? Furthermore, how will communications charges be established, if the industry becomes highly competitive, if local jurisdictions are given regulatory power, and as sophisticated communications permits elaborate routing procedures that cut across regulatory boundaries?

• How will the recent AT&T settlement affect competition and regulation in telecommunications?

The domestic treatment of the industries has a direct relation to their international competitiveness. In addition, the domestic treatment of the industries will affect foreign imports. Finally, similar types of issues are being debated throughout the world, as technological change leads to a rethinking of traditional attitudes and approaches elsewhere.

A Model Regulatory Code for US States?   One solution to the regulatory problems resulting from technological developments could be the formulation of a model code covering information areas such as cable television, satellites, videotex, and other information products. The code could cover currently overlapping areas of jurisdiction and laws, competitive issues, and standards among stages. This approach could be adopted for the international community as well in order to reduce the confusion and other problems created by widely different approaches. The standards issues are addressed by the Consultative Committee for International Telephone and Telegraph (CCITT) in international forums.

US Antitrust Guidelines. We need innovation-oriented antitrust guidelines, based on review of the effect antitrust policy (as practiced in the United States) has had on the development of information sector industries. The study should weigh the anticompetitive aspects of certain practices against their effect on a more viable information sector. For example, was the 1956 Consent Decree that kept AT&T out of the computer business short-sighted or did it encourage competition that would not have otherwise occurred? Similarly, in the 13-year IBM case, was IBM prevented from increasing its competitiveness because of the pending court decision or did more competition result from the case?

In view of technological developments and competitive conditions, antitrust concepts for relevant markets, competition and market share need to be reconsidered. Although the US industries are highly competitive in the domestic market, there is intense international competition. Competition for the information sector occurs on a global rather than a domestic scale. Yet traditional antitrust policy in the United States defines relevant markets and other competitive concerns in domestic terms.

Antitrust policy could have a very positive effect on research and development in the information sector. The competitive success of these industries is based on an ability to continue building a technological research base as well as doing applied research. However, it is questionable whether US companies have in the semiconductor and certain information technology products the resources to match the efforts of the foreign government-supported integrated industries in the future. This is particularly important in these industries, which are becoming more research- and capital-intensive. The leaders of a new joint research effort in the United States feel that the amount of funding, manpower, and range of technology required for the United States to maintain its competitiveness in the semiconductor field are beyond the capability of most US companies.

Yet current antitrust may be an impediment to effective competition. Research policy is considered an important element in the overall competitive process, but joint research frequently raises antitrust questions. The complexity of antitrust attitudes toward joint research has frequently discouraged such activities from taking place. In recognition of this problem, President Carter directed the Justice Department to produce a guide to its antitrust policies upon the conclusion of the White House Domestic Policy Review of Industrial Innovation. Accordingly, the Justice Department issued the *Antitrust Guide Concerning Research Joint Ventures* in November

1980.[6] This is a positive first step, but the subject requires more fundamental examination.

Several efforts for joint research arrangements by US firms in direct response to the Japanese challenge have been evident recently. However, the antitrust implications are not totally clear. The following examples portray the ferment in the US semiconductor industry.

William Norris, Chairman of Control Data Corporation, is sponsoring an initiative that would permit producers to pool research activities under university auspices. Private investors have also established a new venture, tentatively named Megaram, which will be a semiconductor research laboratory for the private sector. This project is an attempt for companies to share research costs without seeking government assistance. Megaram's general objective is to chip makers. The Semiconductor Industry Association (SIA) recently established cooperative research funding for basic research at several US research universities.

US Tax Policy. In contrast to Japan, where tax policy is one of the strongest incentives for its information industries, in the United States, tax policy for innovation is not a priority. The unique needs of the high technology information industries are just beginning to be addressed here. Tax policy can and should play a more positive and central role in the encouragement of US competitiveness. A thorough examination of these issues should be undertaken.

There are several areas where tax policy can promote innovation in these industries through the free market mechanism. Depreciation allowances and depreciation periods should reflect the fact that many of these industries are characterized by low profitability and short product cycles. In addition, tax allowances for research and development are needed incentives. The computer equipment and software suppliers are expected to benefit from the R&D tax credit and accelerated depreciation sections of the Economy Recovery Tax Act of 1981, but more measures along these lines are needed.

In addition, tax benefits for educational purposes could lead to the increased education of citizens about the value of the information sector. Apple Computer has recently encountered problems in obtaining tax credits for educational donations of its products. At present Congress is considering a Technology Act which would allow a 30 percent tax deduction, rather than the standard 10 percent for

---

[6] US Department of Justice, *Antitrust Guide Concerning Research Joint Ventures* (Washington: Government Printing Office, November 1980).

educational donations. Ironically, one of the main casualties of the IBM antitrust case was the ending of large educational discounts that universities and schools once received from IBM. Tax benefits could also encourage the training of additional personnel for these industries, which is badly needed.

The programming (software) industry faces potential problems because it is taxed differently from hardware in the United States and several countries. Programs are increasingly being viewed as a commodity in themselves. More than 30 US states currently tax programs, and several foreign countries have adopted such provisions.

Finally, current tax laws and proposals that affect the US competitive position overseas should be considered in the context of promoting/development of the information industries. The issues of foreign tax credits and the Domestic International Sales Corporation (DISC), pending the outcome of international negotiations, should be assessed.

US Patent and Copyright Laws.   The development of new technology and products and the transformation of old technology and products have resulted in a host of complex patent and copyright questions. Because of the inadequacy of established policy and policy structures to resolve many of the new leading issues, policy questions are more frequently resolved in the courts, which are inappropriate forums for these issues. As a result, decisions are segmented, inconsistent, and frequently ill-guided in developing national technology policy. This area has an important effect on US domestic competition and the success of foreign companies in the US market as well as the US position abroad.

Program sales is the best example of the problems in this area. Programs (software) will be one of the most important growth fields in the near future. Programming costs will contribute approximately 65 percent of total user costs. The expected astronomical growth in personal computers will cause the demand for programs to explode. A variety of program packages permits the owner of a *single* personal computer to undertake limitless tasks.

Despite the importance of programming, patent and copyright protection is very poor. Programs are very easy to duplicate. The Apple Computer Company has estimated that it loses from 10 percent to 50 percent of its potential program business through illegal program distribution. This problem has intensified with the appearance of new "decipher" programs, which can copy most programs within 15 minutes. The lack of protection has been an important disincentive for advances in programming.

The history of protection for programs is limited and fragmentary. Initially, programs were provided free to customers to promote the sale of computers in the early days of the industry. It was not until 1968 that the US Court of Customs and Patent Appeals ruled that "truly novel" computer programs are to be considered inventions and are therefore patentable. However, the US Copyright Act was not amended until December 1980 to cover computer program protection. Now users are permitted to copy programs for "archival purposes" only, but there is little enforcement. Engineers are designing "booby-traps" to prevent their programs from being illegally used or pirated, but these efforts are limited.

The issue has a great international significance as well. Patent and copyright protection abroad is also poor. The Office of the US Trade Representative estimates that 21 countries do not have protection and, as a result, infringements occur. In addition, France and the United Kingdom provide export subsidies to their domestic programming industries. In Brazil, the government is nationalizing the program industry.

Market Access Abroad and "Unfair" Trade. One of the main obstacles to the continued strength of the US information sector is the protectionism of key information industries abroad, particularly in the communications field, that restrict US markets by foreign industries that have had the advantages of strong government support. Examples of these issues are covered below. These activities are incompatible with US interests in maintaining a free trade policy. As part of its overall public policy to encourage the emergence of a strong information sector, US policymakers should adopt an active trade policy through existing trade bodies, including GATT and the OECD, to protect its interests.

There are indications that the concerns for selected high technology trade is now understood. The US administration is considering taking "unfair trade" actions against several other countries for complaints of dumping and subsidies of information industries. Reciprocity bills concerning high technology industries abroad have started to appear on Capitol Hill. The Semiconductor Industry Association (SIA) has urged that Congress adopt legislation authorizing the United States to negotiate with other countries for freer market access for high technology goods and services and investment, and a bill to that effect was recently introduced in the House of Representatives Ways and Means Committee.[7] Recently, testimony before the Senate Finance

[7] Robert Lawrence, "US Semiconductor Group Seeks Freer Market Access," *Journal of Commerce,* 18 March 1982.

Committee's international trade subcommittee concerned the problems that computer companies face abroad in maintaining majority ownership.[8] This is particularly a problem for young, export-oriented companies.

In order to defuse trade tensions between the United States and Japan over market access in Japan and Japanese market penetration in the United States, the two countries recently agreed to a subcabinet level working group. In addition, the United States apparently hopes to raise these issues in appropriate international forums.

Regulatory and Social Restraints.   As a result of legal custom, regulation, contracts or tradition, the development of numerous industry sectors is restricted, despite the availability of technology whose applications would transform those industries.

Banking is one of the best examples. Through the application of information technology, the nature of banking itself has changed. The use of Electronic Funds Transfer (EFT) and Automatic Teller Machines (ATMs) have meant that money could be shifted globally within a few seconds. The interstate and international capabilities of banking have far exceeded the regulatory bounds. Further, the development of these new financial services by unregulated concerns has placed banks at a disadvantage. How meaningful and appropriate is current regulation under these conditions? Furthermore, the question of what constitutes a bank is no longer easily answered because of computer linkages, electronic credit facilities, ATMs, and other innovations in the information sector.

Technology has made an international electronic stock market possible. Interconnection of the various markets could actually enhance the efficiency of the marketplace by instantaneously matching up supply and demand. A computerized network would provide a clearinghouse for the market.

Other examples include the legal questions surrounding the need for an original document versus the efficiency of providing a facsimile document, in light of today's rapid electronic transmission capabilities. Workplace safety rules may change appreciably when robots become a greater part of the workplace. Education is changing as well, but there is resistance to these changes among teachers, who do not understand the technology and are worried about their job security. Computer technology is increasingly becoming part of curricula. Finally, the nature of publishing is changing with the use of

[8] Ibid.

electronic transmission, but regulations still regard the media in traditional terms.

Educational Aid.   Policymakers should consider what role, if any, public policy should play in information education. Should the government, either at the local, state, or federal level, become involved with the issue? Should the government offer companies incentives to educate the population about the importance of the information sector? The significance of the sector to the US economy suggests that the government should adopt some measures.

National Security and Privacy.   Since the Reagan administration took office, the national security rationale has been used more frequently to support restrictive actions toward the export and import of dual use technology, as well as certain major domestic policy questions. The administration has adopted Operation Exodus in the Customs Service to prevent critical US technology from reaching the Soviet Union. The Japanese company Fujitsu was not awarded the contract for the Northeast Corridor fiber optics project ostensibly on the grounds of national security. Secretary of Defense Caspar Weinberger argued that splitting up AT&T would not be in the American national security interest because of the need for a unified, reliable communications infrastructure.

The United States is not well-served if the government restricts the export of technology that the Soviet Union can purchase elsewhere. If the government limits the US export of advanced microchips, the Soviet Union will probably be able to buy them from the Japanese or elsewhere. The administration is attempting to solve this problem by placing pressure on US allies to revise their guidelines for technology exports to the Soviet Union. The United States has pressed Germany to ban its sales of high-grade silicon which can be used to make chips in the guidance system of the Russian SS-20s missiles. As technology increases, there will be increased conflict between the national security and commercial interests of the United States in this area.

In addition, the role of the government in the protection of citizens' right to privacy must be weighted against the other advantages accruing from the free flow of information. Health, work-related, and other types of data have been the most frequently discussed issues in connection with the right to privacy. Adequate safeguards in these areas must be found, while the positive benefits of information technology are not restricted.

United States: Conclusion

The United States should attempt to formulate a coherent and well-integrated policy within its market-driven economy along the lines and the issues suggested. Any policy should recognize the dynamic features and international diffusion of the technology. In addition, policy should concern the adjustment problems that are taking place as the economy shifts from traditional industries to the high technology industries. Measures for education, employment, and retraining should be considered. These will be the major challenges for those who embark on a more comprehensive study of the public policy problems for this sector.

Other Advanced Industrial Nations

The public policy agenda for other advanced industrial nations is different from that for the United States in that it is manifested in the costs of protection and promotion of the information sector through active government intervention. The central issue is to weigh benefits of protection and promotion of the information sector against competitive costs of those policies to the economy and to society. National goals should be examined very carefully in the context of priorities. Is it more important to have domestic information industries at all costs or are there other strategies to be followed to establish a competitive information economy?

In the other advanced industrial countries (as in the United States and less developed countries), there has frequently been confusion between political and technical goals. Technological independence has been a common goal of information policies, but it has been defined and sought in an inappropriate manner. As a result, political objectives have frequently undermined technical objectives. The strongest national interest of these countries lies in obtaining superior and applicable technology and applying it throughout the economy. The goals of developing a domestic industry should be closely weighed against the resources available to promote the industry and an appreciation of the determinants of success for the particular industry. National strategies should reflect a country's comparative advantage. In addition, they should be based on the recognition of the country's role as a cooperative member of the international community.

Government-Owned Monopolies

In Europe and Japan, the governments owned the postal, telephone, and telegraph services in order to regulate communications services and to provide a reliable infrastructure for national security, commercial, and consumer interests. These objectives are generally not satisfied because the overriding goal of the governments is to protect its domestic companies, even if that means that the best technical equipment will not be used. For example, costs of telephone calls from Paris to New York are two times more than calls from New York to Paris; the difference is a factor of three from West Germany. Even intra-European telephone rates are costly because of PTT policies. European business and consumers bear the brunt of the costs.

Government-owned monopolies have frequently chose political over economic considerations. There is a need to study the political benefits, as opposed to the economic costs. Is the restriction on competition artificial? Would the domestic industries actually be stronger if competition were allowed? Alternatively, if deregulation took place, would communications infrastructure be unreliable? The issue of standards could become very important. Another problem would be the incompatibility of products, which is already appearing in the cases of rival videotex and facsimile products.

Government telecom procurement policies are the most important trade barrier. Market access is generally permitted only to national telecommunications suppliers through preferential purchasing arrangements. This is particularly important to countries whose telecommunications industries are export-oriented. Public telephone equipment comprises roughly 50 percent of the world market for telecommunications equipment of all types. Yet most of these markets are closed to imports. In France, the power of the PTT is unrivaled. The 1981 budget of Giscard's DGT (Direction Générale des Télécommunications) was $5.8 billion.[9] DGT director Thiéry limited the role of foreign suppliers in Giscard's program to modernize the French communications network. Protectionist procurement policies are applied to intra-European trade as well. The EC Commission is currently attempting to convince governments to open their trade but this has been a sore point. In Japan, despite the 1980 three-year bilateral agreement to permit US suppliers to compete with Japanese suppliers for the Japanese market, procurement for NTT is limited to Japanese-owned companies, with only minor exceptions. Recently, Motorola was placed on NTT's approved supplier list for mobile

---

[9] Kenneth Dreyfack, "The Heavy Hands of Politics on French Industrial Policy," *Business Week,* 26 January 1981.

paging equipment and ROLM for PBXs, but observers are skeptical about meaningful changes.

Performance requirements, including standards and designs and national content, are used to keep foreign goods out of the markets. In the United Kingdom, proposed applications for connection to British Telecom must pass the scrutiny of the British Standards Institute and then the British Electrical Approval Board. In France, domestic product content is monitored closely.

Telecommunications rates and rate increases are based on considerations other than costs in order to prevent private networks, to promote domestic data processing and to promote public data communications networks. What are the costs to users versus the competitive benefits for local firms? The restriction on private lines affecting international communications is found in Japan and throughout the European Community. In some cases, increased revenue, which is the means of regulation, provides increased revenue for the PTTs. In general, the local industries are promoted. What are the disadvantages to the users versus the revenue gains to the PTTs? Does the restriction in data flow discourage foreign investment?

Other Areas of Intervention

Much discussion has taken place on the question of transborder data flows. Canada is an example of recent market restrictions. The Canadian government has recommended that data processing be performed within the country. The Canadian Banking Act of 1980 requires that banks operating in Canada keep and process all data concerning a bank customer in Canada. Are these regulations discouraging foreign investment in these countries? What are the costs of investment as opposed to the benefits for the protection of local industries?

Most European countries and Japan provide their information industries with substantial financial incentives assistance to promote development. These countries need to consider whether the assistance has helped or hindered its development, and whether the industries are more or less competitive because of it. Are the political objectives worth the cost?

France picked computers as its "national champion" in the 1960s and 1970s. Mitterrand has also targeted the information sector for special development assistance. In Japan, particular products and industries are selected for government aid. Does this sectoral approach distort the economy? Does this depend on the type of sectoral assistance given? What are the disadvantages of selecting the wrong "winner?"

The European Community maintains a tariff of 17 percent on integrated circuits and refuses to negotiate the levels in order to protect its industry and to prevent additional US and Japanese imports. What are the costs of protection for the Europeans? The Japanese recently reduced their tariffs on integrated circuits to 4 percent, as did the United States.

The United Kingdom places a 4 percent duty and an 8 percent value-added tax (VAT) on all microfilm documents and publications imported from non-Community countries. France has considered a tax on information, similar to a tax on imports or exports, but has not adopted one.

Canada, Belgium, Brazil, Germany, and Switzerland place restrictions on commercial visas which limit firms' abilities to market and maintain their services. In addition, other discriminatory regulations make it difficult for qualified people to work in the country. Finally, foreign investment or foreign ventures are often flatly prohibited.

In general, traditional forms of government protectionism and promotion should be examined in terms of their economic and technical costs as well as their political benefits. Is there another approach that these countries could use to build up their industries and to avoid issues concerning dominance by the United States?

Public Policy Issues for Developing Countries

The developing countries face situations in which they would like to take advantage of the new information technologies to improve their standards of life through telecommunications changes and the use of other high technology items. They also face the issue of specialization in information technology to build their economies. Numerous countries have already made key public policy decisions on these matters. Have the decisions been a mistake or benefit? What can we learn from these experiences?

Several Third World countries have skipped a stage of the telecommunications process by adopting satellite technology rather than constructing a terrestrial long-distance communications infrastructure. India has already launched its own satellite and plans to launch a second in July 1983 in order to provide nationwide communication. Indonesia is developing a satellite communications system as well. Do these countries need the most advanced technologies? What should the criteria be? These are fertile areas for public policy study.

With the large economic requirement of creating and sustaining information industries, countries should be very careful in policies to promote domestic industries. Mexico and Brazil have adopted protectionist policies to promote the development of local industries. In Mexico, the rapidly expanding market has been restricted as the government is trying to build up a domestic industry. The government has informed foreign manufacturers either to produce in Mexico under certain conditions or to leave the country. Brazil has followed similar policies for similar reasons. However, in Brazil, the business community has complained that it must utilize outdated equipment that costs more than foreign-made equivalents. The government responds that a period of adjustment is necessary before the industry becomes competitive. Are these appropriate industries to be developing with limited resources? Will there be economic costs that will undermine technical goals, similar to the earlier French example in computers?

The policymakers in the developing countries should carefully consider their comparative advantage and develop industry based on that advantage. A potential area of great growth for the developing countries is in the area of software, which is labor-intensive. How could these countries take advantage of the growing software market?

Many developing countries have actively pushed for a politically oriented New World Information Order in journalism, satellite agreements, and other areas. What are the economic and political costs and benefits of this issue? How are they to be viewed by the political authorities in the developing countries?

Conclusion

The purpose of this chapter has been to illustrate the kinds of international economic problems posed by the information technology industry and to highlight a few of the policy questions that must be addressed in considering this new industry.

Several other areas should be studied:

• Do discriminatory trade practices hurt developing countries more than they help? Regulation of foreign investment and import protection and export promotion are the main examples.

• What are the costs of politicizing issues? How do countries separate legitimate technological and economic concerns from political objectives?

• The protection of the right to privacy versus economic benefits from the unimpeded flow of information.

In the determination of competitiveness and industrial policy for the information sector, public policy does make a difference, as we have seen from the various examples above. Government policy can have an impact that is positive, negative, or both. Even the lack of an explicit government policy can affect the development of the industries, as indicated by the US case. The precise relation between government policy and particular information industries is not well understood, and this chapter has merely suggested the starting points for a thorough discussion.

There is a need to study both methodically and opportunistically in a project-mode the role public policy has and can play in the shaping of the information industries as those industries assume a greater importance in the world's economies and, indeed, the quality of life. Based on the experiences of others, each county needs to develop policies that accommodate and enhance its progress of future technological growth. Although public policies for the information sector have been prevalent since the computer industry developed, there has never been a thorough study of the role of public policy in the competitive success of the information industries. What is needed now is an integrated look at the problems of competitiveness, with domestic and international factors carefully weighed. As has been emphasized, the public policy agenda must be recognized to vary for each country. The current tendency to point to Japan and to try to produce some pale policy copy can lead only to misfortune! This study has attempted to highlight the issues and also to illustrate by example a project approach to establishing national policies for the information industries.

Bibliography

John Diebold. "Business, Government and Science: The Need for a Fresh Look." *Foreign Affairs*, vol. 51 (April 1973), pp. 555–72.

John Diebold. "Is the Gap Technological?" *Foreign Affairs*, vol. 46 (January 1968), p. 276–91.

Organization for Economic Cooperation and Development (OECD). Science and Technology Policies for the 1980s, 1981, pp. 82, 84.

Recent *New York Times* and *Washington Post* articles.

Semiconductor Industry Association (SIA). *International Microelectronics Challenge*, p. 35. Quoted in Department of Commerce, *A Report on the US Semiconductor Industry*. Washington: Government Printing Office, 1979, p. 29.

USTR Computer Group.

CHAPTER 20

The Economic Effects of Complete Elimination of Post-Tokyo Round Tariffs

Alan V. Deardorff and Robert M. Stern

As the result of the Tokyo Round and preceding rounds of multilateral negotiations, tariff rates in the major industrial countries have been reduced to relatively low levels. It seems natural in this light to ask whether tariffs might not be eliminated altogether. In order to evaluate this question, we need estimates of the important economic effects involved by sector and country. The purpose of our chapter is to provide such estimates, using the University of Michigan disaggregated model of world production and trade.

Our chapter is organized as follows. We first consider post-Tokyo Round tariffs by sector and country, the codes covering selected nontariff barriers (NTBs), and the NTBs that were not dealt with in the Tokyo Round. We next discuss briefly the political economy of protection and implications for post-Tokyo Round negotiating options. A brief description of the University of Michigan model will then be given, along with the results of our analysis and some concluding comments.

The Tokyo Round Negotiations

The Tokyo Round of Multilateral Trade Negotiations (MTN) was concluded in 1979. Since then, the process of implementation has involved the first phases of tariff reductions, which are to be spread over a period of up to eight years. In addition, a series of codes covering particular NTBs has been established under GATT auspices, and these codes are currently operational.

TABLE 20.1   TOKYO ROUND OFFER RATE TARIFFS ON INDUSTRIAL
PRODUCTS, BY SECTOR, MAJOR INDUSTRIAL
COUNTRIES
(percentage; weighted by own-country imports, excluding
petroleum)

	Australia[a]	Austria	Benelux	Canada[a]	Denmark	Finland	France	West Germany
Textiles	21.2	15.9	7.2	16.7	8.7	22.5	7.3	7.4
Wearing apparel	61.8	36.2	13.4	24.2	13.2	35.5	13.2	13.4
Leather products	20.3	7.7	2.5	6.3	1.8	9.3	1.6	3.2
Footwear	33.8	23.4	11.4	21.9	11.5	17.4	11.3	11.7
Wood products	12.5	3.7	2.4	3.2	3.4	0.4	2.4	2.9
Furniture and fixtures	31.2	22.1	5.6	14.3	5.5	5.5[b]	5.6	5.6
Paper and paper products	7.1	12.3	6.9	6.7	7.9	4.5	5.5	5.2
Printing and publishing	1.8	1.5	1.5	1.0	2.8	1.1	2.2	2.1
Chemicals	5.4	4.7	8.0	7.5	8.5	1.8	7.6	8.0
Rubber products	11.2	9.9	4.2	6.7	4.4	13.5	3.5	3.8
Nonmetal mineral products	11.5	5.9	3.7	6.4	5.0	2.9	4.7	3.6
Glass and glass products	15.2	12.9	8.0	7.2	7.5	22.3	7.4	7.9
Iron and steel	10.8	5.8	4.6	5.4	5.5	4.2	4.9	4.7
Nonferrous metals	4.2	3.3	1.6	2.0	6.6	0.8	2.6	1.9
Metal products	23.7	10.4	5.4	8.5	5.5	7.7	5.4	5.5
Nonelectrical machinery	13.9	6.4	4.3	4.5	4.4	6.1	4.4	4.5
Electrical machinery	21.6	14.7	7.4	5.8	7.1	6.0[b]	7.7	8.3
Transportation equipment	21.2	22.1	7.9	1.6	7.2	3.8[b]	7.9	7.7
Miscellaneous manufactures	12.8	8.7	3.0	5.4	6.1	12.6	5.8	5.6
All industries	16.5	12.1	5.9	5.2	6.6	7.1	6.0	6.3

In table 20.1, we provide an indication of the average post-Tokyo
Round nominal tariff levels by major industrial sector and country.
These are the tariffs that will exist once the annually phased reductions have been completed in 1987. The tariffs are weighted averages
based on own-country imports, excluding petroleum, for 1976, which
was the reference year used for the MTN and is the year that we
shall use as the benchmark for our model calculations below. The

Ireland	*Italy*	*Japan*	*Netherlands*	*New Zealand*	*Norway*	*Sweden*	*Switzerland*	*United Kingdom*	*United States*	*All*
7.8	5.6	3.3	8.5	12.3	13.3	10.3	6.6	6.7	9.2	8.5
13.2	13.2	13.8	13.5	58.5	21.7	14.2	12.4	13.3	22.7	17.5
1.8	0.7	3.0	3.0	15.3	5.8	4.0	2.1	1.2	4.2	3.0
11.9	10.4	15.7	11.2	40.7	21.7	13.7	9.0	12.5	8.8	12.1
2.5	0.8	0.3	2.8	11.4	1.6	0.7	3.2	3.1	1.7	1.9
5.7	5.6	5.1	5.6	38.3	5.1	4.0	9.2	5.6	4.1[b]	7.3
8.0	2.6	2.1	6.2	20.5	1.9	2.4	4.3	4.9	0.2	4.2
1.5	1.8	0.1	2.2	1.1	4.3	0.2	0.7	2.1	0.7	1.5
7.6	8.1	4.8	8.1	8.1	6.2	4.8	0.9	7.9	2.4	6.7
3.7	2.7	1.1	4.1	9.5	6.6	6.1	1.7	2.7	2.5	4.1
4.5	2.8	0.5	3.3	12.7	2.4	2.8	2.5	2.4	5.3	4.0
7.3	7.6	5.1	7.5	13.5	8.0	7.1	3.1	7.9	6.2	7.9
5.9	3.5	2.8	5.6	5.2	1.7	3.7	1.7	4.7	3.6	4.4
6.5	1.8	1.1	3.6	4.1	0.9	0.7	2.4	1.7	0.7	1.6
5.4	5.5	5.2	5.4	26.5	4.4	4.0	2.8	5.6	4.8	6.3
4.3	4.5	4.4	4.3	22.1	5.2	3.5	1.2	4.2	3.3	4.7
7.2	8.0	4.3	7.8	19.6	6.9	4.5	1.6	8.1	4.4	7.1
10.2	8.8	1.5	9.0	26.8	2.2	5.1	6.1	7.2	2.5	6.0
6.5	5.8	4.6	5.2	18.2	7.4	4.6	1.1	3.0	4.2	4.7
6.9	5.4	2.9	6.8	16.7	5.2	5.0	3.1	5.2	4.3	5.8

Source: Based on data supplied by office of US Trade Representative.
a. Prevailing rates, which include unilateral reductions in post-Kennedy Round tariff rates.
b. Estimated from incomplete data.

weighted post-Tokyo Round average tariff on industrial products is 4.3 percent for the United States, 5.2 percent to 6.9 percent for the nine-member European Economic Community (EEC-nine), and 2.9 percent for Japan. Canada, Finland, Norway, Sweden, and Switzerland have comparably low average tariffs, while those for Australia, Austria, and New Zealand are significantly higher. There is a fair amount of dispersion across sectors, with the highest rates generally in wearing apparel, footwear, and textiles. This in turn suggests that tariff escalation is still present in the tariff structures of the major industrial countries and that post-Tokyo Round effective rates of protection are in many cases higher than the nominal rates shown.

Much attention was devoted in the Tokyo Round to the discussion and formulation of codes and agreements concerning nontariff measures. The principal items negotiated include codes covering customs valuation, government procurement, import-licensing procedures, subsidies, and countervailing duties and standards. There was an attempt to draft a safeguards code governing policies to deal with market disruption due to sudden upsurges in imports, but agreement could not be reached on the principle of applying safeguards selectively by product and supplying country. Besides these NTB codes, the Tokyo Round agreement contained provisions for reform of the GATT framework, arrangements designed to encourage more trade in selected agricultural products, and a sectoral agreement to remove trade impediments affecting civil aircraft.

The failure to negotiate an acceptable safeguards code in the Tokyo Round was not its only omission. The Tokyo Round left intact a wide variety of NTBs governing imports of agricultural products and foodstuffs, textiles and wearing apparel, footwear, iron and steel products, consumer electronic products, and shipbuilding. These NTBs are especially important in the United States and many of the other industrial countries. To the extent that imports especially from developing countries are affected, the Tokyo Round may be of relatively little significance to these countries. We shall return to this point below.

The Political Economy of Protection and Post-Tokyo Round Negotiating Options

The post-Tokyo Round tariff rates for the particular sectors and countries listed in table 20.1 reflect a variety of historical circumstances involving protection and the changes that countries have negotiated multilaterally in successive GATT rounds. It is of interest in this regard to note the work by Baldwin (1981) on the political economy of protection in order to obtain some insight into the forces that shaped the US negotiating position in the Tokyo Round. According to Baldwin, the demand for protection by an industry will depend upon various industry characteristics that determine the extent of its lobbying efforts and the size of the losses that may be experienced if existing protection is reduced. The supply of protection reflects the government's perceptions of voter support and the pressures brought to bear by the interested public on their elected representatives.

Baldwin estimated empirically the determinants of several variants of the Tokyo Round tariff reductions, including the actual average tariff cuts, the average percentage reduction in the prices of domestically produced goods, the difference between the Swiss formula and the rates proposed by the United States, and the proportion of Swiss-formula cuts actually offered. In general, his regression results suggested that the demand for protection across industries in the United States reflected already high tariff rates, a small ratio of exports to shipments, a high import-penetration ratio, a low ratio of value added to shipments, and a high labor share of value added. On the supply side, the proportion of unskilled labor in an industry, the level of industry employment, and the level of import penetration were apparently instrumental in shaping government responses. There was also evidence that industries tended to be protected by both tariffs and NTBs.[1]

These results are indicative of the forces at work in the United States that shaped the outcome of the Tokyo Round negotiations. Presumably, similar forces would be present in the other major industrial countries, although allowance would have to be made for differences in industry structure and in the mode and responsiveness of government officials to protectionist pressures. If post-Tokyo Round tariffs were to be eliminated, a major effort would be required by governments to withstand the pressures from those sectors that might lose the most. It would be necessary furthermore to prevent countries from using NTBs to make up for what they might lose from tariff elimination.

The question of NTBs is one perhaps that should be addressed in its own right. We indicated earlier that some significant progress was

[1] Cline (1982) has estimated a logit model for NTB protection for the United States, Canada, United Kingdom, France, and Germany, using data for the late 1970s. That model fits best for the US-related NTB protection to import penetration and the sectoral share in total manufacturing labor.

made in the Tokyo Round in terms of the various NTB codes that
were negotiated, but that practically nothing was done to reduce or
eliminate existing NTBs covering a wide variety of agricultural and
industrial products. The domestic interest groups that benefit from
NTBs are obviously politically very important and deeply entrenched,
and governments have been, it seems, increasingly responsive to these
pressures. The stakes involved may indeed be substantial. Brown and
Whalley (1980) have estimated, for example, that the abolition of
existing NTBs in the United States, EEC, and Japan would lead to
an estimated increase in world economic welfare of $16 billion per
year (in 1973 prices). This is in contrast to an estimated gain in welfare
of $1.5 billion per year as the result of the tariff reductions negotiated
in the Tokyo Round.

It is beyond the scope of our chapter to deal with negotiating
options for reducing or eliminating NTBs. We shall therefore take
NTBs as given and proceed with our analysis of the economic effects
of tariff elimination. In this regard, we shall abstract from the measures that governments might find necessary to engender support domestically for the elimination of tariffs. By the same token, our results
for individual sectors could be helpful in devising policies for adjustment for those sectors that will be affected adversely and in seeking support from the ones that will benefit from tariff elimination.

Before turning to our results, a brief description of the model on
which they rest is worthwhile.

The Michigan Model of World Production and Trade

The estimated economic effects of complete tariff elimination to
be presented below are based on a disaggregated microeconomic
model of world production and trade that we have developed for this
and related purposes. The technical details of the model are contained
in Deardorff and Stern (1981). Here we shall describe briefly the
main features of the model for those not familiar with it.

Description of the Model

The model incorporates supply and demand functions and market-
clearing conditions for 22 tradable industries, plus markets for another
7 nontradable industries, in each of 34 countries. The number of
industries was dictated by data availability with the 22 tradable industries classified according to three-digit International Standard Industrial Classification (ISIC) categories and the nontradable industries classified by one-digit ISIC categories. The industries are identified

by name and ISIC number in table 20.3. Originally, the model covered the 18 major industrial countries listed in table 20.1[2] We have subsequently added 16 major developing countries: Argentina, Brazil, Chile, Colombia, Greece, Hong Kong, India, Israel, South Korea, Mexico, Portugal, Singapore, Spain, Taiwan, Turkey, and Yugoslavia.[3] There is also an aggregated sector representing the rest of the world.

The supply and demand functions interact with one another on both national and world markets to determine equilibrium values of prices and quantities traded and produced. Labor-demand functions also determine employment in each industry and country. The model abstracts from such macroeconomic determinants of aggregate output and employment as levels of government spending, taxes, and the money stock. Instead, for the calculations to be reported here, aggregate expenditure is adjusted endogenously to maintain aggregate employment constant in each country.[4]

The size of the model precludes our obtaining a meaningful and general analytical solution. We have therefore restricted the functional forms to ones that have been estimated by others using econometric techniques. Within these constraints, however, we have tried to select functional forms, which permit a rich variety of behavior and which experience suggests provide a reasonable description of economic reality.

In order to specify the supply and demand functions of the model, we needed data on trade, tariffs, NTBs, production, and employment

---

[2] The 18-country version of the model was used to analyze changes in tariffs and other trade policies in Deardorff, et al. (1977 and 1979b), to analyze the industrial sensitivity of exchange rate changes in Deardorff, et al. (1979a), and to make a preliminary analysis of the effects of the Tokyo Round in Deardorff and Stern (1979).

[3] The present 34-country version of the model has been used in Deardorff and Stern (1980, 1983a, and 1983b) to analyze changes in trade and employment, assess the structure of protection under fixed and flexible exchange rates in the major industrial countries, and analyze the economic effects of the Tokyo Round.

[4] This is a change from what we have done in earlier applications of the model for this and other purposes, where we have held nominal aggregate expenditure essentially constant. By endogenizing expenditure in this way, we hope to direct attention more to the sector effects of tariff elimination than to the effects on economic aggregates. The latter, to which our model is not well suited, depend more on choices about accompanying macroeconomic policy than on the intersectoral and country interactions focused on here.

for each of these industries and countries. All of these data were available or could be constructed readily for the industrial countries, except for NTBs. For want of a better measure, we have represented NTBs in terms of the fraction of 1976 trade that was covered by NTBs of all kinds in particular sectors and countries. We then model these sectors as somewhat less sensitive to tariff changes than would otherwise be the case. Specifically, the model includes, for each industry and country, an endogenous tariff-equivalent variable that adjusts to reduce changes in imports to only a fraction of what they would be in the absence of NTBs. That fraction is taken to be the fraction of trade not covered by NTBs in 1976.

For the developing countries, we have data on trade, production, and employment by sector, but there are no systematic and easily accessible data on their tariffs and NTBs. This may not be much of a drawback if we can assume that these countries would make few, if any, changes in their existing policies in response to the elimination of post-Tokyo Round tariffs by the major industrial countries. We have, however, attempted to capture important elements of existing nontariff controls in the developing countries by modeling a system of import licensing with exchange rate pegging as characterizing the foreign exchange régime in most of these countries. We assume in this connection that all the industrial countries, except for New Zealand, follow a régime of flexible exchange rates.

In addition to the foregoing data, we required estimates of import-demand elasticities and elasticities of substitution between capital and labor in each industry. These estimates were obtained from the literature. Finally, to implement the model, we needed input-output tables for each of the countries. Limitations of time and resources have prevented us to date from collecting such tables for all countries. We therefore have used the 1972 input-output table for the US economy and applied it to describe technology in all the industrial countries, and the 1970 input-output table for Brazil and applied it to all the developing countries. This undoubtedly introduces some errors into our analysis, the size and importance of which cannot be assessed until the tables for other countries are available for comparison.

Solution Procedure

Since tariffs constitute exogenous variables in our model, the elimination of post-Tokyo Round tariffs is entered as changes in these variables. The assumption is that the tariffs will be eliminated all at once rather than being phased out over a period of years. The model is then solved by computer to obtain the resulting percentage changes in all of the variables that are determined endogenously within the system.

Absolute changes in variables are determined by multiplying these percentage changes times the initial 1976 levels taken as the reference point for all calculations. In addition, we calculate the change in economic welfare by country using the results of the model to estimate changes in consumer and producer surplus and tariff revenues.

Results

The overall results are summarized in table 20.2 for the major industrial and developing countries. The principal findings are as follows.

Based upon 1976 levels, exports will rise by over $29 billion for all the countries listed, which is about a 3.9 percent increase. All of this increase is accounted for by the major industrial countries, since the exports of the major developing countries fall by a small $66 million. US exports rise by $4.5 billion and imports by $3.9 billion.[5]

We have already noted that expenditure has been endogenized to prevent any aggregate change in employment from occurring. As an indicator of labor-market dislocation, we have therefore calculated the "gross change in employment" in the third column of table 20.2. This is the sum of all positive sectoral employment changes and is also shown as a percentage of each country's 1976 labor force in column 4. The former figure represents the total number of workers in each country who would have to change jobs if post-Tokyo Round tariffs were eliminated. It includes those who might have to move only between the export and home sectors of their industries. For the United States, the gross change in employment is 141 thousand workers, which is 0.16 percent of the 1976 US labor force. The total for the European Community (EC) is 855 thousand workers, which is 0.85 percent of 1976 employment. For individual EC-member countries, the percentages range from 0.68 percent for the United Kingdom to 2.03 percent for Belgium-Luxembourg. The total for Japan

[5] As noted in Deardorff and Stern (1983b), the Tokyo Round reductions in tariffs and selected NTBs, chiefly government procurement and certain agricultural concessions, were estimated to increase exports by $13 billion for all the countries. For the United States, exports were estimated to rise by $3.3 billion and imports by $2.3 billion.

TABLE 20.2 SUMMARY OF EFFECTS OF ELIMINATION OF TARIFFS
REMAINING AFTER THE TOKYO ROUND, MAJOR
INDUSTRIAL AND DEVELOPING COUNTRIES

	Change in		Gross change in employment[a]	
	Exports (million dollars)	Imports (million dollars)	(thousand workers)	(percentage)
Industrial countries				
Australia	1,188.3	1,966.7	42.53	0.73
Austria	1,308.9	1,272.5	82.06	2.78
Canada	1,739.4	1,745.8	46.54	0.49
European Community				
Belgium-Luxembourg	1,431.6	1,416.2	78.65	2.03
Denmark	649.7	641.0	36.82	1.53
France	3,246.5	3,329.4	147.79	0.71
Germany	4,888.6	5,080.0	217.65	0.89
Ireland	233.4	233.0	14.65	1.43
Italy	1,739.7	1,710.6	132.58	0.70
Netherlands	1,877.1	1,942.1	59.65	1.31
United Kingdom	3,263.3	3,199.4	166.98	0.68
Total EC	17,330.0	17,551.8	854.76	0.85
Finland	605.1	395.2	34.63	1.62
Japan	1,438.8	1,658.3	116.98	0.22
New Zealand	− 148.8	− 157.9	4.63	0.38
Norway	319.2	372.7	13.18	0.74
Sweden	769.6	666.4	31.89	0.78
Switzerland	163.3	477.1	10.68	0.38
United States	4,467.2	3,926.2	141.31	0.16
Total industrial	29,180.9	29,874.8	1,379.20	0.51
Developing countries				
Argentina	10.5	58.3	17.78	0.17
Brazil	31.0	84.5	44.37	0.11
Chile	1.4	− 18.8	6.59	0.24
Colombia	7.8	29.1	17.48	0.22
Greece	− 32.2	− 64.9	7.16	0.18
Hong Kong	− 0.4	− 36.3	3.98	0.30
India	− 13.5	− 21.5	93.74	0.04
Israel	− 3.1	− 12.7	1.30	0.12
South Korea	30.0	25.3	19.51	0.16
Mexico	− 29.0	− 27.2	24.92	0.14
Portugal	− 21.3	− 50.6	7.53	0.24
Singapore	2.7	− 24.0	2.14	0.25
Spain	− 53.2	− 82.7	10.00	0.08
Taiwan	37.6	30.4	15.93	0.28
Turkey	− 24.5	− 35.3	11.35	0.08
Yugoslavia	− 9.9	− 18.2	5.32	0.11
Total developing countries	− 66.1	− 164.6	289.09	0.08
All countries	29,114.8	29,710.2	1,668.28	0.26

	Change in welfare		Percentage change in effective exchange rate[b]	Percentage change in prices[c]
	(million dollars)	(percentage of GDP)		
Industrial countries				
Australia	729.5	0.72	0.00	−1.05
Austria	−472.8	−1.17	0.26	−3.01
Canada	249.3	0.13	0.66	−0.76
European Community				
Belgium-Luxembourg	−664.6	−0.94	2.08	−3.31
Denmark	−378.1	−0.92	0.88	−2.30
France	−511.4	−0.15	−0.54	−0.95
Germany	−1,039.4	−0.23	−0.21	−1.44
Ireland	−17.7	−0.22	1.23	−2.31
Italy	25.4	0.01	−0.31	−0.84
Netherlands	−91.1	−0.10	1.01	−2.44
United Kingdom	1,386.7	0.63	−0.25	−0.72
Total EC	−1,290.4	−0.09	−0.07	−1.32
Finland	−218.8	−0.77	0.00	−1.64
Japan	704.9	0.12	−0.29	−0.39
New Zealand	−7.9	−0.06	−0.00	−0.79
Norway	7.2	0.02	0.00	−0.94
Sweden	−274.9	−0.37	0.00	−1.12
Switzerland	292.4	0.51	0.08	−0.70
United States	1,045.6	0.06	−0.72	−0.10
Total industrial	764.1	0.02	−0.32	−0.67
Developing countries				
Argentina	17.2	0.03	0.00	−0.30
Brazil	−37.1	−0.03	−0.00	−0.12
Chile	−21.2	−0.25	−0.57	−0.14
Colombia	7.0	0.05	0.00	−0.37
Greece	2.4	0.01	0.00	0.28
Hong Kong	−35.2	−0.38	−0.15	0.07
India	−26.8	−0.03	0.00	0.01
Israel	2.8	0.02	−0.12	0.11
South Korea	11.0	0.04	0.00	−0.18
Mexico	−63.7	−0.08	0.52	−0.07
Portugal	−4.4	−0.03	−0.00	0.45
Singapore	−8.0	−0.14	0.00	0.18
Spain	−19.9	−0.02	0.00	0.06
Taiwan	5.0	0.03	0.00	−0.32
Turkey	−1.7	−0.00	0.00	0.05
Yugoslavia	28.0	0.09	−0.13	0.05
Total developing *countries*	−144.7	−0.02	0.04	−0.04
All countries	619.4	0.01	−0.27	−0.58

a. Refers to sum of changes in the home and export sectors within industries.
b. Positive = Appreciation.
c. Index of import and home prices.

is 117 thousand workers, which is 0.22 percent of the 1976 labor force.[6]

It will be recalled that we have assumed that tariffs will be eliminated all at once. If instead the elimination were phased in over a period of several years, the adjustment of employment might not add materially to normal labor-market turnover, so that any serious disruptions in labor markets would be less likely to occur. However, as noted below, our disaggregated results by sector do not fully support such a conclusion since there are numerous sectors in which the relative changes in employment are sufficiently large to suggest that there could indeed be difficulties in adjustment. As for the major developing countries, the employment changes recorded in table 20.2 are all comparatively small.

Economic welfare will be increased in the United States, Japan, Australia, Canada, Italy, United Kingdom, and Switzerland and reduced in the remaining industrial countries.[7] The reductions in welfare may be due to adverse terms-of-trade effects. That is, when tariffs are eliminated, world prices (exclusive of tariffs) will rise and consumer prices will fall. Depending upon the composition of a country's trade, it is possible that the former effect may predominate. Seven of the developing countries experience a small increase in welfare and the remaining nine a reduction.

The US dollar will depreciate on an effective basis by 0.72 percent, as will the French franc (0.54 percent), German mark (0.21 percent), Italian lira (0.31 percent), British pound (0.25 percent), and Japanese yen (0.29 percent). The remaining industrial-country currencies will appreciate, with the changes most notable for Belgium-Luxembourg (2.08 percent), Ireland (1.23 percent), and the Netherlands (1.01 percent).[8] The exchange rates of most developing countries will remain more or less constant because of controls over foreign exchange licensing.

Import and therefore consumer prices fall by a small 0.10 percent in the United States while the declines for most other industrial coun-

---

[6] The estimated gross changes in employment attributed to the Tokyo Round were 126 thousand workers for the United States, 374 thousand workers for the European Community, and 34 thousand workers for Japan.

[7] The welfare effects attributed to the Tokyo Round, which included both tariff reductions and the liberalization of government procurement and some agricultural concessions, were positive for all the industrial countries except Austria and Denmark.

[8] The estimated changes in exchange rates due to the Tokyo Round were all relatively small in comparison.

tries are significantly greater, ranging from around 1 percent to more than 3 percent.[9] For the developing countries, prices will fall only in Argentina, Brazil, Colombia, South Korea, Mexico, and Taiwan, but these changes and others elsewhere are fairly small.

The country results in table 20.2 mask much industry detail. Indeed, one of the most important features of our model is that we can calculate the absolute and relative employment effects by sector and country. The net changes in employment across the 22 tradable and 7 nontradable sectors in each of the 34 countries are recorded in table 20.3. There are net increases as well as reductions in particular sectors. In the United States, for example, the largest increases are recorded, in thousands of workers, for agriculture (45), transport equipment (17), nonelectric machinery (11), electric machinery (9), and chemicals (7). There are negative employment effects in wearing apparel (-24), textiles (-10), miscellaneous manufactures (-4), nonmetallic mineral produces (-2), and footwear (-2). All of the nontradable sectors except mining and quarrying show net declines in employment. This result is prevalent in most of the countries in the model, and it can be explained by the general substitution towards tradable goods and away from nontradable goods due to the reduction in the prices of tradable goods that would result from the elimination of tariffs.

The effects on the individual sectors in the other countries can be similarly discerned from the detailed results in table 20.3. In West Germany, for example, the increases are concentrated in textiles and wearing apparel, chemicals, and durable manufactures and the declines in agriculture, nonmetallic mineral products, and to a small extent in some other tradable sectors. France has increases in agriculture and food products, textiles and wearing apparel, and durable manufactures, and small declines in several other tradable sectors. The United Kingdom has increases in agriculture and food products, chemicals, fuel products, nonmetallic mineral products, and miscellaneous manufactures and declines especially in textiles and clothing, iron and steel, and transport equipment. Japan has increases in food products, textiles, wood products, rubber products, and durable manufactures and declines especially in agriculture and wearing apparel. Thus, there are some notable differences across the industrial countries in terms of the industries that would experience net employment increases or declines as the result of tariff elimination.

---

[9] All the price reductions due to the Tokyo Round were less than one percent except for Belgium-Luxembourg (-1.22 percent).

TABLE 20.3   NET CHANGES IN EMPLOYMENT DUE TO THE
ELIMINATION OF POST-TOKYO ROUND TARIFFS, BY ISIC
SECTOR, MAJOR INDUSTRIAL AND DEVELOPING
COUNTRIES
(thousand man-years)

	ISIC Code	Australia	Austria	Benelux	Canada
Traded goods					
Agriculture, forestry, and fishing	(1)	10.876	− 6.298	1.576	7.832
Food, beverages and tobacco	(310)	3.260	− 0.905	1.124	− 0.131
Textiles	(321)	8.974	16.989	21.453	− 2.102
Wearing apparel	(322)	− 3.379	20.161	29.082	− 3.998
Leather products	(323)	2.652	1.585	0.119	1.496
Footwear	(324)	− 0.271	5.193	0.042	− 0.195
Wood products	(331)	− 1.447	0.930	− 0.048	0.496
Furniture and fixtures	(332)	− 0.557	− 1.892	− 0.028	− 0.043
Paper and paper products	(341)	− 0.701	2.790	0.685	2.229
Printing and publishing	(342)	− 0.078	− 0.179	− 1.188	− 0.428
Chemicals	(35A)	0.481	0.969	5.926	− 2.310
Petroleum and related products	(35B)	− 0.032	− 0.265	− 1.664	− 0.453
Rubber products	(355)	− 2.339	− 0.751	− 0.053	− 1.128
Nonmetallic mineral products	(36A)	− 0.965	− 1.251	− 3.010	− 0.602
Glass and glass products	(362)	− 0.540	− 0.117	− 0.543	− 0.365
Iron and steel	(371)	− 1.037	2.431	− 1.550	− 0.170
Nonferrous metals	(372)	3.875	0.502	− 0.977	10.609
Metal products	(381)	− 5.060	− 2.404	− 0.199	− 2.718
Nonelectrical machinery	(382)	− 0.539	3.266	− 0.532	1.603
Electrical machinery	(383)	− 4.396	− 0.305	0.460	− 0.351
Transportation equipment	(384)	− 7.457	− 1.502	6.406	6.597
Miscellaneous manufactures	(38A)	− 1.907	3.719	− 0.117	0.116
Total traded		− 0.588	42.665	56.965	15.984
Nontraded goods					
Mining and quarrying	(2)	2.124	− 0.746	− 3.021	0.029
Electricity, Gas, and Water	(4)	− 0.087	− 1.207	− 1.194	− 0.463
Construction	(5)	2.209	− 4.906	− 3.809	0.961
Wholesale and retail trade	(6)	− 3.553	− 14.428	− 17.305	− 5.897
Transportation, storage, and communications	(7)	− 0.428	− 3.495	− 5.093	− 1.659
Finance, insurance, and real estate	(8)	− 1.392	− 5.565	− 8.557	− 2.930
Commercial, social and personal services	(9)	1.715	− 12.319	− 17.986	− 6.025
Total nontraded		0.588	− 42.665	− 56.965	− 15.984
Total, all industries		− 0.000	− 0.000	− 0.000	− 0.000

Denmark	Finland	France	West Germany	Ireland
5.808	− 7.474	20.786	− 3.319	3.953
3.380	− 0.127	3.844	3.882	0.901
3.635	3.758	12.264	23.021	2.159
6.671	18.808	14.989	10.879	2.450
0.467	1.369	1.307	2.354	0.050
0.372	2.146	1.961	− 0.890	− 0.060
− 0.194	0.467	− 1.369	− 1.574	− 0.100
1.770	0.786	− 0.682	3.539	− 0.022
− 0.086	0.749	− 0.925	− 0.648	− 0.168
− 0.356	− 0.382	− 0.502	− 0.343	− 0.119
0.085	0.346	− 2.746	11.656	− 0.001
− 0.116	− 0.022	− 0.037	− 0.409	− 0.102
− 0.107	− 1.289	2.046	− 0.016	− 0.009
− 0.960	− 0.418	− 2.013	− 3.595	− 0.303
− 0.063	− 0.102	− 0.271	− 0.673	− 0.058
0.148	− 0.166	2.433	− 0.450	− 0.213
0.182	− 0.110	0.314	0.029	0.587
0.200	− 0.793	0.745	6.525	0.322
1.399	0.221	8.343	7.127	0.121
0.743	0.186	3.551	8.692	0.041
1.606	1.324	10.316	23.939	− 0.314
2.102	− 0.613	0.484	14.038	0.564
26.686	18.666	74.837	103.762	9.677
− 1.194	− 0.448	− 0.174	− 3.796	− 0.403
− 0.980	− 0.645	− 1.903	− 2.763	− 0.387
− 1.628	− 1.875	− 6.473	− 9.213	− 0.766
− 6.686	− 4.846	− 24.860	− 29.808	− 3.311
− 2.240	− 1.583	− 5.472	− 8.341	− 0.820
− 4.045	− 2.618	− 12.735	− 16.554	− 0.814
− 9.914	− 6.651	− 23.221	− 33.287	− 3.176
− 26.686	− 18.666	− 74.838	− 103.762	− 9.677
− 0.000	− 0.000	− 0.000	− 0.000	− 0.000

TABLE 20.3 (Continued)

	ISIC Code	Italy	Japan	Nether-lands	New Zealand
Traded goods					
Agriculture, forestery, and fishing	(1)	−20.109	−64.411	7.173	0.508
Food, beverages, and tobacco	(310)	2.199	13.001	3.662	−0.094
Textiles	(321)	10.920	5.940	12.867	−2.497
Wearing apparel	(322)	26.264	−8.194	10.716	−0.013
Leather products	(323)	3.274	0.005	0.402	−0.773
Footwear	(324)	24.827	−0.363	0.485	−0.019
Wood products	(331)	−0.113	5.064	−0.971	−0.069
Furniture and fixtures	(332)	4.578	0.255	0.288	0.013
Paper and paper products	(341)	−0.522	1.231	0.109	−0.196
Printing and publishing	(342)	−0.361	1.037	−0.823	0.173
Chemicals	(35A)	−10.122	0.471	4.044	0.394
Petroleum and related products	(35B)	0.212	−1.899	−0.477	0.020
Rubber products	(355)	0.942	4.209	−0.080	0.099
Nonmetallic mineral products	(36A)	−0.562	1.789	−1.221	0.073
Glass and glass products	(362)	−0.733	0.326	0.225	0.031
Iron and steel	(371)	−0.770	10.027	−1.629	0.163
Nonferrous metals	(372)	−0.331	−0.198	0.775	−0.429
Metal products	(381)	3.255	3.135	−0.688	0.178
Nonelectrical machinery	(382)	1.260	3.584	0.038	0.079
Electrical machinery	(383)	−0.241	11.206	1.157	0.245
Transportation equipment	(384)	8.701	20.163	2.957	0.406
Miscellaneous manufactures	(38A)	0.316	13.818	2.190	0.088
Total traded		52.882	20.196	41.199	−1.619
Nontraded goods					
Mining and quarrying	(2)	−0.340	−0.121	−1.075	−0.017
Electricity, gas and water	(4)	−2.496	0.224	−0.898	−0.003
Construction	(5)	−7.167	−4.208	−3.121	−0.081
Wholesale and retail trade	(6)	−14.336	−9.850	−12.271	0.658
Transportation, storage, and communications	(7)	−4.339	−1.747	−3.300	0.033
Finance, insurance, and real estate	(8)	−12.322	−3.869	−6.578	0.454
Commercial, social, and personal services	(9)	−11.882	−0.625	−13.957	0.575
Total nontraded		−52.882	−20.196	−41.199	1.619
Total, all industries		−0.000	0.000	−0.000	0.000

Norway	Sweden	Switzerland	United Kingdom	United States
1.441	− 0.075	0.181	6.642	44.711
− 0.119	− 0.630	0.552	10.806	0.204
1.581	2.420	− 1.337	− 10.610	− 9.953
0.621	4.756	− 0.177	− 2.521	− 24.044
0.393	0.428	− 0.205	− 0.165	− 0.121
0.270	0.845	− 0.020	− 1.547	− 1.970
− 0.097	− 0.016	− 0.407	− 1.356	0.895
0.124	1.067	− 0.424	3.535	0.066
0.242	0.310	− 0.401	− 2.269	2.501
− 0.538	− 0.262	0.032	0.385	0.167
0.135	0.063	1.157	5.860	6.972
− 0.033	− 0.039	− 0.052	5.266	1.149
− 0.092	− 0.762	− 0.100	0.522	− 0.070
− 0.110	− 0.492	0.285	10.567	− 2.380
− 0.101	− 0.083	− 0.066	5.023	0.004
0.290	0.487	− 0.279	− 2.192	1.245
0.157	− 0.113	− 0.515	0.080	− 0.075
− 0.297	0.931	0.500	1.348	1.788
1.125	1.751	− 0.782	− 0.831	10.633
0.015	2.660	1.412	2.019	9.483
2.664	5.877	− 0.174	− 73.130	16.596
0.208	1.598	− 0.335	18.810	− 4.245
6.879	20.721	− 1.746	− 23.758	52.558
− 0.052	− 0.225	− 0.978	15.177	3.957
− 0.192	− 0.431	0.888	1.222	− 0.948
− 0.314	− 1.516	0.758	2.406	− 0.960
− 2.159	− 5.391	0.327	− 7.743	− 21.942
− 0.738	− 1.564	0.096	10.404	− 1.456
− 0.878	− 3.109	0.313	4.670	− 9.029
− 2.545	− 8.485	1.141	− 2.379	− 22.181
− 6.879	− 20.271	1.746	23.758	− 52.558
− 0.000	− 0.000	0.000	− 0.000	0.000

TABLE 20.3 (Continued)

	ISIC Code	Australia	Austria	Benelux	Canada
Traded goods					
Agriculture, forestry, and fishing	(1)	7.688	33.163	4.084	10.509
Food, beverages, and tobacco	(310)	2.293	3.179	−0.656	−0.171
Textiles	(321)	−7.883	−1.501	−0.300	−1.255
Wearing apparel	(322)	0.771	−0.467	−0.008	−0.109
Leather products	(323)	−0.689	−0.936	−0.048	−0.158
Footwear	(324)	0.393	0.109	−0.011	0.082
Wood products	(331)	0.321	−0.253	−0.003	0.004
Furniture and fixtures	(332)	0.483	−0.051	0.001	0.059
Paper and paper products	(341)	−0.267	−0.355	0.090	−0.299
Printing and publishing	(342)	−0.038	−0.199	−0.013	−0.125
Chemicals	(35A)	−0.741	−1.501	0.286	−1.411
Petroleum and related products	(35B)	−0.496	−0.207	0.030	0.000
Rubber products	(355)	−0.039	−0.255	0.088	−0.488
Nonmetallic mineral products	(36A)	−0.176	−0.532	0.058	−0.171
Glass and glass products	(362)	−0.025	−0.080	0.015	−0.106
Iron and steel	(371)	−3.301	−1.793	0.029	−1.610
Nonferrous metals	(372)	−0.952	−0.701	−0.079	−0.540
Metal products	(381)	0.028	−0.150	0.255	0.354
Nonelectrical machinery	(382)	−0.130	−0.811	−0.027	−0.009
Electrical machinery	(383)	−0.027	−0.204	0.041	−0.009
Transportation equipment	(384)	0.554	0.164	0.181	−0.102
Miscellaneous manufactures	(38A)	−0.049	−0.739	0.047	−0.192
Total traded		−2.282	25.879	4.061	4.252
Nontraded goods					
Mining and quarrying	(2)	−0.397	−1.445	0.925	−0.033
Electricity, gas, and water	(4)	−0.299	−1.399	−0.076	−0.199
Construction	(5)	0.563	−1.805	−0.726	0.261
Wholesale and retail trade	(6)	−1.072	−8.018	−1.285	−4.010
Transportation, storage, and communications	(7)	−0.496	−2.056	−0.608	−0.766
Finance, insurance, and real estate	(8)	−0.446	−8.548	−0.355	−0.480
Commercial, social and personal services	(9)	4.430	−2.608	−1.937	0.976
Total nontraded		2.282	−25.879	−4.061	−4.252
Total, all industries		−0.000	−0.000	−0.000	−0.000

Greece	Hong Kong	India	Israel	South Korea
3.621	0.138	69.407	0.641	−1.019
−0.268	−0.261	8.672	−0.364	0.223
−0.855	−1.731	−27.467	−0.274	−3.030
−0.841	1.275	−0.497	−0.037	1.573
−3.322	−0.288	−5.375	−0.078	−0.641
−0.223	0.110	0.319	0.011	0.857
0.219	−0.020	−0.110	−0.017	0.154
−0.131	0.253	0.317	0.013	0.713
0.132	−0.034	−0.087	−0.022	−0.147
0.013	0.004	−0.324	0.003	−0.074
0.312	0.068	0.524	0.105	−0.353
−0.044	0.000	−0.185	−0.011	0.082
0.122	0.045	0.058	0.012	0.636
0.060	0.009	0.749	0.009	0.217
0.047	0.013	0.026	−0.001	0.015
0.046	−0.000	−1.853	−0.012	−0.078
−0.105	−0.016	−3.535	−0.042	−0.093
0.019	1.044	0.753	0.183	1.285
0.027	−0.017	−0.846	−0.014	−0.102
0.065	0.910	−0.305	0.086	2.937
0.158	0.087	0.687	0.167	0.986
0.023	−0.126	−0.503	−0.148	1.365
−0.925	1.465	40.426	0.209	5.506
−0.456	−0.001	−4.458	−0.206	0.573
0.079	−0.034	−0.800	0.000	−0.083
−0.145	−0.198	−2.289	0.010	−0.388
0.608	−0.592	−15.606	−0.016	−4.190
0.170	−0.123	−3.205	−0.019	−0.565
0.821	−0.233	−0.599	0.023	−0.308
−0.152	−0.285	−13.470	−0.001	−0.545
0.925	−1.465	−40.426	−0.209	−5.506
−0.000	−0.000	−0.000	−0.000	0.000

TABLE 20.3 (Continued)

	ISIC Code	Mexico	Portugal	Singapore	Spain
Traded goods					
Agriculture, forestry, and fishing	(1)	16.488	2.874	0.529	5.867
Food, beverages, and tobacco	(310)	−1.715	−0.124	−0.480	−0.164
Textiles	(321)	−4.173	−1.411	−0.394	−1.270
Wearing apparel	(322)	−0.499	−1.946	0.139	−0.493
Leather products	(323)	−0.214	−0.118	−0.111	−0.901
Footwear	(324)	−0.034	−0.259	0.040	−0.120
Wood products	(331)	−0.301	−0.316	−0.127	0.222
Furniture and fixtures	(332)	0.026	−0.038	0.106	−0.755
Paper and paper products	(341)	−0.269	−0.290	−0.024	−0.054
Printing and publishing	(342)	−0.079	0.016	0.022	−0.075
Chemicals	(35A)	2.085	0.296	0.079	0.581
Petroleum and related products	(35B)	−0.120	−0.074	−0.002	−0.135
Rubber products	(355)	0.025	0.076	0.043	0.224
Nonmetallic mineral products	(36A)	−0.132	0.005	0.033	0.062
Glass and glass products	(362)	−0.070	0.009	0.005	0.068
Iron and steel	(371)	−0.470	1.134	−0.011	0.099
Nonferrous metals	(372)	−0.591	0.742	−0.009	0.119
Metal products	(381)	1.553	−0.187	0.201	0.290
Nonelectrical machinery	(382)	−2.064	−0.385	−0.028	−0.685
Electrical machinery	(383)	0.727	−0.033	0.534	0.118
Transportation equipment	(384)	0.778	−0.008	0.404	0.588
Miscellaneous manufactures	(38A)	−0.321	−0.126	−0.051	0.026
Total traded		10.628	−0.165	0.899	3.615
Nontraded goods					
Mining and quarrying	(2)	−2.871	−0.184	−0.002	−1.083
Electricity, gas, and water	(4)	−0.166	0.062	−0.012	−0.037
Construction	(5)	−0.754	−0.533	−0.100	−0.694
Wholesale and retail trade	(6)	−2.485	0.646	−0.341	−0.621
Transportation, storage, and communications	(7)	−0.833	0.230	−0.164	−0.159
Finance, insurance, and real estate	(8)	−0.430	0.228	−0.027	−0.100
Commercial, social, and personal services	(9)	−3.089	−0.283	−0.255	−0.920
Total nontraded		−10.628	0.165	−0.899	−3.615
Total, all industries		−0.000	0.000	0.000	−0.000

Taiwan	Turkey	Yugoslavia
3.162	5.163	0.550
3.041	− 0.011	− 0.076
− 2.706	− 3.824	− 1.565
0.370	− 0.146	− 0.303
− 0.176	− 1.109	− 0.344
0.510	− 0.010	0.017
0.351	− 0.002	− 0.090
0.397	− 0.001	0.287
− 0.169	0.042	− 0.128
− 0.063	− 0.002	0.043
− 1.123	0.584	0.427
0.544	− 0.070	− 0.157
0.036	0.161	0.117
− 0.080	0.006	0.099
0.046	− 0.012	0.010
− 0.757	2.316	− 0.220
0.020	− 0.399	− 0.618
0.490	0.025	0.450
− 0.003	− 0.036	− 0.239
1.616	0.030	0.473
0.306	0.029	0.992
0.240	0.015	− 0.149
6.053	2.750	− 0.424
0.423	− 1.027	− 1.099
− 0.115	− 0.002	− 0.002
− 0.496	− 0.482	0.387
− 2.958	− 0.111	0.401
− 0.908	− 0.055	0.120
− 1.578	0.053	0.106
− 0.421	− 1.126	0.512
− 6.053	− 2.750	0.424
− 0.000	− 0.000	0.000

In several of the developing countries listed in table 20.3, there are net increases in employment in agriculture and declines in textiles. This latter result may reflect the fact that NTBs have been assumed unchanged in carrying out the tariff-elimination exercise. With tariffs being reduced, there is a tendency for world prices to rise and consumer prices to fall. As a consequence, the pattern of world demand shifts somewhat away from the sectors with NTBs and towards those in which tariffs are eliminated. This fall in demand occurs in what may often be an important export sector in developing countries, and its adverse effects may be augmented by the rise in prices of other manufactures which may serve as inputs into these particular sectors. This type of specialization may explain the declines in welfare noted in table 20.2 for many developing countries. By the same token, some developing countries that have been successful in expanding their exports of durable manufactures may be encouraged further along these lines as the result of tariff elimination.

In discussing the overall gross employment results in table 20.2, we noted that there were several cases in which these changes represented sizable percentages of total 1976 employment. In table 20.4, we present the results in terms of the net percentage changes in employment by sector for all the countries. In the United States, for example, agriculture shows a net percentage increase of 1.4 and transport equipment of 0.9, whereas wearing apparel shows a decline of 2.1 percent, footwear of 1.1 percent, and textiles of 0.8 percent. The United States is clearly on the low side as inspection of table 20.4 clearly indicates. Indeed, some of the positive and negative percentage changes are sufficiently large that they might signal sectors in which labor adjustment may present difficulties.[10] This is particularly the case if there are problems of labor mobility and if there is a mismatch in labor skills between the industries that would expand or contract in response to tariff elimination. Again, if tariff elimination were staged over a period of years, the difficulties would be lessened but they might not be fully resolved in certain individual sectors.

The large percentage changes in net employment are much less prevalent for the developing countries, reflecting the fact that these countries in general will not be materially affected by tariff elimination in terms of their production and trade. If, on the other hand,

---

[10] The net percentage changes in employment across sectors due to the Tokyo Round were generally fairly small in comparison to the results obtained here for tariff elimination.

NTBs were to be reduced or eliminated, the developing countries would show much greater responses in their sectors of specialization.

The final set of results that is of interest concerns the percentage changes in value added across sectors that will be experienced as a consequence of tariff elimination. The post-Tokyo Round nominal tariffs recorded in table 20.1 showed evidence of dispersion and escalation, which suggested that effective rates of protection might be significantly higher than nominal rates in some sectors. The complete elimination of tariffs can therefore be expected to encourage expansion of value added in some industries more than others. These changes will be subject of course to the maintenance of existing NTBs and thus do not reflect fully what might occur if all trade barriers were removed. Our model takes into account, it will be recalled, the effects not only of own-country tariff changes but also the effects of changes in foreign tariffs and exchange rates. We have explored these issues theoretically and computationally in Deardorff and Stern (1983a) and space does not permit us to review the relevant considerations here.

In any event, we present in table 20.5 the results based on our model of the ranking of sectors in the major industrial countries and Brazil of the percentage changes in value added that will occur as the result of the complete elimination of post-Tokyo Round tariffs. The results for the industrial countries all reflect the use of the 1972 input-output table for the United States. The only developing country listed is Brazil, for which we used its 1970 input-output table. The results for the remaining developing countries based upon the Brazilian input-output table are available on request. For the United States, the industries with the largest percentage increases in value added are agriculture, transport equipment, chemicals, mining, and quarrying, electrical machinery, nonelectrical machinery, and wood products, while the smallest percentage increases in value added are recorded in wearing apparel, textiles, nonmetallic mineral products, footwear, rubber products, miscellaneous manufactures, and various of the nontradable sectors. The rankings for the other countries can be similarly discerned from table 20.5. The results thus permit identification of the sectors that will expand or contract the most as tariffs are eliminated. To the extent that sectors are protected both by tariffs and NTBs, the elimination of all trade barriers might not change these results appreciably.

In the case of Brazil, the largest percentage increases in value added are recorded in agriculture and foodstuffs, transport equipment, footwear, fuel products, and furniture and fixtures, while the smallest percentage increases occur in nonferrous metals, leather products, chemicals, iron and steel, mining and quarrying, textiles, and rubber

TABLE 20.4   NET PERCENTAGE CHANGES IN EMPLOYMENT DUE TO
THE ELIMINATION OF POST-TOKYO ROUND TARIFFS, BY
ISIC SECTOR, MAJOR INDUSTRIAL AND DEVELOPING
COUNTRIES

	ISIC Code	Australia	Austria	Benelux	Canada
Traded goods					
Agriculture, forestry, and fishing	(1)	2.908	− 1.730	1.151	1.384
Food, beverage, and tobacco	(310)	1.601	− 1.085	1.047	− 0.049
Textiles	(321)	14.826	22.281	20.524	− 1.956
Wearing apparel	(322)	− 5.490	44.654	51.173	− 3.427
Leather products	(323)	43.046	25.738	1.799	15.426
Footwear	(324)	− 2.400	26.362	0.354	− 0.967
Wood products	(331)	− 2.693	8.379	− 0.190	0.407
Furniture and fixtures	(332)	− 2.073	− 6.318	− 0.181	− 0.077
Paper and paper products	(341)	− 2.307	8.817	2.210	1.538
Printing and publishing	(342)	− 0.106	− 0.648	− 2.693	− 0.417
Chemicals	(35A)	0.828	1.832	6.880	− 2.430
Petroleum and related products	(35B)	− 0.525	− 4.375	− 12.484	− 2.260
Rubber products	(355)	− 12.294	− 5.898	− 0.653	− 3.728
Nonmetallic mineral products	(36A)	− 2.171	− 2.840	− 5.533	− 1.285
Glass and glass products	(362)	− 6.530	− 0.929	− 1.699	− 2.563
Iron and steel	(371)	− 1.445	2.892	− 1.430	− 0.232
Nonferrous metals	(372)	14.740	3.503	− 3.517	19.150
Metal products	(381)	− 4.533	− 2.690	− 0.175	− 1.794
Nonelectrical machinery	(382)	− 0.487	4.934	− 0.805	1.443
Electrical machinery	(383)	− 5.347	− 0.350	0.461	− 0.256
Transportation equipment	(384)	− 5.175	− 4.152	8.448	3.531
Miscellaneous manufactures	(38A)	− 3.291	10.245	− 0.322	0.145
Total traded		− 0.036	3.449	4.513	0.637
Nontraded goods					
Mining and quarrying	(2)	2.722	− 3.242	− 7.990	0.020
Electricity, gas, and water	(4)	− 0.101	− 3.657	− 3.329	− 0.414
Construction	(5)	0.446	− 1.939	− 1.194	0.150
Wholesale and retail trade	(6)	− 0.266	− 2.987	− 2.418	− 0.356
Transportation, storage, and communication	(7)	− 0.097	− 1.774	− 1.832	− 0.230
Finance, insurance, and real estate	(8)	− 0.308	− 4.092	− 3.546	− 0.585
Commercial, social, and personal services	(9)	0.135	− 2.106	− 1.844	− 0.184
Total nontraded		0.014	− 2.495	− 2.189	− 0.226
Total, all industries		− 0.000	− 0.000	− 0.000	− 0.000

	Denmark	Finland	France	West Germany	Ireland
Traded goods					
Agriculture, forestry, and fishing	2.604	−2.517	0.918	−0.190	1.627
Food, beverage, and tobacco	3.552	−0.177	0.622	0.699	1.660
Textiles	14.760	13.666	3.354	5.598	10.293
Wearing apparel	31.768	53.983	5.591	3.279	18.174
Leather products	19.000	41.120	2.823	5.240	2.251
Footwear	10.533	35.351	2.403	−1.380	−1.657
Wood products	−1.271	1.206	−0.797	−0.803	−2.524
Furniture and fixtures	8.833	7.540	−0.663	3.014	−0.536
Paper and paper products	−0.640	1.348	−0.739	−0.330	−2.806
Printing and publishing	−0.962	−1.148	−0.226	−0.158	−1.123
Chemicals	0.291	1.407	−0.696	1.722	−0.011
Petroleum and related products	−3.519	−0.683	−0.026	−1.143	−5.489
Rubber products	−2.427	−22.932	2.305	−0.012	−0.454
Nonmetallic mineral products	−3.422	−2.152	−1.020	−1.264	−3.363
Glass and glass products	−1.650	−2.307	−0.364	−0.653	−1.702
Iron and steel	1.791	−0.958	1.059	−0.074	−3.526
Nonferrous metals	5.115	−1.754	0.508	0.026	32.783
Metal products	0.489	−2.575	0.149	1.059	4.073
Nonelectrical machinery	1.963	0.334	1.741	0.534	2.503
Electrical machinery	1.932	0.567	0.633	0.726	0.342
Transportation equipment	3.500	3.371	1.483	2.806	−2.333
Miscellaneous manufactures	7.156	−3.883	0.155	3.115	4.534
Total traded	3.502	2.212	0.935	1.009	2.165
Nontraded goods					
Mining and quarrying	−3.362	−1.430	−0.102	−1.026	−4.025
Electricity, gas, and water	−2.783	−2.304	−1.046	−1.201	−2.762
Construction	−0.835	−1.172	−0.349	−0.478	−1.009
Wholesale and retail trade	−1.894	−1.519	−0.708	−0.837	−1.959
Transportation, storage, and communication	−1.350	−0.983	−0.464	−0.558	−1.281
Finance, insurance, and real estate	−2.715	−2.257	−1.012	−1.230	−2.907
Commercial, social, and personal services	−1.406	−1.372	−0.493	−0.623	−1.491
Total nontraded	−1.628	−1.436	−0.581	−0.727	−1.686
Total, all industries	−0.000	−0.000	−0.000	−0.000	−0.000

TABLE 20.4 (Continued)

	ISIC Code	Italy	Japan	Nether-lands	New Zealand
Traded goods					
Agriculture, forestry, and fishing	(1)	− 0.687	− 1.002	2.431	0.358
Food, beverage, and tobacco	(310)	0.527	0.850	2.038	− 0.128
Textiles	(321)	1.809	0.502	26.502	− 13.373
Wearing apparel	(322)	7.292	− 1.405	34.236	− 0.062
Leather products	(323)	6.675	0.009	13.845	− 24.224
Footwear	(324)	17.073	− 0.913	8.585	− 0.328
Wood products	(331)	− 0.113	0.798	− 2.666	− 0.391
Furniture and fixtures	(332)	3.377	0.116	1.473	0.209
Paper and paper products	(341)	− 0.396	0.316	0.373	− 1.868
Printing and publishing	(342)	− 0.238	0.172	− 1.059	0.912
Chemicals	(35A)	− 2.103	0.079	5.350	2.784
Petroleum and related products	(35B)	0.629	− 3.478	− 4.776	2.193
Rubber products	(355)	0.789	2.725	− 0.433	1.726
Nonmetallic mineral products	(36A)	− 0.181	0.336	− 3.856	0.872
Glass and glass products	(362)	− 0.801	0.379	2.233	1.330
Iron and steel	(371)	− 0.182	1.540	− 3.146	5.222
Nonferrous metals	(372)	− 0.341	− 0.107	5.050	− 13.158
Metal products	(381)	0.872	0.307	− 1.016	0.713
Nonelectrical machinery	(382)	0.239	0.264	0.038	0.673
Electrical machinery	(383)	− 0.040	0.757	1.282	1.372
Transportation equipment	(384)	1.290	1.654	3.670	2.072
Miscellaneous manufactures	(38A)	0.099	1.577	3.712	0.761
Total traded		0.583	0.102	3.084	− 0.368
Nontraded goods					
Mining and quarrying	(2)	− 0.104	− 0.067	− 5.167	− 0.333
Electricity, gas, and water	(4)	− 1.010	0.068	− 1.995	− 0.020
Construction	(5)	− 0.408	− 0.086	− 0.714	− 0.087
Wholesale and retail trade	(6)	− 0.544	− 0.086	− 1.506	0.341
Transportation, storage, and communication	(7)	− 0.394	− 0.051	− 1.065	0.030
Finance, insurance, and real estate	(8)	− 0.900	− 0.224	− 2.164	0.582
Commercial, social, and personal services	(9)	− 0.491	− 0.006	− 1.095	0.213
Total nontraded		− 0.537	− 0.061	− 1.285	0.211
Total, all industries		− 0.000	0.000	− 0.000	0.000

	Norway	Sweden	Switzer-land	United Kingdom	United States
Traded goods					
Agriculture, forestry, and fishing	0.858	−0.029	0.074	1.006	1.356
Food, beverage, and tobacco	−0.227	−0.710	0.788	1.391	0.012
Textiles	11.213	8.499	−2.086	−2.035	−0.847
Wearing apparel	5.477	17.657	−0.595	−0.745	−2.066
Leather products	26.214	13.417	−6.131	−0.394	−0.134
Footwear	12.959	20.207	−0.175	−1.822	−1.126
Wood products	−0.398	−0.022	−1.709	−1.065	0.168
Furniture and fixtures	1.212	5.387	−3.295	2.941	0.016
Paper and paper products	0.904	0.452	−1.793	−1.000	0.376
Printing and publishing	−1.297	−0.524	0.059	0.115	0.016
Chemicals	0.655	0.135	1.285	1.331	0.642
Petroleum and related products	−1.181	−1.243	−4.312	14.122	0.652
Rubber products	−2.603	−4.701	−1.617	0.439	−0.409
Nonmetallic mineral products	−0.890	−1.490	−1.406	4.786	−0.542
Glass and glass products	−4.015	−1.217	−1.583	7.640	0.003
Iron and steel	1.751	0.654	−1.649	−0.558	0.160
Nonferrous metals	1.290	−0.710	−2.992	0.073	−0.024
Metal products	−1.014	0.894	0.686	0.234	0.117
Nonelectrical machinery	0.385	1.102	−0.597	−0.096	0.468
Electrical machinery	0.058	2.751	1.187	0.279	0.517
Transportation equipment	4.653	3.943	−1.319	−8.130	0.926
Miscellaneous manufactures	1.324	4.649	−0.307	4.787	−0.330
Total traded	1.180	1.530	−0.153	−0.294	0.236
Nontraded goods					
Mining and quarrying	−0.470	−1.069	−1.643	4.412	0.505
Electricity, gas, and water	−1.013	−1.307	0.146	0.355	−0.129
Construction	−0.212	−0.516	0.386	0.145	−0.027
Wholesale and retail trade	−0.730	−0.911	0.096	−0.189	−0.106
Transportation, storage, and communication	−0.458	−0.569	0.038	0.666	−0.040
Finance, insurance, and real estate	−1.071	−1.290	0.113	0.332	−0.117
Commercial, social, and personal services	−0.520	−0.665	0.234	−0.034	−0.079
Total nontraded	−0.570	−0.758	0.104	0.146	−0.081
Total, all industries	−0.000	0.000	−0.000	0.000	−0.000

TABLE 20.4   (Continued)

	ISIC Code	Argentina	Brazil	Chile	Colombia
Traded goods					
Agriculture, forestry, and fishing	(1)	0.479	0.218	0.613	0.341
Food, beverage, and tobacco	(310)	0.494	0.288	−0.686	−0.069
Textiles	(321)	−2.146	−0.229	−0.525	−0.528
Wearing apparel	(322)	3.505	−0.131	−0.057	−0.103
Leather products	(323)	−7.920	−1.910	−0.971	−0.829
Footwear	(324)	5.038	0.095	−0.082	0.332
Wood products	(331)	0.432	−0.098	−0.021	0.018
Furniture and fixtures	(332)	1.666	−0.030	0.016	0.307
Paper and paper products	(341)	−0.404	−0.237	0.887	−0.975
Printing and publishing	(342)	−0.054	−0.107	−0.102	−0.255
Chemicals	(35A)	−0.451	−0.472	1.066	−1.329
Petroleum and related products	(35B)	−0.483	−0.360	0.801	0.001
Rubber products	(355)	−0.080	−0.290	1.117	−1.850
Nonmetallic mineral products	(36A)	−0.105	−0.118	0.266	−0.245
Glass and glass products	(362)	−0.090	−0.102	0.231	−0.547
Iron and steel	(371)	−2.002	−0.501	0.147	−4.423
Nonferrous metals	(372)	−4.784	−1.985	−0.651	−8.851
Metal products	(381)	0.084	−0.052	0.815	0.421
Nonelectrical machinery	(382)	−0.322	−0.136	−0.163	−0.021
Electrical machinery	(383)	−0.101	−0.061	0.330	−0.025
Transportation equipment	(384)	0.169	0.047	0.771	−0.196
Miscellaneous manufactures	(38A)	−0.060	−0.230	0.546	−0.299
Total traded		−0.058	0.120	0.375	0.097
Nontraded goods					
Mining and quarrying	(2)	−0.801	−0.565	0.999	−0.129
Electricity, gas, and water	(4)	−0.184	−0.232	−0.294	−0.442
Construction	(5)	0.086	−0.064	−0.405	0.115
Wholesale and retail trade	(6)	−0.065	−0.206	−0.352	−0.374
Transportation, storage, and communication	(7)	−0.069	−0.126	−0.324	−0.195
Finance, insurance, and real estate	(8)	−0.120	−0.155	−0.223	−0.316
Commercial, social, and personal services	(9)	0.154	−0.065	−0.278	0.059
Total nontraded		0.035	−0.138	−0.238	−0.119
Total, all industries		0.000	−0.000	−0.000	−0.000

	Greece	Hong Kong	Indo-nesia	Israel	South Korea
Traded goods					
Agriculture, forestry, and fishing	0.238	1.362	0.044	0.882	− 0.018
Food, beverage, and tobacco	− 0.161	− 2.933	0.223	− 1.001	0.065
Textiles	− 0.725	− 1.493	− 0.570	− 1.205	− 0.646
Wearing apparel	− 1.274	0.479	− 0.747	− 0.156	0.692
Leather products	− 12.828	− 11.988	− 7.734	− 8.682	− 4.029
Footwear	− 1.160	2.194	0.503	0.376	2.695
Wood products	0.537	− 0.264	− 0.070	− 0.253	0.131
Furniture and fixtures	− 0.390	2.981	0.502	0.349	2.796
Paper and paper products	1.059	− 0.375	− 0.033	− 0.438	− 0.233
Printing and publishing	0.056	0.019	− 0.065	0.029	− 0.105
9.6Chemicals	1.059	1.240	0.045	0.880	− 0.342
Petroleum and related products	− 1.213	0.190	− 0.224	− 0.621	0.284
Rubber products	1.901	0.708	0.030	0.226	0.388
Nonmetallic mineral products	0.135	0.677	0.095	0.102	0.209
Glass and glass products	1.011	0.536	0.013	− 0.027	0.088
Iron and steel	0.431	− 0.010	− 0.116	− 0.391	− 0.116
Nonferrous metals	− 2.328	− 1.297	− 2.059	− 1.446	− 0.458
Metal products	0.025	1.496	0.098	0.672	1.209
Nonelectrical machinery	0.107	− 0.140	− 0.082	− 0.119	− 0.101
Electrical machinery	0.252	1.033	− 0.036	0.349	1.141
Transportation equipment	0.608	0.737	0.043	0.703	0.703
Miscellaneous manufactures	0.075	− 0.107	− 0.158	− 0.858	0.669
Total traded	− 0.040	0.189	0.023	0.064	0.067
Nontraded goods					
Mining and quarrying	− 1.628	− 0.258	− 0.330	− 0.844	0.454
Electricity, gas, and water	0.192	− 0.326	− 0.111	0.004	− 0.225
Construction	− 0.060	− 0.382	− 0.081	0.011	− 0.073
Wholesale and retail trade	0.161	− 0.336	− 0.095	− 0.011	− 0.223
Transportation, storage, and communication	0.056	− 0.268	− 0.066	− 0.024	− 0.145
Finance, insurance, and real estate	0.236	− 0.171	− 0.059	0.030	− 0.196
Commercial, social, and personal services	− 0.044	− 0.219	− 0.070	− 0.000	− 0.045
Total nontraded	0.055	− 0.266	− 0.087	− 0.026	− 0.127
Total, all industries	0.000	− 0.000	− 0.000	− 0.000	0.000

TABLE 20.4   (Continued)

	ISIC Code	Mexico	Portugal	Singapore	Spain
Traded goods					
Agriculture, forestry, and fishing	(1)	0.236	0.341	2.687	0.221
Food, beverage, and tobacco	(310)	− 0.189	− 0.233	− 3.312	− 0.036
Textiles	(321)	− 1.549	− 0.886	− 2.645	− 0.417
Wearing apparel	(322)	− 0.180	− 2.106	0.715	− 0.361
Leather products	(323)	− 0.619	− 1.970	− 11.124	− 2.129
Footwear	(324)	− 0.166	− 0.746	1.831	− 0.130
Wood products	(331)	− 0.440	− 0.409	− 1.166	0.333
Furniture and fixtures	(332)	0.048	− 0.107	3.431	− 0.338
Paper and paper products	(341)	− 0.411	− 1.519	− 0.627	− 0.066
Printing and publishing	(342)	− 0.080	0.124	0.221	− 0.067
Chemicals	(35A)	0.422	1.167	1.339	0.257
Petroleum and related products	(35B)	− 0.671	− 1.238	− 0.048	− 0.732
Rubber products	(355)	0.046	1.492	0.830	0.329
Nonmetallic mineral products	(36A)	− 0.066	0.018	0.638	0.030
Glass and glass products	(362)	− 0.123	0.152	0.406	0.151
Iron and steel	(371)	− 0.442	3.883	− 0.667	0.071
Nonferrous metals	(372)	− 1.903	6.450	− 1.793	0.334
Metal products	(381)	0.437	− 0.394	1.548	0.082
Nonelectrical machinery	(382)	− 0.768	− 0.708	− 0.247	− 0.462
Electrical machinery	(383)	0.563	− 0.328	0.961	0.058
Transportation equipment	(384)	0.500	− 0.011	1.275	0.254
Miscellaneous manufactures	(38A)	− 0.464	− 0.230	− 0.265	0.022
Total traded		0.099	− 0.010	0.354	0.060
Nontraded goods					
Mining and quarrying	(2)	− 1.135	− 1.659	− 0.084	− 1.083
Electricity, gas, and water	(4)	− 0.218	0.283	− 0.104	− 0.023
Construction	(5)	− 0.094	− 0.204	− 0.237	− 0.061
Wholesale and retail trade	(6)	− 0.184	0.209	− 0.169	− 0.031
Transportation, storage, and communication	(7)	− 0.163	0.129	− 0.161	− 0.024
Finance, insurance, and real estate	(8)	− 0.114	0.266	− 0.047	− 0.009
Commercial, social, and personal services	(9)	− 0.096	− 0.052	− 0.127	− 0.075
Total nontraded		− 0.162	0.012	− 0.146	− 0.056
Total, all industries		− 0.000	0.000	0.000	− 0.000

	Taiwan	Turkey	Yugo-slavia
Traded goods			
Agriculture, forestry, and fishing	0.192	0.055	0.222
Food, beverage, and tobacco	1.656	− 0.003	− 0.051
Textiles	− 0.808	− 1.061	− 0.709
Wearing apparel	0.820	− 0.629	− 0.358
Leather products	− 3.673	− 8.876	− 1.631
Footwear	2.628	− 0.111	0.039
Wood products	0.473	− 0.007	− 0.105
Furniture and fixtures	5.096	− 0.015	0.357
Paper and paper products	− 0.274	0.116	− 0.315
Printing and publishing	− 0.237	− 0.008	0.067
Chemicals	− 0.538	0.628	0.508
Petroleum and related products	0.368	− 0.594	− 0.716
Rubber products	0.124	0.626	0.348
Nonmetallic mineral products	− 0.161	0.006	0.135
Glass and glass products	0.654	− 0.052	0.062
Iron and steel	− 1.051	1.552	− 0.354
Nonferrous metals	0.093	− 0.613	− 1.414
Metal products	2.475	0.041	0.435
Nonelectrical machinery	− 0.005	− 0.051	− 0.250
Electrical machinery	1.125	0.068	0.306
Transportation equipment	0.497	0.032	0.568
Miscellaneous manufactures	0.777	0.044	− 0.366
Total traded	0.186	0.025	− 0.022
Nontraded goods			
Mining and quarrying	0.557	− 0.925	− 0.894
Electricity, gas, and water	− 0.425	− 0.003	− 0.003
Construction	− 0.141	− 0.090	0.078
Wholesale and retail trade	− 0.392	− 0.017	0.061
Transportation, storage, and communication	− 0.272	− 0.011	0.033
Finance, insurance, and real estate	− 0.367	0.029	0.078
Commercial, social, and personal services	− 0.097	− 0.069	0.050
Total nontraded	− 0.251	− 0.075	0.015
Total, all industries	− 0.000	0.000	0.000

TABLE 20.5 RANKINGS OF SECTORS ACCORDING TO PERCENTAGE CHANGES IN VALUE ADDED DUE TO THE ELIMINATION OF POST-TOKYO ROUND TARIFFS, MAJOR INDUSTRIAL COUNTRIES AND BRAZIL

	ISIC Code	*Australia*	*Austria*	*Benelux*	*Canada*
Traded goods					
Agriculture, forestry, and fishing	(1)	2	28	5	4
Food, beverage, and tobacco	(310)	6	16	7	12
Textiles	(321)	3	2	3	25
Wearing apparel	(322)	21	1	2	23
Leather products	(323)	1	4	8	3
Footwear	(324)	17	6	10	18
Wood products	(331)	24	3	14	7
Furniture and fixtures	(332)	19	24	11	11
Paper and paper products	(341)	20	8	6	6
Printing and publishing	(342)	11	13	24	19
Chemicals	(35A)	7	9	4	29
Petroleum and related products	(35B)	12	15	25	20
Rubber products	(355)	28	25	15	28
Nonmetallic mineral products	(36A)	22	22	27	24
Glass and glass products	(362)	26	14	19	27
Iron and steel	(371)	18	11	17	13
Nonferrous metals	(372)	4	10	23	1
Metal products	(381)	25	21	12	26
Nonelectrical machinery	(382)	16	7	18	5
Electrical machinery	(383)	27	12	9	17
Transportation equipment	(384)	29	29	1	2
Miscellaneous manufactures	(38A)	23	5	13	8
Nontraded goods					
Mining and quarrying	(2)	5	26	29	10
Electricity, gas, and water	(4)	13	23	26	21
Construction	(5)	8	17	16	9
Wholesale and retail trade	(6)	14	20	21	16
Transportation, storage, and communication	(7)	10	18	22	15
Finance, insurance, and real estate	(8)	15	27	28	22
Commercial, social, and personal services	(9)	9	19	20	14

	Denmark	Finland	France	West Germany	Ireland	Italy
Traded goods						
Agriculture, forestry, and fishing	4	28	2	24	4	28
Food, beverage, and tobacco	8	13	10	10	8	9
Textiles	3	5	3	2	2	6
Wearing apparel	1	1	5	7	3	3
Leather products	5	2	7	6	9	4
Footwear	9	3	8	19	14	17
Wood products	25	8	28	26	26	17
Furniture and fixtures	7	6	21	5	12	5
Paper and paper products	16	9	24	16	22	20
Printing and publishing	19	18	17	15	16	18
Chemicals	15	7	26	4	11	29
Petroleum and related products	18	12	15	17	17	11
Rubber products	24	29	6	13	13	8
Nonmetallic mineral products	27	22	25	25	25	16
Glass and glass products	23	21	19	23	21	25
Iron and steel	13	14	11	14	23	14
Nonferrous metals	10	20	12	12	1	19
Metal products	14	24	13	8	6	7
Nonelectrical machinery	12	11	4	11	7	10
Electrical machinery	11	10	9	9	10	13
Transportation equipment	2	4	1	1	29	2
Miscellaneous manufactures	6	27	14	3	5	12
Nontraded goods						
Mining and quarrying	29	23	16	28	28	15
Electricity, gas, and water	26	25	27	27	24	26
Construction	17	15	18	18	15	21
Wholesale and retail trade	21	17	23	22	20	22
Transportation, storage, and communication	22	16	22	21	18	23
Finance, insurance, and real estate	28	26	29	29	27	27
Commercial, social, and personal services	20	19	20	20	19	24

TABLE 20.5 (Continued)

	ISIC Code	Japan	Nether- lands	New Zealand	Norway
Traded goods					
Agriculture, forestry, and fishing	(1)	29	4	6	5
Food, beverage, and tobacco	(310)	7	10	23	16
Textiles	(321)	9	1	27	3
Wearing apparel	(322)	28	2	19	6
Leather products	(323)	18	6	28	2
Footwear	(324)	26	9	20	4
Wood products	(331)	6	28	24	21
Furniture and fixtures	(332)	16	13	14	11
Paper and paper products	(341)	13	14	25	12
Printing and publishing	(342)	14	19	10	26
Chemicals	(35A)	15	5	2	9
Petroleum and related products	(35B)	27	20	26	17
Rubber products	(355)	4	16	5	28
Nonmetallic mineral products	(36A)	12	27	9	23
Glass and glass products	(362)	11	11	7	29
Iron and steel	(371)	3	24	3	8
Nonferrous metals	(372)	24	7	29	10
Metal products	(381)	10	21	11	24
Nonelectrical machinery	(382)	8	15	16	13
Electrical machinery	(383)	2	12	4	14
Transportation equipment	(384)	1	3	1	1
Miscellaneous manufactures	(38A)	5	8	21	7
Nontraded goods					
Mining and quarrying	(2)	22	29	22	22
Electricity, gas, and water	(4)	17	25	17	25
Construction	(5)	23	17	18	15
Wholesale and retail trade	(6)	21	22	12	20
Transportation, storage, and communication	(7)	20	23	15	18
Finance, insurance, and real estate	(8)	25	26	8	27
Commercial, social, and personal services	(9)	19	18	13	19

	Sweden	Switzerland	United Kingdom	United States	Brazil
Traded goods					
Agriculture, forestry, and fishing	15	5	2	1	1
Food, beverage, and tobacco	23	3	5	13	2
Textiles	4	23	29	28	24
Wearing apparel	3	14	25	29	17
Leather products	5	26	24	19	28
Footwear	2	13	27	26	4
Wood products	14	28	28	7	16
Furniture and fixtures	8	25	7	14	6
Paper and paper products	12	19	26	8	20
Printing and publishing	18	11	18	12	19
Chemicals	13	1	4	3	27
Petroleum and related products	16	17	8	9	5
Rubber products	29	20	14	25	23
Nonmetallic mineral products	25	21	10	27	13
Glass and glass products	24	22	6	15	12
Iron and steel	11	18	22	11	26
Nonferrous metals	19	24	19	16	29
Metal products	10	4	16	10	9
Nonelectrical machinery	9	16	21	6	21
Electrical machinery	7	2	11	5	15
Transportation equipment	1	29	1	2	3
Miscellaneous manufactures	6	15	3	24	22
Nontraded goods					
Mining and quarrying	27	27	9	4	25
Electricity, gas, and water	26	9	17	22	18
Construction	17	6	15	17	8
Wholesale and retail trade	22	10	23	21	14
Transportation, storage, and communication	20	12	13	18	10
Finance, insurance, and real estate	28	8	12	23	11
Commercial, social, and personal services	21	7	20	20	7

products. These changes do not take into account the existing structure of Brazil's tariffs and domestic taxes and subsidies, although some of these effects may be captured through our modeling of foreign-exchange licensing. The results for Brazil are thus only broadly suggestive of the reallocation that might occur domestically in response to the elimination of post-Tokyo Round tariffs by the major industrial countries.

Conclusion

If post-Tokyo Round tariffs in the major industrial countries were to be eliminated, our findings are that the exports of these countries would increase by 3.9 percent over 1976 levels. There would be relatively small gross employment effects in the United States and Japan and somewhat larger effects in the European Community especially which might signal some adjustment difficulties in particular sectors. Economic welfare would increase in the United States and Japan but decline in the European Community, except for Italy. The British pound, the US dollar, and other major currencies would depreciate somewhat, and consumer prices would fall to a small extent in the United States but to a much greater extent in most other industrial countries. The effects on the major developing countries would in general be comparatively small. It should be emphasized that these results are based on the assumption that existing NTBs are left unchanged. If both tariffs and NTBs were to be eliminated, the effects would be significantly larger and presumably much more beneficial to the developing countries.

We also presented results on the rankings of sectors according to the percentage changes in value added that might occur as a consequence of tariff elimination. Subject again to the assumption about NTBs and to limited coverage of national input-output tables, these results are suggestive of the allocative effects across sectors that might be experienced if tariffs were eliminated.

It should be emphasized that these conclusions are based upon a computational model of world production and trade that has been constructed to analyze the likely effects of multilateral changes in tariffs and other exogenous events. Our results must be interpreted therefore in the light of the particular model that we have constructed, the behavioral parameters that determine the responses involved,[11] and the data available to us.

[11] We report on some experiments involving the sensitivity of results to changes in parameters in Deardorff and Stern (1983b). In general, the dou-

Finally, we have abstracted from the domestic political environment in the United States and other countries. This environment has a great bearing on the nature and determinants of changes in trade policies. Our model has the merit of identifying the particular sectors that may expand or contract in response to policy changes. Accordingly, results such as those presented above can help to shape policy options for trade liberalization and the associated measures that may be implemented domestically to facilitate adjustment within or between sectors.

---

bling of all elasticities of supply and of substitution between imports and home goods did not materially affect the employment results calculated for the Tokyo Round. The welfare calculation was more noticeably affected, however, and since this is based on a more ad hoc procedure it should be interpreted more cautiously.

References

Baldwin, Robert E. *The Political Economy of US Import Policy*. In process, 1981.

Brown, Fred, and John Whalley. "General Equilibrium Evaluations of Tariff-Cutting Proposals in the Tokyo Round and Comparisons to More Extensive Liberalization of World Trade." *Economic Journal*, vol. 90 (December 1980).

Cline, William R. *Exports of Manufactures from Developing Countries: Performance and Prospects for Market Access*. In process, 1982.

Deardorff, Alan V., and Robert M. Stern. *An Economic Analysis of the Effects of the Tokyo Round of Multilateral Trade Negotiations on the United States and the Other Major Industrialized Countries*. MTN Studies 5, Committee on Finance, US Senate, 96th Cong., 1st sess. Washington: US Government Printing Office, 1979.

———. "Changes in Trade and Employment in the Major Industrialized Countries, 1970–76." Paper presented at the International Economic Association's Sixth World Congress of Economists, August 1980, Mexico City. Processed.

———. "A Disaggregated Model of World Production and Trade: An Estimate of the Impact of the Tokyo Round." *Journal of Policy Modeling*, vol. 3 (1981).

———. "Tariff and Exchange-Rate Protection under Fixed and Flexible Exchange Rates in the Major Industrialized Countries." In *Economic Interdependence and Flexible Exchange Rates*, ed. J. Bhandari and B. Putnam. Cambridge: MIT Press, 1983a.

———. "Economic Effects of the Tokyo Round." *Southern Economic Journal*, vol. 49 (January 1983b).

Deardorff, Alan V., Robert M. Stern, and Christopher F. Baum. "A Multi-Country Simulation of the Employment and Exchange-Rate Effects of Post-Kennedy Round Tariff Reductions." In *Trade and Employment in Asia and the Pacific*, ed. N. Akrasanee, et al. Honolulu: University of Hawaii, 1977.

Deardorff, Alan V., Robert M. Stern, and Mark N. Greene. "The Implications of Alternative Trade Strategies for the United States." In *An American Response to the New International Economic Order*, ed. D. B. H. Denoon. New York: New York University Press, 1979a.

———. "The Sensitivity of Industrial Output and Employment to Exchange-Rate Changes in the Major Industrialized Countries." In *Trade and Payments Adjustment Under Flexible Exchange Rates*, ed. J. P .Martin and M. A. M. Smith. London: Macmillan, 1979b.

Bela Balassa

The session on "New Issues in the 1980s" at the Conference on Trade Policies in the 1980s extends the traditional discourse beyond policies concerning merchandise trade. The four papers presented at the session cover a wide range of issues. To establish some logic in the presentation, I will organize my comments by proceeding from merchandise trade to trade in services. Following time-honored custom, I will emphasize points of disagreement rather than agreement.

In chapter 20, Alan V. Deardorff and Robert M. Stern examine the economic effects of complete elimination of post-Tokyo Round tariffs on the major industrialized and developing countries by the use of a model incorporating supply and demand functions for 22 tradable and 7 nontradable industries in 18 industrial and 16 developing countries. The model has much increased in sophistication since the earlier efforts made by the Deardorff-Stern team. However, greater sophistication also increases the difficulties of understanding how certain results have been obtained in the model.

In particular, questions arise about the authors' conclusions that 9 of the 16 developing countries would experience welfare losses, in the event of the elimination of tariffs on industrial goods by the industrialized countries. These results conflict with estimates made by Robert E. Baldwin and Tracy Murray (1977), Thomas B. Birnberg (1979), and again by Tracy Murray (1979), all of which showed that developing countries would gain from most-favored-nation (MFN) type tariff reductions undertaken by the industrialized countries. At the same time, the Deardorff-Stern results rest on questionable assumptions.

According to the authors, "with tariffs being reduced, there is a tendency for world prices to rise and consumer prices to fall. As a consequence, the pattern of world demand shifts somewhat away from the sectors with NTBs [nontariff trade barriers] and towards those in which tariffs are eliminated. This fall in demand occurs in what may

711

often be an important export sector in developing countries. . . ."
According to the model results, such would be the case in particular
for textiles, where employment in all developing countries would
decline, and for clothing, where a fall in employment would occur in
the large majority of the developing countries.

These results have been obtained by assuming that the developing
countries would maintain their share in the reduced consumption of
textiles and clothing, owing to the increase in the relative prices of
these commodities in the industrialized countries. Such an assumption
does not appear realistic, however. As NTBs are defined in absolute
terms in the form of quotas, increases in the relative prices of textiles
and clothing would not affect NTB-constrained imports from the
developing countries but would rather lead to a decline in high-cost
domestic production in the industrialized countries.

Furthermore, Deardorff and Stern assume low supply elasticities
in the developing countries. This assumption again lacks realism. In
the long run, which is the relevant period for the estimates, developing
countries could greatly increase their exports of industrial goods in
response to the elimination of tariffs in the industrialized countries
by shifting resources from agriculture to industry. Results obtained
by J. Michael Finger (1976) on the effects of the Kennedy Round of
tariff reductions show that supply elasticities tend to be high in the
developing countries even in the short run. Thus, according to Finger's estimates, quantity and value elasticities of export supply in
these countries were 10.6 and 14.8 to US, 3.5 and 3.9 to European,
and 11.9 and 11.9 to Japanese markets, exceeding export supply
elasticities in the industrialized countries by a considerable margin,
the exception being exports to West Europe.

In addition, the model does not incorporate two important advances made in the study of international trade in the mid–1960s that
have modified the traditional theory of international specialization:
the introduction of the concept of effective protection and the analysis
of trade in differentiated products in the form of intraindustry specialization. Yet, integrating these innovations in the estimation procedure would considerably increase the favorable effects for the developing countries of the elimination of tariffs in the industrialized
countries.

To begin with, owing to the escalation of tariffs from lower to
higher levels of fabrication, effective rates of protection are considerably higher than nominal rates, thereby raising the estimated effects
of the elimination of tariffs on total imports. Moreover, the extent
of escalation is greater for products of interest to the developing
countries than for products of interest to the industrialized countries,

further increasing these effects for the former group of countries. Thus, nominal and effective rates of protection on industrial goods imported by the industrial countries from the developing countries averaged 11.8 percent and 22.6 percent, respectively, after the Kennedy Round, compared to protection rates of 6.5 percent and 11.1 percent on their overall industrial imports (Balassa 1968). These relationships do not appear to have changed following the tariff reductions undertaken in the framework of the Tokyo Round.

Also, product differentiation that characterizes much of international trade in manufactured goods leads to gains through the exploitation of economies of scale, which are not captured in calculations of the effects of tariff reductions based on the traditional model of international trade (Balassa 1966). While a number of theoretical models have been developed in recent years to capture this phenomenon (Krugman 1979; Lancaster 1980; and Helpman 1981), the only empirical study, by Richard Harris at the University of Vancouver, is in a draft stage. Harris' preliminary results indicate that the gains from trade in differentiated products following trade liberalization are rather large.

But how important is intraindustry trade between industrialized and developing countries? In chapter 2 C. Fred Bergsten and William R. Cline suggest: "close analysis would probably show that the trade of Japan and the NICs [newly industrializing countries] with the industrial countries tends to be interindustry (exports in different product sectors from imports) rather than intraindustry . . ." and provide some data to support this proposition. However, the data used by Bergsten and Cline are rather aggregated. They refer only to the United States and they do not show changes over time.

I have examined the sources of intraindustry trade through horizontal specialization (that is, trade in different varieties of a particular product) and vertical specialization (that is, trade in parts, components, and accessories in the framework of the international division of the production process) between the industrialized and the developing countries, and have provided estimates for four industrialized countries. The results obtained in a 91–industry classification scheme show that the extent of intraindustry trade in the four countries increased much more rapidly with the developing countries than with the other industrialized countries.

This is indicated by calculating the ratio of the 1979 index of intraindustry specialization to the corresponding 1969 index. For trade with the other industrialized countries, the newly industrializing developing countries, and the less developed countries, respectively, these ratios are 1.12, 1.19, and 1.82 for the United States; 1.10, 1.81, and 2.45 for Germany; 1.43, 1.40, and 2.48 for the United Kingdom; and 1.04, 1.80, and 1.93 for Japan. In the case of Britain, the large increase in intraindustry trade with the other industrialized countries reflects the effects of entry into the European Economic Community (EEC). As a result of these changes, in 1979 the ratio of the index of intraindustry trade with the newly industrialized developing countries to that with the other industrialized countries was in the 48–80 percent range in the four countries while the corresponding ratio for the less developed countries was between 22 percent and 54 percent.

It follows that Deardorff and Stern seriously underestimate the benefits developing countries may obtain through the elimination of tariffs by the industrialized countries. Thus, the statement made by Deardorff in presenting the paper at the conference that "we have gone as far as we can usefully go in tariff reduction, and maybe we have gone too far" is not defensible. Indeed, if we further consider that the lack of progress in tariff reductions can easily lead to backsliding, multinational negotiations aimed at further tariff reductions would be highly desirable from the point-of-view of the developing countries.

Further benefits would be derived through the elimination of nontariff barriers. According to Deardorff and Stern, "to the extent that sectors are protected both by tariffs and NTBs, the elimination of all trade barriers might not change the results appreciably." This statement appears to reflect a misinterpretation of the model results which adjust for the effects of the NTBs. Thus, "the model includes, for each industry and country, an endogenous tariff-equivalent variable that adjusts to reduce changes in imports to only a fraction of what they would be in the absence of NTBs. That fraction is taken to be the fraction of trade not covered by NTBs in 1976."

At the same time, given the observed large differences between the tariff equivalents of NTBs and the rate of tariffs (Baldwin 1970), the developing countries could obtain considerable welfare gains if the industrialized countries abolished their NTBs. In fact, according to the estimates by Fred Brown and John Whalley (1980) which the authors cite, the abolition of NTBs would provide a welfare gain more than 10 times greater than that owing to the elimination of tariffs. The resulting gains could be estimated in the framework of the model by assuming that the tariff equivalents of NTBs would be reduced to zero.

While Deardorff and Stern have examined the effects of tariff and nontariff barriers on international trade in "Trade-Related Investment Issues," A. E. Safarian considers trade distortions that result from rules imposed on the subsidiaries of foreign companies or are the consequence of fiscal incentives. Safarian's emphasis is understandably on Canada. Consistent with my comparative advantage, I will concentrate on questions relating to developing countries.

Trade-related performance requirements may take the form of minimum export targets or domestic content rules for production for home markets. Safarian suggests that "with resources fully employed in the countries concerned, one could argue, with some exceptions, that what occurs is a decline in efficiency of resource use rather than direct employment effects as such. In a world of unemployed resources , international shifts are more likely to happen."

In developing countries where performance requirements are by far the most important, physical capital, labor skills, and managerial know-how are scarce, and hence resource allocative effects are very important. Additional effects relate to the transfer of incomes from domestic users to foreign companies. Finally, in the case of domestic content requirements, there is loss of economies of scale.

Minimum export requirements involve an economic cost, inasmuch as the implicit subsidies involved distort the allocation of scarce resources. At the same time, these subsidies are generally financed by domestic users who pay higher prices in the protected home market in order to permit exports to take place. To the extent that the profits of the foreign subsidiaries are increased as a result, their transfer abroad will add to the cost of inefficient resource allocation in the country concerned.

Export requirements are imposed in larger developing countries, such as Brazil, where the size of the domestic market limits the cost borne by the individual user. In the smaller developing countries, domestic content requirements predominate, with the automobile industry being a prime example. The imposition of these requirements leads to the loss of economies of scale as parts, components, and accessories are manufactured in small production runs, thereby forgoing the advantages of vertical specialization. The resulting excess cost may reach as much as 100 percent (Baranson 1969).

While fiscal incentives may be granted to firms that meet certain performance requirements, in most developing countries they are provided independently from such requirements. Trade distortions will occur in the second case if investment incentives are provided on a selective rather than an across-the-board basis or if the particular measures applied affect the choice of factor proportions. Both are prevalent in developing countries, which have often used investment incentives to favor certain sectors, and have applied measures that reduce the cost of capital, thereby providing inducements for capital-intensive activities (Balassa 1981).

At the same time, Safarian correctly emphasizes the need for increased transparency in regard to trade-related investment policies. He is also correct in noting that "in terms of existing accords, GATT [General Agreement on Tariffs and Trade] offers the best means to tackle performance requirements and investment incentives which are directly related to trade" through the application of the Articles of Agreement. But, one may be less sanguine as regards the chances of introducing a new "section in GATT which explicitly applies to a defined set of trade-related investment policies," inasmuch as many developing countries—but also Canada and France—consider these issues to fall within the domain of their national sovereignty.

I come next to John Diebold's "The Information Technology Industries: A Case Study of High Technology Trade" that straddles the areas of trade in goods and services. My purpose is to extend the discussion to high technology industries in general and to put into sharper focus the differences between the French and the Japanese approaches to these industries.

Prestige projects have played an important role in high technology industries in France, unlike Japan. These projects aim at national-political objectives, with economic considerations taking second place. A prime example is the Concorde that has been a *succès d'estime* but a failure commercially, with no foreign sales occurring and Air France being unable to cover its variable costs.

Furthermore, the French policy has generally been to select a single firm in each industry, as exemplified by the *Plan Calcul* that proved to be unsuccessful, eventually leading to the involvement of an American firm, which it had been designed to avoid. By contrast, in Japan, several firms compete in the computer industry as well as in semiconductors, integrated circuits, and high technology industries in general. Neither does the Japanese government interfere with technological and product choices by individual firms, as has the French government in some industries.

Support to high technology industries also tends to be firm-specific in France, while in Japan it is industry-specific and is available to all firms that meet certain criteria. Such support takes the form of the financing of research and development, fiscal incentives through accelerated depreciation provisions, and tax holidays, as well as low-interest loans.

Last but not least, whereas Japanese firms have to fend for themselves in domestic and foreign markets and compete with each other in the process, French firms in high technology industries often produce largely for sheltered markets. Government procurement for military and for civilian purposes, as well as subsidized exports to socialist and developing countries in the framework of bilateral agreements, often play an important role in the industries in question. This fact, in turn, limits the role of commercial consideration and competitive pressures for technological advance.

According to a careful study of French electronics industries, "state support appears to have reduced the pressure on firms under its tutelage to adopt structures more suited to their technological and market problems" and the technological goals of the state weakened the competitive position of these firms" (Zysmann 1973, pp. 88, 207). Such has been the case, in particular, for state-owned firms while private firms have had more room for maneuver and have achieved greater success in world markets.

In the mid-1970s a partial reversal of the policies occurred, with greater emphasis given to market processes. However, the socialist government of François Mitterrand has nationalized large private firms in high technology industries, it is reorganizing these industries by selecting firms to manufacture particular products in the framework of "filières," and it interferes with product decisions made by the remaining private firms.

Finally, William Diebold, Jr., and Helena Stalson have reviewed "Negotiating Issues in International Service Transactions." In this connection, the first question concerns the character of service transactions. According to the authors, "there is at least a strong similarity between some service transactions and the activities of foreign investors," when the "analogy with investment emphasizes that to an important degree what is involved is the right of establishment and how it is provided." "In addition to the common complaint of US service firms that they are denied the right of establishment abroad, the difficulties of doing business, once established, center on onerous licensing and certification requests, limitations on the range of services that may be offered to the public, restrictions on employee nationality and on foreign equity, and discrimination in government contracts in favor of national firms."

While these statements emphasize differences between merchandise and service transactions, closer inspection reveals considerable similarities between the two. Just like industries producing goods, service industries may undertake international transactions either by exporting or by establishing subsidiaries abroad. Sales by domestic resident firms to foreign residents are dominant in areas such as freight and other transportation, communication, insurance, and engineering. In turn, sales by subsidiaries of domestic firms located abroad to foreign residents are of particular importance in banking and advertising.

Sapir (1982) cites estimates, according to which foreign sales by subsidiaries abroad represent about 70 percent of the international transactions of US services industries; the corresponding figure is about 75 percent for merchandise. There is thus little difference in this regard between merchandise and service transactions. Both furthermore are subject to similar barriers.

The difficulties involved in establishing abroad and in operating foreign subsidiaries apply equally to merchandise and service activities. Also, nontariff barriers have assumed increased importance in regard to merchandise trade in recent years, and the scope of these barriers is rather similar in the two cases. Thus, accounting, advertising, and banking often encounter quantitative restrictions; maritime transport and insurance may be subject to import licensing; government procurement rules apply to transportation, construction, and engineering; data processing and motion pictures are subject to customs valuation procedures of a protective character; and containers encounter technical barriers in the form of national norms and specifications.

A further question relates to the relevance of comparative advantage to trade in services. According to Diebold and Stalson, "when it comes to international comparisons, it is less clear how one might know in advance what competitive advantages one country had over another." This observation may apply more to trade in manufactured goods than to trade in services, however. In chapter 4, Cline notes that "for a range of manufactured goods, comparative advantage is made, not given." In turn, research done at the World Bank indicates the importance of comparative advantages in service trade (Sapir-Lutz 1981).

Thus, international differences in physical capital endowment and, to a lesser extent country size, affect transportation services, while the availability of human capital influences insurance transactions. Furthermore, technical services, as well as the sales of know-how in the form of patents and copyrights, are largely a function of research and development expenditures. While, according to Diebold and Stalson, "many services are highly labor-intensive," this appears to be the case for domestic nontraded services rather than for traded services. Data processing and construction abroad are the only cases where the availability of cheap labor provides an advantage, but even in these cases it is skilled rather than unskilled labor that is important.

Similarities in the character of international transactions in goods and services, the barriers they face, and their basic determinants suggest the need for similar actions in reducing barriers to trade in regard to both. This conclusion applies to all internationally traded services, including banking. While Diebold and Stalson suggest "treating banking separately from other services" largely because of "its close links with monetary policy and credit control," this should not be an obstacle to liberalization in regard to banking. Thus, foreign-owned banks, which dominate in a number of developing countries, apply central bank regulations in the same way as domestically owned banks do. And, given the interdependence of the various banking services, it would hardly be feasible to limit negotiations to nontraditional banking services, as Diebold and Stalson propose.

The question arises, however, as to why the issue of trade in services has assumed importance most recently in international discussions. On the basis of available data, it would appear that the explanation does not lie in the increased importance of service transactions, taken together. According to estimates made by the Office of the US Trade Representative, the share of service transactions in the world exports of goods and services increased only from 16.8 percent in 1974 to 17.2 percent in 1980. And this ratio fell from 14.7 percent to 13.4 percent in the United States, which has put forward proposals for liberalizing international trade in services.

Larger increases are shown for the category of other private services that includes accounting, advertising, banking, construction and engineering, data processing, nonmerchandise insurance, motion pictures, and royalties and fees as well as workers' remittances. The share of this category in the world exports of goods and services increased 5.5 percent in 1974 to 6.1 percent in 1980. Excluding service exports from developing countries, which consist largely of workers' remittances, the increase is from 6.1 percent to 6.7 percent. Growth was lower than the average in the United States, however, leading to a reduction in the share of the other private services category from 5.3 percent to 4.1 percent of US exports of goods and services between 1974 and 1980.

The relative decline of US exports of other private services may be related to increased restrictions on these exports abroad. In the absence of a breakdown of the data, changes in the composition of this category are not known, however. Also, the available data underestimate the increases that have occurred as they cover only partially some of the most rapidly growing private services, including data processing and information as well as professional services. Also some service activities, such as reinsurance and foreign contract operation are measured on a net rather than a gross basis.

Apart from the development of a new range of services, the increased attention given to services may be explained by the internationalization of financial markets as well as by the growing interaction between goods and service trade. The internationalization of financial markets affects banking and insurance, as well as data processing. In turn, some of the rapidly growing services, such as data processing, engineering design, and construction abroad are often linked to transactions in goods, with one or the other being the primary transaction, or the two forming a package.

Thus, the export of computers tends to be accompanied by the sale of computer software, and engineering design often brings with it the sale of machinery, while construction abroad and the sale of construction equipment frequently go hand-in-hand. It should be added that all high technology areas, and in particular data processing and telecommunications, are expected to grow rapidly during the 1980s.

Before international negotiations are undertaken on services, however, there is need for more information on the barriers they face. As regards the content of the negotiations, there is need to ensure that countries apply a "due process," under which foreign entities can pursue their own interests. There is further need to establish a dispute-settlement mechanism on issues related to services trade. These objectives may be served through the application of existing GATT rules and Multilateral Trade Negotiations (MTN) codes as well as through the negotiation of new codes that could also provide a framework for reductions in existing barriers to trade in services.

The question has been raised as to whether an across-the-board or a sectoral approach should be followed in regard to negotiations on trade in services. The sectoral approach has the important disadvantage that it does not allow for the balancing of interests either among sectors in the individual countries or among countries. It would be more desirable, therefore, to pursue an across-the-board approach, with additional rules—or codes—established in cases when a particular service industry has special problems.

The balancing of interests among countries also favors a multilateral over a bilateral approach. As regards the latter, the question of reciprocity needs to be considered. According to Diebold and Stalson, "if foreign governments are not prepared to treat American companies the way the US government treats foreign companies, then reciprocity will require the imposition of restrictions in the United States to match those abroad. Whether this is a sensible arrangement that will give either economic gains or true bargaining power to the United States is not something that can be settled in the abstract."

The imposition of restrictions to match restrictions abroad is called "aggressive reciprocity" by Cline. Aggressive reciprocity should not be invoked even if liberalization of services progresses slowly, both because its use may jeopardize the chances for future negotiations and because of the danger of "spillover" to merchandise trade. More generally, particular care should be exercised to avoid a situation when bilateral agreements become an obstacle to the pursuit of multilateral negotiations. The former should rather be a steppingstone to the latter.

A further consideration is that the use of aggressive reciprocity by the United States may easily backfire, although the United States stands to gain from service negotiations, given its comparative advantage in a number of modern services. A related question is the interest in service negotiations of the developing countries, which do not appear to possess comparative advantage in any of the major services.

Part of the answer is that the newly industrialized countries, which represent an increasingly important factor in merchandise trade, are acquiring comparative advantage in certain services as they accumulate physical and human capital. This trend is apparent in the success of Korea and Turkey to provide construction services in the Middle East and in recent development in the provision of professional services (the Philippines), printing (India), and data processing (Singapore). At the same time, the importation of modern services adds to technological and organizational know-how in the developing countries.

Still, references to future interests may not suffice to induce the developing countries to participate in multilateral negotiations on trade in services. Thus, the industrialized countries and, in particular, the United States may have to offer concessions on merchandise trade for the negotiations to proceed.

Bibliography

Balassa, Bela. "Tariff Reductions and Trade in Manufactures Among Industrial Countries." *American Economic Review* (June 1966).

———. "The Structure of Protection in Industrial Countries and Its Effects on the Exports of Processed Goods from Developing Countries." *Kennedy Round: Estimated Effects on Tariff Barriers.* New York: United Nations, 1968.

———. "Industrial Prospects and Policies in the Developing Countries." World Bank Staff Working Paper, no. 453. Washington: World Bank, April 1981.

———. "Disequilibrium Analysis in Developing Countries: An Overview." Development Research Department (DRD) Discussion Papers, no. 36. Washington: World Bank, June 1982. Also in *World Development* (December 1982), pp. 1027–38.

Baldwin, Robert E. *Nontariff Distortions of International Trade.* Washington: Brookings Institution, 1970.

Baldwin, Robert E., and Tracy Murray. "MFN Tariff Reductions and Developing Country Trade Benefits under the GSP." *Economic Journal* (March 1977).

Baranson, Jack. *Automotive Industries in Developing Countries.* World Bank Occasional Papers, no. 8. Washington: World Bank, 1969.

Birnberg, Thomas B. "Tariff Reform Option Economic Effects on Developing and Developed Countries." In *Policy Alternatives for a New International Economic Order,* ed. William R. Cline. New York: Praeger Publications for the Overseas Development Council, 1979.

Finger, J. Michael. "The Effects of the Kennedy Round Tariff Concessions on the Exports of Developing Countries." *Economic Journal* (March 1976).

Helpman, Elhanan. "International Trade in the Presence of Product Differentiation, Economies of Scale, and Monopolistic Competition: A Chamberlin-Heckscher-Ohlin Approach." *Journal of International Economics* (August 1981).

Krugman, Paul R. "Increasing Returns, Monopolistic Competition, and International Trade." *Journal of International Economics* (November 1979).

Lancaster, Kelvin. "Intra-Industry Trade under Perfect Monopolistic Competition." *Journal of International Economics* (May 1980).

Murray, Tracy. "The 'Tokyo Round' and Latin America." Paper presented at the Annual Meeting of the Eastern Economics Association, May 1979, Washington. Processed.

Sapir, Andre. "Trade in Services: Policy Issues for the Eighties." *Columbia Journal of World Business* (Summer 1982).

Sapir, Andre, and Ernst Lutz. "Trade in Services: Economic Determinants and Development-Related Issues." World Bank Staff Working Paper, no. 480. Washington: World Bank, November 1981.

Zysmann, John. *Political Strategies for Industrial Order. State, Market, and Industry in France.* Berkeley: University of California Press, 1973.

Alan Deardorff in his oral presentation suggested that it might be better not to seek further tariff reductions. Their welfare benefits would be small, while tariff elimination might force policymakers to erect new nontariff barriers. Nontariff barriers are the main obstacle to trade today.

Rodney de C. Grey argued that Canada's Foreign Investment Review Agency (FIRA) was no more restrictive, only more transparent, than practices of other countries restricting investment. He considered it a mistake for the United States to have taken the FIRA to the General Agreement on Tariffs and Trade (GATT) in complaint.

Roberto Fendt noted that in services several new industrial countries were doing well in competition against industrial countries even though they faced subsidies by those countries. As for performance criteria in developing countries, at least they are transparent; multinational companies know what the rules of the game will be.

Åke Lindén remarked that unlike Deardorff, he read the Deardorff-Stern paper to imply that further tariff liberalization was desirable. It would be wrong to think that maintenance of current tariffs could avoid new nontariff barriers (NTBs), or that tariff reduction automatically would cause additional NTBs. In the past, several proposals for major tariff cuts have emerged; for example, in preparations for the Tokyo Round the United States, Japan, Sweden, and Switzerland advanced proposals to eliminate tariffs in manufacturing trade, although the European Community (EC) was opposed. Such proposals could resurface.

C. Fred Bergsten favored tariff reduction or elimination as a useful component to any future major round of trade negotiations, for its own sake and as a catalyst for liberalization in other areas. Such negotiations could be important because they would help hold the line against new protection. Their welfare benefits would include not only those of actual liberalization but also the avoidance of costs from new protection.

723

In addition to the conference discussion, *Deardorff* and *Stern* submitted the following written reply.

Reply by Deardorff and Stern to Comments by Balassa

In our chapter we note that our results suggest net decreases in employment in textiles in several developing countries. To the extent that developing countries specialize in industries such as textiles that are exempted from tariff reductions and NTBs are not completely binding, some of the effects that we describe will be present. Further, these countries may be squeezed on the cost side by the increases in world prices that will come from tariff reductions even if NTBs are assumed to be completely binding in absolute terms.

Balassa claims that the supply elasticities in the developing countries in our model are too low. This may well be, but we lack the data to verify Balassa's contention based on his reference to Finger's work on the Kennedy Round. Our model does capture differences in effective rates of protection, contrary to Balassa's statement. It is true that we do not model scale economies derived from specializing on differentiated products. We are aware of the possible theoretical importance of such specialization, but it is not clear how and why it derives from intraindustry trade.

Deardorff's statement at the conference about the usefulness of further tariff reductions should be understood in the context that many important NTBs were left intact during the Tokyo Round. It does not seem useful therefore to devote too much time and effort to developing a new negotiating authority for tariff reduction when the real problems lie in NTBs.

Balassa's reference to our statement about the elimination of all trade barriers (concluding our discussion of table 20.5) is taken out of context. Our discussion here refers to the ranking of sectors by percentage changes in value added. We were simply noting that many sectors were protected by both tariffs and NTBs so that elimination of all trade barriers would not change the rankings appreciably in the sense of effective protection. Finally, we are very explicit in the chapter about the importance of NTBs and of their impact on developing countries.

PART V

Policy Synthesis

Trade policy making requires two steps: identification of the desired features of the future trading régime in terms that approximate the economic ideal of free trade on the one hand but lie within the bounds of feasibility on the other; and design of a strategy for action likely to achieve this régime. With few exceptions the conference participants shared a common view with respect to the first step. The future trading régime should permit gradual unwinding of the major protection from the past and in addition should make the greatest possible allowance for incorporation of areas of trade not now covered by GATT into an open international trading system.

In chapter 21, panelists Jagdish Bhagwati (Columbia University), Richard Cooper (Harvard University and formerly US Under Secretary of State), and W. Max Corden (Australian National University) derive their respective policy syntheses from the conference. Their view of the feasible ideal share broad areas but includes variations, such as Cooper's more ambitious call for free trade in industrial products among industrial and other willing countries, and Corden's more permissive attitude toward subsidies on grounds that they are self-limiting by virtue of their cost.

In the concluding chapter 22, C. Fred Bergsten and I attempt to spell out the form of a "constrained ideal" for the trade régime in the later 1980s, and in addition we set forth a possible program of action to achieve this result. Informed by the additional retrospective experience of the November 1982 GATT Ministerial (whereas the other contributions to this volume date from mid-1982), this chapter proposes a four-point strategy that features a standstill on protection (with substantial implementing force), a major new round of trade negotiations covering both the old and the new issues, a resuscitation and improvement in trade adjustment assistance, and integration of trade and exchange rate policy with a move toward a more effective exchange rate régime. The GATT Ministerial, which prompted the initial convening of the conference reported here (from which an earlier policy monograph was drawn prior to the Ministerial),[1] made only modest inroads in the direction of such a program. A more forceful program along the lines suggested in chapter 22 seems essential if the drift toward protection is to be arrested and reversed, and if the potential gains from trade in newly emerging fields are to be realized through consolidation of open trading rules before protection encroaches in these new areas as well.

[1] C. Fred Bergsten and William R. Cline, *Trade Policy in the 1980s*, POLICY ANALYSES IN INTERNATIONAL ECONOMICS, NO. 3 (Washington: Institute for International Economics, November 1982).

CHAPTER **21**

Toward A Policy Synthesis: Panel Discussion

1 Jagdish N. Bhagwati

The presumption, shared by many at this conference, is that an open trading system is a desirable objective. This presumption follows both from economic theory and from experience. Many economists, since the days of Adam Smith and David Ricardo, have agreed on the benefits to be derived from an open trading system. Today, economic ideology lends its weight fully to this doctrine, although economic theory of the same mold does *not* support the seemingly similar proposition that free international mobility of capital also enriches each of the countries participating in that process.

The theoretical presumption in favor of an open trading system has also been reinforced by the experience of the postwar period. As Bergsten and Cline have noted in their chapter, the remarkable growth of income in the postwar period was accompanied also by an equally remarkable growth of trade. There is, of course, an identification problem here: did trade serve as an "engine of growth," or was it a wagon hitched to the engine of growth? But the general trade liberalization of the postwar period certainly fueled the growth of that period in more than a marginal fashion. Besides, we now know from the work of many, including the work of Bela Balassa, Irving Kravis, and the recent National Bureau of Economic Research (NBER) project that Anne Krueger and I directed, that the developing countries that maintained an outward orientation, thus seizing the trading opportunity that the postwar expansion of the world economy provided, performed substantially better than those that continued with an inward orientation.

Since the GATT oversaw this postwar expansion of trade and provided the "rule of law" that this required, the question before us today is: what can be done to preserve this open trading system? In this context I address three major issues that have emerged, in my judgment, as the principal focal points of concern.

MFN versus Selectivity

An important question has been raised, in relation to Article XIX, concerning the advisability of modifying it in the direction of selectivity. Alan Wolff has argued for this solution; and Martin Wolf has argued against it, equally cogently. There is little disagreement about the intrinsic desirability of MFN. The argument is, in essence, about the advisability of having on the statutes an article which has increasingly been *bypassed* in favor of bilateral, or multilateral, action outside the framework of GATT because it does not permit selectivity.

The most compelling argument for bringing selectivity into Article XIX is that it will recognize reality and increase therefore the use of GATT by members. In this regard, it is important to note that the GATT has already been seriously compromised on its MFN provision in many important directions: argiculture and textiles have been taken out; customs unions have been permitted; the developing countries have been exempted; and the current contention of at least some of the contracting parties that the obligation of Article I on nondiscrimination does not apply to NTB reductions in the Tokyo Round. GATT has certainly "bent" therefore in the direction of selectivity in important ways. There seem then to have been two major classes of such exceptions to MFN. *Either*, as with Article XXIV and Part IV, the coalitions in favor of these changes were not effectively opposed by other contracting parties: the United States, in particular, supported the European Community's (EC) political objectives; and the developing countries' demands were considered to possess legitimacy while not being expensive. *Or*, virtually all important members of the GATT agreed on the need to infringe on the MFN principle (as with the Multi-Fiber Arrangement, MFA, and agriculture) simply because domestic political difficulties made it impossible to do anything else.

Few would argue that the GATT has been destroyed by bending to reality in these ways, although they and others might wish to bring some of these exclusions (e.g., agriculture and MFA, for instance) back into the GATT fold in some way. Can we view amending Article XIX to accommodate selectivity as a similar "realistic" step that will not fatally compromise GATT in its MFN objectives any more than the other exclusions did? I suppose that GATT could survive even this. But I would come down in favor of those who oppose this amendment. Many contracting parties have already found a way around Article XIX, when their domestic political difficulties required them to do so and their external political muscle permitted them to do so, by imposing voluntary export restraints (VERs) on selected export- ers. But let us not forget that the executives in the Organization for Economic Cooperation and Development (OECD) countries are gen- erally loath to invoke such VERs and that, having GATT Article XIX in its present form, does provide some legitimacy and effective argumentation supportive of their efforts to ward off special interests seeking protection on grounds of market disruption and injury. Why deprive them of this useful prop by legitimating selective protectionist intervention? The war against legislative protectionist pressures in pluralistic societies plagued by high levels of unemployment such as today is such a serious business that we should hesitate to legitimate the practices that reflect a reluctant surrender to these pressures.

Reciprocity, Subsidies, and Fairness

Serious threats to the GATT system come from other directions. In particular, the growing feeling about the need for "reciprocity" in trading arrangements, allegations about subsidies that distort com- parative advantage in favor of one's competitors, and charges of dumping have raised major new concerns about the viability of the GATT system.

Interestingly, most economists have traditionally failed to see why anyone should worry about why the foreigner's prices to you are what they are: the cheaper they supply you with your imports, the better off you are. Somehow, the "systemic" aspects of the question have not impressed themselves on their consciousness. Thus, on his "Free to Choose" TV program on the tyranny of controls, Friedman argued precisely the traditional position that we ought to trade freely re- gardless of what the foreigners were doing, whereas I countered by saying that I would not necessarily receive stolen property at a cheaper price since that could have a systemic effect by undermining the rule of law.

The problem with other countries subsidizing their exports (which doubtless hurts them and helps us, if we believe economic theory on this as we should) or indulging in dumping (which is not simply a temporary, offensive device), is that (i) it does imply a distortion of world efficiency, a value that liberal economists hold in high regard and which they expect an agency such as GATT to uphold; and, far more seriously, (ii) it offends the sense of "fairness" or "fair play" that different economic agents within the importing country expect their governments to embrace. Once that sense of fairness is violated, it becomes easier to unleash the protectionist sentiments that are always present in the shape of pressure groups. The systemic effects of these protectionist sentiments, if translated into action, undermine the liberal trading system itself.

Unfortunately, the threshold at which the sense of fairness is perceived to be violated has been lowered significantly in recent years: as we know from recent attempts at establishing "aggressive reciprocity," for instance. Also, matters have been made worse since I also note an increasing sense that "fairness" in trade further implies that the members of a society should not profit from cheaper imports if that means that the workers in the import-competing industries are seriously hurt. This is *not* simply a Luddite reaction. It is rather a sense of "social contract" which says that, if any efficiency improvement comes to an *outside* factor, such as lower import prices, that should not be accepted if it hurts someone badly; whereas if it comes from an *inside* factor, such as technical change, it is kosher. This kind of social contract has already been accepted by modern societies in relation to immigration restrictions. I would like to import a Haitian maid and this would increase American productivity, but I would not be allowed to do this, of course, since I would be "depriving" a local New Yorker of a maid's job. But if I were to import a maid from Georgia, that *would* be accepted and the "deprivation" of a job for a local New Yorker does not matter. (Will we be able to fight off this outside-inside dichotomy in our reactions to trade any more than we have managed to do it in regard to immigration? In my dark moments, I wonder whether the rise of immigration quotas at the turn of the last century is not simply the handwriting on the wall: that restrictions on trade will also arise at the turn of *this* century, with access to markets being regarded as a privilege, to be doled out according to national criteria rather than agreed-upon GATT-type rules of law. And, then again, in my optimistic moods, I think instead of immigration restrictions and policies being brought under the rule of law, in an augmented international economic order.

What does all this imply for our successful management of an open trading system? It would appear to me that it must make us particularly careful about not giving comfort to the special interest groups *via* arguments that can be so misused. Thus, for example, the great concern that has been expressed repeatedly by some of the conference participants that Japan has inscrutable, invisible barriers to trade simply because the ex post bilateral balance between the United

States and Japan is in large deficit, and because American business-men complain about not being able to sell effectively in Japan, should be resolutely countered and exposed for the fallacies on which it is based, even though there may be some limited validity to the fear that Japan's governmental policies may be detrimental to imports. Again, we ought to curb our natural enthusiasm for a trading system that does not distort comparative advantage and yields world effi-ciency by looking benignly at subsidies of several kinds that are con-ceived to be primarily domestic in their objectives but which do, after all in general-equilibrium analysis, affect comparative advantage. Once you bring them into the realm of discourse, you are really opening up a Pandora's Box. Where would you draw the line? After all, leaving aside conflicting views of the role of the state in regard to ownership and attendant subsidization, there are also *implicit* sub-sidies. Energy policy can affect energy prices and hence affect com-parative advantage. Differences in exercise of income tax jurisdictions over citizens working abroad, as between the US "global" system and the European "schedular" system, can adversely affect (US) comparative advantage in tendering for construction contracts abroad and so on. A perfectionist will want to harmonize everything and scream every time that harmonization does not exist. But the net effect of this, in a world of conflicting views about the other goals of these policies, would simply be to fuel further the possibly growing sense in the trading countries that the trading system is unfair and that protection to the offended sectors, in each instance, should be the answer. Cleverness would have been the enemy of wisdom; the best would have been the enemy of the good.

New versus Old Issues

That brings me to a similar sense of caution against getting hastily into the new areas of concern that have been raised, principally by the United States, in regard to high technology trade and services. I am impressed by the fact that the United States has to have a direct interest in these issues since the comparative advantage of the United States has increasingly shifted toward such activities as against man-ufacturing. It is only natural therefore that the United States should have growing worries about these areas and should want to bring them somehow into the ambit of GATT's rules of law.

But this does not reduce in any way the serious dangers that one would face in feeding protectionist pressures, *via* the fueled sense of unfairness noted by me, if these types of issues were brought into the arena of negotiation prematurely. Take the matter of trade in services. As has been noted by many already, it raises issues that directly touch on national regulations and concerns reflecting political and cultural factors. Admittedly, trade in goods does this too from time to time. But, by and large, it does not, and we have learned over the years to consider political and cultural concerns in regard to trade in goods as something rather comic, if not ludicrous. Besides, consider also the desire expressed by many to free up the international flow of investments on the ground that it is necessary to support free trade in goods (and services). But suppose that you do start down that road, impinging on national concerns of a political nature that are not simply a Canadian fetish but fairly widespread (and spreadable to the US itself as we realized when Arab OPEC investments began to flow into the US and led to widespread political unease and even demands for restrictions). In what way will we be able then to say that such trade-related investment of capital should not also be accompanied by similar freedom to export trade-related labor? Will we permit free migration simply to support the claims of NIC (or what I call SOUTHNIC) exporters who would assert that, as in the Middle East, they wish to bring in hundreds of thousands of their native laborers, skilled people, and others? I have no doubt that all these questions have to be increasingly raised. I just do not feel that now is the time to do anything except raise them, to contemplate them in study groups, and to suggest to GATT that they keep track of progress in sorting out the full implications of the demands for freer trade in services and in trade-supporting investments and labor flows.

Instead, I am with Wolf and others at this conference in thinking that we should rather explore the possibility of getting GATT to reestablish control over MFA, to explore systematically the question of getting agricultural policy of the OECD countries into coherence and compatibility in stages with the principles of an open trading system, and to explore the possibility of getting the SOUTHNICs to accept reciprocity in trade negotiations now that their exports have grown and it is difficult to argue for their "infancy" without creating protectionist responses on grounds of unfair competition. It should be easier to look again at old *lapses* from GATT than to start negotiating new areas of *extension* of GATT.

So, in the end, I come down suggesting that Article XIX be left alone in regard to selectivity, that the growing focus on countervailing duties to offset domestic subsidies by foreign governments be rejected, that the new areas of concern relating to services and foreign investments are too politically sensitive to start up on now, and that it would be ideal if we simply focused on putting many of the old matters back on the GATT agenda.

2 Richard N. Cooper

The discussion during the past two days has been incrementalist in approach—improving the existing GATT system here and there, piecemeal. No doubt that is a sound approach. But the trading system is now, under serious threat of erosion, and it behooves a group such as this to think of possible major and not just incremental changes to preserve an open trading system. In speaking of major changes, I am addressing the objectives of the decade, not simply the next few years. It will take at least a decade to develop any major new approach to the point of implementation, so we are really speaking of the trading system as it will look toward the end of the century.

The trading system is under threat for two reasons. The first is the current world recession, which I do not think will end quickly, and which is putting enormous strain on the system of liberal trade. The main reversals so far have been in the advanced developing countries. But all of the major industrial countries are experiencing substantial protectionist pressures, and the question is how long a thin line of officials can hold them before they break. The liberal trading system may be a major casualty of the attempt to beat back inflation with negligible growth and high unemployment.

The second threat to the trading system is more deep-seated. Many of the "subsidies" and other actions of government that influence trade are, in my view, responses to two basic forces. The first is that governments are increasingly held responsible by democratic publics for economic conditions and economic welfare. The second involves changes in economic trade-related structure that make actions more attractive relative to traditional aggregate demand management. With greater interdependence among countries, monetary and fiscal measures become relatively less effective than they once were, and this problem has been compounded by the dilemma created for macroeconomic policy by the apparent trade-off between inflation and unemployment, with governments vascillating between the two in their attempts to keep national economies on an even keel. Moreover, the increased mobility of factors of production—both establishments and certain kinds of labor—make more attractive both "regional" policies and "industrial" policies as measures to preserve economic growth and employment. These developments, more than declining tariff barriers, push governments in the direction of sectoral policies, and these developments are fundamental, not superficial.

What are possible solutions—in the nature of changes in the trading régime—to the erosion of a liberal world trading system?

One is to reduce greatly the public expectations of government and therefore the role of government. This would involve a reversion back toward laissez faire. If governments are not expected to control economic conditions, they will not meddle in regional and sectoral affairs. That is the rhetoric of the Reagan administration in the United States and the Thatcher administration in Britain, although it is not the pattern of many of their actions. In any case a reversion to laissez faire is unlikely to succeed. If economic conditions are not going well, the publics are more likely to blame their leaders for those developments, rather than the ineffectiveness of governments in influencing them, and will replace the leaders.

A second major proposal would be a move to free trade in industrial products among all the countries willing to make that commitment. (Agriculture involves too many inconsistent domestic policies to make free trade in agricultural products thinkable at this stage.) The advantage of free trade in industrial products could be threefold. First, it would signal to the relevant publics that trade among the participating countries is not a variable to be tampered with lightly. There would be a heavy presumption that trade would continue unimpeded although highly constrained escape clause action might still be possible. This commitment would thus be designed to change the public psychology about trade flows.

Second, it would compel consultation among participating countries on all policies that could be expected to have a major influence on trade, for example, major regional or sectoral policies. This consultation would become a normal feature in framing such policies. At the same time, it would be quite unnecessary to coordinate closely or harmonize these policies completely. The system could tolerate country-by-country variations in such policies, just as the United States tolerates variations among states in their policies toward business activity and taxation. There might, however, be international agreement on the outer limits of direct or indirect subsidies that could be introduced under the name of regional or industrial policies.

Third, nonparticipating countries would still have to pay tariffs in order to export to the free trade area, but safeguard and counter-vailing action would be based on the presumption of a zero tariff, so that the existing tariff would be deemed to provide some protective relief in the absence of special action, and a heavier burden of proof would have to be met for additional relief of a countervailing or safeguard character.

One feature of this suggestion is worth pointing out. It involves conditional most-favored-nation (MFN) treatment, though of a form sanctioned by Article XXIV of the GATT. In view of the heavy criticism that conditional MFN has come under, I would like to say a word in its favor, although I would not want this to be interpreted as favoring the reciprocity legislation that is now before the Congress. The liberalization of trade that has taken place over the last thirty years has depended heavily on "reciprocity" in the liberalizing ne-gotiations. This reciprocity has made it possible to persuade demo-cratic publics that trade liberalization is in the national interest. MFN creates the possibility of "free riders" on any trade negotiation, and with the number and economic importance of countries now members of the GATT having increased sharply, this free rider aspect may well stifle further progress toward trade liberalization. Conditional MFN permits the formation of clubs smaller than the full GATT membership that are willing to take on stronger obligations; but the perceived rewards need to be commensurate to the obligations. An industrial free trade area, like the government procurement code, offers an example of mutual rights and obligations that go consid-erably further than those involved in the GATT itself.

I would permit any member of the GATT willing to commit itself to industrial free trade to join in the free trade area. What about the Generalized System of Tariff Preferences (GSP)? This is something we must deal with in any case. US legislation authorizing GSP expires in early 1985, so action needs to be taken in 1983, a nonelection year, if GSP is to be extended. I was never enthusiastic about GSP, on two grounds. First, I felt that the price in terms of "safeguards" would exceed the rewards to developing countries in terms of tariff gains. Secondly, I felt that sooner or later officials in advanced developing countries would desire international pressure to reduce their own excessive protection, and would therefore welcome the role of reci-procity in achieving trade liberalization in the face of domestic po-litical opposition. For the next decade I would confine GSP to the poorest developing countries, and would restore reciprocity—in the traditional, trade negotiating sense—for middle-income countries, with an invitation to join the industrial free trade area. Prolonged (e.g., 10-year) and asymmetrical transition periods might be permitted to an advanced developing country that chose to join the industrial free trade area.

If a move to an industrial free trade area is considered too radical a step in terms of liberalizing trade and reducing national autonomy in the pursuit of diverse objectives, I have another suggestion. The present industrial countries should impose a uniform minimum tariff of 5 percent or even 10 percent and treat this tariff as the basic protection that domestic economic activity would have from the actions of foreign firms and governments. Straight export subsidies would be prohibited, but a very heavy burden of proof would have to be met by any party wanting additional protection beyond the minimum uniform tariff, either through safeguard action or through antidumping or countervailing duties. Developing countries would be better off than they now are with such a duty combined with strong safeguards against safeguards. A uniform duty would be designed not to protect particular industries but to preserve some degree of national autonomy in economic policy. It would also generate revenue at a cost not too great in allocational terms relative to the other taxes that we now impose.

The emphasis that the US government now places on liberalization of trade in services is an aggressive initiative of the type that I believe is necessary in order to preserve a liberal trading system. I fear, however, that on close inspection the emphasis on services will crumble in our hands. "Services" is too diverse a group of things, many of which (civil aviation, banking, insurance), like agriculture, are regulated industries with extremely diverse national regulations. Others, such as motion pictures, copyrights, patents, and international civil aviation, already are covered by international agreement. I take seriously Rodney de C. Grey's observation that multilateral negotiations of services will very likely result in more restrictive régimes than the ones we have today. The United Nations Conference on Trade and Development (UNCTAD) liner code provides an example of this. It is a highly protectionist arrangement, reserving 80 percent of international carriage of general trade to the importing and exporting nations together, leaving only 20 percent for international competition. There is no doubt in my mind that an international negotiation on liberalization of civil aviation would have resulted in less change than the bilateral approach that the US government took in 1977 to liberalize and make more competitive international civil aviation. I would therefore approach these topics piecemeal, identify the problems of each, and try to ascertain the best approach for liberalization in each of the areas, rather than launch a major multilateral negotiation on all of them. There may, however, be some merit in a multilateral fact-gathering exercise, since one of the problems in this area is lack of readily available information about what is actually happening.

Similar problems prevail with direct investment. National views are too diverse and conflicting to make a multilateral negotiation promising. I like Professor A. E. Safarian's suggestion of treating trade-related investment issues—investment requirements involving local content or export targets—in the GATT. That is a more limited and manageable domain, and we already have some presumption with respect to the direction of international discussions, at least insofar as they represent impairment of obligations undertaken in the GATT.

Finally, I revert to the interaction between monetary developments and trade policy, emphasized by C. Fred Bergsten and John Williamson in their chapter, (ch. 3, this volume). One does not have to go so far as they do to acknowledge the strong influence of exchange rate developments on trade flows and hence on perceptions about trade policy. Major movements in real exchange rates, only partly related to correction of imbalances in payments, have changed radically the competitiveness of some countries' goods relative to those of other countries. They have greatly reinforced the perception that trade flows are a major source of disturbance to domestic economies. I believe that we should begin discussions soon on an effort to establish target exchange rate zones or reference rates among the major currencies of the world. These discussions will not go very quickly, and it is quite likely that it will not be possible to agree on reference rates or a target zone. But such discussions might well lead to some looser but still useful form of management of exchange rates. They would also represent one way to begin harmonization of national monetary policies.

3 W. Max Corden

We have had a large number of impressive, fact-packed and argument-packed papers. Little has been left unsaid and many different practical recommendations have been made. In addition there is the thoroughly balanced Bergsten-Cline summary. So I shall not try to summarize. Furthermore, I have not been able to disentangle all the issues to the extent I would have liked. Rather I propose to deal briefly with five topics: the so-called problem of Japan, exchange rate changes, recession as sources of protectionist pressures, the role of free trade ideology, and, finally, an attempt to classify various approaches to GATT reform.

The Question of Japan

To start with, I must point out that I come from a country that has a current account surplus with Japan. Nevertheless we protect our motor car industry against Japanese imports. Similarly we protect our clothing industry against imports from Hong Kong, even though Hong Kong itself pursues a free trade policy. There is a lesson in this: fundamental protectionist forces are at work in Australia and other countries, and these have very little to do with whether there is a bilateral surplus or deficit with the country generating the import "threat," or whether this country itself pursues protectionist policies or not.

There seems to be an American and European paranoia about Japan. This is reminiscent of concerns in the 1950s that the United States' productivity growth rate was permanently higher than European growth rates. We all recall the time when it was fashionable to believe that the United States was better at everything and that a US surplus was a permanent "problem." These attitudes forgot both the law of comparative advantage and that few things in history go on forever. In any case, the current paranoia about Japan seems to me to be the inevitable result of Japanese economic success just as paranoia about the United States was the consequence of US success. Jealousy and fear are common human failings. I think we should take a broad and historical view of the current situation.

Let me turn first to the matter of Japanese protectionism. The evidence presented by Gary Saxonhouse suggests that Japan's trade volume and trade patterns are, in fact, close to something like a free trade outcome. It is readily explainable that Japan does not import many manufactures from the United States and Europe. This reflects the particular pattern of her comparative advantage and geography. If Japan moved toward complete free trade it would probably not make a great deal of difference to her trade volume, but no doubt, with a constant current account being maintained, it would lead to some more exports and more imports, and this would improve the terms of trade of her trading partners. It is important to note that the same result ensues from a high Japanese growth rate (unless this were highly import-substituting, which it has not been). A fast-growing country is likely to improve the terms of trade of its trading partners. And Japan has been the highest growth rate country in the OECD. Both the reduction of protection and a high growth rate tend to improve the rest of the world's terms of trade relative to the country concerned, as evidenced by improved quality and reduced real prices of Japan's export products.

I come now to the much discussed question of bilateral balances. In an audience full of economists it should hardly be necessary to say that it is ridiculous to focus on bilateral current account balances, and even worse to focus just on trade and not on services. A US-Japan bilateral balance in motor cars is an extraordinarily narrow, if not meaningless, balance on which to focus. I hope no one will complain about the fact that Australia has a permanent bilateral surplus in wool, not to speak of the export of kangaroo tail soup. Japan has substantial deficits, for example, with Australia and Indonesia, and both these countries have deficits with Germany. In turn Germany has a deficit with Japan. I use these cases just as examples. Of course balances need not cancel out triangularly.

The real problems concern firstly the shock effects and secondly the sectoral effects of Japanese trade expansion. There have in recent times been large increases in export volumes by Japan, primarily to pay for worse terms of trade owing to oil price rises. Also there have been some rather sharp shifts in trade patterns. I think the Japanese are well aware of the adverse repercussions of sudden and large export pushes. But we should always remember that, if Japan moves into one field, it is likely to gradually move out of another. With regard to sectoral effects, it is obvious that some industries or sections of industries in the United States and Europe do lose from Japanese trade expansion. But we should not forget the beneficiaries—the European exporters of capital goods to Australia, whose markets would certainly be smaller if Australia did not have the income it received as a result of Japan's high exports to Europe. Nor should we forget European consumers who are the beneficiaries of Japanese technical, design, and quality control successes.

I turn now to the question of the Japanese current account and of the overall balance. It should first of all be noted that Japan has not been in surplus in every year. Its current account goes up and down. In the 12 years 1970–81 there were 4 deficit years, 1 year of balance (1973), and 7 surplus years. Focusing on the tendency to surplus, I would observe that Japan, when running a current account surplus, is simply buying financial assets rather than goods and services. What is wrong with that? Surely there are gains from trade, including trade

in the exchange of assets for goods. The Japanese household sector
has an exceptionally high savings propensity. A large part of these
savings is absorbed by the Japanese government's large budget deficit,
but there is still something left for the rest of the world. The Japanese
net savings help to keep world interest rates down a little. Surely we
should welcome this.

Distinct from the question of the current account is the question
of an overall surplus. It is often argued that the Japanese ought to
be engaging in more direct investment abroad so as to reduce the
Bank of Japan's accumulation of foreign exchange reserves. In fact
there has been a large increase in Japanese direct investment, but it
is not obvious to me that the rest of the world benefits when Japan
accumulates long-term foreign assets rather than short-term assets.
The excess Japanese savings get recycled in one way or another.
Direct investment carries with it Japanese control of foreign enterprises, and there may come a point when resistance to this will emerge.
Here again I would refer to the experience of the 1950s when there
were plenty of complaints about the American "takeover" of European industry. I feel that it is probably better for the rest of the
world that the Japanese invest some part of their excess savings in
short-term assets which are then recycled by the world's international
banks.

To conclude on Japan, it seems to me that we should welcome the
economic success of our neighbors. This success improves our terms
of trade, even though it does have some sectoral adverse effects and
it does not improve the terms of trade of everyone. But such success
sets us a good example, and perhaps teaches us how to improve our
own economic arrangements.

Exchange Rates and Protectionist Pressures

Bergsten and Williamson have made an important point, and I
thoroughly agree with it. Protectionist pressures in the United States
seem to be closely related to the real yen/dollar exchange rate. There
have been at least three episodes when there was a real appreciation
of the dollar leading to strong protectionist pressures, one being the
current one. In other words, macroeconomic events create industrial
policy pressures. One lesson I derive from this is that we should be
patient. These real exchange rate changes are temporary. We are
talking here about fluctuations, not permanent changes. In the past
the pressures have gone away.

Can such medium-run large fluctuations in real exchange rates be moderated? This is a difficult subject which clearly cannot be pursued at this conference, but there are not simple answers. The fluctuations are caused by divergences in monetary and fiscal policies, both in their effects on aggregate demand and in the policy mix. The key point is that the causes are *real* and not just nominal divergences. These differences in policies lead to pressures for international capital movements. There would be no problem if the steady state rates of inflation diverged, and this were all.

The current situation is clearly caused by US policy. If Japan reduced its fiscal deficit this would depreciate the yen even more, even though it would have the welcome effect of lowering world interest rates. On the other hand, if Japan increased its fiscal deficit it would have the welcome effect of appreciating the yen but the undesirable effect of raising world interest rates. The high savings of Japan, which lead to yen depreciation (as capital flows out), are to be welcomed from a world interest rate point of view. It should be noted that the fluctuations in the real exchange rate are *not* just explained by false expectations, and therefore cannot just be remedied by governments intervening on the basis of having knowledge or judgment that is superior compared with the private sector. Essentially they are caused by marcoeconomic policy fluctuations which, in the main, have political origins in different countries.

My own feeling is that trade policy must learn to live with these exchange rate fluctuations because there are no simple solutions to this exchange rate problem. Firstly, governments do not have better forecasting ability than the private sector, and secondly, there are inevitable divergences in policies between countries for domestic reasons. In any case divergences may be desirable. Sometimes real adjustments are required, for example to accommodate the high savings tendency of Japan and the need to channel these savings to the rest of the world.

Recession as a Cause of Protectionist Pressures

Recessions are obvious causes of protectionist pressures, along with real exchange rate changes. This has been true right through history. For example, the agricultural recession in the latter part of the nineteenth century gave rise to European agricultural protectionism. One hardly need mention the Great Depression. Currently protection of the steel industry all around the world is the result of a reduced growth rate having cut demand for steel products. Here I should mention that our current problems are not just caused by the recession but also by the lower growth rate, which may be a more long-term phenomenon. In any case I am inclined to the view that the causes of protection are primarily domestic, not external (though the recession, itself, may originally have been transmitted from abroad).

Free Trade Ideology and International Agreements

The free trade or "liberal" ideology runs right through the discussion and the papers at this conference. It is, of course, prevalent in the United States. Subject to qualifications I happen to subscribe to it myself. But not everyone does. Oversimplifying a little, one might say that Japan accepts the gains from trade proposition, but not necessarily the "liberal" approach. Economists, of course, are widely agreed on this ideology and urge it at every opportunity. I think we are right to stress that it is in the *national* interest—independent of what foreigners do—to have free or freer trade. It is one of the great historic fallacies that protection by foreigners justifies our own protection.

How does this issue relate to trade policy for the 1980s? Firstly, we cannot impose this ideology internationally. Different beliefs prevail in different countries and at different times. We can try to persuade ministers to make agreed statements, but I do not think we can make rules to impose a single ideology on all the world. Secondly, we can keep on spreading the message that a move to free trade is generally in the national interest, especially as this is one of the few propositions on which there is wide agreement among economists. Thirdly, we need to temper all this with realism, to accept the existence of pressure groups and of various national attitudes or ideologies that go counter to the "liberal" approach. The priest who preaches against sin has heard plenty of confessions. I also conclude that we should not negotiate over trivialities in pursuit of this ideology. We should focus on key areas where there is high protection and/or much international tension. Perhaps we should forget about free trade in services, since there is no clear-cut problem there. It is also important to avoid politicizing too many international trade issues.

Practical Recommendations: Three Approaches

I am still agnostic as to what are the appropriate policies to recommend, but have some sympathy for Harald Malmgren's ideas. I also wonder whether it would not be better if the ministers did not meet at all. We have one recent example (the Versailles summit) where international meetings of politicians seem to have led to more ill will and misunderstandings than if they had never faced each other across a table. In any case, on the basis of all the points of view advanced in the various chapters, I would now like to set out three broad approaches to the question of GATT reform.

Complex Rules

Firstly, there is the "complex rules" approach which appeals particularly in the United States. It means that one extends the present rules in considerable detail to services and one tries to eliminate many loopholes, for example with regard to subsidies. There is a tendency now towards this approach, but the rules get ignored. I do not think that this somewhat legalistic approach has a widespread appeal in other countries, for example Britain and Japan.

Decentralized Complex Negotiations

This is a messy and pragmatic approach. It leads to a sort of equilibrium with governments and pressure groups as actors. It could even be modeled formally. Pressure groups act on governments, and then governments negotiate. It is a model of decentralized decision making, with mainly bilateral bargains. The aim of this approach is to attain harmony, not some kind of world optimum. It means that one has loose rules and lots of exceptions and loopholes. GATT is thought of as providing only a forum and a framework, and perhaps a broad philosophy. This approach in practice seems to dominate the present situation. It may be the best that is possible. Success is measured by the degree of harmony (absence of friction) achieved.

Economists, with their free trade ideology, are just pressure groups among others in each country. Their particular objective is to press for the national interest as against sectoral interests. It might be added that when they urge more study, more research, and more calculations they become an *interested* pressure group.

Simple Rules

The third approach of "simple rules" appeals to economists but perhaps goes against reality, especially against the reality of pressure groups. The question is how to impose the rules. Nevertheless it may be worth trying this approach, while at the same time accepting the reality that there will be backsliding in the direction of the second approach above.

Various people will have proposals involving simple rules. Let me conclude with my package.

- Abolish quantitative restrictions (QRs) and tariffs completely— i.e., all trade restrictions proper. Without the threat of QRs no supplying country need agree to voluntary export restraints. All this would have major results on international trade.
- Permit subsidies—especially employment subsidies and adjustment assistance. Every country would be free to subsidize as much or as little as it likes. It would be permitted to counter foreign subsidies with its own. Alternatively one might accept the qualification that subsidies that obviously discriminate against foreigners should be prohibited, though this would detract from the simplicity of this "subsidy freedom." It should be noted that the effect of subsidies on trade is not always bad. Export subsidies improve the terms of trade of a country's trading partners for example. The case for permitting subsidies is that there are built-in restraints—the increasing costs to the budget of the subsidizing government. Perhaps this "subsidy freedom" should be associated with an insistence on transparency in the form of annual reports on subsidies, as exists now in Germany and Australia.
- Safeguards. Possibly, the first rule might be qualified to allow for safeguard arrangements, but they must definitely be temporary and be associated with transparency. Of course the danger is that this loophole would open the floodgates again and detract from the simplicity of the rules.

CHAPTER 22

Conclusion and Policy Implications

C. Fred Bergsten and William R. Cline

The broad objective of the trade policy of the industrial countries in the postwar period has been to progress steadily toward the ideal of free trade while making those exceptions necessary to maintain domestic political support. The survey of trade issues provided by the conference papers presented in this volume serves as a basis for drawing the outlines of the next phase of this historical process for the rest of this decade.

This section first sets forth the authors' view of a "constrained ideal" for the world trading régime in the late 1980s. This policy profile describes what we see as feasible goals for the trading régime, recognizing that some observers will consider them too constrained and others too idealistic. The discussion then turns to the negotiating strategies best suited for achieving these policy goals.

A Policy Blueprint

The trading system in the late 1980s should have the following broad features.

Standstill and Phasedown

There should be an immediate halt to the protectionist drift that began in the mid-1970s with self-restraint on the imposition of new protection in both goods and services; we make specific proposals for a new Standstill Agreement in the concluding section of this chapter. In addition, there should be phased liberalization of the major sectors where protection has been a serious problem, as discussed below.

Macroeconomic Policy

Clearly, the prospects for achieving both a standstill on new protection and a phasedown of old protection will be much greater if the

747

world economy enters a period of sustained recovery rather than remaining in prolonged recession. Lower levels of unemployment would reduce the pressures for trade restrictions, and faster growth would enable adjustment of displaced workers and firms to occur much more readily. Moreover, faster economic growth on a global basis would blunt the export pushes of countries seeking to escape from domestic stagnation by selling abroad, with resultant pressures for subsidies and other unfair trade practices that trigger restrictions and trade conflict. Skillful macroeconomic policy is an essential element of a successful open trade policy.

Integration with the Monetary System

International monetary arrangements that preserve a much greater degree of equilibrium among the major currencies are another prerequisite for maintaining an open trading system. To that end, trade policy must become more integrated with monetary policy.

In the period immediately ahead, the most urgent need is to correct the severe overvaluation of the dollar and undervaluation of other key currencies, especially the yen. For the longer run, the constrained ideal will probably also have to include an international monetary system that is reformed sufficiently to avoid severe overshooting of exchange rates from their fundamental equilibrium levels, perhaps through the use of target zones or reference exchange rates. We will make further comments on this issue in the concluding section.

Other structural changes will also be needed to link money and trade effectively. At the national level, the United States and other major countries should institute new arrangements to ensure that the bureaucratic departments responsible for trade policy and those charged with exchange rate and monetary policy cooperate in determining (if not administering) policy in these areas.

At the international level, it would be desirable to have an annual joint review by the General Agreement on Tariffs and Trade (GATT) and the International Monetary Fund (IMF) of the protectionist trade pressures being generated by imbalances in the international monetary system. Where appropriate, protectionist pressures and actions should be identified as related to overvalued exchange rates (or previously undervalued rates). In its periodic surveillance discussions with member countries, the IMF should continue to incorporate discussion of trade tensions brought on by exchange rate and related economic policies.

A Strong GATT

GATT as an institution and its role in the trading system should be strengthened. Its staff should be enlarged and given initiatory powers to monitor compliance by member countries with their obligations under the General Agreement. It should become a full-fledged international institution like the World Bank and International Monetary Fund, and less a temporary secretariat (despite its historical origins as an executive agreement—the sole survivor of the proposed postwar International Trade Organization, ITO—rather than a formal treaty organization).

An important and eminently feasible reform is to give GATT a mandate to seek out and publicize existing trade barriers in both goods and services. GATT surveillance committees should be established to provide annual reviews of protection in each area (agriculture, industrial safeguards, high technology goods, special régimes such as textiles, services, perhaps investment). These committees should request formal statements from national governments (and the European Community, EC) on the rationale for the protection in question, and on planned steps to reduce the protection and to obtain domestic adjustment.

The Multilateral Trade Negotiations (MTN) codes on nontariff barriers should be implemented faithfully and developed rapidly through a growing body of case law, under GATT auspices. Trade disputes, especially those among the EC, the United States, Canada, and Japan should be taken to the GATT and channeled through its appropriate codes or articles. The major countries should consciously reverse their tendency to make deals outside the GATT on an ad hoc basis, and instead strengthen the GATT by resolving conflicts through its provisions, codes, and committees.

Major Negotiations

The postwar record shows that the existence of a major international trade negotiation, in addition to its substantive merits in dealing with new or outstanding trade issues, has a crucial dynamic impact on the politics of trade policy: the existence of such a negotiation deters new protectionist actions and even pressures, while its absence fosters such pressures and their prospects for success. The reason is that the effort needed to launch and sustain a far-reaching trade negotiation has galvanized, about once per decade, a major effort in each of the participating countries (especially those which lead the enterprise) to seek further opening of the trading system in pursuit of their overall national interests. Sectoral or other protectionist pressures that seek new trade barriers are thus clashing with a realized national consensus, in ways that might jeopardize successful implementation of its major policy thrust. Political leaders, at a minimum, thus find it much easier to resist such pressures.

Conversely, the absence of any such national consensus in favor of further trade liberalization—as revealed by the absence of any new movement toward such an objective—makes it much easier for specific pleas for import relief to succeed. The "constrained ideal" thus encompasses continuous multilateral efforts to negotiate further liberalization of the trading system, or at least the launching and implementation of such negotiations frequently enough to avoid long periods where this barricade against protection is absent.

Incorporation of Developing Countries

The developing countries, and especially the newly industrialized countries (NICs), should be drawn more fully into the GATT system. The phasedown in existing protection suggested already should help induce such cooperation since it would include textiles and apparel, agriculture, and other areas of interest to developing countries (including the reduction of tariffs that are especially high on a value-added basis because of tariff escalation). This liberalization should be offered on a basis that reduces the current discrimination of some régimes (especially the Multi-Fiber Arrangement) against developing countries.[1] The industrial countries should encourage Mexico and other nonmembers to join GATT, and should conduct negotiations in a way that gives effective participation to the developing countries.

For their part, the developing countries should make offers of tariff and NTB concessions of their own in exchange for the desired liberalization in industrial countries. They should accept gradually increased responsibilities for management of the trading system, "graduating" to the maximum extent permitted by their external debt and other constraints. In many cases reduced protection, even on a uni-

---

[1] According to one approach under discussion in the United States, industrial countries might offer to extend some portion or all of their current tariff preferences to the NICs, rather than phase out those preferences, as many legislators would prefer, if the NICs offer liberalization of their own. Because the preferences tend to be limited already, with many NIC exports ineligible because of product sensitivity or the surpassing of "competitive need" thresholds, this approach seems unlikely to work because the incentive being offered is so meager.

lateral basis, would stimulate balanced long-run growth although it would typically have to be accompanied by currency devaluation.

Subsidies

Policy on subsidies by the late 1980s ideally should delineate more clearly those practices that are permissible and those that are not, as well as define more clearly accepted methods of evaluating the extent of a subsidy. Administrative application of countervailing duties not only should be subject to international review but also conducted in such a way that these duties do not establish an inherent nontariff barrier through implementation in an arbitrary or punitive way. Agricultural subsidies should be treated more similarly to those in manufactures. Third countries should facilitate the submission of countervailing duty charges against subsidized exports from one country (or group of countries) that are displacing exports of other, nonsubsidizing countries. Export credit interest rates should be tied to domestic market rates in each country to eliminate subsidies, or all export credits should be extended in the same currency (perhaps Special Drawing Rights). The United States should eliminate the Domestic International Sales Corporation (DISC) as part of the overall bargain, and to increase credibility in its demands for reform in the subsidy practices of other countries.

Safeguards

Any new code should have tight multilateral controls on selectivity, limitation to cases where the exporting country agrees to such discriminatory treatment, and provisions for phasing down the protection in question within a strictly limited time period. For example, a country imposing selective safeguards on a particular product and failing to obtain multilateral approval of them within a prescribed period (such as 90 days) could be subjected to retaliation. A new code should also involve payment of compensation, or retaliation (providing an incentive for the protecting country's other import industries and exporters to exert political pressure to avoid the protection). A weak safeguards code with many loopholes for "legitimized" protection would be worse than no code at all.

In addition to a new safeguards code, ideally it would be desirable for the United States and other major countries, whenever possible, to eschew additional voluntary export restraints or orderly marketing agreements in the future and instead return to the framework of Article XIX of the GATT. New safeguard protection would be on a most-favored-nation (MFN) basis.

It would also be desirable to have safeguard protection be in the form of tariffs rather than quotas (and to have the proceeds, perhaps along with those from existing tariffs, earmarked for use in adjustment programs as discussed below). This approach would make the cost of protection more visible and eliminate the incentive of established foreign suppliers to accept the quotas as a source of windfall rent because the rent would now be appropriated by the importing country. Such safeguards, combined with selectivity, would mean violation of MFN tariffs (by a supplier-specific surcharge, for example) but MFN is already violated where bilateral quotas are applied.

Trade Adjustment Policies

Positive adjustment policies will be needed in the 1980s to promote evolution in the structure of production and trade toward comparative advantage and thereby to foster the kind of trade policies advocated here. In the United States, it will be essential to revive some form of trade adjustment assistance. Any new program should emphasize effective adjustment, including retraining and employment subsidies, rather than simple income transfers.

Two conceptual innovations could strengthen adjustment programs. First, as a general principle, nontariff barrier (NTB) protection could be converted to tariffs. The resulting revenue, perhaps along with revenue from preexisting tariffs, could be earmarked for purposes of financing adjustment.[2] financial incentives funded by the tariff receipts could be offered to affected workers for retraining and relocation on the condition that they leave the industry unless it clearly could be revived. Firms could receive financial assistance for research and development aimed at diversifying their production, perhaps wholly out of import-displaced product lines.

Second, eligibility for adjustment assistance could be strictly time-dated. Only workers who could prove they were employed in the affected industry *before* the implementation of new safeguard protection (or adoption of new adjustment assistance) would be eligible for adjustment benefits; no others could become eligible for at least several years. Future employees would enter the industry at their

---

[2] This approach is recommended by Gary Clyde Hufbauer, ed., *US International Economic Policy 1981: A Draft Report* (Washington: International Law Institute, 1982), p. 1–13, and by William H. Branson and J. David Richardson, "Capacity, Competitiveness, and Capital Mobility in the World Economy: Challenges to US Policy" (Washington: Report of a National Science Foundation project, 1982; processed).

own risk, considering that it would be designated for a phasing down in size to meet the changing structure of comparative advantage. Whatever its exact nature, it seems highly likely that a revived trade adjustment assistance program will be necessary for the United States in the 1980s—along with effective adjustment programs in other countries—if further protectionist drift is to be avoided.

Agriculture

By the late 1980s, all major countries should be moving toward a restructuring of domestic farm programs that would inter alia cause minimum interference with international trade, or at least with trade in third countries. Ideally this approach would mean reliance on unemployment insurance and general domestic support programs to deal with farm-income maintenance, and the phasing out of special price support programs (which tend to benefit richer farmers in any event). In practice, about all that could be hoped for would be a shift from farm-purchase programs that spur surplus production through excessive floor prices, causing the need for subsidized exports of the surplus, to alternative programs (such as acreage set asides) that do not cause surpluses. In parallel to such a shift, application of countervailing duties against agricultural subsidies would be appropriate.

In addition, new norms could be developed to deal with state trading as suggested by Hathaway. And the quest for international or coordinated national grain reserves for purposes of price stabilization warrants new efforts, partly because abrupt explosions in food prices can help touch off worldwide inflation (as in 1973).

Textiles and Apparel

Here our view of the régime for the late 1980s is perhaps most radical. The MFA has come to be accepted as a permanent feature of world trade. But it is time to change the MFA fundamentally. As a number of conference participants advocated, the world should begin to move toward a complete dismantling of the MFA and a transfer of the task of safeguard protection in textiles to the normal channels that all other industries must use. Under this approach, those textile or apparel sectors that could demonstrate injury from rising imports could obtain normal safeguard protection (ideally, under the norms of GATT Article XIX). In the United States, for example, apparel sectors affected by imports could apply for temporary safeguard protection in the same way that other industries (steel, footwear, television sets) have been required to do in the past.

Conversion of the MFA into a normal safeguards approach would be far-reaching. It is highly likely that many textile (as opposed to apparel) products would no longer receive protection because they would not be judged to need it. For textile fabrics, in a meaningful sense, the battle has been won. Conversion to capital-intensive techniques has made US and other industrial-country producers competitive again. Thus, in 1980 the United States had a trade *surplus* of $1.25 billion in textiles (excluding clothing); the EC had a surplus of $780 million.[3] There is no economic reason for protection of textiles in general (although individual subsectors may have a basis for safeguard protection); only the massive political alliance of the textiles-apparel bloc explains continued textile protection.

In apparel the situation is the reverse. The United States had a trade deficit of $5.3 billion in 1980 and the EC had a deficit of $6.1 billion.[4] The normal safeguard procedures would be likely to provide a continued protective umbrella for large parts of the apparel sector even if the MFA were abolished, but on an economically more rational and politically more equitable basis.

Conversion to the safeguard mechanism, if done in the spirit of GATT Article XIX, would mean a return to the MFN principle instead of open markets for rich-country suppliers but closed markets to suppliers from poor countries. Conversion to tariffs instead of quotas, with tariff revenue earmarked for adjustment, would make the system much more equitable among suppliers and adjustment oriented—and would provide the funds to finance substantial improvements in the apparel sector itself.

Because these changes would be fundamental, a phase-in period would be necessary. The 1986 renewal of the MFA might encompass a general conversion of quotas to tariff protection with phased reduction to levels of 10 percent to 15 percent by 1990, when the MFA itself would be abolished, and further protection for the sector would be entrusted to the normal safeguard mechanism.

Steel

The paramount task for the coming years, especially in light of the new US-EC restraint agreement, will be to avoid the creation of a new MFA-like régime of organized trade. The Reagan administration has played with fire by negotiating a new "voluntary" restraint régime

---

[3] GATT, *International Trade 1980/81* (Geneva: GATT, 1981), table A6.
[4] Ibid.

that is acceptable to US and EC producers. Quotas may have been preferred by the majority of the EC producers because, under countervailing and antidumping measures by the United States, the more numerous inefficient producers (in the United Kingdom and France) would lose much more in market shares than the fewer efficient producers (especially those in Germany).

The central point is that any temporary convenience of a US quota would be far outweighed by the high likelihood that such a régime would become frozen into a lasting protective device, despite protestations to the contrary. This in fact occurred in 1968–74, with very high costs to the United States from the immediate escalation of steel wages and prices during that period. The EC has pledged to phase out subsidies by the mid-1980s, when its adjustment should be completed. Until then the United States should have relied on countervailing duties and antidumping levies, and done so in a way that made the calculated duties subject to international concurrence in the GATT. Instead, the US-EC agreement on voluntary export restraints through 1985 is an open invitation to the development of a new international quota régime.

There is a further problem in steel. If Japan has in fact been exercising a voluntary export restraint for the past few years, which seems highly likely given the uncannily constant level of its exports to the United States,[5] there will remain hidden protection in the system as long as this voluntary quota persists. At a minimum, the administration should resist strongly any industry attempt to force an even lower voluntary quota on Japan—which, in light of the quota agreed by the EC, would go even further than the current network of trade restraints toward effectively cartelizing the world steel market.

Other Traditional Industries

The constrained ideal here for the late 1980s involves continuation of the 1981 US decision not to renew protection in footwear and television sets. It would involve a new commitment on the part of other countries to phase out their protection in these sectors, now that the US market is more open. And the device of converting quotas to tariffs with revenue earmarked for adjustment should be used in

---

[5] Except for a brief rise to 8 million tons in 1976 and 1977, steel imports from Japan have been virtually unchanged at 6 million tons annually since 1974. American Iron and Steel Institute, *Annual Statistical Report,* various issues.

these and similar industries as well. In shipbuilding, the constrained ideal might be a reduction in construction subsidies to the more moderate levels (relative to sales) of a previous benchmark period.

Automobiles

The paramount goals should be rejection of the local content bill or any similar approaches, and nonrenewal of the current "voluntary" export quotas from Japan in the US market. (The problem of performance requirements in the auto sector needs to be addressed frontally, however; see the section on trade-related investment practices below). Canada, Germany, and other countries that imposed new barriers against Japan at the time of the 1981 US restriction should dismantle these barriers when the US quota expires, because there would no longer be ricochet market pressure from diversion out of the US market. At the same time, major pressure should be brought on Italy, France, and the United Kingdom to liberalize their highly restrictive treatment of Japanese automobiles; otherwise they will force the burden of market absorption onto the United States and other more open markets.

For both automobiles and steel, world economic recovery and a restoration of equilibrium exchange rates will be important factors in the feasibility of liberalization. Recession hits capital goods (steel) and consumer durables (automobiles) especially hard. The current trend toward a stable or weakening real oil price could help automobile recovery and liberalization, although political disruption could always cause another energy crisis.

Services

By the late 1980s trade rules for services would also be desirable. Emerging new service areas such as those associated with the information industry would be open to international trade; there would be, at a minimum, a standstill against any new barriers in the services sector. Much spadework remains to be done before a meaningful régime can be developed, however. At the conceptual level it remains to be established that the many disparate activities in this field can be grouped together meaningfully for a unified negotiation. In addition, considerable preparatory work is necessary to establish the information base on barriers to trade in services. Nevertheless, the inventory of foreign trade barriers in services compiled by the US Trade Representative (USTR) should be a sufficient basis for including services in a new MTN, although actual negotiations in the field would have to be preceded by further preparation.

Trade-Related Investment Practices

Here the constrained ideal for the late 1980s would involve the development of new rules of the game to limit trade distortions arising from investment policies, primarily incentives that lure investments across national borders in the first place and performance requirements (especially local content and minimum export rules) that direct their activities once in place. Among the industrial countries, it would be desirable to develop a new code to this end—perhaps by beefing up the existing Organization for Economic Cooperation and Development (OECD) arrangements. Failing development of a code, extension of countervailing duties to address the implicit export subsidy in investment incentives and performance requirements may be necessary to impose more discipline on the system.

Among the developing countries, there are probably only a few NICs (such as Brazil and Mexico) with sufficiently large domestic markets that they have the necessary bargaining clout to induce multinational corporations to accept performance requirements that seriously alter the patterns of world trade—although a much larger number of them engage in such practices. Thus, it may be more effective to deal with the NICs in bilateral discussions, and to bring them into as much conformity with the code among industrial countries as possible, than to attempt to design an investment performance code for all developing countries.

High Technology Trade

The GATT should develop an ongoing review of the trade impact of national programs to stimulate high technology development. There should be a complaints procedure in the GATT whereby countries can protest practices they consider to be trade distorting, such as subsidies and particular R&D expenditures. A new GATT code limiting distortive practices in high technology could be developed. Alternatively, discipline could be established in this area by extension of countervailing duty enforcement to cover government interventions that distort trade.

To be sure, before pressing for new trade arrangements in the high technology field, it is necessary to establish more thoroughly the nature of trade barriers in this sector. Many countries consider development of high technology sectors to be essential for reasons of national security, making it ambiguous whether the resulting subsidies or even import restrictions should be regarded as subject to international complaint in view of the GATT tradition of exceptions for national security purposes. Similarly, it remains unclear whether or at which point government subsidies to research and development should be interpreted as trade barriers rather than as legitimate enactment of a normal role of government in compensating for market failure in the private provision of research with major externalities. For example, few would argue that the history of US government sponsorhip of agricultural research constituted a nontariff barrier artificially increasing US agricultural exports. And the extent to which US defense research has conferred an advantage on high technology industries that offsets foreign subsidies to the sector remains a central issue.

Even more fundamentally, it remains unresolved whether countries have the right under an equitable international trading régime to pursue a conscious industrial policy with the subsidies and other government interventions that such a policy usually entails. An increasingly contentious issue may be the frustration of US industries over the trade consequences of foreign "industrial policy" programs that "target" the development of certain sectors. The problem is compounded by the differences in political philosophy between greater adherence to the market process in some countries (at least in principle) and a greater tendency toward at least indicative planning in others.

The international régime for high technology remains to be developed and it remains to be seen whether the United States and other countries will emulate Japan, France, and certain other countries by developing conscious industrial policies of their own for high technology goods. But the central theme in this sector should be to seek, by the late 1980s, subscription by the major trading partners to an open trading approach that takes advantage of the newness of the industry to avoid the protectionism that has spread in several critical older industries.

Tariffs

Finally, all existing tariffs on industrial products should be eliminated by the industrial countries. Average tariff levels are now low, ranging between 3 percent to 5 percent for the major trading countries after completion (in 1987, except for Japan in 1983) of the cuts agreed in the Tokyo Round. Hence their phased elimination should not be difficult. (Conversion of current NTBs to tariffs would mean that some tariffs on industrial products would remain, but these tariffs would have to be handled apart from those which carry over from the past.)

At the same time, these low averages mask some remaining substantial tariffs on some products. Moreover, tariff escalation is still substantial with adverse effects on producers of primary products (especially developing countries). Elimination of existing tariffs would also go far to moot the increasingly thorny issue of preferences for developing countries, providing a binding (and thus much firmer) foundation for their own export-expansion efforts in the future.

A Strategy for the 1980s

It will obviously be difficult to achieve the "constrained ideal" just described. World trade is in decline. Protectionist pressures are severe and increasing. The open trading system is eroding.

The environment for trade policy could hardly be worse. All of the major industrial economies are stagnating. The outlook is for anemic recoveries, at best. Unemployment is the highest since the Great Depression and appears likely to stay high, especially in Europe, throughout much of the 1980s. Severe exchange rate misalignments intensify the pressure for import barriers, especially in the United States due to a substantially overvalued dollar. Japan's record trade surplus with the United States will probably rise sharply over the next year or so. Also in the United States, the virtual dismemberment of trade adjustment assistance has eliminated the only government program that offered a conscious alternative to import relief.

In short, the outlook for maintaining an open trading system is poor. Most observers expect continuing erosion, if not a sharp outbreak in protectionism—which could be triggered by congressional passage of the automobile local content legislation, for example, or complete cartelization of the world steel market. Because the trading system is under such far-reaching assault, we believe it is imperative that GATT members adopt dramatic new initiatives to repel the drift toward protectionism and begin a renewed thrust toward liberalizing the trade régime.

We take this view for three reasons. First, the economic stakes are enormous. The share of trade in the economies of almost all industrial countries has virtually doubled since the last round of negotiations, the MTN, was launched in the early 1970s. As a result, declines in world trade add substantial impetus to the world recession and, as described in the first part of this chapter, generate a downward spiral reminiscent of the early 1930s. Any further trade shrinkage due to protectionist measures would add substantial risks to an already shaky world economy. Moreover, any retardation of the exports of developing countries would further jeopardize their ability to repay their foreign debts and thereby contribute to even greater international financial instability.

Second, the foreign policy stakes are enormous. The severe trade disputes, between the United States and Europe and between the United States and Japan, have badly frayed overall relations within the world's major alliances. The economic ills just cited top the domestic political agenda in every country in the world and seem likely to do so for some time into the future. Actions that deepen those ills can only add further trouble to international relationships. Hence, it is essential in terms of overall foreign policy concerns—indeed, national security—to halt the escalation of trade restraints.

Third, as already indicated, trade policy is like a bicycle: it either moves forward toward greater freedom or it falls into greater protection. Hence the economic and foreign policy costs of erosion of the open trading régime will grow, perhaps rapidly, if the erosion is not reversed.

So the outlook for trade policy is for rapid deterioration over the next year or so, and perhaps throughout the 1980s, unless the current trend is arrested. Unemployment is likely to remain at record postwar levels for some time, with increasing political effect as it resists correctional efforts. The trade balance impact of the overvalued dollar will come home to roost in the United States once the economy begins to pick up, especially vis-à-vis Japan, leading numerous additional industries to join autos and steel in seeking import restraint.

Fortunately, we believe that it is feasible to achieve the needed turnaround in trade policy—if decisive action is taken quickly. Our analysis shows that actual protectionist actions have been remarkably limited, given the underlying circumstances. Political leaders in all countries seem genuinely to want to resist the pressure to restrict trade. It is clear to almost all groups in all industrial countries that external trade developments are *not* the source of their current economic difficulties, and that responding in that direction would be not only misplaced but probably counterproductive. (Even in some of the key developing countries, the external constraints which *are* central to their debt and hence growth problems have derived more from international monetary and macroeconomic considerations than from trade barriers.) Consultative channels remain open and are being extensively used.

The GATT Ministerial of 1982

The Geneva meeting of trade ministers from GATT member countries in November 1982 offered a rare opportunity for halting the slide toward protection and setting the trade agenda for the coming years. In the event, the Ministerial achieved only a modest outcome, far more modest than the type of program outlined subsequently in this chapter.[6]

The United States had taken the initiative in calling for the meeting, but even its goals were relatively limited. The US position emphasized a pledge to refrain from new protection; establishment of a work program to extend GATT to cover services, trade-related investment requirements, and high technology; the tightening of discipline on agricultural export subsidies; the development of a safeguards code; and convening of a North-South round of trade negotiations. The US program was constructive as far as it went but paid little if any attention to the need for correcting the sizable monetary imbalances which underlie contemporary trade problems, to further steps to limit the use of subsidies, and to GATT action for liberalizing textiles and apparel, steel, and automobiles.

Among other delegations, the Australians stood out as pressing for a standstill on further protection as well as for limits on agricultural export subsidies. In contrast, the EC position was much less ambitious than even the limited US program. The EC viewpoint was broadly that, in the face of high unemployment and world recession, it would be unrealistic to expect any substantial commitment to further liberalization, and that governments would be fortunate if they managed merely to resist demands for new protection. The French Minister of Foreign Trade Michel Jobert was the most conspicuous voice opposing new liberalization efforts.[7]

The most heated controversey at the Ministerial concerned agricultural export subsidies. The dominance of representatives from agricultural states in the highly vocal US congressional delegation (which included Senators Jesse Helms, R-NC, and Robert Dole, R-Kan.) heightened the profile of the agricultural issue. Other schisms in the Ministerial included unwillingness of developing countries to accept selectivity in safeguards and their stout resistance to extension of GATT to cover services or investment performance requirements.

After near failure to agree on a communiqué, the ministers reached agreement on the following program. Adopting a form of standstill on protection, they pledged "to refrain from taking or maintaining any measures inconsistent with GATT and to make determined ef-

---

[6] A useful review can be found in Jeffrey J. Schott, "The GATT Ministerial: A Postmortem," *Challenge* (May/June 1983), pp. 40–45.

[7] *New York Times,* 5 December 1982.

forts to avoid measures which would limit or distort international trade."[8] In a compromise widely regarded as a victory for EC resistence to tighter controls on agricultural export subsidies, the ministers merely agreed to a two-year study by a special GATT committee on agriculture.

Firmer progress was achieved on safeguards. The ministers outlined the characteristics of a desirable safeguards code (transparency, objective criteria for action, barriers that are only temporary and decline over time, provision for structural adjustment, compensation and retaliation, and multilateral surveillance) and called for the GATT Council to draft such a code during 1983. On services, the United States did not achieve commitment to a comprehensive GATT study as hoped, but the ministers did agree to recommend that each interested nation carry out its own study and that "international organizations such as GATT" exchange the results of such studies, for examination by GATT within two years. At the insistence of the developing countries, the communiqué also pledged to "examine ways. . . of . . . liberalizing trade in textiles and clothing, including the eventual application of the general agreement, after the expiry of the 1981 protocol extending the arrangement regarding international trade in textiles."[9] The communiqué did not address the issues of high technology trade and investment performance requirements. In addition, the ministers did not pursue the US initiative toward a new North-South round of negotiations.

Many observers had warned that inadequate success at the Ministerial could intensify protectionist sentiment in the US Congress. For his part, US Trade Representative William E. Brock judged the Ministerial to be a qualified success.[10] But the Australian delegation refused to associate itself with the agreement because the trade pledge was too ambiguous and because of inadequate progress on agricultural trade.[11] The net effect of the Ministerial in acting as a restraint to protectionism was unclear, but some US legislators[12] interpreted the meeting as evidence that GATT was ineffective. Giving some substance to that view, the EC commission returned from a visit to Japan in early 1983 proudly waving voluntary restraint agreements in nine

---

[8] General Agreement on Tariffs and Trade, "Ministerial Declaration," Gatt Press Release no. 1328, November 29, 1982.

[9] Ibid.

[10] *New York Times*, 30 November 1982.

[11] *New York Times*, 5 December 1982.

[12] Including Senators Robert Dole and William Roth. *Journal of Commerce*, 26 January 1983.

new product areas—despite the pledge signed at Geneva only a few weeks earlier.

More disturbingly, the conflict over agricultural export subsidies threatened to create yet another severe trade conflict between the United States and the EC, following the conflicts over steel and the Soviet gas pipeline that had only recently been resolved. After initial heated rhetoric, cabinet-level meetings between the United States and the EC temporarily deescalated the agricultural issue from a trade war.[13] But by early 1983 the United States appeared to be initiating a new policy of softer words combined with louder actions; the US government decided to subsidize the sale of 1 million metric tons of wheat flour to Egypt, a move expected to shift a large portion of Egypt's purchases away from the EC.[14] And in the other major area of trade conflict, demands for protection against Japan remained intense, as did US political pressure on Japan to advance liberalizing measures.

In sum, the GATT Ministerial took a correct posture toward stemming new protection and laying the initial groundwork for further liberalization. But because of the intensity of the current forces leading towards protection, a much stronger GATT program is required. The trade pledge in particular would hold more promise if it contained implementing mechanisms and sanctions against violation. Moreover, there is a need for a longer term agenda for the 1980s that, in our view, must include a new major round of trade negotiations. The remainder of this chapter presents a four-point program for an effective trade strategy in the 1980s. Such a program could have been launched at the November 1982 GATT Ministerial. Because that opportunity has passed, it would now behoove the major trading countries to consider recovening the GATT Ministerial within one or at most two years to begin more serious work along the lines suggested below.

A Standstill on Trade Restrictions

The most essential, and most urgent, step is to curb the creeping erosion of the international trading system. The only effective way to do so, in the short run, is to reach a Standstill Agreement on the creation of any new trade barriers or distortions (for example, export subsidies). To be effective, such an agreement must go beyond the trade pledge adopted at the 1982 GATT Ministerial. An effective

---

[13] *Washington Post,* 11 December 1982.
[14] *Wall Street Journal,* 19 January 1983.

agreement would obligate all participating countries to avoid imposing new trade barriers (or other distortions) for its duration. To
implement the agreement, a Standstill Monitoring Committee would
be created within the GATT. Any country that believed another
country had violated its standstill commitment could file a protest
with the committee, and so could any third country even if not directly
affected. Moreover, the GATT Secretariat would be given a mandate
to monitor the trading system and bring to the committee any possible
violations of the agreement.

The committee would be required to reach a decision on each
complaint within 30 days. (It could seek recommendations on the
proper response from an existing GATT committee, for example, the
Committee of Signatories of the Code on Subsidies and Countervailing Measures, but would still have to reach its final judgment in
30 days). If the committee found a country in violation, that country
would be required either to withdraw its new measure or extend
compensation to all aggrieved parties by reducing its other import
barriers (or export aids), on a comparable scale, within 15 days. If
it did neither, affected countries would retaliate automatically against
the original restrictive action. This provision deliberately goes beyond
the existing GATT rule under which countries frequently fail to retaliate, even when authorized to do so, because of pressure from the
offending country or other extraneous considerations—thereby eroding substantially the deterrent force of the rules.

As with all major international trade arrangements, a standstill
could be enacted only if agreed and accepted by the Big Four—the
United States, the European Community, Japan, and Canada. All
countries would be given maximum incentive to join the agreement,
however, by limiting recourse to the Standstill Monitoring Committee
to those countries which decided to participate in the Standstill Agreement itself—a positive form of conditional MFN treatment, with some
exceptions (or phase-in of the commitment) for NICs and possibly
automatic eligibility for the poorest developing countries.

The Standstill Agreement could be made valid until reviewed by
the following GATT Ministerial, to be set approximately one year
after the agreement, or until the successful negotiation of a new
safeguards code which would henceforth (along with Article XIX)
govern the imposition of import barriers. In any event, annualizing
the GATT Ministerial should be an integral part of the response to
the current trade crisis to be decided at the meeting in late November.
The governing body of the international monetary system, the Interim
Committee, meets twice yearly and there is an annual meeting of the
Governors of the International Monetary Fund. The closest approx-

imation to a governing body on world development issues, the Development Committee, meets twice a year and the governors of the World Bank meet annually. There are annual summit meetings on the international economy. The OECD meets annually at ministerial level.

It is thus striking that the GATT did not meet at the ministerial level for almost a decade, despite the enormous difficulties confronting the world trading system. Annual meetings on trade policy would thus be quite appropriate, and could be given the explicit task inter alia of reviewing developments under the Standstill Agreement and deciding on its continuation.

A number of technical issues would have to be decided in constructing the Standstill Agreement. The standstill should begin immediately to avoid giving countries an incentive to adopt new barriers quickly to "get in under the wire." (If detailed negotiation of the agreement were to prevent its immediate commencement, the starting date should nevertheless be set retroactively to the date of the Ministerial for the same reason.) Coverage would include all new import restrictions, except those carried out to implement national laws against unfair trade practices by other countries. (This exception would cover mainly antidumping and countervailing duties; they could be reported to the Standstill Monitoring Committee only when their implementation was viewed as incompatible with existing GATT rules.) A national "action," such as passage of the "reciprocity" legislation currently before the US Congress, would not be viewed as a violation per se, but any implementation of such an action that created a new import barrier would violate the agreement. To limit the risk that the Standstill Agreement might have to be invoked against such contentious actions, however, as well as to set a useful precedent for the longer run, countries would be encouraged to consult with the committee prior to taking steps that might trigger a subsequent complaint.

One possible objection to any standstill on imposing new trade restrictions, which might be heard especially in the United States, is that it would freeze the existing pattern of barriers, representing a kind of "reward" (in mercantilist terms) for countries that had already imposed more than the average level of protection and imposing an unfair penalty on countries with more open markets. There are four responses to this concern. First, the evidence developed in this study (and an earlier analysis of the proposed "reciprocity" legislation[15])

---

[15] William R. Cline, *"Reciprocity": A New Approach to World Trade Policy*, POLICY ANALYSES IN INTERNATIONAL ECONOMICS, no. 2 (Washington: Institute for International Economics, 1982).

casts considerable doubt on the view that the United States, or any other national market, is substantially more open to imports than the markets of the other industrial countries. Second, countries could continue to pursue redress of violations alleged to exist prior to the Standstill Agreement via normal GATT channels, as they are already doing in a number of cases. Third, as indicated below, our proposed package for the Ministerial includes launching a new trade-liberalizing negotiation to get at precisely such barriers. Fourth, all countries— whatever the relative standing of their protective devices at the current time—would benefit enormously from an effective prohibition on the imposition of new barriers.

A Standstill Agreement would raise several unique, and potentially troublesome, problems for the United States in view of its tripartite system of government—and, correspondingly, the United States would raise several unique problems for the Standstill Agreement. First, no administration could legally bind the Congress not to adopt new legislation whose provisions would violate the agreement. Second, it would be impossible to deny US citizens their rights under current law to apply for import relief—either to the executive branch, under provisions such as sections 201 and 301 of the Trade Act, or (in some cases) to the courts.

These difficulties, however, should neither preclude US adherence to such an agreement nor its acceptance by the other trading nations. The most important step to that end would be the strongest possible congressional support for the agreement, preferably indicated through a Joint Congressional Resolution (or even an amendment to the Trade Act of 1974.) Obviously, the administration would have to consult closely with the Congress in advance to plan such a scenario. It would still be necessary to deal with the problem directly, however, because no Congress can commit a succeeding Congress (or, technically, even itself).

Hence the US administration's commitment under the agreement should include pledges to veto any legislation that imposed new trade barriers (or subsidies) and to reject any new barriers recommended by the US International Trade Commission (USITC) or anyone else, under existing statutes, in favor of using trade adjustment assistance (as revised, see below). (Exception would be made for cases that responded to unfair trade practices by other countries in a manner consistent with existing GATT rules.) These suggestions, fortunately, are not nearly as radical as they sound: Congress has in fact passed only two pieces of legislation to protect a specific industry since 1945 (the authorization of meat quotas in the Agricultural Adjustment Act of 1956, and Meat Import Act of 1964), and the proviso concerning executive actions permits ongoing determination of "injury" with a limitation applying only to the nature of the remedy.

If a US violation of the agreement nevertheless occurred, such as congressional passage (and overriding of a presidential veto) of a new Hawley-Smoot bill or even local content legislation for the automobile industry, the compensation or retaliation features of the agreement would go into effect—as would be called for under the GATT rules anyway, but much more quickly and much more automatically. Provision might also have to be made for permitting other countries to denounce the whole agreement, however, in the case of any such extreme violation of its basic approach.

Such a Standstill Agreement would be quite different from the successive "trade pledges" which emerged from OECD ministerial meetings after 1974, the somewhat similar (if less formal) declarations issued at several economic summits, and even the November 1982 GATT Ministerial. Those pledges created no enforcement mechanisms. They made no effort to define the terms and conditions for their implementation. The earlier pledges were limited, of course, to OECD countries, and they failed totally—particularly in recent years— to halt the steady drift toward increasing trade barriers (and subsidies), as evidenced by the state of the world trading system today.

A comprehensive Standstill Agreement should thus be the centerpiece of the management of the international trading system for the next several years. Only such a dramatic commitment is likely to halt the erosion of the system and avoid the risk of severe deterioration into protectionism at levels not seen since the 1930s.

Launching a New "MTN"

A Standstill Agreement, however, would represent only a temporary response to the problems of the trading system. Moreover, it would do nothing to resolve either the long-standing problems still besetting the system (such as agriculture and textiles) or the new problems (such as services and investment) that are likely to emerge as major policy issues during this decade. A Standstill Agreement would be a critical holding action, which could avert further deterioration and buy time for dealing with the underlying problems, but by itself it would not resolve those problems. Moreover, some countries (including the United States) might be unwilling to accept a Standstill Agreement unless they had companion assurance that existing barriers would be tackled as well. To do so, it will be necessary to launch another major international trade negotiation—an "MTN" for the 1980s.

The Kennedy Round was an essential response to the trade problems of the 1960s, notably continuing high tariffs and discrimination against nonmembers by the new European Economic Community. The Tokyo Round was an essential response to the problems of the 1970s: emerging nontariff barriers, some aspects of the newly important role in world trade of the developing countries. Both were integral elements of the response to the protectionist pressures of the day—fed, in the United States, by the high unemployment of the early 1960s and the severe overvaluation of the dollar in the early 1970s. They also had an important place in the overall foreign policy strategies of this period, especially in the context of relations between the United States and Western Europe (and, to a lesser extent, Japan).

A similar case applies today. According to the "bicycle theory," trade policy must move ahead or it will topple. A new set of important and difficult trade issues clearly looms ahead. Important issues from the past remain difficult, and are much more likely to be resolved— for both substantive and political reasons—if placed in the broader context of a comprehensive negotiation. Hence there is a strong case for launching a "new MTN" as soon as possible. This venture could take the form of a decision in principle, or a political commitment, to begin the process of analyzing the issues and obtaining needed domestic authorities in order to begin the actual negotiations at a specific time, say January 1984.

An opposite school of thought, however, argues that such a strategy would be counterproductive in terms of trade policy itself. One segment of that school argues that, contrary to the conventional wisdom, the major trade negotiations of the 1960s and 1970s were themselves counterproductive. This is because, it is said, the concessions to protectionism necessary to win authorization for (especially US) participation in those negotiations—such as the increasingly restrictive régime for textiles and apparel, and the US Trade Act of 1974—set world trade back further than the "rounds" themselves advanced it. Some also argue that the very process of tariff liberalization fostered the creation of NTBs, whose trade effect was more restrictive than the duties they replaced.

A less extreme variant of this view accepts the conventional wisdom that the Kennedy and Tokyo Rounds made net contributions to an open trading system, but believes that the price of launching another "round" now would be unacceptably high—especially in obtaining authorizing legislation in the United States in light of its high unemployment, overvalued dollar, deteriorating trade balance, and absence of alternative policy responses to trade dislocations. The mildest version of this approach, while more sanguine about the possibilities for launching the enterprise, believes that any negotiated agreements that might emerge would on balance be protectionist—ratifying, and thereby encouraging, existing protectionist steps, if not adding new ones to the régime. For evidence, proponents of this view point to the renegotiation of the Multi-Fiber Arrangement in late 1981 and the course of the effort to negotiate a safeguards code over the past three years.

There is substantial merit in these arguments, and there is clearly a risk in seeking to launch a new multilateral trade negotiation in such an environment. To do so, even greater skill and perseverance will be needed than in the efforts of the two previous decades. The domestic political hurdles will be harder to overcome in all countries, including the United States.

Indeed, there might be a case for delaying the next trade-negotiation initiative if there was good reason to expect an early pickup in the world economy with a sharp reduction in unemployment rates, an early end to the major exchange rate misalignments and correction of the severe trade imbalances which will inevitably result, and early restoration of effective adjustment programs in the major countries. Unfortunately, there is little reason for optimism on any of these fronts. Moreover, the possibility is strong that the environment will worsen—with unemployment remaining at record levels and rising further in some countries, with sharp rises in trade imbalances (especially in the United States) and perhaps continued currency misalignments, and with continued (even growing) resistance to "positive adjustment" both because of slow growth and underlying structural rigidities.

If the underlying situation were to brighten substantially, launching the process now would entail no significant costs because the actual talks would not begin until a later date—when, by hypothesis, the climate would have improved. But, more centrally, none of the alternatives to launching a major new negotiation appears adequate to stem the protectionist pressures. It is already clear that a "business as usual" approach, focused on implementing the MTN codes and trying to strengthen the GATT machinery, lacks sufficient political impact in any of the major countries to reverse the basic policy trends. A commissioning of new studies might work if there were time and sufficient resiliency elsewhere in the system.[16] Again, however, the

---

[16] However, such temporizing did not even work in 1969–72: new restrictive régimes appeared for textiles/apparel and steel, and Congress almost passed

dismal outlook suggests that no such modest approach will be adequate.

If it proves impossible to agree in principle to the launching of a new MTN in the near term, at the very minimum there should be adopted, in addition to some form of Standstill Agreement, an approach advocated by several former negotiators at the conference: establishment of a new process of notification and justification of all existing barriers. Under such an approach, countries would have to defend their barriers in the GATT, indicate their intended duration, and outline the "positive adjustment" steps being taken to permit such phaseouts to occur. Within this mechanism the GATT Secretariat would be charged with a mandate to seek out and publicize existing trade barriers. This dual approach would at least begin to address seriously the array of existing barriers, thereby perhaps both producing some remedial action per se and paving the way for future liberalizing negotiations. However, the launching of a "new MTN" would be far preferable and constitutes the second key component of the trade strategy that we envisage for the 1980s, accompanying the Standstill Agreement to halt the immediate erosion of the trading environment.

What Kind of MTN?

Broadly speaking, there are two alternative strategies for structuring and pursuing the "MTN of the 1980s." One is to focus on the new trade problems that are likely to emerge over the decade and beyond, and which represent likely sources of major policy trouble in the years ahead. The most suitable issues for treatment under this concept are the interrelated areas of services, investment-related trade issues, and high technology. This is the approach officially favored by the United States.

There is an alternative, however, which was strongly supported at the conference. Rather than focusing on "new" areas of emerging and future difficulty, this alternative would go back to key issues of trade policy that have been addressed in the past, sometimes repeatedly, without yielding to satisfactory solutions. Each of these areas—textiles and apparel, agriculture, steel, subsidies, safeguards, perhaps automobiles—demonstrably represents a very significant element of world trade. Each presents a thorny problem of trade policy

---

the Mills Bill in 1970 and seriously contemplated the Burke-Hartke Bill in 1971–72.

on which there has been no shortage of effort, but relatively little in the way of coherent results. Each is an important element in the creeping erosion of the international trading system. In addition, heavy emphasis would be placed on developing effectively the codes negotiated in the Tokyo Round and implementing faithfully other existing GATT rules.

According to the alternative view, some or all of these issues should be the focus of any major new trade-negotiation effort. Even partial successes in resolving them, it is argued, would constitute important progress in rolling back protection and restoring momentum to trade liberalization. Conversely, ignoring them would forgo the major available opportunities for reaping additional gains from trade; such side-stepping would even represent a kind of "cop out" from dealing with the tough problems facing the system, thus undermining the credibility of the entire effort.

In our view, there is no need to choose between these alternative approaches. The "new MTN" should encompass both. Indeed, only through addressing all major outstanding issues of trade policy can the negotiation fulfill its twofold purpose of resuming the liberalization of world trade and combatting protectionist pressures by seizing the initiative for the opposite course of action.

But the "new MTN" should strive to go even further. As the logical culmination of the Kennedy and Tokyo Rounds in the area of tariff reductions, it should seek to eliminate all existing duties on industrial products in the industrial countries.[17] Hence it would have three major objectives, outlined in detail in the previous section of this chapter:

• liberalization of the existing import régimes for textiles and apparel, agriculture, steel, and automobiles, including conversion of existing NTBs to tariffs with some or all of the new revenues (perhaps along with existing tariff revenues) devoted to financing programs of positive adjustment to trade dislocations with each industry henceforth eligible for (but limited to) normal protection under Article XIX and any new safeguards code as well as the standard provisions of US trade law
• creation of new codes or trading régimes for services, investment-related performance requirements and high technology trade

---

[17] However, in view of the moderate levels of existing tariffs, it would be a serious mistake to make major concessions to legislative demands for new NTB protection if such demands were the quid pro quo for authority to eliminate tariffs.

- elimination of all tariffs on industrial products by industrial countries.

Such an agenda is obviously ambitious. It would take most of the decade to complete. But, more immediately, it would dramatically alter the thrust of world trade policy by again putting it firmly on the path of liberalization and international rule making—rather than on the current path of creeping restrictionism and unilateral action. It should thus be the second component of an effective trade strategy for the 1980s, joining the Standstill Agreement to halt the erosion immediately while the planning and preparation for the "new MTN" go into effect.

An Effective Program of Trade Adjustment

Both these steps will be economically viable and politically credible, however, only if they are accompanied by a third step: creation of an effective trade adjustment program in the United States (and perhaps elsewhere). Some current changes in trade patterns clearly cause adjustment problems. Dislocations will continue to arise in the future, for reasons including results of the liberalization envisaged above, and will require further adjustment. Rejection of the option of trade restrictions, in the Standstill Agreement, and subsequently via the new negotiations, requires the creation of an alternative program through which government help will be provided to obtain the needed adjustment.

We do not now have a detailed blueprint for such a program although the suggestions advanced by J. David Richardson represent a beginning.[18] However, we remain unconvinced that the previous Trade Adjustment Assistance effort was as bad as its current reputation implies. To be sure, its rules were initially drawn too tightly (in 1962) and subsequently may have been excessively loosened (in 1974). But it was never given full-scale and high-level support by any administration, nor was its own administration centralized and operated effectively. And it did prove successful, in terms of both compensating trade-affected workers and neutralizing political opposition to trade liberalization, for a dozen years until ideological hostility and overriding budgetary concerns dismantled it.

For the future, in any event, it seems highly dubious that the United States will be able to maintain an open trading policy without con-

---

[18] J. David Richardson, "Worker Adjustment to US International Trade: Programs and Prospects," Chapter 12, this volume.

structing a viable alternative to deal effectively with the adjustment problems faced by trade-affected workers, firms, and entire industries. Virtually all other countries deal with such problems within the framework of their overall industrial policies and manpower programs. The United States has no such programs, however, and it would take many years to put them in place—if doing so were to prove feasible at all, given traditional American reliance on market forces and arms'-length attitudes toward relations among business, labor, and government.

Hence, the premise on which the Trade Adjustment Assistance program was based in 1962, and substantially liberalized in 1974, seems valid: that a trade-specific adjustment program is needed both to cope with the real problems of trade-affected Americans and to enable US society as a whole to continue to reap the benefits of an open trading system. It thus seems imperative either to resuscitate the Trade Adjustment Assistance program, or replace it with a new approach aimed at the same purpose, in constructing a viable US trade policy for the 1980s. As indicated, at least partial financing of such a program could be generated by earmarking tariff revenues for adjustment purposes—including revenues obtained by converting existing nontariff restrictions on imports (for example, quotas on apparel items) to tariffs.

The need to improve adjustment programs is not unique to the United States (although the gap between need and reality is probably greatest in the United States for the reasons just cited). Rigid real wages, for example, are a potent force for import restrictions in Europe. All nations will have to review their adjustment programs to see whether they are adequate to cope with the much greater strains that exist today and which may well continue to exist in acute form throughout the 1980s in the face of slower growth and intensifying international competition.

Indeed, it would be possible to add this issue area to the agenda for international trade negotiations. Countries could accept an international obligation to adopt effective national adjustment programs, which would be monitored internationally on an ongoing basis (presumably in the GATT) to see whether the agreed objectives were being met in practice.[19] Such a commitment would be a logical cor-

---

[19] To our knowledge, the idea of internationalizing trade adjustment obligations was first proposed by the Trades Union Congress of the United Kingdom in 1967, then recommended by the Trade Union Advisory Committee of the OECD in 1968, and again (to the OECD High Level Trade Group under Jean Rey) in 1972. See David Lea, "International Adjustment

ollary to the commitment undertaken, in the original GATT and through the additional steps proposed in this study, to maintain open markets for imports—because "positive adjustment" is necessary to cope with the domestic problems sometimes caused by imports, and therefore to preserve the political credibility of the trade commitments themselves. Such linkage in the trade area would be parallel to the linkage in international monetary arrangements between the commitments to maintain a stable domestic economy and to avoid disruptive exchange rate policies. Whether or not international obligations are negotiated in this area, however, improved domestic adjustment programs will be an essential component of an effective trade policy for the 1980s—especially in the United States.

The Link to International Money

The final component of a fundamental strategy for trade policy in the 1980s is to incorporate international monetary considerations into that strategy, indeed to view trade and international monetary affairs as closely linked elements which must be largely determined in concert, and to improve the functioning of international monetary arrangements in ways that will support maintenance of an open trading system.

As indicated throughout this study, severe misalignments in exchange rates are an understandable source of major pressure for a retreat from open trading arrangements. The substantial overvaluation of the dollar, for example, is badly undermining the international price competitiveness of the US economy—as in the late 1960s and early 1970s, during the only previous postwar episode of such extreme dollar overvaluation—and thus swelling pressures to restrict imports. As indicated by industry leaders and top industry analysts, for example, the overvalued dollar is a (if not *the*) chief cause of increased import penetration in the steel and automobile industries.

In fact, linking trade and money is nothing new. For example, the US actions that triggered the international monetary crisis of late 1971—arguably the single greatest threat to the maintenance of cooperative international economic arrangements in the postwar pe-

---

Assistance," in C. Fred Bergsten, ed., *Toward a New World Trade Policy: The Maidenhead Papers* (Lexington, Mass.: D.C. Heath and Co., 1975). Because that proposal was aimed primarily at creating an international funding mechanism for adjustment assistance in support of increased exports from the developing countries, however, it went far beyond the idea advanced here.

riod—deliberately linked the import surcharge and the cessation of dollar convertibility into gold. The resolution of that crisis, at US insistence, encompassed a commitment by other countries to launch major new international trade negotiations (which eventually became the MTN) in return for US dropping of the surcharge and agreement on a new structure of currency parities. The shoe was soon on the other foot, however; at French insistence, the Tokyo Declaration which launched the MTN in 1973 encompassed a commitment (aimed *at* the United States) to promote international monetary stability as an essential element in permitting trade negotiations to proceed in a meaningful way.

The nexus between trade and money has intensified over the past decade, particularly because of the growing failure of the flexible exchange rate system to avoid major currency misalignments with their distorting effects on trade patterns and the level of trade balances. Hence improvements in international monetary arrangements remain an essential counterpoint to further liberalization of the trading system, and indeed to avoiding future erosion of the system currently in place.

Analysis of the specific means for reforming the monetary system to this end is beyond the scope of the current study although, as indicated in the previous section, it will probably be necessary to move in the direction of adopting a "target zone" or "reference rate" approach to limit the severe overshooting of exchange rates which so badly undermines the prospects (and even case) for an open trading system.[20] It is clear, moreover, that much more systematic linkage between trade and money will be needed, on an ongoing basis, both domestically and internationally.

Domestically, governments will have to systematize the interaction between their policy-making machineries for money and trade. This problem is particularly acute in the United States, where primary responsibility for the two issues is assigned to completely different parts of the government—the Treasury and Federal Reserve System for money, USTR and the Commerce Department for trade. Effective coordination between the two has been achieved only when a single individual or department has dominated the entire range of international economic policy, as with Treasury Secretary John M. Connally in the early 1970s, or when the responsible officials in one or

---

[20] See John Williamson, *The Exchange Rate System,* POLICY ANALYSES IN INTERNATIONAL ECONOMICS, no. 7 (Washington: Institute for International Economics, forthcoming September 1983).

both of these areas were fully attuned to the need to achieve such linkage (as in Treasury and USTR under the Carter administration).

Despite the periodic creation of cabinet committees and councils, none has yet provided a mechanism that links the two areas comprehensively and continuously. Any number of methods to do so could be devised, but the most effective is probably to include top trade officials in the key deliberations on international monetary policy and vice versa. White House coordination will be needed to achieve such a result in some administrations, whereas informal approaches may suffice in others.

At the international level, much more extensive coordination is needed between the GATT and the IMF. GATT now holds periodic consultations with member countries—primarily developing countries, which maintain import controls for balance of payments measures—and receives advice from the Fund on the balance of payments position of those countries, with a view toward judging whether their situations justify continuing the controls. For its part, the IMF usually insists that a country eschew import restrictions (or other trade controls) as one of the conditions required to establish its eligibility to draw resources from the Fund.

However, the overarching interrelations between trade and money, as addressed repeatedly in this study, are discussed inadequately within or between the institutions. For example, there is no GATT pressure on the IMF to exercise its multilateral surveillance responsibilities more effectively to correct (or at least reduce) the huge currency imbalances plaguing the trading system. Neither is there IMF pressure on GATT to resist more effectively the imposition of trade barriers by developing countries, which would facilitate the efforts of the Fund (and the World Bank) to induce such countries to adopt fundamental adjustment measures rather than rely on trade constraints, which are at best temporary palliatives and at most counterproductive.

To be sure, such interaction between GATT and the IMF will have to be promoted primarily by the member countries of both which play a leading role in managing the international trade and monetary system. This emphasizes the need for industrial countries to coordinate their trade and monetary policies much more effectively, both internally and among each other. In addition, however, the managements and staffs of the two organizations should be much more active in establishing links between their operations. As a starter, GATT and IMF staff members should participate in country surveillance discussions (at least of major countries) of the *other* organization. In that context, for example, a GATT representative on an IMF team could ask the United States how it planned to maintain its commitments under the GATT (and, in the future, under the Standstill Agreement proposed here) if its overvalued currency provided such a substantial subsidy to imports. And the two organizations might conduct a joint annual review of trends in trade restrictions and policies, including the impact of international monetary arrangements on that topic.

Conclusion

This chapter, and the conference on which it is based, have stressed the severity of the threats to the open trading system which exist at present and are likely to persist well into the 1980s. Yet we believe that the desired course of responding to these threats can be seen with reasonable clarity, as developed in the individual conference papers and in our effort to draw policy conclusions from them, in terms of both overall systemic strategy and dealing with individual sectors. A good deal of political foresight and courage will be needed to adopt such approaches, to be sure, but the needed vision emerged in both the 1960s and 1970s, and it is reasonable to believe that it can also appear in the 1980s.

The specific strategy recommended here calls for four major steps: a comprehensive Standstill Agreement to bar any imposition of new trade barriers; the launching of an "MTN for the 1980s" to eliminate tariffs and address both carryover issues from the past (textiles and apparel, agriculture, steel, autos, safeguards, subsidies) and newly emerging issues in this decade (services, investment-related trade problems, high technology trade); institution of a new trade adjustment assistance program in the United States (and perhaps other countries); and much closer integration of trade and international monetary policy, to relieve trade policy of the major burden created by the recurrence of severe exchange rate misalignments.

The GATT Ministerial of November 1982 offered a critical opportunity to reverse the creeping erosion besetting the international trading system and likely to persist unless consciously reversed by a program of the type suggested here. Unfortunately, its results were modest. Renewed efforts, perhaps through a reconvening of the Ministerial in 1984 or early 1985, will be necessary for effective resistence to protectionist pressures. Beyond any particular meeting, however, perseverance and foresight will be needed for many years to cope with the variety of major problems confronting world trade. The economic and political stakes are enormous. The major nations will have to adopt steps along the lines suggested here to preserve the system. The alternative is to risk losing the gains of almost forty years, which have been so crucial to the prosperity and political stability of the entire postwar period.

Participants at the conference on Trade Policy in the 1980s, June 23–25, 1982, Institute for International Economics, Washington

The participants and their affiliations at the time of the conference, which was partially supported by a grant from the Rockefeller Foundation, are listed below.

Dragoslav Avramovíc
United Nations Conference on
Trade and Development

Bela Balassa
World Bank and Johns Hopkins
University

Robert E. Baldwin
University of Wisconsin

C. Fred Bergsten
Institute for International
Economics

Yves Berthelot
Centre d'Etudes Prospectives et
d'Informations Internationales

Jagdish N. Bhagwati
Columbia University

William R. Cline
Institute for International
Economics

Robert B. Cohen
New York University

Richard N. Cooper
Harvard University

W. Max Corden
The Australian National
University

John Curtis
The Institute for Research on
Public Policy

Gerard Curzon
Graduate Institute of
International Studies (Geneva)

Alan V. Deardorff
University of Michigan

Carlos Diaz-Alejandro
Yale University and PUC/Rio
de Janeiro

John Diebold
The Diebold Group, Inc.

William Diebold, Jr.
Council on Foreign Relations

Juergen B. Donges
Institut für Weltwirtschaft

Asim Erdilek
National Science Foundation

Roberto Fendt
Fundação Central de Estudos
do Comercio Exterior

J. Michael Finger
World Bank

Lawrence Fox
National Association of
Manufacturers

Isaiah Frank
The Johns Hopkins University

Wynne Godley
University of Cambridge

Rodney de C. Grey
Grey, Clark, Shih & Associates

Gottfried Haberler
American Enterprise Institute

Dale E. Hathaway
Consultants International
  Group

Gary Clyde Hufbauer
Institute for International
  Economics

Helen Hughes
World Bank

John H. Jackson
University of Michigan

Hideo Kanemitsu
Sophia University (Tokyo) and
  Stanford University

Åke Lindén
General Agreement on Tariffs
  and Trade

Harald B. Malmgren
Malmgren, Inc.

Robert L. McNeill
Emergency Committee for
  American Trade

Stanley Nehmer
Economic Consulting Services,
  Inc.

Yusuki Onitsuka
Yokohama National University

Gardner Patterson
Consultant, Washington

Rolf Piekarz
National Science Foundation

J. David Richardson
University of Wisconsin

Howard F. Rosen
Institute for International
  Economics

A. E. Safarian
Université de Nice

Sang-mok Suh
Korean Development Institute

Gary M. Saxonhouse
University of Michigan

Jeffrey J. Schott
Carnegie Endowment for
  International Peace

Helena Stalson
Council on Foreign Relations

Robert M. Stern
University of Michigan

Brian Turner
Industrial Unions Department,
  AFL-CIO

Ingo Walter
New York University

Leonard Weiss
Consultant, Arlington, Va.

John Williamson
Institute for International
  Economics

Martin Wolf
Trade Policy Research Centre
  (London)

Alan Wm. Wolff
Verner, Liipfert, Bernhard &
  McPherson

Yoshie Yonezawa
Aoyama Gakuin University
  (Tokyo)

GLOSSARY

ASEAN Association of South East Asian Nations

BIAC Business and Industry Advisory Committee to the OECD

BPS Basis price system

CAP Common agricultural policy of the European Community

CBI Caribbean Basin Initiative

COCOM Coordinating Committee responsible for all aspects of the multilateral export controls system to Sino-Soviet bloc. Members are the United States, the United Kingdom, France, Italy, Belgium, Luxembourg, the Netherlands, Norway, Denmark, Canada, Germany (FR), Greece, Portugal, Turkey, and Japan.

COMECON Council for Mutual Economic Assistance. Participants are: Bulgaria, Czechoslovakia, Hungary, Poland, Romania, USSR, Cuba, German Democratic Republic, Mongolia, Vietnam, Yugoslavia. Observers are China and North Korea.

Comsat Communications Satellite Corporation

CVD Countervailing duty

DCE Domestic credit expansion

DISC Domestic International Sales Corporation. A US international corporation that is permitted to postpone payment of federal taxes on income from export profits until distribution to its shareholders.

Dumping Sale of a commodity in a foreign market at "less than fair value." See GATT, Article VI.

EC European Community. The short-form designation of adherents to the treaties forming the European Coal and Steel Community (ECSC), the European Economic Community (EEC), the European Atomic Energy Community (Euratom), and the treaties amending those treaties. Members are Belgium, France, Denmark, Federal Republic of Germany, Greece, Ireland, Italy, Luxembourg, the Netherlands, and United Kingdom.

EFTA European Free Trade Association. Current members are Austria, Finland, Iceland, Portugal, Sweden, and Switzerland.

Exportkleb USSR buying agency

FIRA Canada's Foreign Investment Review Agency

GATT General Agreement on Tariffs and Trade Article I, *see* MFN. Article XIX, *see* Safeguards. Article XXIII "Nullification and impairment" of former tariff liberalization

GATT Ministerial Meeting of the trade ministers of the GATT member countries

GSP Generalized System of Tariff Preferences. A worldwide system of national, nonreciprocal tariff preferences in favor of developing countries.

IMF International Monetary Fund

ITO International Trade Organization

Kennedy Round The sixth round of trade negotiations under the GATT

LDC Less developed country

LTFV Less than fair value

LICIT Labor–Industry Coalition for International Trade

LTA Long-Term Agreement on International Trade in cotton textiles

MFA Multi-Fiber Arrangement. An agreement allowing participants to limit all textile and apparel imports when the importing country considers restrictions necessary to end internal market disorder. Replaced LTA in 1974.

781

MFN Most favored nation. The policy whereby a trade concession extended by one country to another is granted to all other GATT trading partners, conditionally or unconditionally.

MITI Japan's Ministry of International Trade and Industry

MTN Multilateral Trade Negotiations

NIC Newly industrialized country; newly industrializing country; new industrial country

NTB Nontariff trade barrier

OECD Organization for Economic Cooperation and Development. Members are Australia, Austria, Belgium, Canada, Denmark, Finland, France, Federal Republic of Germany, Greece, Iceland, Ireland, Italy, Japan, Luxembourg, the Netherlands, New Zealand, Norway, Portugal, Spain, Sweden, Switzerland, Turkey, United Kingdom, United States.

OMA Orderly Marketing Agreement

PPA Protocol of Provisional Application, GATT

PTT Postal, Telephone and Telegraph Ministry

Safeguards Import controls or restrictions imposed on the grounds of protecting a domestic industry from injury. GATT Article XIX allows a country to withdraw or modify concessions or impose new controls if it can prove that a product is "being imported in such increased quantities as to cause or threaten serious injury to domestic producers."

SDR Special Drawing Right. A monetary reserve asset established by the International Monetary Fund in 1969. Its current value is based on a basket of the five major industrial countries' currencies.

SIA Semiconductor Industry Association

TAA Trade adjustment assistance. Originally legislated under the Trade Act of 1962 and extended under the Trade Act of 1974, Trade Adjustment Assistance is a program designed to provide workers who are displaced on account of increased imports with training and financial benefits in order to help them adjust.

Tokyo Round The seventh round of trade negotiations under the GATT

TPM Trigger price mechanism. The US system of monitoring milled steel imports for possible dumping based on the estimated landed cost of an import from the world's most efficient maker of a given product.

UNCTAD United Nations Conference on Trade and Development

USTR US Trade Representative, the President's main advisor on international trade policy

VER Voluntary export restraint

VRA Voluntary restraint agreement

INDEX

Authors

Ahmed, A.A. 626, 637
Aho, C. Michael 393, 394 (n.1), 395, 396 (n.5), 397, 399, 418, 422
Amano, A. 280 (n.20, 21)
American Chamber of Commerce in Japan (ACCJ) 21 (n.23), 128 (n.15)
American Iron and Steel Institute 485 (t.15.1), 487, 488 (t.15.2), 516, 523 (t.15A.3), 755 (n.5)
Anderson, Martin 554 (t.16.10), 555, 560
Anderson, R.G. 516
Anjaria, Shailendra J. 69 (n.17, 18), 124 (n.5)
Armington, Paul 99
Arthur D. Little, Inc. 263 (n.7), 278 (n.18)
Avramovíc, Dragoslav 779
Aylen, Jonathan 516, 521 (t.15A.2), 523 (t.15A.3)

Balassa, Bela 44, 59 (n.2), 81 (n.35), 216, 341, 359, 431, 711–22, 713, 715, 724, 729, 779
Baldwin, Robert E. 31, 65 (n.11), 72 (n.22), 407 (t.12.1), 408 (t.12.2), 411 (t.12.3), 412 (t.12.4), 422, 425–30, 431, 677, 710, 711, 714, 721, 779
Ball, R.J. 281 (n.23)
Ban, K. 280 (n.20, 21)
Banerjee, Sumitra 337 (n.6), 359
Baranson, Jack 715, 722
Barcelo, John J., III 356, 359
Basevi, G. 281 (n.23)
Baum, Christopher F. 710
Bayard, Thomas O. 393, 394 (n.1), 395, 396 (n.5), 397, 399, 418, 422
Bell, Joel 611, 637
Bergsten, C. Fred 5 (n.4, 6), 6 (n.8), 12, 13, 52, 53, 56, 59–98, 62 (n.6), 67 (n.14), 68 (n.16), 85 (n.43), 86 (n.45), 89 (n.47), 99–120, 100 (n.1), 101 (n.2, 4), 110, 111 (n.18), 112 (n.19), 114, 117, 118 (n.25), 129 (n.18), 203, 205, 206, 208, 211, 212, 216, 279 (n.19),

319, 346, 359, 574, 611, 623, 633, 634, 636, 637, 713, 723, 726, 727 (n.1), 729, 739, 742, 747–78, 774, 779
Berthelot, Yves 310–11, 574, 779
Bhagwati, Jagdish N. 50, 51, 319, 422, 423, 424, 726, 729–35, 779
Birnberg, Thomas B. 711, 722
Blackhurst, Richard 107 (n.11), 400, 422
Bloomfield, Gerald T. 549 (n.34), 560
Borrus, Michael 129 (n.17)
Bradford, Charles 498, 516
Branson, William H. 403, 422, 752 (n.2)
Brock, William S. 60 (n.3), 159, 398, 599, 595 (n.12), 762
Brookings Institution 64 (t.2.1)
Brown, Craig M. 359
Brown, Fred 262 (n.5), 678, 710, 714
Bryan, Greyson 359
Bulletin of the European Communities 229 (n.7), 230 (n.8)
Bureau of National Affairs 135 (n.31), 159 (n.1), 174 (n.19), 180 (n.25), 184 (n.36), 186 (n.38), 348 (n.15)
Bureau of Labor Statistics (BLS) 485 (t.15.1), 554 (t.16.10)
Business and Industry Advisory Committee (BIAC) to OECD 637
Business International 534 (t.16.1), 618
Business Week 547 (n.31), 561
Byron, George 538 (n.16), 561

Canada Department of Industry, Trade and Commerce 476 (n.16), 477
Carlson, G.N. 359
Chase, D.P. 586 (n.6)
Chenery, Hollis B. 272
Christensen, L. 292 (n.14)
Citrin, Daniel 556, 560
Claybrook, Joan 555 (n.43)
Cline, William R. 1–54, 2 (n.1), 5 (n.4, 5, 6), 6 (n.8), 11 (n.14), 16 (n.19), 23 (n.24), 24 (n.25), 30 (n.32), 52 (n.51), 59–98, 63 (n.8), 64 (t.2.1), 65, 66, 70 (n.20), 75 (n.29), 76 (n.30), 82, 89 (n.47), 95, 99, 101 (n.4), ·121–58, 124 (n.4), 125 (n.6), 137 (n.34), 142

INDEX

Subject

Agricultural trade, 435–36; credit for exports in, 449; domestic programs relation to, 443; food security as issue in, 450–53; foreign policy and, 449–50; GATT rules for, 445, 446, 453; government agencies effect on, 445–46; LTAs in, 448–50; subsidies in, 27, 444–45, 751, 763; trends in, 436–41

Agriculture: government intervention in domestic, 442–43; protection for, 33–35, 125, 126, 325; restructured domestic programs for, 52–53, 753

American Chamber of Commerce in Japan (ACCJ), 128n

American Telephone and Telegraph (AT&T), 649, 656, 658–59, 665

Antidumping, 7, 247; GATT rules on, 249; steel, 39; against subsidies, 28–29

Antitrust policy, for information industries, 660–61

Argentina, 90

Article XIX, GATT. *See* Escape clause; Safeguard protection

Australia, 240–41, 740

Automobiles: country shares of world production, 535; internationalization of industry, 41, 541–50; proposed bills to insure reciprocity in trade, 532, 534–35; shifting competitive advantage for, 527–28; trade policy predictions for, 42, 558–60; trends in world production, 535–37; trends in world trade, 537–41; US versus European protection for, 20, 256; voluntary export restraints on Japanese, 8, 41, 70, 84, 124, 263–64, 529–30

Balance of payments: effect on trade policy, 84–85, 125–27; exchange rates effect on, 279–80; GATT rule on trade restrictions for, 379–80; for services, 583

Banking: information technology for,

664; in services trade, 585–86, 587, 719

Brazil: complaints on EC trade policy, 240–41; export requirements, 627, 715; incentives to US auto industry, 543, 547; indebtedness, 300; information technology industry, 670; phase-out of subsidies, 341; potential effects of tariff elimination on, 695, 708; reciprocity, 130; share of world manufacturing production, 80

Bretton Woods system, 87, 103, 109, 112, 114, 120, 204–5

Burke-Hartke bill, 13, 67, 79, 110, 113, 395

Canada: cattle war between US and, 138; cultural protectionism, 597n; import barriers, 84; restrictions on information technology imports, 668; trucking policy, 594–95. *See also* Foreign Investment Review Agency

Capital: controls over, 117–18; formation, 329, 403

Caribbean Basin Initiative (CBI), 137, 199

Carter administration: automobile protection, 529; steel protection, 491, 495

Commerce, US Department of, 45, 530, 649; study of direct foreign investment, 613, 615–16, 623, 624

Commodity Credit Corporation (CCC), 449

Common Agricultural Policy, 64, 125, 199; objectives and operations, 227–29

Communications Act, *1934*, 647

Communications Satellite Act of *1962*, 652

Communications Satellite Corporation (COMSAT), 644, 653–54

Comparative advantage: general equilibrium theory of, 272–73, 314; Japanese, 272–75; reciprocity to deal

Composed in Times Roman by FotoTypesetters, Inc., Baltimore, Md.
Printed, and bound, by Thomson–Shore, Inc., Dexter, Mich.
Text 50# Champion Pinehurst 540 PPI. Smyth-sewn.
Cloth Joanna Kennett black.